*Probability and Mathematical Statistics (Continued)*

SERFLING • Approximation Theorems of Mathematical Statistics
TJUR • Probability Based on Radon Measures
WILLIAMS • Diffusions, Markov Processes, and Martingales, Volume I: Foundations
ZACKS • Theory of Statistical Inference

*Applied Probability and Statistics*

ANDERSON, AUQUIER, HAUCK, OAKES, VANDAELE, and WEISBERG • Statistical Methods for Comparative Studies
ARTHANARI and DODGE • Mathematical Programming in Statistics
BAILEY • The Elements of Stochastic Processes with Applications to the Natural Sciences
BAILEY • Mathematics, Statistics and Systems for Health
BARNETT • Interpreting Multivariate Data
BARNETT and LEWIS • Outliers in Statistical Data
BARTHOLOMEW • Stochastic Models for Social Processes, *Third Edition*
BARTHOLOMEW and FORBES • Statistical Techniques for Manpower Planning
BECK and ARNOLD • Parameter Estimation in Engineering and Science
BELSLEY, KUH, and WELSCH • Regression Diagnostics: Identifying Influential Data and Sources of Collinearity
BENNETT and FRANKLIN • Statistical Analysis in Chemistry and the Chemical Industry
BHAT • Elements of Applied Stochastic Processes
BLOOMFIELD • Fourier Analysis of Time Series: An Introduction
BOX • R. A. Fisher, The Life of a Scientist
BOX and DRAPER • Evolutionary Operation: A Statistical Method for Process Improvement
BOX, HUNTER, and HUNTER • Statistics for Experimenters: An Introduction to Design, Data Analysis, and Model Building
BROWN and HOLLANDER • Statistics: A Biomedical Introduction
BROWNLEE • Statistical Theory and Methodology in Science and Engineering, *Second Edition*
BURY • Statistical Models in Applied Science
CHAMBERS • Computational Methods for Data Analysis
CHATTERJEE and PRICE • Regression Analysis by Example
CHOW • Analysis and Control of Dynamic Economic Systems
CHOW • Econometric Analysis by Control Methods
CLELLAND, BROWN, and deCANI • Basic Statistics with Business Applications, *Second Edition*
COCHRAN • Sampling Techniques, *Third Edition*
COCHRAN and COX • Experimental Designs, *Second Edition*
CONOVER • Practical Nonparametric Statistics, *Second Edition*
CONOVER and IMAN • Introduction to Modern Business Statistics
CORNELL • Experiments with Mixtures: Designs, Models and The Analysis of Mixture Data
COX • Planning of Experiments
DANIEL • Biostatistics: A Foundation for Analysis in the Health Sciences, *Third Edition*
DANIEL • Applications of Statistics to Industrial Experimentation
DANIEL and WOOD • Fitting Equations to Data: Computer Analysis of Multifactor Data, *Second Edition*
DAVID • Order Statistics, *Second Edition*
DAVISON • Multidimensional Scaling
DEMING • Sample Design in Business Research
DODGE and ROMIG • Sampling Inspection Tables, *Second Edition*
DOWDY and WEARDEN • Statistics for Research
DRAPER and SMITH • Applied Regression Analysis, *Second Edition*
DUNN • Basic Statistics: A Primer for the Biomedical Sciences, *Second Edition*

*continued on back*

# ADVANCED ECONOMETRICS
## A Bridge to the Literature

# ADVANCED ECONOMETRICS

## A Bridge to the Literature

**Edward Greenberg**

*Washington University, St. Louis*

**Charles E. Webster, Jr.**

*Washington University, St. Louis*

**John Wiley & Sons**

*New York* *Chichester* *Brisbane* *Toronto* *Singapore*

**To Joan and Lesley**



***Library of Congress Cataloging in Publication Data:***

Greenberg, Edward, 1936–
Advanced econometrics.

(Wiley series in probability and mathematical statistics. Probability and mathematical statistics, ISSN 0271-6232)
Includes bibliographical references and indexes.
1. Econometrics. I. Webster, Jr. Charles E. (Charles Edward), 1950– II. Title. III. Series.
HB139.G73 1983 330′.028 82-23770
ISBN 0-471-09077-8

Printed in the United States of America

10 9 8 7 6 5 4 3 2 1

# Preface

Many articles appearing in the current econometrics literature are inaccessible to students with a background of one or two semesters in mathematical statistics and an introductory course in econometrics. Our book bridges the gap between an introductory course and such journal articles. It presents background material on selected topics in mathematics and mathematical statistics and provides fairly detailed reviews of three areas of econometric research. The book is intended for courses that continue beyond an introductory econometrics course in a theoretical direction. To a great extent, it is keyed to significant articles in the field to encourage the reading of the original articles.

Part I consists of two chapters that present probabilistic concepts of convergence, maximum likelihood estimation, asymptotic expansions of probability functions, and methods of approximating moments. These widely used large sample and approximation techniques are not adequately covered in most introductory econometrics texts. We present relationships between plims, asymptotic moments, and moments of limiting distributions. An introduction to Edgeworth approximations to distribution and density functions is included, along with a discussion of methods of approximating moments. Although the material on convergence and maximum likelihood estimation is primarily a review of topics covered in mathematical statistics and econometrics courses, the discussion of approximation techniques is likely to be the student's first exposure to these topics. In view of their widespread use, particularly in connection with distributions of estimators of parameters in simultaneous equation models, it is important that students know about them. Appendixes on order of magnitude ($o$ and $O$), complex variables, and characteristic functions provide necessary background.

Part II consists of three chapters on the analysis of time series models. The first two of these present the theory and estimation methods for the ARIMA models popularized by Box and Jenkins. Numerous graphs depict the typical pattern of data generated by low order autoregressive and moving average models and the autocovariance and partial autocovariance functions of these models. The fundamental theoretical concepts of stationarity and invertibility are explained both intuitively and formally. The third chapter of this part takes up the Zellner-Palm synthesis of time series and standard econometric simultaneous equation models, and an illustration of the approach is provided. The chapter concludes with an explanation and a critique of causality tests of the type proposed by Granger and Sims.

Part III is concerned with estimation, particularly of regression coefficients, under a mean squared error (quadratic loss function) criterion. After presenting background material on decision theory concepts and the noncentral $\chi^2$ distribution, we turn to the mean squared error performance of a number of estimators: ordinary least squares, restricted least squares, James-Stein and variants, preliminary test, double $k$-class, and ridge regression. The emphasis is on analytical results and comparisons of the estimators' performances. A discussion of the use of these estimators in econometric research is included.

Part IV examines the estimation of parameters of simultaneous equation models. It emphasizes topics that are not covered in most introductory textbooks because they require considerably more mathematical and statistical technique than most econometric students possess. Appendixes on the ratio of normal variates, the noncentral Wishart distribution, and hypergeometric and confluent hypergeometric functions provide background material. The first chapter deals with identification and contains results that generalize the one equation, linear restriction case that is included in most introductory texts. The next chapter considers the special case of two included endogenous variables. It derives in detail the exact distribution of ordinary least squares and two-stage least squares estimators and the moments of $k$-class estimators. In addition, references are provided for results with other estimators, and approximation methods are applied to derive relatively tractable expressions for distributions and moments. The third chapter presents in detail a theorem on existence of moments of $k$-class estimators with an arbitrary number of included endogenous variables. It also includes a summary of and reference to other topics found in the current literature.

We are happy to acknowledge Professor Arthur Denzau and the help of several of our students, who made comments at various stages: Alvin Hsieh, Dosung Chung, Mark Stover, Blair Harcourt, and Howard Neiman. We also thank Professors R. Carter Hill, Albert Link, Malcolm Dowling, and Jan Kmenta for their very useful comments on the project in its early stages, and Professor Jerry Thursby who made many detailed comments on our completed draft.

Typing was expertly and (usually) cheerfully done by Mary Kastens, Patricia Curtis, Anne Schroeder, and Candace Schap.

**Edward Greenberg**

**Charles E. Webster, Jr.**

# Contents

# LIST OF ABBREVIATIONS, FUNCTIONS, AND SYMBOLS

## Abbreviations

| | |
|---|---|
| a.b.p. | Asymptotically bounded in probability |
| ACF | Autocorrelation function |
| AR | Autoregressive |
| ARIMA | Autoregressive integrated moving average |
| ARMA | Autoregressive moving average |
| c.f. | Characteristic function |
| c.r. | Characteristic root |
| c.v. | Characteristic vector |
| CLT | Central limit theorem |
| CRLB | Cramer-Rao lower bound |
| d.f. | Distribution function |
| i.i.d. | Identically, independently distributed |
| IV | Instrumental variables |
| LIML | Limited information maximum likelihood |
| MA | Moving average |
| m.g.f. | Moment generating function |
| MLE | Maximum likelihood estimator |
| $N'_\epsilon(x)$ | Deleted neighborhood of $x$; $\{u: \|u - x\| < \epsilon$ and $u \neq x\}$ |
| $o(b_t)$ | "$a_t = o(b_t)$" indicates $a_t$ is of *smaller order* than $b_t$ |
| $O(b_t)$ | "$a_t = O(b_t)$" indicates $a_t$ is *at most of order* $b_t$ |
| $o_p(a_t)$ | "$Y_t = o_p(a_t)$" indicates $Y_t$ is of smaller order in probability than $a_t$ |
| $O_p(a_t)$ | "$Y_t = O_p(a_t)$" indicates $Y_t$ is at most of order in probability as $a_t$ |
| OLS | Ordinary least squares |
| PACF | Partial autocorrelation function |
| $P[A]$ | Probability of the event A |
| plim | Probability limit |
| $r(A)$ | Rank of matrix A |
| r.v. | Random variable |

| | |
|---|---|
| SLLN | Strong law of large numbers |
| 3SLS | Three-stage least squares |
| 2SLS | Two-stage least squares |
| WLLN | Weak law of large numbers |

## Functions

| | |
|---|---|
| arg $Z$ | Argument of the complex number $Z$ |
| $B(a, b)$ | Beta function |
| $\chi_k^2$ | Central $\chi^2$ distribution with $k$ degrees of freedom |
| $\chi'^2(n, \lambda)$ | Noncentral $\chi^2$ distribution with $n$ degrees of freedom and noncentrality parameter $\lambda$ |
| $\text{Cov}(\mathbf{X})$ | Covariance matrix of the random vector $\mathbf{X}$ |
| $E(X)$ | Expected value of $X$ (scalar or vector) |
| $F(k, n)$ | Central $F$-distribution with $k$ and $n$ degrees of freedom |
| ${}_1F_1(a, b; z)$ | Confluent hypergeometric function |
| ${}_2F_1(a, b; c; z)$ | Hypergeometric function |
| $\Gamma(a)$ | Gamma function |
| $I(\boldsymbol{\theta})$ | Information matrix |
| Im $Z$ | Imaginary part of the complex number $Z$ |
| $l(\boldsymbol{\theta}; \mathbf{x})$ | Log-likelihood function |
| $\hat{l}(\boldsymbol{\theta}; \mathbf{x})$ | Log-likelihood function evaluated at the maximum likelihood estimator |
| $L(\boldsymbol{\theta}; \mathbf{x})$ | Likelihood function |
| $\hat{L}(\boldsymbol{\theta}; \mathbf{x})$ | Likelihood function evaluated at the maximum likelihood estimator |
| $N(\mu, \sigma^2)$ | Normal distribution with expected value $\mu$ and variance $\sigma^2$ |
| $N_p(\boldsymbol{\mu}, \Sigma)$ | $p$-dimensional multivariate normal distribution with expected value $\boldsymbol{\mu}$ and covariance matrix $\Sigma$ |
| Re $Z$ | Real part of the complex number $Z$ |
| $\text{row}(V, W)$ | The $1 \times mn$ vector formed from the $m \times p$ matrix $V$ and the $p \times n$ matrix $W$ as $(\mathbf{V}_1W, \mathbf{V}_2W, \ldots, \mathbf{V}_mW)$, where $\mathbf{V}_i$ is the $i$th row of $V$ |
| $\text{Var}(X)$ | Variance of the random variable $X$ |
| $\text{vec}(A)$ | The $1 \times mn$ vector formed from the $m \times n$ matrix $A$ as $(\mathbf{a}_1, \mathbf{a}_2, \ldots, \mathbf{a}_m)$, where $\mathbf{a}_i$ is the $i$th row of $A$ |
| $W_p(\Sigma, N)$ | $p$-dimensional Wishart distribution with scale matrix $\Sigma$ and $N$ degrees of freedom |
| $W_p'(\Sigma, N, T)$ | $p$-dimensional noncentral Wishart distribution with scale matrix $\Sigma$, means sigma matrix $T$ and $N$ degrees of freedom |

## Symbols

| | |
|---|---|
| $\sim$ | i. "$x \sim f(x)$" indicates that the random variable $x$ (scalar or vector) has the density function $f(x)$. |
| | ii. "$h(x) \sim \Sigma a_n \phi_n(x)$, $x \to c$" indicates that $\Sigma a_n \phi_n(x)$ is an asymptotic expansion for $h(x)$ as $x \to c$ |
| $\xrightarrow{\text{a.s.}}$ | Convergence almost surely |
| $\xrightarrow{\text{d}}$ | Convergence in distribution |
| $\xrightarrow{\text{p}}$ | Convergence in probability |
| $\xrightarrow{\text{q.m.}}$ | Convergence in quadratic mean |
| $\|Z\|$ | Modulus of the complex number $Z$ |
| $\|\mathbf{X}\|$ | Euclidean norm of vector $\mathbf{X}$; $(\mathbf{X}'\mathbf{X})^{1/2}$ |
| $(a)_n$ | $\dfrac{\Gamma(a+n)}{\Gamma(a)} = (a+n-1)(a+n-2)\ldots a$ |

# PART I

# Topics in Large Sample Theory and Approximation Methods

Chapter 1 is primarily a review of convergence concepts used in probability theory and of the maximum likelihood method of estimation. Chapter 2 illustrates a number of methods that are used to approximate probability distributions and moments of functions of random variables.

Although only a few of those topics are extensively used in the remainder of the book, a basic knowledge of the topics covered in Part I is necessary for understanding and contributing to current research in econometrics.

# CHAPTER 1

# A Review of Asymptotic Distribution Theory and Maximum Likelihood Estimation

We begin our study of asymptotic distribution theory with an examination of sequences of random variables. Several features of such sequences may be studied: Are there concepts of convergence which might be applied to random variables (r.v.'s)? Can anything be said about the behavior of the sequence of corresponding distribution functions, $\{F_T(x)\}$? Can anything be said about the sequence of moments, $\{E(X_t^r)\}$? Can approximations be found to complicated distribution functions as $T \rightarrow \infty$? Precise definitions for these concepts and the relationships between them have been extensively studied.

Relevance for econometricians arises from the fact that $X_T$ may often be interpreted as an estimator for some parameter based on a sample size of $T$, and the behavior of the sequence for large $T$ may be regarded as the behavior of the estimator for large sample sizes. Since it is often easier to investigate the properties of $X_T$ for large $T$ than to ascertain exact (or small sample) distributions, asymptotic concepts have been extensively utilized in econometrics. The questions of interest are whether $X_T$ has any desirable statistical properties as $T$ increases and, for purposes of establishing confidence intervals or testing hypotheses, what is the distribution of $X_T$ for large $T$.

In the sections that follow we first examine various convergence concepts, the relationships between the convergence concepts, and the conditions necessary for a sequence of random variables to converge. Using these concepts of convergence we then present a number of central limit theorems showing the conditions under which a sequence of random variable converges to a random variable that is normally distributed. In the final section of this chapter we examine the properties of maximum likelihood estimators for large sample size.[1]

## 1.1 Convergence Concepts

Since several of the convergence concepts discussed in detail below are bewilderingly similar, some general introductory comments on probability theory may be useful in understanding the differences between them.[2] We begin by defining $\Omega$ as the set of all possible outcomes of an experiment, and $\omega$ is used to denote a particular outcome. A

[1]Econometrics texts that treat these topics in some detail are Dhrymes (1970, Chapter 3) and Theil (1971, Chapter 8).

[2]Pfeiffer (1978) is an excellent introduction to the basic probability theory used in this book. It contains the necessary restrictions on the structure of subsets of $\Omega$ and on the functions that can be r.v.'s.

random variable, $X(\omega)$, is a real valued function with domain $\Omega$ that assigns a numerical value to each outcome. In statistical applications, $\Omega$ is the sample space, $\omega \in \Omega$ is a possible outcome, and $X(\omega)$ is a numerical value assigned to outcome $\omega$.

As an example, consider the experiment of repeatedly tossing a coin, where the possible outcomes are a head ($H$) or a tail ($T$). Then each $\omega$ is an infinite sequence of $H$'s and $T$'s, and $\Omega$ is the set of all such sequences. An example of a random variable, $X(\omega)$, is the proportion of heads in the first ten tosses, which is computed from the number of $H$'s in the first ten positions of $\omega$.

More than one function (each of which is a r.v.) may be defined for a value of $\omega$. A *sequence of random variables* is a sequence of real valued functions, $X_1(\omega), \ldots,$ $X_T(\omega), \ldots$, each of which has the same $\omega$ as its argument. For example, returning to the coin-tossing experiment, $X_1(\omega)$ might be the proportion of heads in one toss, $X_2(\omega)$ the proportion in two tosses, and $X_T(\omega)$ the proportion in $T$ tosses. Thus, if $\omega = \{H, T, T, T, H, H, \ldots\}$, then $X_1(\omega) = 1.00$, $X_2(\omega) = .50$, $X_3(\omega) = .33$, $X_4(\omega) = .25$, $X_5(\omega) = .40$, and so on. A second example would be to define $\omega$ as a particular outcome of gross national product (GNP) now, next year, and into the future. A particular $\omega$, say $\omega^*$, may refer to a time path of GNP of 85 in period 1, 95 in period 2, 108 in period 3, and so on. $\Omega$ would then refer to all possible time paths of GNP from now into the future. We could then define a sequence of random variables $X_i(\omega)$ where $X_i$ is the average value of GNP after $i$ periods. Hence, for our particular series we would have $X_1(\omega^*) = 85$, $X_2(\omega^*) = 90$, $X_3(\omega^*) = 96$, and so on.

Because it is often of interest to see whether a sequence of random variables converges, we next discuss several senses in which the sequence $\{X_T\}$ may be said to converge.

### 1.1.1 Convergence Almost Surely (a.s.)[3]

Before presenting the definition of "convergence almost surely" it is necessary to explain some notation. Consider the sequence of functions, $X_1(\omega), X_2(\omega), \ldots,$ where each $X_i(\omega)$ is a random variable evaluated at the point $\omega$. It may happen that the sequence $\{X_T(\omega)\}$ converges to the point $X(\omega)$ in the sense that, for sufficiently large $T$, the difference $|X_T(\omega) - X(\omega)|$ may be made arbitrarily small and remains arbitrarily small (less than $\epsilon$) as $T$ increases. That is, $|X_{T+i}(\omega) - X(\omega)| \leq \epsilon$ for $i = 0, 1, \ldots$ and $\epsilon > 0$. If that occurs, we write $\lim_{T\to\infty} X_T(\omega) = X(\omega)$. This notation is short for the statement: for every $\epsilon > 0$, there exists a $T_0(\epsilon)$ such that

$$|X_T(\omega) - X(\omega)| \leq \epsilon, \qquad \text{whenever} \quad T > T_0(\epsilon).$$

Now consider the set, $A$, of $\omega$ for which the convergence takes place,

$$A = \{\omega\colon \lim_{T\to\infty} X_T(\omega) = X(\omega)\}.$$

The probability of the occurrence of $A$, $P(A)$, is often expressed as

$$P(A) = P[\lim_{T\to\infty} |X_T(\omega) - X(\omega)| \leq \epsilon].$$

The first concept of convergence is concerned with $P(A)$:

[3]This type of convergence is also called "convergence with probability one."

**Definition**

$X_T(\omega)$ *converges almost surely to* $X$ if $P[\lim_{T\to\infty} |X_T(\omega) - X(\omega)| \leq \epsilon] = 1$, for every $\epsilon > 0$. This will be denoted by $X_T(\omega) \xrightarrow{\text{a.s.}} X$. $X_T(\omega)$ and $X(\omega)$ may be scalars or column vectors; in the latter case, $\mathbf{X}_T(\omega)$ and $\mathbf{X}(\omega)$ will be of the same dimension and $|\mathbf{X}_T(\omega) - \mathbf{X}(\omega)|$ should be interpreted as the Euclidean norm, $[\mathbf{X}_T(\omega) - \mathbf{X}(\omega)]'[\mathbf{X}_T(\omega) - \mathbf{X}(\omega)]^{1/2}$. Moreover, $X$ may be either a constant (or vector of constants) or a r.v. (or vector of r.v.'s).

An equivalent definition of convergence a.s. is helpful in understanding the concept. To develop this, consider the set of $\omega$ for which convergence *fails* to take place. $X_T(\omega)$ does not converge to $X(\omega)$ if for some $\epsilon > 0$, $|X_{T+i}(\omega) - X(\omega)| > \epsilon$ for at least one $i$, no matter how large $T$ is. That is, either $|X_{T+1}(\omega) - X(\omega)| > \epsilon$ or $|X_{T+2}(\omega) - X(\omega)| > \epsilon$ or . . . for every $T$. For convergence a.s., the set of such $\omega$ has probability zero.

An example of convergence a.s. is the "strong law of large numbers" (SLLN): Let $\{Y_i\}$ be a sequence of r.v.'s and $\{X_T\}$ a sequence of partial sums of the $Y_i$; that is, $X_T = 1/T \sum_{i=1}^{T} Y_i$. In addition, assume that $X = \lim_{T\to\infty} E(X_T)$ exists and is finite. If $X_T(\omega) \xrightarrow{\text{a.s.}} X$, the sequence $\{Y_i\}$ is said to obey the SLLN. Two theorems that give sufficient conditions for a sequence of r.v.'s to obey SLLN are next quoted:

**Theorem 1.1.1 (Kolmogoroff)**

If a sequence of mutually independent variables $\{Y_i\}$ satisfies

$$\sum_{n=1}^{\infty} \frac{\text{Var}(Y_n)}{n^2} < \infty,$$

then it obeys the SLLN.

**Proof**

See Gnedenko (1973, p. 215). □

**Theorem 1.1.2**

The existence of $E(Y_i)$ is a necessary and sufficient condition for applying the SLLN to $\{Y_i\}$, where $\{Y_i\}$ is a sequence of identically distributed and mutually independent r.v.'s.

**Proof**

See Gnedenko (1973, p. 216). □

Another example of convergence a.s. is provided by the following:
Let $X \sim N(0, 1)$ and

$$X_T = X + \frac{1}{T}.$$

Since $X_T - X = 1/T$, it is clear that $|X_T(\omega) - X(\omega)| \leqslant \epsilon$ for every $T$ such that $1/T \leqslant \epsilon$. Therefore, the set $\{\omega: \lim|X_T(\omega) - X(\omega)| > \epsilon\}$ is empty. Since the empty set has probability zero, we have $X_T \xrightarrow{\text{a.s.}} X$.

At the risk of belaboring the point, assume $\omega$ is an outcome of an experiment which generates a value from a $N(0, 1)$ variable, $X(\omega)$. If $X_T(\omega) = X(\omega) + 1/T$, a particular outcome, $\omega$, determines $X(\omega)$, and then $X_T(\omega)$ is determined simply by adding $1/T$. Therefore, as $T$ becomes large, $|X_T(\omega) - X(\omega)|$ becomes very small: $X_T(\omega)$ and $X(\omega)$ are virtually the same random variable for large enough $T$; thus $X_T(\omega) \xrightarrow{\text{a.s.}} X(\omega)$, where the latter is a r.v.

Convergence a.s. is a strong convergence concept—any sequence of r.v.'s that converges a.s. also converges "in probability" and "in distribution," two types of convergence discussed below. Since convergence a.s. is a strong property, rather stringent sufficient conditions must be placed on the r.v. to achieve it. Perhaps to avoid such restrictive assumptions, econometricians have preferred to work with the weaker types of convergence discussed in the following sections.

### 1.1.2 Convergence in Probability

**Definition**

The sequence of r.v.'s $\{X_T\}$ *converges in probability to zero* if for all $\epsilon > 0$, $\lim_{T\to\infty} P[|X_T| > \epsilon] = 0$. $X_T$ may be a scalar or a vector; if the latter, the convergence is to the zero vector of suitable dimension. This type of convergence will be denoted by $X_T \xrightarrow{\text{P}} 0$. An equivalent definition is that $X_T$ converges in probability to zero if for all $\epsilon > 0$ and $\delta > 0$, $P[|X_T| \leqslant \epsilon] \geq 1 - \delta$ for sufficiently large $T$.

For this type of convergence we consider the set of points $\{\omega: |X_T(\omega)| > \epsilon\}$ and its probability. To satisfy the definition there must exist a value of $T$, say $T_0$, such that for $T > T_0$, $P[\{\omega: |X_T(\omega)| > \epsilon\}]$ is arbitrarily small. Convergence in probability implies that for $T > T_0$, *each* of the sets of $\omega$ (events), $\{\omega: |X_0| > \epsilon\}$, $\{\omega: |X_{0+1}| > \epsilon\}$, . . . , have arbitrarily small probabilities, but not that the probability of the *union* of these events is arbitrarily small. The latter, as we have seen, is the definition of convergence a.s. To see the relationship between convergence a.s. and convergence in probability, define $S_{i,\epsilon} = \{\omega: |X_{0+i}(\omega) > \epsilon\}$ and assume that $X_T \xrightarrow{\text{a.s.}} 0$. Then there exists a $T_0$ such that $P[S_{0,\epsilon} \cup S_{1,\epsilon} \cup \cdots S_{N,\epsilon} \cup \cdots] < \delta$. But since the probability of the union of a set of events is greater than or equal to the probability of any of the individual events, we must also have $P[S_{i,\epsilon}] < \delta$; hence there exists a $T_0$ that makes $P[|X_T(\omega)| > \epsilon] < \delta$. This proves the following theorem.

**Theorem 1.1.3**

Convergence a.s. implies convergence in probability.

We next provide an example showing that the converse is not true. Although the example is rather difficult, it should be studied to appreciate the difference between the two convergence concepts. This example is a probabilistic interpretation of a standard example in the theory of real variables to show that convergence in measure (which corresponds to convergence in probability) does not imply convergence almost everywhere (which corresponds to convergence a.s.).

Let $\omega$ be uniformly distributed in [0, 1] and define the r.v. $Z_{n,k}$ as follows:

$$Z_{n,k} = \begin{cases} 1, \text{ if } \omega \in \left[\dfrac{k-1}{n}, \dfrac{k}{n}\right) \\ 0, \text{ otherwise.} \end{cases} \qquad k = 1, \ldots n; \quad n = 1, \ldots$$

To utilize the convergence definitions, we first reduce $Z_{n,k}$ to a single subscript as follows:

$$X_1 = Z_{1,1}$$

$$X_2 = Z_{2,1}, \qquad X_3 = Z_{2,2}$$

$$X_4 = Z_{3,1}, \qquad X_5 = Z_{3,2}, \qquad X_6 = Z_{3,3},$$

and so on. First, it is easy to see that $X_T \xrightarrow{\text{P}} 0$. For any $\epsilon$ in [0, 1],

$$P[|X_T| > \epsilon] < \frac{1}{n+1},$$

where $n$ is associated with $T$ as shown above; therefore $\lim_{T\to\infty} P[|X_T| > \epsilon] = 0$.

On the other hand, consider the set $A = \{\omega\colon |X_T(\omega)| > \epsilon \text{ or } |X_{T+1}(\omega)| > \epsilon \text{ or} \ldots\}$. By definition, $X_T$ corresponds to some $Z_{n,k}$. Hence for some value of $s$, $X_{T+s} = Z_{n+1,1}$, $X_{T+s+1} = Z_{n+1,2}, \cdots, X_{T+s+n+1} = Z_{n+1,n+1}$. Because of the way the $Z_{n,k}$ were defined, for every $\omega$ in [0, 1], one of the $Z_{n+1,i} = 1$; hence $X_{T+s+j}(\omega) = 1$ for some $j$, $1 \le j \le n+1$. Therefore the set $A$ has probability one for $\epsilon < 1$. Equivalently, note that every $\omega$ in [0, 1] will make one member of each set $Z_{n,1}, Z_{n,2}, \ldots, Z_{n,n}$ equal to one; therefore the corresponding $|X_T| = 1$. This is true for every $n$—no matter how large—and therefore for every $T$. But the set of every $\omega$ in [0, 1] has probability one. In contrast, note that $P[|Z_{N,i}| = 1] = 1/N$ and $P[|Z_{N,i}| = 0] = 1 - 1/N$. Hence $X_T \xrightarrow{\text{P}} 0$ (as has already been proved).

The reader should verify that by redefining $Z_{n,k}$ in the following way (and defining $X_t$ as above), the resulting r.v. converges a.s. to zero:

$$Z_{n,k} = \begin{cases} 1 \text{ if } \omega \in \left[0, \dfrac{k}{n^2}\right) \\ 0 \text{ otherwise.} \end{cases} \qquad k = 1, \ldots n; \quad n = 1, \ldots$$

Incidentally, it can be shown that convergence in probability does guarantee the existence of an almost surely convergent subsequence; that is, any sequence $\{X_T(\omega)\}$ that converges in probability contains a subsequence that converges a.s.

The dependence on zero in the definition of convergence in probability is removed by the following definition.

**Definition**

The sequence of r.v.'s $\{X_T(\omega)\}$ *converges in probability to* $X$ if $[X_T(\omega) - X(\omega)] \xrightarrow{\text{P}} 0$. $X$ may be a vector or scalar random variable, or a constant vector or scalar.

The SLLN mentioned in (1.1.1) has a counterpart here. From the sequence of r.v.'s $\{Y_i\}$, form the partial sums, $X_T = 1/T \Sigma_{i=1}^T Y_i$. If $X_T \xrightarrow{P} X$ (a constant), $Y_i$ is said to obey the "weak law of large numbers" (WLLN). A necessary and sufficient condition for the application of the WLLN may be found in Gnedenko (1973, p. 207). A sufficient condition for convergence in probability is contained in the following theorem.

**Theorem 1.1.4**

If $\{X_T\}$ is such that as $T \to \infty$, $1/T^2 \text{ Var}[\Sigma_{t=1}^T X_t] \to 0$, then $1/T \Sigma_{i=1}^T (X_i - E[X_i]) \xrightarrow{P} 0$.

**Proof**

See Gnedenko (1973, p. 205). □

Note that this theorem does not require that the $X_i$ be either identically or independently distributed. We next briefly discuss some special topics in convergence to a constant and to a random variable.

**1.1.2a Convergence in Probability to a Constant; Consistency and Plim** In the case that $X_T \xrightarrow{P} k$, where $k$ is a constant, special notation is used.

**Definition**

If $X_T \xrightarrow{P} k$, where $k$ is a constant, then $k$ is said to be the *probability limit* of $X_T$; this is written as plim $X_T = k$.

The following theorem makes working with plims convenient and is in contrast to the fact that $E[g(X)]$ does not generally equal $g[E(X)]$, that is, a function of the expectation does not, in general, equal the expectation of a function. [For example, let $P(X = 0) = \frac{1}{2}$, $P(X = 1) = \frac{1}{2}$, and $g(X) = X^2$. Then $E(X) = \frac{1}{2}$, so that $g[E(X)] = \frac{1}{4}$; but $E[g(X)] = \frac{1}{2}$.]

**Theorem 1.1.5 (Slutsky)**

If $g(x)$ is a continuous function,[4] plim $g(X_T) = g(\text{plim } X_T)$. $X$ may be a vector or scalar and a r.v. or a constant. The proof we present is for the scalar case.

**Proof**

Define $X$ as plim $X_T$; that is, $X_T \xrightarrow{P} X$. Pick an arbitrary $\epsilon > 0$ and $\delta > 0$. Since $g$ is continuous, it is uniformly continuous in the bounded interval $[-M, M]$ where $M$ is a positive finite real number,[5] and since $X$ is a random variable we can choose $M$ such that

[4] $g(X)$ is a *continuous* function if for every $\epsilon > 0$ and every $X_0$ in the domain of $g(X)$ there exists a $\delta$ such that $|g(X) - g(X_0)| < \epsilon$ whenever $|X - X_0| < \delta$.

[5] $g(x)$ is *uniformly continuous* if the value of $\delta$ used in footnote 4 is independent of $X_0$. The fact that a continuous function is uniformly continuous in a bounded closed interval is proved in Kaplan and Lewis (1971, p. 982).

$P[|X| > M] < \delta/2$. In this interval, by the uniform continuity of $g$, there is a $\delta' > 0$ such that if $|X_T - X| < \delta'$, $|g(X_T) - g(X)| < \epsilon$. And since $X_T \xrightarrow{P} X$, we know that for $\epsilon > 0$ and $\delta' > 0$ there is a $T$, call it $T_0$, such that $P[|X_T - X| < \delta'] \geq 1 - \delta$, for $T > T_0$.

Let us now define the following sets:

$$A = \{X: |X| \leq M\},$$

$$B = \{X_T: |X_T - X| < \delta'\},$$

$$C = \{X_T: |g(X_T) - g(X)| < \epsilon\},$$

and let $\bar{A}$ and $\bar{B}$ denote the complements of $A$ and $B$, respectively. By the continuity of $g(X)$ we have that $B$ is a subset of $C$. But $B \subset C$ implies $(A \cap B) \subset C$. This implies

$$\begin{aligned} P[C] &\geq P[A \cap B] \\ &= 1 - P[\bar{A} \cup \bar{B}] \\ &\geq 1 - P[|X| > M] - P[|X_T - X| \geq \delta'] \\ &\geq 1 - \frac{\delta}{2} - P[|X_T - X| \geq \delta']. \end{aligned}$$

But for $T > T_0$, the right-hand side probability can be made less than $\delta/2$. Thus

$$\begin{aligned} P[g(X_T) - g(X)| \leq \epsilon] &\geq 1 - \frac{\delta}{2} - \frac{\delta}{2} \\ &= 1 - \delta \end{aligned}$$

for $T > T_0$. Hence we have that $g(X_T)$ converges in probability to $g(X)$. □

Convergence in probability to a constant has special importance in statistics. If we regard $X_T$ as an estimator of an unknown parameter, $\theta$, then the property that $\text{plim}\, X_T = \theta$ is often considered desirable; it is called "consistency":

**Definition**

$X_T$ is a *consistent estimator* for $\theta$ if $\text{plim}\, X_T = \theta$.

**Example**

If the $Y_i$ are drawn from the same distribution with $E(Y_i) = \mu$ and are independent, then Theorem 1.1.6 states that $X_T = 1/T\ \Sigma_1^T\, Y_i \xrightarrow{P} \mu$. That is, under the conditions of the theorem, the arithmetic mean of a r.v. is a consistent estimator of the expected value of that r.v. (By applying Theorem 1.1.4 we also have that $X_T \xrightarrow{\text{a.s.}} \mu$ in this example.)

**1.1.2b Convergence to a Random Variable** The following theorem generalizes the Slutsky theorem of the previous section.

**Theorem 1.1.6**

If $X_T \xrightarrow{p} X$ and $g(X)$ is a continuous function, then $g(X_T) \xrightarrow{p} g(X)$, where $X$ is a random variable.

**Proof**

Define $h(X_T, X) = g(X_T) - g(X)$; then $h(X_T, X)$ is continuous because $g(X)$ is. By the vector form of the previous theorem, if $X_T \xrightarrow{p} X$ (and, trivially, $X \xrightarrow{p} X$), then $h(X_T, X) \xrightarrow{p} h(X, X) = 0$. Therefore, $g(X_T) - g(X) \xrightarrow{p} 0$, or $g(X_T) \xrightarrow{p} g(X)$. □

Thus, if $g(X_T)$ is an estimator for some parameter and if it is difficult to determine the distribution of $g(X_T)$, this theorem allows us to approximate it by $g(X)$ if we know that $X_T \xrightarrow{p} X$.

**Example**

Let $Y_T \xrightarrow{p} Y$, where $Y \sim N(0, 1)$; then $Y^2 \xrightarrow{p} Y^2$, and $Y^2 \sim \chi^2_1$.

### 1.1.3 Convergence in *r*th Moment

**Definition**

The sequence of scalar r.v.'s $\{X_T\}$ *converges in rth moment* $(r \geq 1)$ to the r.v. $X$ If $E[X_t^r]$ and $E[X^r]$ exist for all $T$ and if $\lim_{T\to\infty} E[|X_T - X|^r] = 0$. To generalize this definition to vector r.v.'s, $\mathbf{X}' = (X_{T1}, \ldots, X_{Tn})$, let $|X_T - X|^r = [\Sigma_{i=1}^n (X_{Ti} - X_i)^2]^{r/2}$.

The case where $r = 2$ is most frequently encountered and is given a special name:

**Definition**

$X_T$ *converges in quadratic mean to* $X$ if $X_T$ converges in the second moment to $X$. This is denoted by $X_T \xrightarrow{\text{q.m.}} X$.

**Theorem 1.1.7**

$X_T \xrightarrow{\text{q.m.}} X$ implies $X_T \xrightarrow{p} X$.

**Proof**

By the Chebycheff inequality [Gnedenko (1973, p. 240)], $P[|X_T - X| \geq \epsilon] \leq E(|X_T - X|^2)/\epsilon^2$. Since $X_T \xrightarrow{\text{q.m.}} X$, the right-hand term goes to zero as $T \to \infty$. □

The converse is not true, that is, convergence in probability does not imply convergence in quadratic mean, as the following example shows.

**Example**

$$P[X = \alpha] = 1 - \frac{1}{T}$$

$$P[X = T^2] = \frac{1}{T}.$$

It is easy to see that plim $X_T = \alpha$, but

$$E[(X_T - \alpha)^2] = 0 \cdot \left(1 - \frac{1}{T}\right) + \frac{(T^2 - \alpha)^2}{T}.$$

As $T \to \infty$, $E[(X_T - \alpha)^2] \to \infty$.

Convergence in probability does not imply convergence in quadratic mean because convergence in probability merely requires that the probability of points different from the probability limit tend to zero. Convergence in quadratic mean, on the other hand, requires that the probability of points different from their limit times the squared distance from the limit be zero. In the above example, although the probability of a point not being equal to $\alpha$ goes to zero, the distance of the point from $\alpha$ grows so large with $T$ that the product of the probability times the squared distance from $\alpha$ does not go to zero. The r.v., therefore, does not converge in quadratic mean.

Lukacs (1968, pp. 32–34) presents examples to show that $X_T \xrightarrow{\text{q.m.}} X$ does not imply $X_T \xrightarrow{\text{a.s.}} X$ and that $X_T \xrightarrow{\text{a.s.}} X$ does not imply $X_T \xrightarrow{\text{q.m.}} X$.

### 1.1.4 Convergence in Distribution

Before defining convergence in distribution, it is necessary to define ''convergence to a function'' as it is used in the theory of real variables.

**Definition**

The sequence of functions $\{F_T\}$ *converges to the function* $F$ if and only if, for all $x$ in the domain of $F(x)$ and for every $\epsilon > 0$, there exists a $T_0$ such that

$$|F_T(x) - F(x)| < \epsilon \quad \text{for} \quad T > T_0.$$

This property is denoted by $F_T \to F$.

The definition requires that, for every value of $x$ in some set, the difference between $F_T(x)$ and $F(x)$ can be made arbitrarily small for sufficiently large $T$. This definition is next used to define a probabilistic counterpart.

**Definition**

The sequence of r.v.'s $\{X_T\}$ with corresponding distribution functions $\{F_T(x)\}$ is said to *converge in distribution* (some authors say ''converge in law'') to the r.v. $X$, with distribution function $F$, if and only if $F_T \to F$ at all continuity points of $F$. As usual, $X_T$ may be a vector. This type of convergence is denoted by $X_T \xrightarrow{d} X$. (Some authors write this as $X_T \xrightarrow{L} X$.) $F(x)$ is called the *limiting* or *asymptotic* distribution of $F_T(x)$.

If we think of $X_T$ as an estimator of a parameter (or a vector of parameters) based on sample size $T$,[6] the knowledge that $X_T \xrightarrow{d} X$ is often very useful. For example, it may be extremely difficult to determine $F_T$ for use in significance tests or confidence intervals, whereas $F$ may be much easier to work with—it may be already tabulated or easily computed. Of course, using $F$ to approximate $F_T$ is valid only for "sufficiently large $T$," and we often do not know how large $T$ must be; nevertheless, in practice it is often necessary to work with approximations. (We devote considerable attention to the "exact" distributions, the $F_T$, for common econometric estimators in Chapters 10 and 11.)

As the next theorem indicates, it may be possible to find a limiting distribution by finding the limit of the characteristic function. (These are discussed in detail in Appendix C.)

**Theorem 1.1.8**

Let $\phi_T(t)$ be the characteristic function of $F_T$. If $X_T \xrightarrow{d} X$, then $\lim_{T\to\infty} \phi_T(t) = \phi(t)$ where $\phi(t)$ is the c.f. of $F$, and $F$ is the distribution function of $X$. Conversely, if $\lim_{T\to\infty} \phi_T(t) = \phi(t)$ and $\phi(t)$ is continuous at $t = 0$, then $X_T \xrightarrow{d} X$ where $\phi(t)$ is the c.f. of $X$.

**Proof**

Rao (1973, p. 119). □

Except for the condition on continuity at 0, this theorem states that $X_T \xrightarrow{d} X$ if and only if the c.f. of $X_T$ converges to the c.f. of $X$ as $T \to \infty$. This theorem is useful because in many cases it is rather easy to determine $\lim_{T\to\infty} \phi_T(t) = \phi(t)$, which either is recognized to be the c.f. of a known distribution function or can be inverted to determine the corresponding $F(t)$. The proof of the central limit theorem presented below exploits this fact.

**Theorem 1.1.9**

If $X_T \xrightarrow{p} X$ then $X_T \xrightarrow{d} X$. That is, convergence in probability implies convergence in distribution.

**Proof**

The random variable $Z$ introduced in this proof is the random variable to which $X_T$ converges in probability. Consider the sets $\{\omega\colon X_T(\omega) \le x\} = [\{\omega\colon X_T(\omega) \le x$ and

[6]In such cases, the estimator is usually denoted by a "hat" over the symbol for the parameter to be estimated—for example, $\hat{\beta}$ or $\hat{\theta}$—and the dependence on sample size is often not explicitly stated.

$Z(\omega) \leq x_2\} \cup \{\omega\colon X_T(\omega) \leq x$ and $Z(\omega) > x_2\}] \subset [\{\omega\colon Z(\omega) \leq x_2\} \cup \{X_T(\omega) \leq x$ and $Z(\omega) > x_2\}]$.

Therefore, $F_T(x) \leq F(x_2) + P[X_T(\omega) \leq x$ and $Z(\omega) > x_2]$. Since this inequality holds for all $T$, it holds for the least upper bound (sup) achieved by $F_T(x)$, that is, sup $F_T(x)$. Accordingly, sup $F_T(x) \leq F(x_2) + P[X_T(\omega) \leq x$ and $Z(\omega) > x_2]$. For the bracketed event, $-X_T(\omega) \geq -x$ and $Z(\omega) > x_2$, so $Z(\omega) - X_T(\omega) > x_2 - x$. If $x_2 - x > 0$, then $Z(\omega) - X_T(\omega) > x_2 - x > 0$, so that $P[X_T(\omega) \leqslant x$ and $Z(\omega) > x_2]$ is no greater than $P[|X_T(\omega) - Z(\omega)| > x_2 - x]$. But this probability goes to 0 as $T \to \infty$. Therefore, we have the following inequality:

$$\limsup F_T(x) \leq F(x_2).$$

By starting with the set

$$\{\omega\colon Z(\omega) \leq x\} = \{\omega\colon Z(\omega) \leq x \quad \text{and} \quad X_T(\omega) \leq x_1\}$$
$$\cup\ \{\omega\colon Z(\omega) \leq x \quad \text{and} \quad X_T(\omega) > x_1\},$$

for $x_1 < x$ we can obtain $F(x_1) \leq \liminf F_T(x)$, where inf is the greatest lower bound. Therefore

$$F(x_1) \leq \liminf F_T(x) \leq \limsup F_T(x) \leq F(x_2).$$

As $x_1$ and $x_2$ approach $x$, assumed to be a continuity point of $F$, it follows that $\lim F_T(x) = F(x)$. □

The converse is not true; convergence in distribution does not, in general, imply convergence in probability. To show this we present an example. (Conditions under which the converse is true appear in the theorem that follows the example.)

**Example**

Let $X_T \sim N(0, 1 + 1/T)$ and $X \sim N(0, 1)$, where $X_T$ and $X$ are independently distributed. (Note carefully that $X_t$ and $X$ are assumed to be *independent*.) Clearly, as $T \to \infty$, $X_T \xrightarrow{d} X$: $X_T$ is normally distributed with zero expected value and variance $1 + 1/T$, which is very close to a random variable with zero expected value and unit variance, especially for large $T$. Accordingly, $X_T$ and $X$ have almost the same distribution function. However, $X_T$ does not converge in probability to $X$. Since $X_T$ and $X$ are independent, there is no reason for a drawing from $X_T$ to be close to a drawing from $X$, even if $T$ is large. Even for very large $T$, this entails drawing values from two independent $N(0, 1)$ variables. The distribution of $X_T - X$ is $N(0, 2 + 1/T)$; neglecting $1/T$, which can be made arbitrarily small, $X_T - X$ is approximately $N(0, 2)$. Therefore,

$$P[|X_T - X| > 2] \approx .32,$$

and since this is true for all $T$, $\lim P\{|X_T - X| > 2\} \approx .32$, implying that $X_T$ does not converge in probability to $X$.

Somewhat loosely, we might say that if $X_T \xrightarrow{p} X$, $X_T$ and $X$ are (approximately) the same r.v. and would be expected to have (approximately) the same distribution function. But r.v.'s that are quite different may nevertheless have the same distribution function.

**Theorem 1.1.10**

$X_T \xrightarrow{d} k$ (a constant) if and only if $X_T \xrightarrow{p} k$.

**Proof**

Because of the previous theorem we need only show that $X_T \xrightarrow{d} k$ implies $X_T \xrightarrow{p} k$. In this case, the distribution function takes the form of a degenerate distribution at $k$:

$$F(x) = \begin{cases} 0 & x < k \\ 1 & x \geq k. \end{cases}$$

Since $X_T \xrightarrow{d} k$,

$$\lim_{T \to \infty} F_T(x) = \begin{cases} 0 & x < k \\ 1 & x \geq k. \end{cases}$$

To show convergence in probability of $X_T$ to $k$ we write, for $\epsilon > 0$,

$$\begin{aligned} P[|X_T - k| < \epsilon] &= P[k - \epsilon < X_T < k + \epsilon] \\ &= P[k - \epsilon < X_T \leq k + \epsilon] - P[X_T = k + \epsilon] \\ &= P[X_T \leq k + \epsilon] - P[X_T \leq k - \epsilon] - P[X_T = k + \epsilon] \\ &= F_T(k + \epsilon) - F_T(k - \epsilon) - P[X_T = k + \epsilon]. \end{aligned}$$

If we take limits on both sides we have

$$\begin{aligned} \lim_T P[|X_T - k| < \epsilon] &= \lim_T F_T(k + \epsilon) - \lim_T F_T(k - \epsilon) - \lim_T P[X_T = k + \epsilon] \\ &= 1 - 0 - 0. \\ &= 1. \end{aligned}$$

□

**Theorem 1.1.11**

If $g$ is a continuous function and $X_T \xrightarrow{d} X$, then $g(X_T) \xrightarrow{d} g(X)$.

**Proof**

See Rao (1973, p. 119). □

The next several theorems, proved in Rao (1973, pp. 119–125), involve mixtures of convergence in probability and convergence in distribution.

**Theorem 1.1.12**

If $|X_T - Y_T| \xrightarrow{p} 0$ and $Y_T \xrightarrow{d} Y$, then $X_T \xrightarrow{d} Y$.

**Theorem 1.1.13**

a. If $X_T \xrightarrow{d} X$ and $Y_T \xrightarrow{p} 0$, then $X_T Y_T \xrightarrow{p} 0$.
b. If $X_T \xrightarrow{d} X$ and $Y_T \xrightarrow{p} C$ (a constant), then
   i. $X_T + Y_T \xrightarrow{d} X + C$ and
   ii. $X_T Y_T \xrightarrow{d} CX$ and
   iii. $X_T / Y_T \xrightarrow{d} X/C$ $(C \neq 0)$.
c. If $X_T \xrightarrow{d} X$ and $Y_T \xrightarrow{p} C$, then the limit of the joint distribution of $(X_T, Y_T)$ exists and equals that of $(X, C)$.

A corollary of this theorem is often useful for finding the limiting distribution of a function of a random variable which has a known limiting distribution.

**Corollary**

Suppose that $\alpha_T$ is a sequence of nonstochastic real numbers tending to $\infty$, $\theta$ is a fixed number, and $\alpha_T(Z_T - \theta) \xrightarrow{d} X$. Let $g$ be a function that possesses at least two continuous derivatives. Then

$$\alpha_T[g(Z_T) - g(\theta)] \xrightarrow{d} g'(\theta)X.$$

**Proof [Bickel and Doksum (1977)]**

First, note that $Z_T \xrightarrow{p} \theta$ because $Z_T - \theta = 1/\alpha_T[\alpha_T(Z_T - \theta)] \xrightarrow{d} 0 \cdot X = 0$, and convergence in distribution to a constant implies convergence in probability. We next apply the mean value theorem to $g(Z_T)$ at $\theta$:

$$g(Z_T) = g(\theta) + g'(\theta)(Z_T - \theta) + \tfrac{1}{2}g''(\theta^*)(Z_T - \theta)^2,$$

where $\theta^*$ is between $Z_T$ and $\theta$. Therefore

$$\begin{aligned}\alpha_T[g(Z_T) - g(\theta)] &= \alpha_T(Z_T - \theta)g'(\theta) + \frac{1}{2}g''(\theta^*)\alpha_T(Z_T - \theta)^2 \\ &= \alpha_T(Z_T - \theta)g'(\theta) + \frac{1}{2}\frac{g''(\theta^*)}{\alpha_T}\alpha^2(Z_T - \theta)^2.\end{aligned}$$

Since $\alpha_T(Z_T - \theta) \xrightarrow{d} X$, by Theorem 1.1.11, $\alpha^2(Z_T - \theta)^2 \xrightarrow{d} X^2$. Moreover, since $\theta^*$ is between $Z_T$ and $\theta$, $\theta^* \xrightarrow{p} \theta$ because $Z_T \xrightarrow{p} \theta$. Finally, $(1/\alpha_T)g''(\theta^*) \xrightarrow{p} 0$, since $\alpha_T \to \infty$. The right-hand side thus converges in distribution to $g'(\theta)X$. □

**TABLE 1.1 Exact and Approximate Values of $P[X_T < K]$**

| $K$ | $P[X_\infty < K]$ | $P[X_1 < K]$ | $P[X_{10} < K]$ | $P[X_{30} < K]$ |
|---|---|---|---|---|
| .1 | .54 | .53 | .54 | .54 |
| .5 | .69 | .64 | .64 | .69 |
| 1.0 | .84 | .76 | .83 | .84 |
| 2.0 | .98 | .92 | .97 | .98 |

An important use of this theorem is in finding the asymptotic distribution of a function of an estimator whose asymptotic distribution is known. For example, let $\hat{\beta}_T$ be an estimator of $\beta$ based on sample size $T$ and suppose it is known that $\sqrt{T}(\hat{\beta}_T - \beta) \xrightarrow{d} N(0, \sigma^2_{\hat{\beta}})$. If we let $\hat{\beta}_T$ play the role of $Z_T$, $\beta$ the role of $\theta$, and $\sqrt{T}$ the role of $\alpha_T$, we can easily find the asymptotic distribution of a function of $\hat{\beta}_T$. For example, if we were interested in the distribution of $\hat{\beta}^2_T$ we would have $\sqrt{T}[\hat{\beta}^2_T - \beta^2] \xrightarrow{d} N[0, 4\beta^2\sigma^2_{\hat{\beta}}]$.

An important application of convergence in distribution is to use the limiting (or asymptotic) distribution as an approximation to $F_T(x)$ for finite $T$. The quality of the approximation depends on the size of $T$ and the form of $F_T$. Before turning to central limit theorems and other methods of approximating distributions, we close this section with two examples of convergence in distribution as an approximation technique.

**Example**

Let $X_T \sim N(0, 1 + 1/T)$ and $X \sim N(0, 1)$ where $X$ is independent of $X_T$ for all $T$. We can use the distribution of $X$ to approximate the distribution of $X_T$. In Table 1.1 we compare the approximated probabilities ($T = \infty$) for different values of $T$.

**Example**

Let $X$ have the $F$-distribution with $k$ and $n$ degrees of freedom, which will be denoted by $F(k, n)$. Consider the limiting distribution of $X$ as $n \to \infty$ with $k$ fixed. Since $X \sim F(k, n)$, it can be written as $n\chi^2_k/k\chi^2_n$, where $\chi^2_k$ and $\chi^2_n$ are independent $\chi^2$ variates with $k$ and $n$ degrees of freedom, respectively. As $n \to \infty$, it can be shown that $\chi^2_n/n \xrightarrow{p} 1$. Applying the above theroem we have that as $n \to \infty$, $F(k, n) \xrightarrow{d} \chi^2_k$. Accordingly, $\chi^2_k/k$ can be used to approximate $F(k, n)$ for large $n$. Table 1.2 contains the 5% critical values for various $n$ and $k = 5$; the approximating value from the $\chi^2_5$ distribution is 2.21.

**TABLE 1.2 5% Critical Values for $F(5, n)$**

| $n$ | Critical Value |
|---|---|
| 10 | 3.33 |
| 20 | 2.71 |
| 30 | 2.53 |
| 60 | 2.37 |
| 120 | 2.29 |
| $\infty$ | 2.21 |

### 1.1.5 Summary: Logical Relations Between Convergence Concepts

Convergence to a Random Variable ($X$)

$$\boxed{X_T \xrightarrow{\text{a.s.}} X} \;\rightarrow\; \boxed{X_T \xrightarrow{\text{p}} X} \;\rightarrow\; \boxed{X_T \xrightarrow{\text{d}} X}$$

$$\uparrow$$

$$\boxed{X_T \xrightarrow{\text{q.m.}} X}$$

Convergence to a Constant ($k$)

$$\boxed{X_T \xrightarrow{\text{a.s.}} k} \;\rightarrow\; \boxed{X_T \xrightarrow{\text{p}} k} \;\leftrightarrow\; \boxed{X_T \xrightarrow{\text{d}} k}$$

$$\uparrow$$

$$\boxed{X_T \xrightarrow{\text{q.m.}} k}$$

## 1.2 Central Limit Theorems

Central limit theorems (CLT's) are concerned with a special case of convergence in distribution: random variables of the form

$$\frac{1}{b_T} \sum_{k=1}^{T} (X_k - a_k)$$

($a_k$, $b_T$ nonstochastic, $X_k$ random) that converge in distribution to $N(0, 1)$.

**Example**

It is shown in introductory mathematical statistics courses that if $X_k \sim b(\theta, T)$ and

$$Y_T = \frac{\sum^{T} (X_k - \theta)}{\sqrt{T\theta(1 - \theta)}},$$

then $Y_T \xrightarrow{\text{d}} Y \sim N(0, 1)$, where $b(\theta, T)$ denotes a binomial distribution with probability of success $\theta$ and $T$ trials. In this example, $b_T = \sqrt{T\theta(1 - \theta)}$ and $a_k = \theta$.

We prove a special case of the central limit theorem and then state and discuss more general conditions.

**Theorem 1.2.1**

Let $\{X_T\}$ be a sequence of i.i.d. r.v.'s with $E(X_T) = \mu$ and $\mathrm{Var}(X_T) = \sigma^2$. Then $\sqrt{T}(\bar{X}_T - \mu) \xrightarrow{d} N(0, \sigma^2)$.

**Proof**

The proof will make use of characteristic functions (see Appendix C). Note that the nature of the distribution of the $X_T$'s is unspecified; this fact is what makes the CLT extremely general and useful.

Let $Y_T = \sqrt{T}(X_t - \mu)$; then $\bar{Y}_T = \sqrt{T}(\bar{X}_T - \mu)$.

$$\begin{aligned}
\phi_{\bar{Y}}(s) &= \phi_{\sqrt{T}(\bar{X} - \mu)}(s) \\
&= E[\exp\{is\sqrt{T}(\bar{X} - \mu)\}] \\
&= E\left[\exp\left\{is\sqrt{T}\,\frac{\Sigma(X_t - \mu)}{T}\right\}\right] \\
&= \left[E\left(\exp\left\{i\left(\frac{s}{\sqrt{T}}\right)(X_t - \mu)\right\}\right)\right]^T \\
&= \left[\phi_{X-\mu}\left(\frac{s}{\sqrt{T}}\right)\right]^T.
\end{aligned}$$

Using the second order approximation to the characteristic function, we obtain

$$\begin{aligned}
[\phi_{\bar{Y}}(s)]^T &= \left[1 + \frac{i \cdot 0 \cdot s}{\sqrt{T}} - \frac{\sigma^2 s^2}{2T} + o\left(\frac{s^2}{T}\right)\right]^T \\
&= \left[1 - \frac{\sigma^2 s^2}{2T} + o\left(\frac{s^2}{T}\right)\right]^T,
\end{aligned}$$

which may be expanded by the binomial theorem to

$$\left(1 - \frac{\sigma^2 s^2}{2T}\right)^T + \sum_{t=1}^{T} \binom{T}{t}\left(1 - \frac{\sigma^2 s^2}{2T}\right)^{T-t}\left[o\left(\frac{s^2}{T}\right)\right]^t.$$

Taking limits as $T \to \infty$, the first term approaches $e^{-s^2\sigma^2/2}$, and each term of the summation goes to zero since $\binom{T}{t}(1 - (\sigma^2 s^2)/2T)^{T-t}$ is less than $T^t$ and $[o(s^2/T)]^t$ is $o(s^{2t}/T^t)$. Hence, $\phi_{\bar{Y}}(s) \to e^{-s^2\sigma^2/2}$, which is the c.f. of a $N(0, \sigma^2)$ variable. □

We now present a theorem that weakens the assumption of identical distributions by allowing the variances of the r.v.'s to be different.

**Theorem 1.2.2**

Let $\{X_T\}$ be a sequence of independently distributed r.v.'s with $E(X_T) = \mu$ and $\mathrm{Var}(X_t) = \sigma_t^2$ and let the third moments exist. Then

$$\sqrt{T}(\bar{X}_T - \mu) \xrightarrow{d} N(0, \bar{\sigma}^2),$$

where

$$\bar{\sigma}^2 = \lim \frac{1}{T} \sum_{t=1}^{T} \sigma_t^2.$$

**Proof**

The proof parallels the proof of Theorem 1.2.1. Following the same logic and using the same notation as in that proof, we can write

$$\begin{aligned} \phi_{\bar{Y}}(s) &= \prod_{t=1}^{T} \left[ E\left( \exp\left\{ i\left(\frac{s}{\sqrt{T}}\right)(X_t - \mu) \right\} \right) \right] \\ &= \prod_{t=1}^{T} \phi_{X_t - \mu}\left(\frac{s}{\sqrt{T}}\right). \end{aligned}$$

Using a second order approximation, $\phi_{\bar{Y}}$ can be approximated as

$$\phi_{\bar{Y}}(s) = \prod_{t=1}^{T} \left[ 1 - \frac{\sigma_t^2 s^2}{2T} + o\left(\frac{s^2}{T}\right) \right],$$

and, after a further approximation,

$$\log \phi_{\bar{Y}}(s) = -\sum_{t=1}^{T} \frac{\sigma_t^2 s^2}{2T} + o\left(\frac{s^2}{T}\right),$$

so that for large $T$ the characteristic function of $\bar{Y}$ is that of a normal distribution with variance $\Sigma_{t=1}^{T} (\sigma_t^2)/T$. □

From the above two theorems it is obvious that several versions of "central limit" theorems exist. Minimal conditions for convergence to a normal distribution are contained in the Lindeberg-Feller theorem, which provides necessary and sufficient conditions for application of the CLT.

**Theorem 1.2.3 (Lindeberg-Feller)**

Let $X_k$ be a sequence of mutually independent random variables having finite means and variances, and let $a_k$ be a sequence of constants. A necessary and sufficient condition that

$$\frac{1}{b_T} \sum_{k=1}^{T} (X_k - a_k)$$

converge in distribution to $N(0, 1)$ is that, for any $t > 0$,

$$\lim \frac{1}{b^2} \sum_{k=1}^{T} \int_{|x-a_k|>tb} (x - a_k)^2 f_k(x)dx = 0, \tag{1.2.1}$$

where $f_k(x)$ is the density function of $X_k$ and $b^2 = \text{Var}(\Sigma X_k)$.

**Proof**

See Gnedenko (1973, chapter 8). □

Intuitively, this condition requires that none of the individual terms in the sequence $(1/b_T)(X_k - a_k)$ be very important. To see this, consider the set

$$A_k = \{\omega: |X_k(\omega) - a_k| > tb_T\}, \qquad k = 1, \ldots, T.$$

It is easy to see that

$$\{\omega: \max[|X_1(\omega) - a_1| > tb_T, |X_2(\omega) - a_2| > tb_T, \ldots, |X_T(\omega) - a| > tb_T]\} = A_1 \cup A_2 \cup \cdots A_T. \quad \textbf{(1.2.2)}$$

[If $\omega$ is contained in the left-hand side of (1.2.2) then at least one of $|X_i(\omega) - a_i| > tb_T$, which means it is in the right-hand side; and if $\omega$ is in the right-hand side, for at least one $i$, $|X_i(\omega) - a_i| > tb_T$.]
Therefore,

$$P[\max_{1\le k\le T} \{|X_k - a_k|\} > tb_T] = P[A_1 \cup A_2 \cup \cdots A_T] \le \sum_{k=1}^{T} P[A_k],$$

and

$$P[A_k] = \int_{|x-a_k|>tb_T} dF_k(x) \le \frac{1}{(tb_T)^2} \sum \int_{|x-a_k|>tb_T} (x - a_k)^2 f_k(x)\, dx,$$

and the latter sum tends to zero by the condition. Accordingly, for each $k$, $P[A_k] \to 0$, which limits the probability of large values of $(1/b_T)(X_k - a_k)$.

An example of the use of the Lindeberg-Feller theorem is next examined.

**Example**

Let each $X_k$ be independent and uniformly distributed,

$$f(X_k) = \begin{cases} \dfrac{1}{2c_k}, & -c_k < X_k < c_k \\ 0, & \text{otherwise,} \end{cases}$$

where the $c_k$ are bounded. Let $b_T^2 = \operatorname{Var}(\Sigma^T X_k) = \frac{1}{3} \Sigma^T c_k^2$, and assume that $b_T^2 \to \infty$ as $T \to \infty$. We show that the conditions of the theorem are satisfied for the variable $Y_T = \Sigma^T X_k/b_T$ (with $a_k = 0$). It is easy to verify that

$$\int_{|x|>tb_T} x^2 f_k(x)\, dx = \frac{1}{2c_k} \int_{|x|>tb_T} x^2\, dx$$

$$= \begin{cases} \dfrac{1}{3c_k}, (c_k^3 - t^3 b_T^3), & tb_T < c_k \\ 0, & tb_T \geqslant c_k. \end{cases}$$

For any $t > 0$, we can choose $T$ (the sample size) such that $tb_T \geqslant \sup c_k$ (because the $c_k$'s are bounded and $b_T \to \infty$). Then each of $\int_{|x|>tb_T} x^2 f_k(x)\, dx$ equals zero; hence,

$$\sum_{k=1}^{T} \int x^2 f_k(x)\, dx = 0,$$

and condition (1.2.1) follows. It is remarkable that even the normalized sum of uniformly distributed variables—which are individually far from being normally distributed—may nevertheless tend to normality.

Multivariate versions of Theorems 1.2.1, 1.2.2, and 1.2.3 exist. As an example we present a multivariate version of (1.2.1):

**Theorem 1.2.4**

If $\{\mathbf{X}_T\}$ is a sequence of i.i.d. random vectors of dimension $p \times 1$, with $E(\mathbf{X}_T) = \boldsymbol{\mu}$ and $\text{Cov}(\mathbf{X}_T) = \Sigma$, then $\sqrt{T}(\overline{\mathbf{X}}_T - \boldsymbol{\mu}) \xrightarrow{d} N_p(\mathbf{0}, \Sigma)$, where $N_p(\mathbf{0}, \Sigma)$ denotes the $p$-dimensional multivariate normal with mean $\mathbf{0}$ and covariance matrix $\Sigma$.

To show the usefulness of these theorems we present an example of convergence of regression coefficients to a normal distribution. Let

$$y_t = \alpha + \beta_1 X_{1t} + \beta_2 X_{2t} + \cdots + \beta_k X_{kt} + \epsilon_t, \qquad t = 1, \ldots, T, \qquad \textbf{(1.2.3)}$$

where we assume that

$$\epsilon_t \sim \text{i.i.d. } (0, \sigma^2)$$

and

$$\lim_{T\to\infty} \frac{1}{\text{T}} X_T' X_T = Q.$$

Equation 1.2.3 can be rewritten in matrix form as

$$\mathbf{y}_T = X_T \beta + \boldsymbol{\epsilon}_T, \qquad \textbf{(1.2.4)}$$

where $\mathbf{y}_T$ and $\boldsymbol{\epsilon}_T$ are $T \times 1$ vectors, $\boldsymbol{\beta}$, a $k \times 1$ vector, and $X_T$, a $T \times k$ matrix. The ordinary least squares estimate of $\boldsymbol{\beta}$ is

$$\begin{aligned}\hat{\boldsymbol{\beta}}_T &= (X' X_T)^{-1} X' \mathbf{y}_T \\ &= \boldsymbol{\beta} + (X' X_T)^{-1} X' \boldsymbol{\epsilon}_T,\end{aligned}$$

or

$$\hat{\boldsymbol{\beta}}_T - \boldsymbol{\beta} = (X' X_T)^{-1} X' \boldsymbol{\epsilon}_T,$$

which upon multiplication by $\sqrt{T}$ becomes

$$\sqrt{T}(\hat{\boldsymbol{\beta}}_T - \boldsymbol{\beta}) = \left(\frac{1}{T} X' X_T\right)^{-1} \frac{1}{\sqrt{T}} X' \boldsymbol{\epsilon}_T. \qquad \textbf{(1.2.5)}$$

We now examine the second term on the right-hand side of (1.2.5). It may be written as

$$\begin{bmatrix} \frac{1}{\sqrt{T}} \sum_{t=1}^{T} X_{1t}\epsilon_t \\ \frac{1}{\sqrt{T}} \sum_{t=1}^{T} X_{2t}\epsilon_t \\ \cdot \\ \cdot \\ \cdot \\ \frac{1}{\sqrt{T}} \sum_{t=1}^{T} X_{kt}\epsilon_t . \end{bmatrix} \tag{1.2.6}$$

It is easily seen that the expected value of each term in (1.2.6) is zero and that

$$\begin{aligned} E\left[\left(\frac{1}{\sqrt{T}} X_T'\epsilon_T\right)\left(\frac{1}{\sqrt{T}} X_T'\epsilon_T\right)'\right] &= \frac{1}{T} E[X_T'\epsilon_T \, \epsilon_T' X_T] \\ &= \sigma^2 \frac{1}{T}(X_T'X_T). \end{aligned}$$

Hence we can apply the multivariate version of Theorem 1.2.1 to obtain

$$\frac{1}{\sqrt{T}} X_T'\epsilon_T \xrightarrow{d} N(\mathbf{0}, \sigma^2 Q). \tag{1.2.7}$$

But from (1.2.5), using (1.2.7) and the fact that $((1/T)X_T'X_T)^{-1} \rightarrow Q^{-1}$, we have that

$$\sqrt{T}(\hat{\boldsymbol{\beta}}_T - \boldsymbol{\beta}) \xrightarrow{d} Q^{-1} \cdot N(\mathbf{0}, \sigma^2 Q),$$

or

$$\sqrt{T}(\hat{\boldsymbol{\beta}}_T - \boldsymbol{\beta}) \xrightarrow{d} N(\mathbf{0}, \sigma^2 Q^{-1}).$$

This is a powerful result for the linear model because it provides distributional results and allows statistical tests to be made on weak assumptions. (Note that this result yields estimates of the regression coefficients that are normally distributed for large $T$. For the coefficients divided by their standard errors to have a $t$-distribution, $\epsilon$ must be normally distributed.)

## 1.3 Maximum Likelihood Estimation

The method of maximum likelihood is a general method for finding estimators for parameters. While the method of maximum likelihood has many desirable features, perhaps its most desirable feature is its appeal to intuition. Maximum likelihood estimators find the parameters that are "most likely to have generated the observed data" given the distribution function.

For example, suppose that a coin tossed three times yields two heads and one tail. The probability of two heads and one tail occurring, given that the probability of a head is .5, is .375. If the probability of a head is .75, the probability of observing two heads and one tail is .422. The probability of observing two heads and one tail, given that the probability of a head is .667, is .444. In fact, the probability of a head equal to .667 maximizes the probability of drawing two heads and one tail. This can be seen as follows:

$$P[3 \text{ heads}] = 3p \cdot p \cdot (1 - p).$$

Differentiating and setting the first derivative to 0 yields

$$3(2p - 3p^2) = 0; \qquad \text{hence} \quad p = \tfrac{2}{3}.$$

The second derivative is

$$6 - 6p,$$

which is negative for $0 \leq p < 1$; the function therefore achieves a maximum at $p = \frac{2}{3}$. We emphasize that $p = \frac{2}{3}$ maximizes the probability that the observed outcome (two heads and one tail) occurs, *given that the distribution is binomial*.

For random variables that are discretely distributed (e.g., the coin-tossing example), we can choose our estimators to be those values that maximize the probability that the observed data are observed, but for a continuous distribution the probability of each point is zero. Instead we maximize the likelihood—that is, we pick those parameters that yield the maximum value of the density function for the observed data. For example, suppose we observe a number, $x^*$, from $N(\mu, \sigma^2)$ with $\sigma^2$ known and $\mu$ unknown. Then the maximum likelihood estimate of $\mu$ is $x^*$ because $\mu = x^*$ maximizes the height of the density function at $x^*$. This can be shown by writing the normal distribution function, evaluated at $x^*$:

$$f(x^*; \mu, \sigma^2) = \frac{1}{\sqrt{2\pi\sigma^2}} \exp\left\{-\frac{1}{2}(x^* - \mu)^2\right\}.$$

Obviously, setting $\mu = x^*$ maximizes the value of the density function evaluated at $x^*$.

If we know the density function we can find and use as estimates those parameter values that maximize the value of the density function evaluated at the observed data values. Such estimators are referred to as maximum likelihood estimators, and they have many desirable properties. We next discuss several of these properties and prove some important results. [Norden (1972, 1973) is an excellent detailed survery of the method of maximum likelihood. See also Hogg and Craig (1978) and Cox and Hinkley (1974) for further discussion and examples.]

### 1.3.1 The Likelihood Function

We formally define the likelihood function as the joint density evaluated at a set of observations.

#### Definition

Let $x_1, \ldots, x_n$ be realizations of the i.i.d. random variable $X$ and let

$$L(\theta; x_1, x_2, \ldots, x_n) = \prod_{i=1}^{n} f(x_i; \theta),$$

where $f(X, \theta)$ is the density function of $X$, and $\theta$ is a parameter. $L(\cdot)$ is called the *likelihood function;* it is regarded as a function of $\theta$ for a given set of observations.

It is often easier to work with the logarithm of the likelihood function—an increasing function of $L$—and we use the notation

$$l = \log(L).$$

Since the logarithm function is monotonic and has a nonzero first derivative, the value of $\theta$ that maximizes the likelihood function also maximizes the logarithm of the likelihood function.

**Definition**

Let $\Omega$ be the parameter space. A *maximum likelihood estimator* of $\theta$ is a $\hat{\theta} \in \Omega$ for which, for all $\tilde{\theta} \in \Omega$,

$$L(\hat{\theta}; x_1, x_2, \ldots, x_n) \geqslant L(\tilde{\theta}; x_1, x_2, \ldots, x_n);$$

equivalently,

$$l(\hat{\theta}; x_1, x_2, \ldots, x_n) \geqslant l(\tilde{\theta}; x_1, x_2, \ldots, x_n).$$

**Definition**

Let $l(\theta; x_1, x_2, \ldots, x_n)$ be the log of the likelihood function. The equation

$$\frac{\partial}{\partial\theta} l(\theta; x_1, x_2, \ldots, x_n) = 0$$

is called the *likelihood equation.*

Because it is often necessary to work with the likelihood function or the log of the likelihood function evaluated at the maximum likelihood estimate, we use the notation

$$\hat{L} = L(\hat{\theta}; x_1, x_2, \ldots, x_n)$$

and

$$\hat{l} = \log(\hat{L}),$$

where $\hat{\theta}$ is the maximum likelihood estimator.

It should be noted that a solution of the likelihood equation does not necessarily maximize the likelihood function. The solution may yield a minimum or saddle point, or the maximum may occur at a boundary of the admissible values of $\theta$. An example is discussed below.

For many statistical results concerning maximum likelihood estimators we need to put mathematical conditions on the density function of the random variables. These are referred to as *regularity conditions*. Following Norden, the regularity conditions for the density function $f(x; \theta)$ are:

**Regularity Conditions 1.3.1–1.3.3**

For almost all $x$, $\dfrac{\partial \log f}{\partial \theta}, \dfrac{\partial^2 \log f}{\partial \theta^2}$, and $\dfrac{\partial^3 \log f}{\partial \theta^3}$ exist for every $\theta \in \Theta$. **(1.3.1)**

For all $\theta \in \Theta$, $\left|\dfrac{\partial f}{\partial \theta}\right| < F_1(x)$, $\left|\dfrac{\partial^2 f}{\partial \theta^2}\right| < F_2(x)$, and $\left|\dfrac{\partial^3 \log f}{\partial \theta^3}\right| < H(x)$, the functions $F_1$ and $F_2$ being integrable over $(-\infty, \infty)$ and $\int_{-\infty}^{\infty} H(x) f(x, \theta)\, dx < M$, where $M$ does not depend on $\theta$. **(1.3.2)**

For all $\theta \in \Theta$, the integral $\int_{-\infty}^{\infty} (\partial \log f/\partial\theta)^2 f\, dx$ is finite and positive. **(1.3.3)**

Serfling (1980, p. 145) explains the role of these assumptions in proofs of the consistency and asymptotic normality of MLE's. Briefly, the first ensures the existence of a Taylor expansion, the second permits differentiation under an integral, and the third states that the r.v. $\partial \log f/\partial\theta$ has a finite variance.

In the multivariate case, we would write the likelihood function as

$$L(\boldsymbol{\theta}; \mathbf{x}_1, \ldots, \mathbf{x}_N) = \prod_{j=1}^{N} f(\mathbf{x}_j; \boldsymbol{\theta}),$$

where $\boldsymbol{\theta}$ is a vector of parameters and $\mathbf{x}_j$ is a vector of the $j$th observation. All the results of this chapter hold for the multivariate case if the assumptions are appropriately changed. We present two examples of multivariate processes below.

We next present several examples that show how maximum likelihood estimates can be obtained; the first example is the exponential distribution. The distribution function is

$$f(x) = \alpha e^{-\alpha x};$$

the likelihood function can be written as

$$L = \prod_{i=1}^{N} \alpha e^{-\alpha x_i};$$

and the log likelihood function is

$$l = \sum_{i=1}^{N} [\log(\alpha) - \alpha x_i]$$

$$= N \log(\alpha) - \alpha \sum_{i=1}^{N} x_i.$$

The likelihood equation is

$$\frac{N}{\alpha} - \sum_{i=1}^{N} x_i = 0,$$

leading to the estimate

$$\hat{\alpha} = \frac{N}{\Sigma x_i}.$$

To show that this yields a maximum, we examine the second derivative of the likelihood function:

$$\frac{\partial^2 l}{\partial \alpha^2} = -\frac{N}{\alpha^2} < 0.$$

Our second example involves finding estimates of the mean and variance from the normal distribution. The distribution function is

$$f(x) = \frac{1}{\sqrt{2\pi\sigma^2}} \exp\left\{ -\frac{1}{2}\frac{(x-\mu)^2}{\sigma^2} \right\}.$$

The likelihood equation can be written as

$$L[\mu, \sigma^2; x_1, \ldots, x_N] = (2\pi\sigma^2)^{-N/2} \exp\left\{ -\frac{1}{2}\sum_{i=1}^{N}\frac{(x_i-\mu)^2}{\sigma^2} \right\},$$

and the log likelihood function as

$$l(\mu, \sigma^2; x_1, \ldots, x_N) = -\frac{N}{2}\log(2\pi) - \frac{N}{2}\log\sigma^2 - \frac{1}{2}\sum_{i=1}^{N}\frac{(x_i-\mu)^2}{\sigma^2}.$$

The likelihood equations are

$$\frac{\partial l}{\partial \mu} = \sum_{i=1}^{N}\frac{(x_i-\hat{\mu})}{\hat{\sigma}^2} = 0,$$

$$\frac{\partial l}{\partial \sigma^2} = -\frac{N}{2}\frac{1}{\hat{\sigma}^2} + \frac{1}{2}\sum_{i=1}^{N}\frac{(x_i-\hat{\mu})^2}{(\hat{\sigma}^2)^2} = 0.$$

These imply that

$$\hat{\mu} = \frac{1}{N}\sum_{i=1}^{N} x_i \quad \text{and} \quad \hat{\sigma}^2 = \frac{1}{N}\sum_{i=1}^{N}(x_i-\hat{\mu})^2.$$

The reader should verify that these values of $\hat{\mu}$ and $\hat{\sigma}$ maximize the likelihood.

The next example is a standard problem in econometrics—the errors in variables problem. It is interesting because it demonstrates how to set up the likelihood function for a general problem and is a case in which the first order conditions are not sufficient for a maximum. Indeed, the likelihood function fails to attain a maximum for any choice of parameters.

Let

$$Z_t = X_t + u_t$$
$$Y_t = \alpha + \beta X_t + \epsilon_t$$
$$u_t \sim N(0, \sigma_u^2)$$
$$\epsilon_t \sim N(0, \sigma_\epsilon^2),$$

where $u$ and $\epsilon$ are independent and where $X_t$ is unobservable. We can write the joint density of $(u_1, u_2, \ldots, u_T; \epsilon_1, \epsilon_2, \ldots, \epsilon_T)$ as

$$f(u_1, \ldots, u_T; \epsilon_1, \ldots, \epsilon_T; \sigma_u^2, \sigma_\epsilon^2)$$
$$= \left(\frac{1}{2\pi\sigma_u^2}\right)^{T/2} \exp\left\{-\frac{\sum_{t=1}^{T} u_t^2}{2\sigma_u^2}\right\}\left(\frac{1}{2\pi\sigma_\epsilon^2}\right)^{T/2} \exp\left\{-\frac{\sum_{t=1}^{T} \epsilon_t^2}{2\sigma_\epsilon^2}\right\}.$$

Transforming variables from $u$ and $\epsilon$ to $Y$ and $X$, the joint density may be written as

$$f(Y_1, \ldots, Y_T, X_1, \ldots, X_T; \alpha, \beta, \sigma_u^2, \sigma_\epsilon^2, Z_1, \ldots, Z_T)$$
$$= \left(\frac{1}{2\pi\sigma_u^2}\right)^{T/2} \exp\left\{-\frac{\sum_{t=1}^{T} (Z_t - X_t)^2}{2\sigma_u^2}\right\} \times \left(\frac{1}{2\pi\sigma_\epsilon^2}\right)^{T/2} \exp\left\{-\sum_{t=1}^{T} \frac{(Y_t - \alpha - \beta X_t)^2}{2\sigma_\epsilon^2}\right\}.$$

Conditional upon observed $Y$ and $Z$ values, $y$ and $z$, the log likelihood function is

$$l(X_1, \ldots, X_T, \sigma_\mu^2, \sigma_\epsilon^2, \alpha, \beta; y_1, \ldots, y_T, z_1, \ldots, z_T) = -T \log(2\pi)$$
$$-\frac{T}{2} \log \sigma_u^2 - \frac{T}{2} \log \sigma_\epsilon^2 - \frac{1}{2\sigma_u^2} \sum_{t=1}^{T} (z_t - X_t)^2 - \frac{1}{2\sigma_\epsilon^2} \sum_{t=1}^{T} (y_t - \alpha - \beta X_t)^2.$$

Taking derivatives of $l$ yields

$$\frac{\partial l}{\partial X_t} = \frac{z_t - X_t}{\sigma_u^2} + \frac{\beta}{\sigma_\epsilon^2}(y_t - \alpha - \beta X_t) \qquad (t = 1, \ldots, T), \tag{1.3.1}$$

$$\frac{\partial l}{\partial \alpha} = \sum_{t=1}^{T} \frac{(y_t - \alpha - \beta X_t)}{\sigma_\epsilon^2}, \tag{1.3.2}$$

$$\frac{\partial l}{\partial \beta} = \sum_{t=1}^{T} \frac{X_t(y_t - \alpha - \beta X_t)}{\sigma_\epsilon^2}, \tag{1.3.3}$$

$$\frac{\partial l}{\partial \sigma_u^2} = -\frac{T}{2\sigma_u^2} + \frac{1}{2\sigma_u^4} \sum_{t=1}^{T} (z_t - X_t)^2, \tag{1.3.4}$$

and

$$\frac{\partial l}{\partial \sigma_\epsilon^2} = -\frac{T}{2\sigma_\epsilon^2} + \frac{1}{2\sigma_\epsilon^4} \sum_{t=1}^{T} (y_t - \alpha - \beta X_t)^2. \tag{1.3.5}$$

Setting these derivatives to zero and solving yields solutions that appear to be maximum likelihood estimators (denoted by ^):

$$\hat{\sigma}_u^2 = \frac{1}{T}\sum_{t=1}^{T}(z_t - \hat{X}_t)^2 \tag{1.3.6}$$

and

$$\hat{\sigma}_\epsilon^2 = \frac{1}{T}\sum_{t=1}^{T}(y_t - \hat{\alpha} - \hat{\beta}X_t)^2. \tag{1.3.7}$$

Setting (1.3.1) to zero, summing, and squaring yields

$$\hat{\beta}^2 \frac{\sum_{t=1}^{T}(y_t - \hat{\alpha} - \hat{\beta}\hat{X}_t)^2}{\hat{\sigma}_\epsilon^4} = \sum_{t=1}^{T}\frac{(z_t - \hat{X}_t)^2}{\hat{\sigma}_\mu^4}, \tag{1.3.8}$$

which, upon substitution of (1.3.6) and (1.3.7), yields

$$\hat{\beta}^2 = \frac{\hat{\sigma}_\epsilon^2}{\hat{\sigma}_u^2}.$$

Hence our estimate of $\beta^2$ is the ratio of the estimated variances. But as we show below, under regularity conditions, MLE's are consistent; this would seem to imply

$$\beta^2 = \frac{\sigma_\epsilon^2}{\sigma_\mu^2}, \tag{1.3.9}$$

but there is no reason to believe that (1.3.9) is true in general. The explanation is that the estimators derived from (1.3.1)–(1.3.5) do not yield a maximum of the likelihood function. Rather, they yield a saddle point, as is shown by Solari (1969).

### 1.3.2 Small Sample Maximum Likelihood Estimation

In this section we briefly review some of the statistical theory concerning maximum likelihood estimation. The presentation is nonrigorous and incomplete. Although maximum likelihood estimators have certain optimality properties to be discussed below, they need not be unbiased. As was shown above, the MLE of the variance of a $N(0, \sigma^2)$ variable is

$$\hat{\sigma}_T^2 = \frac{1}{T}\sum_{t=1}^{T}(X_t - \overline{X}_T)^2,$$

but

$$E[\hat{\sigma}_T^2] = \frac{T-1}{T}\sigma^2.$$

Accordingly, $\hat{\sigma}^2$ is a biased estimator of $\sigma^2$, but in this case a simple transformation of $\hat{\sigma}^2$ yields an unbiased estimate.

Statisticians often make use of *sufficient statistics*.[7] One reason is that if (under appropriate regularity conditions) an unbiased estimator exists that is not a function of the sufficient statistic, it is always possible to use the estimator and the sufficient statistic to obtain an unbiased estimator with a variance that is no larger than the variance of the original estimator. This result, the Rao-Blackwell theorem, guarantees that a minimum variance unbiased estimator is a function of the sufficient statistic, if a sufficient statistic exists. Many desirable properties of estimators based on sufficient statistics also hold for MLE's because of the following result: If a sufficient statistic for an estimator exists, and if a maximum likelihood estimator exists, then the MLE is a function of the sufficient statistic.[8]

We now state a remarkable result that places a lower bound on the variance of an unbiased estimator.

**Theorem 1.3.1 (Cramer-Rao)**

Let $x_1, x_2, \ldots, x_T$ denote a random sample from a distribution with density function $f(x; \theta)$. Then, under certain regularity conditions, for any unbiased estimator of $\theta$ based on $T$ observations, say $\hat{\theta}_T$,

$$E[(\hat{\theta}_T - \theta)^2] \geq \frac{1}{TE\left[\frac{\partial \log f(x, \theta)}{\partial \theta}\right]^2}.$$

This theorem puts a lower bound, referred to as the Cramer-Rao lower bound (CRLB), on the variance of all unbiased estimators.[9] An unbiased estimator of $\theta$ is *efficient* if it attains the Cramer-Rao lower bound, and the *efficiency* of an unbiased statistic is defined as the ratio of its variance to the CRLB.

If an unbiased estimator attains the CRLB, then it can be shown that it is a function of the sufficient statistic. Furthermore, it can be shown [Norden (1972, p. 342)] that, under the appropriate regularity conditions, if there is an estimator that attains the CRLB, it can be expressed as a function of the maximum likelihood estimator.

### 1.3.3 Large Sample Maximum Likelihood Estimation

Under regularity conditions 1.3.1–1.3.3, it can be shown that maximum likelihood estimators are both consistent and asymptotically normally distributed. These are remarkable results in light of the minimal assumptions necessary. We state the theorem on consistency, due to Cramer (1946), and provide a sketch of the theorem on asymptotic normality.[10] Both theorems are presented for scalar random variables but hold for vectors as well.

[7]A sufficient statistic for $\theta$ is a statistic that uses all the information about $\theta$ in the sample. That is, there is no information in the sample that can improve upon the estimate of $\theta$ given by the sufficient statistic. Sufficient statistics are discussed in detail in Hogg and Craig (1978).

[8]See Hogg and Craig (1978, p. 347) for a proof.

[9]This lower bound is sometimes referred to as the minimum variance bound.

[10]Complete proofs of both theorems may be found in Serfling (1980, section 4.2.2). Consistency under a different set of regularity conditions was proved by Wald (1949); a detailed proof of the Wald theorem is in Dudewicz (1976, section 8.3).

**Theorem 1.3.2 (Cramer)**

Under conditions 1.3.1–1.3.3, the solution to $[\partial L(\theta; x)]/\partial\theta = 0$ is a consistent estimator of $\theta$.

To sketch a proof of the asymptotic normality of maximum likelihood estimators we need the following lemma.

**Lemma 1.3.1**

Let $x_1, x_2, \ldots, x_T$ be a random sample from a population characterized by a density function obeying regularity conditions 1.3.1–1.3.3. Then

$$E\left[\frac{\partial \log L}{\partial\theta}\right] = \int_{-\infty}^{\infty} \cdots \int_{-\infty}^{\infty} \left(\frac{\partial \log L}{\partial\theta}\right) f(x_1), \ldots, f(x_T)\, dx_1, \ldots, dx_T = 0$$

and

$$E\left[\left(\frac{\partial \log L}{\partial\theta}\right)^2\right] = -E\left[\frac{\partial^2 \log L}{\partial\theta^2}\right].$$

**Proof**

Denoting $(x_1, x_2, \ldots, x_T)$ by $\mathbf{x}$,

$$L(\theta; \mathbf{x}) = \prod_{i=1}^{T} f(x_i; \theta).$$

Then

$$\log L(\theta; \mathbf{x}) = \sum_{i=1}^{T} \log\,[f(x_i; \theta)]$$

and

$$\frac{\partial \log L(\theta; \mathbf{x})}{\partial\theta} = \sum_{i=1}^{T} \frac{f'(x_i; \theta)}{f(x_i; \theta)}.$$

We can thus write

$$\begin{aligned}
E\left(\frac{\partial \log L}{\partial\theta}\right) &= E\left[\sum_{i=1}^{T} \frac{f'(x_i; \theta)}{f(x_i; \theta)}\right] \\
&= \int_{-\infty}^{\infty} \sum_{i=1}^{T} \frac{f'(x_i; \theta)}{f(x_i; \theta)} \prod_{j=1}^{T} f(x_j; \theta)\, dx_j \\
&= \sum_{i=1}^{T} \int_{-\infty}^{\infty} \frac{f'(x_i; \theta)}{f(x_i; \theta)} \prod_{j=1}^{T} f(x_j; \theta)\, dx_j \\
&= \sum_{i=1}^{T} \prod_{\substack{j=1 \\ i\neq j}}^{T} \int f(x_j; \theta)\, dx_j \cdot \int_{-\infty}^{\infty} f'(x_i; \theta)\, dx_i \\
&= \sum_{i=1}^{T} \int_{-\infty}^{\infty} f'(x_i; \theta)\, dx_i.
\end{aligned}$$

But each of these terms is equal to zero because from

$$\int_{-\infty}^{\infty} f(x_i; \theta)\, dx_i = 1$$

we obtain

$$\int_{-\infty}^{\infty} \frac{\partial f(x_i; \theta)}{\partial \theta}\, dx_i = \frac{\partial}{\partial \theta} \int_{-\infty}^{\infty} f(x_i; \theta)\, dx_i = 0.$$

Thus

$$E\left[\frac{\partial \log L}{\partial \theta}\right] = 0.$$

To prove the second part of the lemma, start from

$$\int_{-\infty}^{\infty} \frac{\partial \log L}{\partial \theta} \Pi f(x_i; \theta)\, dx_i = 0$$

and differentiate with respect to $\theta$. This gives

$$\int_{-\infty}^{\infty} \frac{\partial^2 \log L}{\partial \theta^2} \Pi f(x_i; \theta)\, dx_i + \int_{-\infty}^{\infty} \frac{\partial \log L}{\partial \theta} \frac{\partial}{\partial \theta} \Pi f(x_i; \theta)\, dx_i = 0,$$

which may be rewritten as

$$\begin{aligned} -E\left[\frac{\partial^2 \log L}{\partial \theta^2}\right] &= \int_{-\infty}^{\infty} \frac{\partial \log L}{\partial \theta} \frac{\partial L}{\partial \theta} \Pi\, dx_i \\ &= \int_{-\infty}^{\infty} \frac{\partial \log L}{\partial \theta} \frac{\partial L}{\partial \theta} \frac{1}{L} \Pi f(x_i; \theta)\, dx_i \\ &= \int_{-\infty}^{\infty} \left(\frac{\partial \log L}{\partial \theta}\right)^2 \Pi f(x_i; \theta)\, dx_i \\ &= E\left(\frac{\partial \log L}{\partial \theta}\right)^2. \end{aligned}$$

□

**Theorem 1.3.3**

Assume regularity conditions 1.3.1–1.3.3. Then

$$\sqrt{T}(\hat{\theta} - \theta) \xrightarrow{d} N[0, M(\theta)^{-1}],$$

where

$$M(\theta) = \left[-E\left(\frac{\partial^2 \log L}{\partial \theta^2}\right)\right].$$

**Proof**

We begin by taking a Taylor series expansion of the first derivative of the log likelihood function.

$$\frac{\partial l(\hat{\theta}; \mathbf{x})}{\partial \theta} = \frac{\partial l(\theta; \mathbf{x})}{\partial \theta} + \frac{\partial^2 l(\theta; \mathbf{x})}{\partial \theta^2} (\hat{\theta} - \theta) + \frac{1}{2} \frac{\partial^3 l(\theta^*; \mathbf{x})}{\partial \theta^3} (\hat{\theta} - \theta)^2, \qquad \textbf{(1.3.10)}$$

where $\theta^*$ is between $\theta$ and $\hat{\theta}$. Note that it is a first derivative that is being expanded in terms of $\hat{\theta}$ about $\theta$ and that the third term is the remainder term.

Upon manipulation and multiplication by $\sqrt{T}$,

$$\sqrt{T}(\hat{\theta} - \theta) = \left[\frac{1}{T}\frac{\partial^2 l(\theta; \mathbf{x})}{\partial\theta^2}\right]^{-1}\left[\frac{1}{\sqrt{T}}\frac{\partial l(\hat{\theta}; \mathbf{x})}{\partial\theta} - \frac{1}{\sqrt{T}}\frac{\partial l(\theta; \mathbf{x})}{\partial\theta} - \frac{1}{2\sqrt{T}}\frac{\partial^3 l(\theta^*; \mathbf{x})}{\partial\theta^3}(\hat{\theta} - \theta)^2\right]. \tag{1.3.11}$$

We shall examine each term in the above equation. First,

$$\frac{1}{T}\frac{\partial^2 l(\theta; \mathbf{x})}{\partial\theta^2} = \left(\frac{1}{T}\right)\frac{\partial^2}{\partial\theta^2}\log\prod_{i=1}^{T} f(x_i; \theta)$$
$$= \frac{1}{T}\sum_{i=1}^{T}\frac{\partial^2}{\partial\theta^2}\log f(x_i; \theta).$$

Upon setting $Y_i = (\partial^2/\partial\theta^2)\log f(x_i; \theta)$, it can be seen that the $Y_i$ are independent random variables and that

$$\begin{aligned}
E[Y_i] &= \int_{-\infty}^{\infty}\left(\frac{\partial^2}{\partial\theta^2}\log f(x_i; \theta)\right) f(x_i; \theta)\, dx_i \\
&= \int_{-\infty}^{\infty}\left(\frac{\partial}{\partial\theta}\frac{f'(x_i; \theta)}{f(x_i)}\right) f(x_i; \theta)\, dx_i \\
&= \int_{-\infty}^{\infty}\left(\frac{f''(x_i; \theta)}{f(x_i; \theta)} - \left[\frac{f'(x_i; \theta)}{f(x_i; \theta)}\right]^2\right) f(x_i; \theta)\, dx_i \\
&= \int_{-\infty}^{\infty} f''(x_i; \theta)\, dx_i - \int_{-\infty}^{\infty}\left[\frac{f'(x_i; \theta)}{f(x_i, \theta)}\right]^2 f(x_i; \theta)\, dx_i \\
&= -E\left(\left[\frac{\partial}{\partial\theta}\log f(x_i; \theta)\right]^2\right).
\end{aligned}$$

Thus, the $Y_i$ are independent with identical means, and we can apply the strong law of large numbers to obtain

$$\operatorname{plim}\left(\frac{1}{T}\right)\frac{\partial^2 l(\theta; \mathbf{x})}{\partial\theta^2} = \operatorname{plim}\frac{1}{T}\sum_{i=1}^{T} Y_i = -E\left[\frac{\partial}{\partial\theta}\log f(x_i; \theta)\right]^2. \tag{1.3.12}$$

The next term,

$$\frac{1}{\sqrt{T}}\frac{\partial l(\hat{\theta}; \mathbf{x})}{\partial\theta},$$

is equal to zero because $\hat{\theta}$ is assumed to be a solution of the likelihood equation.

For the expression

$$\frac{1}{\sqrt{T}}\frac{\partial l(\theta; \mathbf{x})}{\partial\theta},$$

let

$$Z_i = \frac{f'(x_i; \theta)}{f(x_i; \theta)};$$

then we have

$$\frac{1}{\sqrt{T}} \frac{\partial l(\theta; \mathbf{x})}{\partial \theta} = \frac{1}{\sqrt{T}} \sum_{i=1}^{T} \frac{\partial}{\partial \theta} \log f(x_i; \theta) = \frac{1}{\sqrt{T}} \sum_{i=1}^{T} Z_i.$$

It was previously shown that $E(Z_i) = 0$ and by the definition of $Z_i$,

$$E(Z_i^2) = E\left[\left[\frac{\partial}{\partial \theta} \log f(x_i; \theta)\right]^2\right].$$

Hence, the sum

$$\frac{1}{\sqrt{T}} \sum_{i=1}^{T} Z_i$$

is a sum of independent r.v.'s with zero means and identical constant variances. We can thus apply Theorem 1.2.1, a central limit theorem, to obtain

$$\frac{1}{\sqrt{T}} \frac{\partial l(\theta; \mathbf{x})}{\partial \theta} = \frac{1}{\sqrt{T}} \sum_{i=1}^{T} Z_i \xrightarrow{d} N\left[0, E\left\{\left(\frac{\partial}{\partial \theta} \log f(x; \theta)\right)^2\right\}\right].$$

We can now examine the final term in (1.3.11),

$$\frac{1}{2\sqrt{T}} \frac{\partial^3 l(\theta^*; \mathbf{x})}{\partial \theta^3} (\hat{\theta} - \theta)^2.$$

By the regularity condition 1.3.1 we have that $\partial^3 l(\theta^*; x)/\partial \theta^3$ is bounded by a constant, and by Theorem 1.3.2 we have $\hat{\theta} \xrightarrow{p} \theta$; therefore, this term converges in probability to zero.

We rewrite (1.3.11) and summarize what has been shown.

$$\begin{array}{ccccccc} \sqrt{T}(\hat{\theta} - \theta) = & \left[\dfrac{1}{T} \dfrac{\partial^2 l(\theta; \mathbf{x})}{\partial \theta^2}\right]^{-1} & \Bigg[\dfrac{1}{\sqrt{T}} \dfrac{\partial l(\hat{\theta}; \mathbf{x})}{\partial \theta} & - & \dfrac{1}{\sqrt{T}} \dfrac{\partial l(\theta; \mathbf{x})}{\partial \theta} & - & \dfrac{1}{2\sqrt{T}} \dfrac{\partial^3 l(\theta^*; \mathbf{x})}{\partial \theta^3} (\hat{\theta} - \theta)^2\Bigg]. \\ & \downarrow p & \| & & \downarrow d & & \downarrow p \\ & -M(\theta)^{-1} & 0 & & N[0, M(\theta)] & & 0 \end{array}$$

Finally, using Theorems 1.1.5 and 1.1.13b.ii, we have

$$\sqrt{T}(\hat{\theta} - \theta) \xrightarrow{d} -M(\theta)^{-1} \cdot N[0, M(\theta)],$$

or

$$\sqrt{T}(\hat{\theta} - \theta) \xrightarrow{d} N[0, M(\theta)^{-1}].$$

□

This result immediately generalizes to the multivariate case. Let $\boldsymbol{\theta}$ and $\hat{\boldsymbol{\theta}}$ be $k \times 1$ vectors of parameters and estimators, respectively, let $\mathbf{x}_1, \mathbf{x}_2, \ldots, \mathbf{x}_T$ be $p \times 1$ vectors of observations, and let the regularity conditions be understood to pertain to vectors. We can then write the following theorem, the proof of which is similar to the proof for the scalar case.

**Theorem 1.3.4**

Under multivariate versions of regularity conditions 1.3.1–1.3.3,

$$\hat{\boldsymbol{\theta}} \xrightarrow{P} \boldsymbol{\theta}$$

and

$$\sqrt{T}(\hat{\boldsymbol{\theta}} - \boldsymbol{\theta}) \xrightarrow{d} N[\mathbf{0}, I(\boldsymbol{\theta})^{-1}],$$

where $I(\boldsymbol{\theta}) = \left\{-E\left[\frac{\partial^2}{\partial\theta_i\,\partial\theta_j} l(\boldsymbol{\theta}; \mathbf{x}_1, \mathbf{x}_2, \ldots, \mathbf{x}_T)\right]\right\}.$

The matrix I($\boldsymbol{\theta}$) is called the *information matrix,* which is easier to understand when written out in detail:

$$I(\boldsymbol{\theta}) = -E\begin{bmatrix} \frac{\partial^2 l(\boldsymbol{\theta})}{\partial\theta_1^2} & \frac{\partial^2 l(\boldsymbol{\theta})}{\partial\theta_1\,\partial\theta_2} & \cdots & \frac{\partial^2 l(\boldsymbol{\theta})}{\partial\theta_1\,\partial\theta_k} \\ \vdots & \ddots & & \vdots \\ \frac{\partial^2 l(\boldsymbol{\theta})}{\partial\theta_k\,\partial\theta_1} & \cdots & \cdots & \frac{\partial^2 l(\boldsymbol{\theta})}{\partial\theta_k^2} \end{bmatrix}. \qquad \textbf{(1.3.13)}$$

Thus, each element of $-I(\boldsymbol{\theta})$ is the expected value of a second partial or cross-partial derivative of the log-likelihood function with respect to the parameters. Theorem 1.3.4 states that $I(\boldsymbol{\theta})^{-1}$ is the covariance matrix of the limiting normal distribution.

### 1.3.4 Examples

As an example of the usefulness of Theorem 1.3.3 let us examine parameter estimation for the exponential distribution discussed in Section 1.3.1:

$$f(X; \theta) = \alpha e^{-\alpha X}.$$

Application of Theorem 1.3.3 shows that asymptotically,

$$\sqrt{T}(\hat{\alpha} - \alpha) \xrightarrow{d} N[0, \alpha^2].$$

Note the power of Theorem 1.3.3—regardless of the original distribution, the maximum likelihood estimator converges to a normally distributed random variable.

At the risk of mentioning an obvious point we should point out that the asymptotic normality result pertains to an estimator whose form depends on the original distribution. That is, the MLE *derived from the initial distribution* is asymptotically normally distributed. But we cannot in general utilize a MLE from one distribution for some other distribution and claim asymptotic normality. For example,

$$\hat{\sigma}_T^2 = \left(\frac{1}{T}\right)\sum_{t=1}^{T}(x_t - \bar{x}_T)^2$$

is the MLE of the variance for several distributions, but is not always a MLE.

To illustrate the multivariate version of the theorem, we present an example of estimation of a second order, autoregressive process where the errors are normally distributed. Let $y_t = \phi_1 y_{t-1} + \phi_2 y_{t-2} + a_t$, where $a_t \sim N(0, \sigma^2)$. For simplicity we will assume that $y_0$ and $y_{-1}$ are nonstochastic and known. We can then write the likelihood function as

$$L(\phi_1, \phi_2, \sigma^2) = f(y_1, \ldots, y_T; \sigma^2, \phi_1, \phi_2, y_0, y_{-1})$$
$$= \left(\frac{1}{\sqrt{2\pi}}\right)^T (\sigma^2)^{-T/2} \exp\left\{\left(-\frac{1}{2\sigma^2}\right) \sum_{t=1}^{T} (y_t - \phi_1 y_{t-1} - \phi_2 y_{t-2})^2\right\}$$

and

$$l = -\frac{T}{2}\ln(2\pi) - \frac{T}{2}\ln(\sigma^2) - \frac{1}{2\sigma^2}\sum_{t=1}^{T}(y_t - \phi_1 y_{t-1} - \phi_2 y_{t-2})^2.$$

The first order conditions for a maximum are

$$\frac{\partial l}{\partial \phi_1} = -\frac{1}{\sigma^2}\sum_{t=1}^{T}(-y_{t-1})(y_t - \phi_1 y_{t-1} - \phi_2 y_{t-2}) = 0,$$

$$\frac{\partial l}{\partial \phi_2} = -\frac{1}{\sigma^2}\sum_{t=1}^{T}(-y_{t-2})(y_t - \phi_1 y_{t-1} - \phi_2 y_{t-2}) = 0,$$

and

$$\frac{\partial l}{\partial \sigma^2} = \frac{-T}{2\sigma^2} + \frac{1}{2\sigma^4}\sum_{t=1}^{T}(y_t - \phi_1 y_{t-1} - \phi_2 y_{t-2})^2 = 0,$$

which yield the following estimators:

$$\begin{bmatrix}\hat{\phi}_1 \\ \hat{\phi}_2\end{bmatrix} = \begin{bmatrix}\Sigma y_{t-1}^2 & \Sigma y_{t-1}y_{t-2} \\ \Sigma y_{t-1}y_{t-2} & \Sigma y_{t-2}^2\end{bmatrix}^{-1} \begin{bmatrix}\Sigma y_{t-1}y_t \\ \Sigma y_{t-2}y_t\end{bmatrix}$$

and

$$\hat{\sigma}^2 = \frac{1}{T}\sum_{t=1}^{T}(y_t - \hat{\phi}_1 y_{t-1} - \hat{\phi}_2 y_{t-2})^2.$$

Estimates of the variances are based on the information matrix 1.3.7. We introduce the notation $\gamma_0 \equiv E[y_t^2]$ and $\gamma_1 \equiv E[y_t y_{t-1}]$. From

$$\frac{\partial^2 l}{\partial \phi_1^2} = -\sum_{t=1}^{T} y_{t-1}^2,$$

we have

$$-E\left[\frac{\partial^2 l}{\partial \phi_1^2}\right] = TE[y_{t-1}^2]$$
$$= TE[y_t^2]$$
$$= T\gamma_0,$$

which supplies the 1, 1 element for the information matrix. For the 1, 2 and 2, 1 elements we examine

$$\frac{\partial^2 l}{\partial \phi_1 \, \partial \phi_2} = -\sum_{t=1}^{T} y_{t-1} y_{t-2}.$$

Taking expectations yields

$$-E \frac{\partial^2 l}{\partial \phi_1 \, \partial \phi_2} = TE[y_t y_{t-1}] = T\gamma_1.$$

For the 1, 3 and 3, 1 elements we have

$$\frac{\partial_2 l}{\partial \phi_1 \, \partial \sigma^2} = -\frac{1}{\sigma^4} \sum_{t=1}^{T} y_{t-1}(y_t - \phi_1 y_{t-1} - \phi_2 y_{t-2}) = -\frac{1}{\sigma^4} \sum_{t=1}^{T} y_{t-1} a_t,$$

and taking expectations yields

$$-E\left[\frac{\partial^2 l}{\partial \phi_1 \, \partial \sigma^2}\right] = 0.$$

The 2, 3 and 3, 2 elements are also zero. By a similar procedure the 2, 2 element can be found to be

$$-E\left[\frac{\partial^2 l}{(\partial \phi_2)^2}\right] = T\gamma_0.$$

For the 3, 3 element of the information matrix we have

$$\frac{\partial^2 l}{\partial (\sigma^2)^2} = \frac{T}{2\sigma^4} - \frac{\Sigma a_t^2}{\sigma^6}$$

and

$$-E\left[\frac{\partial^2 l}{(\partial \sigma^2)^2}\right] = -\frac{T}{2\sigma^4} + \frac{T\sigma^2}{\sigma^6} = \frac{T}{2\sigma^4}.$$

This yields the information matrix

$$I(\boldsymbol{\theta}) = -E\begin{bmatrix} \dfrac{\partial^2 l}{\partial \phi_1^2} & \dfrac{\partial^2 l}{\partial \phi_1 \, \partial \phi_2} & \dfrac{\partial^2 l}{\partial \phi_1 \, \partial \sigma^2} \\ \cdots & \dfrac{\partial^2 l}{\partial \phi_2^2} & \dfrac{\partial^2 l}{\partial \phi_2 \, \partial \sigma^2} \\ \cdots & \cdots & \dfrac{\partial^2 l}{(\partial \sigma^2)^2} \end{bmatrix}$$

$$= \begin{bmatrix} T\gamma_0 & T\gamma_1 & 0 \\ T\gamma_1 & T\gamma_0 & 0 \\ 0 & 0 & \dfrac{1}{2}\dfrac{T}{\sigma^4} \end{bmatrix}$$

$$= T \begin{bmatrix} \gamma_0 & \gamma_1 & 0 \\ \gamma_1 & \gamma_0 & 0 \\ 0 & 0 & \dfrac{1}{2\sigma^4} \end{bmatrix}$$

and

$$I(\boldsymbol{\theta})^{-1} = \frac{1}{T} \begin{bmatrix} \dfrac{\gamma_0}{\gamma_0^2 - \gamma_1^2} & \dfrac{-\gamma_1}{\gamma_0^2 - \gamma_1^2} & 0 \\ \dfrac{-\gamma_1}{\gamma_0^2 - \gamma_1^2} & \dfrac{\gamma_0}{\gamma_0^2 - \gamma_1^2} & 0 \\ 0 & 0 & 2\sigma^4 \end{bmatrix},$$

which is the asymptotic variance-covariance matrix for the estimators. To complete this we note

$$\gamma_0 = E[y_t^2] = \frac{(1 - \phi_2)\sigma^2}{(1 - \phi_2)(1 - \phi_1^2 - \phi_2^2) - 2\phi_1^2\phi_2}$$

and

$$\gamma_1 = E[y_t y_{t-1}] = \frac{\phi_1\sigma^2}{(1 - \phi_2)(1 - \phi_1^2 - \phi_2^2) - 2\phi_1^2\phi_2}.$$

To use these formulae to estimate the variance-covariance matrix, we must assign numerical values to the parameters we are estimating. Since we do not know the true parameter values, the information matrix is evaluated at the estimated parameter values—in this case at $\hat{\phi}_1$, $\hat{\phi}_2$, and $\hat{\sigma}^2$. These estimators are consistent; therefore, evaluating the information matrix at the maximum likelihood estimates yields consistent estimates of the variance-covariance matrix. (In practice, most computer programs calculate the information matrix numerically and provide the variance-covariance matrix evaluated at the estimated parameter values.)

### 1.3.5 MLE and the Cramer-Rao Lower Bound

As remarkable as Theorem 1.3.3 is—that the MLE, under the appropriate regularity conditions, converges in distribution to a normally distributed random variable—the MLE has an even more remarkable property: the covariance matrix of the normal distribution to which the MLE converges is a lower bound for the variances of a class of estimators. As we have seen, this covariance matrix is equal to the inverse of the information matrix. A comparison of Theorems 1.3.2 and 1.3.3 shows that, under the appropriate regularity conditions, the maximum likelihood estimator converges in distribution to a normally distributed random variable that achieves the Cramer-Rao lower bound. The result generalizes immediately to the multivariate case.

### 1.3.6 Asymptotic Efficiency

It is often necessary to compare estimators to determine which estimator is best according to some criterion. This is true with large samples as well as with small samples, but with large samples two special problems arise in defining criteria. We often cannot compare the biases, variances, and so on, of two estimators for each sample size because the inability to find the exact distribution is usually the reason we use an estimator for which large sample properties are known. Second, we cannot compare biases and variances for an infinite sample size because most estimators we are likely to consider have first two moments (at least) that converge to the true parameter values for large $T$. Hence, some other criteria are needed for asymptotic comparisons. Those that have been suggested arise from examining the properties of the limiting distributions of the estimators. We define asymptotic efficiency by restricting ourselves to estimators that are asymptotically normal, that is, for which $\sqrt{T}(\hat{\theta} - \theta) \xrightarrow{d} N[0, \sigma^2]$.

**Definition**

Let $\hat{\theta}$ and $\tilde{\theta}$ be estimators of $\theta$ based on a random sample of size $T$, from a density function $f(x; \theta)$. Then if

$$\sqrt{T}(\hat{\theta} - \theta) \xrightarrow{d} N[0, \sigma^2_{\hat{\theta}}]$$

and

$$\sqrt{T}(\tilde{\theta} - \theta) \xrightarrow{d} N[0, \sigma^2_{\tilde{\theta}}],$$

we say that $\hat{\theta}$ *is asymptotically efficient with respect to* $\tilde{\theta}$ if $\sigma^2_{\tilde{\theta}} \geqslant \sigma^2_{\hat{\theta}}$.

Since the MLE reaches the Cramer-Rao lower bound, it is asymptotically efficient with respect to all estimators of the required form, and we say that the MLE is *asymptotically efficient*. In fact, one way to prove that an estimator is asymptotically efficient is to show that it converges to the MLE. [See Hatanaka (1974) for an example.] The above discussion of asymptotic efficiency generalizes easily from the scalar to vector case if "≥" is replaced with "exceeds by a positive semidefinite matrix."

### 1.3.7 Miscellaneous

The asymptotic distribution can be used to perform the usual statistical tests in much the same way the exact distribution is used. The asymptotic variance-covariance matrix derived from the information matrix can be employed to develop confidence intervals, test for significant differences from zero, and so on. Since the results are not exact distributional results and could be quite misleading in a small sample, the researcher must exercise some judgment in interpreting statistical tests based on large sample approximations.

In this chapter we have examined methods that allow us to approximate the distribution of random variables as the sample size grows large. In the next chapter we consider the relationship between moments of asymptotic distributions and exact moments. In addition, we examine approximations to moments and distributions that hold more generally than those considered above.

## 1.4. References

Bickel, P. J. and K. A. Doksum (1977), *Mathematical Statistics,* San Francisco: Holden-Day.

Cox, D. R. and D. V. Hinkley (1974), *Theoretical Statistics,* London: Chapman and Hall.

Cramer, H. (1946), *Mathematical Methods of Statistics,* Princeton, N.J.: Princeton University Press.

Dhrymes, P. J. (1970), *Econometrics: Statistical Foundations and Applications,* New York: Harper & Row.

Dudewicz, E. J. (1976), *Introduction to Statistics and Probability,* Holt, Rinehart & Winston: New York.

Gnedenko, B. V. (1973), *The Theory of Probability,* Moscow: Mir Publishers.

Hatanaka, M. (1974), "An Efficient Two-Step Estimator for the Dynamic Adjustment Model with Autoregressive Errors," *Journal of Econometrics,* **2,** 199–220.

Hogg, B., and Craig, A. (1978), *Introduction to Mathematical Statistics,* New York: MacMillan.

Kaplan, W. and D. J. Lewis (1971), *Calculus and Linear Algebra,* Vol. II, New York: Wiley.

Lukacs, E. (1968), *Stochastic Convergence,* Lexington, Mass.: D. C. Heath.

Norden, R. H. (1972), "A Survey of Maximum Likelihood Estimation, Part I," *Review of the International Institute of Statistics,* **40,** 329–354.

Norden, R. H. (1973), "A Survey of Maximum Likelihood Estimation, Part II," *Review of the International Institute of Statistics,* **41,** 39–58.

Pfeiffer, P. E. (1978), *Concepts of Probability Theory,* 2nd rev. ed., New York: Dover.

Rao, C. R. (1973), *Linear Statistical Inference and Its Applications,* 2nd ed., New York: Wiley.

Serfling, R. J. (1980), *Approximation Theorems of Mathematical Statistics,* New York: Wiley.

Solari, M. E. (1969), "The 'Maximum Likelihood Solution' of the Problem of Estimating a Linear Functional Relationship," *Journal of the Royal Statistical Society,* Series B, **31,** 372–375.

Theil, H. (1971), *Principles of Econometrics,* New York: Wiley.

Wald, A. (1949), "A Note on the Consistency of Maximum Likelihood Estimates," *Annals of Mathematical Statistics,* **20,** 595–601.

# CHAPTER TWO

# Methods of Approximating Distribution Functions, Density Functions, and Moments

This chapter contains a selection from the large number of techniques that may be used to approximate distribution functions, density functions, and moments, either when the exact distribution is too difficult to derive explicitly or when the exact distribution is known but is too complex to be conveniently analyzed. The approximation techniques discussed in this chapter are illustrated with fairly simple examples; applications to the rather complicated cases that arise in connection with simultaneous equation estimators in econometrics are presented in Chapters 10 and 11.

Some of the approaches to the problem of approximation have been discussed in Chapter 1. For example, it was pointed out that the limiting distribution of a r.v. is often used as an approximation; the widespread use of the normal approximation when conditions of the central limit theorem are met indicates how valuable a tool this is. In addition, the corollary to Theorem 1.1.13 illustrates the use of limiting distributions for the purpose of approximation, this time for a differentiable function of a r.v. with known distribution.

We begin with a section on a mathematical technique—asymptotic expansions—that has many uses in statistics. This is followed by applications of asymptotic expansions to approximate distribution and density functions and then by several methods for approximating moments.

## 2.1 Asymptotic Expansions

### 2.1.1 Introduction

Asymptotic expansions are widely used in various branches of mathematics when it is desired to obtain an approximation to a function, especially in cases where the Taylor series approximations require too many terms before the desired accuracy is attained. This type of approximation has been applied to statistical problems for many years in the form of Edgeworth approximations, which are taken up below, and in more recent years to many of the complicated distribution and density functions that arise in econometrics. Because their use seems likely to grow in the future, it is worthwhile to sketch out the general idea of these expansions and present the main theorems used in working with them before turning to statistical applications.

**Definition**

$\{\phi_n(x)\}$ is an *asymptotic sequence* as $x \to x_0$ if for each $n$, $\phi_{n+1} = o(\phi_n)$ as $x \to x_0$.

By the definition of $o(\phi)$, it may be seen that the definition of an asymptotic sequence requires that

$$\frac{\phi_{n+1}}{\phi_n} \to 0 \quad \text{as} \quad x \to x_0, \qquad \text{for all } n, \tag{2.1.1}$$

in order for $\{\phi_n(x)\}$ to be an asymptotic sequence. This means that all of the terms after the $n$th term are of a smaller order of magnitude than the $n$th term as $x \to x_0$, for each $n$. With this definition, we can define asymptotic expansions:

**Definition**

Suppose

$$f(x) - \sum_{n=0}^{m} a_n\phi_n(x) = o(\phi_m(x)) \tag{2.1.2}$$

for every $m$ as $x \to x_0$. Then $\Sigma_{n=0}^{\infty} a_n\phi_n(x)$ is said to be an *asymptotic expansion* (or *asymptotic approximation*) of $f(x)$ with respect to the asymptotic sequence $\{\phi_n(x)\}$.

The standard notation for an asymptotic expansion is

$$f(x) \sim \sum_{0}^{\infty} a_n\phi_n(x),$$

and this notation is also used when a finite number of terms is contained in the sum in order to approximate $f(x)$:

$$f(x) \sim \sum_{0}^{m} a_n\phi_n(x).$$

Since the definition implies that

$$f(x) - \sum_{0}^{m-1} a_n\phi_n(x) = a_m\phi_m(x) + o(\phi_m(x)), \tag{2.1.3}$$

we see that the difference between $f(x)$ and the sum of the first $m - 1$ terms is of order $O(\phi_m(x))$. From (2.1.3), it can be seen that $a_m$ is given by

$$\lim_{x \to x_0} \frac{f(x) - \sum_{0}^{m-1} a_n\phi_n(x)}{\phi_m(x)} = a_m. \tag{2.1.4}$$

Therefore, if an asymptotic expansion of $f(x)$ exists relative to the asymptotic sequence $\{\phi_n(x)\}$, the coefficients, $a_n$, are unique. It should be noted that a function may have more then one asymptotic expansion, each based on different asymptotic sequences and different sets of coefficients. See Erdelyi (1956, p. 14) for examples.

A special case of the above is contained in the following definition.

**Definition**

As asymptotic expansion of $f(x)$ of the form

$$f(x) \sim a_0 + \frac{a_1}{x} + \frac{a_2}{x^2} + \cdots, \qquad x \to \infty,$$

is called an *asymptotic power series.*

Before proceeding to some examples, it is important to point out that an asymptotic expansion need not converge in the usual sense; that is, it is not necessarily true for an asymptotic expansion, $\Sigma\, a_n \phi_n(x)$, that

$$\lim_{m \to \infty} \left| f(x) - \sum_0^m a_n \phi_n(x) \right| = 0.$$

Note that the test for *convergence* is that, for a given $x$, the difference between $f(x)$ and its representation goes to zero as the number of terms in the approximation goes to infinity. This is not claimed for an *asymptotic expansion*, which requires that the order of magnitude of the approximation error is equal to that of the first omitted term as $x$ tends to $x_0$. Another way of showing the difference is to note that the definition of an asymptotic expansion requires that, for every $m$,

$$\lim_{x \to x_0} \frac{\left| f(x) - \sum_{n=0}^m a_n \phi_n(x) \right|}{\phi_m(x)} = 0.$$

For some functions, the error is reasonably small when $m$ is small, even if it then grows as more terms are included.

In statistical applications, which will be taken up in the following sections, two cases have been examined. Let $F_T(x; \alpha)$ be a distribution function for the r.v. $X_T$, depending on sample size $T$ and a parameter $\alpha$. Asymptotic expansions have been obtained for cases in which $T \to \infty$ and in which $\alpha \to 0$ or $\infty$. It is important to recognize that the $x$ that appears in the definition of asymptotic expansions is not the value of the random variable in statistical applications; in statistical applications, $x$ would be a parameter of the distribution or density function—the sample size or some other parameter. The asymptotic expansion of $F_T(x; \alpha)$, for example, should hold for each $x$, where $x$ is the value of the r.v. [Another type of approximation theory is concerned with large values of the r.v. $x$; it deals with the adequacy of approximation in tail areas by developing "large deviation expansions." See Phillips (1980) for a discussion and further references.]

The main difficulty with the use of asymptotic expansions is finding an appropriate sequence $\{\phi_n(x)\}$. Several general methods and results appear in the literature, but ingenuity is often needed to find an appropriate sequence. In the remainder of this section, we present some basic theorems of asymptotic expansions and show how integration by parts may be used to generate sequences for particular functions. Asymptotic expansions for many important functions are found in Abramowitz and Stegun (1972), and the basic theory is presented in Copson (1965) and Erdelyi (1956).

### 2.1.2 Fundamental Theorems

On the assumption that $f(x) \sim \Sigma a_n/x^n$ and $g(x) \sim \Sigma b_n/x^n$ as $x \to \infty$, the following theorems are proved in Copson (1965, pp. 8–12):

**Theorem 2.1.1**

If $A$ is a constant, $Af(x) \sim \Sigma A a_n/x^n$.

**Theorem 2.1.2**

$f(x) + g(x) \sim \Sigma(a_n + b_n)/x^n$.

**Theorem 2.1.3**

$f(x)g(x) \sim \Sigma c_n/x^n$, where $c_n = a_0 b_n + a_1 b_{n-1} + \cdots + a_n b_0$.

**Theorem 2.1.4**

If $a_0 \neq 0$,

$$\frac{1}{f(x)} \sim \frac{1}{a_0} + \sum \frac{d_n}{x^n}.$$

[The $d_i$ may be found in Copson (1965, p. 9).]

**Theorem 2.1.5**

If $f(x)$ is continuous when $0 < a < x$, then if $a < x$,

$$F(x) = \int_x^\infty \left\{ f(t) - a_0 - \frac{a_1}{t} \right\} dt$$

has the asymptotic power series expansion

$$F(x) \sim \frac{a_2}{x} + \frac{a_3}{2x^2} + \cdots + \frac{a_{n+1}}{nx^n} + \cdots.$$

**Theorem 2.1.6**

If $f(x)$ has a continuous derivative $f'(x)$, and if $f'(x)$ possesses an asymptotic power series expansion as $x \to \infty$,

$$f'(x) \sim -\sum_{2}^{\infty} \frac{(n-1)a_{n-1}}{x^n}.$$

The last two theorems, which deal with derivatives and integrals, are useful for statistical applications because they allow us to move between asymptotic expansions of distribution functions, density functions, and characteristic functions.

### 2.1.3 Asymptotic Expansions of Definite Integrals by the Method of Integration by Parts

In this section we present two examples of the use of integration by parts for finding asymptotic expansions of definite integrals. The example is based on Copson (1965, p. 13). Consider first the function

$$\Gamma(a, x) = \int_x^{\infty} e^{-t} t^{a-1}\, dt, \tag{2.1.5}$$

which is related to the incomplete gamma function,

$$\gamma(a, x) = \int_0^{x} e^{-t} t^{a-1}\, dt.$$

Letting $u = -e^{-t}$, $du = e^{-t}\, dt$, $v = t^{a-1}$, $dv = (a-1)t^{a-2}\, dt$, we have

$$\begin{aligned} \int_x^{\infty} e^{-t} t^{a-1}\, dt &= -e^{-t} t^{a-1}\Big|_x^{\infty} + (a-1)\int_x^{\infty} e^{-t} t^{a-2}\, dt \\ &= e^{-x} x^{a-1} + (a-1)\Gamma(a-1, x). \end{aligned} \tag{2.1.6}$$

Repeating this procedure, we obtain

$$\begin{aligned} \Gamma(a, x) &= e^{-x} x^{a-1} + (a-1)e^{-x} x^{a-2} + \cdots \\ &\quad + (a-1)(a-2)\cdots(a-n+1)e^{-x} x^{a-n} \\ &\quad + (a-1)(a-2)\cdots(a-n)\int_x^{\infty} e^{-t} t^{a-n-1}\, dt \\ &= \sum_{r=1}^{n} \frac{\Gamma(a)}{\Gamma(a-r+1)} e^{-x} x^{a-r} + \frac{\Gamma(a)}{\Gamma(a-n)} \Gamma(a-n, x). \end{aligned} \tag{2.1.7}$$

To show that the first term of (2.1.7) is an asymptotic expansion as $x \to \infty$—note that it is in the form of a power series expansion—consider the order of the final term: for $n > a - 1$,

$$\begin{aligned} \left| \frac{\Gamma(a)}{\Gamma(a-n)} \int_x^{\infty} e^{-t} t^{a-n-1}\, dt \right| &< \left| \frac{\Gamma(a)}{\Gamma(a-n)} x^{a-n-1} \int_x^{\infty} e^{-t}\, dt \right| \\ &= \left| \frac{\Gamma(a)}{\Gamma(a-n)} e^{-x} x^{a-n-1} \right|. \end{aligned} \tag{2.1.8}$$

Thus, the error in stopping at the $n$th term is less than

$$\left| \frac{\Gamma(a)}{\Gamma(a - n)} e^{-x} x^{a-n-1} \right|, \tag{2.1.9}$$

which is the first omitted term. This term is $o(x^{a-n})$ as $x \to \infty$; hence

$$\Gamma(a, x) \sim \sum_{r=1}^{\infty} \frac{\Gamma(a)}{\Gamma(a - r + 1)} e^{-x} x^{a-r}, \qquad \text{as} \quad x \to \infty. \tag{2.1.10}$$

A finite number of terms of the asymptotic expansion may be used to approximate $\Gamma(a, x)$ for large $x$.

As a second example, based on Erdelyi (1956, p. 26), consider

$$f(x) = \int_0^{\infty} \frac{e^{-t}}{1 + xt} \, dt \tag{2.1.11}$$

for $x$ positive and near 0. Repeated use of integration by parts yields

$$f(x) = \sum_{n=0}^{m} (-1)^n n! x^n + (-1)^{m+1}(m + 1)! x^{m+1} \int_0^{\infty} \frac{e^{-t}}{(1 + xt)^{m+2}} \, dt. \tag{2.1.12}$$

For any $x > 0$, the series diverges as $m \to \infty$, but for fixed $m$ the last integral may be shown to be $O(1)$ as $x \to 0$, implying that the remainder term is $o(x^m)$ as $x \to 0$, so that $f(x) \sim \Sigma(-1)^n n! x^n$ as $x \to 0$.

## 2.2 Statistical Applications of Asymptotic Expansions

### 2.2.1 Asymptotic Expansions of Characteristic Functions; Edgeworth Expansions

The approximation methods discussed in this section are based on an asymptotic expansion of the characteristic function. The basic idea is to use the Taylor series expansion of the characteristic function as an asymptotic expansion of the c.f.; the latter is expressed in terms of cumulants (which will be explained), and after further approximations the original c.f. is expressed in terms of the c.f. of another distribution—usually the standard normal—and the cumulants of both distributions. Finally, the inversion theorem that maps the c.f. into its distribution function is applied to yield an approximation to the d.f., which may be differentiated to find an approximation to the density function. This is a rather old technique that has been extensively utilized in recent years for the study of widely used estimators in simultaneous equation models. Applications to these estimators will be found in Chapters 10 and 11; at this point, we discuss the method in general and the particular application studied by Edgeworth. Much of the discussion that follows is based on Wallace (1958); the approximations are also explained in Cramer (1946), Wilks (1962), Kendall and Stuart (1968), Feller (1966), and Phillips (1980).

The Edgeworth expansion is based on the Gram-Charlier series expansion, which expresses the distribution function $F(x)$ in terms of another distribution function (usually the standard normal), $G(x)$, and the derivatives of $G(x)$, $(d^jG(x))/dx^j = G^{(j)}(x)$:

$$F(x) \sim \Sigma c_j G^{(j)}(x). \tag{2.2.1}$$

In many applications the terms in the sum contain powers of $T^{-1/2}$; for the Edgeworth expansion, which will be explained in more detail below, the right-hand side of (2.2.1) is rearranged if necessary to form a sum in powers of $T^{-1/2}$:

$$F(x) \sim \Sigma H_j(x) T^{-j/2}.$$

To explain the Gram-Charlier and Edgeworth series, it is useful to work with *cumulants*.

**Definition**

The $r$th *cumulant* of $F(x)$, $\kappa_r$, is the coefficient of $(it)^r/r!$ in the Taylor series expansion of $\ln \phi_x(t)$, where $\phi_x(t)$ is the characteristic function of $F(x)$.

The cumulants are computed in the following way: From Appendix C, we have

$$\phi_x(t) = 1 + \sum_{j=1}^{k} \frac{(it)^j}{j!} \alpha_j + o(t^k), \qquad \text{as } t \to 0, \tag{2.2.2}$$

where $\alpha_j$ is the $j$th moment of $F(x)$. [Note that this is an asymptotic power series for $\phi_x(t)$.] For small $z$, the Taylor series expansion for $\ln(1 + z)$ is given by

$$\ln(1 + z) = z - \tfrac{1}{2} z^2 + \tfrac{1}{3} z^3 + \cdots. \tag{2.2.3}$$

Applying (2.2.3) to (2.2.2) with $z = \Sigma((it)^j/j!)\alpha_j$, we have

$$\begin{aligned} \ln \phi_x(t) = &\left[\frac{(it)^1}{1!}\alpha_1 + \frac{(it)^2}{2!}\alpha_2 + \cdots\right] \\ &- \frac{1}{2}\left[\frac{(it)^1}{1!}\alpha_1 + \frac{(it)^2}{2!}\alpha_2 + \cdots\right]^2 + \cdots \end{aligned} \tag{2.2.4}$$

It may be seen that the only term in the expansion containing $((it)^1)/1!$ is $\alpha_1((it)^1)/1!$; accordingly, $\alpha_1 = \kappa_1$. To find $\kappa_2$, we need the coefficients of $((it)^2)/2!$, which are

$$\kappa_2 = \alpha_2 - \alpha_1^2.$$

The reader should verify that

$$\kappa_3 = \alpha_3 - 3\alpha_1\alpha_2 + 2\alpha_1^3.$$

Note that $\kappa_r$ is a polynomial of degree $r$ in the $\alpha_j$'s up to and including $\alpha_r$. Additional cumulants may be found in Kendall and Stuart (1963).

The expressions for $\kappa$ may be inverted to express the moments as functions of the cumulants. The first three moments are given by

$$\begin{aligned} \alpha_1 &= \kappa_1 \\ \alpha_2 &= \kappa_2 + \kappa_1^2 \\ \alpha_3 &= \kappa_3 + 3\kappa_1\kappa_2 + \kappa_1^3. \end{aligned}$$

By the definition of cumulants, the c.f. may be expressed as

$$\phi_x(t) = \exp\left\{\Sigma \frac{(it)^j}{j!} \kappa_j\right\}. \tag{2.2.5}$$

We return to the problem of approximating $F(x)$ after stating and proving a lemma that will be needed below:

**Lemma 2.2.1**

Let $\phi(t)$ be the c.f. of $F(x)$, let

$$\phi^{(r)}(t) = \int_{-\infty}^{\infty} e^{itx} \frac{d^{r+1}F(x)}{dx^{r+1}}\, dx, \tag{2.2.6}$$

and assume

$$\frac{d^rF(x)}{dx^r} \to 0 \quad \text{as} \quad x \to \pm\infty, \qquad r = 0, 1, \ldots \tag{2.2.7}$$

Then $(-it)^r\phi(t) = \phi^{(r)}(t)$, or $(-1)^r\phi^{(r)}(t) = (it)^r\phi(t)$. [In this notation, $\phi^{(o)}(t) = \phi_x(t)$.]

**Proof**

Let $u = e^{itx}$ and $v = d^rF(x)/dx^r$. Integrating (2.2.6) by parts, we obtain

$$\int_{-\infty}^{\infty} e^{itx} \frac{d^{r+1}F(x)}{dx^{r+1}}\, dx = e^{itx} \frac{d^rF(x)}{dx^r}\Bigg|_{-\infty}^{\infty} - it\int_{-\infty}^{\infty} e^{itx} \frac{d^rF(x)}{dx^r}\, dx. \tag{2.2.8}$$

(For the purpose of this integration, the imaginary number $i$ may be treated as a constant.) From (2.2.8) it may be seen that $\phi^{(r)}(t) = (-it)\phi^{(r-1)}(t)$. Applying the result $r - 1$ times completes the proof of the lemma. □

To approximate $F(x)$, we introduce a second distribution function, $G(x)$, with c.f. $\psi(t)$ and cumulants $\gamma_j$. From (2.2.5) and the analogous expression for $\psi_x(t)$, we have

$$\phi_x(t) = \exp\left\{\sum(\kappa_j - \gamma_j) \frac{(it)^j}{j!}\right\}\psi_x(t). \tag{2.2.9}$$

Applying the Taylor series expansion for $e^z$,

$$e^z = 1 + z + \frac{1}{2!} z^2 + \cdots,$$

to (2.2.9) with $z = \Sigma(\kappa_j - \gamma_j)[(it)^j/j!]$, we obtain

$$\begin{aligned}\phi_x(t) &= \left\{1 + \Sigma(\kappa_j - \gamma_j)\frac{(it)^j}{j!} + \frac{1}{2}\left[\Sigma(\kappa_j - \gamma_j)\frac{(it)^j}{j!}\right]^2 + \cdots\right\}\psi_x(t)\\ &= \psi_x(t) + \Sigma(\kappa_j - \gamma_j)\frac{(it)^j}{j!}\psi_x(t)\\ &\quad + \frac{1}{2}\left[\Sigma(\kappa_j - \gamma_j)\frac{(it)^j}{j!}\right]^2\psi_x(t) + \cdots\\ &= \psi_x(t) + \Sigma(\kappa_j - \gamma_j)\frac{(-1)^j}{j!}\psi_x^{(j)}(t) + \cdots\end{aligned} \tag{2.2.10}$$

(by Lemma 2.2.1). The inversion theorem (Appendix C) that transforms $\phi_x(t)$ into $F(x)$ transforms $\phi_x^{(j)}(t)$ into $(d^jG(x))/dx^j = D^jG(x)$. After applying the theorem to both sides of (2.2.10), $F(x)$ may be written as

$$\begin{aligned}F(x) &= G(x) + \Sigma(\kappa_j - \gamma_j)\frac{(-1)^j}{j!}D^jG(x) + \cdots\\ &= G(x) + \Sigma(\kappa_j - \gamma_j)\frac{(-D)^j}{j!}G(x) + \cdots\end{aligned} \tag{2.2.11}$$

This representation of $F(x)$ as the sum of terms involving $G(x)$, taken to be the standard normal distribution function, and its derivatives is called a *Gram-Charlier A series*. The reader should verify that the terms in $G(x)$ and its first two derivatives are given by

$$G(x) - (\kappa_1 - \gamma_1)G'(x) + \left[\frac{\kappa_2 - \gamma_2}{2} + (\kappa_1 - \gamma_1)^2\right]G''(x). \tag{2.2.12}$$

Under certain circumstances, the right-hand side of (2.2.11) is an asymptotic expansion of $F(x)$. As an example let

$$X_T = \frac{\sum^T (Y_i - \mu)}{\sqrt{T}\sigma},$$

where $E(Y_i) = \mu$, $\mathrm{Var}(Y_i) = \sigma^2$, and the $Y_i$ are i.i.d. Define

$$\lambda_r' = \frac{\kappa_r'}{\sigma^r}, \qquad r \geq 3, \tag{2.2.13}$$

where $\kappa_r'$ is the $r$th cumulant of the distribution function of $Y_i$, $G(y)$. The distribution function of $X_T$, $F_T(x)$, will be approximated in terms of the standard normal distribution function, $N(x)$, and its derivatives.

To compute the approximation we require the cumulants of $F_T(x)$ and $N(x)$. The latter are easy to obtain: Since the c.f. of $N(x)$ is $e^{-t^2/2} = e^{(it)^2/2}$, $\ln e^{(it)^2/2} = (it)^2/2$, and it follows immediately that $\gamma_1 = 0$, $\gamma_2 = 1$, and $\gamma_r = 0$, $(r > 2)$, where $\gamma_r$ are the cumulants of $N(x)$. The c.f. of $F_T(x)$, $\phi_x(t)$, is derived from that of $G(y)$, $\psi_y(t)$, as follows:

$$\begin{aligned}\phi_x(t) &= E[\exp\{itx\}]\\ &= E\left[\exp\left\{it\,\frac{\Sigma(Y_i-\mu)}{\sqrt{T}\sigma}\right\}\right]\\ &= E\left[\exp\left\{i\left(\frac{t}{\sqrt{T}\sigma}\right)\Sigma(Y_i-\mu)\right\}\right]\\ &= \left[E\exp\left\{i\left(\frac{t}{\sqrt{T}\sigma}\right)(Y_i-\mu)\right\}\right]^T\\ &= \left[\psi_{y-\mu}\left(\frac{t}{\sqrt{T}\sigma}\right)\right]^T.\end{aligned} \tag{2.2.14}$$

Then

$$\ln\phi_x(t) = T\ln\psi_{y-\mu}\left(\frac{\mathrm{t}}{\sqrt{T}\sigma}\right). \tag{2.2.15}$$

Since $E(X_T) = 0$ and $\mathrm{Var}(X_T) = 1$, we have

$$\kappa_1 = 0 \quad\text{and}\quad \kappa_2 = 1,$$

where $\kappa_r$ is the $r$th cumulant of $F_T(x)$. For $r > 2$, the coefficient of $(it)^r/r!$ in the expansion of $\ln\psi_{y-\mu}(t/\sqrt{T}\sigma)$ is $\kappa_r'/(T^{r/2}\sigma^r)$; after multiplying by $T$ and defining $\lambda_r = \kappa_r'/\sigma^r$, we have

$$\kappa_r = \frac{\lambda_r}{T^{(r/2)-1}}.$$

Equation 2.2.11 may be differentiated to obtain an approximation as $T\to\infty$ to $f_T(x)$, the density function of $X_T$, in terms of $n(x) = dN(x)/dx$ and its derivatives, $n^{(j)}(x)$. Upon differentiating and substituting the $\kappa_r$ and $\gamma_r$ derived above, the first few terms of the approximation are given by

$$\begin{aligned}f_T(x) = n(x) &- \frac{1}{3!}\frac{\lambda_3}{T^{1/2}}n^{(3)}(x) + \frac{1}{4!}\frac{\lambda_4}{T}n^{(4)}(x)\\ &- \frac{1}{5!}\frac{\lambda_5}{T^{3/2}}n^{(5)}(x) + \frac{1}{6!}\left[\frac{\lambda_6}{T^2} + \frac{10\lambda_3^2}{T}\right]n^{(6)}(x) + \cdots.\end{aligned} \tag{2.2.16}$$

Conditions under which (2.2.16) is an asymptotic expansion for $f_T(x)$ as $T\to\infty$ are presented in the references cited at the beginning of this section.

Note that $1/T$ appears as a factor in two different terms of (2.2.16). Therefore, if we wish to obtain an approximation to order $T^{-1}$, for example, performing the computations in the order given in (2.2.16) will require evaluating terms in $T^{-3/2}$ and $T^{-2}$. The *Edgeworth expansion* modifies the Gram-Charlier expansion by grouping terms according to powers of $T^{-1/2}$, rather than by the order of the derivative. For the example being considered, the first few terms of the Edgeworth expansion are given by

$$f_T(x) = n(x) - \frac{1}{3!}\frac{\lambda_3}{T^{1/2}}n^{(3)}(x) + \frac{1}{T}\left[\frac{1}{4!}\lambda_4 n^{(4)}(x) + \frac{10}{6!}\lambda_3^2 n^{(6)}(x)\right] + \cdots. \tag{2.2.17}$$

It is interesting to note that the derivatives of $n(x)$ are in the form of signed polynomials times $n(x)$. For example,

$$\begin{aligned} n^{(1)}(x) &= (-1)xn(x) \equiv (-1)H_1(x)n(x) \\ n^{(2)}(x) &= (x^2 - 1)n(x) \equiv H_2(x)n(x) \\ n^{(3)}(x) &= (-1)(x^3 - 3x)n(x) \equiv (-1)H_3(x)n(x). \end{aligned}$$

The $H_i(x)$ defined above are known as the *Hermite polynomials*. In this notation, we may rewrite (2.2.17) as

$$f_T(x) = n(x)\left[1 + \frac{1}{T^{1/2}}\left(\frac{\lambda_3}{3!}H_3(x)\right) + \frac{1}{T}\left(\frac{\lambda_4}{4!}H_4(x) + \frac{10}{6!}\lambda_3^2 H_6(x)\right) + \cdots\right]. \quad \textbf{(2.2.18)}$$

The Edgeworth expansion in this example and in other cases has an interesting interpretation: the first term in the approximation of $f_T(x)$ is $n(x)$, which is the approximation derived from the central limit theorem as $T \to \infty$. Succeeding terms may be regarded as adjustments to the normal approximation when terms of order $T^{-1/2}$ and several of its powers are too large to be neglected.

### 2.2.2 Asymptotic Expansions of Distribution and Density Functions

Another useful technique is to apply asymptotic expansions directly to distribution and density functions. We illustrate this approach with two examples. First, suppose $x^*$ and $y^*$ are jointly normally distributed,

$$\begin{bmatrix} x^* \\ y^* \end{bmatrix} \sim N_2\left(\begin{bmatrix} 0 \\ \mu \end{bmatrix}, \begin{bmatrix} 1 & \rho \\ \rho & 1 \end{bmatrix}\right),$$

and it is desired to approximate the distribution function of $Z = x^*/y^*$ for large $\mu$.[1] [Note that this approximation does not require a large sample size; $E(y^*) = \mu$ may be large for other reasons.]

The first step in deriving an approximation is to transform $(x^*, y^*)$ to independent normal variates.

Let

$$\begin{aligned} x^* &= \sqrt{1 - \rho^2}\, x + \rho y \\ y^* &= y + \mu, \end{aligned}$$

or

$$\begin{aligned} y &= y^* - \mu \\ x &= \frac{x^* - \rho(y^* - \mu)}{\sqrt{1 - \rho^2}}. \end{aligned} \quad \textbf{(2.2.19)}$$

[1]The exact distribution of $Z$ is derived in Appendix D, which also contains an approximation due to Geary. The example in the text is based on Mariano (1973). The problem is also studied by Marsiglia (1965) and Hinkley (1969).

It is then easily verified that

$$\begin{bmatrix} x \\ y \end{bmatrix} \sim N_2\left(\begin{bmatrix} 0 \\ 0 \end{bmatrix}, \begin{bmatrix} 1 & 0 \\ 0 & 1 \end{bmatrix}\right).$$

Therefore

$$z = \frac{x^*}{y^*} = \frac{\sqrt{1 - \rho^2}\, x + \rho y}{y + \mu} \tag{2.2.20}$$

and

$$P\left[z \leq \frac{b}{\mu}\right] = P\left[\frac{\sqrt{1 - \rho^2}\, x + \rho y}{y + \mu} \leq \frac{b}{\mu}\right]. \tag{2.2.21}$$

The transformed variables are independent normal, and we proceed to approximate (2.2.21).

If $y + \mu > 0$, we can rewrite the bracketed term as

$$\sqrt{1 - \rho^2}\, x + \rho y \leq b\,\frac{(y + \mu)}{\mu} = \frac{by}{\mu} + b$$

or

$$\sqrt{1 - \rho^2}\, x - \left(\frac{b}{\mu} - \rho\right) y \leq b. \tag{2.2.22}$$

A similar calculation for $y + \mu < 0$ yields

$$\begin{aligned} P\left[z \leqslant \frac{b}{\mu}\right] &= P\left[\sqrt{1 - \rho^2}\, x - \left(\frac{b}{\mu} - \rho\right) y \leqslant b \text{ and } y + \mu \geqslant 0\right] \\ &\quad + P\left[\sqrt{1 - \rho^2}\, x - \left(\frac{b}{\mu} - \rho\right) y > b \text{ and } y + \mu < 0\right]. \end{aligned}$$

Since we are interested in a large $\mu$ approximation, (2.2.21) will be rewritten to take advantage of the fact that probabilities will be small for events in which $y + \mu < 0$. To do so, set

$$A = \left\{(x, y) \colon \sqrt{1 - \rho^2}\, x - \left(\frac{b}{\mu} - \rho\right) y \leqslant b\right\},$$

$B = \{(x, y) \colon y + \mu \geq 0\}$, $\quad \bar{A}, \bar{B}$ complements of $A$ and $B$, respectively.

In this notation,

$$P\left[z \leqslant \frac{b}{\mu}\right] = P[A \cap B] + P[\bar{A} \cap \bar{B}].$$

From the identity

$$A = (A \cap B) \cup (A \cap \bar{B}),$$

we have

$$P(A) = P(A \cap B) + P(A \cap \bar{B}),$$

from which we may derive

$$P(A \cap B) + P(\bar{A} \cap \bar{B}) = P(A) + P(\bar{A} \cap \bar{B}) - P(A \cap \bar{B})$$

or

$$P\left[z \leq \frac{b}{\mu}\right] = P\left[\sqrt{1-\rho^2}\,x - \left(\frac{b}{\mu} - \rho\right)y \leq b\right] + R, \qquad (2.2.23)$$

where

$$R = P\left[\sqrt{1-\rho^2}\,x - \left(\frac{b}{\mu} - \rho\right)y > b \text{ and } y + \mu \leq 0\right] - P\left[\sqrt{1-\rho^2}\,x - \left(\frac{b}{\mu} - \rho\right)y \leq b \text{ and } y + \mu \leq 0\right]. \qquad (2.2.24)$$

Each term in $R$ is less than or equal to

$$P[y + \mu \leq 0] = \Phi(-\mu) \leqslant \frac{\phi(\mu)}{\mu},$$

where $\Phi(\ )$ is the normal distribution function and $\phi(\ )$ its density function. The inequality is based on the following: First,

$$\Phi(-\mu) = \frac{1}{\sqrt{2\pi}} \int_{-\infty}^{-\mu} e^{-(1/2)t^2}\,dt = \frac{1}{\sqrt{2\pi}} \int_{\mu}^{\infty} e^{-(1/2)t^2}\,dt. \qquad (2.2.25)$$

Ignoring the multiplicative constant temporarily, we have

$$\int_{\mu}^{\infty} e^{-(1/2)t^2}\,dt = \int_{\mu}^{\infty} \frac{1}{t}\, te^{-(1/2)t^2}\,dt = \int_{\mu}^{\infty} u\,dv,$$

where

$$u = \frac{1}{t} \quad \text{and} \quad dv = te^{-(1/2)t^2}\,dt. \qquad (2.2.26)$$

Since $v = -e^{-(1/2)t^2}$ and $du = -1/t^2$, integration by parts yields

$$\int_{\mu}^{\infty} e^{-(1/2)t^2}\,dt = -\frac{1}{t}e^{-(1/2)t^2}\Big|_{\mu}^{\infty} - \int_{\mu}^{\infty} \frac{1}{t^2}\,e^{-(1/2)t^2}\,dt = \frac{1}{\mu}e^{-(1/2)\mu^2} - S, \qquad (2.2.27)$$

where $S = \int_{\mu}^{\infty} 1/t^2\, e^{-(1/2)t^2}\,dt$ is nonnegative and of order $o(\mu^{-3})$. Multiplying (2.2.27) by $1/\sqrt{2\pi}$ and dropping $S$, we have $\phi(-\mu) \leqslant (\phi(\mu))/\mu$. Since $(1/\mu)\phi(\mu) = 1/(\sqrt{2\pi}\,\mu e^{(1/2)\mu^2})$ can be made arbitrarily small, for sufficiently large $\mu$ it follows from (2.2.23) that

$$P\left[z \leq \frac{b}{\mu}\right] = P\left[\sqrt{1-\rho^2}\,x - \left(\frac{b}{\mu} - \rho\right)y \leq b\right]. \qquad (2.2.28)$$

The random variable

$$\omega = \sqrt{1 - \rho^2}\, x - \left(\frac{b}{\mu} - \rho\right) y$$

is distributed as $N(0, \xi^{-2})$, where

$$\xi^{-2} = 1 - \frac{2b\rho}{\mu} + \frac{b^2}{\mu^2}. \tag{2.2.29}$$

Therefore,

$$P[\mu z \leq b] = \Phi(b\xi) \qquad \text{as} \quad \mu \rightarrow \infty, \tag{2.2.30}$$

which is the desired approximation.

A second example illustrates the use of an asymptotic expansion of an integral. The integral represents the exact density of an estimator studied by Taylor (1978); it is given by

$$f(\hat{\gamma}_i^*) = \frac{1}{B(\nu, \nu)\sqrt{2\pi}\sqrt{1 + \lambda}} \int_0^\infty \frac{1 + \lambda u}{u\sqrt{1 + \lambda u^2}} \exp\left\{\frac{-(\hat{\gamma}_i^* - \gamma_i)^2}{2} \frac{(1 + \lambda u^2)}{(1 + \lambda)(1 + \lambda u^2)}\right\} \times \left(\frac{u}{(1 + u)^2}\right)^\nu du.$$

To order $1/\nu$, the integral may be approximated by the Laplace approximation, an asymptotic expansion [see Copson (1965, p. 39)], which yields

$$f(\hat{\gamma}_i^*) = \frac{\sqrt{2\pi}}{B(\nu, \nu)\sqrt{\nu}} \left(\frac{1}{4}\right)^\nu \exp\left\{\frac{(\hat{\gamma}_i^* - \gamma_i)^2}{2}\right\}. \tag{2.2.31}$$

In his article Taylor uses an Edgeworth expansion to show that $f(\hat{\gamma}_i^*)$ is reasonably well approximated by the normal distribution. The Laplace approximation yields a similar conclusion, except that the constant factor in the approximation depends on $\nu$; as $\nu \rightarrow \infty$, however, it may be shown that $\sqrt{2}/[B(\nu, \nu)\sqrt{\nu}](\frac{1}{4})^\nu \rightarrow (2\pi)^{-1/2}$. [To do so, write $B(\nu, \nu)$ in terms of gamma functions and use Stirling's formula for $\Gamma(x)$.]

## 2.3 Approximations to the Distribution of Functions of Random Variables; Nonlinear Regression

The approach discussed in this section combines Taylor series approximation with the central limit theorem to derive an approximate distribution for an estimator or a vector of estimators. The method is discussed in the context of least squares estimation in nonlinear regression and then illustrated with a particular function.

The general nonlinear regression problem may be stated as

$$y_t = f(x_t, \boldsymbol{\theta}) + u_t, \tag{2.3.1}$$

where $\boldsymbol{\theta}$ is a vector of $p$ parameters and $u_t$ is an i.i.d. random disturbance, $E(u_t) = 0$, $\text{Var}(u_t) = \sigma^2$. The least squares estimator, $\hat{\theta}$, minimizes

$$S(\boldsymbol{\theta}) = \sum_t [y_t - f(x_t, \boldsymbol{\theta})]^2. \tag{2.3.2}$$

To develop the approximation, we begin with $\partial S/\partial\boldsymbol{\theta}$, a $p \times 1$ column vector of partial derivatives when $\boldsymbol{\theta}$ is a vector; it is a random variable because it depends on the sample of $y_t$. A Taylor series expansion to $\partial S/\partial\boldsymbol{\theta}|_{\boldsymbol{\theta}=\hat{\boldsymbol{\theta}}}$ around $\boldsymbol{\theta}$, denoting $\partial S/\partial\boldsymbol{\theta}|_{\boldsymbol{\theta}=\hat{\boldsymbol{\theta}}}$ by $\partial S/\partial\hat{\boldsymbol{\theta}}$, yields

$$\frac{\partial S}{\partial \hat{\boldsymbol{\theta}}} = \frac{\partial S}{\partial \boldsymbol{\theta}} + \frac{\partial^2 S}{\partial \boldsymbol{\theta}^2}(\hat{\boldsymbol{\theta}} - \boldsymbol{\theta}) + R, \tag{2.3.3}$$

where

$$\frac{\partial^2 S}{\partial \boldsymbol{\theta}^2} = \begin{bmatrix} \dfrac{\partial^2 S}{\partial \theta_1^2} & \dfrac{\partial^2 S}{\partial \theta_1\, \partial \theta_2} & \cdots & \dfrac{\partial^2 S}{\partial \theta_1\, \partial \theta_p} \\ & \dfrac{\partial^2 S}{\partial \theta_2^2} & \cdots & \cdots \\ & & \cdots & \dfrac{\partial^2 S}{\partial \theta_p^2} \end{bmatrix} \tag{2.3.4}$$

and $R$ is a remainder term evaluated at a $\bar{\boldsymbol{\theta}}$ between $\hat{\boldsymbol{\theta}}$ and $\boldsymbol{\theta}$. Under rather general regularity conditions, presented in Jennrich (1969) and Gallant (1975), it can be shown that $\hat{\boldsymbol{\theta}} \xrightarrow{\text{a.s.}} \boldsymbol{\theta}$. Since $\partial S/\partial\hat{\boldsymbol{\theta}} = \mathbf{0}$ is a necessary condition for the minimization of $S(\boldsymbol{\theta})$, (2.3.3) implies

$$\hat{\boldsymbol{\theta}} - \boldsymbol{\theta} = -\left[\frac{\partial^2 S}{\partial \boldsymbol{\theta}^2}\right]^{-1} \frac{\partial S}{\partial \boldsymbol{\theta}} - \left[\frac{\partial^2 S}{\partial \boldsymbol{\theta}^2}\right]^{-1} R \tag{2.3.5}$$

and

$$\sqrt{T}(\hat{\boldsymbol{\theta}} - \boldsymbol{\theta}) = \left[\frac{1}{T}\frac{\partial^2 S}{\partial \boldsymbol{\theta}^2}\right]^{-1} \left[-\frac{1}{\sqrt{T}}\frac{\partial S}{\partial \boldsymbol{\theta}}\right] - \left[\frac{1}{T}\frac{\partial^2 S}{\partial \boldsymbol{\theta}^2}\right]^{-1} \frac{1}{\sqrt{T}} R. \tag{2.3.6}$$

The remainder of the argument consists of showing that $(1/T)(\partial^2 S/\partial\hat{\boldsymbol{\theta}}^2) \xrightarrow{\text{P}} \Sigma$ (a constant matrix) and that the central limit theorem may be applied to $[(-1/\sqrt{T})(\partial S/\partial\boldsymbol{\theta})]$. We assume that $(1/\sqrt{T})R \xrightarrow{\text{P}} 0$. This will yield the result that $\sqrt{T}(\hat{\boldsymbol{\theta}} - \boldsymbol{\theta})$ converges in distribution to a normally distributed random variable with mean $\theta$ and variance-covariance matrix $\sigma^2\Sigma^{-1}$. Details are supplied for a special case in the following example.

**Example**

Let

$$y_t = \theta_1 \exp\{\theta_2 x_t\} + \epsilon_t,$$

where $\epsilon_t (t = 1, \ldots, T)$ are identically, independently distributed random variables, with $E[\epsilon_t] = 0$ and $E[\epsilon_t^2] = \sigma^2$. The least squares estimator is the vector, $\hat{\boldsymbol{\theta}}' = (\hat{\theta}_1, \hat{\theta}_2)$, that minimizes $S(\boldsymbol{\theta}) = \Sigma(y_t - \theta_1 \exp\{\theta_2 x_t\})^2$. Since the estimator is a complicated nonlinear function of the $y_t$'s, it is desirable to find an approximation to its distribution function.

It may be verified that

$$\frac{1}{T}\frac{\partial^2 S}{\partial \boldsymbol{\theta}^2} = \frac{2}{T}\begin{bmatrix} \Sigma \exp\{2\theta_2 x_t\} & \Sigma[\theta_1 x_t \exp\{2\theta_2 x_t\} - x_t \exp\{\theta_2 x_t\}\epsilon_t] \\ \Sigma[\theta_1 x_t \exp\{2\theta_2 x_t\} - x_t \exp\{\theta_2 x_t\}\epsilon_t] & \Sigma[\theta_1^2 x_t^2 \exp\{2\theta_2 x_t\} - \theta_1^2 x_t^2 \exp\{\theta_2 x_t\}\epsilon_t] \end{bmatrix}.$$

In practice, this matrix is evaluated at $\boldsymbol{\theta} = \hat{\boldsymbol{\theta}}$, the least squares estimator. To study its limiting behavior as $T \to \infty$, we assume that the sequence $\{x_t\}$ is such that

$$\frac{1}{T}\Sigma \exp\{2\hat{\theta}_2 x_t\} \xrightarrow{p} \sigma_{11} = \lim \frac{1}{T}\Sigma \exp\{2\theta_2 x_t\}, \qquad \textbf{(2.3.7)}$$

$$\frac{1}{T}\Sigma[\hat{\theta}_1 x_t \exp\{2\hat{\theta}_2 x_t\} - x_t \exp\{2\hat{\theta}_2 x_t\}\epsilon_t] \xrightarrow{p} \sigma_{12} = \lim \frac{1}{T}\Sigma\theta_1 x_t \exp\{2\theta_2 x_t\}, \qquad \textbf{(2.3.8)}$$

and

$$\frac{1}{T}\Sigma[\hat{\theta}_1^2 x_t^2 \exp\{2\hat{\theta}_2 x_t\} - \hat{\theta}_1 x_t^2 \exp\{2\hat{\theta}_2 x_t\}\epsilon_t] \xrightarrow{p} \sigma_{22} = \lim \frac{1}{T}\Sigma\theta_1^2 x_t^2 \exp\{2\theta_2 x_t\}. \qquad \textbf{(2.3.9)}$$

Consistent estimators of $\sigma_{11}$, $\sigma_{12}$, and $\sigma_{22}$, respectively, are given by

$$\frac{1}{T}\Sigma \exp\{2\hat{\theta}_2 x_t\}, \qquad \textbf{(2.3.10)}$$

$$\frac{1}{T}\Sigma\hat{\theta}_1 x_t \exp\{2\hat{\theta}_2 x_t\}, \qquad \textbf{(2.3.11)}$$

and

$$\frac{1}{T}\Sigma\hat{\theta}_1^2 x_t^2 \exp\{2\hat{\theta}_2 x_t\}. \qquad \textbf{(2.3.12)}$$

In addition, it should be verified that

$$\left[-\frac{1}{\sqrt{T}}\frac{\partial S}{\partial \boldsymbol{\theta}}\right] = \frac{2}{\sqrt{T}}\begin{bmatrix} \Sigma \exp\{\theta_2 x_t\}\epsilon_t \\ \Sigma\theta_1 x_t \exp\{\theta_2 x_t\}\epsilon_t \end{bmatrix}.$$

Under appropriate conditions on the $x_t$ and $\epsilon_t$, the multivariate version of the central limit theorem may be applied to $[(-1/\sqrt{T})(\partial S/\partial\boldsymbol{\theta})]$ to obtain

$$\left[-\frac{1}{\sqrt{T}}\frac{\partial S}{\partial \boldsymbol{\theta}}\right] \xrightarrow{d} N_2(\mathbf{0}, \sigma^2\Sigma).$$

Therefore,

$$\sqrt{T}[\hat{\boldsymbol{\theta}} - \boldsymbol{\theta}] \xrightarrow{d} N_2[\mathbf{0}, \sigma^2\Sigma^{-1}]. \qquad \textbf{(2.3.13)}$$

A consistent estimator of $\sigma^2$ is

$$\frac{1}{T}\sum_{t=1}^{T}(y_t - \hat{\theta}_1 \exp\{2\hat{\theta}_2 x_t\})^2. \tag{2.3.14}$$

In summary, for large samples, $\sqrt{T}(\hat{\boldsymbol{\theta}} - \boldsymbol{\theta})$ may be approximated by a normal distribution when assumptions are made to ensure that $\hat{\boldsymbol{\theta}} \xrightarrow{\text{p}} \boldsymbol{\theta}$ and that $\{x_t\}$ is well behaved. Note that this procedure does not require an explicit expression for $\hat{\boldsymbol{\theta}}$; the results are derived from a Taylor series expansion using only the property that $\hat{\boldsymbol{\theta}}$ minimizes $S$, implying

$$\left.\frac{\partial S}{\partial \boldsymbol{\theta}}\right|_{\boldsymbol{\theta}=\hat{\boldsymbol{\theta}}} = \mathbf{0}.$$

This is in contrast to applications of the CLT discussed in Chapter 1 and to Theorem 1.1.11, both of which assume that the r.v. whose distribution is to be approximated is an explicit function of other random variables.

## 2.4 Methods of Approximating Moments

The previous sections were concerned with approximations to the density and distribution functions of random variables. This one discusses the approximation of moments of distributions, which may provide useful information about location and spread. We first examine several possible measures of location and discuss some relationships between them. We then turn to the approximation of moments of functions of random variables.

### 2.4.1 Asymptotic Moments and Moments of Limiting Distributions

The subject of this section causes more confusion than any other single topic in large sample theory. Most of the difficulty arises from not distinguishing carefully between concepts that are similar, but not identical.

**Definition**

The *rth asymptotic moment of* $X_T$, denoted by $AE(X_T^r)$, is defined by

$$\lim_{T\to\infty} E(X_T^r) \equiv AE(X_T^r).$$

To interpret this definition, note that $E(X_T^r)$ is not a random variable; rather, it is a nonstochastic function of $T$. The limiting operation is the usual calculus idea of a limit. For example, if $X_T \sim N(1/T,\ 1 + 1/T)$, then $E(X_T) = 1/T$, so $\lim E(X_T) = 0$. Also, since

$$E(X_T^2) = \text{Var}(X_T) + [E(X_T)]^2 = 1 + \frac{1}{T} + \frac{1}{T^2}, \qquad AE(X_T^2) = 1.$$

For statistical applications, two additional definitions are useful:

**Definition**

$X_T$ is an *asymptotically unbiased estimator* for $\theta$ if $AE(X_T) = \theta$.

**Definition**

The *asymptotic variance* of $X_T$ is denoted by $AV(X_T)$, where

$$AV(X_T) = AE\{[X_T - E(X_T)]^2\}.$$

**Theorem 2.4.1**

If $AE(X_T) = k$ and $AV(X_T) = 0$, then plim $X_T = k$.

The statistical interpretation is that an asymptotically unbiased estimator with zero asymptotic variance is also a consistent estimator. The theorem is useful because it is sometimes easier to show that the sufficient conditions of the theorem hold than to prove consistency directly.

**Proof**

$$\begin{aligned} E[(X_T - k)^2] &= E\{[(X_T - E(X_T)) + (E(X_T) - k)]^2\} \\ &= E[(X_T - E(X_T))^2] + [E(X_T) - k]^2. \end{aligned}$$

Upon taking the limit as $T \to \infty$, the conditions of the theorem imply that the right-hand side goes to zero. Therefore lim $E[(X_T - k)^2] = 0$, or $X_T \xrightarrow{\text{q.m.}} k$, which implies $X_T \xrightarrow{\text{p}} k$. □

Another type of moment is easily confused with $AE(X_T^r)$.

**Definition**

If $X_T \xrightarrow{\text{d}} X$, the $r$th moment of the limiting distribution of $X_T$ is sometimes used to approximate $E(X_T^r)$. In such cases, we define

$$LE(X_T^r) = E(X^r),$$

where $X_T \xrightarrow{\text{d}} X$.

We next present several theorems and examples that indicate some of the possible relationships between the plim, $E(X_T)$, $AE(X_T)$, and $LE(X_T)$. Much of this discussion is based on Srinivisan (1970) and Dhrymes (1970).

**Example**

[plim $X_T$ may not equal $AE(X_T)$.]

Let

$$P[X_T = \alpha] = 1 - \frac{1}{T}$$

$$P[X_T = T^{\nu}] = \frac{1}{T}.$$

In Section (1.1.3) it was shown that plim $X_T = \alpha$ (for $\nu = 2$). However, $E[X_T] = \alpha(1 - 1/T) + T^{\nu-1}$, and for $\nu > 1$, $AE(X_T) = \infty$. Therefore, $X_T$ is a consistent estimator for $\alpha$, but it is not asymptotically unbiased. In this example, all but a small part of the distribution becomes concentrated at $\alpha$, but the weight in computing $E(X_T)$ that is given to the density not concentrated at $\alpha$ grows faster than the probability diminishes. Hence, $E(X_T)$ has no limit as $T \to \infty$. Note that plim $X_T = \alpha \neq \alpha + 1 = AE(X_T)$ when $\nu = 1$; that is, even when they both exist, the plim may not equal the asympototic expectation.

**Example**

[$E(X_T) = k$ but plim $X_T \neq k$.]

Let

$$P[X_T = k + \alpha_1 T] = \tfrac{1}{3}$$

$$P[X_T = k - \alpha_2 T] = \tfrac{2}{3}, \qquad \alpha_1, \alpha_2 \neq 0.$$

As $T$ increases, this variable does not converge in probability to $k$, but consider $E[X_T] = \frac{1}{3}(k + \alpha_1 T) + \frac{2}{3}(k - \alpha_2 T)$. If $2\alpha_2 = -\alpha_1$, $E[X_T] = k$ for all $T$, and so $AE(X_T) = k$. In this case, $X_T$ is unbiased and asymptotically unbiased, but not consistent for $k$.

**Example**

[$LE(X_T^r)$ is well defined—that is, moments of the limiting distribution exist—but the $E(X_T^r)$ are infinite, so that $AE(X_T^r)$ does not exist.]

Let the denisty function for $X_T$ be

$$f_T(x) = \begin{cases} \alpha^T(\delta - 1)x^{-\delta} + \dfrac{(1 - \alpha^T)}{\sqrt{2\pi}\theta_T} \exp\left\{-\dfrac{1}{2}\left[\dfrac{x - \beta_T}{\theta_T}\right]^2\right\} & (x \geq 1) \\ \dfrac{1 - \alpha^T}{\sqrt{2\pi}\theta_T} \exp\left\{-\dfrac{1}{2}\left[\dfrac{x - \beta_T}{\theta_T}\right]^2\right\} & (x < 1) \end{cases}$$

$$0 < \alpha < 1, \qquad 1 < \delta < 2.$$

For finite $T$ and $r > \delta$ it is easy to see that $\alpha^T(\delta - 1) \int_1^\infty x^{-\delta+r}\,dx$ is infinite, and the integral of $x^r$ times the other two terms is finite. Therefore, $E(X_T^r) = \infty$, $r > \delta$. But as $T \to \infty$, $(X_T - \beta_T)/\theta_T \xrightarrow{d} Y \sim N(0, 1)$, because $\lim \alpha^T(\delta - 1)x^{-\delta} = 0$ and $\lim 1 - \alpha^T = 1$. All moments of $Y$ are finite.

**Example**

[$AE(X_T)$ may not equal $LE(X_T)$ although both exist.]

Let

$$f_T(z) = \frac{1}{\sqrt{2\pi}}\left(\alpha^T \exp\left\{-\frac{1}{2}(z - \alpha^{-T})^2\right\}\right.$$
$$\left. + (1 - \alpha^T)\exp\left\{-\frac{1}{2}z^2\right\}\right), \qquad 0 < \alpha < 1.$$

Then, since

$$\begin{aligned} E(Z_T) &= \frac{1}{\sqrt{2\pi}}\left(\alpha^T \int_{-\infty}^{\infty} z \exp\left\{-\frac{1}{2}(z - \alpha^{-T})^2\right\} dz\right. \\ &\quad \left. + (1 - \alpha^T)\int_{-\infty}^{\infty} z \exp\left\{-\frac{1}{2}z^2\right\} dz\right) \\ &= 1, \qquad \text{for all } T,\ AE(Z_T) = 1. \end{aligned}$$

But $Z_T \xrightarrow{d} Y \sim N(0, 1)$, so that $LE(Z_T) = 0$.

The reader should take no comfort from the fact that these examples seem artificial and conclude that in "routine" cases, plims, $AE(X_T)$'s, and $LE(X_T)$'s may be interchanged more or less at will. They cannot be *assumed* equal to each other in general, and proof of equality must be provided before they are interchanged.

After this series of negative results, we conclude this section with a few positive ones.

**Theorem 2.4.2**

If $X_T \xrightarrow{\text{q.m.}} X$, then $\lim E(X_T) = E(X)$ and $\lim E(X_T^2) = E(X^2)$.

**Proof**

$$\begin{aligned} E(X_T - X)^2 &= \mathrm{Var}(X_T - X) + [E(X_T - X)]^2 \\ &= \mathrm{Var}(X_T - X) + [E(X_T) - E(X)]^2 \\ &\geq [E(X_T) - E(X)]^2. \end{aligned}$$

Since $E[(X_T - X)^2] \to 0$, $E(X_T) \to E(X)$. □

The proof of the second statement may be found in Lukacs (1968, p. 38).

**Theorem 2.4.3**

If $X_T \xrightarrow{d} X$ and $m_T$ is a median of $X_T$, then $\lim m_T$ is a median of $X$.

**Proof**

Lukacs (1968, p. 39). □

**Theorem 2.4.4**

If $g(y)$ is a nonnegative continuous function, $X_T \xrightarrow{p} X$, and $E[g(X_T)]$ and $E[g(X)]$ exist, then $E[g(X_T)] = E[g(X)]$ if and only if $\int_a^b g(x)f_T(x)\,dx$ converges uniformly to $\int_{-\infty}^{\infty} g(x)f_T(x)\,dx$ as $a \to -\infty$ and $b \to \infty$, where $f_T(x)$ is the density function of $X_T$.[2]

**Proof**

Lukacs (1968, p. 41). □

### 2.4.2 Approximations to Moments of Functions of Random Variables

Given a random variable, $u_T$, this section discusses methods of approximating $E[h(u_T)^r]$ based on Taylor series expansions. It may be possible in some cases to obtain an approximation through the use of one of the methods discussed above; for example, calculating the desired expected values from the limiting distribution. As will be illustrated, approximations based on different methods may be quite different from each other.

This discussion is based on Bickel and Doksum (1977, pp. 30–31), who also present other applications. Let $\theta$ be a parameter for which $h(u_T)$, $u_T$ random, is an estimator. Assuming that the necessary derivatives exist and are continuous, one may expand $h(u_T)$ around $\theta$:

$$h(u_T) = h(\theta) + (u_T - \theta)h^{(1)}(\theta) + \frac{(u_T - \theta)^2 h^{(2)}(\theta)}{2} + \cdots + \frac{(u_T - \theta)^n h^{(n)}(\theta)}{n!} + \frac{(u_T - \theta)^{n+1} h^{(n+1)}(\xi)}{(n+1)!}, \quad \textbf{(2.4.1)}$$

where $\xi$ is between $u_T$ and $\theta$. Expected values of both sides can be taken, yielding $E[h(u_T)]$ in terms of moments of $u_T$ and derivatives of $h(u_T)$ evaluated at $u_T = \theta$. Higher order moments may be obtained by raising $[h(u_T) - Eh(u_T)]$ to the desired power. (In practice the derivatives are evaluated at the estimated value of $\theta$.) This approach is especially useful if the derivatives of $h(u_T)$ are bounded and the moments of $u_T$ are of order $1/T$.

As an example, let $u_T = \bar{x}_T = 1/T\,\Sigma x_i$, where $E[x_i] = \theta$, $\mathrm{Var}(x_i) = \sigma^2$, and $E[(x_i - \theta)^3] = \mu_3 < \infty$. In addition, assume that $E[(x_i - \mu)^4]$ is finite and that $|h^{(4)}(x)| \le M$

[2]The uniform convergence condition requires that there exist constants $A$ and $B$, independent of $T$, such that

$$\left| \int_a^b g(x)f_T(x)\,dx - \int_{-\infty}^{\infty} g(x)f_T(x)\,dx \right| < \epsilon \quad \text{for} \quad a < A \quad \text{and} \quad b < B.$$

for all $x$. For $\hat{\mu}$ between $\mu$ and $\bar{x}$, the first three terms of the Taylor series for $h(\bar{x})$ around $\mu$ give us

$$\left| h(\bar{x}) - h(\mu) - h^{(1)}(\mu)(\bar{x} - \mu) - \frac{h^{(2)}(\mu)}{2}(\bar{x} - \mu)^2 - \frac{h^{(3)}(\mu)}{6}(\bar{x} - \mu)^3 \right| = \frac{|h^{(4)}(\hat{\mu})|}{24}(\bar{x} - \mu)^4 \leq \frac{M}{24}(\bar{x} - \mu)^4. \quad \textbf{(2.4.2)}$$

Since $|E(y)| \leq E(|y|)$, upon taking expectations of both sides we have

$$|E[h(\bar{x})] - h(\mu) - h^{(1)}(\mu)E(\bar{x} - \mu) - \frac{h^{(2)}(\mu)}{2} E[(\bar{x} - \mu)^2] - \frac{h^{(3)}(\mu)}{6} E[(\bar{x} - \mu)^3]| \leq \frac{M}{24}[E(\bar{x} - \mu)^4].$$

And since $|a - b| \geq |a| - |b|$ implies $|a| \leq |a - b| + |b|$,

$$|E[h(\bar{x})] - h(\mu) - h^{(1)}(\mu)E(\bar{x} - \mu) - \frac{h^{(2)}(\mu)}{2} E[(\bar{x} - \mu)^2]| \leq \frac{M}{24} E(\bar{x} - \mu)^4 + \frac{|h^{(3)}(\mu)|}{6} |E[(\bar{x} - \mu)^3]|.$$

Finally, since $E(\bar{x} - \mu) = 0$, $E[(\bar{x} - \mu)^2] = \sigma^2/T$, $E[(\bar{x} - \mu)^3] = \mu_3/T^2$, and $E[(\bar{x} - \mu)^4] = (\mu_4 + 3(T - 1)\sigma^4)/T^3$, we are justified in stating

$$E[h(\bar{x})] = h(\mu) + \frac{h^{(2)}(\mu)\sigma^2}{2T} + R_T,$$

where

$$R_T = o(T^{-1}).$$

Before approximating $\text{Var}[h(\bar{x})]$, it is worthwhile to take a closer look at the approach used in deriving this approximation. Under the assumed conditions, the Taylor series expansion is valid. Upon taking expectations, we obtained $E[h(\bar{x})]$ equal to $h(\mu)$ plus an explicit term of order $1/T$ plus a remainder term of smaller order. Obviously, as $T \to \infty$, $E[h(\bar{x})] \to h(\mu)$, which suggests that $h(\mu)$ may be regarded as an approximation to $AE[h(\bar{x})]$. It may also be tempting to regard the term of order $1/T$ as the ''bias to order $1/T$.'' We return to this issue after deriving $\text{Var}[h(\bar{x})]$.

Combining the expressions for $h(\bar{x})$ and $E[h(\bar{x})]$, we have

$$h(\bar{x}) - E[h(\bar{x})] = h^{(1)}(\mu)(\bar{x} - \mu) + \frac{h^{(2)}(\mu)}{2}(\bar{x} - \mu)^2 - \frac{h^{(2)}(\mu)}{2}\frac{\sigma^2}{T} + R(\bar{x}, \mu) - R_T,$$

where

$$R(\bar{x}, \mu) \equiv \frac{h^{(3)}(\mu)(\bar{x} - \mu)^3}{6}.$$

Upon squaring both sides and taking expected values, an approximation to $\text{Var}[h(\bar{x})]$ is given by

$$\mathrm{Var}[h(\bar{x})] = \frac{1}{T}[h^{(1)}(\mu)]^2\sigma^2 + \frac{1}{T^2}h^{(1)}(\mu)h^{(2)}(\mu)\mu_3 + \frac{1}{2T^2}[h^{(2)}(\mu)]^2\sigma^4 + o(T^{-2}).$$

Returning to an earlier point regarding the use of the term of order $1/T$ as a measure of bias, we discuss an article by Srinivisan (1970), who analyzes a procedure introduced by Nagar (1959). Nagar's aim was to choose a value for $k$ that eliminated the bias of the $k$-class estimator to order $1/T$. To present these ideas, we first define two concepts of boundedness.

**Definition**

A random variable, $u_T$, is said to be *asymptotically bounded in probability* (a.b.p.) if for each $\delta > 0$, there exists an $M$ such that $P[|u_T| > M] < \delta$ for $T$ sufficiently large.

**Theorem 2.4.5**

If plim $u_T$ exists, then $u_T$ is a.b.p.

**Proof**

Let plim $u_T = \theta$. Then for every $\delta$ and $\epsilon > 0$, there exists a $T$ sufficiently large such that

$$P[|u_T - \theta| > \epsilon] < \delta.$$

By choosing $M = \epsilon + |\theta|$, it can be seen that the existence of plim $u_T$ implies that $u_T$ is a.b.p. □

**Definition**

Let $\{u_T\}$ be a sequence of random variables and let $H$ be the set of real numbers $h$ such that $\{T^h X_T\}$ is a.b.p. If $H$ is nonempty and bounded above, the sequence $\{u_T\}$ is said to be of *order* $T^{-k}$ *in probability*, where $k = \sup H$. (We shall use the notation $u_T = O_p(T^{-k})$ for this concept in the rest of this section.)

The Nagar approach is to expand $h(u_T)$ in an infinite sum in $u_T^k$, where $u_T = O_p(T^{-1})$, and to interpret $E[\Sigma_{k=0}^m \alpha_k u_T^k]$ as the bias to the order $T^{-m}$. Srinivisan provides a number of examples to show that this method is not generally applicable. Additional discussion of these points may be found in Srinivisan (1970) and Dhrymes (1970).

**Example**

Let $Z_T = X_T - \theta = u_T/(1 - u_T)$, where for all $T > 1$,

$$P\left[u_T = \frac{\beta}{T}\right] = 1 - \frac{1}{T}$$

$$P[u_T = T] = \frac{1}{T}, \qquad 0 < \beta < 1.$$

Accordingly,

$$P\left[z_T = \frac{\beta}{(T - \beta)}\right] = 1 - \frac{1}{T}$$

$$P\left[z_T = \frac{T}{(1 - T)}\right] = \frac{1}{T}.$$

It is easy to see that plim $X_T = \theta$ and $AE(X_T) = \theta$. The latter follows from $EZ_T = (\beta - 1)/T + (\beta^2 - \beta - 1)/T^2 + \cdots$, which also shows that the true bias to order $1/T$ is $(\beta - 1)/T$. Moreover, since plim $Tu_T = \beta$, it follows that $u_T = O_p(T^{-1})$ and $u_T^r = O_p(T^{-r})$. Since $u_T/(1 - u_T) = u_T(1 + u_T + u_T^2 + \cdots)$, the "Nagar bias" to order $1/T$ is $Eu_T = 1 + \beta/T$, which is not equal to the true bias.

**Example**

For $Z_T$ defined as above, let

$$P\left[u_T = -\frac{\beta}{T}\right] = 1 - \frac{1}{T}$$

$$f_T(u) = \begin{cases} \dfrac{1}{T}\dfrac{\beta}{T} u_T^{-2}, & u < -\dfrac{\beta}{T} \\ 0, & u > -\dfrac{\beta}{T} \end{cases} \qquad \beta \geq 0.$$

Then it may be verified that the true bias to order $1/T$ is $-\beta/T$, while the Nagar bias is not defined.

Other examples provided by Srinivisan show cases in which (1) the true bias does not exist but the Nagar bias does, and (2) all even moments of $u_T$ are of order $1/T$, so that one cannot obtain the true bias to order $1/T$ by taking the expectation of a finite number of the terms in $\Sigma\alpha_k u_T^k$. Kadane (1971) and Brown, Kadane, and Ramage (1974) use an approach similar to that of Nagar for small $\sigma$ rather than large $T$. Use of the Nagar approach in econometrics is discussed in Chapter 11.

## 2.5 Concluding Remarks

This brief review of asymptotic theory should serve to convince the reader that great care is needed when dealing with approximations to probability functions and moments. A large number of asymptotic techniques exist, and it is often difficult to determine exactly what is being approximated or how good the approximation is. Which technique is most useful for a particular purpose is frequently not obvious; to make matters worse, the values of plim $X_T$, $E(X_T)$, $AE(X_T)$, and $LE(X_T)$ may differ greatly from each other. Accordingly, great care must be taken in proofs to make sure that illegitimate substitutions are not made. An interesting example of an incorrect substitution is discussed by McCallum (1973).

Our survey of recent econometric literature reveals a revival of interest in techniques for approximating distributions. For estimators whose exact distributions are too complicated to analyze effectively, it is often possible to obtain approximations for moderate to large samples without invoking the central limit theorem, which requires very large samples. The Edgeworth approximation, for example, may provide a better approximation to the small sample distribution of an estimator than does the normal distribution. Unfortunately no hard and fast rules can be given about when the central limit theorem will be an unsatisfactory approximation. An approximation to the distribution is needed for such statistical procedures as hypothesis testing and confidence intervals. In such cases the availability of a reasonably tractable approximation may make statistical inference possible. Indeed, even if the exact distribution has no moments it may be possible to compute approximate probabilities from an approximating distribution, the first moment of which may be a useful indicator of location.

We expect interest in approximation theory to grow as econometricians attempt to understand more fully the nature of the estimators with which they have been working—to go beyond the computation of an estimator's plim and to avoid the use of the normal approximation when better approximations are available. Applications to econometric problems of several of the techniques discussed in the chapter are contained in Chapters 10 and 11.

## 2.6 References


Abramowitz, M. and I. A. Stegun (1972), *Handbook of Mathematical Functions,* New York: Dover.

Bickel, P. J. and K. A. Doksum (1977), *Mathematical Statistics,* San Francisco: Holden-Day.

Brown, G. F. Jr., J. B. Kadane, and J. G. Ramage (1974), "The Asymptotic Bias and Mean-Squared Error of Double *k*-Class Estimators when the Disturbances are Small," *International Economic Review*, **15,** 667–679.

Copson, E. T. (1965), *Asymptotic Expansions,* Cambridge: Cambridge University Press.

Cramer, H. (1946), *Mathematical Methods of Statistics,* Princeton, N.J.: Princeton University Press.

Dhrymes, P. J. (1970), *Econometrics,* New York: Harper & Row.

Erdelyi, A. (1956), *Asymptotic Expansions,* New York: Dover.

Feller, W. (1966), *An Introduction to Probability Theory and Its Applications,* Vol. II, New York: Wiley.

Gallant, A. R. (1975), "Nonlinear Regression," *The American Statistician,* **29,** 73–81.

Gnedenko, B. V. (1969), *The Theory of Probability,* Moscow: Mir Publishers.

Hinkley, D. V. (1969), "On the Ratio of Two Correlated Normal Random Variables," *Biometrika,* **56,** 635–639.

Jennrich, R. I. (1969), "Asymptotic Properties of Non-Linear Least Squares Estimators," *The Annals of Mathematical Statistics,* **40,** 633–643.

Kadane, J. B. (1971), "Comparisons of $k$-Class Estimators When the Disturbances are Small," *Econometrica,* **39,** 723–737.

Kendall, M. G. and A. Stuart (1963), *The Advanced Theory of Statistics,* Vol. 1, *Distribution Theory,* 2nd ed., New York: Hafner.

Lukacs, E. (1968), *Stochastic Convergence,* Lexington, Mass.: D. C. Heath.

Mariano, R. S. (1973), "Approximations to the Distribution Functions of the Ordinary Least-Squares and Two-Stage Least-Squares Estimators in the Case of Two Included Endogenous Variables," *Econometrica,* **41,** 67–77.

Marsiglia, G. (1965), "Ratios of Normal Variables and Ratios of Sums of Uniform Variables," *Journal of the American Statistical Association,* **60,** 193–204.

McCallum, B. T. (1973), "A Note Concerning Asymptotic Covariance Expressions," *Econometrica,* **41,** 581–583.

Nagar, A. L. (1959), "The Bias and Moment Matrix of the General $k$-Class Estimators of the Parameters in Simultaneous Equations," *Econometrica,* **27,** 575–595.

Phillips, P. C. B. (1980), "The Exact Distribution of Instrumental Variable Estimators in an Equation Containing $n + 1$ Endogenous Variables," *Econometrica,* **48,** 861–878.

Rao, C. R. (1973), *Linear Statistical Inference and Its Applications,* 2nd ed., New York: Wiley.

Sargan, J. D. (1974), "The Validity of Nagar's Expansion for the Moments of Econometric Estimators," *Econometrica,* **42,** 169–176.

Sargan, J. D. (1976), "Econometric Estimators and the Edgeworth Approximation," *Econometrica,* **44,** 421–448.

Srinivisan, T. N. (1970), "Approximations to Finite Sample Moments of Estimators Whose Exact Sampling Distributions are Unknown," *Econometrica,* **38,** 533–541.

Taylor, W. E. (1978), "The Heteroscedastic Linear Model: Exact Finite Sample Results," *Econometrica,* **46,** 663–675.

Wallace, D. L. (1958), "Asymptotic Approximations to Distributions," *Annals of Mathematical Statistics,* **29,** 635–654.

Wilks, S. S. (1962), *Mathematical Statistics,* New York: Wiley.

# PART II

# Topics in Time Series Analysis

The three chapters in this part are concerned with various aspects of time series analysis. In Chapter 3 a parametric model for the analysis of time series is described. In Chapter 4, we discuss identification, prediction, and forecasting using the parametric model of Chapter 3. Chapter 5 takes up the relationship between econometric and time series modeling, ending with an extensive discussion of Granger-Sims causality.

# CHAPTER 3

# An Introduction to Time Series Analysis

In the past ten years a set of statistical procedures, often called time series methods or "Box-Jenkins methods," Box and Jenkins (1970), have become widely used for the analysis and prediction of time series data. While in some ways these procedures are similar to standard econometric procedures, in many ways they are quite different, both in techniques used and in underlying philosophy. Because of these differences and because of the increasingly widespread use of Box-Jenkins models in econometrics, we present a fairly lengthy excursion into time series methodology. In this chapter we first discuss the nature of time series analysis and its relationship to standard econometric methods. We then discuss the basic theory of time series analysis, including discussions of autoregressive, moving average, and autoregressive moving average processes. Excellent treatments of time series analysis can be found in Anderson (1971), Box and Jenkins (1970), and Fuller (1976).

## 3.1 Introduction

We begin by explaining why time series data are different from other types of data and why the analysis of time series data requires different techniques than those used to analyze other data. The main difference is that for time series data the ordering of the data is important: the value of a variable at time $t$ is likely to depend on the value of the variable at some earlier time, $s$. A time series of length $T$ is not $T$ different observations of a random variable, but is *one* observation of a multivariate random variable. This dependence over time is a mixed blessing. On the one hand, standard methods requiring independently, identically distributed observations cannot be used directly; on the other hand the dependence over time can be exploited for several purposes, not the least of which is forecasting.

Time series methods can be distinguished from standard econometric models in a number of ways, but the two most important distinctions are in the purpose of the model and in the use of theory. Time series methods are usually used to build models that are useful for prediction. In this application parameter estimates, tests of significance of parameters, and so on, are important only to the extent that they aid in forecasting; there is no intrinsic reason to know the parameter values. Econometric models are often built for purposes of testing theory rather than for purposes of forecasting; moreover, an interest in the values of parameters is often the reason that models are built, unlike the case in time series models. This distinction is not empty—it is not always the case that the best parameter estimates yield the best forecasts. The second major difference between econometric and time series methods has to do with the role of theory. Econometricians take pride in the ways they have developed to incorporate information from both theory and data into parameter estimates, for example, simultaneous equation estimation. Time series methods, on the other hand, rarely incorporate theory into parameter estimates, and it is hard to see how theory would ever develop in a way that could yield restrictions useful in estimating simple time series models.[1]

For these two reasons, econometric and time series methods have been considered essentially different. This is not to say that econometricians would not find time series methods useful—for "quick and dirty" forecasts, for forecasts where little theory is available, for the analysis and modeling of error processes, for building naive models to test predictive power with more sophisticated models—but time series models have usually been considered to be outside of the mainstream of conventional econometrics. Fortunately, recent theoretical developments have brought time series models and standard econometric methods closer together. These are discussed in Chapter 5.

## 3.2 Background Material

In this section we introduce methods and definitions needed for the analysis of time series data that are not likely to be covered in an econometrics course. We discuss lag operators, stationarity, autocovariance, and autocorrelation.

### 3.2.1 Lag Operators

Before working with time series models it is useful to introduce the notions of lag operators and polynomials in the lag operator. The treatment here will not be completely rigorous; a good discussion of the mathematical validity of using lag operators can be found in Dhrymes (1971).

Let us call the lag operator $L$. It operates on the variable $Y_t$ as follows:

$$\begin{aligned} LY_t &= Y_{t-1}, \\ LLY_t &= L^2Y_t = LY_{t-1} = Y_{t-2}, \\ L^kY_t &= Y_{t-k}. \end{aligned}$$

That is, the lag operator $L$ takes $Y_t$ into its past value $Y_{t-1}$. The lag operator is often referred to as the "backshift operator." $L$ is said to have an inverse $F$, the lead operator, where

$$\begin{aligned} F &= L^{-1}, \\ F \cdot L &= 1, \\ FY_t &= Y_{t+1}, \\ L(FY_t) &= LY_{t+1}, = Y_t. \end{aligned}$$

The lead operator is often referred to as the "forward shift" operator. If we formally

[1]There are some situations in which theory can be of use in time series models, for example, rational expectation and efficient market models where parameter restrictions are implied. It is conceivable that the Zellner-Palm (1974) approach (see Chapter 5) could be used to bring economic theory to bear on the estimation of time series models, but this would be very difficult.

treat $L$ as a variable we can write a (possibly infinite) polynomial in $L$, $\phi(L)$, called a lag polynomial. The lag operators in the lag polynomial operate linearly upon a variable as is shown below.

If

$$\phi(L) = \phi_0 + \phi_1 L + \phi_2 L^2 + \cdots + \phi_p L^p,$$

then

$$\begin{aligned}\phi(L)Y_t &= (\phi_0 + \phi_1 L + \phi_2 L^2 + \cdots + \phi_p L^p)Y_t \\ &= \phi_0 Y_t + \phi_1 Y_{t-1} + \phi_2 Y_{t-2} + \cdots + \phi_p Y_{t-p} \\ &= \sum_{i=0}^{p} \phi_i Y_{t-i}.\end{aligned}$$

The use of lag polynomials leads to a compact notation, but that is not the only gain from their use. As shown in Dhrymes, many complicated operations can be performed on time series processes simply by manipulation of the lag operator. These include multiplication and division. For example, if

$$Y_t = (\phi_0 + \phi_1 L + \phi_2 L^2)X_t$$

and

$$X_t = (\theta_0 + \theta_1 L)\epsilon_t,$$

$Y_t$ may be expressed as

$$\begin{aligned}Y_t &= (\phi_0 + \phi_1 L + \phi_2 L^2)(\theta_0 + \theta_1 L)\epsilon_t \\ &= [\phi_0\theta_0 + (\phi_1\theta_0 + \phi_0\theta_1)L + (\phi_2\theta_0 + \phi_1\theta_1)L^2 + \phi_2\theta_1 L^3]\epsilon_t \\ &= \phi_0\theta_0\epsilon_t + (\phi_1\theta_0 + \phi_0\theta_1)\epsilon_{t-1} + (\phi_2\theta_0 + \phi_1\theta_1)\epsilon_{t-2} + \phi_2\theta_1\epsilon_{t-3},\end{aligned}$$

where the coefficients of the lag polynomial operator are obtained by straightforward polynomial multiplication. Solving by substitution yields the same answer. As the above example suggests, transformations of variables can be handled by simply treating polynomials in the lag operator as polynomials in the *variable* $L$, doing the manipulation, and then using the fact that $L$ is the lag operator.

As another example, polynomial lag operators can be manipulated as polynomials for purposes of division. If

$$Y_t = \phi(L)X_t,$$

we may write

$$\phi^{-1}(L)Y_t = X_t,$$

where $\phi^{-1}(L)$ is the inverse of the polynomial $\phi(L)$.

Polynomials are easily inverted. If $\phi(L)$ is a polynomial, let $\psi(L)$ be its inverse, that is,

$$\phi(L)\psi(L) = 1.$$

Multiplying and collecting terms we get

$$(\phi_0 + \phi_1 L + \phi_2 L^2 + \cdots)(\psi_0 + \psi_1 L + \psi_2 L^2 + \cdots)$$
$$= 1 + 0L + 0L^2 + \cdots$$

$$(\phi_0\psi_0) = 1 \quad \Rightarrow \psi_0 = \frac{1}{\phi_0},$$

$$(\phi_0\psi_1 + \psi_1\phi_0)L = 0 \quad \Rightarrow \psi_1 = -\frac{\phi_1}{\phi_0^2},$$

$$(\phi_0\psi_2 + \phi_1\psi_1 + \phi_2\psi_0)L^2 = 0 \Rightarrow \psi_2 = \frac{\phi_1^2}{\phi_0^3} - \frac{\phi_2}{\phi_0^2},$$

$$\vdots \qquad\qquad \vdots$$

Note that the inverse of a finite polynomial is an infinite polynomial. Polynomials can also be inverted by the "long division" technique.

Polynomial multiplication and division allows us to write the lag relationship

$$\phi(L)Y_t = \theta(L)X_t$$

as

$$\begin{aligned} Y_t &= \frac{\theta(L)}{\phi(L)}X_t \\ &= \phi^{-1}(L)\theta(L)X_t \\ &= \left[\frac{1}{\phi_0} - \frac{\phi_1}{\phi_0^2}L + \left(\frac{\phi_1^2}{\phi_0^3} - \frac{\phi_2}{\phi_0^2}\right)L^2 + \cdots\right]\theta(L)X_t \\ &= [\alpha_0 + \alpha_1 L + \alpha_2 L^2 + \cdots]X_t. \end{aligned}$$

As another example, if

$$(1 - \rho L)Y_t = \epsilon_t,$$

then

$$Y_t = (1 - \rho L)^{-1}\epsilon_t,$$

which can be inverted by the above technique to yield

$$Y_t = (1 + \rho L + \rho^2 L^2 + \rho^3 L^3 + \cdots)\epsilon_t.$$

### 3.2.2 Stationarity

An important assumption for purposes of time series analysis is that of stationarity. We define stationarity in the strong sense as follows:

**Definition**

A time series is said to be *stationary in the strong sense* if the distribution function

$$F(Y_t, Y_{t+1}, \ldots, Y_{t+k}) = F(Y_{t+s}, Y_{t+s+1}, \ldots, Y_{t+s+k})$$

for all $s$ and $k$.

This is a strong assumption on a time series; it requires that the joint distribution of $k$ consecutive observations be identical regardless of when the $k$ observations occur. Since this assumption is so strong, a weaker assumption, that of weak stationarity is often made.

**Definition**

A time series is said to be *weakly stationary* if

$$EY_t = EY_s < \infty, \qquad \text{for all } s, t$$

$$EY_tY_{t+k} = EY_{t+s}Y_{t+s+k} < \infty, \qquad \text{for all } s, t, k.$$

Weak stationarity is often referred to as *stationarity of order two* or *second order stationarity* due to the restrictions placed on the second moments. The definition of stationarity of order $n$ should be obvious. If the second moments of the probability distribution exist, weak stationarity is much less restrictive than strong stationarity, since weak stationarity requires only that the second moments be independent of time of occurrence, whereas strong stationarity requires identical density functions. Weak stationarity is a strong enough assumption for most statistical analyses of data. While a general analysis of nonstationary time series is beyond the scope of this book, in many cases a simple transformation can be made on a nonstationary process to make the transformed process stationary. This will be discussed below.

### 3.2.3 Autocovariance and Autocorrelation

Useful tools for analyzing a time series are the *autocovariance function* and the *autocorrelation function.*

**Definition**

Let $Y_t$ and $Y_{t-k}$ be observations from a time series with mean zero. The *autocovariance function* $\gamma(k)$, or $\gamma_k$, is defined as

$$\gamma(k) \equiv \gamma_k \equiv E[Y_tY_{t-k}], \qquad k = 0, 1, 2, \ldots.$$

For a stationary time series the *autocorrelation function*, $\rho(k)$, or $\rho_k$, is

$$\rho(k) \equiv \rho_k \equiv \frac{\gamma_k}{\gamma_0}.$$

Obviously, the autocovariance function is just the covariance between current and lagged values of the time series in question, and the autocorrelation function is the autocovariance function standardized by division by $\gamma_0$. Since we normally do not know the autocovariances, they must be estimated. Consistent estimates are given by

$$c_k \equiv \hat{\gamma}_k = \frac{1}{T} \sum_{t=k+1}^{T} (Y_t - \bar{Y})(Y_{t-k} - \bar{Y})$$

$$r_k \equiv \hat{\rho}_k = \frac{c_k}{c_0} = \frac{\hat{\gamma}_k}{\hat{\gamma}_0}.$$

Note that the estimates use the divisor $T$ rather than $T - k$. Although this leads to biased small sample estimators of the population moments, it is done to get simple results for the distribution of the estimates. The autocorrelation function (ACF) is often plotted, and the plot is referred to as the *correlogram*. The autocorrelation function, when combined with the partial autocorrelation function (to be defined below), is useful for identifying the nature of the time series model to be fitted to the data. Many examples of autocorrelation functions are given below.

### 3.2.4 Time Series Models

To analyze a time series we need to specify time series models. These models impose a structure on the time series that allows us, using a finite number of parameters, to characterize, analyze, and forecast from a time series. We now proceed to develop three different, although related, parameterizations of time series: the autoregressive model, the moving average model, and the autoregressive moving average model. In an autoregressive model, the current value of a time series depends upon past values of a time series and a random error. In a moving average model, the current value of a random variable depends upon current and past random errors. Finally, in an autoregressive moving average model, the current value of a time series depends upon past values of the time series and current and past random errors. We proceed to develop these three types of models in turn.

## 3.3 The Autoregressive Model

In this section we impose an autoregressive structure upon a time series. The autoregressive structure is a relatively simple, but amazingly powerful, model for the analysis of a time series. The autoregressive process assumes that the current value of a time series depends upon past values of the time series and a random shock. It is essentially a model that transforms a statistical problem involving highly dependent random variables into one involving identically, independently distributed random variables.

### 3.3.1 Autoregressive Representation

An autoregressive model of order $p$, AR($p$), is expressed as

$$Y_t = \phi_1 Y_{t-1} + \phi_2 Y_{t-2} + \cdots + \phi_p Y_{t-p} + a_t, \tag{3.3.1}$$

or,

$$Y_t - \phi_1 Y_{t-1} - \phi_2 Y_{t-2} - \cdots - \phi_p Y_{t-p} = a_t,$$

where

$$a_t \sim \text{i.i.d.}(0, \sigma_a^2).$$

Equation 3.3.1 can also be written with a polynomial lag operator as

$$\phi(L)Y_t = a_t. \tag{3.3.2}$$

In 3.3.1 and 3.3.2 we write $Y_t$ as a function of past $Y$ values and a random error term $a_t$. Since the $a_t$ term represents the part of the time series that cannot be predicted from the past, it is often referred to as the *innovation* in the time series.

### 3.3.2 Stationarity in Autoregressive Models

Stationarity in the weak sense requires that the second moments of a time series are both independent of time and are finite. In this section we manipulate the AR representation of a time series into a form in which we can easily see the requirements that stationarity puts on the coefficients of an AR process.

The time series $Y$ can, under certain assumptions, be represented as a function only of past innovations. Thic can be seen by starting with the autoregressive form of the model

$$Y_t - \phi_1 Y_{t-1} - \phi_2 Y_{t-2} - \cdots - \phi_p Y_{t-p} = a_t,$$

or,

$$Y_t = \phi_1 Y_{t-1} + \phi_2 Y_{t-2} + \cdots + \phi_p Y_{t-p} + a_t,$$

and substituting the expression for $Y_{t-1}$ into the process:

$$Y_t = \phi_1(\phi_1 Y_{t-2} + \phi_2 Y_{t-3} + \cdots + \phi_p Y_{t-p-1} + a_{t-1}) + \phi_2 Y_{t-2} + \cdots + a_t. \tag{3.3.3}$$

This yields

$$Y_t = (\phi_2 + \phi_1^2)Y_{t-2} + (\phi_3 + \phi_1\phi_2)Y_{t-3} + \cdots \phi_p Y_{t-p-1} + a_t + \phi_1 a_{t-1}.$$

Continuing this process (and making assumptions to be discussed below) we obtain

$$Y_t = a_t + \psi_1 a_{t-1} + \psi_2 a_{t-2} + \cdots. \tag{3.3.4}$$

Making any finite number of substitutions of 3.3.1 lagged $n$ times into 3.3.3 requires no additional assumptions. However, making the infinite number of substitutions that results in 3.3.4 does require restrictions on the $\phi_i$; these are discussed below. This derivation is much easier in lag operator notation. The autoregressive representation can be written as

$$\phi(L)Y_t = a_t.$$

Premultiplication by the inverse of $\phi(L)$ yields

$$Y_t = \phi^{-1}(L)a_t,$$

and setting $\phi^{-1}(L) = \psi(L)$, we have $Y_t = \psi(L)a_t$.

This procedure can be better understood with the aid of a simple example,

$$Y_t - \phi_1 Y_{t-1} = a_t,$$

or

$$Y_t = \phi_1 Y_{t-1} + a_t.$$

Substitution yields

$$\begin{aligned} Y_t &= \phi_1(\phi_1 Y_{t-2} + a_{t-1}) + a_t \\ &= \phi_1^2 Y_{t-2} + \phi_1 a_{t-1} + a_t \\ &= \phi_1^2(\phi_1 Y_{t-3} + a_{t-2}) + \phi_1 a_{t-1} + a_t \\ &= \phi_1^3 Y_{t-3} + \phi_1^2 a_{t-2} + \phi_1 a_{t-1} + a_t \qquad (3.3.5) \\ &\cdot \\ &\cdot \\ &\cdot \\ Y_t &= a_t + \phi_1 a_{t-1} + \phi_1^2 a_{t-2} + \phi_1^3 a_{t-3} + \cdots. \end{aligned}$$

In terms of the lag operator, we have

$$(1 - \phi_1 L)Y_t = a_t,$$

which implies that

$$\begin{aligned} Y_t &= (1 + \phi_1 L + \phi_1^2 L^2 + \phi_1^2 L^3 + \cdots)a_t \qquad (3.3.6) \\ &= a_t + \phi_1 a_{t-1} + \phi_1^2 a_{t-2} + \cdots. \end{aligned}$$

A similar procedure can be used to find the autoregressive weights (the $\phi_i$'s), given the $\psi_i$'s:

$$\begin{aligned} Y_t &= a_t + \phi_1 a_{t-1} + \phi_1^2 a_{t-2} + \cdots \\ \psi_0 &= 1, \\ \psi_1 &= \phi_1, \\ \psi_2 &= \phi_1^2, \qquad (3.3.7) \\ &\cdot \\ &\cdot \\ &\cdot \end{aligned}$$

Since we have shown that under unspecified assumptions an AR process can be represented as a weighted sum of past innovations, it is of interest to determine when such a representation exists. To do so we first examine the simple AR(1) process and ask when $Y_t$, as represented in (3.3.6), is stationary. To examine the stationarity of the $Y_t$ series we first examine the variance of $Y_t$:

$$E[Y_t^2] = E[(a_1 + \phi_1 a_{t-1} + \phi_1^2 a_{t-2} + \cdots)^2] \qquad \textbf{(3.3.8)}$$
$$= [1 + \phi_1^2 + \phi_1^4 + \phi_1^6 + \cdots]\sigma_a^2.$$

Obviously the variance of $Y$ is finite if and only if $|\phi_1| < 1$. Therefore stationarity is equivalent to $\phi_1$ being between $-1$ and 1. In terms of the lag operator $1 - \phi_1 L$, this requires that the root of the equation $1 - \phi_1 L = 0$, which is $L = 1/\phi_1$, be greater than 1 in absolute value.

In the more general case, similar results can be obtained. We show this for the special case in which $\phi(L)$ is a $p$th order polynomial in $L$. From the theory of equations it is known that the lag polynomial $\phi(L)$ can be written as a product of first degree polynomials. Accordingly,

$$\phi(L) = \prod_{i=1}^{p} (1 - \lambda_i L),$$

where the $\lambda_i$ terms may be complex. Therefore,

$$\psi(L) = \phi^{-1}(L) = \prod_{i=1}^{p} (1 - \lambda_i L)^{-1}$$
$$= \prod_{i=1}^{p} (1 + \lambda_i L + \lambda_i^2 L^2 + \lambda_i^3 L^3 + \cdots),$$

and for $k > p$

$$\psi_k = \sum_{i=1}^{p} \left[ \lambda_i^k + \lambda_i^{k-1} \sum_{j \neq i} \lambda_j + \lambda_i^{k-2} \left( \sum_{j \neq i} \lambda_j^2 + \sum_{j \neq i} \sum_{l \neq j} \lambda_j \lambda_l \right) + \cdots \right].$$

From this equation it can be seen that, if all the $\lambda_i$ were real, stationarity would require that all $|\lambda_i| < 1$. Including the possibility of complex $\lambda_i$, stationarity requires that all the $\lambda_i$ have moduli less than 1, or that the $\lambda_i$ be inside the unit circle. (Appendix A contains a short review of complex numbers.)

The stationarity condition is usually phrased in terms of roots of the $\phi(L)$ polynomials. Setting $\phi(L)$ to zero,

$$\phi(L) = 0,$$

implies that

$$\prod_{i=1}^{p} (1 - \lambda_i L) = 0,$$

which has roots

$$L = \frac{1}{\lambda_i}, \qquad i = 1, \ldots, p.$$

Thus the stationarity condition can be phrased in terms of the roots of the above equation; if $\lambda_i$ is inside the unit circle, the root $1/\lambda_i$ is outside the unit circle. Therefore, the process is stationary if the roots of the AR lag polynomial are outside the unit circle.

An intuitive reason for assuming stationarity is the belief that the effects of the past become less important the further in the past they occurred. As can be seen from (3.3.8), in a nonstationary series, the effect of past innovations does not diminish with time and actually grows.

### 3.3.3 Stationarity and Stability

At this point, we present a short digression to clear up a point concerning roots of polynomial equations that may be confusing. An AR($p$) process is stationary if the roots of the polynomial equation

$$1 + \phi_1 L + \phi_2 L^2 + \cdots + \phi_p L^p = 0$$

are outside the unit circle. However, if we think of the AR($p$) equation 3.3.1, written in terms of the $Y_t$'s, as a difference equation we would get [e.g., see Chiang (1967), p. 532] a characteristic equation of the form

$$X^p + \phi_1 X^{p-1} + \phi_2 X^{p-2} + \cdots + \phi_p = 0,$$

which is said to be stable only if its roots are inside the unit circle.

This may lead to some confusion between conditions for stability in difference equations and conditions for stationarity in autoregressive equations. Fortunately the confusion is easily dispelled. Notice that in the AR form, the powers of the variable, $L$, are the same as the index of the coefficient, while in the difference equation form of the model the coefficient index and the power of the variable always sum to $p$. This turns out to be the key in explaining the apparent contradiction.

The roots of the equation

$$1 + \alpha_1 W + \alpha_2 W^2 + \cdots + \alpha_k W^k = 0$$

are inverses of the roots of the equation

$$Z^k + \alpha_1 Z^{k-1} + \alpha_2 Z^{k-2} + \cdots + \alpha_{k-1} Z + \alpha_k = 0.$$

This is easily seen by dividing both sides of the second form of the above equation by $Z^k$, which yields

$$1 + \alpha_1 Z^{-1} + \alpha_2 Z^{-2} + \cdots + \alpha_k Z^{-k} = 0.$$

Substituting $W$ for $Z^{-1}$ yields

$$1 + \alpha_1 W + \alpha_2 W^2 + \cdots + \alpha_k W_k = 0.$$

From this form it is obvious that any solution for $W$ in the first equation is the inverse of a solution for $Z$. Hence the requirements placed on the $\phi_i$ coefficients for stability of a difference equation are exactly the same as those placed upon an autoregressive equation for stationarity.

We now return to our discussion of autoregressive models.

### 3.3.4 Autocovariance Function of an Autoregressive Process

The autocovariance and the autocorrelation functions can be used to shed some light on the dynamic properties of the Ar($p$) process. Writing out the AR($p$) process and multiplying by $Y_t$ yields

$$Y_tY_t = \phi_1 Y_tY_{t-1} + \phi_2 Y_tY_{t-2} + \cdots + \phi_p Y_tY_{t-p} + Y_ta_t.$$

Upon taking expectations, remembering that $E[Y_tY_{t-k}] = \gamma_k$, we have

$$\gamma_0 = \phi_1\gamma_1 + \phi_2\gamma_2 + \cdots + \phi_p\gamma_p + \sigma_a^2.$$

Multiplying $Y_t$ by $Y_{t-1}$ and taking expectations yields

$$\gamma_1 = E[Y_tY_{t-1}] = \phi_1\gamma_0 + \phi_2\gamma_1 + \phi_3\gamma_2 + \cdots + \phi_p\gamma_{p-1}.$$

For $\gamma_2$ we have

$$\gamma_2 = E[Y_tY_{t-2}] = \phi_1\gamma_1 + \phi_2\gamma_0 + \phi_3\gamma_1 + \phi_4\gamma_2 + \cdots + \phi_p\gamma_{p-2}.$$

Multiplying $Y_t$ by $Y_{t-k}$, after taking expectations, we have for $k \geq p$

$$\gamma_k = \phi_1\gamma_{k-1} + \phi_2\gamma_{k-2} + \cdots + \phi_p\gamma_{k-p}. \qquad \textbf{(3.3.9)}$$

For $k \geq p$ we have the rather remarkable result that the autocovariances (and the autocorrelations) satisfy the same difference equation as the data. This is very useful since it helps us determine the nature of the actual series from the behavior of the autocovariances and autocorrelations. Because of this, we can write, for $k \geq p$,

$$\gamma_k = \sum_{i=1}^{p} c_i\lambda_i^k,$$

where the $\lambda_i$ are the roots of the difference equation of the autoregressive process. As with any difference equation, its behavior as $k$ gets large is determined by its largest root. If the largest root is less than one in modulus and is positive, the autocovariances will decay exponentially as $k$ gets large.[2] If the largest root is less than one in modulus and complex, the autocovariances will decay sinusoidally. If the largest root is less than one in modulus and negative, the autocovariances will flip-flop from positive to negative and decay as $k$ gets large.

[2]For a discussion of the properties of difference equations, see Goldberg (1958) or Chiang (1967).

Dropping the assumption of $k > p$, we can now write out explicitly the relationship between the AR coefficients and the autocorrelations:

$$\begin{aligned}
\gamma_1 &= \phi_1\gamma_0 + \phi_2\gamma_1 + \phi_3\gamma_2 + \cdots + \phi_p\gamma_{p-1} \\
\gamma_2 &= \phi_1\gamma_1 + \phi_2\gamma_0 + \phi_3\gamma_1 + \cdots + \phi_p\gamma_{p-2} \\
&\vdots \\
\gamma_k &= \phi_1\gamma_{k-1} + \phi_2\gamma_{k-2} + \cdots + \phi_p\gamma_{k-p}
\end{aligned} \tag{3.3.10}$$

where $\gamma_i = \gamma_{-i}$ if $i < 0$. The equations in (3.3.10) are referred to as the *Yule-Walker equations*.

The first $p$ Yule-Walker equations can be written in matrix form as

$$\begin{bmatrix} \gamma_1 \\ \gamma_2 \\ \cdot \\ \cdot \\ \cdot \\ \gamma_p \end{bmatrix} = \begin{bmatrix} \gamma_0 & \gamma_1 & \cdots & \gamma_{p-1} \\ \gamma_1 & & & \\ \gamma_2 & & & \\ \cdot & & & \\ \cdot & & & \\ \cdot & & & \\ \gamma_{p-1} & & \cdots & \gamma_0 \end{bmatrix} \begin{bmatrix} \phi_1 \\ \phi_2 \\ \cdot \\ \cdot \\ \cdot \\ \phi_p \end{bmatrix}. \tag{3.3.11}$$

Note that since the matrix in (3.3.11) is invertible, the Yule-Walker equations allow us to solve for values of the AR coefficients using only the autocovariances. This yields the correct values for the AR coefficients for $k \geq p$, but for $k < p$ it does not. To see this we write the Yule-Walker equations for $k < p$ as

$$\begin{bmatrix} \gamma_1 \\ \gamma_2 \\ \cdot \\ \cdot \\ \cdot \\ \gamma_k \end{bmatrix} = \begin{bmatrix} \gamma_0 & \gamma_1 & \cdots & \gamma_{k-1} \\ \cdot & & & \\ \cdot & & & \\ \cdot & & & \\ \gamma_{k-1} & & \cdots & \gamma_0 \end{bmatrix} \begin{bmatrix} \phi_1 \\ \phi_2 \\ \cdot \\ \cdot \\ \cdot \\ \phi_k \end{bmatrix} + \begin{bmatrix} \gamma_k & \cdots & \gamma_{p-1} \\ \gamma_{k-1} & & \\ \cdot & & \\ \cdot & & \\ \cdot & & \\ \gamma_{p-1} & \cdots & \gamma_{k-p} \end{bmatrix} \begin{bmatrix} \phi_{k+1} \\ \cdot \\ \cdot \\ \cdot \\ \phi_p \end{bmatrix}$$

or in matrix notation

$$\boldsymbol{\gamma}_k = \Gamma_{kk}\boldsymbol{\phi}_k + \Gamma_{pk}\boldsymbol{\phi}_p. \tag{3.3.12}$$

Manipulation yields

$$\boldsymbol{\phi}_k = \Gamma_{kk}^{-1}\boldsymbol{\gamma}_k - \Gamma_{kk}^{-1}\Gamma_{pk}\boldsymbol{\phi}_p. \tag{3.3.13}$$

Let $\tilde{\boldsymbol{\phi}}_k$ be the solution to the Yule-Walker equations based upon only $k$ terms. $\tilde{\boldsymbol{\phi}}_k$ can be written as

$$\tilde{\boldsymbol{\phi}}_k = \Gamma_{kk}^{-1}\boldsymbol{\gamma}_k. \qquad \textbf{(3.3.14)}$$

Obviously $\tilde{\boldsymbol{\phi}}_k$ in (3.3.14) is not the same as $\boldsymbol{\phi}_k$. Because of this dependence on $k$, the solutions to the Yule-Walker equation are indexed as follows: $\phi_{ik}$ is the solution for $\phi_i$ from the Yule-Walker equation system of size $k$. It is shown below that $\phi_{ik} = \phi_i$ if $k \geq p$ and that $\phi_{ik} = 0$ if $k > p$ and $i > p$. The $\phi_{ik}$ are used to define the partial autocorrelation function, to which we turn next.

### 3.3.5 The Partial Autocorrelation Function

Regarding $\phi_{kk}$ as a function of $k$ yields the partial autocorrelation function. If $\phi_{kk}$ is the $k$th $\phi$ term of the Yule-Walker equation system of order $k$, we say PACF($k$) $= \phi_{kk}$.

**Definition**

Let $\boldsymbol{\phi}_k$ be the solution to the Yule-Walker equations of order $k$ for a stationary time series as defined in (3.2). Let $\phi_{kk}$ be the $k$th element of $\boldsymbol{\phi}_k$. We define $\phi_{kk}$ as the *kth order partial autocorrelation* and PACF($k$) as the *partial autocorrelation function.*

For example, if the autocovariances are

$$\begin{aligned} \gamma_0 &= 10 \\ \gamma_1 &= 4 \\ \gamma_2 &= 3 \\ \gamma_3 &= 2, \end{aligned}$$

then the first order Yule-Walker equations have the solution

$$\begin{aligned} \phi_{11} &= \Gamma_{11}^{-1}\gamma_1 \\ &= \frac{\gamma_1}{\gamma_0} \\ &= 0.4. \end{aligned}$$

For the second order Yule-Walker equations we have

$$\begin{aligned} \boldsymbol{\phi}_2 &= \Gamma_{22}^{-1}\boldsymbol{\gamma}_2 \\ &= \begin{bmatrix} 10 & 4 \\ 4 & 10 \end{bmatrix}^{-1} \begin{bmatrix} 4 \\ 3 \end{bmatrix} \\ &= \begin{bmatrix} 0.333 \\ 0.167 \end{bmatrix}, \end{aligned}$$

and

$$\phi_{22} = 0.167.$$

For the third order system

$$\phi_3 = \begin{bmatrix} 10 & 4 & 3 \\ 4 & 10 & 4 \\ 3 & 4 & 10 \end{bmatrix}^{-1} \begin{bmatrix} 4 \\ 3 \\ 2 \end{bmatrix}$$

and

$$\phi_{33} = 0.060.$$

Therefore, the PACF is

$$\begin{aligned} \text{PACF}(1) &= \phi_{11} = 0.400 \\ \text{PACF}(2) &= \phi_{22} = 0.167 \\ \text{PACF}(3) &= \phi_{33} = 0.060 \end{aligned}$$

One useful way of thinking of the PACF is as a series of marginal regression coefficients. If we were to regress $Y_t$ on $Y_{t-1}$ and replace the sample moments with the population moments, the coefficient on $Y_{t-1}$ would be the first PACF term; if we were to regress $Y_t$ on $Y_{t-1}$ and $Y_{t-2}$, and replace the sample moments by the population moments, the regression coefficient on $Y_{t-2}$ would be the second PACF term; the $k$th PACF term would be the coefficient on $Y_{t-k}$ in a regression of $Y_t$ on $Y_{t-1}, Y_{t-2}, \ldots, Y_{t-k}$ using population moments. The PACF and the marginal regression coefficients are approximately the same when actual data are used to calculate the regression coefficients and the PACF.

A particularly useful property of the partial autocorrelation function is that $\phi_{kk} = 0$ for $k > p$ for an AR($p$) process; that is, for an AR($p$) process the $p$ + first, $p$ + second, and so on, PACF terms are zero. This is easily shown by the following argument. Let the Yule-Walker equations be shown below, assuming $k > p$:

$$\begin{bmatrix} \gamma_1 \\ \gamma_2 \\ \cdot \\ \cdot \\ \cdot \\ \gamma_p \\ \gamma_{p+1} \\ \cdot \\ \cdot \\ \cdot \\ \gamma_k \end{bmatrix} = \begin{bmatrix} \gamma_0 & \gamma_1 & \cdots & \gamma_{p-1} & \gamma_p & & \gamma_{k-1} \\ \gamma_1 & \gamma_0 & \cdots & \gamma_{p-2} & \gamma_{p-1} & & \gamma_{k-2} \\ \cdot & & & & & & \\ \cdot & & & & & & \\ \cdot & & & & & & \\ \gamma_{p-1} & & & \gamma_0 & \gamma_1 & & \gamma_{k-p} \\ \gamma_p & \gamma_{p-1} & \cdots & \gamma_1 & \gamma_0 & \cdots & \gamma_{k-p-1} \\ \gamma_{p+1} & \gamma_p & & \cdot & \cdot & & \cdot \\ \cdot & & & \cdot & \cdot & & \cdot \\ \cdot & & & \cdot & \cdot & & \cdot \\ \gamma_{k-1} & & & \gamma_{k-p} & \gamma_{k-p-1} & & \gamma_0 \end{bmatrix} \begin{bmatrix} \phi_1 \\ \phi_2 \\ \cdot \\ \cdot \\ \cdot \\ \phi_p \\ \phi_{p+1} \\ \cdot \\ \cdot \\ \cdot \\ \phi_k \end{bmatrix}. \quad \textbf{(3.3.15)}$$

Equation 3.3.15 is a system of $k$ equations in $k$ unknowns. It is easy to show that the system is nonsingular, so there is a unique solution; hence if we can find a solution, it is the only solution. But notice that if $\phi_{p+1}, \ldots, \phi_k$ are set to zero, each equation is of the form

$$\gamma_i = \phi_1\gamma_{i-1} + \phi_2\gamma_{i-2} + \cdots + \phi_p\gamma_{i-p},$$

where

$$\gamma_{i-1} = \gamma_{|i-1|}, \qquad i < 0.$$

Now these equations are solved by the coefficients of the AR($p$) process, the $\phi_i$ terms. This gives a solution to the equation, and shows that the $\phi_i$ terms must be zero for $i > p$. And since solution terms of order greater than $p$ must be zero, no PACF term higher than the $p$th can be nonzero.

The ACF's and PACF's for stationary autoregressive processes have characteristic patterns: the ACF goes to zero as a function of its largest characteristic root, either exponentially or in an oscillatory fashion. The PACF, on the other hand, can be nonzero for the first $p$ terms, but is zero for terms after that. These patterns are very useful in determining both whether a time series is an AR process, and if so, what the value of $p$ is. (Unfortunately, things are not quite so simple when there is sampling error, as we shall see below.)

To use the ACF and PACF for determining the order of an AR process, we must have some idea of the patterns of ACF's and PACF's generated by particular time series models. Accordingly we present the ACF's and PACF's associated with a few AR models; these appear in Figures 3.1 to 3.4. Note that in all cases the PACF terms are nonzero where the number of lags is less than or equal to the number of nonzero AR terms. The ACF, on the other hand, approaches zero either exponentially or as a damped sinusoidal term as the number of lags becomes large, depending upon the value of the AR coefficients. Note that the speed with which the ACF goes to zero depends upon the value of the coefficients. For $\phi_1$ close to one in the AR(1), the ACF remains far from zero for a large number of lags.

## 3.4 The Moving Average Model

In this section we introduce a second type of model that imposes a structure upon a time series, the moving average. The moving average model represents a time series as a weighted sum of current and past white noise random errors.

### 3.4.1 Moving Average Representation

Let $Y_t$ be expressed as a linear function of past $a_t$ terms; this is called a *moving average process*.

$$\begin{aligned} Y_t &= \theta_0 a_t + \theta_1 a_{t-1} + \theta_2 a_{t-2} + \cdots + \theta_q a_{t-q} \\ &= \sum_{i=0}^{q} \theta_i a_{t-i} \\ &= \theta(L) a_t \end{aligned} \tag{3.4.1}$$

where

$$a_t \sim \text{i.i.d.}(0, \sigma_a^2).$$

A moving average process that depends upon lagged $a_t$ terms, where the largest lag is $q$, is referred to as an MA($q$) process. We will use the convention that $\theta_0 = 1$, which merely entails a scaling of the $a_t$ term. Notice that this representation of $Y_t$ expresses the time series as a (possibly infinite) linear combination of white noise terms. (A white noise process is a series of independently, identically distributed random variables.)

As with the AR process, the white noise term, $a_t$, is often referred to as the *innovation* of the time series—that part of the time series that cannot be predicted from its own past. The variance of $a_t$ is referred to as the innovation variance of the series to distinguish it from $\gamma_0$, the variance of the $Y_t$ series.

A theoretical justification for the moving average process is given by the Wold decomposition theorem [Wold (1954)]. This theorem states that any stationary time series can be uniquely represented by the sum of two mutually uncorrelated processes, where the first process is linearly deterministic, and the second is a moving average process.

From the above representation we can easily calculate the autocovariance and autocorrelation functions.

$$\begin{aligned} \gamma_0 &= E[Y_t Y_t] \\ &= E[(a_t + \theta_1 a_{t-1} + \theta_2 a_t + \cdots + \theta_q a_{t-q})^2] \\ &= \sigma_a^2(1 + \theta_1^2 + \theta_2^2 + \cdots + \theta_q a_{t-q}) \\ &= \sigma_a^2 \sum_{i=0}^{q} \theta_i^2; \end{aligned} \tag{3.4.2}$$

$$\begin{aligned} \gamma_1 &= E[(a_t + \theta_1 a_{t-1} + \theta_2 a_{t-2} + \cdots + \theta_q a_{t-q}) \\ &\times (a_{t-1} + \theta_1 a_{t-2} + \theta_2 a_{t-3} + \cdots \theta_q a_{t-q-1})] \\ &= \sigma_a^2(\theta_1 + \theta_1\theta_2 + \theta_2\theta_3 + \cdots + \theta_{q-1}\theta_q) \\ &= \sigma_a^2 \sum_{i=1}^{q} \theta_{i-1}\theta_i; \end{aligned}$$

$$\begin{aligned} \gamma_k &= E[(a_t + \theta_1 a_{t-1} + \theta_2 a_{t-2} + \cdots + \theta_q a_{t-q}) \\ &\times (a_{t-k} + \theta_1 a_{t-k-1} + \cdots + \theta_q a_{t-q-k})] \\ &= \sigma_a^2(\theta_k + \theta_1\theta_{k+1} + \cdots + \theta_{k-q}\theta_k) \\ &= \sigma_a^2 \sum_{i=k}^{q} \theta_i\theta_{i-k}. \end{aligned} \tag{3.4.3}$$

```
AUTOCORRELATION FUNCTION
LAG      ACF      -1                   0                   +1
                  I--------------------+--------------------I
  1     0.500     I                    +         *
  2     0.250     I                    +    *
  3     0.125     I                    + *
  4     0.063     I                    +*
  5     0.031     I                    +*
  6     0.016     I                    *
  7     0.008     I                    *
  8     0.004     I                    *
  9     0.002     I                    *
 10     0.000     I                    *
 11     0.000     I                    *
 12     0.000     I                    *
 13     0.000     I                    *
 14     0.000     I                    *
 15     0.000     I                    *
 16     0.000     I                    *
 17     0.000     I                    *
 18     0.000     I                    *
 19     0.000     I                    *
 20     0.000     I                    *
                  I--------------------+--------------------I

PARTIAL AUTOCORRELATION FUNCTION

LAG     PACF      -1                   0                   +1
                  I--------------------+--------------------I
  1     0.500     I                    +         *
  2     0.000     I                    *
  3     0.000     I                    *
  4     0.000     I                    *
  5     0.000     I                    *
  6     0.000     I                    *
  7     0.000     I                    *
  8     0.000     I                    *
  9     0.000     I                    *
 10     0.000     I                    *
 11     0.000     I                    *
 12     0.000     I                    *
 13     0.000     I                    *
 14     0.000     I                    *
 15     0.000     I                    *
 16     0.000     I                    *
 17     0.000     I                    *
 18     0.000     I                    *
 19     0.000     I                    *
 20     0.000     I                    *
                  I--------------------+--------------------I
```

**FIGURE 3.1** ACF and PACF of $Y_t = 0.5Y_{t-1} + a_t$.

```
AUTOCORRELATION FUNCTION
LAG        ACF      -1                   0                   +1
                    I--------------------+--------------------I
   1       0.900    I                    +                *
   2       0.810    I                    +              *
   3       0.729    I                    +             *
   4       0.656    I                    +            *
   5       0.590    I                    +           *
   6       0.531    I                    +         *
   7       0.478    I                    +        *
   8       0.430    I                    +       *
   9       0.387    I                    +       *
  10       0.349    I                    +      *
  11       0.313    I                    +     *
  12       0.282    I                    +    *
  13       0.254    I                    +    *
  14       0.229    I                    +   *
  15       0.206    I                    +   *
  16       0.185    I                    +  *
  17       0.167    I                    +  *
  18       0.150    I                    +  *
  19       0.135    I                    + *
  20       0.118    I                    + *
                    I--------------------+--------------------I

PARTIAL AUTOCORRELATION FUNCTION

LAG        PACF     -1                   0                   +1
                    I--------------------+--------------------I
   1       0.900    I                    +                *
   2       0.000    I                    *
   3       0.000    I                    *
   4       0.000    I                    *
   5       0.000    I                    *
   6       0.000    I                    *
   7       0.000    I                    *
   8       0.000    I                    *
   9       0.000    I                    *
  10       0.000    I                    *
  11       0.000    I                    *
  12       0.000    I                    *
  13       0.000    I                    *
  14       0.000    I                    *
  15       0.000    I                    *
  16       0.000    I                    *
  17       0.000    I                    *
  18       0.000    I                    *
  19       0.000    I                    *
  20       0.000    I                    *
                    I--------------------+--------------------I
```

**FIGURE 3.2** ACF and PACF of $Y_t = 0.9Y_{t-1} + a_t$.

```
AUTOCORRELATION FUNCTION
LAG        ACF      -1                    0                    +1
                    I--------------------+--------------------I
  1     -0.500      I          *          +
  2      0.250      I                     +    *
  3     -0.125      I                 *   +
  4      0.063      I                     +*
  5      0.031      I                    *+
  6      0.016      I                     *
  7      0.008      I                     *
  8      0.004      I                     *
  9      0.002      I                     *
 10      0.000      I                     *
 11      0.000      I                     *
 12      0.000      I                     *
 13      0.000      I                     *
 14      0.000      I                     *
 15      0.000      I                     *
 16      0.000      I                     *
 17      0.000      I                     *
 18      0.000      I                     *
 19      0.000      I                     *
 20      0.000      I                     *
                    I--------------------+--------------------I

PARTIAL AUTOCORRELATION FUNCTION

LAG       PACF      -1                    0                    +1
                    I--------------------+--------------------I
  1     -0.500      I          *          +
  2      0.000      I                     *
  3      0.000      I                     *
  4      0.000      I                     *
  5      0.000      I                     *
  6      0.000      I                     *
  7      0.000      I                     *
  8      0.000      I                     *
  9      0.000      I                     *
 10      0.000      I                     *
 11      0.000      I                     *
 12      0.000      I                     *
 13      0.000      I                     *
 14      0.000      I                     *
 15      0.000      I                     *
 16      0.000      I                     *
 17      0.000      I                     *
 18      0.000      I                     *
 19      0.000      I                     *
 20      0.000      I                     *
                    I--------------------+--------------------I
```

**FIGURE 3.3** ACF and PACF of $Y_t = -0.5Y_{t-1} + a_t$.

```
AUTOCORRELATION FUNCTION
LAG       ACF    -1                  0                  +1
                 I-------------------+-------------------I
  1     0.600    I                   +           *
  2     0.040    I                   +*
  3    -0.264    I              *    +
  4    -0.258    I              *    +
  5    -0.100    I                 * +
  6     0.039    I                   +*
  7     0.085    I                   + *
  8     0.057    I                   +*
  9     0.009    I                   *
 10     0.020    I                  *+
 11     0.023    I                  *+
 12     0.010    I                   *
 13     0.002    I                   *
 14     0.007    I                   *
 15     0.005    I                   *
 16     0.000    I                   *
 17     0.000    I                   *
 18     0.000    I                   *
 19     0.000    I                   *
 20     0.000    I                   *
                 I-------------------+-------------------I

PARTIAL AUTOCORRELATION FUNCTION

LAG       PACF   -1                  0                  +1
                 I-------------------+-------------------I
  1     0.600    I                   +           *
  2    -0.500    I         *         +
  3     0.000    I                   *
  4     0.000    I                   *
  5     0.000    I                   *
  6     0.000    I                   *
  7     0.000    I                   *
  8     0.000    I                   *
  9     0.000    I                   *
 10     0.000    I                   *
 11     0.000    I                   *
 12     0.000    I                   *
 13     0.000    I                   *
 14     0.000    I                   *
 15     0.000    I                   *
 16     0.000    I                   *
 17     0.000    I                   *
 18     0.000    I                   *
 19     0.000    I                   *
 20     0.000    I                   *
                 I-------------------+-------------------I
```

**FIGURE 3.4** ACF and PACF of $Y_t = 0.5Y_{t-1} - 0.5Y_{t-2} + a_t$.

The autocorrelation function is then obtained by dividing each $\gamma_i$ term by $\gamma_0$.

From Equation 3.4.3 we can see that the second moments of the $Y_t$ series do not change over time; hence, the $Y_t$ series is weakly stationary if the second moment exists. Using the fact that $|\gamma_0| > |\gamma_k|$ for all $k$, if $\gamma_0$ is finite,[3] the series is stationary if the power series in $\theta_i$ (3.4.2) in converges. Note that convergence implies that the $\theta_i$ coefficients get smaller as $i$ increases, so that the importance of past random shocks to the current variable diminishes. This is an intuitively appealing property.

It is obvious from (3.4.3) that the autocorrelation function for the MA($q$) process is (in general) nonzero for the first $q$ terms, but zero for terms higher than $q$. The partial autocorrelation function, on the other hand, is nonzero for all terms. This can be seen by writing the MA($q$) process in terms of its roots,

$$y_t = \prod_{i=1}^{q} (1 - \omega_i L)a_t,$$

which, upon inversion, becomes

$$\prod_{i=1}^{q} (1 + \omega_i L + \omega_i^2 L^2 + \cdots)Y_t = a_t.$$

This represents the MA process as an infinite autoregressive process, where the sizes of the coefficients decrease as the lag gets large. Since the AR representation is infinite, the MA process has a PACF that approaches zero asymptotically.

To give the reader some idea of what the ACF and PACF of an MA($q$) process look like, we present plots of the ACF and PACF for several MA processes. See Figures 3.5 to 3.8. Note that in all cases the ACF is zero for lags that exceed $q$ and that in all cases the PACF approaches zero, but that the speed and manner with which it approaches zero depends upon the particular coefficients.

### 3.4.2 Invertibility

A random variable which has a moving average representation can, under certain conditions, be represented as a linear combination of its past values. This can best be seen using the simple MA(1) model,

$$Y_t = a_t + \theta_1 a_{t-1} = (1 + \theta_1 L)a_t, \tag{3.4.4}$$

which can be written as

$$a_t = Y_t - \theta_1 a_{t-1}. \tag{3.4.5}$$

Substituting (3.4.5) with lagged subscripts into (3.4.4) yields

$$Y_t = \theta_1 Y_{t-1} - \theta_1^2 a_{t-2} + a_t. \tag{3.4.6}$$

Repeated substitution of (3.4.5) with lagged subscripts into (3.4.6) yields

$$Y_t = \theta_1 Y_{t-1} - \theta_1^2 Y_{t-2} + \theta_1^3 Y_{t-3} - \cdots + (-1)^{i-1}\theta_1^i Y_{t-i} + \cdots + a_t. \tag{3.4.7}$$

[3]This is easily seen by examining the covariance matrix of $Y_t$ and $Y_{t-k}$. Positive definiteness requires that $\gamma_0^2 - \gamma_k^2 > 0$, which in turn requires $|\gamma_0| > |\gamma_k|$.

```
AUTOCORRELATION FUNCTION
LAG       ACF      -1                  0                   +1
                   I-------------------+--------------------I
  1        0.400   I                   +       *
  2        0.000   I                   *
  3        0.000   I                   *
  4        0.000   I                   *
  5        0.000   I                   *
  6        0.000   I                   *
  7        0.000   I                   *
  8        0.000   I                   *
  9        0.000   I                   *
 10        0.000   I                   *
 11        0.000   I                   *
 12        0.000   I                   *
 13        0.000   I                   *
 14        0.000   I                   *
 15        0.000   I                   *
 16        0.000   I                   *
 17        0.000   I                   *
 18        0.000   I                   *
 19        0.000   I                   *
 20        0.000   I                   *
                   I-------------------+--------------------I
```

```
PARTIAL AUTOCORRELATION FUNCTION

LAG       PACF     -1                  0                   +1
                   I-------------------+--------------------I
  1        0.400   I                   +       *
  2       -0.190   I               *   +
  3        0.094   I                   + *
  4        0.047   I                  *+
  5        0.023   I                   *
  6        0.012   I                   *
  7        0.006   I                   *
  8        0.003   I                   *
  9        0.001   I                   *
 10        0.001   I                   *
 11        0.000   I                   *
 12        0.000   I                   *
 13        0.000   I                   *
 14        0.000   I                   *
 15        0.000   I                   *
 16        0.000   I                   *
 17        0.000   I                   *
 18        0.000   I                   *
 19        0.000   I                   *
 20        0.000   I                   *
                   I-------------------+--------------------I
```

**FIGURE 3.5** ACF and PACF of $Y_t = a_t + 0.5a_{t-1}$.

```
AUTOCORRELATION FUNCTION
LAG        ACF   -1                  0                   +1
                 I-------------------+-------------------I
   1    -0.497  I         *         +
   2     0.000  I                   *
   3     0.000  I                   *
   4     0.000  I                   *
   5     0.000  I                   *
   6     0.000  I                   *
   7     0.000  I                   *
   8     0.000  I                   *
   9     0.000  I                   *
  10     0.000  I                   *
  11     0.000  I                   *
  12     0.000  I                   *
  13     0.000  I                   *
  14     0.000  I                   *
  15     0.000  I                   *
  16     0.000  I                   *
  17     0.000  I                   *
  18     0.000  I                   *
  19     0.000  I                   *
  20     0.000  I                   *
                I-------------------+-------------------I

PARTIAL AUTOCORRELATION FUNCTION

LAG       PACF   -1                  0                   +1
                I-------------------+-------------------I
   1    -0.497  I         *         +
   2    -0.328  I            *      +
   3    -0.243  I              *    +
   4    -0.191  I               *   +
   5    -0.156  I                *  +
   6    -0.131  I                *  +
   7    -0.112  I                 * +
   8     0.096  I                 * +
   9     0.084  I                 * +
  10     0.073  I                 * +
  11     0.065  I                  *+
  12     0.057  I                  *+
  13     0.051  I                  *+
  14     0.045  I                  *+
  15     0.041  I                  *+
  16     0.036  I                  *+
  17     0.032  I                  *+
  18     0.029  I                  *+
  19     0.026  I                  *+
  20     0.023  I                  *+
                I-------------------+-------------------I
```

**FIGURE 3.6** ACF and PACF of $Y_t = a_t - 0.9a_{t-1}$.

```
AUTOCORRELATION FUNCTION
LAG        ACF   -1                  0                   +1
                 I-------------------+-------------------I
  1      0.500   I                   +         *
  2      0.333   I                   +      *
  3      0.000   I                   *
  4      0.000   I                   *
  5      0.000   I                   *
  6      0.000   I                   *
  7      0.000   I                   *
  8      0.000   I                   *
  9      0.000   I                   *
 10      0.000   I                   *
 11      0.000   I                   *
 12      0.000   I                   *
 13      0.000   I                   *
 14      0.000   I                   *
 15      0.000   I                   *
 16      0.000   I                   *
 17      0.000   I                   *
 18      0.000   I                   *
 19      0.000   I                   *
 20      0.000   I                   *
                 I-------------------+-------------------I

PARTIAL AUTOCORRELATION FUNCTION

LAG       PACF   -1                  0                   +1
                 I-------------------+-------------------I
  1      0.500   I                   +         *
  2      0.111   I                   + *
  3     -0.275   I             *     +
  4      0.087   I                   + *
  5      0.091   I                   + *
  6      0.088   I                 * +
  7      0.001   I                   *
  8      0.044   I                   +*
  9      0.022   I                  *+
 10      0.011   I                   *
 11      0.017   I                   *
 12      0.003   I                   *
 13      0.007   I                   *
 14      0.005   I                   *
 15      0.001   I                   *
 16      0.003   I                   *
 17      0.001   I                   *
 18      0.001   I                   *
 19      0.001   I                   *
 20      0.000   I                   *
                 I-------------------+-------------------I
```

**FIGURE 3.7** ACF and PACF of $Y_t = a_t + 0.5a_{t-1} - 0.5a_{t-2}$.

```
AUTOCORRELATION FUNCTION
LAG       ACF     -1                  0                  +1
                  I-------------------+-------------------I
  1        0.261  I                   +    *
  2       -0.224  I              *    +
  3        0.000  I                   *
  4        0.000  I                   *
  5        0.000  I                   *
  6        0.000  I                   *
  7        0.000  I                   *
  8        0.000  I                   *
  9        0.000  I                   *
 10        0.000  I                   *
 11        0.000  I                   *
 12        0.000  I                   *
 13        0.000  I                   *
 14        0.000  I                   *
 15        0.000  I                   *
 16        0.000  I                   *
 17        0.000  I                   *
 18        0.000  I                   *
 19        0.000  I                   *
 20        0.000  I                   *
                  I-------------------+-------------------I
```

```
PARTIAL AUTOCORRELATION FUNCTION

LAG      PACF     -1                  0                  +1
                  I-------------------+-------------------I
  1        0.261  I                   +    *
  2       -0.313  I             *     +
  3        0.189  I                   +   *
  4       -0.165  I                *  +
  5        0.127  I                   + *
  6       -0.107  I                 * +
  7        0.088  I                   + *
  8        0.074  I                 * +
  9        0.062  I                   +*
 10        0.052  I                  *+
 11        0.044  I                   +*
 12        0.037  I                  *+
 13        0.032  I                   +*
 14        0.027  I                  *+
 15        0.023  I                   *
 16        0.020  I                   *
 17        0.017  I                   *
 18        0.014  I                   *
 19        0.012  I                   *
 20        0.010  I                   *
                  I-------------------+-------------------I
```

**FIGURE 3.8** ACF and PACF of $Y_t = a_t + 0.5a_{t-1} - 0.3a_{t-2}$.

From (3.4.7) we can clearly see that $Y$ can be represented as a function of past $Y$ terms only if $|\theta_1| < 1$. Note the importance of $|\theta_1| < 1$; if $|\theta_1| \geq 1$ then the contribution of past $Y$ terms to the current value of $Y$ grows as the distance from the present grows. Rather than allow this to happen we typically require that the coefficients on the past $Y$ terms converge, a requirement called *invertibility*.

In general, we can write an MA($q$) process as

$$Y_t = \theta(L)a_t, \tag{3.4.8}$$

or

$$Y_t = \prod_{i=1}^{q} (1 - \omega_i L)a_t, \tag{3.4.9}$$

where (3.4.9) expresses (3.4.8) in terms of the roots of $\theta(L)$. If $\theta^{-1}(L)$ exists, we can write

$$\theta^{-1}(L)Y_t = a_t,$$

or

$$\prod_{i=1}^{q} (1 - \omega_i L)^{-1} Y_t = a_t, \tag{3.4.10}$$

which gives $Y_t$ as a function of $a_t$ and past $Y$. From (3.4.10) we can see that a minimal requirement for $Y_t$ to have a representation as a function of past $Y$ is that all the $\omega_i$ be less than 1 in absolute value (or modulus). Therefore, a MA process is invertible if $|\omega_i| < 1$ for all $i$, or if the roots of the polynominal lag operator, the $1/\omega_i$ terms, are outside the unit circle.

The intuitive meaning of invertibility can be seen from (3.4.7) and (3.4.10). If a time series is not invertible then past $Y$ values can have increasing (or at least nondecreasing) importance on the current values of $Y$.

The importance of invertibility to the MA process can be seen in the following example. Suppose we have a time series that is an MA(1) process with known coefficient $\theta_1$, and we are interested in finding the $a_t$ terms.[4] Writing a few terms from the time series and then converting to matrix notation, we have

$$\begin{aligned} Y_t &= a_t + \theta_1 a_{t-1} \\ Y_{t-1} &= a_{t-1} + \theta_1 a_{t-2} \\ Y_{t-2} &= a_{t-2} + \theta_1 a_{t-3}, \end{aligned}$$

and

$$\begin{bmatrix} Y_t \\ Y_{t-1} \\ Y_{t-2} \end{bmatrix} = \begin{bmatrix} 1 & \theta_1 & 0 & 0 \\ 0 & 1 & \theta_1 & 0 \\ 0 & 0 & 1 & \theta_1 \end{bmatrix} \begin{bmatrix} a_t \\ a_{t-1} \\ a_{t-2} \\ a_{t-3} \end{bmatrix}.$$

[4]There are a number of reasons why we may be interested in finding the $a_t$ term that will be discussed in detail below. These include estimation, forecasting, and diagnostic checks of a model.

If we think of the $a_t$'s as the unknowns for which we solve, we have three equations and four unknowns; regardless of the number of observations, we will have one more unknown than equations. Thus we will not be able to write the $a_t$'s as exact functions of the $Y_t$'s. If we had one more equation [or $q$ more in an MA($q$) process], there would be as many equations as unknowns. But where is that one equation going to come from? A frequently used method is to start with a value for $a_0$, say $\hat{a}_0$, the initial white noise term, and then estimate the rest of the $a_t$'s conditional upon $\hat{a}_0$. For $t = 3$ we have

$$\begin{bmatrix} Y_3 \\ Y_2 \\ Y_1 \end{bmatrix} = \begin{bmatrix} 1 & \theta_1 & 0 & 0 \\ 0 & 1 & \theta_1 & 0 \\ 0 & 0 & 1 & \theta_1 \end{bmatrix} \begin{bmatrix} a_3 \\ a_2 \\ a_1 \\ \hat{a}_0 \end{bmatrix}.$$

This gives three equations in three unknowns and allows a solution for the $a_t$'s. The value for $a_0$ is often set at zero, but need not be. (Box and Jenkins present a method of "backcasting" that is just a sophisticated way of getting estimates of the $a_0$ term. It is discussed in Chapter 4.)

It would be comforting to know that for an observation fairly far from $t = 0$, the effect of the value of $a_0$ makes little difference. This is the case if the process is invertible. For example, the MA(1) process,

$$Y_t = (1 + \theta_1 L)a_t,$$

can be written as

$$(1 - \theta_1 L + \theta_1^2 L^2 - \theta_1^3 L^3 + \theta_1^4 L^4 - \cdots)Y_t = a_t,$$

or

$$Y_t - \theta_1 Y_{t-1} + \theta_1^2 Y_{t-2} - \cdots = a_t.$$

This can be rewritten as

$$a_t = [Y_t - \theta_1 Y_{t-1} + \theta_1^2 Y_{t-2} - \cdots + (-1)^{t-1}\theta^{t-1} Y_1] + (-1)^t(\theta_1)^t a_0,$$

from which it is easily seen that the second part of the above equation becomes negligible as $t$ gets large if $|\theta_1| < 1$. If the second part becomes small, $a_t$ can be written as a linear function of past (observable) $Y_t$ terms with an error that gets small as $t$ gets large. But $|\theta_1| < 1$ is the condition for invertibility, so one property of invertibility is that it allows us to solve for the white noise shocks as a linear function of current and past $Y_t$ terms, where the error shrinks with the sample size. [This generalizes to invertibility with an MA($q$) process.]

## 3.5 The Autoregressive Moving Average Model

The most useful of the time series models is the autoregressive moving average model in which both the autoregressive and moving average portions are of finite length. The following process is said to be an autoregressive moving average process of order $p$, $q$, or an ARMA($p$, $q$) process:

$$Y_t - \phi_1 Y_{t-1} - \cdots - \phi_p Y_{t-p} = a_t + \theta_1 a_{t-1} + \cdots + \theta_q a_{t-q}, \quad \textbf{(3.5.1)}$$

or

$$Y_t = \phi_1 Y_{t-1} + \cdots + \phi_p Y_{t-p} + a_t + \theta_1 a_{t-1} + \cdots + \theta_q a_{t-q},$$

or

$$\phi(L)Y_t = \theta(L)a_t. \tag{3.5.2}$$

An alternative form for (3.5.2) is

$$\prod_{i=1}^{p} (1 - \lambda_i L)Y_t = \prod_{i=1}^{q} (1 - \omega_i L)a_t,$$

where the $\lambda_i$ are the inverses of the roots of the AR lag polynomial and the $\omega_i$ are the inverses of the roots of the MA lag polynomial. The process is said to be stationary if the roots of the AR polynomial are outside the unit circle, and the process is said to be invertible if the roots of the MA lag polynomial are outside the unit circle. It should be noted that stationarity of a process is independent of invertibility of a process. For example, the ARMA(1, 1) process,

$$Y_t = \phi_1 Y_{t-1} + a_t + \theta_1 a_{t-1},$$

is stationary if $\phi_1$ is less than unity in absolute value, regardless of the value of $\theta_1$. It is invertible if $\theta_1$ is less than unity in absolute value, regardless of the value of $\phi_1$. An ARMA process can be written either as a pure AR process if $\theta(L)$ is invertible—

$$\theta^{-1}(L)\phi(L)Y_t = a_t,$$

or as a pure MA process if $\phi(L)$ is stationary—

$$Y_t = \phi^{-1}(L)\theta(L)a_t.$$

Although both the autocorrelation function and the partial autocorrelation function are of infinite length, the ACF and PACF still yield information about the order of the ARMA process. Writing out the ARMA($p$, $q$) process and multiplying by $Y_{t-k}$ yields

$$Y_t Y_{t-k} = \phi_1 Y_{t-1} Y_{t-k} + \phi_2 Y_{t-2} Y_{t-k} + \cdots + \phi_p Y_{t-p} Y_{t-k} + a_t Y_{t-k} + \theta_1 a_{t-1} Y_{t-k} + \cdots + \theta_q a_{t-q} Y_{t-k}.$$

If $k > q$, the moving average parts of $Y_t$ and $Y_{t-k}$ are independent. Taking expectations on both sides of the above equation yields

$$\gamma_k = \phi_1 \gamma_{k-1} + \gamma_2 \gamma_{k-2} + \cdots + \phi_p \gamma_{k-p}, \qquad k > q.$$

This is the same relationship that is obtained from an AR($p$) process, so the ACF of an ARMA($p$, $q$) process behaves the same way as the ACF for an AR($p$) process beyond the $q$th term. For the first $q$ terms the ACF of an AR($p$) and ARMA($p$, $q$) will behave differently, but beyond the first $q$ terms the ACF of an ARMA($p$, $q$) process will behave just like the ACF of an AR($p$) process. That is, for a stationary process, the ACF decays exponentially or sinusoidally as determined by the largest root of the difference equation shown above.

For the ARMA(1, 1) process,

$$Y_t = \phi_1 Y_{t-1} + a_t + \theta_1 a_{t-1},$$

the autocovariances are

$$\gamma_0 = \frac{1 + \theta_1^2 + 2\theta_1\phi_1}{1 - \phi_1^2}\sigma_a^2$$

$$\gamma_1 = \frac{(1 + \phi_1\theta_1)(\phi_1 + \theta_1)}{1 - \phi_1^2}\sigma_a^2$$

$$\gamma_2 = \phi_1\gamma_1$$

$$\vdots$$

$$\gamma_k = \phi_1\gamma_{k-1} = \phi_1^{k-1}\gamma_1.$$

Here it can be seen that for $k \leq q$ (in this case $k \leq 1$) there is no discernible pattern in the ACF, but for $k > q$ the ACF behaves exactly as the ACF of an AR(1). Division by $\gamma_0$ yields the autocorrelation function, and the Yule–Walker equations yield the partial autocorrelation function.

Figures 3.9 through 3.11 show the ACF and PACF for ARMA processes with various parameter values. Notice how the ACF decays just like an AR(1) process for lags greater than $q$, with the speed and type of decay determined by the AR coefficient.

## 3.6 Nonzero Mean, Nonstationarity, Differencing, and ARIMA Models

In this section we clear up a few points that were mentioned earlier but put off until enough theory was developed to discuss them. These include the problems raised by a time series with a nonzero mean and a nonstationary time series.

### 3.6.1 Nonzero Mean

For ease of exposition we have assumed that the time series of interest have a zero mean or that the data series have had their means removed. The effect of removing the mean of a time series can be seen by examining an ARMA($p$, $q$) model from which the mean has not been removed. Let $Y_t'$ refer to such a data series. We can then write

$$Y_t' = \phi_0 + \phi_1 Y_{t-1}' + \cdots + \phi_p Y_{t-p}' + a_t + \cdots + \theta_q a_{t-q}. \qquad \textbf{(3.6.1)}$$

Taking expectations yields

$$E[Y_t'] = \phi_0 + E[Y_t'][\phi_1 + \phi_2 + \cdots + \phi_p],$$

or

$$E[Y_t'] = \frac{\phi_0}{1 - \phi_1 - \phi_2 - \cdots - \phi_p}. \qquad \textbf{(3.6.2)}$$

```
AUTOCORRELATION FUNCTION
LAG      ACF     -1                   0                   +1
                 I--------------------+--------------------I
  1      0.714   I                    +             *
  2      0.357   I                    +      *
  3      0.179   I                    +   *
  4      0.089   I                    + *
  5      0.045   I                    +*
  6      0.022   I                    *
  7      0.011   I                    *
  8      0.005   I                    *
  9      0.003   I                    *
 10      0.001   I                    *
 11      0.000   I                    *
 12      0.000   I                    *
 13      0.000   I                    *
 14      0.000   I                    *
 15      0.000   I                    *
 16      0.000   I                    *
 17      0.000   I                    *
 18      0.000   I                    *
 19      0.000   I                    *
 20      0.000   I                    *
                 I--------------------+--------------------I

PARTIAL AUTOCORRELATION FUNCTION

LAG      PACF    -1                   0                   +1
                 I--------------------+--------------------I
  1      0.714   I                    +             *
  2     -0.313   I              *     +
  3      0.152   I                    +   *
  4      0.075   I                  * +
  5      0.038   I                    +*
  6      0.019   I                    *
  7      0.009   I                    *
  8      0.005   I                    *
  9      0.002   I                    *
 10      0.001   I                    *
 11      0.000   I                    *
 12      0.000   I                    *
 13      0.000   I                    *
 14      0.000   I                    *
 15      0.000   I                    *
 16      0.000   I                    *
 17      0.000   I                    *
 18      0.000   I                    *
 19      0.000   I                    *
 20      0.000   I                    *
                 I--------------------+--------------------I
```

**FIGURE 3.9** ACF and PACF of $Y_t = 0.5Y_{t-1} + a_t + 0.5a_{t-1}$.

```
AUTOCORRELATION FUNCTION
LAG      ACF     -1                   0                    +1
                  I-------------------+--------------------I
  1     0.628     I                   +            *
  2     0.565     I                   +          *
  3     0.508     I                   +         *
  4     0.457     I                   +        *
  5     0.411     I                   +       *
  6     0.370     I                   +      *
  7     0.332     I                   +      *
  8     0.299     I                   +     *
  9     0.268     I                   +    *
 10     0.241     I                   +    *
 11     0.216     I                   +   *
 12     0.194     I                   +   *
 13     0.174     I                   +  *
 14     0.155     I                   +  *
 15     0.139     I                   +  *
 16     0.124     I                   + *
 17     0.111     I                   + *
 18     0.098     I                   + *
 19     0.087     I                   + *
 20     0.077     I                   +*
                  I-------------------+--------------------I
```

```
PARTIAL AUTOCORRELATION FUNCTION

LAG      PACF    -1                   0                    +1
                  I-------------------+--------------------I
  1     0.628     I                   +            *
  2     0.282     I                   +     *
  3     0.137     I                   +  *
  4     0.068     I                   +*
  5     0.034     I                   +*
  6     0.017     I                   *
  7     0.008     I                   *
  8     0.004     I                   *
  9     0.002     I                   *
 10     0.000     I                   *
 11     0.000     I                   *
 12     0.001     I                   *
 13     0.001     I                   *
 14     0.001     I                   *
 15     0.001     I                   *
 16     0.001     I                   *
 17     0.001     I                   *
 18     0.001     I                   *
 19     0.002     I                   *
 20     0.002     I                   *
                  I-------------------+--------------------I
```

**FIGURE 3.10** ACF and PACF of $Y_t = 0.9Y_{t-1} + a_t - 0.5a_{t-1}$.

```
AUTOCORRELATION FUNCTION
LAG      ACF    -1                  0                  +1
                I-------------------+-------------------I
  1     0.958   I                   +                  *
  2     0.882   I                   +                 *
  3     0.795   I                   +               *
  4     0.714   I                   +             *
  5     0.642   I                   +            *
  6     0.577   I                   +           *
  7     0.519   I                   +         *
  8     0.466   I                   +        *
  9     0.418   I                   +       *
 10     0.375   I                   +      *
 11     0.336   I                   +      *
 12     0.301   I                   +     *
 13     0.269   I                   +    *
 14     0.241   I                   +    *
 15     0.214   I                   +   *
 16     0.191   I                   +   *
 17     0.169   I                   +  *
 18     0.149   I                   +  *
 19     0.131   I                   +  *
 20     0.115   I                   + *
                I-------------------+-------------------I

PARTIAL AUTOCORRELATION FUNCTION

LAG     PACF    -1                  0                  +1
                I-------------------+-------------------I
  1     0.958   I                   +                  *
  2    -0.450   I          *        +
  3     0.012   I                   *
  4     0.092   I                   + *
  5     0.038   I                  *+
  6     0.007   I                   *
  7     0.010   I                   *
  8     0.004   I                   *
  9     0.003   I                   *
 10     0.000   I                   *
 11     0.002   I                   *
 12     0.002   I                   *
 13     0.002   I                   *
 14     0.002   I                   *
 15     0.002   I                   *
 16     0.002   I                   *
 17     0.003   I                   *
 18     0.003   I                   *
 19     0.003   I                   *
 20     0.004   I                   *
                I-------------------+-------------------I
```

**FIGURE 3.11** ACF and PACF of $Y_t = 0.9Y_{t-1} + a_t + 0.5a_{t-1} + 0.3a_{t-2}$.

Note that $E[Y_t'] \neq 0$ requires $\phi_0 \neq 0$. If we let $Y_t = Y_t' - E[Y_t']$ we can rewrite (3.6.1) as

$$Y_t + E[Y_t'] = \phi_0 + E[Y_t'][\phi_1 + \phi_2 + \cdots + \phi_p] + \phi_1 Y_{t-1} + \cdots + \phi_p Y_{t-p} + a_t + \cdots + \theta_q a_{t-q},$$

or

$$Y_t = \phi_0 - E[Y_t][1 - \phi_1 - \phi_2 - \cdots - \phi_p] + \phi_1 Y_{t-1} + \cdots + \phi_p Y_{t-p} + a_t + \cdots \theta_q a_{t-q};$$

substitution of (3.6.2) yields

$$Y_t = \phi_0 - \phi_0 + \phi_1 Y_{t-1} + \cdots \phi_p Y_{t-p} + a_t + \cdots + \theta_q a_{t-q},$$

or

$$Y_t = \phi_1 Y_{t-1} + \phi_2 Y_{t-2} + \cdots + \phi_p Y_{t-p} + a_t + \cdots + \theta_q a_{t-q}. \quad \textbf{(3.6.3)}$$

Comparing (3.6.1) and (3.6.3) shows that a time series with a nonzero mean can easily be transformed into a time series which has had its mean removed, that is, which has a zero mean. This justifies dropping the constant term in theoretical work.

### 3.6.2 Nonstationarity

In the next chapter, we discuss the identification and estimation of actual time series, and many of the methods used depend critically on the assumption of stationarity in the time series. But even a casual look at many economic time series is sufficient to bring into question this assumption. For example, Figures 3.12 and 3.13 show plots of two economic time series from 1954 to 1981. It is obvious that the first moments of the series are not constant for the entire time period, and the series are thus nonstationary. It is therefore legitimate to question the usefulness of a set of techniques based upon stationarity when many of the data series we wish to analyze may be nonstationary.

A possible solution to this problem is to transform the data in such a way that the transformed data set is stationary even if the initial data set is not. As an example consider

$$\begin{aligned} Y_t &= (Y_0 + \epsilon_t)t^k \\ &= Y_0 t^k + \epsilon_t t^k, \end{aligned}$$

where $\epsilon_t$ is a white noise process. This series has expectation

$$E[Y_t] = Y_0 \cdot t^k$$

and variance

$$E[(Y_t - E(Y_t))^2] = \sigma_\epsilon^2 t^{2k}.$$

Since both of these change with time, the process is nonstationary. However, if we define the series

$$X_t = \frac{Y_t}{t^k},$$

the $X$ series is stationary and may be analyzed with the methods we discuss. In this example, a simple transformation allows us to turn a nonstationary series into a stationary series.

Unfortunately, finding a transformation that makes the series stationary is not easy in practice and is very much an art. A frequently used method that seems to give reasonable results in a wide variety of circumstances is the method of *differencing*. If $Z_t$ is the initial series, call $Y$ the $d$th differenced series, where

$$Y_t = (1 - L)^d Z_t.$$

For $d = 1$ (first order differencing) we have

$$\begin{aligned} Y_t &= (1 - L)Z_t \\ &= Z_t - Z_{t-1}. \end{aligned}$$

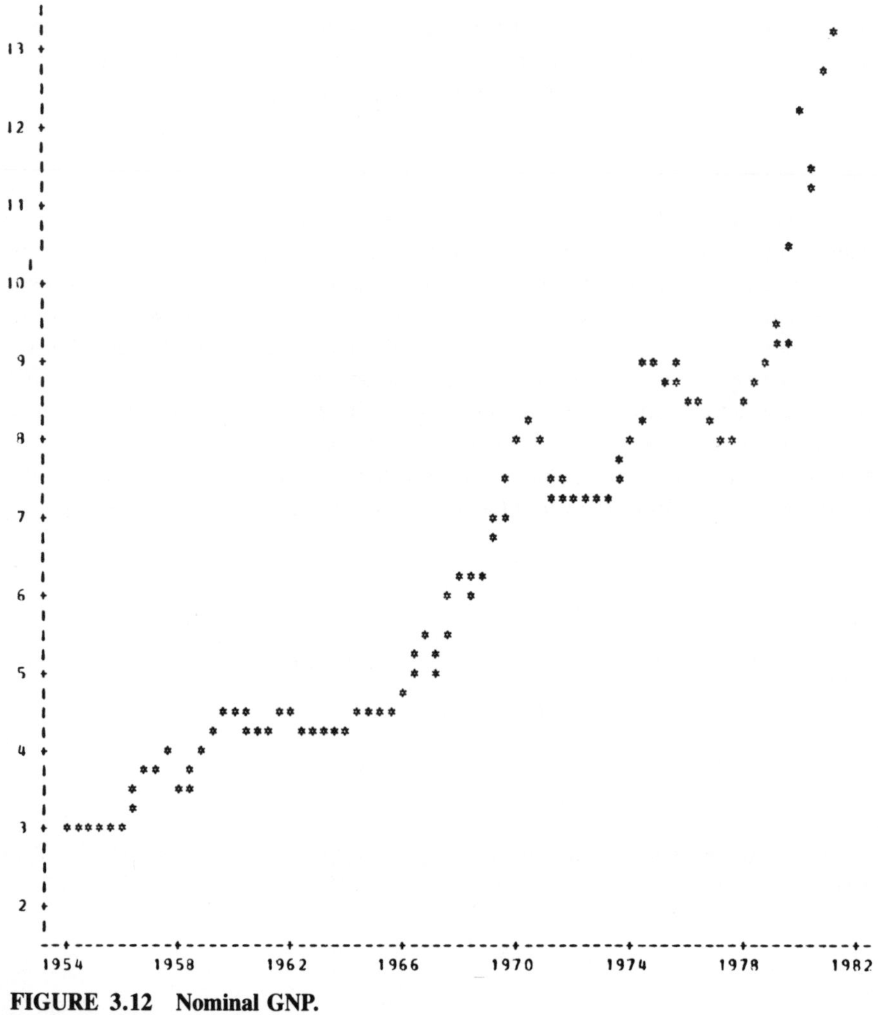


**FIGURE 3.12 Nominal GNP.**

Many economic time series must be differenced, and then ARMA models are fit to the differenced series. So frequently is this done that a special name is given to models fit to differenced data. An ARMA($p$, $q$) model fit to the $d$th difference of a data series is called an *autoregressive integrated moving average* (ARIMA) model of order ($p$, $d$, $q$), written as ARIMA($p$, $d$, $q$). Notice that an observation is lost each time a series is differenced.

For a wide variety of series, differencing does seem to make the series stationary. Judgment is often required in applying the correct amount of differencing, and, unfortunately, a data series can be differenced too many times with misleading results. [For example, see Plosser and Schwert (1978).]

In most applied work, nonstationarity is dealt with by transforming the data series to a stationary series. However, some work has been done on the properties of estimators when nonstationary time series are used. For examples, see Stigum (1976), and Fuller (1976).

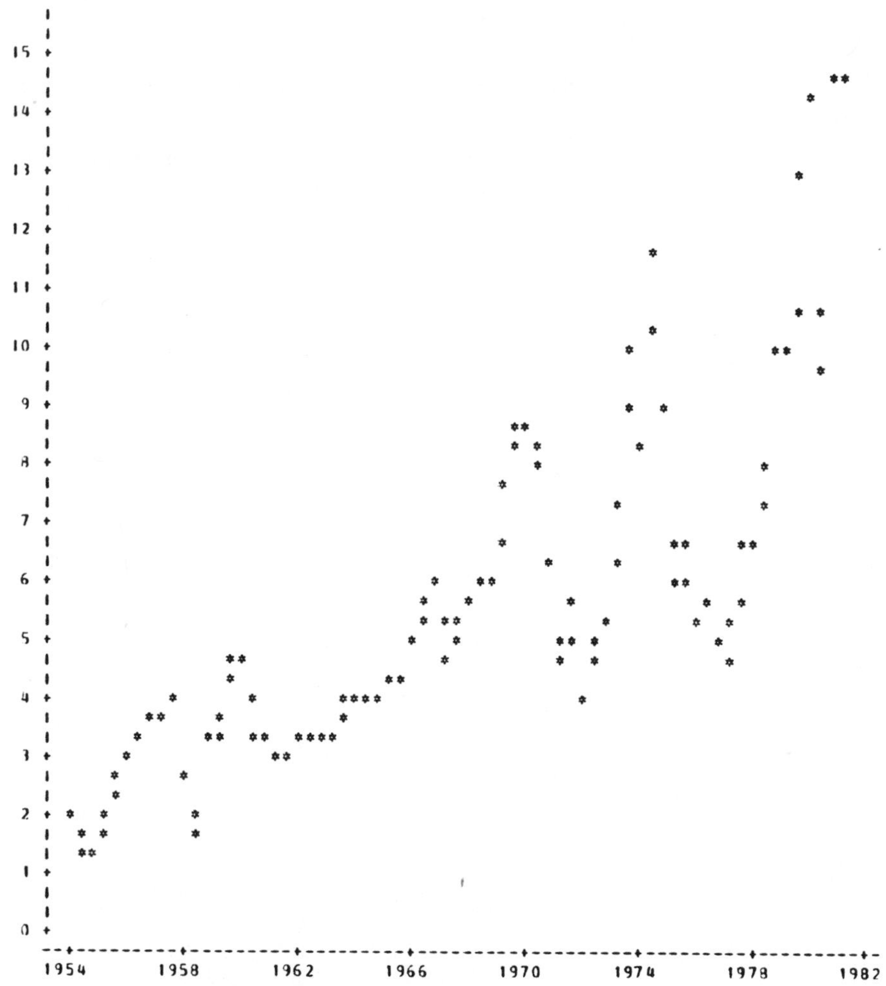


**FIGURE 3.13 First difference of nominal GNP.**

## 3.7 References


Anderson, T. W. (1971), *The Statistical Analysis of Time Series,* New York: Wiley.

Box, G. E. P. and G. Jenkins (1970), *Time Series Analysis: Forecasting and Control,* San Francisco: Holden-Day.

Chiang, A. (1967), *Fundamental Methods of Mathematical Economics,* New York: McGraw-Hill.

Dhrymes, P. (1971), *Distributed Lags: Problems of Estimation and Formulation,* San Francisco: Holden-Day.

Fuller, W. (1976), *Introduction to Statistical Time Series,* New York: Wiley.

Goldberg, S. (1958), *Introduction to Difference Equations,* New York: Wiley.

Plosser, C. and C. W. Schwert (1977), ''Estimation of a Noninvertible Moving Average Process: The Case of Over-Differencing,'' *Journal of Econometrics,* **6,** 199–216.

Stigum, B. (1976), ''Least Squares and Stochastic Difference Equations,'' *Journal of Econometrics,* **4,** 349–371.

Wold, H. (1938), *The Analysis of Stationary Time Series,* Uppsala, Sweden: Almquist and Wicksell.

Zellner, A. and F. Palm (1974), ''Time Series Analysis and Simultaneous Equation Econometric Models,'' *Journal of Econometrics,* **2,** 17–54.

# CHAPTER 4

# Identification, Estimation, and Prediction in Time Series Models

In this chapter we discuss identification and estimation of time series models from data, and prediction from the estimated models. Except for a few introductory remarks, we restrict ourselves to stationary time series with a zero mean.

So far in the discussion of ARMA and ARIMA models we have dealt only with models with known parameters. Realistically, we must work with estimated parameters, but before we can estimate an ARIMA($p$, $d$, $q$) model we must know the order of the process, that is, $p$, $d$, and $q$. It is, of course, possible in principle to search over "all reasonably likely" specifications of the model to see which process fits best. But even restricting the order of the AR and MA processes to be less than 5 and the differencing to 2 or less, the number of possible models is 75, which is clearly too many to search over. To overcome this problem, Box and Jenkins developed a set of techniques known as identification techniques.[1] These techniques are used to infer the order of the order of the ARIMA process from the autocorrelation and partial autocorrelation functions.

We divide this process up into four parts—identification, estimation, diagnostics, and forecasting. In the first step, identification, we will assume the correct order of differencing, $d$, is known and will concentrate on determining the order of the ARMA model ($p$ and $q$) from the data, using the autocorrelation function and the partial autocorrelation function. Having tentatively identified $p$ and $q$, we estimate $\phi_1, \phi_2, \ldots, \phi_p$, $\theta_1, \ldots, \theta_q$ conditional upon our choice of $p$ and $q$. We then apply diagnostic tests to see if the model "makes sense" or "holds together." If it does we proceed to forecast; if it does not, we begin again. The process is shown diagrammatically in Figure 4.1.

## 4.1 Identification of ARMA Models

Since identification of the order of an ARMA($p$, $q$) process involves making judgments about the order of the process from the ACF and PACF, we begin by reviewing what the ACF and PACF of various processes look like. For the remainder of this discussion we assume that the data have zero mean and that the process has already been transformed

[1]The term "identification" as used in the time series literature is not the same as the identification problem in econometrics. Identification, when used in the context of ARIMA models, refers to the determination of the order of the process ($p$, $d$, and $q$) from the data. In contrast, identification in econometric models is largely accomplished by a priori information and takes the form of specifying constraints on particular parameters. See Chapter 9 for more details.

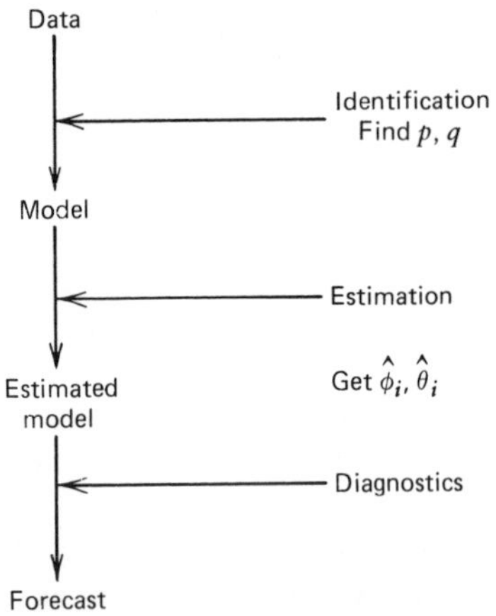


**FIGURE 4.1 Forecasting from ARIMA models.**

to stationarity. For an AR($p$) process, the first $p$ terms of the PACF are nonzero and the ACF is of infinite length, but ultimately goes to zero with the inverse of the smallest root (in modulus) of the lag operator of the process. If the root is positive, convergence is an exponential decline in the ACF terms; if the root is negative, convergence is exponential with the terms of the ACF alternating in sign. If the smallest root is complex then the ACF converges to zero, but cycles around zero. For an MA($q$) process the ACF is finite with $q$ nonzero terms, but the PACF is infinite. The PACF terms behave, relative to the smallest root of the lag operator, in much the same way as the ACF terms for an AR process.

For an ARMA($p$, $q$) process the ACF and PACF are more complicated. Since an ARMA process has both an infinite autoregressive and moving average representation, both the PACF and the ACF are infinite. After $q$ terms the ACF acts just like the ACF of an AR process; it consists of terms that behave as damped exponentials or sine waves after $q$ lags. If $p > q$, the PACF behaves just like the PACF of an MA process, after $p - q$ lags, consisting of terms that behave as damped exponentials and sine waves after $p - q$ lags.

Making identification difficult, when real data are used, is the fact that we observe estimates of the actual ACF and PACF, estimates that contain sampling variability. While under the proper conditions each estimated value converges in probability to its respective parameter value, we are never sure when the sample is large enough. Therefore we need to take into consideration the sampling distributions of the ACF and PACF.

Unfortunately [see Bartlett (1946), Quenouille (1949), or Fuller (1976)], the distributions of the ACF and PACF terms depend upon the values of the parameters of the ARMA process, so that unless we know the parameter values we do not know the true sampling distribution. However, if we are interested in determining whether *any* of the $\phi_i$ or $\theta_i$ are nonzero, we can perform a test based on the null hypothesis that all the $\phi_i$ and $\theta_i$ are zero. On the assumption that the $\phi_i$ and $\theta_i$ are zero, we can approximate the distribution of the ACF and PACF in the following way.

If all the $\theta_i$ and $\phi_i$ are zero, the ARMA model can be written as

$$Y_t = a_t,$$

where $a_t$ is an independently, identically distributed r.v. with a zero mean. Under this assumption, the $k$th sample autocorrelation coefficient,

$$r_k = \frac{\sum_{t=k+1}^{T} Y_t Y_{t-k}}{\sum_{t=1}^{T} Y_t^2}$$

converges in probability to the least squares estimator from the regression of $Y_t$ on $Y_{t-k}$, $b$, where

$$b = \frac{\sum_{t=k+1}^{T} Y_t Y_{t-k}}{\sum_{t=k+1}^{T} Y_{t-k}^2}.$$

Since the asymptotic distribution of $r_k$ converges in probability to that of the least squares estimator, we can derive the asymptotic distribution of the estimator of the ACF terms by deriving the asymptotic distribution of the least squares estimator.[2]

The least squares estimator minimizes the sum of squared errors as a function of $b$, $S(b)$:

$$S(b) = \sum_{t=k+1}^{T} (Y_t - bY_{t-k})^2.$$

Taking a Taylor series expansion of $S'(b)$ around 0 yields

$$S'(b) = S'(0) + S''(0)\,(b - 0) + R.$$

Ignoring the remainder term, $R$, and noting that $S'(b) = 0$, we have that

$$b \approx -[S''(0)]^{-1}\, S'(0).$$

We can find $S''(0)$ and $S'(0)$ easily. From

$$S(b) = \sum_{t=k+1}^{T} (Y_t - bY_{t-k})^2,$$

it follows that

$$S'(b) = -2 \sum_{t=k+1}^{T} Y_{t-k}(Y_t - bY_{t-k})$$

$$S'(0) = -2 \sum_{t=k+1}^{T} Y_{t-k}Y_t,$$

[2]We are, strictly speaking, dealing with a least squares estimator conditional upon the first $k$ observations.

where $Y_t$ and $Y_{t-k}$ are i.i.d. $(0,\sigma^2)$. By the central limit theorem (Theorem 1.2.1) we have, on the null hypothesis that $b = 0$,

$$\frac{S'(0)}{\sqrt{T}} \xrightarrow{d} N[0,\ 4\sigma^4].$$

Moreover,

$$S''(b) = 2 \sum_{t=k+1}^{T} Y_{t-k}^2 = S''(0).$$

From Theorem 1.1.4 and the fact that on the null hypothesis the $Y_t$ are i.i.d. $(0,\sigma^2)$, we have that

$$\frac{S''(0)}{T} \xrightarrow{p} 2\sigma^2.$$

Therefore, since

$$b \approx -[S''(0)]^{-1}\, S'(0),$$

we have

$$\sqrt{T}b \approx -\left[\frac{S''(0)}{T}\right]^{-1} \frac{S'(0)}{\sqrt{T}},$$

where the first right-hand side term converges in probability and the second right-hand side term converges in distribution. Using Theorem 1.1.3 on the product of two r.v.'s, one of which converges in probability and the other in distribution, we can write

$$\sqrt{T}b \xrightarrow{d} \left[\frac{1}{2\sigma^2}\right] \cdot N[0,\ 4\sigma^4],$$

which implies

$$\sqrt{T} \cdot b \xrightarrow{d} N[0,\ 1].$$

Since the estimated autocorrelation function converges in probability to $b$, we have an asymptotic distribution for $r_k$ and can use $1/\sqrt{T}$ as an approximate standard error.[3]

Since an approximate asymptotic standard error is $1/\sqrt{T}$ for any correlation coefficient, given the other correlation coefficients are zero, we have an approximate 5% test for *any* one of the $\phi_i$ and $\theta_i$ being nonzero, that is, for the presence of serial correlation. We examine the ACF terms to see whether any of the ACF or PACF terms exceed, in absolute value, twice the asymptotic standard error. In practice, it should be noted that on the null hypothesis of no serial correlation, each estimated ACF term is independent in large samples, so that in the limit the expected proportion of ACF terms that exceed $2/\sqrt{T}$ in absolute value is $\frac{1}{20}$ if a 5% significance level is used. For example, if ten ACF

[3]The distribution of the autocorrelation function has received a substantial amount of attention in the time series literature. Early work includes that of Bartlett (1946), and Quenouille (1949). Fuller (1976) has an excellent discussion on the distribution of the sample autocorrelation function.

terms are examined, there is a 50% chance that one of the autocorrelations will appear significantly different from zero because of sampling error alone.

Another test for the absence of serial correlation is due to Box and Pierce (1970), who develop a test for serial correlation based on the autocorrelation coefficients.[4] Box and Pierce find that, on the null hypothesis of no serial correlation, for sample size $T$,

$$T \sum_{k=1}^{m} r_k^2 \sim \chi_m^2.$$

One of the implications of the work of Box and Pierce is that approximating the standard error of an autocorrelation by $1/\sqrt{T}$ leads to an overly conservative test—that is, a test that does not reject the null hypothesis of $\rho_k = 0$ as often as it should. [See Box and Pierce (1970) or Box and Jenkins (1970) on this point.]

With the exception of these two tests for serial correlation, identification proceeds as if the sample ACF and PACF were the actual ACF and PACF. This results in uncertainty over whether the model identified is the true model; in practice, identification is used to rule out certain models and narrow the number of possible model types rather than to identify a "true" model at the end of the identification process. Model builders typically fit more than one model to the data and make their model selection on the basis of sample fit.

Figures 4.2 to 4.6 contain the ACF and PACF of a number of generated ARMA models, all of which are assumed to be stationary. The processes that generated the data are specified on the graphs, and all the innovations (the $a_t$ terms) are normally distributed with zero mean and unit variance. For 100 observations the 95% confidence interval is approximately $(-.2, .2)$ on the null hypothesis of no serial correlation. Notice that in almost all cases the process is easily identified from the ACF and PACF.

From these examples, it may appear that identification is a relatively easy process. The generated series lead to fairly easy identification. However, when real data are used, the ACF's and PACF's are much more complicated. This is shown in the next group of examples, where the ACF's and PACF's are from actual data series.

As can be seen from Figures 4.7 to 4.10, identifying the order of ARMA processes is very inexact and is much more of an art than a science. Thus, more than one ARMA model should usually be estimated and the resulting estimated models compared. Fitting multiple models (as well as looking at the ACF and PACF before estimating the model) may appear to be "data-mining" and a violation of the classical precept that the data should be looked at only once. However, in the typical case in which we want to fit an ARIMA model, there is almost no a priori information on the correct model form. Searching over different models is therefore necessary. Fortunately, models that cannot be differentiated in the identification step are likely to lead to similar forecasts.

## 4.2 Estimation of ARMA Models

In this section we discuss estimation of previously identified ARMA models. For a fuller treatment of the estimation of ARMA models we refer readers to other sources, for

[4]This test will be discussed in great detail later.

```
AUTOCORRELATION FUNCTION
LAG      ACF     -1                  0                   +1
                 I-------------------+-------------------I
  1   -0.03262   I                  *+
  2   -0.07885   I                 * +
  3    0.00045   I                   *
  4    0.26340   I                   +    *
  5    0.01134   I                   *
  6   -0.00143   I                   *
  7    0.11051   I                   + *
  8   -0.05524   I                  *+
  9   -0.14310   I                *  +
 10   -0.02227   I                  *+
 11    0.05815   I                   +*
 12   -0.17098   I               *   +
 13   -0.10876   I                 * +
 14   -0.07199   I                 * +
 15    0.02153   I                   *
 16   -0.06203   I                  *+
 17   -0.03002   I                  *+
 18    0.02741   I                   *
 19   -0.05648   I                  *+
 20    0.00132   I                   *
                 I-------------------+-------------------I
```

```
PARTIAL AUTOCORRELATION FUNCTION

LAG      PACF    -1                  0                   +1
                 I-------------------+-------------------I
  1   -0.03262   I                  *+
  2   -0.08000   I                 * +
  3   -0.00497   I                   *
  4    0.25887   I                   +    *
  5    0.03152   I                   +*
  6    0.03920   I                   +*
  7    0.12284   I                   + *
  8   -0.12210   I                *  +
  9   -0.16256   I                *  +
 10   -0.06343   I                  *+
 11   -0.03277   I                  *+
 12   -0.15755   I                *  +
 13   -0.04747   I                  *+
 14   -0.08569   I                 * +
 15    0.01869   I                   *
 16    0.05043   I                   +*
 17    0.02007   I                   *
 18    0.07220   I                   +*
 19   -0.01772   I                   *
 20    0.00906   I                   *
                 I-------------------+-------------------I
```

**FIGURE 4.2** Sample ACF and PACF of $Y_t = a_t$.

```
AUTOCORRELATION FUNCTION
LAG       ACF     -1                  0                  +1
                  I-------------------+-------------------I
   1    0.66886   I                   +            *
   2    0.50636   I                   +         *
   3    0.33496   I                   +      *
   4    0.21256   I                   +   *
   5    0.16731   I                   +  *
   6    0.16858   I                   +  *
   7    0.09728   I                   + *
   8   -0.00906   I                   *
   9   -0.07910   I                 * +
  10   -0.15385   I                *  +
  11   -0.22383   I              *    +
  12   -0.15716   I                *  +
  13   -0.16091   I                *  +
  14   -0.20207   I               *   +
  15   -0.25332   I              *    +
  16   -0.26525   I              *    +
  17   -0.20432   I               *   +
  18   -0.12541   I                *  +
  19   -0.05724   I                  *+
  20   -0.04388   I                  *+
                  I-------------------+-------------------I
```

```
PARTIAL AUTOCORRELATION FUNCTION

LAG       PACF    -1                  0                  +1
                  I-------------------+-------------------I
   1    0.66886   I                   +            *
   2    0.10673   I                   + *
   3   -0.07132   I                 * +
   4   -0.03318   I                  *+
   5    0.06566   I                   +*
   6    0.08757   I                   + *
   7   -0.10302   I                 * +
   8   -0.15489   I                *  +
   9   -0.03615   I                  *+
  10   -0.05707   I                  *+
  11   -0.11581   I                 * +
  12    0.11369   I                   + *
  13   -0.04508   I                  *+
  14   -0.13272   I                *  +
  15   -0.11432   I                 * +
  16    0.01297   I                   *
  17    0.12885   I                   + *
  18    0.01804   I                   *
  19   -0.03427   I                  *+
  20   -0.03266   I                  *+
                  I-------------------+-------------------I
```

**FIGURE 4.3** Sample ACF and PACF of $Y_t = 0.9Y_{t-1} + a_t$.

```
AUTOCORRELATION FUNCTION
LAG       ACF  -1                  0                  +1
               I-------------------+-------------------I
  1   0.36141  I                   +      *
  2  -0.01539  I                   *
  3  -0.07596  I                 * +
  4  -0.02445  I                  *+
  5   0.05983  I                   +*
  6  -0.04009  I                  *+
  7  -0.05788  I                  *+
  8  -0.06725  I                  *+
  9  -0.15917  I                *  +
 10  -0.05394  I                  *+
 11   0.04310  I                   +*
 12  -0.07161  I                 * +
 13  -0.04856  I                  *+
 14   0.01285  I                   *
 15   0.07132  I                   +*
 16   0.01910  I                   *
 17   0.03661  I                   +*
 18  -0.05374  I                  *+
 19  -0.13690  I                *  +
 20  -0.29685  I             *     +
               I-------------------+-------------------I
```

```
PARTIAL AUTOCORRELATION FUNCTION

LAG      PACF  -1                  0                  +1
               I-------------------+-------------------I
  1   0.36141  I                   +      *
  2  -0.16795  I                *  +
  3  -0.01037  I                   *
  4   0.01030  I                   *
  5   0.06377  I                   +*
  6  -0.11029  I                 * +
  7   0.00939  I                   *
  8  -0.05571  I                  *+
  9  -0.14968  I                *  +
 10   0.05621  I                   +*
 11   0.03450  I                   +*
 12  -0.15623  I                *  +
 13   0.04940  I                   +*
 14   0.04101  I                   +*
 15   0.01016  I                   *
 16  -0.05099  I                  *+
 17   0.10669  I                   + *
 18  -0.16983  I                *  +
 19  -0.09266  I                 * +
 20  -0.25003  I              *    +
               I-------------------+-------------------I
```

**FIGURE 4.4** Sample ACF and PACF of $Y_t = 0.5Y_{t-1} + a_t$.

```
AUTOCORRELATION FUNCTION
LAG       ACF   -1                   0                   +1
                I--------------------+--------------------I
  1    0.47111  I                    +        *
  2   -0.09441  I                  * +
  3   -0.13352  I                 *  +
  4   -0.10262  I                  * +
  5   -0.06142  I                   *+
  6    0.06045  I                    +*
  7    0.09592  I                    + *
  8    0.00948  I                    *
  9    0.04880  I                    +*
 10    0.07936  I                    +*
 11   -0.00655  I                    *
 12   -0.08013  I                  * +
 13   -0.07097  I                  * +
 14   -0.02153  I                   *+
 15    0.01615  I                    *
 16    0.05741  I                    +*
 17   -0.02652  I                   *+
 18   -0.17780  I                *   +
 19   -0.21396  I                *   +
 20   -0.13100  I                 *  +
                I--------------------+--------------------I
```

```
PARTIAL AUTOCORRELATION FUNCTION

LAG      PACF   -1                   0                   +1
                I--------------------+--------------------I
  1    0.47111  I                    +        *
  2   -0.40660  I            *       +
  3    0.18569  I                    +   *
  4   -0.22574  I               *    +
  5    0.12026  I                    + *
  6    0.01654  I                    *
  7    0.01653  I                    *
  8   -0.04072  I                   *+
  9    0.16283  I                    +  *
 10   -0.07731  I                  * +
 11    0.03604  I                    +*
 12   -0.09617  I                  * +
 13    0.02719  I                    *
 14   -0.01451  I                    *
 15    0.01688  I                    *
 16    0.01680  I                    *
 17   -0.13053  I                 *  +
 18   -0.10258  I                  * +
 19   -0.10331  I                  * +
 20   -0.03353  I                   *+
                I--------------------+--------------------I
```

**FIGURE 4.5 Sample ACF and PACF of $Y_t = a_t + 0.5a_{t-1}$.**

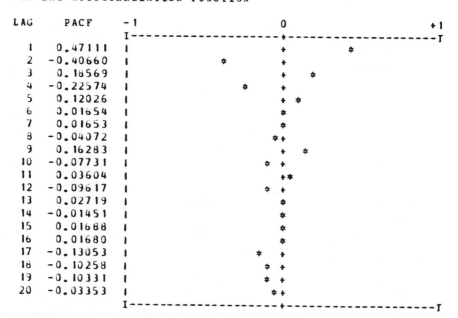

```
AUTOCORRELATION FUNCTION
LAG      ACF       -1                   0                   +1
                   I--------------------+--------------------I
  1   -0.52865     I         *          +
  2    0.05234     I                    +*
  3   -0.00478     I                    *
  4   -0.02638     I                   *+
  5   -0.01540     I                    *
  6    0.12273     I                    + *
  7   -0.11331     I                  * +
  8    0.07923     I                    +*
  9   -0.05736     I                   *+
 10   -0.06654     I                   *+
 11    0.10229     I                    + *
 12   -0.01052     I                    *
 13   -0.01176     I                    *
 14   -0.04844     I                   *+
 15    0.06190     I                    +*
 16   -0.00419     I                    *
 17   -0.08043     I                  * +
 18    0.09991     I                    + *
 19   -0.12096     I                 *  +
 20    0.18594     I                    +   *
                   I--------------------+--------------------I
```

```
PARTIAL AUTOCORRELATION FUNCTION

LAG      PACF      -1                   0                   +1
                   I--------------------+--------------------I
  1   -0.52865     I         *          +
  2   -0.31523     I              *     +
  3   -0.20809     I               *    +
  4   -0.18677     I               *    +
  5   -0.19946     I               *    +
  6    0.00709     I                    *
  7   -0.03473     I                   *+
  8    0.04486     I                    +*
  9    0.01396     I                    *
 10   -0.12867     I                *   +
 11   -0.05151     I                   *+
 12   -0.00939     I                    *
 13    0.01094     I                    *
 14   -0.09294     I                  * +
 15   -0.01085     I                    *
 16    0.06041     I                    +*
 17   -0.09344     I                  * +
 18   -0.00677     I                    *
 19   -0.15446     I                 *  +
 20    0.09418     I                    + *
                   I--------------------+--------------------I
```

**FIGURE 4.6** Sample ACF and PACF of $Y_t = a_t - 0.5a_{t-1}$.

```
AUTOCORRELATION FUNCTION
LAG       ACF     -1                  0                  +1
                  I-------------------+-------------------I
  1     0.89133   I                   +                *
  2     0.75972   I                   +              *
  3     0.72066   I                   +             *
  4     0.66877   I                   +            *
  5     0.54615   I                   +          *
  6     0.42744   I                   +       *
  7     0.36194   I                   +      *
  8     0.32171   I                   +     *
  9     0.26761   I                   +    *
 10     0.21921   I                   +   *
 11     0.21193   I                   +   *
 12     0.22602   I                   +   *
 13     0.23668   I                   +    *
 14     0.24624   I                   +    *
 15     0.27006   I                   +    *
 16     0.30396   I                   +     *
 17     0.33104   I                   +      *
 18     0.33500   I                   +      *
 19     0.32748   I                   +     *
 20     0.33693   I                   +      *
                  I-------------------+-------------------I


PARTIAL AUTOCORRELATION FUNCTION

LAG      PACF     -1                  0                  +1
                  I-------------------+-------------------I
  1     0.89133   I                   +                *
  2    -0.16901   I                *  +
  3     0.39914   I                   +       *
  4    -0.25110   I              *    +
  5    -0.16871   I                *  +
  6    -0.06866   I                  *+
  7     0.02444   I                   *
  8     0.10983   I                   + *
  9     0.01887   I                   *
 10     0.06392   I                   +*
 11     0.08464   I                   + *
 12     0.03293   I                   +*
 13     0.08087   I                   + *
 14     0.00985   I                   *
 15     0.05499   I                   +*
 16     0.03991   I                   +*
 17     0.03589   I                   +*
 18    -0.05118   I                  *+
 19    -0.02488   I                  *+
 20     0.07905   I                   +*
                  I-------------------+-------------------I
```

**FIGURE 4.7 ACF and PACF for the commercial paper rate.**

```
AUTOCORRELATION FUNCTION
LAG        ACF      -1                   0                   +1
                    I--------------------+--------------------I
  1     0.94476     I                    +                 *
  2     0.88832     I                    +                *
  3     0.84798     I                    +               *
  4     0.80652     I                    +              *
  5     0.74949     I                    +             *
  6     0.70915     I                    +            *
  7     0.68256     I                    +            *
  8     0.65332     I                    +           *
  9     0.62398     I                    +          *
 10     0.59791     I                    +          *
 11     0.57541     I                    +         *
 12     0.55517     I                    +         *
 13     0.53836     I                    +         *
 14     0.52678     I                    +        *
 15     0.51877     I                    +        *
 16     0.50977     I                    +        *
 17     0.49795     I                    +        *
 18     0.48318     I                    +        *
 19     0.46535     I                    +       *
 20     0.44741     I                    +       *
                    I--------------------+--------------------I

PARTIAL AUTOCORRELATION FUNCTION

LAG        PACF     -1                   0                   +1
                    I--------------------+--------------------I
  1     0.94476     I                    +                 *
  2    -0.03954     I                   *+
  3     0.12034     I                    + *
  4    -0.03696     I                   *+
  5    -0.14888     I                 *  +
  6     0.13013     I                    +  *
  7     0.06565     I                    +*
  8    -0.00650     I                    *
  9     0.02602     I                    *
 10    -0.03066     I                   *+
 11     0.01770     I                    *
 12     0.04229     I                    +*
 13     0.02891     I                    *
 14     0.05131     I                    +*
 15     0.03188     I                    +*
 16    -0.00546     I                    *
 17    -0.01545     I                    *
 18    -0.03073     I                   *+
 19    -0.02786     I                   *+
 20     0.00810     I                    *
                    I--------------------+--------------------I
```

**FIGURE 4.8** ACF and PACF of the AAA corporate bond rate.

```
AUTOCORRELATION FUNCTION
LAG      ACF    -1                   0                   +1
                I--------------------+--------------------I
  1    0.81246  I                    +               *
  2    0.79088  I                    +               *
  3    0.76854  I                    +              *
  4    0.73844  I                    +              *
  5    0.71434  I                    +             *
  6    0.68908  I                    +             *
  7    0.66574  I                    +            *
  8    0.63922  I                    +            *
  9    0.61520  I                    +           *
 10    0.59243  I                    +           *
 11    0.56913  I                    +          *
 12    0.54904  I                    +          *
 13    0.52696  I                    +         *
 14    0.50405  I                    +         *
 15    0.48370  I                    +         *
 16    0.46267  I                    +        *
 17    0.44343  I                    +        *
 18    0.42226  I                    +       *
 19    0.40087  I                    +       *
 20    0.38009  I                    +       *
                I--------------------+--------------------I

PARTIAL AUTOCORRELATION FUNCTION

LAG      PACF   -1                   0                   +1
                I--------------------+--------------------I
  1    0.81246  I                    +               *
  2    0.38477  I                    +       *
  3    0.20929  I                    +   *
  4    0.08871  I                    + *
  5    0.05103  I                    +*
  6    0.02303  I                    *
  7    0.01399  I                    *
  8   -0.00629  I                    *
  9   -0.00614  I                    *
 10   -0.00338  I                    *
 11   -0.00603  I                    *
 12    0.00233  I                    *
 13   -0.00494  I                    *
 14   -0.01263  I                    *
 15   -0.00691  I                    *
 16   -0.00837  I                    *
 17   -0.00383  I                    *
 18   -0.01145  I                    *
 19   -0.01589  I                    *
 20   -0.01530  I                    *
                I--------------------+--------------------I
```

**FIGURE 4.9 ACF and PACF of GNP in 1972 dollars.**

```
AUTOCORRELATION FUNCTION
 LAG       ACF  -1                  0                  +1
                I-------------------+-------------------T
   1   0.28076  I                   +     *
   2   0.17069  I                   +  *
   3   0.00811  I                   *
   4   0.01754  I                   *
   5  -0.07964  I                 * +
   6  -0.04672  I                  *+
   7  -0.06316  I                  *+
   8  -0.21387  I               *   +
   9  -0.16824  I                *  +
  10  -0.01917  I                   *
  11  -0.05225  I                  *+
  12  -0.07979  I                 * +
  13  -0.08372  I                 * +
  14   0.00467  I                   *
  15   0.00148  I                   *
  16   0.06012  I                   +*
  17   0.02363  I                   *
  18   0.07664  I                   +*
  19   0.00172  I                   *
  20   0.08780  I                   + *
                I-------------------+-------------------T


PARTIAL AUTOCORRELATION FUNCTION

 LAG      PACF  -1                  0                  +1
                I-------------------+-------------------T
   1   0.28076  I                   +     *
   2   0.09973  I                   + *
   3  -0.06911  I                  *+
   4   0.01634  I                   *
   5  -0.08510  I                 * +
   6  -0.01102  I                   *
   7  -0.02698  I                  *+
   8  -0.21018  I               *   +
   9  -0.05960  I                  *+
  10   0.09803  I                   + *
  11  -0.06657  I                  *+
  12  -0.08182  I                 * +
  13  -0.06480  I                  *+
  14   0.03690  I                   +*
  15   0.01086  I                   *
  16   0.00022  I                   *
  17  -0.05773  I                  *+
  18   0.08022  I                   + *
  19  -0.02751  I                  *+
  20   0.03955  I                   +*
                I-------------------+-------------------T
```

**FIGURE 4.10 ACF and PACF of the first difference of GNP in 1972 dollars.**

example, Box and Jenkins (1970), Anderson (1971), or Fuller (1976). Rather than cover the estimation of ARMA models in detail we explain the method and some of the problems that arise by the use of a simple example.

### 4.2.1 The Initial Value Problem

ARMA models are usually estimated by assuming that the innovations are normally distributed and then maximizing the likelihood function or by minimizing the sum of the squared errors. To illustrate, we examine a simple ARMA(1, 1) model, assuming both stationarity and invertibility. Let

$$Y_t = \phi Y_{t-1} + a_t + \theta a_{t-1}.$$

The sum of squares to be minimized is given by

$$\sum_{t=1}^{T} a_t^2 = \sum_{t=1}^{T} [Y_t - \phi Y_{t-1} - \theta a_{t-1}]^2 \tag{4.2.1a}$$

$$= \sum_{t=1}^{T} \left[ \sum_{s=0}^{t-1} (-\theta)^s (Y_{t-s} - \phi Y_{t-s-1}) + (-\theta)^t a_0 \right]^2. \tag{4.2.1b}$$

From (4.2.1) we can see that the sum of squared errors contains $Y_0$ and $a_0$, that is, values for $Y_t$ and $a_t$ at a time before data are available. This presents the problem of determining values for both $Y_0$ and $a_0$, the "initial values." We now discuss three ways of handling the initial problem: (1) setting the values prior to time period one to their unconditional expectations; (2) starting at an observation with $t > 1$; and (3) backcasting. We discuss each of these in turn.

The first method of handling the initial value problem is to set $Y_t$ and $a_t$ equal to their unconditional expectations, zero, for $t < 1$. (Remember that in this chapter we have assumed a zero mean for the $Y$ series.) Given values for $a_t$ and $Y_t$, $t < 1$, (4.2.1a) or (4.2.1b) can be minimized with respect to $\phi$ and $\theta$. While minimization of (4.2.1b) is nonlinear, but straightforward, minimization of (4.2.1a) is not. Minimization of (4.2.1a) requires initial estimates of $\phi$ and $\theta$, which, along with $a_0$, are used to calculate the other $a_t$ terms. From the $a_t$ terms, the sum of squared errors can be calculated. The values of $\phi$ and $\theta$ that minimize the sum of squared errors is determined by iteration.

Setting the initial values to their unconditional expectation allows estimation to proceed, but has one undesirable aspect—the values for $Y_t$ and $a_t$, $t < 1$ were probably not zero, and setting them to zero introduces the errors in variables problem, which results in biased estimates. However, the impact of setting these values to zero declines as the sample size increases.

A second way to handle the initial value problem is to start at observation 2 and minimize

$$\sum_{t=2}^{T} a_t^2 = \sum_{t=2}^{T} \left[ \sum_{s=0}^{t-2} (-\theta)^s (Y_{t-s} - \theta Y_{t-s-1}) + (-\theta)^{t-1} a_1 \right]^2, \tag{4.2.2}$$

which solves the problem of the initial value for $Y$ but not for $a$; we still need to come up with a value for the initial innovation. A common procedure is to set the initial value of $a_t$ to its unconditional expectation of zero. Given a value for $Y_1$ and setting $a_1 = 0$ we can minimize (4.2.1) with respect to $\phi$ and $\theta$ to get estimates of $\phi$ and $\theta$. These estimators, however, are conditional upon the given value of $Y_1$ and upon $a_1 = 0$. Conditioning upon $Y_1$ is not seen as a serious problem, but conditioning upon $a_1 = 0$ is.

To overcome this problem, $a_1$ can be treated as an unknown parameter and estimated jointly with $\phi$ and $\theta$ by the method of *backcasting*, presented in Box and Jenkins (1970), to estimate the initial conditions for an ARMA model conditional only upon the observed data series, the $Y$'s.

Backcasting is based upon a rather strange looking result that states that if a time series can be written as

$$\phi(L)Y_t = \theta(L)a_t,$$

where $a_t$ is i.i.d.$(0,\sigma_a^2)$, it can also be written as

$$\phi(F)Y_t = \theta(F)e_t,$$

where $e_t$ is i.i.d. $(0,\sigma_a^2)$ and $F = L^{-1}$.[5] This means that the ARMA(1, 1) process

$$Y_t = \phi Y_{t-1} + a_t + \theta a_{t-1}$$

or

$$(1 - \phi L)Y_t = (1 + \theta L)a_t,$$

can be written as

$$(1 - \phi F)Y_t = (1 + \theta F)e_t,$$

or

$$Y_t - \phi Y_{t+1} = e_t + \theta e_{t+1}.$$

The dual representation of ARMA models is useful because it permits us to assign values to the $Y$ and $a$ that occurred before time period one that are consistent with the rest of the data.

The general method of attack is to set future $e$ values to zero and solve for past $Y$ values, conditional upon the future and past $e$ values being zero and upon observed $Y$ values. The computed $Y$ values are then used to find past $a$ values conditional upon the data and to find noninitial $a$ values. As an example, the MA(1) process has the following two representations:

$$Y_t = a_t + \theta a_{t-1}$$
$$Y_t = e_t + \theta e_{t+1}.$$

Assume that observations are available for $t = 1, \ldots, 5$. If we start by setting $e_0 = e_6 = 0$, we can solve for the remaining $e$'s and $a$'s as follows.

[5]This result is discussed by Box and Jenkins (1970, pp. 196–198). Its proof is difficult and is omitted.

$$
\begin{aligned}
e_5 &= Y_5 - \theta e_6 \\
&= Y_5; \\
e_4 &= Y_4 - \theta e_5 \\
&= Y_4 - \theta Y_5; \\
e_3 &= Y_3 - \theta e_4 \\
&= Y_3 - \theta Y_4 + \theta^2 Y_5; \\
e_2 &= Y_2 - \theta e_3 \\
e_1 &= Y_1 - \theta e_2; \\
e_0 &= Y_0 - \theta e_1.
\end{aligned}
$$

On the assumption that $e_0 = 0$,

$$Y_0 = \theta e_1,$$

which is a numerical value for $Y_0$. We can then work forward through the equations as follows. First set $a_{-1} = 0$;[6] we then have

$$
\begin{aligned}
a_0 &= Y_0 - \theta a_{-1} \\
&= \theta e_1; \\
a_1 &= Y_1 - \theta a_0; \\
a_2 &= Y_2 - \theta a_1; \\
&\ \ \vdots \\
a_5 &= Y_5 - \theta a_4.
\end{aligned}
$$

This procedure can be repeated. That is, the $a_t$ series can be used to generate a $Y_6$ and then a second set of $e_t$'s can be calculated. But in practice the series generated by a second or third run through the above process is almost identical to the series generated by the first. The $a_t$ series generated by the backcasting process can then be used for past values of the $a_t$'s in the forecasting process.[7]

### 4.2.2 Estimating the General ARMA Model

In the general ARMA$(p, q)$ case we have

$$\phi(L)Y_t = \theta(L)a_t,$$

or

$$Y_t = \phi_1 Y_{t-1} + \cdots \phi_p Y_{t-p} + a_t + \theta_1 a_{t-1} + \cdots + \theta_q a_{t-q}.$$

[6]Setting $a_{-1} = 0$ and solving for the other $a_t$ terms may not seem to be much of an improvement over setting $a_0 = 0$ and solving, but it is because $a_0$, not $a_{-1}$, is used in calculating the other $a_t$ terms. For an MA$(q)$ or an ARMA$(p, q)$ we would solve for $q$ initial values: $a_{1-q}, a_{2-q}, \ldots, a_0$.

[7]Backcasting is also used in estimation for purposes of calculating the minimum sum of squared errors of the $a_t$ series for different parameter values.

For $T$ observations, we have

$$
\begin{bmatrix}
1 & 0 & 0 & 0 & \cdots & & & 0 \\
-\phi_1 & 1 & 0 & 0 & \cdots & & & 0 \\
-\phi_2 & -\phi_1 & 1 & 0 & \cdots & & & \vdots \\
\vdots & & & & 0 & & & \vdots \\
-\phi_p & -\phi_{p-1} & \cdots & \cdots & 1 & 0 & & \vdots \\
 & & & & \cdot & 1 & & \vdots \\
\vdots & & & & \cdot & \cdot & 1 & \vdots \\
\cdot & & & & & & & 1
\end{bmatrix}
\begin{bmatrix}
Y_1 \\ Y_2 \\ \vdots \\ \\ \\ \\ \\ Y_T
\end{bmatrix}
$$

$$
= \begin{bmatrix}
1 & 0 & \cdot & \cdots & & 0 \\
\theta_1 & 1 & 0 & \cdots & & 0 \\
\theta_2 & \theta_1 & 1 & 0 & & 0 \\
\vdots & & & & & \\
\theta_q & \theta_{q-1} & & & & \\
0 & \theta_q & & & & \\
\vdots & \vdots & & & & \\
\cdot & \cdot & & & & 0 \\
0 & 0 & \cdots & \theta_q & \cdots \ \theta_1 & 1
\end{bmatrix}
\begin{bmatrix}
a_1 \\ a_2 \\ \vdots \\ \\ \\ \\ \\ \\ a_T
\end{bmatrix}
$$

$$
+ \begin{bmatrix}
\phi_p & \phi_{p-1} & \cdots & \cdots & \phi_1 \\
0 & \phi_p & \phi_{p-1} & \cdots & \phi_2 \\
0 & 0 & \phi_p & & \vdots \\
\cdot & & & & \\
\cdot & & & & 0 \\
\cdot & & & & 0 \\
 & & & & \vdots \\
0 & 0 & \cdot & \cdots & 0
\end{bmatrix}
\begin{bmatrix}
Y_{-p+1} \\ Y_{-p+2} \\ \vdots \\ \\ \cdot \\ Y_0
\end{bmatrix}
$$

$$+\begin{bmatrix} \theta_q & \theta_{q-1} & \cdots & \theta_1 \\ 0 & \theta_q & & \theta_2 \\ 0 & & \cdot & \cdot \\ \cdot & & \cdot & \cdot \\ \cdot & & \cdot & \cdot \\ \cdot & & \cdot & \cdot \\ 0 & \cdots & \cdots & \theta_q \\ \cdot & & & 0 \\ \cdot & & & \cdot \\ \cdot & & & \cdot \\ \cdot & & & \cdot \\ 0 & \cdots & \cdots & 0 \end{bmatrix} \begin{bmatrix} a_{-q+1} \\ a_{-q+2} \\ \cdot \\ \cdot \\ \\ a_0 \end{bmatrix}. \qquad \textbf{(4.2.3)}$$

The above can be written in matrix form as

$$\phi \mathbf{Y}_T = \theta \mathbf{a}_T + \phi_0 \mathbf{Y}_0 + \theta_0 \mathbf{a}_0,$$

where $\mathbf{Y}_0$ and $\mathbf{a}_0$ are data values that occurred before the period for which the estimates are to be made, and $\phi$, $\theta$, $\phi_0$ and $\theta_0$ are the appropriate matrices in (4.2.3). Equation 4.2.3 yields a solution for $\mathbf{a}_T$,

$$\mathbf{a}_T = \theta^{-1}[\phi \mathbf{Y}_T - \phi_0 \mathbf{Y}_0 - \theta_0 \mathbf{a}_0]. \qquad \textbf{(4.2.4)}$$

We can now write the sum of squared errors as

$$\begin{aligned} \sum_{t=1}^{T} a_t^2 &= \mathbf{a}_T' \mathbf{a}_T \\ &= (\phi \mathbf{Y}_T - \phi_0 \mathbf{Y}_0 - \theta_0 \mathbf{a}_0)'(\theta^{-1})'(\theta^{-1})(\phi \mathbf{Y}_T - \phi_0 \mathbf{Y}_0 - \theta_0 \mathbf{a}_0). \end{aligned} \qquad \textbf{(4.2.5)}$$

Equation 4.2.5 shows the sum of squared errors as a function of the parameter values, past observed values of $Y$, and past values of $Y$ and $a$ that occurred before $t = 0$. Equation 4.2.5 can be minimized to yield least squares estimates once we deal with values of $\mathbf{Y}_0$ and $\mathbf{a}_0$. Conditional on specified values for $\mathbf{a}_0$ and $\mathbf{Y}_0$ (e.g., $\mathbf{a}_0 = \mathbf{0}$ and $\mathbf{Y}_0 = \mathbf{0}$), (4.2.5) can be minimized in a relatively straightforward (if nonlinear) way. If we are unwilling to specify values for $\mathbf{a}_0$ and $\mathbf{Y}_0$ there are a number of ways to proceed. We can treat $\mathbf{Y}_0$ and $\mathbf{a}_0$ as parameters and minimize (4.2.5) with respect to $\mathbf{a}_0$ and $\mathbf{Y}_0$ as well as with respect to $\phi$ and $\theta$.[8] Alternatively, we can begin the minimization at time $t = p$ in which case $\mathbf{Y}_0$ is a vector containing the first $p$ observations of the $Y_t$ series. Given $\mathbf{Y}_0$, (4.2.5) can then be minimized, either conditional upon $\mathbf{a}_0$ or by treating $\mathbf{a}_0$ as a vector of unknown parameters.

The relationship between minimum sum of squared error estimates and maximum likelihood estimators can easily be seen by writing the likelihood function of $\mathbf{a}_T$, where

[8]In practice we can minimize (4.2.5) with respect to $\phi$, $\theta$, $\mathbf{a}_0$, and $\mathbf{Y}_0$ as follows: start with values of $\phi$ and $\theta$ and use those parameter values to calculate $\mathbf{Y}_0$ and $\mathbf{a}_0$ via backcasting. Given $\mathbf{Y}_0$ and $\mathbf{a}_0$, $\mathbf{a}_T$ can be calculated and (4.2.5) can be minimized.

$a_t \sim N(0, \sigma^2)$, i.i.d., as

$$f(a_1, \cdots, a_T; \sigma^2) = \left(\frac{1}{\sqrt{2\pi}}\right)^T \sigma^{-T} \exp\left\{\left(\frac{-1}{2}\right) \sum_{t=1}^{T} \frac{a_t^2}{\sigma^2}\right\}. \qquad \textbf{(4.2.6)}$$

Transforming from the random vector $\mathbf{a}_T$ to $\mathbf{Y}_T$ involves replacing $\Sigma_{t=1}^{T} a_t^2$ with (4.2.5) in (4.2.6); the Jacobian of the transformation is one.

The large sample properties of the estimated $\phi$, $\theta$, and $\sigma^2$ depend, of course, on the assumptions made. If we assume normality and find maximum likelihood estimators, then all properties of MLE's discussed in Chapter 1 hold—that is, $\hat{\phi}$, $\hat{\theta}_T$, and $\hat{\sigma}_T^2$ are consistent, efficient, and have an asymptotic distribution that is multivariate normal [e.g., see Bloomfield (1972), Walker (1962)]. Without the assumption of normal innovations it can be shown, under the appropriate conditions, that the least squares coefficients are asymptotically normal; see Anderson (1971) or Fuller (1976).

### 4.2.3 AR(1) Example

To illustrate the estimation procedure, we derive analytic expressions for the estimators and their estimated variances for an AR(1) process. (In practice, the maximization, differentiation, and estimation would be done numerically.)

Let

$$Y_t = \phi Y_{t-1} + a_t,$$

where the $a_t$ terms are normally distributed:

$$f(a_1, \cdots, a_T; \sigma^2) = \left(\frac{1}{\sqrt{2\pi}}\right)^T \sigma^{-T} \exp\left\{\sum_{t=1}^{T} \frac{a_t^2}{\sigma^2}\right\}.$$

Transforming variables from $a_t$ to $Y_t$, where the Jacobian of the transformation is 1, and treating $Y_0$ as a parameter, we have the likelihood function for the vector $\mathbf{Y}$:

$$f(\mathbf{Y}; \sigma^2, Y_0, \phi) = \left(\frac{1}{\sqrt{2\pi}}\right)^T (\sigma^2)^{-T/2} \times \exp\left\{\left(-\frac{1}{2}\right) \sum_{t=1}^{T} (Y_t - \phi Y_{t-1})^2\right\}.$$

Taking the logarithm yields the log likelihood function,

$$\ln f = -\frac{T}{2} \ln(2\pi) - \frac{T}{2} \ln(\sigma^2) - \frac{1}{2} \sum_{t=1}^{T} \frac{(Y_t - \phi Y_{t-1})^2}{\sigma^2}.$$

Differentiation of the log likelihood function yields the first order conditions,

$$\frac{\partial \ln f}{\partial Y_0} = \frac{\phi}{\sigma^2}(Y_1 - \phi Y_0)$$

$$\frac{\partial \ln f}{\partial \phi} = \frac{1}{\sigma^2} \sum_{t=1}^{T} Y_{t-1}(Y_t - \phi Y_{t-1})$$

$$\frac{\partial \ln f}{\partial \sigma^2} = -\frac{T}{2\sigma^2} + \sum_{t=1}^{T} \frac{(Y_t - \phi Y_{t-1})^2}{2\sigma^4}.$$

Setting the derivatives to zero and solving these three equations yields the maximum likelihood estimates,

$$\hat{Y}_0 = \frac{Y_1}{\hat{\phi}},$$

$$\hat{\phi} = \frac{\sum_{t=2}^{T} Y_t Y_{t-1}}{\sum_{t=2}^{T} Y_{t-1}^2},$$

and

$$\hat{\sigma}^2 = \sum_{t=2}^{T} \frac{(Y_t - \hat{\phi} Y_{t-1})^2}{T}.$$

Notice that $\hat{Y}_0$ does not appear in the latter two expressions. This is because substitution of the condition $Y_1 - \hat{Y}_0\hat{\phi} = 0$ in the second and third first order conditions makes the $t = 1$ term zero.

Large sample standard errors can be obtained by inverting the information matrix, the $i$, $j$ element of which is

$$I_{ij}(\boldsymbol{\theta}) = -E\left[\frac{\partial^2 \ln f}{\partial \theta_i \, \partial \theta_j}\right],$$

where the $\theta$'s are the parameters of the likelihood function. For this problem, these are given by

$$E\left[\frac{\partial^2 \ln f}{(\partial Y_0)^2}\right] = -E\left[\frac{\phi^2}{\sigma^2}\right] = -\frac{\phi^2}{\sigma^2},$$

$$E\left[\frac{\partial^2 \ln f}{\partial Y_0 \, \partial \phi}\right] = E\left[-\frac{\phi Y_0}{\sigma^2} + \frac{(Y_1 - \phi Y_0)}{\sigma^2}\right] = -\frac{\phi Y_0}{\sigma^2},$$

$$E\left[\frac{\partial^2 \ln f}{\partial Y_0 \, \partial \sigma^2}\right] = -E\left[\frac{Y_1 - \phi Y_0}{\sigma^4}\right] = 0$$

$$E\left[\frac{\partial^2 \ln f}{(\partial \sigma^2)^2}\right] = E\left[\frac{T}{2\sigma^4} - \frac{2}{\sigma^6}\Sigma(Y_t - \phi Y_{t-1})^2\right]$$

$$= \frac{T}{2\sigma^4} - \frac{T\sigma^2}{\sigma^6} = -\frac{T}{2\sigma^4},$$

$$E\left[\frac{\partial^2 \ln f}{\partial \sigma^2 \, \partial \phi}\right] = -E\left[\frac{\Sigma Y_{t-1}(Y_t - \phi Y_{t-1})}{\sigma^4}\right] = 0$$

$$E\left[\frac{\partial^2 \ln f}{(\partial \phi)^2}\right] = -E\left[\frac{1}{\sigma^2}\sum_{t=1}^{T} Y_{t-1}^2\right]$$

$$= -\frac{1}{\sigma^2}\sum_{t=1}^{T} E(Y_{t-1}^2)$$

$$= -\frac{1}{\sigma^2}\sum_{t=1}^{T} \frac{\sigma^2}{1 - \phi^2}$$

$$= -\frac{T}{1 - \phi^2}.$$

The information matrix for $Y_0$, $\phi$, and $\sigma^2$ is

$$I(Y_0, \phi, \sigma^2) = \begin{bmatrix} \dfrac{\phi^2}{\sigma^2} & \dfrac{\phi Y_0}{\sigma^2} & 0 \\ \dfrac{\phi Y_0}{\sigma^2} & \dfrac{T}{1 - \phi^2} & 0 \\ 0 & 0 & \dfrac{T}{2\sigma^4} \end{bmatrix}$$

$$= \frac{1}{\sigma^2} \begin{bmatrix} \phi^2 & \phi Y_0 & 0 \\ \phi Y_0 & \dfrac{T\sigma^2}{1 - \phi^2} & 0 \\ 0 & 0 & \dfrac{T}{2\sigma^2} \end{bmatrix},$$

and

$$[I(Y_0, \phi, \sigma^2)]^{-1} = \sigma^2 \begin{bmatrix} \dfrac{T^2}{2D(1 - \phi^2)} & \dfrac{-T\phi Y_0}{2D\sigma^2} & 0 \\ \dfrac{-T\phi Y_0}{2D\sigma^2} & \dfrac{T\phi^2}{2D\sigma^2} & 0 \\ 0 & 0 & \dfrac{2\sigma^2;}{T} \end{bmatrix},$$

where

$$D = \frac{T}{2\sigma^2}\left[\frac{T\phi^2\sigma^2}{1 - \phi^2} - \phi^2 Y_0^2\right].$$

Obviously, all the elements of the asymptotic covariance matrix other than $\text{Var}(Y_0)$ go to zero as $T$ increases.

For ARMA processes more complicated than AR(1), the derivation of analytic expressions for the parameter estimates and the elements of the information matrix is substantially more difficult. In practice the estimators and information matrix are calculated numerically.

## 4.3 Diagnostic Tests

Once a model has been identified and estimated we want to determine how much faith to put in it by subjecting it to as rigorous a testing as possible. While there are no general tests for all forms of model inadequacy, there are tests against several specific alternatives. The most widely used test is to examine the residuals of the model for serial correlation, since the presence of serially correlalted errors is obvious evidence of model inadequacy.

### 4.3.1 The Box-Pierce Test

Box and Pierce (1970) have developed a test for the presence of serial correlation in ARIMA model residuals. Their test is based upon the sample autocorrelation function of the residuals from an estimated ARMA($p$, $q$) process. Let $\hat{r}_k$ be the $k$th sample autocorrelation computed from residuals from an estimated ARMA($p$, $q$) model based on a sample of size $T$; on the null hypothesis of no serial correlation the statistic

$$T\sum_{k=1}^{m} \hat{r}_k^2$$

has a chi-square distribution with $m$-$p$-$q$ degrees of freedom. Thus to test for the presence of serial correlation we need merely calculate this statistic and compare it to published chi-square tables.

Since this result is of such importance in time series analysis, it is useful to examine it in detail. To do this we derive the basic result for an autoregressive process.

The derivation proceeds in the following manner: First, the relationship between the correlation coefficients estimated from the actual innovations and the correlation coefficients estimated from the estimated innovations is found. Second, this relationship is used to derive an expression for the difference between the estimated autocorrelations and the true autocorrelations. Finally, this difference is manipulated to a point where a central limit theorem can be applied.

We begin by considering an AR($p$) process,

$$Y_t = \phi_1 Y_{t-1} + \phi_2 Y_{t-2} + \cdots + \phi_p Y_{t-p} + a_t, \tag{4.3.1}$$

or

$$\phi(L)Y_t = a_t, \qquad t = 1, \ldots, N,$$

where $a_t$ is distributed i.i.d.(0, $\sigma_a^2$), and the process $\phi(L)$ is stationary. Equation 4.3.1 has a moving average representation

$$Y_t = a_t + \psi_1 a_{t-1} + \psi_2 a_{t-2} + \cdots. \tag{4.3.2}$$

If we estimate the AR($p$) process by minimizing the sum of the squared errors

$$\text{SSE} = \sum_{t=p+1}^{N} (Y_t - \phi_1 Y_{t-1} - \cdots - \phi_p Y_{t-p})^2,$$

the first order conditions for minimization are

$$\frac{\partial \text{SSE}}{\partial \phi_j} = -2 \sum_{t=p+1}^{N} Y_{t-j}(Y_t - \hat{\phi}_1 Y_{t-1} - \cdots - \hat{\phi}_p Y_{t-p}) = 0 \qquad j = 1, 2, \ldots, p. \tag{4.3.3}$$

Solution of (4.3.3) yields estimates $\hat{\phi}_1, \hat{\phi}_2, \ldots, \hat{\phi}_p$ and estimated innovations $\hat{a}_t$, where

$$\hat{a}_t = Y_t - \hat{\phi}_1 Y_{t-1} - \cdots - \hat{\phi}_p Y_{t-p}. \tag{4.3.4}$$

Substituting (4.3.4) into (4.3.3) yields

$$0 = \sum_{t=p+1}^{N} Y_{t-j}\hat{a}_t, \qquad j = 1, \ldots, p. \tag{4.3.5}$$

The estimates of $\phi_i$ obtained from minimizing the sum of squared errors can be used to find the estimated $\hat{\psi}_i$ values corresponding to (4.3.2), which allow us to write

$$Y_t = \hat{a}_t + \hat{\psi}_1\hat{a}_{t-1} + \hat{\psi}_2\hat{a}_{t-2} + \cdots .$$
$$= \sum_{i=0}^{\infty} \hat{a}_{t-i}\hat{\psi}_i.$$

The $k$th term of the autocorrelation function for $a_t$ can be written as

$$r_k \equiv \frac{\sum_{t=k+1}^{N} a_t a_{t-k}}{\sum_{t=k+1}^{N} a_t^2}; \tag{4.3.6}$$

its sample counterpart, using estimated $a_t$'s, is

$$\hat{r}_k \equiv \frac{\sum_{t=k+1}^{N} \hat{a}_t \hat{a}_{t-k}}{\sum_{t=k+1}^{N} \hat{a}_t^2}. \tag{4.3.7}$$

Substitution for $Y_t$ into (4.3.5) yields

$$0 = \sum_{t=p+1}^{N} \hat{a}_t \left( \sum_{k=0}^{\infty} \hat{\psi}_k \hat{a}_{t-j-k} \right) \tag{4.3.8}$$

$$= \sum_{k=0}^{N} \hat{\psi}_k \left( \sum_{t=p+1}^{N} \hat{a}_t \hat{a}_{t-j-k} \right) + \sum_{k=N+1}^{\infty} \hat{\psi}_k \left( \sum_{t=p+1}^{N} \hat{a}_t \hat{a}_{t-j-k} \right), \tag{4.3.9}$$

$j = 1, \ldots, p.$

Dividing both sides of (4.3.9) by $\Sigma_{t=p+1}^{N} \hat{a}_t^2$ allows us to write

$$0 = \sum_{k=j}^{N} \hat{\psi}_k \frac{\sum_{t=p+1}^{N} \hat{a}_t \hat{a}_{t-j-k}}{\sum_{t=p+1}^{N} \hat{a}_t^2} + O_p\left(\frac{1}{N}\right), \tag{4.3.10}$$

where the expression $O_p(1/N)$ means "order in probability"; it is explained in Appendix B. From the definition of the correlation coefficient we have

$$0 = \sum_{k=j}^{N} \hat{\psi}_k \hat{r}_{k+j} + O_p\left(\frac{1}{N}\right). \tag{4.3.11}$$

We now define

$$\Delta_k \equiv \psi_k - \hat{\psi}_k. \tag{4.3.12}$$

Since the $\hat{\phi}_i$ terms are estimated by minimizing the sum of squared errors we have

[Anderson (1971)] that

$$\hat{\phi}_k \xrightarrow{p} \phi_k,$$

and it is easily shown that

$$\hat{\psi}_k \xrightarrow{p} \psi_k.$$

Thus we can say that $\Delta_k$ is of order in probability $1/N$ that is, $\Delta_k = O_p(1/N)$. Combining (4.3.11) and (4.3.12) yields

$$\begin{aligned} 0 &= \sum_{k=0}^{N} \psi_k \hat{r}_{k+j} + \sum_{k=0}^{N} \Delta_k \hat{r}_{k+j} \\ &= \sum_{k=0}^{M} \psi_k \hat{r}_{k+j} + O_p\left(\frac{1}{N}\right), \end{aligned} \tag{4.3.13}$$

where $M$ is a number such that $\psi_h$ is sufficiently close to 0 for $h > M$.

The next step in Box and Pierce's derivation is to expand, via a Taylor series expansion, the sample correlation coefficients. We can write, using (4.3.6) and (4.3.1),

$$\begin{aligned} r_k &= \frac{\sum_{t=k+1}^{N} a_t a_{t-k}}{\sum_{t=k+1}^{N} a_t^2} \\ &= \frac{\sum_{t=k+1}^{N} (Y_t - \phi_1 Y_{t-1} - \cdots - \phi_p Y_{t-p})(Y_{t-k} - \phi_1 Y_{t-k-1} - \cdots - \phi_p Y_{t-p-k})}{\sum_{t=k+1}^{N} (Y_t - \phi_1 Y_{t-1} - \cdots - \phi_p Y_{t-p})^2}. \end{aligned} \tag{4.3.14}$$

Since $\hat{r}_k$ is defined the same way as $r_k$ but with estimated $\phi_i$'s in place of actual $\phi_i$'s, we may expand $\hat{r}_k$ via a Taylor series expansion as

$$\hat{r}_k = r_k(\phi) + \sum_{j=1}^{p} (\phi_j - \hat{\phi}_j) \frac{\partial r_k(\phi)}{\partial \phi_j} + O_p\left(\frac{1}{N}\right). \tag{4.3.15}$$

Through an involved argument that will not be repeated here, Box and Pierce are able to show that

$$\frac{-\partial r_k(\phi)}{\partial \phi_j} = -\hat{\psi}_{k-j};$$

therefore

$$r_k = \hat{r}_k + \sum_{j=1}^{p} (\phi_j - \hat{\phi}_j)\psi_{k-j} + O_p\left(\frac{1}{N}\right), \qquad k = 1, \ldots, M. \tag{4.3.16}$$

Equation 4.3.16 can be rewritten as

$$r_k = \hat{r}_k + (\psi_{k-1}, \psi_{k-2}, \ldots, \psi_{k-p})(\phi_1 - \hat{\phi}_1, \phi_2 - \hat{\phi}_2, \ldots, \phi_p - \hat{\phi}_p)' + O_p\left(\frac{1}{N}\right),$$

where $\psi_k = 0$ for $k < 0$. Writing this in matrix form, where

$$\mathbf{r}' = (r_1, r_2, \ldots, r_m),$$

we have, ignoring the $O_p(1/N)$ term,

$$\mathbf{r} = \hat{\mathbf{r}} + \begin{bmatrix} 1 & 0 & 0 \ldots 0 \\ & & \cdot \\ \psi_1 & 1 & 0 \ldots . \\ & & \cdot \\ \psi_2 & \psi_1 & 1 \ldots 0 \\ & & \psi_1 \\ \cdot & \cdot & \cdot \\ \cdot & \cdot & \cdot \\ \cdot & \cdot & \cdot \\ \psi_{m-1} & \psi_{m-2} & \psi_{m-p} \end{bmatrix} \begin{bmatrix} \phi_1 - \hat{\phi}_1 \\ \phi_2 - \hat{\phi}_2 \\ \cdot \\ \cdot \\ \cdot \\ \phi_p - \hat{\phi}_p \end{bmatrix} \tag{4.3.17}$$

or

$$\mathbf{r} = \hat{\mathbf{r}} + X(\boldsymbol{\phi} - \hat{\boldsymbol{\phi}}), \tag{4.3.18}$$

where $\mathbf{r}$ is $m \times 1$, $X$ is $m \times p$, $(\boldsymbol{\phi} - \hat{\boldsymbol{\phi}})$ is $p \times 1$, and $X$ is implicitly defined. Multiplying both sides of (4.3.18) by $X(X'X)^{-1}X'$ yields

$$X(X'X)^{-1}X'\mathbf{r} = X(X'X)^{-1}X'\hat{\mathbf{r}} + X(\boldsymbol{\phi} - \hat{\boldsymbol{\phi}}). \tag{4.3.19}$$

Rewriting (4.3.10) in the notation of (4.3.18) yields

$$X'\mathbf{r} = \mathbf{0};$$

therefore, (4.3.19) becomes

$$X(X'X)^{-1}X'\mathbf{r} = \mathbf{0} + \mathbf{r} - \hat{\mathbf{r}}$$

or

$$\hat{\mathbf{r}} = (I_m - X(X'X)^{-1}X')\mathbf{r}, \tag{4.3.20}$$

where $I_m$ is the $m \times m$ identity matrix.

Box and Pierce now claim that, on the null hypothesis of no serial correlation, $\mathbf{r}$ is approximately distributed as

$$\sqrt{N}\mathbf{r} \sim N[\mathbf{0}, I_m].$$

Accordingly, $\hat{\mathbf{r}}$ is a linear transformation of a normally distributed random variable, and

$$\begin{aligned} N \cdot \sum_{k=1}^{M} \hat{r}_k^2 &= (\sqrt{N}\hat{\mathbf{r}})'(\sqrt{N}\hat{\mathbf{r}}) \\ &= \sqrt{N}\mathbf{r}'[I - X(X'X)^{-1}X'][I - X(X'X)^{-1}X']\mathbf{r}\sqrt{N} \\ &= (\sqrt{N}\mathbf{r}')[I - X(X'X)^{-1}X'](\mathbf{r}\sqrt{N}) \\ &\sim \chi^2_{m-p}, \end{aligned}$$

where the last step follows from a theorem on quadratic forms and idempotent matrices [see, e.g., Anderson (1958)]. We now have the desired result

$$N \cdot \sum_{k=1}^{m} \hat{r}_k^2 \sim \chi^2_{m-p} \tag{4.3.21}$$

for the AR($p$) case. Box and Pierce go on to show that

$$N \sum_{k=1}^{m} \hat{r}_k^2 \sim \chi^2_{m-(p+q)} \tag{4.3.22}$$

for the ARMA($p$, $q$) case.

Equation 4.3.21 provides a test for serially correlated residuals. On the null hypothesis of no serial correlation in the residuals of a time series model (estimated with $p + q$ parameters), the sum of the squares of the first $M$ autocorrelations is asymptotically distributed as shown in (4.3.22).[9]

### 4.3.2 Other Diagnostic Tools

While the Box–Pierce test for serially correlated residuals is the most widely used diagnostic test, there are other tests that should be mentioned. First and foremost, model residuals should be plotted and examined. Oftentimes, the forecaster's eye will see evidence of model inadequacy that no formal test could ever pick up. A second method that is suggested as a test against model inadequacy is that of overfitting. Overfitting involves reestimation of a model and testing whether parameters assumed to be zero are in fact zero. For example, if a forecaster has identified and estimated an ARMA(1, 1) model, the forecaster might also estimate an ARMA(2, 1) and an ARMA(1, 2) model to check against model inadequacy. A third method that is often used as a test for model inadequacy is to test the model residuals for serial correlation using Durbin's (1967) cumulated periodogram test.

## 4.4 Forecasting

This section discusses forecasting with ARIMA models, the main reason for which ARIMA models are built. For ease of exposition, we assume that all the time series of concern are stationary and have zero mean. Since adequate computer programs exist for forecasting, we will not go into great detail on the mechanics.

Stationary and invertible ARMA models can be represented in the following three equivalent ways:

$$\phi(L)Y_t = \theta(L)a_t;$$

$$Y_t = \psi(L)a_t, \quad \text{where} \quad \psi(L) = \phi^{-1}(L)\theta(L);$$

and

$$\pi(L)Y_t = a_t, \quad \text{where} \quad \pi(L) = \theta^{-1}(L)\phi(L).$$

[9]Pierce (1971) derives similar results for autocorrelations based on residuals from a regression model.

The third form is the most useful for forecasting, but the second form is often used for theoretical work.

To begin our discussion of forecasting we introduce, following Box and Jenkins, some notation for conditional expectations. Let

$$E_t[X_{t+k}]$$

be the expectation of $X_{t+k}$ conditional upon information up to and including time period $t$. We will often shorten the notation to either

$$E[X_{t+k}] \quad \text{or} \quad [X_{t+k}]$$

when the meaning is clear from the context. Under suitable conditions (which we assume) it can be shown that a variable's conditional expectation is the best forecast in a mean square error sense.[10]

### 4.4.1 Forecasts for Simple Models

A few examples will make clear how conditional expectations are used in forecasting from ARMA models. Assume a first order AR process,

$$Y_t = \phi Y_{t-1} + a_t, \qquad |\phi| < 1,$$

where we observe the variable $Y$ up to time $t$. Then

$$\begin{aligned} E_t[Y_{t+1}] &= \phi E_t[Y_t] + E_t[a_{t+1}] \\ &= \phi Y_t + 0. \end{aligned}$$

Similarly,

$$\begin{aligned} E_t[Y_{t+2}] &= \phi E_t[Y_{t+1}] + E_t[a_{t+2}] \\ &= \phi^2 Y_t. \end{aligned}$$

Continuing this procedure yields

$$E_t[Y_{t+k}] = \phi^k Y_t.$$

Note that if $Y$ is a zero mean series, the expectation of $Y_{t+k}$ at time $t$ goes to zero as $k$ gets large. This is true of all stationary time series with zero mean: as the forecast length increases, the conditional expectation goes to zero.[11]

Taking conditional expectations for a moving average process is not difficult if we assume that the actual values of the past innovations can be recovered—an assumption discussed earlier. The MA(1) process is given by

$$Y_t = a_t + \theta a_{t-1}, \qquad |\theta| < 1.$$

[10]See Astrom (1970) for more detail.

[11]If the time series does not have a zero mean, the conditional expectation for a stationary time series tends to a constant as the forecast length increases, which is a function of the ARMA process coefficients and the mean of the time series.

If we assume knowledge of the $a_t$ series up to and including time $t$, we have

$$E_t[Y_{t+1}] = \theta a_t$$

and

$$\begin{aligned} E_t[Y_{t+2}] &= E_t[a_{t+2}] + \theta E_t[a_{t+1}] \\ &= 0. \end{aligned}$$

In general, for a moving average process the conditional expectation is the mean of the series if the forecast length exceeds the order of the process.

For an ARMA(1, 1) process,

$$Y_t = \phi Y_{t-1} + a_t + \theta a_{t-1}, \qquad |\phi| < 1, \quad |\theta| < 1,$$

forecasts are made in a similar fashion. We have that

$$\begin{aligned} E_t[Y_{t+1}] &= \phi E_t[Y_t] + E_t[a_{t+1}] + \theta E_t[a_t] \\ &= \phi Y_t + \theta a_t. \end{aligned}$$

For a two period ahead forecast, we have

$$\begin{aligned} E_t[Y_{t+2}] &= \phi E_t[Y_{t+1}] + E_t[a_{t+2}] + \theta E_t[a_{t+1}] \\ &= \phi[\phi Y_t + \theta a_t] \\ &= \phi^2 Y_t + \phi\theta a_t. \end{aligned}$$

And for $k > 0$, the forecast is given by

$$\begin{aligned} E_t[Y_{t+k}] &= \phi^{k-1}[Y_{t+1}] \\ &= \phi^{k-1}[\phi Y_t + \theta a_t] \\ &= \phi^k Y_t + \phi^{k-1}\theta a_t. \end{aligned}$$

From the above we can see that for forecasts of length greater than the order of the MA process, the conditional expectation of an ARMA process behaves as the conditional expectation of an AR process.

### 4.4.2 Forecast Error Variance

When forecasts are made, it is useful to know the forecast variance in order to have some idea of the distribution of the actual value of the variable being forecast. We will do this first on the assumption that the forecast is based on the true coefficients. If the coefficients are known, forecast variances can best be calculated from the MA version of the model,

$$\begin{aligned} Y_t &= \psi(L)a_t \\ &= a_t + \psi_1 a_{t-1} + \psi_2 a_{t-2} + \cdots, \end{aligned}$$

where $\psi(L)$ may be either finite or infinite. From this form, the $k$-period ahead forecast is given by

$$E_t[Y_{t+k}] = E_t[a_{t+k}] + \psi_1 E_t[a_{t+k-1}] + \cdots + \psi_k E_t[a_t] + \cdots$$
$$= \psi_k a_t + \psi_{k+1} a_{t-1} + \cdots;$$

therefore,

$$Y_{t+k} - E_t[Y_{t+k}] = a_{t+k} + \psi_1 a_{t+k-1} + \cdots + \psi_{k-1} a_{t+1},$$

and the $k$-period ahead forecast variance, $\sigma^2(k)$, is

$$\sigma^2(k) = E\{Y_{t+k} - E_t[Y_{t+k}]\}^2$$
$$= \sigma_a^2(1 + \psi_1^2 + \psi_2^2 + \cdots + \psi_{k-1}^2).$$

Notice that as $k$ gets large, the variance of the forecast approaches the overall variance of the series, $\sigma^2$. Using this method it is possible to calculate the variance of a forecast for any length from which 95% confidence intervals may be calculated and plotted in a graph such as Figure 4.11.

A word of caution should be added in interpreting Figure 4.11. The confidence intervals are the confidence intervals for any individual $k$-period ahead forecast. Since the forecast errors are not independent, it is not a joint confidence interval and should not be interpreted as such. That is, the probability that the forecast for time period $t + k$ is inside the 95% confidence interval is 95%; the probability that the forecast for time period $t + i$ is in the 95% confidence interval is 95%. But the probability that the forecasts for both time period $t + k$ and $t + i$ are in *both* individual 95% confidence intervals is not 95%. Moreover, the forecasts and forecast errors will be correlated, so that the probability that the time $t + k$ forecast is outside the 95% confidence depends on whether or not the forecast for time period $t + i$ is outside the 95% confidence interval.

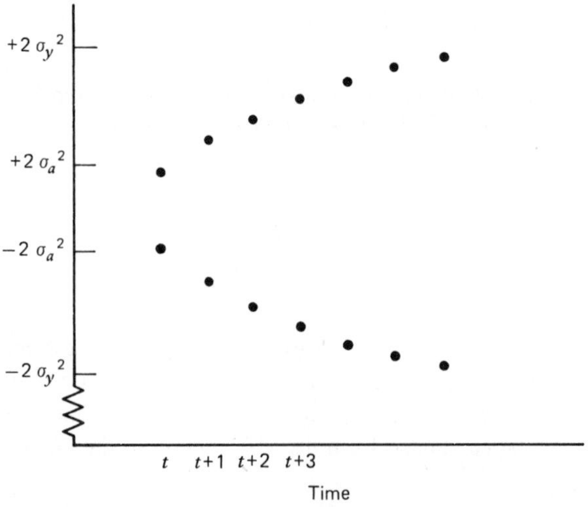


**FIGURE 4.11 Variances of ARIMA forecasts.**

We have thus far ignored the contribution of parameter error to the forecast error variance. This is in part due to convenience, in part due to the inherent difficulty of the problem, and in part due to lack of consideration of parameter error by practitioners of ARIMA models. It is often thought that for any reasonably large sample, the increase in forecast error variance due to parameter error is likely to be quite small. Fuller (1976), in fact, is able to show that the addition to the forecast error variance due to parameter estimation is $O_p(1/\sqrt{T})$. [Bloomfield (1972) presents similar asymptotic results on the sample forecast error variance.] Nevertheless, it is worthwhile to discuss the problem of forecast error variance caused by parameter error.

The difficulty is perhaps most easily seen using the MA form of an ARMA model, where the forecast is

$$\hat{Y}_{t+k} = \hat{a}_t\hat{\psi}_k + \hat{a}_{t-1}\hat{\psi}_{k-1} + \cdots;$$

this yields a forecast error of

$$Y_{t+k} - \hat{Y}_{t+k} = (a_{t+k} + \psi_1 a_{t+k-1} + \cdots + \\ + (a_t\psi_k - \hat{a}_t\hat{\psi}_k) + (a_{t-1}\psi_{k+1} - \hat{a}_{t-1}\hat{\psi}_{k+1}) + \cdots.$$

From the above, the difficulties involved in finding the true forecast error variance can be seen. First, we have only asymptotic expressions for the variance of the estimated ARMA coefficients—those from the information matrix. Second, since estimated coefficients, which depend on past values of the time series, and future forecast errors are correlated, we must find the variance of the derived estimates of the innovations and the covariances between the estimates of the innovations and the estimates of the parameters. Third, the problem will involve moments of higher than second order. Finally, when using the MA form of the model, the $\psi$ terms are not estimated directly; estimates of their variances and covariances must therefore be derived in another way, for example, by a Taylor series expansion. The problem of the variance of the $\psi$ terms does not arise if we forecast directly from the ARMA form of the model, but there we must take into account the lack of independence between past observations, future observations, and the estimated coefficients.

## 4.5 Conclusion

In our short discussion of time series analysis we have left out a number of important topics. Chief among these are seasonal adjustment using time series models and the relationship between time series models of the sort we have discussed and the analysis of time series using spectral methods. ARIMA models are used to analyze data in the presence of seasonality by a number of authors: for example, Box and Jenkins (1970) and Bowerman and O'Connell (1979). The relationship between ARIMA models and spectral analysis is also discussed by Box and Jenkins (1970), Anderson (1971), Fuller (1976), and others.

## 4.6 References


Anderson, T. W. (1958), *An Introduction to Multivariate Statistical Analysis,* New York: Wiley.

Anderson, T. W. (1971), *The Statistical Analysis of Time Series,* New York: Wiley.

Astrom, K. J. (1970), *Introduction to Stochastic Control Theory,* New York: Academic Press.

Bartlett, M. S. (1946), "On the Theoretical Specification and Sampling Properties of Autocorrelated Time Series," *Journal of the Royal Statistical Society,* Series B, **8**, 27–41.

Bloomfield, P. (1972), "On the Prediction Error of a Time Series," *Biometrika,* **59**, 501–507.

Bowerman, B. L. and R. T. O'Connell (1979), *Time Series and Forecasting,* Belmont, Calif.: Duxbury.

Box, G. E. P. and G. M. Jenkins (1970), *Time Series Analysis: Forecasting and Control,* San Francisco: Holden-Day.

Box, G. E. P. and D. A. Pierce (1970), "Distribution of Residual Autocorrelation in Autoregressive Integrated Moving Average Time Series Models," *Journal of the American Statistical Association,* **65**, 509–526.

Durbin, J. (1967), "Tests for Serial Independence based on the Cumulated Periodogram," *Bulletin of the International Statistical Institute,* **49**, 1039–1049.

Fuller, W. A. (1976), *Introduction to Statistical Time Series,* New York: Wiley.

Pierce, D. A. (1971), "Distribution of Residual Autocorrelation in the Regression Model with Autoregressive Moving Average Error," *Journal of the Royal Statistical Society,* Series B, **33**, 140–146.

Quenouille, M. H. (1949), "The Joint Distribution of Serial Correlation Coefficients," *Annals of Mathematical Statistics,* **20**, 561–571.

Walker, A. M. (1962), "Large-Sample Estimation of Parameters for Auto Regressive Processes with Moving Average Residuals," *Biometrika,* **49**, 117–131.

# CHAPTER 5

# The Relationship Between Time Series Models and Econometric Models

The time series methods and models examined in Chapters 3 and 4 seem quite different from standard econometric methods and models. Economists pride themselves on their ability to use economic theory in their empirical work, but the methods described above model a variable as a function only of its own past and random errors. Although this may lead one to believe that time series analysis and econometrics have little in common, recent work has shown that the interface between time series analysis and econometric analysis is quite large. In this chapter we concentrate on two aspects of that interface. The first, developed by Theil and Boot (1962) and Zellner and Palm (1974), shows how ARIMA models may be regarded as "reduced forms" of econometric models. We discuss this relationship in Sections 5.2 and 5.3. The second aspect of this interface, developed by Granger (1969) and Sims (1972), attempts to determine the presence or absence of causality between two time series. We discuss causality and tests for causality in Section 5.4. Before we examine these topics, however, we extend our analysis of ARIMA models to include multivariate ARIMA models.

## 5.1 Multivariate ARIMA Models

A natural extension of univariate ARIMA models is to multivariate ARIMA models, which can be written as

$$\begin{aligned} \phi_0\mathbf{Y}_t &= \phi_1\mathbf{Y}_{t-1} + \cdots + \phi_p\mathbf{Y}_{t-p} + \theta_0\mathbf{a}_t + \theta_1\mathbf{a}_{t-1} + \cdots + \theta_q\mathbf{a}_{t-q}, \\ t &= 1, \ldots, \infty, \qquad\qquad (\mathbf{5.1.1}) \\ E[\mathbf{a}_t\mathbf{a}_t'] &= \Sigma_a, \end{aligned}$$

where $\mathbf{Y}_t$ and $\mathbf{a}_t$ are $k \times 1$ vectors, $\phi_i$ and $\theta_j$ are $k \times k$ matrices, and we assume that $\mathbf{Y}_t$ is a stationary time series with mean zero. Equation 5.1.1 can be written in lag operator notation (with $L$, a scalar lag operator, operating on each element of $\mathbf{Y}_t$ and $\mathbf{a}_t$) as follows:

$$(\phi_0 - \phi_1 L - \cdots - \phi_p L^p)\mathbf{Y}_t = (\theta_0 + \theta_1 L + \theta_2 L^2 + \cdots + \theta_q L^q)\mathbf{a}_t. \qquad (\mathbf{5.1.2})$$

In a more convenient notation, (5.1.2) can be written as

$$\phi(L)\mathbf{Y}_t = \theta(L)\mathbf{a}_t, \qquad (\mathbf{5.1.3})$$

where each element of the $\phi(L)$ and $\theta(L)$ matrices in (5.1.3) is a polynomial in the lag operator $L$, that is,

$$[\phi(L)]_{ij} = \phi_{ij}^0 + \phi_{ij}^1 L + \cdots + \phi_{ij}^p L^p$$

and

$$[\theta(L)]_{ij} = \theta_{ij}^0 + \theta_{ij}^1 L + \cdots + \theta_{ij}^q L^q,$$

where $\phi_{ij}^r$ is the $ij$ element of $\phi_r$ and $\theta_{ij}^s$ is the $ij$ element of $\theta_s$. Operations can be performed on the matrix lag operators in (5.1.2) or (5.1.3) in the same fashion as they can be performed on scalar lag operators, except that matrix operations are substituted for the corresponding scalar operations.

On the usual assumption that only the $\mathbf{Y}_t$ series is observed, a problem arises in the specification of multivariate ARIMA models: the possibility that many models are consistent with the empirically observed $\mathbf{Y}_t$ series, that is, the problem of identification.[1]

For example, $\phi_0$ is not unique—premultiplication of (5.1.1) by $A\phi_0^{-1}$, where $A$ is an arbitrary nonsingular matrix, results in

$$A\mathbf{Y}_t = (A\phi_0^{-1}\phi_1)\mathbf{Y}_{t-1} + \cdots + (A\phi_0^{-1}\phi_p)\mathbf{Y}_{t-p} + (A\phi_0^{-1}\phi_0)\mathbf{a}_t + \cdots + (A\phi_0^{-1}\theta_q)\mathbf{a}_{t-q}, \quad \textbf{(5.1.4)}$$

which yields a set of coefficients that are observationally equivalent to the coefficients in (5.1.1). This problem is usually dealt with by the convention of specifying $\phi_0$ to be the identity matrix.

A second problem is the nonuniqueness of the $\mathbf{a}_t$ terms. If between each $\theta$ and $\mathbf{a}_t$ term we insert $A^{-1}A$, where $A$ is an arbitrary nonsingular matrix, we have

$$\mathbf{Y}_t - \phi_1\mathbf{Y}_{t-1} - \cdots - \phi_p\mathbf{Y}_{t-p} = \theta_0 A^{-1}A\mathbf{a}_t + \cdots + \theta_q A^{-1}A\mathbf{a}_{t-q}$$

with

$$E[\mathbf{a}_t\mathbf{a}_t'] = \Sigma_a, \quad \textbf{(5.1.5)}$$

or

$$\mathbf{Y}_t - \cdots - \phi_p\mathbf{Y}_{t-p} = \psi_0\mathbf{e}_t + \cdots + \psi_q\mathbf{e}_{t-q}$$

with

$$\mathbf{e}_t = A\mathbf{a}_t,$$

$$\psi_i = \theta_i A^{-1},$$

and

$$E[\mathbf{e}_t\mathbf{e}_t'] = A\Sigma_a A'. \quad \textbf{(5.1.6)}$$

That is, we can write a process observationally equivalent to (5.1.2) in terms of $\mathbf{e}_t$. From (5.1.6) we can see that unless there exists some prior information about $\theta_i$, $\theta_i A^{-1}$ will be indistinguishable from $\theta_i$. To remove this problem, a standardization requiring that $\theta_0$ be the identity matrix is typically imposed. From (5.1.5) and (5.1.6) it is apparent that if $\theta_0$ is the identity matrix, there would exist no matrix $A^{-1}$, other than the identity matrix, for which $\theta_j A^{-1}$ was indistinguishable from $\theta_j$. Hence, we assume that $\theta_0 = I$. (Note that restricting $\Sigma_a$ to be the identity matrix is *not* sufficient for identification.)

Multivariate ARIMA models are very difficult to fit to data, both because of the

[1]The identification problem in econometrics is discussed in Chapter 9.

large number of parameters and the lack of theoretical restrictions on parameters. A $k$-variable ARMA($p$, $q$) system has $[p + q + (k + 1)/2k]k^2$ parameters to estimate. A simple AR(2), five variable system requires, in general, the estimation of 65 parameters.[2]

An interesting way in which multivariate ARIMA models are now being used stems from criticisms of attempts to model macroeconomic phenomena with econometric techniques.[3] This critique, often associated with Sims (1974, 1980) and described by Wallis (1980), is based on the fact that much of macroeconomic theory utilizes future expectations of endogenous and (especially under the rational expectations assumption) exogenous variables. Because of the inherent difficulty of specifying the way in which future expectations are formed, the attempt to model macroeconomic relationships entails a nontrivial possibility of confusing the impact of exogenous variables on endogenous variables with the impact of expected future exogenous variables on endogenous variables. Unless theory is strong enough to differentiate between these effects, which Sims and others doubt, theoretical restrictions placed on empirically estimated models are incorrect. What Sims has suggested is that macroeconomic prediction and policy analysis (to the extent that policy analysis can be done) should be based on multivariate ARIMA models; see Sims (1980).

## 5.2 Multiple Equation Simultaneous Equation Models

Having introduced multivariate ARIMA models, we are now in a position to discuss the way in which ARIMA models can be thought of as reduced forms of structural econometric models. Let us begin with a general ARIMA model:

$$\begin{bmatrix} A(L) & -B(L) \\ -C(L) & D(L) \end{bmatrix} \begin{bmatrix} \mathbf{Y}_t \\ \mathbf{X}_t \end{bmatrix} = \begin{bmatrix} \boldsymbol{\epsilon}_t \\ \boldsymbol{\delta}_t \end{bmatrix}, \tag{5.2.1}$$

where $\boldsymbol{\epsilon}_t$ and $\boldsymbol{\delta}_t$ are unobservable serially uncorrelated white noise processes[4] with diagonal variance-covariance matrices, $\mathbf{Y}_t$ and $\boldsymbol{\epsilon}_t$ $n \times 1$ vectors, and $\mathbf{X}_t$ and $\boldsymbol{\delta}_t$ $m \times 1$ vectors. The matrices $A(L)$, $B(L)$, $C(L)$, and $D(L)$ are matrix lag polynomials of size $n \times n$, $n \times m$, $m \times n$, and $m \times m$, respectively; that is, each element of these matrices is a polynomial in the lag operator. The matrices can be represented as

$$\begin{aligned} A(L) &= A_0 - A_1L - A_2L^2 - A_3L^3 - \ldots \\ B(L) &= B_0 + B_1L + B_2L^2 + B_3L^3 + \ldots \\ C(L) &= C_0 + C_1L + C_2L^2 + C_3L^3 + \ldots \\ D(L) &= D_0 - D_1L - D_2L^2 - D_3L^3 - \ldots \end{aligned} \tag{5.2.2}$$

[2]Nelson (1973) and Granger and Newbold (1977) have done some work on fitting multivariate ARIMA models. Sims (1980) estimates and uses a number of multivariate ARIMA models.

[3]The critique also applies to many econometric studies in microeconomics that utilize time series data.

[4]The restriction that the error process be serially uncorrelated introduces no loss of generality if the lag operators in the matrices of lag polynomials are allowed to be infinite.

where $A(L)$, $B(L)$, $C(L)$, and $D(L)$ may or may not be finite.

Economists often believe that variables can be classified into endogenous and exogenous variables. This distinction can be represented by setting $C(L) = 0$ in (5.2.1). Equation 5.2.1 can then be written as[5]:

$$A(L)\mathbf{Y}_t = B(L)\mathbf{X}_t + \boldsymbol{\epsilon}_t \tag{5.2.3}$$

$$D(L)\mathbf{X}_t = \boldsymbol{\delta}_t. \tag{5.2.4}$$

If we express (5.2.3) in terms of the $A(L)$ polynomial matrix, we have

$$\begin{aligned} A_0\mathbf{Y}_t &= [A_1L + A_2L^2 + \cdots]\mathbf{Y}_t + B(L)\mathbf{X}_t + \boldsymbol{\epsilon}_t \\ &= A_1\mathbf{Y}_{t-1} + A_2\mathbf{Y}_{t-2} + \cdots + B(L)\mathbf{X}_t + \boldsymbol{\epsilon}_t. \end{aligned} \tag{5.2.5}$$

Equation 5.2.5 is the form of the model that econometricians usually formulate and try to estimate—it is the *structural form* of an econometric model in which each equation is called a structural equation. Each equation of (5.2.5) is a relationship between endogenous, lagged endogenous, exogenous, and lagged exogenous variables.

Premultiplication of (5.2.5) by $A_0^{-1}$ yields

$$\mathbf{Y}_t = A_0^{-1}[A_1L + A_2L^2 + \cdots]\mathbf{Y}_t + A_0^{-1}B(L)\mathbf{X}_t + A_0^{-1}\boldsymbol{\epsilon}_t, \tag{5.2.6}$$

which represents the endogenous variables as functions of the lagged endogenous, exogenous, and lagged exogenous (often jointly referred to as predetermined) variables. Equation 5.2.6 is often referred to as the *reduced form* of the system of Equations 5.2.5.

If we premultiply both sides of (5.2.3) by $A^{-1}(L)$ we obtain

$$\mathbf{Y}_t = A^{-1}(L)B(L)\mathbf{X}_t + A^{-1}(L)\boldsymbol{\epsilon}_t, \tag{5.2.7}$$

which is referred to as the *final form* of the econometric model. In this form of the model, each current endogenous variable is expressed as a function of current and past exogenous variables and white noise terms.[6] The coefficients of this form give information on how much different the value of a current endogenous variable would be if a past exogenous variable or white noise variable had been different. The coefficients attached to each exogenous variable [the elements of $A^{-1}(L)B(L)$] are called *dynamic multipliers*.

Further analysis of the dynamic properties of an econometric model can be accomplished by writing

$$A(L) \cdot A^*(L) = |A(L)| \cdot I, \tag{5.2.8}$$

where $I$ is the identity matrix of order $n$, $A^*(L)$ is the adjoint of $A(L)$, and $|A(L)|$ is the determinant of $A(L)$.[7] Upon multiplying (5.2.3) by $A^*(L)$, we have

[5]Writing $\mathbf{X}_t$, the exogenous variable, with an autoregressive representation is a point of some controversy to which we return later.

[6]The final form could also be obtained by repeatedly lagging $\mathbf{Y}_t$ in (5.2.6) and substituting into (5.2.6).

[7]For a discussion of the adjoint of a matrix, see Hohn (1972). It is here legitimate to deal with the matrix lag operators [the $A(L)$] as if they were ordinary matrices; see Gantmacher (1959).

$$|A(L)|\mathbf{Y}_t = A^*(L)B(L)\mathbf{X}_t + A^*(L)\boldsymbol{\epsilon}_t, \tag{5.2.9}$$

where $|A(L)|$ is a *scalar* lag polynomial. Note that Equation 5.2.9 implies that each equation has the same autoregressive form in the endogenous variable. Each individual equation in (5.2.9) is called the *fundamental dynamic equation* for that variable by Kmenta (1974).

We now present as an example a simple income-expenditure model, consisting of two structural equations and one identity. $C$, $I$, $Y$, and $G$ refer to first differences in consumption, investment, income, and government spending, respectively, all in real terms. For purposes of exposition, it is assumed that the model is the "true" structure. (The model was estimated by the authors using National Income Accounts data.)

$$C_t = 3.66 + 0.167Y_t + 0.121C_{t-1} + \epsilon_{1t} \tag{5.2.10}$$

$$I_t = -3.16 + 0.521Y_t - 0.201I_{t-1} + \epsilon_{2t} \tag{5.2.11}$$

$$Y_t = C_t + I_t + G_t \tag{5.2.12}$$

$$\sigma_{11} = 16.08, \qquad \sigma_{22} = 17.22, \qquad \sigma_{12} = -11.10 \tag{5.2.13}$$

$$G_t = \delta_t + 0.319\delta_{t-1} + 0.407\delta_{t-2} \tag{5.2.14}$$

$$\sigma_a^2 = 4.15.$$

Equations 5.2.10–5.2.11 represent the endogenous variables, and Equation 5.2.14 is a moving average representation of government spending. The model has the *reduced form* representation:

$$\begin{bmatrix} C_t \\ I_t \\ Y_t \end{bmatrix} = \begin{bmatrix} 2.281 \\ -1.729 \\ 1.618 \end{bmatrix} + \begin{bmatrix} 0.186 & -0.107 & 0.096 & 0.535 \\ 0.202 & -0.536 & 0.481 & 1.667 \\ 0.238 & 0.643 & 0.577 & 3.201 \end{bmatrix} \begin{bmatrix} C_{t-1} \\ I_{t-1} \\ Y_{t-1} \\ G_t \end{bmatrix} + \begin{bmatrix} u_{1t} \\ u_{2t} \\ u_{3t} \end{bmatrix},$$

where

$$\begin{bmatrix} u_{1t} \\ u_{2t} \\ u_{3t} \end{bmatrix} = \begin{bmatrix} 1.123 & 0.123 \\ -0.385 & 0.615 \\ 0.739 & 0.739 \end{bmatrix} \begin{bmatrix} \epsilon_{1t} \\ \epsilon_{2t} \end{bmatrix} \tag{5.2.15}$$

and

$$E(u_t u_t') = \begin{bmatrix} 23.37 & 5.179 & 28.54 \\ 5.179 & 41.67 & 46.84 \\ 28.54 & 46.84 & 75.38 \end{bmatrix}.$$

The *final form* of this model can be computed for each variable. For example, using (5.2.7) we can solve for $C_t$ as a function of past $G_t$,

$$C_t = \bar{\alpha} + \sum_{i=0}^{\infty} \alpha_i G_{t-i} + e_t, \tag{5.2.16}$$

where $\overline{\alpha}$ and the $\alpha_i$ depend upon the parameters of the model. The final form for the model is presented in Table 5.1. Rewriting (5.2.16) with the coefficients from Table 5.1 yields

$$C_t = 2.281 + 0.535G_t + 0.229G_{t-1} + 0.056G_{t-2} + \cdots e_t.$$

The row denoted ''cumulative'' in Table 5.1 presents the long run multipliers, which are the sums of the short run multipliers. They indicate the total cumulative effect on $C$, $I$, and $Y$ of a one unit increase in $G$.

Using (5.2.9) we can solve for the *fundamental dynamic equations* of this simple income expenditure model:

$$(1 - 0.349L - 0.080L^2)C_t = 2.281 + (0.535 + 0.279L)G_t + u_{1t}^* \tag{5.2.17}$$

$$(1 - 0.349L - 0.080L^2)I_t = -1.729 + (1.670 + 0.202L)G_t + u_{2t}^* \tag{5.2.18}$$

$$(1 - 0.349L - 0.080L^2)Y_t = 1.618 + (3.201 + 0.356L - 0.0779L^2)G_t + u_{3t}^*, \tag{5.2.19}$$

where the $u_i^*$ terms depend upon the $u_i$ terms and $A(L)$.

## 5.3 Multiple Equation ARIMA Models as Derived from Simultaneous Equation Models

In this section, the work of Zellner and Palm (1974) is used to show the sense in which ARIMA models can be thought of as derived from, or as types of, ''reduced forms'' of econometric models.

### 5.3.1 Basic Relationships

We begin by rewriting (5.2.4) as

$$\mathbf{X}_t = D^{-1}(L)\boldsymbol{\delta}_t \tag{5.3.1}$$

**TABLE 5.1 Final Form of the Income Expenditure Model**

| $i$ | $\Delta C_t/\Delta G_{t-1}$ | $\Delta I_t/\Delta G_{t-1}$ | $\Delta Y_t/\Delta G_{t-i}$ |
|---|---|---|---|
| 0 | 0.535 | 1.667 | 3.201 |
| 1 | 0.229 | 0.758 | 0.982 |
| 2 | 0.056 | 0.115 | 0.171 |
| 3 | 0.015 | 0.032 | 0.047 |
| 4 | 0.004 | 0.008 | 0.012 |
| 5 | 0.000 | 0.001 | 0.001 |
| 6 | . | . | . |
| | . | . | . |
| | . | . | . |
| Cumulative | 0.835 | 2.581 | 4.414 |

and substituting (5.3.1) into (5.2.7), which yields

$$\mathbf{Y}_t = A^{-1}(L)B(L)D^{-1}(L)\boldsymbol{\delta}_t + A^{-1}(L)\boldsymbol{\epsilon}_t. \quad \textbf{(5.3.2)}$$

Equation 5.3.2 shows that the endogenous variables can be written as a function of white noise shocks.

A more interesting way of examining the ARIMA representations of an economic model is to substitute (5.3.1) into (5.2.9), which yields

$$|A(L)|\mathbf{Y}_t = A^{*-1}(L)B(L)D^{-1}(L)\boldsymbol{\delta}_t + A^{*-1}(L)\boldsymbol{\epsilon}_t. \quad \textbf{(5.3.3)}$$

Equation 5.3.3 shows the way in which the economic model determines the autoregressive structure of each variable. The $i$th individual equation in (5.3.3) can be written as

$$|A(L)|Y_{it} = \sum_{j=1}^{M} [A^{*-1}(L)B(L)D^{-1}(L)]_{ij}\delta_{jt} + \sum_{j=1}^{N} [A^{*-1}(L)]_{ij}\epsilon_{jt}, \quad \textbf{(5.3.4)}$$

where $[F(L)]_{ij}$ is the $i, j$ element of $[F(L)]$. Equation 5.3.4 shows that each variable can be represented as an autoregressive process with an error term that is the sum of two moving average terms. Since moving average processes (if they are invertible) can be aggregated [see Ansley, Spivey and Wrobleski (1977)], (5.3.4) may be written as

$$|A(L)|Y_{it} = h_i(L)u_{it}, \quad \textbf{(5.3.5)}$$

where both $h_i(L)$ and $u_{it}$ can be derived from (5.3.4), and where $u_{it}$ is a white noise term.

Hence we have shown that the endogenous variables have ARIMA representations that can be derived from the economic representation. This allows us to conclude that ARIMA models, rather than being substantially different from econometric models, are actually another representation of econometric models. Moreover, ARIMA representations for different variables from the same econometric model have the particular structure of (5.2.9); that is, the reduced form ARIMA process has the same AR process for the endogenous variables.

### 5.3.2 The Time Series Representation of the Exogenous Variables

An important step in deriving the ARIMA reduced form is the substitution of the ARIMA process of the exogenous variables into the final form. Exogenous variables, which include nonstochastic variables, time trends, dummy variables, and nonautocorrelated variables, are not usually assumed to have ARIMA representations. In this section we discuss some of the problems raised by exogenous variables of these types in simple models; this discussion can be extended to more complicated models.

Let us first examine a time trend. Let (5.3.6) and (5.3.7) below be, respectively, the structural relationship for $Y$ and the time series representation of $X$, where the variable $t$ is a time trend and $p(L)$ a polynomial in the lag operator $L$. Substituting (5.3.7) into (5.3.6) yields (5.3.8); collecting the moving average terms into the aggregate moving average process, $d(L)v_t$, yields (5.3.9); and further manipulation yields (5.3.10) and (5.3.11). Both $K_0$ and $K_1$ are finite if $-1 < a < 1$.

$$Y_t = aY_{t-1} + bX_t + ct + e_t \tag{5.3.6}$$

$$E(e_t^2) = \sigma_e^2, \qquad E(e_t e_s) = 0, \quad s \neq t$$

$$E(v_t^2) = \sigma_v^2, \qquad E(v_t v_s) = 0, \quad s \neq t$$

$$X_t = p(L)\mu_t \tag{5.3.7}$$

$$Y_t = (1 - aL)^{-1} bp(L)\mu_t + c(1 - aL)^{-1} t + (1 - aL)^{-1} e_t \tag{5.3.8}$$

$$= ct + ca(t - 1) + ca^2(t - 2) + \cdots + d(L)v_t \tag{5.3.9}$$

$$= -c(a + 2a^2 + 3a^3 + \cdots) + c(1 + a + a^2 + a^3 + \cdots)t + d(L)v_t \tag{5.3.10}$$

$$= K_0 + K_1 t + d(L)v_t, \tag{5.3.11}$$

$$K_0 = -c(a + 2a^2 + 3a^3 + \cdots)$$

$$K_1 = c(1 + a + a^2 + \cdots),$$

$$\Delta Y_t = K_1 + (1 - L)\, d(L)v_t. \tag{5.3.12}$$

From (5.3.11) it can be seen that the time trend in the ARIMA structure shows up as a time trend in the ARIMA "reduced form." This procedure can be generalized to higher order trends and more complicated systems.

Another type of variable that may be thought to create problems for the ARIMA representation of the exogenous variables is the dummy variable; that is, a variable that takes on only two values (usually 0 and 1). The effect of dummy variables can be seen in Equations 5.3.13 through 5.3.15. Let (5.3.13) and (5.3.14) below be the structure of the true model, with $d_t$ being either 1 or 0 for each time period; then (5.3.15) is the time series representation of the $Y$ series.

$$Y_t = aY_{t-1} + bX_{t-1} + cd_t + e_t \tag{5.3.13}$$

$$X_t = p(L)\mu_t \tag{5.3.14}$$

$$Y_t = aY_{t-1} + cd_t + p(L)\mu_t + e_t. \tag{5.3.15}$$

Although dummy variables can easily be added to ARIMA models, this would lead to a problem of interpretation.[8] Since dummy variables are usually specified in the structural model, that is, (5.3.13), each dummy variable would, in general, show up in each ARIMA reduced form equation. Consequently, the restrictions on the structural econometric model necessary to result in a dummy variable in one implied ARIMA equation and not in others are hard to specify, and even harder to defend theoretically. Hence, dummy variables may lead to some practical modeling difficulties, but they lead to no theoretical difficulties.[9]

A third type of nonstandard variable is one that has no correlation across time, for

[8]Some research has been done on dummy-type variables in ARIMA models by Box and Tiao (1975) in what they call "intervention models."

[9]On a somewhat more fundamental level, questions about the use of dummy variables can be raised. In particular, it can be argued that dummy variables are often just a "quick and dirty" way of

example, a "cross section" variable. This presents no theoretical difficulty because a variable that cannot be forecast from its own past can be modeled as a time series, with its innovation variance equal to the series total variance and all AR and MA terms equal to zero. This variable then enters the equations as any other time series variable would. It can easily be shown, however, that a system containing many such variables implies an ARIMA reduced form with a large innovation variance relative to the overall variance of the dependent variable.

A fourth type of variable that may be thought to create problems for the ARIMA representation is an exogenous variable that is not considered stochastic. An example is a policy variable set by the government. By assuming the variable is nonstochastic, we have ruled out policy that depends on the values of the (stochastic) endogenous variables of the system. But some variables that we think of as nonstochastic can, upon deeper investigation, be considered stochastic. Part of the problem is that, in their model building, economists spend much time and effort specifying relationships between endogenous variables and between endogenous and exogenous variables, and very little time and effort modeling relationships between exogenous variables. But the stochastic nature of many exogenous variables seems obvious (at least to us), suggesting that the stochastic specification of the exogenous variables is ignored either as an oversight or because of the belief that the stochastic nature of the exogenous variables makes little difference in estimation.

## 5.4 Causality

A major goal of economic research is to determine which economic variables depend upon (or are caused by) other economic variables. Until recently, the identification of causal relationships was viewed as a task for theory alone; or perhaps more correctly it was thought that even the cleverest statistical tests, unless they embodied substantial economic theory, would be unable to distill a chain of causal relationships from a set of correlations. Recently, however, a set of methods has been introduced that purports to determine whether one variable "causes" another variable without employing economic theory in any way. If these methods do in fact provide tests for what is customarily regarded as causality, a substantial amount of work that had been considered to be the responsibility of theorists can be done with relatively simple statistical tests. Because of this, the issue of causality and these methods deserve careful examination. In this section, the issue of causality is approached from the point of view of the researcher who has two data series that he or she wishes to examine for causal ordering. In Section 5.4.1 the definition of causality is presented and discussed; in Section 5.4.2 causality is discussed within the structure of a bivariate time series model; in Sections 5.4.3, 5.4.4, and 5.4.5 several tests of causality are discussed; and in Section 5.4.6 conclusions are drawn.

---

modeling terribly complicated phenomena that could, at least in theory, be correctly modeled; dummy variables for seasons and strikes are obviously of this type. If this is the case, the ARIMA reduced form will reflect the underlying structure of the world, and the dummy variables will reflect the "quick and dirty" simplification.

### 5.4.1 Introduction

In this section we present Granger's (1969) definition of causality. The initial definitions of causality, feedback, and so forth, are general in nature; testable forms will be introduced later.

Let $A_t$ be a stationary stochastic process, let $\overline{A}_t$ represent the set of past values $\{A_{t-j}, j = 1, 2, \ldots, \infty\}$, and $\overline{\overline{A}}_t$ represent the set of past and present values $\{A_{t-j}, j = 0, 1, \ldots, \infty\}$. Further, let $\overline{A}(k)$ represent the set $\{A_{t-j}, j = k, k + 1, \ldots, \infty\}$.

Denote the optimum, unbiased, least squares predictor of $A_t$ that uses the set of values of $B_t$ by $P_t(A|B)$. Thus, for instance, $P_t(X|\overline{X})$ will be the optimum predictor of $X_t$ using only past $X_t$. The predictive error series will be denoted by $\epsilon_t(A|B) = A_t - P_t(A|B)$. Let $\sigma^2(A|B)$ be the variance of $\epsilon_t(A|B)$. Let $U_t$ be all the information in the universe accumulated as of time $t$, and let $U_t - Y_t$ denote all this information other than the series $Y_t$. We then have the following definitions.

**Definition**

*Causality.* If $\sigma^2(Y|\overline{U}) < \sigma^2(Y|\overline{U} - \overline{X})$, we say that $X$ is causing $Y$, denoted by $X \rightarrow Y$; that is, $X$ is causing $Y$ if we are better able to predict $Y_t$ using all available information than if all information other than $X$ had been used.

**Definition**

*Feedback.* If

$$\sigma^2(X|\overline{U}) < \sigma^2(X|\overline{U} - \overline{Y}),$$
$$\sigma^2(Y|\overline{U}) < \sigma^2(Y|\overline{U} - \overline{X}),$$

we say that feedback is occurring, which is denoted $Y \leftrightarrow X$, that is, feedback is said to occur when $X$ is causing $Y$ and $Y$ is causing $X$.

**Definition**

*Instantaneous Causality.* If $\sigma^2(Y|\overline{U} - \overline{\overline{X}}) < \sigma^2(Y|\overline{U})$, we say that instantaneous causality between $X$ and $Y$ is occurring. In other words, the current value of $Y_t$ is better "predicted" if the present value of $X_t$ is included in the "prediction" than if it is not.

**Definition**

*Causality Lag.* If $X \rightarrow Y$, we define the (integer) causality lag $m$ to be the least value of $k$ such that $\sigma^2[Y|U - X(k)] < \sigma^2[Y|U - X(k + 1)]$. Thus, knowing the values $X_{t-j}, j = 0, 1, \ldots, m - 1$, will be of no help in improving the prediction of $Y_t$.

Note that the definition of causality is in terms of the variance of the optimal unbiased least squares predictor using all the information in the universe before some point in time. If the universe consists of just two variables, $X$ and $Y$, $X$ is said to cause $Y$ if current values of the variable $Y$ are better predicted by both past values of $X$ and $Y$ than by past values of $Y$ alone. $X$ is said to cause $Y$ instantaneously if the current value of $X$ and lagged values of $X$ and $Y$ lead to a better prediction of $Y$ than just lagged values of $X$ and $Y$. Notice that the properties of causality and instantaneous causality are independent properties. Causality does not imply instantaneous causality, nor does instantanteous causality imply causality.

The above definition is a very restrictive way in which to define causality; it is unworkable in practice for a number of reasons. To begin with, the definition of causality is in terms of the variance of unbiased forecasts. In practice, optimal forecasting is not even attempted, but is usually replaced by linear least squares prediction. Second, since the true distributions of $X$ and $Y$ are rarely known, neither is the actual minimum variance unbiased predictor. Third, an estimator based on the universe of information is impossible; at best any estimator will be based upon a set of variables that are thought, for a priori reasons, to have some chance of improving the forecast of the variable in question. In practice, tests for causality are performed within a specific structure that has been assumed. Within this structure the tests for causality make sense, but the validity of the structure is open to question. The structure usually imposed is that of a multivariate stationary time series process where the number of different time series is small, and the prediction technique employed is linear least squares prediction.

At a more fundamental level, questions may be raised about how well this definition of causality corresponds to either common sense or philosophical notions of causality. A discussion of these issues is covered in detail in Sims (1977) and Zellner (1979), but is beyond the scope of this work. If the reader is disturbed by our equating of "causality" and "causality in the sense of Granger and Sims," then the reader should replace the word "causality" with "causality in the sense of Granger and Sims" or "Granger-Sims causality" in what follows.

Three approaches to testing for Granger-Sims causality appear in the literature: cross-spectral methods, Granger (1969); regression methods, Sims (1972); and cross-correlation methods, Haugh and Pierce (1977). In the next section we examine the latter two methods; we do not discuss spectral methods.

### 5.4.2 The Structure of Causality in a Bivariate Time Series Model

We begin with a characterization of causality due to Sims (1972). Consider the bivariate process shown in (5.4.1) where $a(L)$, $b(L)$, $c(L)$, and $d(L)$ are polynomials in the lag operator $L$, and $u_t$ and $v_t$ are mutually uncorrelated white noise processes.

$$\begin{aligned} X_t &= a(L)u_t + b(L)v_t \\ Y_t &= c(L)u_t + d(L)v_t, \end{aligned} \tag{5.4.1}$$

or

$$\begin{bmatrix} X_t \\ Y_t \end{bmatrix} = \begin{bmatrix} a(L) & b(L) \\ c(L) & d(L) \end{bmatrix} \begin{bmatrix} u_t \\ v_t \end{bmatrix}. \tag{5.4.2}$$

For this process,[10] Sims shows that $Y$ does not cause $X$ if either $a(L)$ or $b(L)$ can be chosen identically zero; that is, if the process can be characterized in such a way that either $a(L)$ or $b(L)$ is zero.[11]

For simplicity we will always have $a(L) \neq 0$ and will characterize $Y$ not causing $X$ by setting $b(L) = 0$.

The relationship between causality and instantaneous causality can be seen from Equation 5.4.3, which is just a rewriting of (5.4.2),

$$\begin{bmatrix} X_t \\ Y_t \end{bmatrix} = \begin{bmatrix} a_0 & b_0 \\ c_0 & d_0 \end{bmatrix} \begin{bmatrix} u_t \\ v_t \end{bmatrix} + \begin{bmatrix} a_1 & b_1 \\ c_1 & d_1 \end{bmatrix} \begin{bmatrix} u_{t-1} \\ v_{t-1} \end{bmatrix} + \cdots + \begin{bmatrix} a_q & b_q \\ c_q & d_q \end{bmatrix} \begin{bmatrix} u_{t-q} \\ v_{t-q} \end{bmatrix} \tag{5.4.3}$$

It turns out that without loss of generality (5.4.3) can be written with $b_0 = 0$, so that $b(L)$ being zero or nonzero says nothing about instantaneous causality. Instantaneous causality turns on $c_0$ not being zero. [See Sargent (1979, Chapter 11) for more details.]

At this point it may be useful to look at an example of a simple system and to characterize the causal relationships: Let (5.4.4) generate $Y_t$, and (5.4.5) generate $X_t$, where both $\epsilon_t$ and $a_t$ are independent white noise.

$$Y_t = B_0 X_t + B_1 X_{t-1} + \epsilon_t \tag{5.4.4}$$

$$X_t = a_t + \theta a_{t-1}. \tag{5.4.5}$$

This system can be rewritten as

$$\begin{bmatrix} X_t \\ Y_t \end{bmatrix} = \begin{bmatrix} (1 + \theta L) & 0 \\ (B_0 + B_1 L)(1 + \theta L) & 1 \end{bmatrix} \begin{bmatrix} a_t \\ \epsilon_t \end{bmatrix}. \tag{5.4.6}$$

The system shown in (5.4.6) is obviously a system in which $X$ is exogenous and $Y$ is dependent upon $X$. From (5.4.4) and (5.4.6), we can see that past values of $Y$ are of no use in predicting current values of $X$ in the presence of past values of $X$; however, current values of $Y$ do aid in the prediction of current values of $X$. As is easily seen, past and current values of $X$ help in the prediction of current values of $Y$, even in the presence of past values of $Y$; moreover past values of $X$ aid in the prediction of current values of $Y$ even in the presence of past $Y$. Therefore, in this simple system, it is clear that $X$ causes $Y$, $X$ causes $Y$ instantaneously, $Y$ does not cause $X$, but $Y$ does cause $X$ instantaneously. Comparing Equations 5.4.2 and 5.4.6, which are of the same form, we can see that the causality structure is implied by zero in the appropriate place in the system. We can also see that there is, at least in this example, a relationship between exogeneity and causality.

[10]Justification for the structure of the model assumed in (5.4.2) comes from a multivariate version of the Wold decomposition theorem, Hannan (1970). This theorem states that any stationary bivariate (or multivariate) time series can be decomposed into a deterministic component and a component of the form (5.4.2).

[11]Sims's proof is not presented because it employs methods that are beyond the scope of this work. Sargent (1979, Chapter 11) presents a version of Sims's proof.

From Equation 5.4.1, if $b(L) = 0$, that is, $Y$ does not cause $X$, then (5.4.1) can be rewritten as

$$X_t = a(L)u_t \qquad \textbf{(5.4.7)}$$
$$Y_t = c(L)u_t + d(L)\, v_t.$$

From (5.4.7), we can see the crux of causality. Although current $Y$ contains information from current and past values of both $u_t$ and $v_t$, and hence from current and past values of both $X$ and $Y$, $X$ contains no information from current or past values of $Y$ that is not contained in past values of $X$. Thus, past values of $Y$ contain no information about $X$ that past values of $X$ do not already contain. This means that past $Y$ is of no use in predicting future values of $X$ once the information in past values of $X$ has been taken into account.[12] In the absence of past values of $X$, current and past values of $Y$ will be useful in predicting $X$, but once past values of $X$ have been introduced, past values of $Y$ are of no use.

### 5.4.3 Sims's Test for Causality

Sims has developed a practical test for causal relationships based upon regressions involving current and future values of $X$ and $Y$. Although a formal derivation is beyond the scope of this book, we provide an intuitive explanation of his test.

If $b(L)$ is zero and if $a(L)$ is invertible, we can manipulate (5.4.7) into the form

$$a^{-1}(L)X_t = u_t \qquad \textbf{(5.4.8)}$$

$$Y_t = c(L)a^{-1}(L)X_t + d(L)v_t \qquad \textbf{(5.4.9)}$$

$$d^{-1}(L)Y_t = d^{-1}(L)c(L)a^{-1}(L)X_t + v_t. \qquad \textbf{(5.4.10)}$$

In (5.4.9), $Y_t$ is expressed as a distributed lag of $X_t$ and a random noise process, where the random noise process is uncorrelated with $X_t$. The lack of correlation between $X$ and $v$ in (5.4.9) means that a regression of $Y_t$ upon *future, current,* and *lagged* $X$ will result (in large samples) in regression coefficients of zero for future $X$ terms. This is because that part of the variation in $Y$ that can be explained by variations in $X$ can be explained perfectly by variation in *current* and *lagged* $X$; hence, the inclusion of future $X$ values can explain no part of the variation in $Y$. Furthermore, since $X$ is uncorrelated with $v$ at any lag, future $X$ is uncorrelated with current and lagged $v$. Hence, a necessary condition for $Y$ *not* to cause $X$ is for future $X$ terms to have zero coefficients in a regression of $Y$ on future, current, and lagged $X$. Note that the zero value of future $X$ variables in Equation 5.4.10 results from the fact that $X$ and $v$ are uncorrelated. But $X$ and $v$ are uncorrelated because $b(L)$ is zero, and $b(L)$ being zero is a characterization of $Y$ not causing $X$. Therefore, because $Y$ does not cause $X$, future values of $X$ will have zero coefficients in a regression of $Y$ upon future, current, and past $X$.[13]

[12]However, as we will see below, if $b(L) = 0$ and if $c(L) \neq 0$, then $X$ will be of use in predicting $Y$.

[13]In practice, since coefficients must be estimated, small sample difficulties with actual tests for causality arise. These are discussed below.

From (5.4.2), after assuming that $b(L) = 0$, we can write $X_t$ as a distributed lag in $Y_t$. This is shown in (5.4.11) and (5.4.12):

$$u_t = c^{-1}(L)Y_t - c^{-1}(L)d(L)v_t \tag{5.4.11}$$

$$X_t = a(L)c^{-1}(L)Y_t - a(L)c^{-1}(L)d(L)v_t. \tag{5.4.12}$$

Equation 5.4.12 appears to be a distributed lag equation like (5.4.10) (with, of course, the roles of $X$ and $Y$ reversed), but there is a major difference. In (5.4.12), unlike (5.4.10), the distributed lag variable, $Y$, and the white noise variable, $u$, are correlated. This means that both current and future $Y$ values are correlated with $u_t$. Thus, when current $X$ is regressed upon future, current, and past $Y$ variables, future values of $Y$ should enter the regression equation with nonzero coefficients. On the assumption that $b(L) = 0$, that is, $X$ causes $Y$ in the sence of Granger and Sims, a regresion of current $X$ upon past, current, and future $Y$ will show nonzero coefficients for future $Y$ terms.

Sims's procedure is a simple way to test for causality for stationary random variables. Current values of $Y$ should be regressed upon current, past, and future values of $X$; a joint test of significance on coefficients of future $X$ values will determine whether $Y$ causes $X$. If the test concludes that all coefficients of future $X$ terms are zero and past $X$ terms nonzero, we can say that $X$ causes $Y$ and that $Y$ does not cause $X$. If the test concludes that the coefficients for future $X$ values are significantly different from zero, we would be unable to conclude that $Y$ does not cause $X$.

Unfortunately, practical difficulties (which Sims identifies) are likely to be encountered when actually performing this test for causality. This can be seen by examining Equation 5.4.9, the equation that holds if $Y$ does not cause $X$. The presence of lagged $v$ values means that ordinary least squares regression will be inefficient for estimating (5.4.9) and will yield an incorrect estimate of the variance-covariance matrix, and hence incorrect $t$ and $F$ statistics.

To remedy the serially correlated residual problem, Sims suggests either prewhitening[14] the $X$ and $Y$ series and regressing the prewhitened $Y$ series on past, current, and future prewhitened $X$, or employing a generalized least squares procedure.[15] If we follow the prewhitening approach, then all the problems attendant with prewhitening occur. We must be sure that we have used the appropriate prewhitening filter and that the series is, in fact, prewhitened. The importance of care in prewhitening cannot be overemphasized. Feige and Pearce (1979) provide an example in which different prewhitening filters change the direction of causal ordering.[16]

In testing for causality from $Y$ to $X$ without prewhitening (by regressing $Y$ on future,

[14]*Prewhitening* a series means transforming the series to a white noise process. For example, if $Y_t = \phi Y_{t-1} + \epsilon_t$, prewhitening $Y_t$ is accomplished by subtracting $\phi Y_{t-1}$ from $Y_t$. Transforming data with a lag polynomial is also called *filtering* the data.

[15]It is, of course, assumed in both cases that the variables are from stationary time series.

[16]Sims (1972) uses the filter $(1 - 0.75L)^2$ to prewhiten his data; that is, $Z_t = (1 - 0.75L)^2 Y_t$ is the prewhitened version of $Y$. He claims that this filter ". . . approximately flattens the spectral density of most economic time series"; that is, prewhitens most economic data. This may be true, but far too many researchers have used this particular filter on far too many data series.

current, and past $X$), we must test for serial correlation in the residuals and take it into account if it exists. This means that generalized least squares, maximum likelihood, or some other method must be used and that the degree and type of serial correlation in the residuals must be specified. This leads to potential misspecification.

Whether $Y$ is prewhitened or an adjustment is made for serial correlation, we must also resolve the problem of specifying the lengths of leads and lags. That is, we must specify (1) the number of future and lagged $X$ terms to include in the equations to be estimated and (2) the number of serially correlated terms to include if serial correlation is to be corrected for. This can, of course, be a serious problem, since incorrectly excluding lags or leads biases coefficients, while including too many lags or leads uses up degrees of freedom.[17] An examination of (5.4.9) reveals that even on the null hypothesis that $Y$ does not cause $X$, the distributed lag of $X$ may be infinite. If the lag is infinite, the distributed lag must be truncated at some point, leading to the problem of omitted variables.[18] Another practical problem with the Sims test is that of multicollinearity. On the assumption that $Y$ does not cause $X$, Equation 5.4.9 implies that the lagged $X$ variables will be correlated with one another since they are serially correlated; the extent to which they are correlated is determined by the structure of $a(L)$. The correlation between future, current, and past $X$ varibles makes it difficult to separate the effects of the individual right-hand side variables. These correlations may lead to the usual effects of multicollinearity—an estimated equation with a high $R^2$, but low $t$-statistics for the individual variables, and a low $F$-statistic for test of significance of a subset of the right-hand side variables, for example, the future $X$ variables. In addition, the use of this method to test for causality raises the usual problems involved in estimating distributed lag equations, for example, seasonality.[19]

### 5.4.4 A Second Regression Based Test for Causality

A second, perhaps the simplest, method of testing for causality from $X$ to $Y$ can be developed by rewriting (5.4.1) as

$$\begin{bmatrix} A(L) & 0 \\ C(L) & D(L) \end{bmatrix} \begin{bmatrix} X_t \\ Y_t \end{bmatrix} = \begin{bmatrix} u_t \\ v_t \end{bmatrix}, \tag{5.4.13}$$

where

$$\begin{aligned} A(L) &= a^{-1}(L) \\ C(L) &= -d^{-1}(L)c(L)a^{-1}(L) \\ D(L) &= d^{-1}(L), \end{aligned}$$

[17]Feige and Pearce (1979) provide an example in which the choice of lag length affects the results of the causality test.

[18]Granger (1969) suggests a method of testing for causality in the frequency domain in a manner that avoids some of these problems, although it does raise a new set of problems. This method, in essence, substitutes truncation of lags in the time domain for truncation of frequencies in the frequency domain.

[19]For a discussion of many of these problems, see Sims (1974).

and where we have assumed that $Y$ does not cause $X$, that is, $b(L) = 0$. The first equation in (5.4.13) reveals that if $Y$ does not cause $X$, then $X$ can be written as a function of past $X$ and a white noise term. Hence, regressing current $X$ on past $X$ and past $Y$ should yield nonzero coefficients on past $X$ and zero coefficients on past $Y$. On the other hand, rewriting the second part of (5.4.13),

$$D(L)Y_t = -C(L)X_t + v_t \tag{5.4.14}$$

or

$$Y_t = \sum_i D_i Y_{t-i} - \sum_i C_i X_{t-i} + v_t,$$

we can see that if $X$ causes $Y$, then coefficients on past $X$ should show up as nonzero in a regression of current $Y$ on past $X$ and past $Y$. This gives an apparently very simple test for causality—regress $Y$ on lagged $Y$ and lagged $X$. If the coefficients on lagged $X$ are significantly different from zero, then $X$ causes $Y$; if not, then $X$ does not cause $Y$. (This same method can be used to test for instantaneous causality; use current and lagged $X$ values rather than just lagged $X$ values.) This test for causality is natural in view of the definition put forth by Granger (see Section 5.4.1). In this test, $X$ and $Y$ are assumed to be the only relevant variables and the predictions from a regression model for the dependent variable to be the optimal predictions. If the lagged $X$ variables lower the prediction error variance—measured as a degrees of freedom adjusted change in the residual sum of squares—we say that $X$ causes $Y$.

Unfortunately, this test is not valid if, while testing to see whether $X$ causes $Y$, we admit the possibility that $Y$ causes $X$. If this is the case and we regress $Y$ on $X$, then the right-hand side variable, $X$, will be correlated with the residual term; biased coefficients will result and the tests for zero coefficients will be inaccurate. This can be seen by taking (5.4.1) and (5.4.2) and solving for $Y$ in terms of $X$:

$$a(L)Y_t = c(L)X_t + [a(L)d(L) - b(L)c(L)]v_t. \tag{5.4.15}$$

From (5.4.15) with $b(L) \neq 0$, we can clearly see the correlation between the error term and the regressors, which causes problems for estimation. There are, of course, methods to deal with this correlation. In addition to this problem, the standard problems involved in estimation with distributed lag and lagged dependent variables still exist, for example, multicollinearity, seasonality, determination of lag length, and testing for serial correlation.

The test for causality discussed in this section, like the test for causality mentioned in the previous section, attempts to test statistically whether $b(L) = 0$. Like the previous test, this test is a regression-based test that uses techniques familiar to econometricians. The next test to be discussed introduces techniques that are not commonly used by econometricians.

### 5.4.5 Haugh's Characterization of Causality

Another characterization of causality between two time series has been proposed by Haugh (1972). Using the same definition of causality as Granger and Sims, Haugh's method entails taking the two series of interest and prewhitening each one separately. The cross-correlation function of the two series is then calculated, and the test for causality is based on whether the correlations are jointly different from zero. Significant correlation between current prewhitened $Y$ and past prewhitened $X$ indicates that $X$ causes $Y$; correlation between current prewhitened $X$ and current prewhitened $Y$ indicates instantaneous causality. Because the prewhitening removes the influence of past values of a variable from its current value, the cross-correlation function provides information about the explanatory power of the second variable after all of the explanatory power of the first variable has been taken into account.

To examine Haugh's test, we begin by writing expression 5.4.1 in autoregressive form by inverting the lag polynomials in (5.4.1):

$$\begin{bmatrix} A(L) & B(L) \\ C(L) & D(L) \end{bmatrix} \begin{bmatrix} X_t \\ Y_t \end{bmatrix} = \begin{bmatrix} u_t \\ v_t \end{bmatrix}. \tag{5.4.16}$$

The lag polynomial in (5.4.16) can be expressed in terms of the lag polynomials in (5.4.1) by defining

$$\begin{aligned} \Delta(L) &= a(L)d(L) - b(L)c(L) \\ A(L) &= \Delta^{-1}(L)d(L) \\ B(L) &= -\Delta^{-1}(L)b(L) \\ C(L) &= -\Delta^{-1}(L)c(L) \\ D(L) &= \Delta^{-1}(L)a(L). \end{aligned}$$

If we assume that $X$ and $Y$ can be prewhitened into white noise residuals, then we can write

$$\begin{bmatrix} F(L) & 0 \\ 0 & G(L) \end{bmatrix} \begin{bmatrix} X_t \\ Y_t \end{bmatrix} = \begin{bmatrix} r_t \\ s_t \end{bmatrix}, \tag{5.4.17}$$

where $r_t$ and $s_t$ are prewhitened $X$ and prewhitened $Y$, respectively.

To examine the causal relationships in terms of prewhitened $X$ and $Y$, Haugh (1972) shows that $(r_t, s_t)$ has a bivariate representation as shown in (5.4.18), where $(u_t, v_t)$ is the same white noise error process as in (5.4.2) and (5.4.15):

$$\begin{bmatrix} \alpha(L) & \beta(L) \\ \gamma(L) & \delta(L) \end{bmatrix} \begin{bmatrix} r_t \\ s_t \end{bmatrix} = \begin{bmatrix} u_t \\ v_t \end{bmatrix}. \tag{5.4.18}$$

Combining (5.4.17) and (5.4.18) yields

$$\begin{bmatrix} \alpha(L)F(L) & \beta(L)G(L) \\ \gamma(L)F(L) & \delta(L)G(L) \end{bmatrix} \begin{bmatrix} X_t \\ Y_t \end{bmatrix} = \begin{bmatrix} u_t \\ v_t \end{bmatrix}. \tag{5.4.19}$$

From (5.4.19), it is clear that current and lagged $Y$ will be of use in predicting current $X$ only if $\beta(L)$ is not zero. But from (5.4.17) and (5.4.19), it is clear that $\beta(L)$ will be zero if and only if $B(L)$ is zero in (5.4.16) and if $b(L)$ is zero in (5.4.1), Sims's criterion for lack of causality. But from (5.4.18), we see that testing for $\beta(L)$ being different from zero using the prewhitened series $r_t$ and $s_t$ is equivalent to testing for causality. [This is a special case of a result mentioned by Haugh and Pierce (1977) that linear transformations are causality preserving.] Hence, testing for $\beta(L) = 0$ is equivalent to testing for causality.

Showing that $\beta(L)$ is zero if and only if certain autocorrelations are zero is now easily done. We can write

$$\begin{aligned}\gamma_{rs}(k) &= E[r_{t+k}s_t] \\ &= E\{\alpha^{-1}(L)[u_{t+k} - \beta(L)s_{t+k}]s_t\} \\ &= \alpha^{-1}(L)E[u_{t+k}s_t] - \alpha^{-1}(L)\beta(L)E[s_{t+k}s_t].\end{aligned} \tag{5.4.20}$$

From (5.4.18) we can see that if $\beta(L)$ is zero, $u_{t+k}$ and $s_t$ are uncorrelated; hence $\gamma_{rs}(k)$ is zero if $\beta(L) = 0$. This forms the basis for the cross-correlation test.[20]

In practice, testing for causality using the cross-correlation function presents a number of difficulties. The first problem is that of prewhitening the individual series. Finding the correct lag polynomial structure to prewhiten a time series correctly is no easy matter; it involves substantial subjective elements, admitting the possibility of misspecification of the prewhitening process. Fortunately, a general test for the absence of serial correlation in the prewhitened residuals does exist [see Box and Pierce (1970)], but it is unknown how well this test performs as the first step in a general test for causality. If the model is correctly specified, Haugh and Pierce (1977) have been able to show that on the null hypothesis $\gamma_{rs}(k) = 0$, the cross correlations based upon estimated $r_t$ and $s_t$ have the same asymptotic distribution as the cross correlations based upon the actual $r_t$ and $s_t$; hence the use of residuals presents no real problem, at least asymptotically.

A more serious problem with tests of causality based upon the cross correlations has to do with the distribution of the cross correlations. On the assumption that all cross correlations are zero, the probability distributions are known. However, when some of the population cross correlation are nonzero, the distribution of any of the cross correlations will depend upon the value of the nonzero cross correlations. In particular, if $X$ causes $Y$, but if $Y$ does not cause $X$, the distribution of the sample cross correlations between current $Y$ and future $X$ depends upon the values of the cross correlations between current $Y$ and past $X$, which will not, in general, be zero. This is a disturbing gap in knowledge that makes causality testing with the cross correlations very difficult.

### 5.4.6 Conclusions

The literature on testing for causality is now voluminous and is constantly growing.[21] However, there remain substantial unanswered questions about the nature of causality in the sense of Granger and Sims. The most fundamental of these equations concerns the relationship between Granger-Sims causality and exogeneity in the economic sense.

Sims, among others, argues quite strongly that tests for causality are indeed tests for exogeneity. While Sims (1979, p. 109) admits that there are some instances in which what is meant by causality is not what is meant by exogeneity, he argues that the statistical properties of an exogenous variable are exactly those of a causally prior variable. On the

[20]Since the cross spectrum is nothing but a transformation of the cross-correlation function, it is easily seen how causality can be characterized in terms of the cross spectrum.

[21]Although written for other purposes, articles by Zellner (1979) and Schwert (1979) contain a good review of much of the causality literature, including excellent discussions of problems with tests for causality.

other hand it can be argued, as Zellner (1979) does effectively, that causality and exogeneity are similar but different concepts that should not be confused.

How this controversy is resolved, as a philosophical argument, remains to be seen. As a practical matter it is apparent that tests for causality do not suffice as tests for exogeneity. This is not to say that tests of causality yield no information about exogeneity, but that, with the current state of knowledge, tests for causality cannot determine exogeneity. In this section we have discussed various tests of causality, each of which requires the imposition of a structure on the data and the imposition of rather arbitrary restrictions on the relevant parameter space (at minimum to reduce the dimensionality) before causality tests can be performed. Given that this must be done, there seems little doubt that carefully derived restrictions from economic theory can be of at least as much use in the determination of exogeneity as tests for causality.

## 5.5 Conclusion

In this chapter we have briefly examined the relationship between econometric models and time series models. The integration of time series methods into econometrics has already been accomplished, and we are currently seeing the integration of time series methods into macroeconomic theory. The importance of time series models to economists can only continue to grow.

## 5.6 References

Ansley, C. F., W. A. Spivey and W. Wrobleski (1977), "On the Structure of Moving Average Processes," *Journal of Econometrics,* **6**, 121–134.

Box, G. E. P. and D. A. Pierce (1970), "Distribution of Residual Autocorrelations in Autocorrelated Moving Average Models," *Journal of the American Statistical Association,* **65**, 1509–1526.

Box, G. E. P. and G. Tiao (1975), "Intervention Analysis with Applications to Economic and Environmental Problems," *Journal of the American Statistical Association*, **70**, 70–79.

Feige, E. L. and D. K. Pearce (1979), "The Casual Causal Relationship Between Money and Income: Some Caveats for Time Series Analysis," *Review of Economics and Statistics,* **61**, 521–533.

Gantmacher, F. R. (1959), *The Theory of Matrices,* Vols. I and II, New York: Chelsea.

Geweke, J. (1977), "Testing the Exogeneity Specification in the Complete Dynamic Simultaneous Equation Model," *Journal of Econometrics,* **7**, 163–185.

Granger, C. W. J. (1969), "Investigating Causal Relations by Econometric Models and Cross Spectral Methods," *Econometrica,* **37**, 424–438.

Granger, C. W. J. and P. Newbold (1977), *Forecasting Economic Time Series,* New York: Academic Press.

Hannan, E. J. (1970), *Multiple Time Series,* New York: Wiley.

Haugh, L. D. (1972), *The Identification of Time Series Interrelationships with Special Reference to Dynamic Regression,* Ph. D. Thesis (Department of Statistics, University of Wisconsin, Madison).

Haugh, L. D. and D. A. Pierce (1977), "Causality in Temporal Systems," *Journal of Econometrics,* **5**, 265–293.

Hohn, F. E. (1972), *Introduction to Linear Algebra,* New York: MacMillan.

Kmenta, J. (1974), *Elements of Econometrics,* New York: McMillan.

Neftci, S. (1979), "Lead-Lag Relations, Exogeneity and Prediction of Economic Time Series," *Econometrica,* **47**, 101–114.

Nelson, C. R. (1973), *Applied Time Series Analysis,* San Francisco: Holden-Day.

Plosser, C. and G. W. Schwert (1977), "Estimation of a Noninvertible Moving Average Process: The Case of Overdifferencing," *Journal of Econometrics,* **6**, 199–224.

Sargent, T. (1979), *Macroeconomic Theory,* New York: Academic Press.

Schwert, G. W. (1979), "Tests of Causality: The Message in the Innovations," in *Carnegie Rochester Conference Series on Public Policy,* **10**, edited by Brunner, K. and A. Meltzer, 55–96.

Sims, C. A. (1972), "Money, Income, and Causality," *American Economic Review,* **62**, 540–52.

Sims, C. A. (1974), "Distributed Lags," in M. D. Intriligator and D. A. Kendrick, eds., *Frontiers of Quantitative Economics,* Amsterdam: North-Holland.

Sims, C. A. (1977), "Exogeneity and Causal Ordering in Macroeconometric Models," *New Methods in Business Cycle Research*, edited by C. A. Sims, Minneapolis: Federal Reserve Bank of Minneapolis.

Sims, C. A. (1980), "Macroeconomics and Reality," *Econometrica,* **48**, 1–48.

Theil, H. and J. Boot (1962), "The Final Form of Econometric Equation Systems," *Review of the International Statistical Institute,* **30**, 136–152.

Wallis, K. F. (1980), "Econometric Implications of the Rational Expectations Hypothesis," *Econometrica,* **48**, 49–73.

Zellner, A. (1979), "Causality and Econometrics," in *Carnegie Rochester Conference Series on Public Policy*, edited by Brunner, K. and A. Meltzer, **10**, 9–54.

Zellner, A. and F. Palm (1974), "Time Series Analysis and Simultaneous Equation Econometric Models," *Journal of Econometrics,* **2**, 17–54.

# PART III

# Topics in Estimation Under a Quadratic Loss Criterion

The three chapters in this part are concerned with various aspects of estimation under a quadratic loss function. The estimation criterion usually adopted in econometrics is that of minimum variance in the class of unbiased estimators. A number of interesting estimators, however, are biased, and these are eliminated from consideration when the usual criterion is adopted. One example is the group of estimators proposed by James and Stein—nonlinear biased estimators that may outperform ordinary least squares under a quadratic loss function. Moreover, some mathematical results obtained in the study of these estimators are useful for the analysis of preliminary test estimators, which are widely used in practice, but whose statistical properties are little understood; these are also taken up in this part. We begin with some introductory material and an analysis of the performance under quadratic loss of the constrained least squares estimator.

# CHAPTER 6

# Introduction to Estimation Under a Quadratic Loss Function

## 6.1 Introduction

The standard econometric analysis of the linear regression model is concerned with the properties of the linear unbiased estimator that has the smallest variance. In that approach, therefore, attention is restricted at the outset to linear and unbiased estimators, even though "better" estimators might be available. Linearity is desirable because such estimators are usually easy to compute and because their statistical properties can often be analyzed without the need for rather advanced mathematics. The criterion of unbiasedness is attractive both because it seems intuitively desirable that the mathematical expectation of an estimator be equal to what is being estimated and because it expresses complete ignorance of the parameter to be estimated—the criterion must hold for any conceivable value of the unknown parameter, even values that the statistician believes to be unlikely.[1]

But the price to be paid, in terms of variance, by concentrating on linear unbiased estimators may be unacceptably high. For example, many empirical investigators deal with a form of this problem by dropping an insignificant variable from a regression when a high correlation between it and another variable causes a large standard error for both—the problem of multicollinearity. Of course, if the original model is "correct," estimates based on the reduced model will be biased. (This procedure results in an estimator whose value depends on the outcome of a hypothesis test. Estimators of this type are called preliminary test estimators and are discussed in Chapter 8.)

To analyze a wider class of estimators, therefore, we need a criterion that is not confined to linear unbiased estimators. An attractive choice is the "mean squared error" or "quadratic loss function":

$$L(\hat{\boldsymbol{\theta}}, \boldsymbol{\theta}) = [(\hat{\boldsymbol{\theta}} - \boldsymbol{\theta})'(\hat{\boldsymbol{\theta}} - \boldsymbol{\theta})], \qquad \textbf{(6.1.1)}$$

where $\hat{\boldsymbol{\theta}}$ is an estimator of $\boldsymbol{\theta}$, which may be a scalar or a vector. It is easy to see that

$$E[L(\hat{\boldsymbol{\theta}}, \boldsymbol{\theta})] = [E(\hat{\boldsymbol{\theta}}) - \boldsymbol{\theta}]'[E(\hat{\boldsymbol{\theta}}) - \boldsymbol{\theta}] + \mathrm{Cov}(\hat{\boldsymbol{\theta}}) = B^2(\hat{\boldsymbol{\theta}}) + \mathrm{Cov}(\hat{\boldsymbol{\theta}}), \qquad \textbf{(6.1.2)}$$

where $B^2(\hat{\boldsymbol{\theta}})$ is the squared bias of $\hat{\boldsymbol{\theta}}$ as an estimator for $\boldsymbol{\theta}$. Under this criterion a biased estimator will perform better than an unbiased estimator if the resulting reduction in variance is sufficient to offset the increase in squared bias.

The loss function (6.1.1) may be expressed as $\Sigma(\hat{\theta}_i - \theta_i)^2$, and in this form it is clear that $L(\hat{\boldsymbol{\theta}}, \boldsymbol{\theta})$ depends on units of measurement of the individual $\theta_i$. Squared errors for parameters measured in large units will be given larger weight than those for parameters measured in small units, but these weights may not reflect the researcher's perceived losses. To avoid this problem, the loss function may be modified by introducing explicit

[1] On this point, see Chipman (1964).

weights—for example, $\Sigma a_i(\hat{\theta}_i - \theta_i)^2$, $a_i \geq 0$; more generally, a positive semidefinite matrix $A$ may be included to weight the losses:

$$L(\hat{\boldsymbol{\theta}}, \boldsymbol{\theta}; A) = [(\hat{\boldsymbol{\theta}} - \boldsymbol{\theta})'A(\hat{\boldsymbol{\theta}} - \boldsymbol{\theta})]. \quad \textbf{(6.1.3)}$$

The performance of estimators and other statistics under an explicit loss criterion, such as the quadratic loss function, has been extensively studied in the area of statistical decision theory. Although in principle there is considerable flexibility regarding the choice of loss function, the quadratic loss function has been the most popular for estimation problems. Two reasons for this popularity are its intuitive reasonableness—it increases with the distance between $\hat{\boldsymbol{\theta}}$ and $\boldsymbol{\theta}$—and the relative ease with which it can be studied.

Before proceeding to a discussion of the performance of a number of estimators under a quadratic loss criterion, we present some background on statistical decision theory and the noncentral $\chi^2$ distribution. The chapter concludes with a discussion of constrained OLS estimation in regression as an example of estimation under the quadratic loss criterion.

## 6.2 Decision Theory Concepts[2]

### 6.2.1 Introduction

Let $\theta$ be the unknown true value of a parameter, and let $d(X)$ be an estimator for $\theta$, which is a function of the sample data $X$.[3]

**Definition**

$L(\theta, d(X))$ is the *loss function;* it gives the loss from employing the estimator $d(X)$ when the sample outcome is the random variable $X$ and the true parameter value is $\theta$. The functional form of $L(\theta, d(X))$ may be quite general, but it will usually increase with the distance between $d(X)$ and $\theta$.

**Definition**

The *risk* function is

$$R(\theta, d(\cdot)) = E[L(\theta, d(X))] = \int L(\theta, d(x))p(x|\theta)\, dx,$$

that is, it is the expected value of the loss function taken over all possible samples of $X$ when the distribution is evaluated using $\theta$ as the parameter value.

The risk is therefore a function of both $\theta$ and the decision function (estimator) that

[2]A good short treatment of this subject is in Silvey (1970). Barnett (1973) compares decision theory with classical and Bayesian approaches. More extended treatments of decision theory are Ferguson (1967) and DeGroot (1970).

[3]In statistical decision theory, $d(X)$ is called a decision rule, and estimation is a subset of the problems to which the theory may be applied. It will suffice to think of $d(X)$ as an estimator for our purposes.

is used. The object of decision theory is to choose a $d(X)$ that performs well when $\theta$ is unknown. Many principles of choice have been developed and studied; we discuss Bayes' principle and the admissibility and minimax approaches.

### 6.2.2 Bayes' Principle

In this approach, as is common in Bayesian procedures, it is assumed that a prior distribution for $\theta$ exists, denoted by $\pi(\theta)$. *Bayes' risk* of the estimator $d(X)$, $r(d(X), \pi)$, is $E[R(\theta, d(X))]$, where the expectation is taken over $\pi(\theta)$. Since $R(\theta, d(X))$ is found by integrating $L(\theta, d(X))$ with respect to $X$, we have

$$\begin{aligned} r(d(X), \pi) &= E[R(\theta, d(X))] \\ &= \int_\theta \pi(\theta) \int_x L(\theta, d(x))p(x|\theta)\, dx\, d\theta \qquad \textbf{(6.2.1)} \\ &= \int_x p(x) \int_\theta L(\theta, d(x))\pi(\theta|x)\, d\theta\, dx, \qquad \textbf{(6.2.2)} \end{aligned}$$

where

$$\pi(\theta|x) = \frac{\pi(\theta)p(x|\theta)}{p(x)} = \frac{\pi(\theta)p(x|\theta)}{\int \pi(\theta)p(x|\theta)\, d\theta}$$

is the posterior probability of $\theta$ given $x$.

**Definition**

A decision rule $d$ is *Bayes with respect to* $\pi(\theta)$ if

$$r(d(X), \pi) \leq r(d'(X), \pi)$$

for all $d'(X)$ in the set of decision rules.

Equation 6.2.2 indicates that $d(X)$ may be found by minimizing, for each $x$, the integral $\int L(\theta, d(x))\pi(\theta|x)\, d\theta$ with respect to $d(X)$.

**Example [Silvey (1970, p. 168)]**

Assume

$$\begin{aligned} L(d(X), \theta) &= (d(X) - \theta)^2, \\ \pi(\theta) &= 1, \qquad 0 < \theta < 1, \\ x &= 0, 1, \ldots, n \end{aligned}$$

and

$$p(x|\theta) = \binom{n}{x}\theta^x(1 - \theta)^{n-x}.$$

Letting $d(X) = \hat{\theta}(X)$, we have

$$r(\hat{\theta}(X), \pi) = \int_0^1 d\theta \sum_{x=0}^{n} [\hat{\theta}(x) - \theta]^2 \binom{n}{x} \theta^x (1 - \theta)^{n-x}$$

$$= \sum_{x=0}^{n} \binom{n}{x} \int_0^1 [\hat{\theta}(x) - \theta]^2 \theta^x (1 - \theta)^{n-x}\, d\theta.$$

Since $\binom{n}{x} > 0$, the problem reduces to minimizing the integral for each $x$. Differentiating with respect to $\hat{\theta}(X)$ and setting the derivative equal to zero, we obtain

$$2 \sum_{x=0}^{n} \binom{n}{x} \int_0^1 [\hat{\theta}(x) - \theta] \theta^x (1 - \theta)^{n-x}\, d\theta = 0,$$

which implies, for each $x$,

$$\hat{\theta}(x) \int_0^1 \theta^x (1 - \theta)^{n-x}\, d\theta = \int_0^1 \theta^{x+1} (1 - \theta)^{n-x}\, d\theta,$$

or

$$\hat{\theta}(x) B(x + 1, n - x + 1) = B(x + 2, n - x + 1)$$

or

$$\hat{\theta}(x) \frac{\Gamma(x + 1)\Gamma(n - x + 1)}{\Gamma(n + 2)} = \frac{\Gamma(x + 2)\Gamma(n - x + 1)}{\Gamma(n + 3)}$$

or

$$\hat{\theta}(x) \frac{\Gamma(x + 1)}{\Gamma(n + 2)} = \frac{(x + 1)\Gamma(x + 1)}{(n + 2)\Gamma(n + 2)},$$

so that

$$\hat{\theta}(x) = \frac{x + 1}{n + 2}.$$

The Bayes' risk associated with this $\hat{\theta}$ and the assumed prior density [$\theta$ uniformly distributed over (0, 1)] is computed as follows: By definition,

$$r(\hat{\theta}, \pi) = \int_0^1 \sum \binom{n}{x} \left[\frac{x + 1}{n + 2} - \theta\right]^2 \theta^x (1 - \theta)^{n-x}\, d\theta,$$

and

$$\left(\frac{x + 1}{n + 2} - \theta\right)^2 = \frac{1}{(n + 2)^2} [(x - n\theta) + (1 - 2\theta)]^2.$$

Since $E(X) = n\theta$, and $\mathrm{Var}(X) = n\theta(1 - \theta)$, we have

$$\sum_x \binom{n}{x} \left[\frac{x + 1}{n + 2} - \theta\right]^2 \theta^x(1 - \theta)^{n-x}$$

$$= \frac{1}{(n + 2)^2} \sum \binom{n}{x}[(x - n\theta) + (1 - 2\theta)]^2 \theta^x(1 - \theta)^{n-x}$$

$$= \frac{1}{(n + 2)^2} [n\theta(1 - \theta) + (1 - 2\theta)^2]. \qquad \textbf{(6.2.3)}$$

Equation 6.2.3 must be integrated with respect to $\theta$:

$$r(\hat{\theta}, \pi) = \frac{1}{(n + 2)^2} \int_0^1 [n\theta(1 - \theta) + (1 - 2\theta)^2]\, d\theta = \frac{1}{6(n + 2)}.$$

By way of comparison, the maximum likelihood estimator of $\theta$, $t$, is given by $t = x/n$. This is an unbiased minimum variance estimator; its Bayes' risk relative to the uniform prior is

$$\int_0^1 \sum \binom{n}{x} \left[\frac{x}{n} - \theta\right]^2 \theta^x(1 - \theta)^{n-x}\, d\theta = \int_0^1 n\theta(1 - \theta)\, d\theta = \frac{1}{6n},$$

and it is easily seen that

$$r[\hat{\theta}, \pi] < r[t, \pi].$$

Other choices for the prior distribution would lead to different estimators.

### 6.2.3 Admissibility and Minimax Approaches

Another approach to decision theory may be taken if the researcher is unwilling or unable to specify a prior distribution. In the absence of a prior distribution, the risk function is a function of $\theta$, and it is usually impossible to find an estimator that is better than every other estimator for all values of the unknown $\theta$. However, some estimators may be worse than others for all values of $\theta$, which leads to the next principle.

**Definition**

The decision $d$ *strictly dominates* $d'$ if $R(d, \theta) \leq R(d', \theta)$, for all $\theta$, and the inequality is strict for some $\theta$.

**Definition**

Any decision rule that is strictly dominated by another is *inadmissible;* any rule that is not strictly dominated is *admissible.*

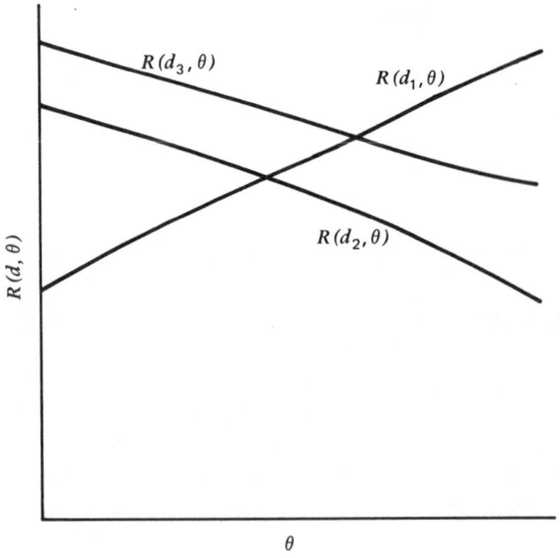


**FIGURE 6.1 Risk functions.**

Figure 6.1 illustrates the principle. Clearly, $R(d_3, \theta) > R(d_2, \theta)$ for all $\theta$, so that $d_3$ is dominated by $d_2$ and is therefore inadmissible. As a practical matter, adoption of the risk function given by $R(d, \theta)$ would seem to rule out the use of $d_3$ since, for every possible value of $\theta$, $d_2$ yields a smaller risk. The choice between $d_1$ and $d_2$, however, is not clear. Note that $d_1$ performs better than $d_2$ for small values of $\theta$, and the opposite is true for large values. Bayes' principle solves this choice problem because the prior distribution for $\theta$ weighs the risk function by the researcher's prior beliefs about values of $\theta$. An informal Bayes' approach to choosing between $d_1$ and $d_2$ would require the researcher to state a belief regarding the relative probability of high and low values of $\theta$. As a more concrete example, consider the following.

**Example**

Assume $\theta$ is the expected value of a distribution with variance equal to one, $0 \leq \theta \leq 5$, and compare the two estimators, $d_1(X) = \bar{X}$ and $d_2(X) = 3$. [Any constant value would do for $d_2(X)$.] Then $d_1(X)$ is unbiased and its variance is $1/n$, while the bias of $d_2(X)$ is $\theta - 3$, but $\text{Var}(d_2) = 0$. Accordingly, with a quadratic loss function, $R(d_1, \theta) = 1/n$, and $R(d_2,\theta) = (\theta - 3)^2$. Clearly, $(\theta - 3)^2 \leq 1/n$ if $3 - 1/\sqrt{n} \leq \theta \leq 3 + 1/\sqrt{n}$. For other values of $\theta$, $R(d_1,\theta) < R(d_2,\theta)$. See Figure 6.2.

One way to shorten the list of estimators when more than one is admissible is to restrict the set of decision rules to a class and find the one with smallest risk in that class. For example, in the standard regression theory attention is restricted to linear unbiased

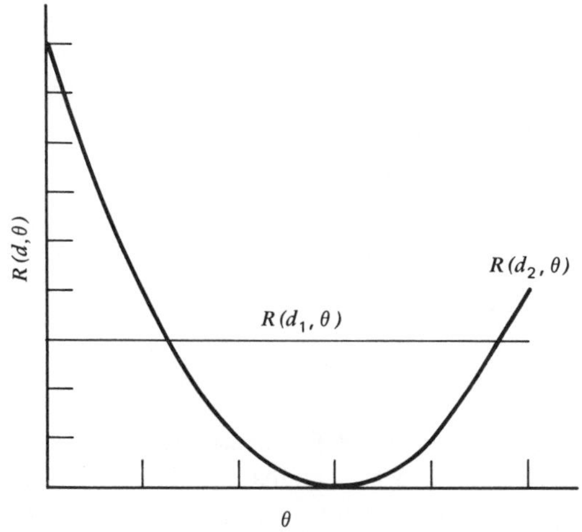


**FIGURE 6.2 Risk functions for $d_1 = X$ and $d_2 = 3$.**

estimators, and the minimum variance estimator within that class is chosen. In this class, minimum variance corresponds to minimum risk.

Another approach to estimator selection is the conservative one of choosing on the basis of the largest value of $R(d, \theta)$ as a function of $\theta$. [Note that in the previous example, $\max R(d_1, \theta) = 1/n$, while $\max R(d_2, \theta) = 9$.] A decision rule that minimizes the maximum value of $R(d, \theta)$ is called a minimax decision rule.

**Definition**

The decision rule $\delta$ is *minimax* if

$$\max_\theta R(\delta, \theta) \leq \max_\theta R(\delta', \theta)$$

for all $\delta'$.

An extensive discussion of the relationships between Bayes' and minimax decision rules is contained in Ferguson (1967). We conclude this section with an interesting application of the minimax approach to regression from Judge and Bock (1978, pp. 18–20). Assume the standard regression model

$$\mathbf{y} = X\boldsymbol{\beta} + \boldsymbol{\epsilon},$$

where $E(\boldsymbol{\epsilon}) = 0$, $E(\boldsymbol{\epsilon}\boldsymbol{\epsilon}') = \sigma^2 I$, $\mathbf{y}$ is $T \times 1$, $X$ is $T \times k$, $\boldsymbol{\beta}$ is $k \times 1$, and $\boldsymbol{\epsilon}$ is $T \times 1$. Suppose it is desired to find a linear estimator, $\hat{\boldsymbol{\beta}} = A\mathbf{y}$, where the risk function is quadratic loss,

$$R(\hat{\boldsymbol{\beta}}, \boldsymbol{\beta}) = E[(\hat{\boldsymbol{\beta}} - \boldsymbol{\beta})'(\hat{\boldsymbol{\beta}} - \boldsymbol{\beta})].$$

Then we have

$$\begin{aligned}
E[(\hat{\boldsymbol\beta} - \boldsymbol\beta)'(\hat{\boldsymbol\beta} - \boldsymbol\beta)]& \\
&= E\{[(\hat{\boldsymbol\beta} - E(\hat{\boldsymbol\beta})) - (\boldsymbol\beta - E(\hat{\boldsymbol\beta}))]'[(\hat{\boldsymbol\beta} - E(\hat{\boldsymbol\beta})) - (\boldsymbol\beta - E(\hat{\boldsymbol\beta}))]\} \\
&= E[(\hat{\boldsymbol\beta} - E(\hat{\boldsymbol\beta}))'(\hat{\boldsymbol\beta} - E(\hat{\boldsymbol\beta}))] + (E(\hat{\boldsymbol\beta}) - \boldsymbol\beta)'(E(\hat{\boldsymbol\beta}) - \boldsymbol\beta) \\
&= E[(A\mathbf{y} - AX\boldsymbol\beta)'(A\mathbf{y} - AX\boldsymbol\beta)] + (AX\boldsymbol\beta - \boldsymbol\beta)'(AX\boldsymbol\beta - \boldsymbol\beta) \\
&= E[(\mathbf{y} - X\boldsymbol\beta)'A'A(\mathbf{y} - X\boldsymbol\beta)] + \boldsymbol\beta'(AX - I)'(AX - I)\boldsymbol\beta \\
&= \sigma^2 \text{tr}AA' + \boldsymbol\beta'(AX - I)'(AX - I)\boldsymbol\beta. \qquad \textbf{(6.2.4)}
\end{aligned}$$

Note that the first term in (6.2.4) is independent of $\boldsymbol\beta$ and the second is a positive semidefinite quadratic form in $\boldsymbol\beta$. As the elements of $\boldsymbol\beta \to \infty$, this term will grow without bound. Since the risk of an estimator that is independent of $\boldsymbol\beta$ will not be affected by large values of $\boldsymbol\beta$, setting $AX = I$ will yield a linear estimator that is minimax in the class of linear estimators. Clearly, $A = (X'X)^{-1}X'$ will do the trick, and thus the least squares estimator is minimax in the class of linear estimators.

## 6.3 The Noncentral $\chi^2$ Distribution

Analysis of the James-Stein and related estimators makes extensive use of the noncentral $\chi^2$ distribution. Since this distribution is not usually covered in a first course in mathematical statistics or econometrics, we present several of its main properties. More detail may be found in Johnson and Kotz (1972) and in Graybill (1961). We begin with a brief review of the central $\chi^2$ distribution.

Let $\mathbf{Y}$ be a $p$-dimensional column vector, $\mathbf{Y} \sim N_p(\mathbf{0}, \sigma^2 I)$. Then $X = \mathbf{Y}'\mathbf{Y}/\sigma^2$ is distributed as $\chi^2$ with $p$ degrees of freedom, denoted by $\chi^2_p$. Its density is given by

$$f(x) = \frac{x^{(p-2)/2}}{2^{p/2}\Gamma(p/2)} e^{-x/2}. \qquad \textbf{(6.3.1)}$$

If $X \sim \chi^2_p$, then $E(X)$ is given by

$$\begin{aligned}
\int_0^\infty xf(x)\,dx &= \frac{1}{2^{p/2}\Gamma(p/2)} \int_0^\infty x \cdot x^{(p-2)/2} e^{-x/2}\,dx \\
&= \frac{1}{2^{p/2}\Gamma(p/2)} \int_0^\infty x^{p/2} e^{-x/2}\,dx \\
&= 2\left(\frac{p}{2}\right)\left[\frac{1}{2^{(p+2)/2}\Gamma[(p+2)/2]} \int_0^\infty x^{p/2} e^{-x/2}\,dx\right] \\
&= p, \qquad \textbf{(6.3.2)}
\end{aligned}$$

since the bracketed term in (6.3.2) is the density function of a $\chi^2_{p+2}$ variate integrated over its possible values. For future reference, we also need the result that $E(X^2) = p(p + 2)$:

$$
\begin{aligned}
E(X^2) &= \frac{1}{2^{p/2}\Gamma(p/2)} \int_0^\infty x^2 \cdot x^{(p-2)/2} e^{-x/2}\, dx \\
&= 2^2 \left(\frac{p}{2}\right) \left(\frac{p+2}{2}\right) \left[\frac{1}{2^{(p+4)/2}\Gamma[(p+4)/2]} \int_0^\infty x^{(p+2)/2} e^{-x/2}\, dx\right] \\
&= p(p + 2).
\end{aligned}
$$

Finally, we require $E(1/X)$:

$$
\begin{aligned}
E\left(\frac{1}{X}\right) &= \frac{1}{2^{p/2}\Gamma(p/2)} \int_0^\infty \frac{1}{x} \cdot x^{(p-2)/2} e^{-x/2}\, dx \\
&= \frac{1}{2^{p/2}\Gamma(p/2)} \int_0^\infty x^{(p-4)/2} e^{-x/2}\, dx \qquad (6.3.3)
\end{aligned}
$$

[since the integral in (6.3.3) converges if and only if $p > 2$, this condition is assumed for the remainder of the derivation]

$$
\begin{aligned}
&= \frac{1}{2[(p-2)/2]} \left[\frac{1}{2^{(p-2)/2}\Gamma[(p-2)/2]} \int_0^\infty x^{(p-4)/2} e^{-x/2}\, dx\right] \\
&= \frac{1}{p-2}, \qquad p > 2.
\end{aligned}
$$

We now turn to the noncentral $\chi^2$: Let $\mathbf{Y} \sim N_p(\boldsymbol{\mu}, \sigma^2 I)$. Then $\omega = \mathbf{Y}'\mathbf{Y}/\sigma^2$ has the *noncentral* $\chi^2$ *distribution* with $p$ degrees of freedom and noncentrality parameter $\theta = \boldsymbol{\mu}'\boldsymbol{\mu}/2$; it will be denoted by $\chi'^2(p, \theta)$. Note that $\chi'^2(p, 0) = \chi_p^2$. (Some authors define the noncentrality parameter as $\boldsymbol{\mu}'\boldsymbol{\mu}$.) The density of $\omega$ is given by

$$
\begin{aligned}
f(\omega) &= \sum_{i=0}^{\infty} \frac{e^{-\theta}\theta^i}{i!} \frac{\omega^{(p+2i)/2-1} e^{-\omega/2}}{2^{(p+2i)/2}\Gamma[(p+2i)/2]} \\
&= \sum_{i=0}^{\infty} \frac{e^{-\theta}\theta^i}{i!} g_{p+2i}(\omega), \qquad (6.3.4)
\end{aligned}
$$

where $g_{p+2i}(\omega)$ is the density of a *central* $\chi^2$ with $p + 2i$ degrees of freedom, $\chi_{p+2i}^2$. Thus, for given values of $p$ and $\omega$, $f(\omega)$ may be interpreted as the expected value of a central $\chi^2$ variate with $p + 2i$ degrees of freedom, where $i$ has a Poisson distribution with parameter $\theta$. This interpretation is exploited in the derivation of the James–Stein estimator.

The characterization of $\chi'^2(p, \theta)$ as a Poisson weighted average of central $\chi^2$ variates facilitates the derivation of $E(\omega)$ and $E(1/\omega)$. First,

$$\begin{aligned} E(\omega) &= \int_0^\infty \omega f(\omega)\, d\omega \\ &= \sum_{i=0}^\infty \frac{e^{-\theta}\theta^i}{i!} \int_0^\infty \omega g_{p+2i}(\omega)\, d\omega \\ &= \sum_{i=0}^\infty \frac{e^{-\theta}\theta^i}{i!} (p + 2i) \\ &= E(p + 2i) = p + 2E(i) = p + 2\theta. \end{aligned} \tag{6.3.5}$$

And

$$\begin{aligned} E\left(\frac{1}{\omega}\right) &= \sum \frac{e^{-\theta}\theta^i}{i!} \int_0^\infty \frac{1}{\omega} g_{p+2i}(\omega)\, d\omega \\ &= \sum \frac{e^{-\theta}\theta^i}{i!} \frac{1}{p + 2i - 2} \qquad (p > 2) \\ &= E\left[\frac{1}{p + 2i - 2}\right], \end{aligned} \tag{6.3.6}$$

where the expectation in (6.3.6) is taken over the Poisson variate, $i$. Incidentally, Ullah (1974) shows that $E(1/(p + 2i - 2)^r)$ may be written in terms of the confluent hypergeometric function (see Appendix F):

$$E\left[\left(\frac{1}{p + 2i - 2}\right)^r\right] = 2^{-r} \frac{\Gamma(p/2 - r)}{\Gamma(p/2)} e^{-\theta} {}_1F_1(p/2 - r, p/2; \theta). \tag{6.3.7}$$

This is a useful relationship for deriving exact and approximate moments of James–Stein estimators.

To conclude this section, we state without proof the reproductive property of the noncentral $\chi^2$ distribution: Let $\omega_i \sim \chi'^2(p_i, \theta_i)$, $i = 1, \ldots, n$, and let the $\omega_i$ be jointly independent. Then $\omega = \Sigma\omega_i$ is distributed as $\chi'^2(\Sigma p_i, \Sigma\theta_i)$.

## 6.4 Estimation under Linear Restrictions; Principal Component Regression

To conclude our introduction to estimation under the quadratic loss criterion, we consider constrained least squares estimators.[4] As an example, assume the model,

$$\begin{gathered} y_i = \beta_1 x_{1i} + \beta_2 x_{2i} + u_i, \qquad i = 1, \ldots, N, \\ E(u_i) = 0, \qquad E(u_i^2) = \sigma^2, \qquad E(u_i u_j) = 0, \qquad i \neq j. \end{gathered}$$

[4]This theory was developed by Wallace and his associates; see Toro-Vizcarrondo and Wallace (1968) and Wallace (1972). It is also discussed in Judge and Bock (1978) and in references cited there.

For convenience, let $\Sigma y_i = \Sigma x_{1i} = \Sigma x_{2i} = 0$ and $\Sigma y_i^2 = \Sigma x_{1i}^2 = \Sigma x_{2i}^2 = 1$, and assume nonstochastic $x_{ji}$'s. Suppose the investigator is particularly interested in $\beta_1$ and therefore adopts the loss function

$$L(b_1, \boldsymbol{\beta}) = (b_1 - \beta_1)^2.$$

Let us first derive

$$E[L(\hat{\beta}_1, \boldsymbol{\beta})] = \hat{R}(\beta_1, \boldsymbol{\beta}),$$

where $\hat{\beta}_1$ is the first component of the ordinary least squares (OLS) multiple regression estimator

$$\hat{\boldsymbol{\beta}} = (X'X)^{-1}X'\mathbf{y}.$$

Since $\hat{\boldsymbol{\beta}}$ is unbiased, the risk reduces to the variance, $\sigma^2_{\hat{\beta}_1} = \sigma^2/(1 - r_{12}^2)$ where $r_{12}$ is the correlation between $x_1$ and $x_2$. If $r_{12}^2$ is close to 1, $\sigma^2_{\hat{\beta}_1}$ will be large.

On the other hand, consider the constrained OLS estimator of $\beta_1$, $\beta_1^c$, defined by setting $\beta_2 = 0$:

$$\beta_1^c = \frac{\sum x_{1i}y_i}{\sum x_{1i}^2} = \sum x_{1i}y_i.$$

This estimator is biased:

$$\begin{aligned} E\left[\sum x_{1i}y_i\right] &= E\left[\sum x_{1i}(\beta_1 x_{1i} + \beta_2 x_{2i} + u_i)\right] \\ &= \beta_1 + \beta_2 r_{12}. \end{aligned}$$

Its variance is given by

$$E[\sum x_{1i}y_i - (\beta_1 + \beta_2 r_{12})]^2 = \sigma^2.$$

Therefore,

$$\begin{aligned} R(\beta_1^c, \boldsymbol{\beta}) &= (\beta_2 r_{12})^2 + \sigma^2 \\ &= \frac{\sigma^2 r_{12}^2}{1 - r_{12}^2} \frac{\beta_2^2}{\sigma^2/(1 - r_{12}^2)} + \sigma^2 \\ &= \frac{2\sigma^2\, r_{12}^2}{1 - r_{12}^2} \frac{\beta_2^2}{2\sigma^2_{\hat{\beta}_2}} + \sigma^2. \end{aligned}$$

The two risks are displayed as functions of $\beta_2^2/2\sigma^2_{\hat{\beta}_2}$ in Figure 6.3. As the figure reveals, the risk of the constrained estimator increases linearly with $\beta_2^2/2\sigma^2_{\hat{\beta}_2}$, but there is an interval, if $r_{12}^2 \neq 0$, in which $R^c(\beta_1, \boldsymbol{\beta}) < R(\beta_1, \boldsymbol{\beta})$. Note that it is not necessary that $\beta_2 = 0$ to make $\beta_1^c$ preferred to $\hat{\beta}_1$;$\beta_2^2/2\sigma^2_{\hat{\beta}_2} < \frac{1}{2}$ is sufficient for this purpose.

It is a relatively straightforward matter to extend this analysis to more general restrictions: Let $\mathbf{y} = X\boldsymbol{\beta} + \boldsymbol{\epsilon}$, $E(\boldsymbol{\epsilon}) = 0$, $E(\boldsymbol{\epsilon\epsilon}') = \sigma^2 I$, and $R(\mathbf{b}, \boldsymbol{\beta}) = E[(\mathbf{b} - \boldsymbol{\beta})'(\mathbf{b} - \boldsymbol{\beta})]$. Then one can compare the risk functions of the OLS estimator $\hat{\boldsymbol{\beta}} = (X'X)^{-1}X'\mathbf{y}$ with the constrained OLS estimator, $\boldsymbol{\beta}^c$, which minimizes $(\mathbf{y} - X\boldsymbol{\beta}^c)'(\mathbf{y} - \mathbf{X}\boldsymbol{\beta}^c)$ under

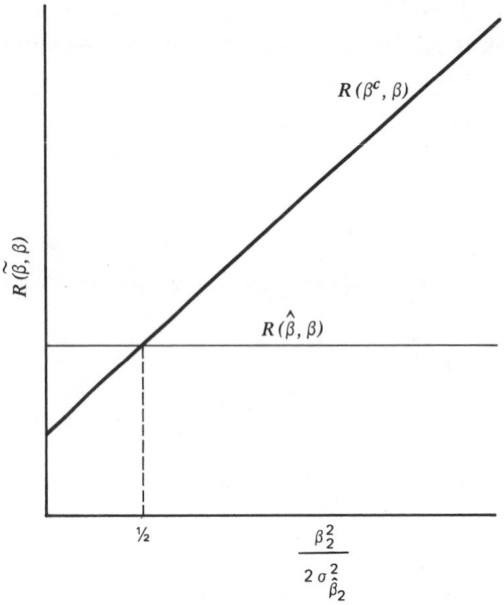


**FIGURE 6.3 Risk functions for OLS and constrained estimators.**

the constraints $H'\boldsymbol{\beta} = \mathbf{h}$, where $r(H) < r(X)$. As shown by Yancey, Bock, and Judge (1973), the constrained estimator has a lower risk if

$$\frac{(H'\boldsymbol{\beta} - \mathbf{h})'(H'(X'X)^{-1}H)^{-1}(H'\boldsymbol{\beta} - \mathbf{h})}{2\sigma^2} \leq \frac{1}{2d_L} \operatorname{tr}[(X'X)^{-1}H(H'(X'X)^{-1}H)^{-1} H'(X'X)^{-1}],$$

where $d_L$ is the largest characteristic root of a matrix defined in the above mentioned article. As in the simple case, the risk of the constrained estimator depends on how seriously the constraint is violated: in the illustrative case, it depended on $\beta_2^2 = (\beta_2 - 0)^2$, and in the general case, on a quadratic form in the difference between the constrained and true values,

$$(H'\boldsymbol{\beta} - \mathbf{h})'(H'(X'X)^{-1}H)^{-1}(H'\boldsymbol{\beta} - \mathbf{h}).$$

Yancey, Bock, and Judge also show that additional information is needed to determine the point at which $R(\boldsymbol{\beta}^c, \boldsymbol{\beta}) = R(\hat{\boldsymbol{\beta}}, \boldsymbol{\beta})$; the above result is the greatest bound for which $R(\boldsymbol{\beta}^c, \boldsymbol{\beta}) < R(\hat{\boldsymbol{\beta}}, \boldsymbol{\beta})$ that can be determined with knowledge only of $H$, $\mathbf{h}$, and $X$.

Toro-Vizcarrondo and Wallace (1968) suggest a type of preliminary test estimator. In the simple case described above, this estimator is found by using $\beta_1^c$ if the hypothesis $\beta_2^2/2\sigma^2_{\hat{\beta}_2} < \frac{1}{2}$ is accepted and $\hat{\beta}_1$ if it is rejected. The noncentral $F$ distribution may be used for the test. As will be shown in Section 8.1, the risk function of this test is not $R(\beta_1^c, \boldsymbol{\beta})$ for $\beta_2^2/2\sigma^2_{\hat{\beta}_2} \leq \frac{1}{2}$ and $R(\hat{\beta}_1, \boldsymbol{\beta})$ for $\beta^2_{\hat{\beta}_2} > \frac{1}{2}$. Because the same data are used both to test the hypothesis and to estimate the parameters, the risk function is not simply the envelope of $R(\boldsymbol{\beta}_1^c, \boldsymbol{\beta})$ and $R(\hat{\boldsymbol{\beta}}_1, \boldsymbol{\beta})$.

A special case of restricted estimators, sometimes suggested for dealing with multicollinearity, is *principal component regression*. In that approach, we again assume that the observations are normalized so that $\Sigma y_t = 0$, $\Sigma x_{ti} = 0$, $\Sigma y_t^2 = 1$, and $\Sigma_t x_{ti}^2 = 1$

where $i = 1, \ldots, k$ denotes the independent variables and $t = 1, \ldots, T$ denotes the individual observations. With these assumptions, $X'X$ is the matrix of correlation coefficients, $r_{ij}$, between $X_i$ and $X_j$.

Starting from

$$\mathbf{y} = X\boldsymbol{\beta} + \boldsymbol{\epsilon}, \qquad E(\boldsymbol{\epsilon}) = 0, \qquad E(\boldsymbol{\epsilon\epsilon}') = \sigma^2 I,$$

we introduce the $k \times k$ orthogonal matrix $P$, with the property that

$$P'X'XP = \Lambda = \text{diag}\{\lambda_i\},$$

where the $\lambda_i$ are the characteristic roots of $X'X$ arranged so that

$$\lambda_1 \geq \lambda_2 \geq \cdots \lambda_k.$$

Then we reparameterize the model,

$$\begin{aligned} \mathbf{y} &= XPP'\boldsymbol{\beta} + \boldsymbol{\epsilon} \\ &= Z\boldsymbol{\alpha} + \boldsymbol{\epsilon}, \qquad \text{where} \quad Z = XP \quad \text{and} \quad \boldsymbol{\alpha} = P'\boldsymbol{\beta}. \end{aligned}$$

The least squares estimator of $\boldsymbol{\alpha}$, $\hat{\boldsymbol{\alpha}}$, is given by

$$\begin{aligned} \hat{\boldsymbol{\alpha}} &= (Z'Z)^{-1} Z'\mathbf{y} \\ &= \Lambda^{-1} Z'\mathbf{y} \end{aligned}$$

and

$$\text{Cov}(\hat{\boldsymbol{\alpha}}) = \sigma^2\Lambda^{-1}.$$

From the estimate $\hat{\boldsymbol{\alpha}}$, we can return to $\hat{\boldsymbol{\beta}}$ by the relationship

$$\hat{\boldsymbol{\beta}} = P\hat{\boldsymbol{\alpha}}.$$

The $\mathbf{Z}_i = X\mathbf{P}_i$ are called the *principal components* of the matrix $X'X$, and the $\hat{\alpha}_i = 1/\lambda_i \mathbf{Z}_i'\mathbf{y}$ are the *principal component regression coefficients,* where $\mathbf{Z}_i$ and $\mathbf{P}_i$ are the $i$th columns of $Z$ and $P$, respectively. [Since $(Z'Z)^{-1} = \Lambda^{-1}$, a diagonal matrix, each $\hat{\alpha}_i$ may be computed independently of the others.] From $\hat{\boldsymbol{\beta}} = P\hat{\boldsymbol{\alpha}}$, we have

$$\hat{\boldsymbol{\beta}} = \hat{\alpha}_1\mathbf{P}_1 + \hat{\alpha}_2\mathbf{P}_2 \cdots + \hat{\alpha}_k\mathbf{P}_k, \tag{6.4.1}$$

that is, $\hat{\boldsymbol{\beta}}$ may be regarded as a weighted average of the $\mathbf{P}_i$, with the $\hat{\alpha}_i$'s serving as weights. It may be verified that

$$\text{Cov}(\hat{\boldsymbol{\beta}}) = \sigma^2\text{P}\Lambda^{-1}\text{P}'.$$

Next, consider the effect of multicollinearity, which may be defined as the existence of one or more near-linear dependencies among the columns of $X$; that is, for one or more $(k \times 1)$ vectors, $\mathbf{b}$,

$$X\mathbf{b} = \boldsymbol{\psi} \tag{6.4.2}$$

where $\boldsymbol{\psi}$ is an $(n \times 1)$ vector whose elements are close to zero.

Such dependencies imply that one or more characteristic roots are close to zero, as may be seen by the following argument. Premultiplying (6.4.2) by $X'$, we have

$$X'X\mathbf{b} = \text{X}'\boldsymbol{\psi}, \tag{6.4.3}$$

where the elements of the $n \times 1$ vector $X'\boldsymbol{\psi}$ are close to zero because the elements of $\boldsymbol{\psi}$ are small by assumption and the elements of $X$ are small because of the constraint that $\Sigma x_{ti}^2 = 1$, $i = 1, \ldots, k$. Therefore, $X'\boldsymbol{\psi} = \delta\mathbf{b}$, where $\delta$ is close to zero, which tells us that $\mathbf{b}$ is a characteristic vectot of $X'X$ with a characteristic root $\delta$ that is close to zero. [See Belsley, Kuh, and Welsch (1980, Chapter 3) for an extensive discussion of the definition and implications of small characteristic roots and the general problem of collinearity.]

To determine the effect of a small characteristic root on the variance of $\hat{\boldsymbol{\beta}}$, recall

$$\text{Cov}(\hat{\boldsymbol{\beta}}) = \sigma^2 P\Lambda^{-1}P' = \sigma^2 \sum_{i=1}^{k} \frac{1}{\lambda_i} \mathbf{P}_i\mathbf{P}_i'. \tag{6.4.4}$$

In this form, it may be seen that a small value of $\lambda_i$, which leads to a large value of $1/\lambda_i$, results in large values of the diagonal elements of $\text{Cov}(\hat{\boldsymbol{\beta}})$; these, of course, are the $\text{Var}(\hat{\boldsymbol{\beta}}_i)$. To avoid such large variances, it has been proposed to estimate $\hat{\boldsymbol{\beta}}$ from the first $r < k$ components—those associated with the $r$ largest characteristic roots. Specifically, let

$$P_{(r)} = [\mathbf{P}_1, \mathbf{P}_2, \ldots, \mathbf{P}_r],$$
$$\overline{\mathrm{P}}_{(r)} = \mathbf{P}_{r+1}, \ldots, \mathbf{P}_k],$$
$$\hat{\boldsymbol{\alpha}}_r' = [\hat{\alpha}_1, \ldots, \hat{\alpha}_r],$$

The estimate of $\boldsymbol{\beta}$ based on the first $r$ principal components, $\hat{\boldsymbol{\beta}}_r^+$ is

$$\begin{aligned} \hat{\boldsymbol{\beta}}_r^+ &= \hat{\alpha}_1\mathbf{P}_1 + \cdots + \hat{\alpha}_r\mathbf{P}_r \\ &= P_{(r)}\hat{\alpha}_{(r)} \\ &= P_{(r)}P'_{(r)}\hat{\boldsymbol{\beta}} \\ &= P_{(r)}P'_{(r)}(X'X)^{-1}X'X\hat{\boldsymbol{\beta}} \\ &= P_{(r)}\Lambda_{(r)}^{-1}P'_{(r)}X'X\hat{\boldsymbol{\beta}}. \end{aligned} \tag{6.4.5}$$

Thus, in this notation, (6.4.1) shows that $\hat{\boldsymbol{\beta}} = \hat{\boldsymbol{\beta}}_k^+$, $\hat{\boldsymbol{\beta}}_r^+$ may be interpreted as the OLS, estimator subject to the restrictions that $\hat{\alpha}_{r+1} = \cdots = \hat{\alpha}_k = 0$. The mean squared error of $\hat{\boldsymbol{\beta}}_r^+$ is

$$\text{tr Cov}(\hat{\boldsymbol{\beta}}_r^+) + \boldsymbol{\beta}'\overline{\mathrm{P}}'_{(r)}\boldsymbol{\beta}.$$

Now

$$\text{tr Cov}(\hat{\boldsymbol{\beta}}_r^+) = \sigma^2[1/\lambda_1 + \cdots + 1/\lambda_r];$$

this is smaller than

$$\text{tr Cov}(\hat{\boldsymbol{\beta}}) = \sigma^2[1/\lambda_1 + \cdots + 1/\lambda_k],$$

and if $\lambda_j \approx 0$ for one or more $j$, $r + 1 \leqslant j \leqslant k$, the former will be substantially smaller. Of course, the bias term,

$$\boldsymbol{\beta}'\,\overline{P}_r\overline{P}_r'\boldsymbol{\beta},$$

may be large—and it is unknown. Thus, principal component regression is a form of restricted least squares: the problem is to estimate $\boldsymbol{\alpha}$ subject to

$$[0_{(k-r)xr}, I_{k-r}]\, \alpha = \mathbf{0}_{(k-r)x1}.$$

This can be transformed back to linear restrictions on $\boldsymbol{\beta}$:

$$[0_{(k-r)xr}, I_{k-r}]PP'\boldsymbol{\alpha} = \mathbf{0}$$

implies

$$[0_{(k-r)xr}, I_{k-r}]P\boldsymbol{\beta} = \mathbf{0},$$

or

$$Q\boldsymbol{\beta} = \mathbf{0},$$

where

$$Q = [0_{(k-r)xr}, I_{k-r}]P.$$

Several questions may arise concerning the application of this procedure, for example, (1) do the $\alpha_i$'s have any interpretation in their own right, and (2) are there any good reasons for choosing the restrictions on $\boldsymbol{\beta}$ that result from $\hat{\alpha}_{r+1} = \cdots = \hat{\alpha}_k = 0$.

Greenberg (1975) shows that $\mathbf{P}_1'\boldsymbol{\beta} = \alpha_1$ may be interpreted as that (nontrivial) linear combination of the $\boldsymbol{\beta}$ which can be estimated with smallest variance. That is,

$$\text{Cov}(\mathbf{P}_1'\hat{\boldsymbol{\beta}}) \leq \text{Cov}(\mathbf{C}'\hat{\boldsymbol{\beta}}),$$

where $\mathbf{C}$ is any vector such that $\mathbf{C}'\mathbf{C} = 1$. The latter condition is necessary to avoid a trivial estimator, since $\mathbf{C} = \mathbf{0}$ produces a variance of zero, but estimates all coefficients as zero. The idea here is to view the $X$ matrix as an "unplanned" experiment that may have resulted in a poor matrix for estimating $\boldsymbol{\beta}$. Nevertheless, it may be that certain linear combinations of $\boldsymbol{\beta}$ can be estimated with reasonable variances. Since the variance of $\hat{\alpha}_i$ is proportional to $1/\lambda_i$, the researcher may decide for which $i$ the variance is so high that it is not worthwhile to compute further estimates.

It is also shown that choosing $\hat{\boldsymbol{\beta}}_r^+$ as above minimizes $(1/\sigma^2)$ tr $\text{Cov}(P_{(r)}P_{(r)}'\hat{\boldsymbol{\beta}})$ for all $S_{(r)}S_{(r)}'\hat{\boldsymbol{\beta}}$, where $S_{(r)}$ is a matrix composed of any $r$ columns of $P$. It seems reasonable to confine attention to projections of the unbiased estimator $\hat{\boldsymbol{\beta}}$, and $P_{(r)}P_{(r)}'\hat{\boldsymbol{\beta}}$ minimizes the variance component of the mean squared error.

In addition, Fomby, Hill, and Johnson (1978) extend the above result by proving the following:

**Theorem 6.4.1**

The trace of the covariance matrix for principal component estimators obtained by deleting components associated with the smallest characteristic roots is at least as small as that for any other restricted least squares estimator with an equal or smaller number of restrictions.

This theorem shows that if the researcher's criterion is a small value of tr $\text{Cov}(\boldsymbol{\beta}^c)$, where $\boldsymbol{\beta}^c$ is constrained by $k - r$ linear restrictions, attention can be confined to principal component regressions with no loss in performance.

**TABLE 6.1 Comparison of Estimated Coefficients**

| Attributes* | Expected Sign | Principal Component Analysis | Ordinary Least Squares |
|---|---|---|---|
| LIVAREA | + | 2.07 | 5.60 |
| ROOMS | + | 913.75 | 1361.92 |
| BEDS | + | 1066.99 | −1635.50 |
| BATHS | + | 2570.36 | 2172.14 |
| LOTSIZE | + | 0.17 | 0.35 |
| CRIMRATE | − | −0.15 | −0.15 |
| MEDY | + | 0.32 | 0.87 |
| NWPC | − | −7.40 | 12.01 |
| EXPPUP | + | 4.60 | −0.74 |
| ADJNONPC | − | −9.70 | −3.29 |
| JBSMT | + | 3686.70 | 2307.69 |
| AIR | + | 2456.06 | 3546.91 |
| MEDSCHYR | + | 699.84 | 110.42 |
| PC39 | − | −21.67 | 19.97 |
| BLUEPC | − | −63.24 | −72.74 |
| VACYRPC | − | −17.27 | −36.12 |
| FHDPC | − | −62.17 | 55.65 |
| RENTPC | − | −25.89 | −14.91 |
| POP20PC | + | 52.82 | −46.16 |
| YEARSOLD | − | −30.99 | −121.92 |
| $R^2$ | | 0.73 | 0.81 |

Reprinted from Mark and Parks (1978), with permission of the publisher, Academic Press.

*Definitions of attributes:

| | |
|---|---|
| LIVAREA | Total usable area of unit |
| ROOMS | Number of rooms |
| BEDS | Bedrooms |
| BATHS | Baths |
| LOTSIZE | Total area of parcel |
| CRIMRATE | Crimes per thousand population |
| MEDY | Median income of families |
| NWPC | Percentage of total population nonwhite |
| EXPPUP | Expenditures per pupil |
| ADJNONPC | Highest percentage of nonwhite adjacent tract |
| JBSMT | Full basement dummy |
| AIR | Central air-conditioning dummy |
| MEDSCHYR | Median school years completed |
| PC39 | Percentage of units constructed before 1939 |
| BLUEPC | Percentage of all employed population not employed as professionals or supervisors |
| VACYRPC | Percentage of all units vacant year round |
| FHDPC | Percentage of all units with female head |
| RENTPC | Percentage of all units rented |
| POP20PC | Percentage of population less than 20 years old |
| YEARSOLD | Age of structure |

To conclude this discussion, it should be stressed that the optimal properties of principal component regression are concerned with the variance component of the mean squared error. The squared bias term may be very large for $\hat{\boldsymbol{\beta}}_r^+$, and, although the squared bias is nonincreasing as $r$ increases, it will not decrease if $\boldsymbol{\beta}$ happens to lie in the subspace spanned by the omitted columns of $P$. In short, principal component regression is an approach to the problem of multicollinearity, which, like other approaches, has advantages and disadvantages. For a more detailed examination of multicollinearity, see Belsley, Kuh, and Welsch (1980, Chapters 3 and 4) and Judge, Griffiths, Hill, and Lee (1980, Chapter 12).

As an illustration of principal components regression, Table 6.1 contains the results of a study by Mark and Parks (1978) based on previous work of Little (1976). The observations are housing units, with sales prices plus future discounted taxes as the dependent variable. The principal component regression estimates are based on five components, and the differences between them and the corresponding OLS estimates are sometimes striking. For example, note that the coefficient of BEDS (number of bedrooms) is $-1635.50$ for OLS and 1066.99 for the principal component regression. Other reversals of sign appear in the table, and in each case it is the coefficient based on the principal component regression that has the expected sign. Moreover, the overall $R^2$ for the equation drops only from 0.81 to 0.73, even though there are 15 fewer regressors in the principal component regression.

## 6.5 References

Barnett, V. D. (1973), *Comparative Statistical Inference*, London: Wiley.

Belsley, D. A., E. Kuh, and R. E. Welsch (1980), *Regression Diagnostics,* New York: Wiley.

Chipman, J. S. (1964), "On Least Squares with Insufficient Observations," *Journal of the American Statistical Association,* **59**, 1078–1111.

DeGroot, M. H. (1970), *Optimal Statistical Decisions*, New York: McGraw-Hill.

Ferguson, T. S. (1967), *Mathematical Statistics,* New York: Academic Press.

Fomby, T. B., R. C. Hill, and S. R. Johnson (1978), "An Optimal Property of Principal Components in the Context of Restricted Least Squares," *Journal of the American Statistical Association*, **73**, 191–193.

Graybill, F. A. (1961), *An Introduction to Linear Statistical Models,* Vol. 1, New York: McGraw-Hill.

Greenberg, E. (1975), "Minimum Variance Properties of Principal Component Regression," *Journal of the American Statistical Association,* **70**, 194–197.

Johnson, N. L. and S. Kotz (1972), *Continuous Multivariate Distributions,* New York: Wiley.

Judge, G. G. and M. E. Bock (1978), *The Statistical Implications of Pre-Test and Stein-Rule Estimators in Econometrics,* Amsterdam: North-Holland.

Judge, G. G., W. E. Griffiths, R. C. Hill, and T.-C. Lee (1980), *The Theory and Practice of Econometrics,* New York: Wiley.

Little, J. T. (1976), "Residential Preferences, Neighborhood Filtering and Neighborhood Change," *Journal of Urban Economics,* **3**, 68–81.

Mark, J. H. and R. P. Parks (1978), "Residential Preferences, Neighborhood Filtering and Neighborhood Change: Comment and Corrections," *Journal of Urban Economics,* **5**, 535–537.

Silvey, S. D. (1970), *Statistical Inference,* Harmondsworth: Penguin Books.

Toro-Vizcarrondo, C. and T. D. Wallace (1968), "A Test of the Mean Square Error Criterion for Restrictions in Linear Regression," *Journal of the American Statistical Association,* **63**, 558–572.

Ullah, A. (1974), "On the Sampling Distribution of Improved Estimators for Coefficients in Linear Regression," *Journal of Econometrics,* **2**, 143–150.

Wallace, T. D. (1972), "Weaker Criteria and Tests for Linear Restrictions in Regression," *Econometrica,* **40**, 689–698.

Yancey, T. A., M. E. Bock, and G. G. Judge (1973), "Wallace's Mean Square Error Criterion for Testing Linear Restrictions in Regression: A Tighter Bound," *Econometrica,* **41**, 1203–1206.

# CHAPTER 7

# James-Stein Estimators and Applications to Regression

The first section of this chapter is concerned with a biased nonlinear estimator that, under some conditions, dominates the widely used maximum likelihood estimator for estimating the vector of means of a multivariate normal variable. This estimator and several variants are called James-Stein estimators. We then turn to applications of these estimators to general regression situations and derive conditions under which the ordinary least squares estimator is dominated by a James-Stein type. The last section deals with Bayesian estimators of regression coefficients under a quadratic loss criterion. These are helpful for understanding the James-Stein method and are interesting and important in their own right. A more detailed account of the material in this and the next chapter is contained in the excellent monograph of Judge and Bock (1978).

## 7.1 James-Stein Estimators

In this section we discuss a set of biased, nonlinear estimators that dominate their OLS counterparts under a quadratic loss function if certain conditions are met. We examine these estimators in some detail because both the results and the technique of analysis are instructive and important. To facilitate the reading of the original article, we adopt the notation used by James and Stein (1961) and Stein (1966). Since this notation may cause some confusion for regression applications, before proceeding we note that the random vector $\mathbf{X}$ studied below corresponds to $\hat{\boldsymbol{\beta}}$ in a special case of the standard regression model—the case in which the cross-product matrix of the independent variables is the identity matrix. This restriction is relaxed in the next section.

The following assumptions are made in this section:

1. $\mathbf{X}_{p\times 1} \sim N_p(\boldsymbol{\xi}, \sigma^2 I)$, where $\boldsymbol{\xi}$ is $p \times 1$ and $I$ is $p \times p$.
2. $\sigma^2$ is unknown, but a statistic, $S$, is independent of $\mathbf{X}$ and $S/\sigma^2 \sim \chi^2_n$. (In the regression case $S$ is the sum of the squared residuals.)
3. We are interested in estimating $E(\mathbf{X}) = \boldsymbol{\xi}$ under a quadratic loss criterion.

Adopting the notation $\mathbf{Z}'\mathbf{Z} = \|\mathbf{Z}\|^2$ for the column vector $\mathbf{Z}$, the problem is to find an estimator $\hat{\boldsymbol{\xi}}$ that minimizes $E[\|\boldsymbol{\xi} - \hat{\boldsymbol{\xi}}\|^2]$. The reader should verify that $E[\|\mathbf{X} - \boldsymbol{\xi}\|^2] = p\sigma^2$ and that $\mathbf{X}$ is the maximum likelihood estimator for $\boldsymbol{\xi}$.

James and Stein restrict the class of estimators of $\boldsymbol{\xi}$ to those of the form $\hat{\boldsymbol{\xi}} = \phi(\|\mathbf{X}\|^2)\mathbf{X}$, where $\phi(\ )$ is a scalar function.[1] Then

[1]This restriction is an example of the principle (mentioned in Section 6.2.3) of finding an estimator with smallest risk in a given class. As will be seen below, $\phi(\|\mathbf{X}\|^2)$ is further restricted to be of the

$$\begin{aligned} R(\hat{\boldsymbol{\xi}}, \boldsymbol{\xi}) &= E[\|\phi(\|\mathbf{X}\|^2)\mathbf{X} - \boldsymbol{\xi}\|^2] \\ &= E[\phi^2(\|\mathbf{X}\|^2)\|\mathbf{X}\|^2 - 2\phi(\|\mathbf{X}\|^2)\boldsymbol{\xi}'\mathbf{X}] + \|\boldsymbol{\xi}\|^2. \end{aligned} \quad \textbf{(7.1.1)}$$

We temporarily let $\sigma^2 = 1$ and start by considering the first term. From the assumptions made above, $\|\mathbf{X}\|^2$ is distributed as $\chi'^2(p, \|\boldsymbol{\xi}\|^2/2)$, which may be regarded as a Poisson-weighted sum of central $\chi^2$; that is, $\|\mathbf{X}\|^2$ is distributed as $\chi^2_{p+2K}$, where $K$ has a Poisson distribution with mean $\|\boldsymbol{\xi}\|^2/2$. (See Section 6.3.) Then

$$E[\phi^2(\|\mathbf{X}\|^2)\|\mathbf{X}\|^2] = E[\phi^2(\chi^2_{p+2K})\chi^2_{p+2K}]. \quad \textbf{(7.1.2)}$$

Computation of the second term of (7.1.1), $E[\phi(\|\mathbf{X}\|^2)\boldsymbol{\xi}'\mathbf{X}]$, is the next step. Since $\mathbf{X}$ is a vector in $p$-dimensional space, we are free to choose a coordinate system (or basis) for it. It will prove convenient to use $\boldsymbol{\xi}$ as one of the basis vectors and then take $p - 1$ other vectors that are mutually orthogonal and orthogonal to $\boldsymbol{\xi}$. Accordingly, the vector $\mathbf{X}$ is expressed as

$$\mathbf{X} = \left(\frac{1}{\lambda}\right)x_1\boldsymbol{\xi} + x_2\boldsymbol{\alpha}_2 + \cdots x_p\boldsymbol{\alpha}_p; \quad \textbf{(7.1.3)}$$

the $x_i$ are scalars, $\boldsymbol{\alpha}_i$ are vectors of dimension $p \times 1$, $\boldsymbol{\alpha}_i'\boldsymbol{\xi} = 0$ $(i = 2, \ldots, p)$,

$$\boldsymbol{\alpha}_i'\boldsymbol{\alpha}_j = \begin{cases} 0 & i \neq j \\ 1 & i = j, \end{cases}$$

and $\lambda = \|\boldsymbol{\xi}\|$. In this basis $\boldsymbol{\xi}'\mathbf{X} = x_1\boldsymbol{\xi}'\boldsymbol{\xi}/\lambda = \lambda x_1$. Then

$$\begin{aligned} E[\phi(\|\mathbf{X}\|^2)\boldsymbol{\xi}'\mathbf{X}] &= \lambda E[\phi(\|\mathbf{X}\|^2)x_1] \\ &= \frac{\lambda}{(2\pi)^{p/2}} \int \cdots \int x_1\phi(\|\mathbf{x}\|^2) \exp\left\{-\frac{1}{2}(\mathbf{x} - \boldsymbol{\xi})'(\mathbf{x} - \boldsymbol{\xi})\right\} d\mathbf{x}. \end{aligned} \quad \textbf{(7.1.4)}$$

It is easy to see that

$$-\frac{1}{2}(\mathbf{x} - \boldsymbol{\xi})'(\mathbf{x} - \boldsymbol{\xi}) = -\frac{1}{2}\|\mathbf{x}\|^2 - \frac{\lambda^2}{2} + \lambda x_1. \quad \textbf{(7.1.5)}$$

The integral (7.1.4) can therefore be expressed as

$$\frac{\lambda e^{-\lambda^2/2}}{(2\pi)^{p/2}} \int \cdots \int x_1\phi(\|\mathbf{x}\|^2) \exp\left\{-\frac{1}{2}\|\mathbf{x}\|^2 + \lambda x_1\right\} d\mathbf{x}. \quad \textbf{(7.1.6)}$$

The $x_1$ factor may be removed by the following partial differentiation:

$$\begin{aligned} &\frac{\lambda e^{-\lambda^2/2}}{(2\pi)^{p/2}} \int \cdots \int x_1\phi(\|\mathbf{x}\|^2) \exp\left\{-\frac{1}{2}\|\mathbf{x}\|^2 + \lambda x_1\right\} d\mathbf{x} \\ &= \frac{\lambda e^{-\lambda^2/2}}{(2\pi)^{p/2}} \frac{\partial}{\partial\lambda} \int \cdots \int \phi(\|\mathbf{x}\|^2) \exp\left\{-\frac{1}{2}\|\mathbf{x}\|^2 + \lambda x_1\right\} d\mathbf{x} \\ &= \frac{\lambda e^{-\lambda^2/2}}{(2\pi)^{p/2}} \frac{\partial}{\partial\lambda} \int \cdots \int e^{\lambda^2/2}\phi(\|\mathbf{x}\|^2) \exp\left\{-\frac{1}{2}\|\mathbf{x}\|^2 - \frac{\lambda^2}{2} + \lambda x_1\right\} d\mathbf{x} \\ &= \lambda e^{-\lambda^2/2} \frac{\partial}{\partial\lambda} e^{\lambda^2/2} E[\phi(\|\mathbf{x}\|^2)], \end{aligned} \quad \textbf{(7.1.7)}$$

---

form $1 - cS/\|\mathbf{X}\|^2$. Although the restriction is arbitrary, it does lead to an estimator that both dominates the MLE and is relatively easy to compute.

where the last step is justified by (7.1.5).

Using again the result that $\|\mathbf{X}\|^2$ is distributed as a noncentral $\chi^2$, we continue from (7.1.7):

$$= \lambda e^{-\lambda^2/2} \frac{\partial}{\partial\lambda} e^{\lambda^2/2} \left\{ e^{-\lambda^2/2} \sum_{k=0}^{\infty} \frac{(\lambda^2/2)^k}{k!} E[\phi(\chi^2_{p+2k})|k] \right\}$$

$$= \lambda e^{-\lambda^2/2} \sum_{k=0}^{\infty} \frac{\lambda k(\lambda^2/2)^{k-1}}{k!} E[\phi(\chi^2_{p+2k})|k]$$

$$= \sum_{k=0}^{\infty} \frac{e^{-\lambda^2/2}(\lambda^2/2)^k}{k!} 2kE[\phi(\chi^2_{p+2k})|k]$$

$$= 2E[K\phi(\chi^2_{p+2K})].$$

The expectation in the last equation is taken over the two random variables, $K$ and $\chi^2_{p+2K}$.

The original risk (7.1.1) may therefore be written as

$$E[\|\phi(\|\mathbf{X}\|^2)\mathbf{X} - \xi\|^2] = E[\chi^2_{p+2K}\phi^2(\chi^2_{p+2K})] - 4E[K\phi(\chi^2_{p+2K})] + \|\xi\|^2. \quad \textbf{(7.1.8)}$$

To remove the restriction that $\sigma^2 = 1$, we utilize the statistic $S$, which is independent of $\mathbf{X}$ and therefore of $\|\mathbf{X}\|^2$. This is done by modifying the original risk function to

$$E\left[\|\phi\left(\frac{\|\mathbf{X}\|^2}{S}\right)\mathbf{X} - \xi\|^2\right]. \quad \textbf{(7.1.9)}$$

But since $\|\mathbf{X}\|^2$ is independent of $S$, the only modification needed in the derivation above is to include a term for the density of $S$; this affects none of the results, except that the $S$ appears under each of the $\chi^2$ terms that appear in $\phi(\ \ )$ and $\phi^2(\ \ )$; thus

$$E\left[\|\phi\left(\frac{\|\mathbf{X}\|^2}{S}\right)\mathbf{X} - \xi\|\right]^2 = \sigma^2 E\left[\left\|\phi\left(\frac{\|\mathbf{X}/\sigma\|^2}{S/\sigma^2}\right)\frac{\mathbf{X}}{\sigma} - \frac{\xi}{\sigma}\right\|^2\right]. \quad \textbf{(7.1.10)}$$

Now, $\|\mathbf{X}/\sigma\|^2$ is distributed as a noncentral $\chi^2$ with $p$ degrees of freedom and noncentrality parameter $\xi'\xi/2\sigma^2$, so that (7.1.10) can be written as

$$\sigma^2\left\{E\left[\chi^2_{p+2K}\phi^2\left(\frac{\chi^2_{p+2K}}{S/\sigma^2}\right)\right] - 4E\left[K\phi\left(\frac{\chi^2_{p+2K}}{S/\sigma^2}\right)\right] + \left\|\frac{\xi}{\sigma}\right\|^2\right\}. \quad \textbf{(7.1.11)}$$

James and Stein restrict $\phi(\|\mathbf{X}\|^2/S)$ to be of the form $1 - c/u$, where $c$ is a constant and $u = \|\mathbf{X}\|^2/S$. Then (7.1.11) may be rewritten as

$$\sigma^2\left\{E\left[\chi^2_{p+2K}\left(1 - \frac{cS/\sigma^2}{\chi^2_{p+2K}}\right)^2\right]\right.$$
$$\left. - 4E\left[K\left(1 - \frac{cS/\sigma^2}{\chi^2_{p+2K}}\right)\right] + \left\|\frac{\xi}{\sigma}\right\|^2\right\} \quad \textbf{(7.1.12)}$$

$$= \sigma^2\left\{E[\chi^2_{p+2K}] - 2cE\left[\frac{S}{\sigma^2}\right] + c^2E\left[\frac{S^2/\sigma^4}{\chi^2_{p+2K}}\right]\right.$$
$$\left. - 4E(K) + 4cE\left[\frac{KS/\sigma^2}{\chi^2_{p+2k}}\right] + \left\|\frac{\xi}{\sigma}\right\|^2\right\}. \quad \textbf{(7.1.13)}$$

The above may be simplified with the use of the following results, which are derived in Section 6.3:

$$E(\chi^2_{p+2K}) = p + 2E(K); \qquad E\left(\frac{S}{\sigma^2}\right) = n;$$

$$E(K) = \frac{\|\xi\|^2}{2\sigma^2}; \qquad E\left(\frac{1}{\chi^2_{p+2K}}\right) = E\left(\frac{1}{p + 2K - 2}\right), \qquad p > 2; \qquad \textbf{(7.1.14)}$$

and $E(S^2/\sigma^4) = n(n + 2)$. In addition, since $S$ and $\|\mathbf{X}\|^2$ are independent we have $E(S/\chi^2_{p+2K}) = E(S)E(1/(p + 2K - 2))$.

Using these results, the loss function may be written as

$$\sigma^2\left\{p + 2E(K) - 2nc + c^2n(n + 2)E\left(\frac{1}{p + 2K - 2}\right)\right.$$

$$\left.- 4E(K) + 4cnE\left(\frac{K}{p + 2K - 2}\right) + \left\|\frac{\xi}{\sigma}\right\|^2\right\}$$

$$= \sigma^2\left\{p + cn[c(n + 2) - 2(p - 2)]E\left(\frac{1}{p + 2K - 2}\right)\right\}. \qquad \textbf{(7.1.15)}$$

Note that (7.1.14) requires that there be more than two parameters to estimate. Earlier work of Stein (1956) had shown that the maximum likelihood estimator is admissible when $p \leq 2$.

Since $E(1/(p + 2K - 2)) > 0$ and $E[\|\mathbf{X} - \xi\|^2] = p\sigma^2$, the James-Stein estimator $(1 - c/u)\mathbf{X}$ has a smaller risk than $\mathbf{X}$ if and only if

$$c > 0 \quad \text{and} \quad c(n + 2) - 2(p - 2) < 0,$$

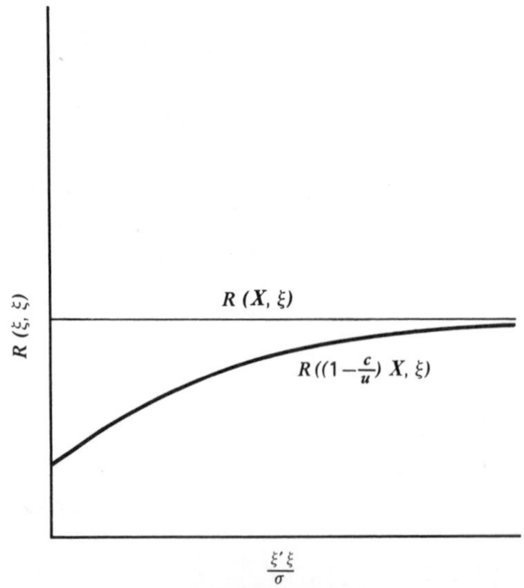


**FIGURE 7.1 Risk functions for maximum likelihood and James-Stein estimators.**

or

$$0 < c < \frac{2(p-2)}{n+2}. \tag{7.1.16}$$

That is, for any choice of $c$ in this interval the James-Stein estimator dominates, under the quadratic loss criterion, the usual estimator (which is the maximum likelihood estimator) for estimating $p$ means, when $p > 2$. It may be verified by differentiating Equation 7.1.15 with respect to $c$ that the risk function is minimized by choosing $c = (p-2)/(n+2)$. If we set $c$ at that value and rewrite the last expression for $E[\|\hat{\boldsymbol{\xi}} - \boldsymbol{\xi}\|^2]$, we have

$$E[\|\hat{\boldsymbol{\xi}} - \boldsymbol{\xi}\|^2] = \sigma^2\left[p - \frac{n(p-2)^2}{n+2}E\left(\frac{1}{p+2K-2}\right)\right]. \tag{7.1.17}$$

Since $E(K) = \|\boldsymbol{\xi}\|^2/2\sigma^2$, $E(1/(p+2K-2))$ is largest when $\|\boldsymbol{\xi}/\sigma\|^2$ is small and goes to zero as $\|\boldsymbol{\xi}/\sigma\|^2 \to \infty$. Accordingly, the difference between $E[\|\mathbf{X} - \boldsymbol{\xi}\|^2]$ and $E[\|(1-(c/u))\mathbf{X} - \boldsymbol{\xi}\|^2]$ is greatest for small $\|\boldsymbol{\xi}/\sigma\|^2$ and goes to zero as $\|\boldsymbol{\xi}/\sigma\|^2 \to \infty$; see Figure 7.1.

Before discussing the James-Stein approach in more detail, a variant of it—the positive part estimator—will be mentioned. Consider Equation 7.1.12:

$$E\left[\left\|\left(1-\frac{c}{u}\right)\mathbf{X} - \boldsymbol{\xi}\right\|^2\right]$$

$$= \sigma^2\left\{E\left[\chi^2_{p+2K}\left(1 - \frac{cS/\sigma^2}{\chi^2_{p+2K}}\right)^2\right] - 4E\left[K\left(1 - \frac{cS/\sigma^2}{\chi^2_{p+2K}}\right)\right] + \left\|\frac{\boldsymbol{\xi}}{\sigma}\right\|^2\right\}.$$

If $\phi < 0$ (i.e., $c > \|\mathbf{X}\|^2/S$), the middle term in (7.1.12) will be positive, causing the risk function to be higher than it would be if $\phi(\|\mathbf{X}\|^2/S) = 0$. Accordingly, if we define

$$a^+ = \begin{cases} a, & \text{if } a > 0 \\ 0, & \text{if } a \leqslant 0 \end{cases}$$

(where $a$ is any function of the random variables $X$ and $S$), the *positive part estimator* is $(1 - (cS/\|\mathbf{X}\|^2))^+\mathbf{X}$, and it dominates the James-Stein estimator since it equals the latter when $\phi > 0$ and has a lower risk if $\phi \leqslant 0$. The positive part estimator is due to Baranchik (1964).

The positive part estimator is closely related to the commonly used preliminary test estimator: Suppose it is decided to estimate a set of coefficients as $\mathbf{0}$ unless they are jointly statistically significant according to the usual test, based on $(\|\mathbf{X}\|^2/p)/(S/n) = f$, which has a central $F$-distribution under the null hypothesis. In this case, the estimator will be $\mathbf{0}$ if $f < f_0$ and $\mathbf{X}$ if $f \geqslant f_0$, where $f_0$ is the critical value. More about this estimator appears in Chapter 8.

Both the James-Stein and the positive part estimators are formed by multiplying the maximum likelihood estimator by a number with absolute value between 0 and 1. For this reason they may be regarded as pulling the maximum likelihood estimator toward the zero vector. A slight modification permits the pulling to be toward an arbitrary $\boldsymbol{\beta}$: $(1-(c/u))(\mathbf{X} - \boldsymbol{\beta}) + \boldsymbol{\beta}$ or $(1-(c/u))^+(\mathbf{X} - \boldsymbol{\beta}) + \boldsymbol{\beta}$.

Ullah (1974) has derived expressions for the exact moments of the James-Stein estimators and approximations of those moments to order $1/T^2$, where there are $T$ observations. The latter are given by

$$E[(\hat{\xi}_i - \xi_i)] = \frac{-a(K-2)}{\xi'\xi/\sigma^2}\,\xi_i\left[1 - \frac{p-2}{\xi'\xi/\sigma^2} - \frac{2}{T}\right]$$

$$E[(\hat{\xi}_i - \xi_i)^2] = \sigma^2 + \frac{a(K-2)}{\xi'\xi/2\sigma^2}\left[\frac{\xi_i^2}{\xi'\xi/2\sigma^2} - \sigma^2\right],$$

where $0 < a \leqslant 2$. Ullah shows that the distribution of $\hat{\xi}_i$ is negatively skewed if $\xi_i > 0$ and positively skewed otherwise. The kurtosis coefficient[2] (up to order $1/T^2$) is 3, the same as that of a normal distribution. The exact distribution of $\hat{\boldsymbol{\xi}}$ has not been derived at the time of this writing.

The James-Stein result is both surprising and counter-intuitive. It is remarkable to find an estimator that dominates the maximum likelihood estimator—one that has a lower risk for any value of the parameter—in view of the generally desirable properties of the latter. This surprise leads to the question of what is the source of the gain. Two possibilities, intuitively appealing, are at once ruled out: the gain is not due to some advantage in estimating $\sigma^2$, since the gain exists even if $\sigma^2$ is known.[3] And it is not due to an interrelationship among the components of $\mathbf{X}$, since those components are assumed independent. Why a joint estimation procedure, such as the James-Stein approach, should lead to a gain over individual estimators when the estimators being combined are statistically independent is a puzzling question. As Hill (1974) puts it:

> Surely it is criminal to use data concerning the temperature on Venus to adjust census data, and yet in principle this is what [the James-Stein estimator] does.

Hill goes on to show that the maximum likelihood estimator is admissible if a reasonable restriction is imposed—the estimator of $\xi_i$ should depend only on the corresponding $X_i$. We return to the source of the gain from using the James-Stein estimator in Section 7.3.

Several interesting empirical applications of the James-Stein procedure are presented by Efron and Morris (1974, 1977). They estimate the batting averages of 18 major league baseball players for the entire 1970 season based on their averages after their first 45 times at bat. If $\bar{y}$ is the overall average for 18 players and $y_i$ the $i$th player's average after 45 times at bat, the estimate of the $i$th player's batting average, $z_i$, was determined by $z_i = \bar{y} + (1 - ((K-3)\sigma^2)/(\Sigma(y_i - \bar{y})^2)(y_i - \bar{y})$; $\sigma^2$ was estimated from the data. It was found that the $z_i$ had a lower mean squared error than the $y_i$ when compared to the batting averages at the end of the season. Other empirical applications are mentioned in Section 8.3.

[2]The kurtosis coefficient for a random variable $X$, where $E[X] = \mu$ and $\mathrm{Var}(X) = \sigma^2$, is defined as $E[(X-\mu)^4]/\sigma^4$.

[3]To see this, refer to the risk function before $S$ is introduced and let $\sigma^2 = 1$. Verify that $E[\|\phi(\|\mathbf{X}\|^2)\mathbf{X} - \boldsymbol{\xi}\|^2] = p + c[c - 2(p-2)]E(1/(p + 2K - 2))$. This is less than $p$ if $0 < c < 2(p-2)$, and the risk is minimized at $c = p - 2$.

## 7.2 Applications of the James-Stein Approach to Regression

In the usual regression setup, with $p$ independent variables and $n + p$ observations, we can restate the James-Stein result as follows: If $\hat{\boldsymbol{\beta}} \sim N(\boldsymbol{\beta}, \sigma^2 I)$, where $\hat{\boldsymbol{\beta}}$ is the ordinary least squares estimator, and if $\boldsymbol{\beta}$ contains more than two components, then $\hat{\boldsymbol{\beta}}$ is dominated by an estimator of the form $(1 - (c\|\mathbf{y} - X\hat{\boldsymbol{\beta}}\|^2)/\|\hat{\boldsymbol{\beta}}\|^2)\hat{\boldsymbol{\beta}}$ which, in turn, is dominated by the positive part estimator $(1 - (c\|\mathbf{y} - X\hat{\boldsymbol{\beta}}\|)^2/\|\hat{\boldsymbol{\beta}}\|^2)^+\hat{\boldsymbol{\beta}}$, $0 < c < 2(p - 2)/(n + 2)$.

However, the assumption that $\text{Cov}(\hat{\boldsymbol{\beta}}) = \sigma^2 I$ is a very special case. In the usual regression model $\text{Cov}(\hat{\boldsymbol{\beta}}) = \sigma^2(X'X)^{-1}$, so that the case we have discussed applies only if the set of independent variables are normalized and orthogonal; that is, $X'X = I$. One possibility [see Sclove (1968)] is to orthogonalize the variables and then apply the above theorem to the transformed variables: Let $P$ be a matrix with the property that $P'X'XP = I$. Then $\mathbf{y} = X\boldsymbol{\beta} + \boldsymbol{\epsilon} = XPP^{-1}\boldsymbol{\beta} + \boldsymbol{\epsilon} = XP\boldsymbol{\gamma} + \boldsymbol{\epsilon}$ where $\boldsymbol{\gamma} = P^{-1}\boldsymbol{\beta}$. In this setup, $\hat{\boldsymbol{\gamma}} = (P'X'XP)^{-1} P'X'\mathbf{y}$ and $\text{Cov}(\hat{\boldsymbol{\gamma}}) = \sigma^2 I$. The James-Stein method can therefore be applied to $\hat{\boldsymbol{\gamma}}$. There is a difficulty with this approach, however. The usual risk function for $\mathbf{g}$ (an estimator of $\boldsymbol{\gamma}$) is $R(\mathbf{g}, \boldsymbol{\gamma}) = E[\|\mathbf{g} - \boldsymbol{\gamma}\|^2] = E[\|P^{-1}\mathbf{b} - P^{-1}\boldsymbol{\beta}\|^2]$, where $\mathbf{b}$ is an estimator of $\boldsymbol{\beta}$. The last expression may be written as

$$R(\mathbf{g}, \boldsymbol{\gamma}) = E[(\mathbf{b} - \boldsymbol{\beta})'(P^{-1})'P^{-1}(\mathbf{b} - \boldsymbol{\beta})] = E[(\mathbf{b} - \boldsymbol{\beta})'X'X(\mathbf{b} - \boldsymbol{\beta})], \quad \textbf{(7.2.1)}$$

which is not the risk function that we would usually consider; the latter would be $E[(\mathbf{b} - \boldsymbol{\beta})'(\mathbf{b} - \boldsymbol{\beta})]$. The orthogonalization of the $X$'s has led to a change in the risk function. Although the James-Stein approach leads to an improved estimator of $\boldsymbol{\gamma}$, it may not improve an estimator of $\boldsymbol{\beta}$. It is therefore necessary to tackle the problem of the risk when the covariance matrix of the estimator is not of the form $\sigma^2 I$. Before discussing this further, we note that the risk function being examined after the transformation, $E[(\mathbf{b} - \boldsymbol{\beta})'X'X(\mathbf{b} - \boldsymbol{\beta})]$, may be of interest in its own right. Rewriting (7.2.1) as $E[(X\mathbf{b} - X\boldsymbol{\beta})'(X\mathbf{b} - X\boldsymbol{\beta})]$, we see that it may be interpreted as a function of the differences between the predicted values and the expected values of the sample $\mathbf{y}$. This risk function has been termed a "prediction goal" by Aigner and Judge (1977), and the previous discussion of the James-Stein and related estimators may be used to show that these dominate the usual estimator (for $p > 2$) under that goal.[4] The original criterion, $E[\|\mathbf{b} - \boldsymbol{\beta}\|^2]$, has been termed the "estimation goal." Since it is shown in what follows that James-Stein estimators may not dominate OLS under the estimation goal even when more than two parameters are to be estimated, the particular quadratic loss function adopted may make a difference in the choice of estimators and the resulting estimates. Some comments about which criterion is preferred are therefore in order.

If the econometric research is being undertaken for the general purpose of parameter estimation without a well-defined objective, the estimation goal (with units of measurement chosen to reflect the relative weight of the coefficients) seems to be the more appropriate of the two. A goal based on the difference between $X\mathbf{b}$ and $X\boldsymbol{\beta}$ seems extraneous, especially if different sets of $X$ will appear in further research. In that case, it is of interest to consider the performance of various estimators under a "forecast goal,"

[4]Note that this risk function does not depend on the measurement units of the independent variables.

one that is concerned with $E[\|\mathbf{X}_f\mathbf{b} - \mathbf{X}_f\boldsymbol{\beta}\|^2]$, where $\mathbf{X}_f$ is to be set and $y_f$ observed. This criterion can alternatively be expressed as $E[\|\hat{y}_f - E(y_f)\|^2]$, which is an out-of-sample forecast problem. Problems of this type are discussed in Judge and Bock (1978, Chapter 12).

We return to the problem of estimating $\boldsymbol{\beta}$ under the risk function $E[\|\mathbf{b} - \boldsymbol{\beta}\|^2]$ when $\text{Cov}(\hat{\boldsymbol{\beta}})$ is assumed known up to a scalar, but is not diagonal. It is necessary to compute $E[\|b(\mathbf{y}) - \boldsymbol{\beta}\|^2]$, where $b(\mathbf{y})$ is an estimator of $\boldsymbol{\beta}$ of the form $h(\hat{\boldsymbol{\beta}}'X'X\hat{\boldsymbol{\beta}})\hat{\boldsymbol{\beta}}$ and $h$ is a nonnegative scalar function of $\hat{\boldsymbol{\beta}}'X'X\hat{\boldsymbol{\beta}}$. We assume the existence of a statistic $S/\sigma^2 \sim \chi^2_n$, independent of $\hat{\boldsymbol{\beta}}'X'X\hat{\boldsymbol{\beta}}$, and assume temporarily that $\sigma^2 = 1$. Then

$$R(\mathbf{b}, \boldsymbol{\beta}) = E[\|h(\ )\hat{\boldsymbol{\beta}} - \boldsymbol{\beta}\|^2] = E[h^2(\ )\hat{\boldsymbol{\beta}}'\hat{\boldsymbol{\beta}}] - 2\boldsymbol{\beta}'E[h(\ )\hat{\boldsymbol{\beta}}] + \boldsymbol{\beta}'\boldsymbol{\beta}. \quad \textbf{(7.2.2)}$$

To evaluate the two expected values, a theorem of Bock (1975) is used[5]:

**Theorem 7.2.1**

Let $\mathbf{Z} \sim N_p(\boldsymbol{\theta}, I)$ and $h(\ )$ be a nonnegative function, where $\boldsymbol{\theta}' = (\theta_1, \ldots, \theta_p)$ and $\mathbf{Z}' = (Z_1, \ldots, Z_p)$. Then $E[h(\mathbf{Z}'\mathbf{Z})Z_i] = \theta_i E\{h(\chi'^2(p + 2, \boldsymbol{\theta}'\boldsymbol{\theta}/2))\}$.

**Proof**

Since the $Z_i$'s are independent,

$$\begin{aligned} E[h(\mathbf{Z}'\mathbf{Z})Z_i] &= E\left\{E\left[h(Z_i^2 + \sum_{i\neq j} Z_j^2)Z_i \,\middle|\, \sum_{i\neq j} Z_j^2\right]\right\} \\ &= E\left\{\frac{1}{(2\pi)^{1/2}}\int_{-\infty}^{\infty} h\left(Z_i^2 + \sum_{i\neq j} Z_j^2\right)Z_i \exp\left\{-\frac{1}{2}(Z_i - \theta_i)^2\right\} dZ_i\right\} \\ &= E\left\{\frac{1}{(2\pi)^{1/2}} e^{-\theta_i^2/2}\int_{-\infty}^{\infty} h\left(Z_i^2 + \sum_{i\neq j} Z_j^2\right)Z_i \exp\left\{-\frac{1}{2}Z_i^2 + \theta_i Z_i\right\} dZ_i\right\}. \end{aligned}$$

Next, separate the range of integration,

$$\begin{aligned} &\int_{-\infty}^{\infty} h\left(Z_i^2 + \sum_{i\neq j} Z_j^2\right)Z_i \exp\left\{-\frac{1}{2}Z_i^2 + \theta_i Z_i\right\} dZ_i \\ &= \int_0^{\infty} h(\ )Z_i \exp\left\{-\frac{1}{2}Z_i^2 + \theta_i Z_i\right\} dZ_i \\ &\quad + \int_{-\infty}^{0} h(\ )Z_i \exp\left\{-\frac{Z_i^2}{2} + \theta_i Z_i\right\} dZ_i, \end{aligned} \qquad \textbf{(7.2.3)}$$

[5]Note that Bock defines the noncentrality parameter without dividing by 2 in the original article and that Bock's notation differs somewhat from ours.

and replace $Z_i$ by $-Z_i$ in the second integral of (7.2.3), which then equals

$$-\int_0^\infty h(\quad)Z_i \exp\left\{-\frac{1}{2}Z_i^2 - \theta_i Z_i\right\} dZ_i. \tag{7.2.4}$$

The transformation $\omega = Z_i^2$ yields

$$E[h(\mathbf{Z}'\mathbf{Z})Z_i] = E\left\{\frac{e^{-\theta_i^2/2}}{2(2\pi)^{1/2}}\int_0^\infty h\left(\omega + \sum_{i\neq j} Z_j^2\right)e^{-\omega/2}\,(e^{\theta_i\omega^{1/2}} - e^{-\theta_i\omega^{1/2}})\,d\omega\right\}; \tag{7.2.5}$$

the term $e^{\theta_i\omega^{1/2}} - e^{-\theta_i\omega^{1/2}}$ may be expanded in a Taylor series:

$$e^{\theta_i\omega^{1/2}} - e^{-\theta_i\omega^{1/2}} = \sum_{k=0}^{\infty}\frac{2(\theta_i\omega^{1/2})^{2k+1}}{(2k+1)!}, \tag{7.2.6}$$

and $(2K+1)! = (2K+1)2K\Gamma(2K) = (2K+1)2K\Gamma(K)\Gamma((2K+1)/2)2^{2K-1}\pi^{-1/2}$.[The fact that $\Gamma(2K) = \Gamma(K)\Gamma((2K+1)/2)2^{2K-1}\pi^{-1/2}$ may be verified by mathematical induction.] Making these substitutions and simplifying, Bock rewrites the expectation as

$$\theta_i E\left\{\int_0^\infty h\left(\omega + \sum_{i\neq j} Z_j^2\right)\left[e^{-\theta_i^2/2}\sum_{k=0}^{\infty}\frac{(\theta_i^2/2)^k\omega^{(2k+3)/2-1}e^{-\omega/2}}{k!\Gamma\left(\dfrac{2k+3}{2}\right)2^{(2k+3)/2}}\right]d\omega\right\}. \tag{7.2.7}$$

The bracketed term in the integral is the density of a noncentral $\chi^2$ variable with 3 degrees of freedom and noncentrality parameter $\theta_i^2/2$, denoted by $\chi'^2(3, \theta_i^2/2)$. Accordingly,

$$E[h(\mathbf{Z}'\mathbf{Z})Z_i] = \theta_i E\left\{h\left(\chi'^2\left(3, \frac{\theta_i^2}{2}\right) + \sum_{i\neq j} Z_j^2\right)\right\}. \tag{7.2.8}$$

Finally, since $\Sigma_{i\neq j} Z_j^2 \sim \chi'^2(p-1, \Sigma_{i\neq j}\theta_j^2/2)$, independent of $Z_i^2$, we have the result

$$E[h(\mathbf{Z}'\mathbf{Z})Z_i] = \theta_i E\left[h\left(\chi'^2\left(p+2, \frac{\boldsymbol{\theta}'\boldsymbol{\theta}}{2}\right)\right)\right]. \tag{7.2.9}$$ □

A similar theorem proved by Bock (1975) is as follows:

**Theorem 7.2.2**

$$E[h(\mathbf{Z}'\mathbf{Z})Z_i^2] = E\left[h\left(\chi'^2\left(p+2, \frac{\boldsymbol{\theta}'\boldsymbol{\theta}}{2}\right)\right)\right] + \theta_i^2 E\left[h\left(\chi'^2\left(p+4, \frac{\boldsymbol{\theta}'\boldsymbol{\theta}}{2}\right)\right)\right]. \tag{7.2.10}$$

To employ these results in evaluating the risk function, let

$$\mathbf{Z} = P\hat{\boldsymbol{\beta}}, \qquad \text{where} \quad P(X'X)^{-1}P' = I. \tag{7.2.11}$$

Therefore $\mathbf{Z} \sim N_p(P\boldsymbol{\beta}, I)$, and the previous theorem may be applied to $P\hat{\boldsymbol{\beta}}$ and $\boldsymbol{\theta} = P\boldsymbol{\beta}$. Turning first to the middle term of the risk function, and making the above transformation, we have

$$\begin{aligned}
-2\boldsymbol{\beta}'E[h(\hat{\boldsymbol{\beta}}'X'X\hat{\boldsymbol{\beta}})\hat{\boldsymbol{\beta}}] &= -2\boldsymbol{\beta}'E[h(\mathbf{Z}'\mathbf{Z})P^{-1}\mathbf{Z}] \\
&= -2\boldsymbol{\beta}'P^{-1}E[h(\mathbf{Z}'\mathbf{Z})\begin{bmatrix} Z_1 \\ Z_2 \\ \cdot \\ \cdot \\ \cdot \\ Z_p \end{bmatrix} \\
&= -2\boldsymbol{\beta}'P^{-1}E\left[h\left[\chi'^2\left(p+2, \frac{\boldsymbol{\theta}'\boldsymbol{\theta}}{2}\right)\right]\right]\boldsymbol{\theta} \\
&= -2\boldsymbol{\beta}'P^{-1}E\left[h\left[\chi'^2\left(p+2, \frac{\boldsymbol{\theta}'\boldsymbol{\theta}}{2}\right)\right]\right]P\boldsymbol{\beta} \\
&= -2\boldsymbol{\beta}'\boldsymbol{\beta}E\left[h\left[\chi'^2\left(p+2, \frac{\boldsymbol{\theta}'\boldsymbol{\theta}}{2}\right)\right]\right]. \qquad \textbf{(7.2.12)}
\end{aligned}$$

The two theorems are next used to compute the first term in the risk function:

$$\begin{aligned}
E[h^2(\hat{\boldsymbol{\beta}}'X'X\hat{\boldsymbol{\beta}})\hat{\boldsymbol{\beta}}'\hat{\boldsymbol{\beta}}] &= E[h^2(\mathbf{Z}'\mathbf{Z})\mathbf{Z}'(P^{-1})'P^{-1}\mathbf{Z}] \\
&= E[h^2(\mathbf{Z}'\mathbf{Z})\mathbf{Z}'A\mathbf{Z}] \\
&= E[h^2(\mathbf{Z}'\mathbf{Z})\ \Sigma_i\ \Sigma_j\ a_{ij}Z_iZ_j] \\
&= \Sigma_i\ \Sigma_j\ a_{ij}E[h^2(\mathbf{Z}'\mathbf{Z})Z_iZ_j], \qquad \textbf{(7.2.13)}
\end{aligned}$$

where $\{a_{ij}\} = A = (P^{-1})'P^{-1}$. For $i \neq j$, we employ Theorem 7.2.1 twice, with $h^2(\ \ )$ in place of $h(\ \ )$:

$$\begin{aligned}
\sum_{i \neq j}\sum a_{ij}E[h^2(\mathbf{Z}'\mathbf{Z})Z_iZ_j] &= \sum_{i \neq j}\sum a_{ij}\theta_i E\left\{h^2\left(\chi'^2\left(p+2, \frac{\boldsymbol{\theta}'\boldsymbol{\theta}}{2}\right)\right)Z_j\right\} \\
&= \sum_{i \neq j}\sum a_{ij}\theta_i\theta_j E\left\{h^2\left(\chi'^2\left(p+4, \frac{\boldsymbol{\theta}'\boldsymbol{\theta}}{2}\right)\right)\right\}. \qquad \textbf{(7.2.14)}
\end{aligned}$$

For $i = j$,

$$\begin{aligned}
\sum a_{ii}E[h^2(\mathbf{Z}'\mathbf{Z})Z_i^2] &= \sum a_{ii}\left\{E\left[h^2\left(\chi'^2\left(p+2, \frac{\boldsymbol{\theta}'\boldsymbol{\theta}}{2}\right)\right)\right]\right. \\
&\quad \left. + \theta_i^2 E\left[h^2\left(\chi'^2\left(p+4, \frac{\boldsymbol{\theta}'\boldsymbol{\theta}}{2}\right)\right)\right]\right\}. \qquad \textbf{(7.2.15)}
\end{aligned}$$

Putting these terms together, we have

$$\begin{aligned}
E[h^2(\hat{\boldsymbol\beta}'X'X\hat{\boldsymbol\beta})\hat{\boldsymbol\beta}'\hat{\boldsymbol\beta}] &= \textstyle\sum_i \sum_j a_{ij}\theta_i\theta_j E\left\{h^2\left(\chi'^2\left(p+4, \frac{\boldsymbol\theta'\boldsymbol\theta}{2}\right)\right)\right\} \\
&\quad + (\operatorname{tr} A)E\left[h^2\left(\chi'^2\left(p+2, \frac{\boldsymbol\theta'\boldsymbol\theta}{2}\right)\right)\right] \\
&= \boldsymbol\theta'A\boldsymbol\theta E\left[h^2\left(\chi'^2\left(p+4, \frac{\boldsymbol\theta'\boldsymbol\theta}{2}\right)\right)\right] \\
&\quad + \operatorname{tr}(P^{-1})'P^{-1}E\left[h^2\left(\chi'^2\left(p+2, \frac{\boldsymbol\theta'\boldsymbol\theta}{2}\right)\right)\right] \\
&= \boldsymbol\beta'P'(P^{-1})'(P^{-1})P\boldsymbol\beta E\left[h^2\left(\chi'^2\left(p+4, \frac{\boldsymbol\beta'X'X\boldsymbol\beta}{2}\right)\right)\right] \\
&\quad + \operatorname{tr}(X'X)^{-1}E\left[h^2\left(\chi'^2\left(p+2, \frac{\boldsymbol\beta'X'X\boldsymbol\beta}{2}\right)\right)\right]. \qquad \textbf{(7.2.16)}
\end{aligned}$$

Substituting these results into (7.2.2) yields

$$\begin{aligned}
R(\mathbf{b}, \boldsymbol\beta) &= \boldsymbol\beta'\boldsymbol\beta E\left[h^2\left(\chi'^2\left(p+4, \frac{\boldsymbol\beta'X'X\boldsymbol\beta}{2}\right)\right)\right] \\
&\quad + \operatorname{tr}(X'X)^{-1}E\left[h^2\left(\chi'^2\left(p+2, \frac{\boldsymbol\beta'X'X\boldsymbol\beta}{2}\right)\right)\right] \\
&\quad - 2\boldsymbol\beta'\boldsymbol\beta E\left[h\left(\chi'^2\left(p+2, \frac{\boldsymbol\beta'X'X\boldsymbol\beta}{2}\right)\right)\right] + \boldsymbol\beta'\boldsymbol\beta \\
&= \operatorname{tr}(X'X)^{-1}E\left[h^2\left(\chi'^2\left(p+2, \frac{\boldsymbol\beta'X'X\boldsymbol\beta}{2}\right)\right)\right] \\
&\quad + \boldsymbol\beta'\boldsymbol\beta\left\{E\left[h^2\left(\chi'^2\left(p+4, \frac{\boldsymbol\beta'X'X\boldsymbol\beta}{2}\right)\right)\right]\right. \\
&\quad \left. - 2E\left[h\left(\chi'^2\left(p+2, \frac{\boldsymbol\beta'X'X\boldsymbol\beta}{2}\right)\right)\right] + 1\right\}. \qquad \textbf{(7.2.17)}
\end{aligned}$$

This result is generalized to the case $\sigma^2 \neq 1$ with the aid of the statistic $S$, which is distributed as $\sigma^2\chi_n^2$ independently of $\hat{\boldsymbol\beta}'X'X\hat{\boldsymbol\beta}$, in the following theorem:

**Theorem 7.2.3**

Let $\mathbf{b}(\mathbf{Y})$ be an estimator of $\boldsymbol\beta$ of the form $h(\hat{\boldsymbol\beta}'X'X\hat{\boldsymbol\beta}/S)\hat{\boldsymbol\beta}$, where $h$ is a nonnegative scalar function of $\hat{\boldsymbol\beta}'X'X\hat{\boldsymbol\beta}/S$, and let $S/\sigma^2 \sim \chi_n^2$ be independent of $\hat{\boldsymbol\beta}'X'X\hat{\boldsymbol\beta}$. Then

$$\frac{R(\mathbf{b}, \boldsymbol{\beta})}{\sigma^2} = \frac{1}{\sigma^2} E[\|\mathbf{b}(\mathbf{Y}) - \boldsymbol{\beta}\|^2]$$

$$= \text{tr}(X'X)^{-1}E[h^2(g'_{p+2})]$$

$$+ \frac{\boldsymbol{\beta}'\boldsymbol{\beta}}{\sigma^2}\{E[h^2(g'_{p+4})] - 2E[h(g'_{p+2})] + 1\}, \qquad \textbf{(7.2.18)}$$

where $g'_k \sim \chi'^2(k, \hat{\boldsymbol{\beta}}'X'X\hat{\boldsymbol{\beta}}/2\sigma^2)/\chi^2_n$, and the $\chi^2$ variates of the numerator and denominator are independent.

**Proof**

See Bock (1975). □

To derive the main result regarding the existence of an $h(\ \ )$ that yields a lower risk than that of the OLS estimator, $R(\hat{\boldsymbol{\beta}},\boldsymbol{\beta})/\sigma^2 = \text{tr}(X'X)^{-1}$, three lemmas are needed.

**Lemma 7.2.1**

Let $\phi$ be a real valued measurable function [which implies that $\phi(k)$ is a r.v.] defined on the integers. Let $K \sim$ Poisson $(\lambda/2)$. Then if both sides exist

$$\lambda E[\phi(K)] = E[2K\phi(K - 1)]. \qquad \textbf{(7.2.19)}$$

**Proof**

For the reader. (Write the left-hand side as

$$\lambda e^{-\lambda} \sum_{K=0}^{\infty} \frac{(\lambda/2)^K}{K!} \phi(K)$$

and rearrange terms.) □

**Lemma 7.2.2**

Let $h(\ \ )$ be a function with domain $(0, \infty)$ and range $(-\infty, \infty)$. Then if both sides exist,

$$E[h(\chi^2_m)] = E\left\{\frac{mh(\chi^2_{m+2})}{\chi^2_{m+2}}\right\}. \qquad \textbf{(7.2.20)}$$

**Proof**

For the reader. (Write the left-hand side as

$$\frac{1}{2^{m/2}\Gamma\left(\frac{m}{2}\right)} \int_0^\infty h(y)y^{m/2-1}e^{-y/2}\, dy,$$

multiply and divide the constant to transform it to $[2^{(m+2)/2}\Gamma((m+2)/2)]^{-1}$, and write $y^{m/2-1} = y^{(m+2)/2-1}/y$.) □

### Lemma 7.2.3

Let $S(W)$ be a monotone nondecreasing nonnegative function, $t(W)$ be a monotone nonincreasing nonnegative function, and $W$ be a nonnegative random variable. Assume $E(W)$, $E[(S(W)]$, $E[WS(W)]$, $E[t(W)]$, and $E[Wt(W)]$ exist and are finite. Then

$$E[S(W)(E(W) - W)] \leqslant 0 \leqslant E[t(W)(E(W) - W)]. \tag{7.2.21}$$

### Proof

We prove the first inequality. Since $S(W)$ is nondecreasing,

$$S(\overline{W}) \geqslant S(W), \qquad W \leqslant \overline{W}$$
$$S(\overline{W}) \leqslant S(W), \qquad W \geqslant \overline{W}.$$

Then

$$\begin{aligned}\int_0^{\infty} S(W)[W - E(W)]f(W)\,dW &= \int_0^{E(W)} S(W)[W - E(W)]f(W)\,dW \\ &\quad + \int_{E(W)}^{\infty} S(W)[W - E(W)]f(W)\,dW \\ &\geqslant \int_0^{E(W)} S(\overline{W})[W - E(W)]f(W)\,dW \\ &\quad + \int_{E(W)}^{\infty} S(\overline{W})[W - E(W)]f(W)\,dW \\ &= S(\overline{W})\int [W - E(W)]f(W)\,dW = 0.\end{aligned} \tag{7.2.22}$$

The inequality follows from $W - E(W) \leqslant 0$ and $S(\overline{W}) \geqslant S(W)$ in the first integral, so that $S(\overline{W})[W - E(W)] \leqslant S(W)[W - E(W)]$; for the second integral, $W - E(W) \geqslant 0$ and $S(\overline{W}) \leqslant S(W)$, implying $S(\overline{W})[W - E(W)] \leqslant S(W)[W - E(W)]$. □

Finally, one other result is needed: $\hat{\boldsymbol\beta}$ is a minimax estimator for $\boldsymbol\beta$ relative to a quadratic loss function; see Girshick and Savage (1951).

### Theorem 7.2.4

Let $\mathrm{tr}(X'X)^{-1} \geqslant 2d_L$, where $d_L$ is the largest characteristic root of $(X'X)^{-1}$, $p > 2$, and $r(\ )$ a function from $[0, \infty)$ to $[0, 1]$. Assume $\sigma^2$ is known. Then $\boldsymbol\theta(\hat{\boldsymbol\beta}) \equiv \hat{\boldsymbol\theta} = [1 - (cr(\hat{\boldsymbol\beta}'X'X\hat{\boldsymbol\beta}))/(\hat{\boldsymbol\beta}'X'X\hat{\boldsymbol\beta})]\hat{\boldsymbol\beta}$ is a minimax estimator for $\boldsymbol\beta$ if $0 \leqslant c \leqslant 2[(\mathrm{tr}(X'X)^{-1}/d_L) - 2]$ and $r$ is monotone nondecreasing.

### Proof

See Bock (1975). Since $(1/\sigma^2)R(\hat{\boldsymbol\beta}, \boldsymbol\beta) = \mathrm{tr}(X'X)^{-1}$, and $\hat{\boldsymbol\beta}$ is minimax as mentioned above, it suffices to show $(1/\sigma^2)R(\hat{\boldsymbol\theta}, \boldsymbol\beta) \leqslant \mathrm{tr}(X'X)^{-1}$ for all $\boldsymbol\beta$. Set $r^*(a) = r(a)/a$ and let $(1/\sigma^2)[R(\hat{\boldsymbol\theta}, \boldsymbol\beta) - \mathrm{tr}(X'X)^{-1}] = Q$.

From Theorem 7.2.3,

$$\begin{aligned} Q &= \operatorname{tr}(X'X)^{-1}E\left\{h^2\left(\chi'^2\left(p+2,\frac{\boldsymbol{\beta}'X'X\boldsymbol{\beta}}{2\sigma^2}\right)\right)\right\} \\ &+ \frac{\boldsymbol{\beta}'\boldsymbol{\beta}}{\sigma^2}\left\{E\left[h^2\left(\chi'^2\left(p+4,\frac{\boldsymbol{\beta}'X'X\boldsymbol{\beta}}{2\sigma^2}\right)\right)\right]\right. \\ &\left. - 2E\left[h\left(\chi'^2\left(p+2,\frac{\boldsymbol{\beta}'X'X\boldsymbol{\beta}}{2\sigma^2}\right)\right)\right] + 1\right\} - \operatorname{tr}(X'X)^{-1}. \end{aligned} \tag{7.2.23}$$

With $h(a) = 1 - cr^*(a)$, (7.2.23) may be rewritten as

$$\begin{aligned} Q &= \operatorname{tr}(X'X)^{-1}E\left[\left[1 - cr^*\left(\chi'^2\left(p+2,\frac{\boldsymbol{\beta}'X'X\boldsymbol{\beta}}{2\sigma^2}\right)\right)\right]^2\right] \\ &+ \frac{\boldsymbol{\beta}'\boldsymbol{\beta}}{\sigma^2}\left\{E\left[\left[1 - cr^*\left(\chi'^2\left(p+4,\frac{\boldsymbol{\beta}'X'X\boldsymbol{\beta}}{2\sigma^2}\right)\right)\right]^2\right]\right. \\ &\left. - 2E\left[1 - cr^*\left(\chi'^2\left(p+2,\frac{\boldsymbol{\beta}'X'X\boldsymbol{\beta}}{2\sigma^2}\right)\right)\right] + 1\right\} \\ &- \operatorname{tr}(X'X)^{-1} \\ &= c^2\operatorname{tr}(X'X)^{-1}E\left\{r^*\left(\chi'^2\left(p+2,\frac{\boldsymbol{\beta}'X'X\boldsymbol{\beta}}{2\sigma^2}\right)\right)^2\right\} \\ &- 2c\operatorname{tr}(X'X)^{-1}E\left[r^*\left(\chi'^2\left(p+2,\frac{\boldsymbol{\beta}'X'X\boldsymbol{\beta}}{2\sigma^2}\right)\right)\right] \\ &+ \frac{\boldsymbol{\beta}'\boldsymbol{\beta}c^2}{\sigma^2}E\left\{r^*\left(\chi'^2\left(p+4,\frac{\boldsymbol{\beta}'X'X\boldsymbol{\beta}}{2\sigma^2}\right)\right)^2\right\} \\ &- 2\frac{\boldsymbol{\beta}'\boldsymbol{\beta}c}{\sigma^2}E\left\{r^*\left(\chi'^2\left(p+4,\frac{\boldsymbol{\beta}'X'X\boldsymbol{\beta}}{2\sigma^2}\right)\right)\right\} \\ &+ 2\frac{\boldsymbol{\beta}'\boldsymbol{\beta}c}{\sigma^2}E\left\{r^*\left(\chi'^2\left(p+2,\frac{\boldsymbol{\beta}'X'X\boldsymbol{\beta}}{2\sigma^2}\right)\right)\right\} \\ &= c^2\operatorname{tr}(X'X)^{-1}E\{r^*(\chi^2_{p+2+2K})^2\} \\ &- 2c\operatorname{tr}(X'X)^{-1}E\{r^*(\chi^2_{p+2+2K})\} \\ &+ \frac{\boldsymbol{\beta}'\boldsymbol{\beta}c^2}{\sigma^2}E\{r^*(\chi^2_{p+4+2K})^2\} \\ &- 2\frac{\boldsymbol{\beta}'\boldsymbol{\beta}c}{\sigma^2}E[r^*(\chi^2_{p+4+2K})] \\ &+ 2\frac{\boldsymbol{\beta}'\boldsymbol{\beta}c}{\sigma^2}E[r^*(\chi^2_{p+2+2K})], \end{aligned} \tag{7.2.24}$$

where $K$ is a Poisson variable with parameter $\boldsymbol{\beta}'X'X\boldsymbol{\beta}/2\sigma^2$.

Taking each term in turn, we have

$$E\{r^*(\chi^2_{p+2+2K})^2\} = E\left\{\frac{r(\chi^2_{p+2+2K})^2}{(\chi^2_{p+2+2K})^2}\right\}$$

$$= E\left\{\frac{(p + 2K)r(\chi^2_{p+2+2K})^2/(p + 2K)\chi^2_{p+2+2K}}{\chi^2_{p+2+2K}}\right\}$$

$$= E\left\{\frac{r(\chi^2_{p+2K})^2}{(p + 2K)\chi^2_{p+2K}}\right\} \qquad \textbf{(7.2.25)}$$

(by Lemma 7.2.2)

$$= E\left\{\frac{(p - 2 + 2K)r(\chi^2_{p+2K})^2}{(p + 2K)(p - 2 + 2K)\chi^2_{p+2K}}\right\}$$

$$= E\{r(\chi^2_{p-2+2K})^2(p + 2K)^{-1}(p - 2 + 2K)^{-1}\} \qquad \textbf{(7.2.26)}$$

(applying Lemma 7.2.2 again). Next, we apply Lemma 7.2.2 twice to the second term:

$$E\{r^*[\chi^2_{p+2+2K}]\} = E\left\{\frac{r(\chi^2_{p+2+2K})}{\chi^2_{p+2+2K}}\right\}$$

$$= E\left\{\frac{(p + 2K)r(\chi^2_{p+2+2K})/(p + 2K)}{\chi^2_{p+2+2K}}\right\}$$

$$= E\{r(\chi^2_{p+2K})/(p + 2K)\}$$

$$= E\left\{\frac{(p - 2 + 2K)r(\chi^2_{p+2K})\chi^2_{p+2K}/(p + 2K)(p - 2 + 2K)}{\chi^2_{p+2K}}\right\}$$

$$= E\left\{\frac{r(\chi^2_{p-2+2K})\chi^2_{p-2+2K}}{(p + 2K)(p - 2 + 2K)}\right\}. \qquad \textbf{(7.2.27)}$$

Applying Lemma 7.2.2 twice to the third term yields

$$E\{[r^*(\chi^2_{p+4+2K})]^2\} = E\left\{\frac{r(\chi^2_{p+2K})^2}{(p + 2 + 2K)(p + 2K)}\right\},$$

and then use Lemma 7.2.1 with

$$\phi(K) = \frac{r(\chi^2_{p+2K})^2}{(p + 2 + 2K)(p + 2K)}$$

to obtain

$$\frac{\sigma^2}{\beta'X'X\beta} E\left\{\frac{2Kr(\chi^2_{p-2+2K})^2}{(p + 2K)(p - 2 + 2K)}\right\}. \qquad \textbf{(7.2.28)}$$

The fourth term is also rewritten using this approach:

$$E[r^*(\chi^2_{p+4+2K})] = \frac{\sigma^2}{\beta'X'X\beta} E\left\{\frac{2Kr(\chi^2_{p-2+2K})\chi^2_{p-2+2K}}{(p + 2K)(p - 2 + 2K)}\right\}. \qquad \textbf{(7.2.29)}$$

The fifth term is simplified by an application of Lemmas 7.2.2 and 7.2.1:

$$E\{r^*(\chi^2_{p+2+2K})\} = \frac{\sigma^2}{\beta' X' X\beta} E\left\{\frac{2Kr(\chi^2_{p-2+2K})}{p-2+2K}\right\}. \tag{7.2.30}$$

These terms are next substituted into (7.2.24), where $\alpha(\boldsymbol{\beta}) \equiv \boldsymbol{\beta}'\boldsymbol{\beta}/\boldsymbol{\beta}'X'X\boldsymbol{\beta}$:

$$Q = c\,\mathrm{tr}(X'X)^{-1}E\left\{\frac{r(\chi^2_{p-2K+2})}{(p+2K)(p-2+2K)}\left[(cr(\chi^2_{p-2+2K}) - 2\chi^2_{p-2+2K})\left(1 + \frac{\alpha(\beta)2K}{\mathrm{tr}(X'X)^{-1}}\right) + \frac{2K\alpha(\beta)2(p+2K)}{\mathrm{tr}(X'X)^{-1}}\right]\right\}. \tag{7.2.31}$$

Since $r(\ ) \leq 1$ by an hypothesis of the theorem, the following inequality may be derived by setting the second $r(\chi^2_{p-2+2K})$in the above expression equal to one:

$$Q \leq c\,\mathrm{tr}(X'X)^{-1}E\left\{\frac{r(\chi^2_{p-2+2K})}{(p+2K)(p-2+2K)} \times \left[2\left(1 + \alpha(\beta)\frac{2K}{\mathrm{tr}(X'X)^{-1}}\right)(p-2+2K-\chi^2_{p-2+2K}) + c - 2(p-2) + \frac{\alpha(\beta)2K}{\mathrm{tr}(X'X)^{-1}}\left(c - 2\left(\frac{\mathrm{tr}(X'X)^{-1}}{\alpha(\beta)} - 2\right)\right)\right]\right\}. \tag{7.2.32}$$

By an hypothesis of the theorem,

$$c \leq 2\left[\frac{\mathrm{tr}(X'X)^{-1}}{d_L} - 2\right], \tag{7.2.33}$$

but since $1/\alpha(\boldsymbol{\beta}) = \boldsymbol{\beta}'X'X\boldsymbol{\beta}/\boldsymbol{\beta}'\boldsymbol{\beta}$ is minimized over $\boldsymbol{\beta}$ at the value $1/\alpha(\boldsymbol{\beta}) = 1/d_L$, that is, $\alpha(\boldsymbol{\beta}) \leq d_L$, (7.2.33) implies

$$c \leq 2\left[\frac{\mathrm{tr}(X'X)^{-1}}{\alpha(\beta)} - 2\right]. \tag{7.2.34}$$

And since

$$\mathrm{tr}(X'X)^{-1} = \sum_{i=1}^{p} d_i \leq pd_L, \tag{7.2.35}$$

where $d_i$ are the characteristic roots of $(X'X)^{-1}$,

$$c \leq 2\left[\frac{\mathrm{tr}(X'X)^{-1}}{d_L} - 2\right]$$

implies

$$c \leq 2\left[\frac{pd_L}{d_L} - 2\right] = 2(p-2). \tag{7.2.36}$$

Therefore the inequality in $Q$ may be further simplified:

$$Q \leqslant \operatorname{tr}(X'X)^{-1} cE\left[\frac{r(\chi^2_{p-2+2K})}{(p+2K)(p-2+2K)} \times \left\{2\left(1+\frac{\alpha(\boldsymbol{\beta})2K}{\operatorname{tr}(X'X)^{-1}}\right)(p-2+2K-\chi^2_{p-2+2K})\right\}\right]. \tag{7.2.37}$$

Letting

$$W = \chi^2_{p-2+2K}, \qquad E[W] = p - 2 + 2K,$$

and

$$S(W) = \frac{r(\chi^2_{p-2+2K})}{(p+2K)(p-2+2K)}\left\{2\left(1+\frac{\alpha(\boldsymbol{\beta})2K}{\operatorname{tr}(X'X)^{-1}}\right)\right\}, \tag{7.2.38}$$

Lemma 7.2.3 implies

$$Q \leqslant 0. \qquad \square$$

Under the given restrictions on $r(\ )$, $p$, and $c$, the theorem indicates that $\mathbf{b(Y)}$ dominates $\hat{\boldsymbol{\beta}}$. For the case $r(\hat{\boldsymbol{\beta}}'X'X\hat{\boldsymbol{\beta}}) = 1$ and $(X'X)^{-1} = I$, this is the James-Stein estimator when $\sigma^2 = 1$. For unknown $\sigma^2$, Bock shows the existence of a minimax estimator of the form

$$\left(1 - \frac{cS}{\hat{\boldsymbol{\beta}}'X'X\hat{\boldsymbol{\beta}}}\right)\hat{\boldsymbol{\beta}}, \tag{7.2.39}$$

where $S/\sigma^2 \sim \chi^2_n$, and $S$ is independent of $\hat{\boldsymbol{\beta}}'X'X\hat{\boldsymbol{\beta}}$. This result requires

$$0 \leq c \leq \frac{2(\operatorname{tr}(X'X^{-1})/d_L - 2)}{n+2}. \qquad \textbf{(7.2.40)}^{6}$$

Bock also shows the necessity of these conditions for certain cases.

It may be seen that the presence of multicollinearity in the $X$ matrix reduces the possibility of improving on $\hat{\boldsymbol{\beta}}$ by an estimator of this type. If there is substantial multicollinearity, $d_L$ [the largest characteristic root of $(X'X)^{-1}$] will be very large (since the smallest characteristic root of $X'X$ will be very small). Accordingly, $tr(X'X)^{-1}/d_L$ will be

[6] This result is sometimes written in a slightly different form. From (7.2.39), we have

$$1 - \frac{cS}{\hat{\boldsymbol{\beta}}'X'X\hat{\boldsymbol{\beta}}} = 1 - \frac{c^*S/n}{\hat{\boldsymbol{\beta}}'X'X\hat{\boldsymbol{\beta}}/p},$$

where $c^* = cn/p$ and the random variables $S$ and $\hat{\boldsymbol{\beta}}'X'X\hat{\boldsymbol{\beta}}$ are divided by their respective degrees of freedom. In this form the condition is

$$0 \leqslant c^* \leqslant \frac{2n[\operatorname{tr}(X'X)^{-1}/d_L - 2]}{p(n+2)}$$

a very small number, possibly less than 2, in which case no choice of $c$ satisfies the required inequality. What happens with typical economic data is discussed in Section 8.3.

In brief, if the researcher is willing to adopt a quadratic loss function, both the James-Stein estimator and its positive part variant improve on the OLS estimator for all values of unknown parameters if $\text{tr}(X'X)^{-1}/d_L > 2$. If another loss function is chosen, of course, the dominance may not continue, which illustrates the importance of choosing between estimators consistently.

## 7.3 Bayesian Approaches to Quadratic Loss Functions in Regression Applications

Bayesian approaches to the concerns of this chapter are not only interesting in their own right, but also help to explain the source of the gain from following the James-Stein procedure. A comprehensive and understandable article on the subject for econometricians is that of Zellner and Vandaele (1974); a more technical paper is by Efron and Morris (1973b).[7] We follow Zellner and Vandaele in the remainder of the section.

For the Bayesian approach to the regression model

$$\mathbf{y} = X\boldsymbol{\beta} + \mathbf{u},$$

where

$$\begin{aligned} &\mathbf{y} \text{ is } T \times 1, \\ &X \text{ is } T \times k, \\ &\boldsymbol{\beta} \text{ is } k \times 1, \\ &\mathbf{u} \text{ is } T \times 1, \end{aligned}$$

and $\mathbf{u} \sim N(\mathbf{0}, \sigma^2 I)$, we must add a prior distribution on $\boldsymbol{\beta}$. It is assumed that $\boldsymbol{\beta} \sim N(\bar{\boldsymbol{\beta}}, \tau^2 A^{-1})$ where $\tau^2 A^{-1}$, a positive definite symmetric matrix, represents the statistician's prior variance on $\boldsymbol{\beta}$. We shall see below that one choice for $A^{-1}$ (or $A$) yields a James-Stein estimator and another gives the ridge regression estimator (discussed in Section 8.2).

As in other Bayes problems, the posterior distribution for $\boldsymbol{\beta}$ (conditional on $\sigma$) is proportional to the product of the prior distribution for $\boldsymbol{\beta}$ and the likelihood function. Accordingly, we can write

$$\begin{aligned} p(\boldsymbol{\beta}|\sigma) = K\tau^{-k}\sigma^{T} \exp\left\{ -\frac{1}{2\tau^2} (\boldsymbol{\beta} - \bar{\boldsymbol{\beta}})'A(\boldsymbol{\beta} - \bar{\boldsymbol{\beta}}) \right. \\ \left. - \frac{1}{2\sigma^2} [\nu S^2 + (\boldsymbol{\beta} - \hat{\boldsymbol{\beta}})'X'X(\boldsymbol{\beta} - \hat{\boldsymbol{\beta}})] \right\}, \end{aligned} \qquad \textbf{(7.3.1)}$$

[7]For more detail on Bayesian methods see Zellner (1971) or Box and Tiao (1973).

where $\nu = T - k$, $\hat{\boldsymbol\beta} = (X'X)^{-1}X'\mathbf{y}$, and $\nu S^2 = (\mathbf{y} - X\hat{\boldsymbol\beta})'(\mathbf{y} - X\hat{\boldsymbol\beta})$. For a reason to be explained below, it is of interest to compute $E[\boldsymbol\beta|\sigma]$. To do so, arrange the terms involving $\boldsymbol\beta$ in the exponential into the form $-(\boldsymbol\beta - \bar{\bar{\boldsymbol\beta}})'C(\boldsymbol\beta - \bar{\bar{\boldsymbol\beta}})/2$. In that form, $E(\boldsymbol\beta) = \bar{\bar{\boldsymbol\beta}}$ and $\text{Cov}(\boldsymbol\beta) = C^{-1}$. To determine $\bar{\bar{\boldsymbol\beta}}$ and $C$, consider first the quadratic form in $\beta$:

$$\boldsymbol\beta'C\boldsymbol\beta = \boldsymbol\beta'\left[\frac{A}{\tau^2} + \frac{X'X}{\sigma^2}\right]\boldsymbol\beta, \tag{7.3.2}$$

implying that

$$C = \frac{A}{\tau^2} + \frac{X'X}{\sigma^2}. \tag{7.3.3}$$

Now consider the bilinear form in $\boldsymbol\beta$ and $\bar{\bar{\boldsymbol\beta}}$,

$$\boldsymbol\beta'C\bar{\bar{\boldsymbol\beta}} = \boldsymbol\beta'\left[\frac{A}{\tau^2}\bar{\boldsymbol\beta} + \frac{X'X}{\sigma^2}\hat{\boldsymbol\beta}\right]$$

for all $\boldsymbol\beta$, so that

$$C\bar{\bar{\boldsymbol\beta}} = \frac{A}{\tau^2}\bar{\boldsymbol\beta} + \frac{X'X}{\sigma^2}\hat{\boldsymbol\beta}$$

and

$$\bar{\bar{\boldsymbol\beta}} = \left[\frac{A}{\tau^2} + \frac{X'X}{\sigma^2}\right]^{-1}\left[\frac{A}{\tau^2}\bar{\boldsymbol\beta} + \frac{X'X}{\sigma^2}\hat{\boldsymbol\beta}\right]. \tag{7.3.4}$$

The original exponential also includes

$$-\frac{1}{2\sigma^2}\nu S^2 - \frac{\bar{\boldsymbol\beta}'A\bar{\boldsymbol\beta}}{2\tau^2} - \frac{\hat{\boldsymbol\beta}'X'X\hat{\boldsymbol\beta}}{2\sigma^2}. \tag{7.3.5}$$

Since (7.3.5) does not involve $\boldsymbol\beta$, it may be absorbed into the constant term along with $\exp\{\bar{\bar{\boldsymbol\beta}}'C\bar{\bar{\boldsymbol\beta}}/2\}$ to offset $\exp\{-\bar{\bar{\boldsymbol\beta}}'C\bar{\bar{\boldsymbol\beta}}/2\}$, which appears in $\exp\{(\boldsymbol\beta - \bar{\bar{\boldsymbol\beta}})'C(\boldsymbol\beta - \bar{\bar{\boldsymbol\beta}})/2\}$. $\bar{\bar{\boldsymbol\beta}}$ may be rewritten as

$$\bar{\bar{\boldsymbol\beta}} = \bar{\boldsymbol\beta} + \left[I - \left(A + \frac{\tau^2}{\sigma^2}X'X\right)^{-1}A\right](\hat{\boldsymbol\beta} - \bar{\boldsymbol\beta}). \tag{7.3.6}$$

The last step is derived by adding and subtracting $\bar{\boldsymbol\beta}$ in (7.3.4):

$$\begin{aligned}
\bar{\bar{\boldsymbol\beta}} &= \bar{\boldsymbol\beta} + \left[\frac{1}{\tau^2}\left(A + \frac{\tau^2}{\sigma^2}X'X\right)\right]^{-1}\left[\frac{A\bar{\boldsymbol\beta}}{\tau^2} + \frac{X'X\hat{\boldsymbol\beta}}{\sigma^2}\right] - \bar{\boldsymbol\beta} \\
&= \bar{\boldsymbol\beta} + \tau^2\left(A + \frac{\tau^2}{\sigma^2}X'X\right)^{-1}\left[\frac{A\bar{\boldsymbol\beta}}{\tau^2} + \frac{X'X\hat{\boldsymbol\beta}}{\sigma^2} - \frac{1}{\tau^2}\left(A + \frac{\tau^2}{\sigma^2}X'X\right)\bar{\boldsymbol\beta}\right] \\
&= \bar{\boldsymbol\beta} + \left[A + \frac{\tau^2}{\sigma^2}X'X\right]^{-1}\frac{\tau^2}{\sigma^2}X'X(\hat{\boldsymbol\beta} - \bar{\boldsymbol\beta}).
\end{aligned} \tag{7.3.7}$$

By rewriting (7.3.7) as

$$\bar{\bar{\boldsymbol{\beta}}} = \left(A + \frac{\tau^2}{\sigma^2}X'X\right)^{-1} A\bar{\boldsymbol{\beta}} + \left[I - \left(A + \frac{\tau^2}{\sigma^2}X'X\right)^{-1} A\right]\hat{\boldsymbol{\beta}},$$

we see that $\bar{\bar{\boldsymbol{\beta}}}$ may be thought of as a weighted average of $\bar{\boldsymbol{\beta}}$ and $\hat{\boldsymbol{\beta}}$. As $\tau^2/\sigma^2$ tends to zero, $\bar{\bar{\boldsymbol{\beta}}}$ approaches $\bar{\boldsymbol{\beta}}$; and as $\tau^2/\sigma^2 \to \infty$, $\bar{\bar{\boldsymbol{\beta}}} \to \hat{\boldsymbol{\beta}}$. Since $\tau^2/\sigma^2$ is the ratio of the variance of the prior distribution to the variance of the error distribution, this result is reasonable. If the prior variance is small relative to the error variance it seems clear that $\bar{\bar{\boldsymbol{\beta}}}$ should be close to $\bar{\boldsymbol{\beta}}$. And if the prior variance is large relative to the error variance, $\bar{\bar{\boldsymbol{\beta}}}$ should be close to $\hat{\boldsymbol{\beta}}$.

The significance of $\bar{\bar{\boldsymbol{\beta}}}$, the mean value of $\boldsymbol{\beta}$ taken over its posterior distribution conditioned on $\sigma$, is that in general, the posterior mean minimizes Bayes' risk under a quadratic loss function. To see this, recall from Section 6.2 that the estimator that minimizes Bayes' risk may be found by minimizing for each $X$, the integral

$$\begin{aligned} r[\hat{\theta}(\ ), \pi] &= \int L[\hat{\theta}, \theta(\mathbf{x})]\pi(\theta|\mathbf{x})\, d\theta \\ &= \int [\hat{\theta}(\mathbf{x}) - \theta]^2\pi(\theta|\mathbf{x})\, d\theta. \end{aligned} \quad \textbf{(7.3.8)}$$

Differentiate (7.3.8) with respect to $\hat{\theta}(\mathbf{x})$ and set it equal to zero to find the minimum:

$$\frac{dr[\hat{\theta}(\mathbf{x})]}{d\hat{\theta}(\mathbf{x})} = 2\int [\hat{\theta}(\mathbf{x}) - \theta]\pi(\theta|\mathbf{x})\, d\theta = 0, \quad \textbf{(7.3.9)}$$

which implies $\hat{\theta}(\mathbf{x}) \int \pi(\theta|\mathbf{x})\, d\theta = \int \theta\pi(\theta|\mathbf{x})\, d\theta$ [since $\hat{\theta}(\mathbf{x})$ does not depend on $\theta$], or $\hat{\theta}(\mathbf{x}) = \int \theta\pi(\theta|\mathbf{x})\, d\theta$, and the right-hand side is the mean of the posterior distribution for $\theta$. Therefore $\bar{\bar{\boldsymbol{\beta}}}$ is optimal for a quadratic loss function.

To relate the above to the James-Stein approach, set $A = X'X$; that is, assume that the prior distribution for $\boldsymbol{\beta}$ has a covariance matrix equal to $\tau^2(X'X)^{-1}$. Then

$$\bar{\bar{\boldsymbol{\beta}}} = \bar{\boldsymbol{\beta}} + \left[1 - \frac{\sigma^2}{\sigma^2 + \tau^2}\right](\hat{\boldsymbol{\beta}} - \bar{\boldsymbol{\beta}}). \quad \textbf{(7.3.10)}$$

This is similar to the James-Stein estimator discussed above. The similarity is more apparent if we replace $\sigma^2$ and $\tau^2$ by reasonable estimates.[8] For $\sigma^2$ it is natural to use $S^2 = (\mathbf{y} - X\hat{\boldsymbol{\beta}})'(\mathbf{y} - X\hat{\boldsymbol{\beta}})/(T - k)$, and for $\tau^2$ use $\{1/[\text{tr}(X'X)^{-1}]\}(\hat{\boldsymbol{\beta}} - \bar{\boldsymbol{\beta}})'(\hat{\boldsymbol{\beta}} - \bar{\boldsymbol{\beta}}) - S^2$ because of the following argument: Under the model specified, $\hat{\beta}_i = \beta_i + u_i$, where $u_i \sim N(0, \sigma^2 a_{ii})$ and $a_{ii}$ is the $ii$th element of $(X'X)^{-1}$. Then

$$\hat{\beta}_i - \bar{\beta}_i = \beta_i - \bar{\beta}_i + u_i, \quad \textbf{(7.3.11)}$$

so that

$$E[(\hat{\beta}_i - \bar{\beta}_i)^2] = E[(\beta_i - \bar{\beta}_i)^2] + E[u_i^2] = \tau^2 a_{ii} + \sigma^2 a_{ii} \quad \textbf{(7.3.12)}$$

and

$$\sum_i E[(\hat{\beta}_i - \bar{\beta}_i)^2] = E[(\hat{\boldsymbol{\beta}} - \bar{\boldsymbol{\beta}})'(\hat{\boldsymbol{\beta}} - \bar{\boldsymbol{\beta}})] = \text{tr}(X'X)^{-1}(\tau^2 + \sigma^2), \quad \textbf{(7.3.13)}$$

[8]Using estimates for $\sigma^2$ and $\tau^2$ in the Bayesian framework is called an "empirical Bayes" approach; see Judge and Bock (1978, pp. 175–176) for more detail and further references.

or

$$\tau^2 = \frac{1}{\mathrm{tr}(X'X)^{-1}} E[(\hat{\beta} - \bar{\beta})'(\hat{\beta} - \bar{\beta})] - \sigma^2.$$

Therefore

$$\frac{(\hat{\beta} - \bar{\beta})'(\hat{\beta} - \bar{\beta})}{\mathrm{tr}(X'X)^{-1}} - S^2 \tag{7.3.14}$$

is an unbiased estimator for $\tau^2$.

Substituting the estimates of $\tau^2$ and $\sigma^2$ into the expression for $\bar{\bar{\beta}}$ yields

$$\bar{\bar{\beta}} = \bar{\beta} + \left[1 - \frac{\mathrm{tr}(X'X)^{-1}}{T - k} \frac{\|\mathbf{y} - X\hat{\beta}\|^2}{\|\hat{\beta} - \bar{\beta}\|^2}\right](\hat{\beta} - \bar{\beta}). \tag{7.3.15}$$

If $X'X = I_k$, (7.3.15) reduces to

$$\bar{\bar{\beta}} = \bar{\beta} + \left[1 - \frac{k}{T - k} \frac{\|\mathbf{y} - X\hat{\beta}\|^2}{\|\hat{\beta} - \bar{\beta}\|^2}\right](\hat{\beta} - \bar{\beta}). \tag{7.3.16}$$

James-Stein showed that substituting

$$\frac{k - 2}{T - k + 2} \quad \text{for} \quad \frac{k}{T - k}$$

improves the performance of the above estimator relative to $\hat{\beta}$.

Before considering another Bayesian approach to estimation under quadratic loss, we return to the question of the source of the gain from James-Stein estimators in light of the Bayesian approach. In doing so, we continue to assume that $X'X = \tau^2 I$, or in general, that the random vectors whose expected values are to be estimated are independently distributed. This case restricts the possibility of gain, since the possession of a priori information on the covariance of random variables would be an obvious reason to estimate them together. The parameter $\tau^2$ is the researcher's prior estimate of the variance of each $\beta_i$. Thus, a restriction in the model and therefore a source of variance reduction is the assumption that each $\beta_i$ has the same prior variance. Pooling the estimates then has the effect of improving the estimate of $\tau^2$. Note that as $\tau^2 \to 0$, the James-Stein estimator departs further from $\hat{\beta}$ and achieves its greatest gain. In fact, $\tau^2$ corresponds to $\xi'\xi$, which played a key role in the fundamental James-Stein result.

In some situations—especially in the $k$-means case, where a vector of means is estimated—use of the average of the maximum likelihood estimates of the individual means as the prior mean for each component has been suggested. In the present problem, this would amount to $\bar{\beta} = (1/k)\Sigma\hat{\beta}_i$. Then $\tau^2 = E[\Sigma(\beta_i - \bar{\beta})^2]$ would be small when the $\beta_i$'s are close to each other. Thus the point made by Hill (see Section 7.1) is a consideration in deciding which parameters should be estimated together: bringing together unrelated problems may decrease the gains made by grouping related ones, where related problems are those for which it is believed that expected values are similar. Efron and Morris have studied various aspects of this issue in a series of papers. See Efron and Morris (1972) and (1973a) for a discussion and further references.

We conclude this section with a brief mention of the "minimum mean square error" (MMSE) approach; see Zellner and Vandaele (1974) for more detail. The MMSE approach starts with the quadratic loss function $L(\boldsymbol{\beta}, \mathbf{b}) = (\mathbf{b} - \boldsymbol{\beta})'Q(\mathbf{b} - \boldsymbol{\beta})$, where $Q$ is a $k \times k$ positive semidefinite matrix. The risk associated with $\hat{\boldsymbol{\beta}}$ is

$$E[L(\boldsymbol{\beta}, \hat{\boldsymbol{\beta}})] = \sigma^2 \operatorname{tr}(X'X)^{-1}Q. \tag{7.3.17}$$

Suppose now we multiply $\hat{\boldsymbol{\beta}}$ by a scalar, $q$, and choose the scalar that minimizes risk:

$$\begin{aligned} E[L(\boldsymbol{\beta}, q\hat{\boldsymbol{\beta}})] &= E[(q\hat{\boldsymbol{\beta}} - \boldsymbol{\beta})'Q(q\hat{\boldsymbol{\beta}} - \boldsymbol{\beta})] \\ &= E[q(\hat{\boldsymbol{\beta}} - \boldsymbol{\beta}) - (1 - q)\boldsymbol{\beta}]'Q[q(\hat{\boldsymbol{\beta}} - \boldsymbol{\beta}) - (1 - q)\boldsymbol{\beta}] \\ &= q^2E(\hat{\boldsymbol{\beta}} - \boldsymbol{\beta})'Q(\hat{\boldsymbol{\beta}} - \boldsymbol{\beta}) + (1 - q)^2\boldsymbol{\beta}'Q\boldsymbol{\beta}. \end{aligned} \tag{7.3.18}$$

Minimizing with respect to $q$ yields

$$q^* = 1 - \frac{\sigma^2 \operatorname{tr}(X'X)^{-1}Q}{\sigma^2 \operatorname{tr}(X'X)^{-1}Q + \boldsymbol{\beta}'Q\boldsymbol{\beta}}. \tag{7.3.19}$$

The unknown $\sigma^2$ and $\boldsymbol{\beta}$ can be approximated by

$$\hat{\sigma}^2 = \frac{\|\mathbf{y} - X\hat{\boldsymbol{\beta}}\|^2}{\nu + 2}$$

and $\hat{\boldsymbol{\beta}}$, respectively. Since

$$E[(\hat{\boldsymbol{\beta}} - \boldsymbol{\beta})'Q(\hat{\boldsymbol{\beta}} - \boldsymbol{\beta})] = \sigma^2 \operatorname{tr}(X'X)^{-1}Q, \tag{7.3.20}$$

it is easy to see that

$$E[\hat{\boldsymbol{\beta}}'Q\hat{\boldsymbol{\beta}}] = \sigma^2 \operatorname{tr}(X'X)^{-1}Q + \boldsymbol{\beta}'Q\boldsymbol{\beta}. \tag{7.3.21}$$

Accordingly, $q^*$ is approximated by

$$1 - \hat{\sigma}^2 \frac{\operatorname{tr}(X'X)^{-1}Q}{\hat{\boldsymbol{\beta}}'Q\hat{\boldsymbol{\beta}}}. \tag{7.3.22}$$

Again, the result is in a James-Stein form. Thus, two different approaches—Bayes and MMSE— lead to James-Stein type estimators.

## 7.4 Conclusion

This chapter has been concerned with the most important theoretical properties of the James-Stein and related estimators and with their interpretation in the Bayesian framework. It has been established that these estimators improve upon the usual maximum likelihood estimator under certain conditions. After discussing several other estimators under the quadratic loss criterion, Section 8.3 considers the possible application of these estimators to econometric research.

## 7.5 References

Aigner, D. J. and G. G. Judge (1977), "Application of Pre-Test and Stein Estimators to Economic Data," *Econometrica,* **45,** 1279–1288.

Baranchik, A. (1964), Multiple Regression and Estimation of the Mean of a Multivariate Normal Distribution, Unpublished Ph.D. Thesis, Stanford University.

Bock, M. E. (1975), "Minimax Estimators of the Mean of a Multivariate Normal Distribution," *The Annals of Statistics,* **3,** 209–218.

Box, G. E. P. and G. C. Tiao (1973), *Bayesian Inference in Statistical Analysis,* Reading: Addison-Wesley.

Efron, B. and C. Morris (1972), "Limiting the Risk of Bayes and Empirical Bayes Estimators—Part II: The Empirical Bayes Case," *Journal of the American Statistical Association,* **67,** 130–139.

Efron, B. and C. Morris (1973a), "Combining Possibly Related Estimation Problems," *Journal of the Royal Statistical Society,* Ser. B, **35,** 379–421.

Efron, B. and C. Morris (1973b), "Stein's Estimation Rule and Its Competitors—An Empirical Bayes Approach," *Journal of the American Statistical Association,* **68,** 117–130.

Efron, B. and C. Morris (1974), "Data Analysis Using Stein's Estimator and Its Generalizations," R-1394-OEO, The RAND Corporation, Santa Monica.

Efron, B. and C. Morris (1977), "Stein's Paradox in Statistics," *Scientific American,* **236,** 119–127.

Girshick, M. A. and L. J. Savage (1951), "Bayes and Minimax Estimates for Quadratic Loss Functions," *Proceedings of the Second Berkeley Symposium on Mathematical Statistics and Probability,* 53–73, Berkeley and Los Angeles: University of California Press.

Hill, B. M. (1974), "On Coherence, Inadmissibility and Inference About Many Parameters in the Theory of Least Squares," in S. E. Fienberg and A. Zellner, eds., *Studies in Bayesian Econometrics and Statistics,* 555–584, Amsterdam: North-Holland.

James, W. and C. Stein (1961), "Estimation With Quadratic Loss," *Proceedings of the Fourth Berkeley Symposium on Mathematical Statistics and Probability,* 361–379, Berkeley: University of California Press.

Judge, G. G. and M. E. Bock (1978), *The Statistical Implications of Pre-Test and Stein-Rule Estimators in Econometrics,* Amsterdam: North-Holland.

Sclove, S. L. (1968), "Improved Estimators for Coefficients in Linear Regression," *Journal of the American Statistical Association,* **63,** 597–606.

Stein, C. (1956), "Inadmissibility of the Usual Estimator for the Mean of a Multivariate Normal Distribution," *Proceedings of the Third Berkeley Symposium on Mathematical Statistics and Probability,* **1,** 197–206, Berkeley and Los Angeles: University of California Press.

Stein, C. (1966), "An Approach to the Recovery of Inter-Block Information in Balanced

Incomplete Block Designs,'' in F. N. David, ed., *Research Papers in Statistics: Festschrift for J. Neyman,* 351–366, New York: Wiley.

Ullah, A. (1974), ''On the Sampling Distribution of Improved Estimators for Coefficients in Linear Regression,'' *Journal of Econometrics,* **2,** 143–150.

Zellner, A. (1971), *An Introduction to Bayesian Inference in Econometrics,* New York: Wiley.

Zellner, A. and W. Vandaele (1974), ''Bayes-Stein Estimators for *K*-means, Regression and Simultaneous Equation Models,'' in S. E. Fienberg and A. Zellner, eds., *Studies in Bayesian Econometrics and Statistics,* 627–653, Amsterdam: North-Holland.

# CHAPTER 8

# Preliminary test and Other Estimators Under a Quadratic Loss Function

The first two sections of this chapter discuss properties of the preliminary test estimator, ridge regression, and the double $k$-class estimator under a quadratic loss criterion. The third section briefly reviews several applications to econometric problems of the techniques discussed in Chapters 6, 7, and 8. Many of the topics are covered in greater detail in Judge and Bock (1978).

## 8.1 Preliminary Test Estimators in Regression

In the course of their research, econometricians frequently eliminate insignificant variables from a regression and then estimate an equation that includes only significant variables. This procedure is regarded by some as an attempt to extract impressive statistical results from the data at hand, results which may not hold up in other samples. Viewed in that light the procedure seems objectionable; it overemphasizes the importance of obtaining good results with a particular body of data and does not appear to be justified by more general statistical criteria. Statistical properties of this estimator (it is called a preliminary test estimator because parameter estimates are partly determined by the outcome of an hypothesis test) have been examined under the criterion of quadratic loss.

In two situations frequently encountered when working with economic data, use of this procedure may seem appropriate: (1) the presence of considerable collinearity between the independent variables prevents them from achieving statistical significance, and (2) the economic theory being utilized may not yield clear-cut implications regarding which variables belong in the equation. In either case, the preliminary test procedure cannot be justified as a minimum variance unbiased estimator. In particular, the estimator is not unbiased. In situations of the first type, it is possible to compare properties of the preliminary test estimator with others—for example, OLS and James-Stein—by adopting the more general criterion of quadratic loss in place of minimum variance, linear unbiased estimators. Situations of the second type are more problematic: most estimation procedures assume a known model. Indeed, unbiasedness has no clear meaning when the model is unknown. See Leamer (1978) for an approach to estimation in such cases and Cooley and Leroy (1981) for an application to the estimation of money demand.

For simplicity in the following discussion we deal with a special case of the preliminary test estimator. Starting with the usual regression setup ($\mathbf{y} = X\boldsymbol{\beta} + \boldsymbol{\epsilon}$, where $\boldsymbol{\beta}$ is $p \times 1$, $E[\boldsymbol{\epsilon}] = 0$, and $E[\boldsymbol{\epsilon}\boldsymbol{\epsilon}'] = \sigma^2 I$), the preliminary test estimator ($\boldsymbol{\beta}^*$) is constructed as follows: the researcher estimates the OLS estimator, $\hat{\boldsymbol{\beta}}$, and then tests the hypothesis

$\boldsymbol{\beta} = \mathbf{0}$ with the usual $F$-statistic. If the hypothesis is accepted, $\boldsymbol{\beta}^*$ is set equal to $\mathbf{0}$; if the hypothesis is rejected, $\boldsymbol{\beta}^*$ is set equal to $\hat{\boldsymbol{\beta}}$. More general preliminary test estimators may be analyzed in the above framework after reparametrization; see the appendix to this chapter for details and references.

The risk function is assumed quadratic,

$$R(\mathbf{b}(\mathbf{y}), \boldsymbol{\beta}) = E[\|\mathbf{b}(\mathbf{y}) - \boldsymbol{\beta}\|^2], \tag{8.1.1}$$

where $\mathbf{b}(\mathbf{y})$ is an estimator of $\boldsymbol{\beta}$ of the form $\mathbf{b}(\mathbf{y}) = h(\hat{\boldsymbol{\beta}}'X'X\hat{\boldsymbol{\beta}}/S)\hat{\boldsymbol{\beta}}$ and $h(\quad)$ is a scalar function of $\hat{\boldsymbol{\beta}}'X'X\hat{\boldsymbol{\beta}}/S$.

Equation 7.2.18 gives the result

$$\frac{1}{\sigma^2} R(\mathbf{b}(\mathbf{y}), \boldsymbol{\beta}) = \operatorname{tr}(X'X)^{-1}E\{h^2[g'_{p+2}]\} + \frac{\boldsymbol{\beta}'\boldsymbol{\beta}}{\sigma^2}\{E[h^2(g'_{p+4})] - 2E[h(g'_{p+2})] + 1\}, \tag{8.1.2}$$

where $g'_k$ is defined in the statement of Theorem 7.2.3. To see how $\boldsymbol{\beta}^*$ may be written in this form, let

$$\boldsymbol{\beta}^* = I_{(c,\infty)}(g'_k)\hat{\boldsymbol{\beta}},$$

where

$$I_{(c,\infty)}(g'_k) = \begin{cases} 0, & \text{if } g'_k \leqslant c \\ 1, & \text{if } g'_k > c \end{cases}.$$

That is, for $g'_k < c$, $\boldsymbol{\beta}^* = \mathbf{0}$, and for $g'_k \geqslant c$, $\boldsymbol{\beta}^* = \hat{\boldsymbol{\beta}}$. $\boldsymbol{\beta}^*$ is a *preliminary test estimator,* where the test is based on the random variable $g'_k$. If $\hat{\boldsymbol{\beta}}$ is not significantly different from zero, where $c$ is chosen to set the level of significance, the estimator is taken to be the zero vector. Otherwise the estimator is $\hat{\boldsymbol{\beta}}$. Since

$$g'_k \sim \frac{\chi'^2(k, \boldsymbol{\beta}'X'X\boldsymbol{\beta}/2)}{\chi^2_n},$$

under the null hypothesis $\boldsymbol{\beta} = \mathbf{0}$, $g'_k \sim (k/n)F(k, n)$. Hence $(k/n)F(k, n) < c$ implies $F(k, n) < cn/k$, so the test can be based on the usual $F$-statistic, with $c$ chosen to reflect degrees of freedom and significance level. With the aid of Theorem 7.2.1, it may be shown that $E[\boldsymbol{\beta}^*] = \boldsymbol{\beta}P[g'_{k+2} > c]$, which is closer to zero than $\boldsymbol{\beta}$ for $c < \infty$, and so $\boldsymbol{\beta}^*$ is biased. For details see Bock, Yancey, and Judge (1973).

We next set $h(g'_k) = I_{(c,\infty)}(g'_k)$ to use (8.1.2) for $\boldsymbol{\beta}^*$. From the facts that $I^2(\quad) = I(\quad)$ and $E[I_{(c,\infty)}(g'_k)] = P(g'_k > c)$, the risk may be expressed as

$$\frac{1}{\sigma^2} R(\boldsymbol{\beta}^*, \boldsymbol{\beta}) = \operatorname{tr}(X'X)^{-1}P[g'_{p+2} > c] + \frac{\boldsymbol{\beta}'\boldsymbol{\beta}}{\sigma^2}\{\mathrm{P}[\mathrm{g}'_{p+4} > \mathrm{c}] - 2P[g'_{p+2} > c] + 1\}. \tag{8.1.3}$$

This risk will now be compared with the risk of the ordinary least squares estimator,

$R(\hat{\boldsymbol\beta}, \boldsymbol\beta)/\sigma^2 = \text{tr}(X'X)^{-1}$, following Sclove, Morris, and Radhakrishnan (1972). First, it is shown that $R(\boldsymbol\beta^*, \boldsymbol\beta) > R(\hat{\boldsymbol\beta}, \boldsymbol\beta)$ for $\boldsymbol\beta'\boldsymbol\beta/\sigma^2 > \text{tr}(X'X)^{-1}$:

$$\begin{aligned}
\frac{1}{\sigma^2} R(\boldsymbol\beta^*, \boldsymbol\beta) &= \left[\text{tr}(X'X')^{-1} - \frac{2\boldsymbol\beta'\boldsymbol\beta}{\sigma^2}\right] P[g'_{p+2} > c] \\
&\quad + \frac{\boldsymbol\beta'\boldsymbol\beta}{\sigma^2} P[g'_{p+4} > c] + \frac{\boldsymbol\beta'\boldsymbol\beta}{\sigma^2} \\
&> \left[\text{tr}(X'X)^{-1} - \frac{2\boldsymbol\beta'\boldsymbol\beta}{\sigma^2}\right] P[g'_{p+2} > c] \\
&\quad + \frac{\boldsymbol\beta'\boldsymbol\beta}{\sigma^2} P[g'_{p+2} > c] + \frac{\boldsymbol\beta'\boldsymbol\beta}{\sigma^2} \\
&= \left\{\text{tr}(X'X)^{-1} - \frac{\boldsymbol\beta'\boldsymbol\beta}{\sigma^2}\right\} P[g'_{p+2} > c] + \frac{\boldsymbol\beta'\boldsymbol\beta}{\sigma^2} \\
&= \text{tr}(X'X)^{-1} + \left[\frac{\boldsymbol\beta'\boldsymbol\beta}{\sigma^2} - \text{tr}(X'X)^{-1}\right] P[g'_{p+2} \leqslant c]. \qquad \textbf{(8.1.4)}
\end{aligned}$$

(The inequality follows from

$$P\left[\chi'^2\left(p + 4, \frac{\boldsymbol\beta'X'X\boldsymbol\beta}{2}\right) > c\right] > P\left[\chi'^2\left(p + 2, \frac{\boldsymbol\beta'X'X\boldsymbol\beta}{2}\right) > c\right],$$

and the last step uses

$$P[g'_k > c] = 1 - P[g'_k \leqslant c].)$$

Since $P[g'_{p+2} \leq c] > 0$ for $c > 0$, we have the result that $\boldsymbol\beta'\boldsymbol\beta/\sigma^2 > \text{tr}(X'X)^{-1}$ implies $R(\boldsymbol\beta^*, \boldsymbol\beta) > R(\hat{\boldsymbol\beta}, \boldsymbol\beta)$.

Moreover, as $\boldsymbol\beta'\boldsymbol\beta/\sigma^2 \to \infty$, $P[g'_{p+2} \leqslant c] \to 0$, so that $R(\boldsymbol\beta^*, \boldsymbol\beta) \to R(\hat{\boldsymbol\beta}, \boldsymbol\beta)$.[1] Upon replacing $g'_{p+2}$ by $g'_{p+4}$ in (8.1.3), the reader should verify that there is a range of $\boldsymbol\beta'\boldsymbol\beta/\sigma^2$ over which $R(\boldsymbol\beta^*, \boldsymbol\beta) < R(\hat{\boldsymbol\beta}, \boldsymbol\beta)$. The qualitative relationship is displayed in Figure 8.1. The mean squared error performance of the preliminary test estimator relative to that of the OLS estimator is similar to that pictured in Figure 8.1 for more general cases, for example when the risk function is of the form $E[(\boldsymbol\beta^* - \boldsymbol\beta)'W(\boldsymbol\beta^* - \boldsymbol\beta)]$, for positive semidefinite $W$. The risk for the preliminary test estimator—as a function of a quadratic

[1]It is sufficient to show that the second term in (8.1.4) tends to zero. Thus,

$$\begin{aligned}
\frac{\boldsymbol\beta'\boldsymbol\beta}{\sigma^2} P[g'_{p+2} \leqslant c] &= 2\lambda \sum_{i=0}^{\infty} \frac{e^{-\lambda}\lambda^i}{i!} \int_0^c \frac{\chi^2_{p+2i}(W)}{\chi^2_n(W)}\, dW \\
&= \sum_{i=0}^{\infty} C_i \frac{e^{-\lambda}\lambda^{i+1}}{i!},
\end{aligned}$$

where $C_i$ does not depend on $\lambda$, and $\lambda = \boldsymbol\beta'\boldsymbol\beta/\sigma^2$. Using L' Hospital's rule, it can be shown that

$$\lim_{\lambda\to\infty} \frac{e^{-\lambda}\lambda^{i+1}}{i!} = 0 \qquad \text{for every } i.$$

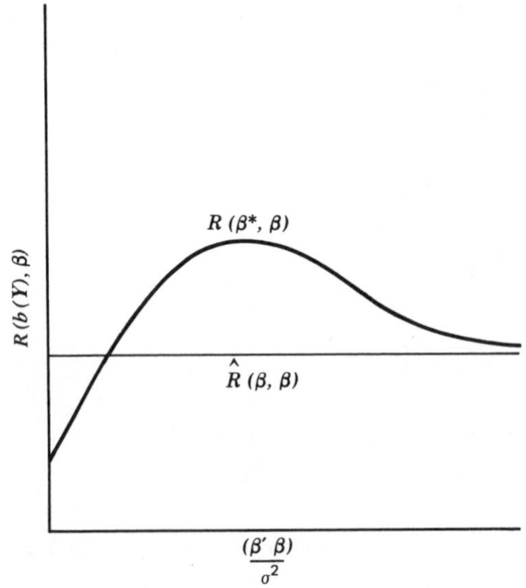


**FIGURE 8.1 Risk functions for preliminary test and maximum likelihood estimators.**

form involving $\boldsymbol{\beta}$, $X$, $W$, and $\sigma^2$—is below that of OLS for small values of the quadratic form, rises above it, and then approaches it asymptotically from above. The exact relationship depends primarily upon the largest and smallest c.r.'s of $X'X$ and the level of significance employed in the preliminary test. Detailed comparisons are presented in Judge and Bock (1978, Chapter 4) both algebraically and graphically, and the question of whether there is an optimal level of significance to employ is considered.

In addition to comparisons between OLS and preliminary test estimators, the relationships between these and James-Stein estimators have been investigated. Moreover, various combinations of preliminary test estimators and James-Stein estimators have been proposed. For example, Sclove, Morris, and Radhakrishnan (1972) define a modified James-Stein estimator that dominates the preliminary test estimator. In the simple case that $X'X = I$, the estimator takes the form

$$\left(1 - \frac{ac_0}{F}\right) I_{(ac_0,\infty)}(F)\hat{\boldsymbol{\beta}}. \qquad \textbf{(8.1.5)}$$

They also show that (8.1.5) is dominated by its positive part variant if $c < ac_0$. Further detail appears in Judge and Bock (1978, Chapter 8).

Other types of preliminary test estimators have been studied. Judge and Bock (1978, Chapter 7) utilize Monte Carlo techniques to study preliminary test estimators when serial correlation in the disturbance term is suspected. Two preliminary tests for serial correlation are employed along with several alternative procedures that may be used when serial correlation is present. As another example, Greenberg (1980) and Ohtani and Toyoda (1980) examine a preliminary test estimator when heteroscedasticity may be present.

## 8.2 Other Estimators Under a Quadratic Loss Function

Two types of estimators are taken up in this section. The family of double $k$-class estimators, although more recent, is taken up first because it is as a useful framework in which to study the second—ridge regression.

### 8.2.1 Double $k$-Class Estimators

Ullah and Ullah (1978) introduced a family of biased estimators and computed the mean squared errors for special cases of that family. Their starting point is the estimator of $\boldsymbol{\beta}$, $\boldsymbol{\beta}^* = A\mathbf{y}$, that minimizes $E[\|\boldsymbol{\beta}^* - \boldsymbol{\beta}\|^2]$. From Equation 6.2.4, we have

$$E[\|\boldsymbol{\beta}^* - \boldsymbol{\beta}\|^2] = E[\|A\mathbf{y} - \boldsymbol{\beta}\|^2] = \sigma^2 \operatorname{tr} AA' + \boldsymbol{\beta}'[AX - I]'[AX - I]\boldsymbol{\beta}. \quad \textbf{(8.2.1)}$$

This expression is differentiated with respect to $A$, and the derivative set equal to zero. Thus,

$$\begin{aligned}\frac{\partial E[\|A\mathbf{y} - \boldsymbol{\beta}\|^2]}{\partial A} &= \sigma^2 \frac{\partial}{\partial A} \operatorname{tr} AA' + \frac{\partial}{\partial A}[\boldsymbol{\beta}'X'A'AX\boldsymbol{\beta}] \\ &\quad - 2\frac{\partial}{\partial A}[\boldsymbol{\beta}'X'A'\boldsymbol{\beta}] = 0.\end{aligned} \quad \textbf{(8.2.2)}$$

First, since $\operatorname{tr} AA' = \Sigma_s\Sigma_t a_{st}^2$ implies $\partial/\partial a_{ij} (\operatorname{tr} A) = 2a_{ij}$, we have

$$\frac{\partial}{\partial A} \operatorname{tr} AA' = 2A. \quad \textbf{(8.2.3)}$$

Next, let $\mathbf{b} = X\boldsymbol{\beta}$. Then

$$\boldsymbol{\beta}'X'A'AX\boldsymbol{\beta} = \mathbf{b}'A'A\mathbf{b} = (A\mathbf{b})'(A\mathbf{b}) = [\Sigma a_{1s}b_s \cdots \Sigma a_{ms}b_s]\begin{bmatrix}\Sigma a_{1s}b_s \\ \cdot \\ \cdot \\ \cdot \\ \Sigma a_{ms}b_s\end{bmatrix} = \Sigma_t(\Sigma_s a_{ts}b_s)^2.$$

Therefore,

$$\left\{\frac{\partial}{\partial a_{ij}} \mathbf{b}'A'A\mathbf{b}\right\} = \{2\Sigma_s a_{is}b_s b_j\} = 2A\mathbf{b}\mathbf{b}' = 2AX\boldsymbol{\beta}\boldsymbol{\beta}'X. \quad \textbf{(8.2.4)}$$

Finally,

$$\boldsymbol{\beta}'XA'\boldsymbol{\beta} = \mathbf{b}'A'\boldsymbol{\beta} = \Sigma_s a_{st}b_t\beta_s;$$

thus

$$\frac{\partial}{\partial a_{ij}} \mathbf{b}'A\boldsymbol{\beta} = b_j\beta_i,$$

and

$$\frac{\partial}{\partial A}\mathbf{b}'A\boldsymbol{\beta} = \boldsymbol{\beta}\mathbf{b}' = \boldsymbol{\beta}\boldsymbol{\beta}'X'. \tag{8.2.5}$$

Substituting (8.2.3), (8.2.4), and (8.2.5) into (8.2.2) yields

$$2\sigma^2 A + 2AX\boldsymbol{\beta}\boldsymbol{\beta}'X' = 2\boldsymbol{\beta}\boldsymbol{\beta}'X', \tag{8.2.6}$$

which implies

$$A[X\boldsymbol{\beta}\boldsymbol{\beta}'X' + \sigma^2 I] = \boldsymbol{\beta}\boldsymbol{\beta}'X',$$

or

$$A = \boldsymbol{\beta}\boldsymbol{\beta}'X'[X\boldsymbol{\beta}\boldsymbol{\beta}'X' + \sigma^2 I]^{-1} \tag{8.2.7}$$

and

$$\boldsymbol{\beta}^* = \boldsymbol{\beta}\boldsymbol{\beta}'X'[X\boldsymbol{\beta}\boldsymbol{\beta}'X' + \sigma^2 I]^{-1}\mathbf{y}. \tag{8.2.8}$$

Equation 8.2.8 may be rewritten with

$$(I + \mathbf{a}\mathbf{a}')^{-1} = I - \mathbf{a}(1 + \mathbf{a}'\mathbf{a})^{-1}\mathbf{a}', \tag{8.2.9}$$

where $\mathbf{a}$ is $p \times 1$ and $I$ is $p \times p$. [Equation 8.2.9 is easily verified by showing that $[I + \mathbf{a}\mathbf{a}'][I - \mathbf{a}(1 + \mathbf{a}'\mathbf{a})^{-1}\mathbf{a}'] = I$.] From (8.2.9) it follows that

$$\begin{aligned}[X\boldsymbol{\beta}\boldsymbol{\beta}'X' + \sigma^2 I]^{-1} &= \frac{1}{\sigma^2}\left[I - \frac{X\boldsymbol{\beta}}{\sigma}\left(1 + \frac{\boldsymbol{\beta}'X'X\boldsymbol{\beta}}{\sigma^2}\right)^{-1}\frac{\boldsymbol{\beta}'X'}{\sigma}\right] \\ &= \frac{1}{\sigma^2}\left[I - \frac{X\boldsymbol{\beta}\boldsymbol{\beta}'X'}{\sigma^2 + \boldsymbol{\beta}'X'X\boldsymbol{\beta}}\right].\end{aligned} \tag{8.2.10}$$

Accordingly,

$$\begin{aligned}\boldsymbol{\beta}^* &= \frac{\boldsymbol{\beta}\boldsymbol{\beta}'X'}{\sigma^2}\left[I - \frac{X\boldsymbol{\beta}\boldsymbol{\beta}'X'}{\sigma^2 + \boldsymbol{\beta}'X'X\boldsymbol{\beta}}\right]\mathbf{y} \\ &= \frac{\boldsymbol{\beta}}{\sigma^2(\sigma^2 + \boldsymbol{\beta}'X'X\boldsymbol{\beta})}[(\sigma^2 + \boldsymbol{\beta}'X'X\boldsymbol{\beta})\boldsymbol{\beta}'X' - \boldsymbol{\beta}'X'X\boldsymbol{\beta}\boldsymbol{\beta}'X']\mathbf{y} \\ &= \left[\frac{\boldsymbol{\beta}'X'\mathbf{y}}{\sigma^2 + \boldsymbol{\beta}'X'X\boldsymbol{\beta}}\right]\boldsymbol{\beta};\end{aligned} \tag{8.2.11}$$

and from $X\boldsymbol{\beta} = \mathbf{y} - \mathbf{u}$,

$$\boldsymbol{\beta}^* = \left[\frac{(\mathbf{y} - \mathbf{u})'\mathbf{y}}{\sigma^2 + (\mathbf{y} - \mathbf{u})'(\mathbf{y} - \mathbf{u})}\right]\boldsymbol{\beta}. \tag{8.2.12}$$

Although $\boldsymbol{\beta}$ and $\mathbf{u}$ are not observable, estimates are available in the form of the OLS estimator of $\boldsymbol{\beta}$, denoted by $\mathbf{b}$, and $\hat{\mathbf{u}} = \mathbf{y} - X\mathbf{b}$. Accordingly, define

$$\tilde{\mathbf{b}} = \left[\frac{(\mathbf{y} - \hat{\mathbf{u}})'\mathbf{y}}{(1/n)\hat{\mathbf{u}}'\hat{\mathbf{u}} + (\mathbf{y} - \hat{\mathbf{u}})'(\mathbf{y} - \hat{\mathbf{u}})}\right]\mathbf{b}$$

$$= \left[1 - \frac{\hat{\mathbf{u}}'\hat{\mathbf{u}}/n}{\mathbf{y}'\mathbf{y} - \hat{\mathbf{u}}'\hat{\mathbf{u}}(1 - 1/n)}\right]\mathbf{b}. \qquad \textbf{(8.2.13)}$$

The reader should verify that

$$0 < \frac{\hat{\mathbf{u}}'\hat{\mathbf{u}}/n}{\mathbf{y}'\mathbf{y} - \hat{\mathbf{u}}'\hat{\mathbf{u}}(1 - 1/n)} < 1.$$

Ullah and Ullah generalize the expression for $\tilde{\mathbf{b}}$ to

$$\tilde{\mathbf{b}}_{k1,k2} = \left[1 - \frac{k_1\hat{\mathbf{u}}'\hat{\mathbf{u}}}{\mathbf{y}'\mathbf{y} - k_2\hat{\mathbf{u}}'\hat{\mathbf{u}}}\right]\mathbf{b}. \qquad \textbf{(8.2.14)}$$

A choice of $k_1 = 1/n$ and $k_2 = 1 - 1/n$ yields $\tilde{\mathbf{b}}$; $k_1 = 0$ results in the OLS estimator; and $k_2 = 1$ yields the James-Stein estimator for an appropriate choice of $k_1$. They derive the first and second moments of the double $k$-class estimators for nonstochastic $k_1$ and $k_2$. These are shown to exist, but the expressions are extremely complicated. In order to compare $R(\tilde{\mathbf{b}}_{k_1,k_2})$ to $R(\mathbf{b})$, they complete an asymptotic expansion of $R(\tilde{\mathbf{b}}_{k_1,k_2})$ for large $\theta$ in powers of $1/\theta$, where $\theta = \boldsymbol{\beta}'X'X\boldsymbol{\beta}/2\sigma^2$. It is found that $R(\tilde{\mathbf{b}}_{k_1,k_2}) < R(\mathbf{b})$ when

$$0 < k_1 < \frac{2}{n + 2}(d - 2)$$

and

$$0 \leqslant k_2 \leqslant 1, \qquad \text{where} \qquad d = \sum \frac{\lambda_i}{\lambda_L} > 2, \qquad \textbf{(8.2.15)}$$

provided $K \geqslant 3$ when $k_2 = 1$; $\lambda_L$ is the largest c.r. of $(X'X)^{-1}$ and $n = T - K$. [The $d$ that appears in (8.2.15) is similar to an expression that appears in ridge regression theory, which is discussed below.] Note that multicollinearity is likely to result in a large value of $\lambda_L$ and fairly small values for the other c.r.'s. Accordingly it is quite likely that $d < 2$, in which case the OLS estimator is preferred.

The Ullah and Ullah article contains further results on the double $k$-class estimator and comparisons with other estimators. The double $k$-class framework is used by Vinod (1980) to investigate the properties of several James-Stein type estimators. Monte Carlo results that compare several of these are presented.

### 8.2.2 Ridge Regression[2]

There are several ways to introduce the ridge regression approach. One is to begin with

[2]For further information and many references see the review article by Vinod (1978).

the expression for $\bar{\boldsymbol{\beta}}$, Equation 7.3.4, and set $A = I$ and $\bar{\boldsymbol{\beta}} = \mathbf{0}$; this yields

$$\bar{\bar{\boldsymbol{\beta}}} = \left[X'X + \frac{\sigma^2}{\tau^2} I\right]^{-1} X'\mathbf{y}. \tag{8.2.16}$$

With $k = \sigma^2/\tau^2$, the ridge regression estimator, $\hat{\boldsymbol{\beta}}_R$, is defined as

$$\hat{\boldsymbol{\beta}}_R = [X'X + k\,I]^{-1}X'\mathbf{y}. \tag{8.2.17}$$

This approach provides a Bayesian interpretation for $\hat{\boldsymbol{\beta}}_R$: it is the posterior mean of $\hat{\boldsymbol{\beta}}$ when the prior distribution of $\boldsymbol{\beta}$ is $N(\mathbf{0}, \tau^2 I)$. The prior mean of zero appears to be a strong assumption and is likely to be unreasonable as a general rule.

In other derivations of the ridge regression estimator, $\hat{\boldsymbol{\beta}}_R$ has been recommended when $X'X$ is close to being singular. In such cases the addition of a small value of $k$ to each diagonal element permits an inverse to be calculated more accurately. (Accuracy here is used in a computational sense.)

In the following discussion, $\mathbf{y}$ is $T \times 1$, $X$ is $T \times p$, $\boldsymbol{\beta}$ is $p \times 1$, $\mathbf{u}$ is $T \times 1$, $E(u_i) = 0$ and $E(u_i^2) = \sigma^2$. To establish properties of $\hat{\boldsymbol{\beta}}_R$ it is useful to reparameterize from $\mathbf{y} = X\boldsymbol{\beta} + \mathbf{u}$ to $\mathbf{y} = XCC'\boldsymbol{\beta} + \mathbf{u} = XC\boldsymbol{\alpha} + \mathbf{u}$, where $\boldsymbol{\alpha} = C'\boldsymbol{\beta}$ and $C$ is an orthogonal matrix such that

$$C'X'XC = \Lambda = \text{diag}\{\lambda_1, \cdots \lambda_p\}.$$

With the definition

$$\hat{\boldsymbol{\alpha}}_R = C'\hat{\boldsymbol{\beta}}_R, \quad \text{or} \quad \hat{\boldsymbol{\beta}}_R = C\hat{\boldsymbol{\alpha}}_R, \tag{8.2.18}$$

it is easy to see that $R(\hat{\boldsymbol{\beta}}_R, \boldsymbol{\beta}) = R(\hat{\boldsymbol{\alpha}}_R, \boldsymbol{\alpha})$:

$$\begin{aligned} R(\hat{\boldsymbol{\beta}}_R, \boldsymbol{\beta}) &= E[(\hat{\boldsymbol{\beta}}_R - \boldsymbol{\beta})'(\hat{\boldsymbol{\beta}}_R - \boldsymbol{\beta})] \\ &= E[(C\hat{\boldsymbol{\alpha}}_R - C\boldsymbol{\alpha})'(C\hat{\boldsymbol{\alpha}}_R - C\boldsymbol{\alpha})] \\ &= E[(\hat{\boldsymbol{\alpha}}_R - \boldsymbol{\alpha})'C'C(\hat{\boldsymbol{\alpha}}_R - \boldsymbol{\alpha})] \\ &= R(\hat{\boldsymbol{\alpha}}_R, \boldsymbol{\alpha}). \end{aligned} \tag{8.2.19}$$

The OLS estimator of $\boldsymbol{\alpha}$ is

$$\begin{aligned} \hat{\boldsymbol{\alpha}} &= (C'X'XC)^{-1}C'X'\mathbf{y} \\ &= \Lambda^{-1}C'X'\mathbf{y}, \end{aligned} \tag{8.2.20}$$

and

$$\begin{aligned} \hat{\boldsymbol{\alpha}}_R &= C'\hat{\boldsymbol{\beta}}_R \\ &= C'[X'X + kI]^{-1}X'\mathbf{y} \\ &= C'[X'X + kI]^{-1}CC'X'\mathbf{y} \\ &= [C'X'XC + kCC']^{-1}\Lambda\hat{\boldsymbol{\alpha}} \\ &= [\Lambda + kI]^{-1}\Lambda\hat{\boldsymbol{\alpha}}, \end{aligned} \tag{8.2.21}$$

or

$$\hat{\alpha}_{R,i} = \left[\frac{\lambda_i}{\lambda_i + k}\right]\hat{\alpha}_i,$$

where the $i$ subscript indicates the $i$th component of the relevant vector.

Since $E(\hat{\alpha}_i) = \alpha_i$, we may compute the bias of $\hat{\alpha}_{R,i}$ by

$$\begin{aligned} E(\hat{\alpha}_{R,i} - \alpha_i) &= \frac{\lambda_i}{\lambda_i + k}\alpha_i - \alpha_i \\ &= \frac{-k\alpha_i}{\lambda_i + k}; \end{aligned}$$

the squared bias is therefore

$$b_i^2(k) = E[(\hat{\alpha}_{R,i} - \alpha_i)^2] = \frac{k^2\alpha_i^2}{(\lambda_i + k)^2}, \tag{8.2.22}$$

and the sum of the squared bias terms is

$$b^2(k) = \sum b_i^2(k) = \sum \frac{k^2\alpha_i^2}{(\lambda_i + k)^2}. \tag{8.2.23}$$

By differentiating (8.2.24) with respect to $k$, it may be verified that $b^2(k)$ increases with $k$. Since the mean squared error is $b^2(k) + \Sigma \operatorname{Var}(\hat{\alpha}_{R,i})$, we next compute the latter:

$$\begin{aligned} \sum \operatorname{Var}(\hat{\alpha}_{R,i}) &= \sum \left(\frac{\lambda_i}{\lambda_i + k}\right)^2 \operatorname{Var}(\hat{\alpha}_i) \\ &= \sum \left(\frac{\lambda_i}{\lambda_i + k}\right)^2 \frac{\sigma^2}{\lambda_i} \\ &= \sigma^2 \sum \frac{\lambda_i}{(\lambda_i + k)^2}; \end{aligned} \tag{8.2.24}$$

clearly $\Sigma \operatorname{Var}(\hat{\alpha}_{R,i})$ decreases with $k$. From (8.2.23) and (8.2.24) the mean squared error is

$$\begin{aligned} R(\hat{\boldsymbol{\alpha}}_R, \boldsymbol{\alpha}) &= k^2 \sum \frac{\alpha_i^2}{(\lambda_i + k)^2} + \sigma^2 \sum \frac{\lambda_i}{(\lambda_i + k)^2} \\ &= \sum \frac{k^2\alpha_i^2 + \sigma^2\lambda_i}{(\lambda_i + k)^2}. \end{aligned} \tag{8.2.25}$$

To establish the fact that $R(\hat{\boldsymbol{\alpha}}_R, \boldsymbol{\alpha})$ is less than $R(\hat{\boldsymbol{\alpha}}, \boldsymbol{\alpha})$ for some values of $k$, note first that $\hat{\boldsymbol{\alpha}}_R = \hat{\boldsymbol{\alpha}}$ when $k = 0$. We next show that

$$\left.\frac{dR(\hat{\boldsymbol{\alpha}}_R)}{dk}\right|_{k=0} < 0,$$

indicating that $R(\hat{\boldsymbol{\alpha}}_R, \boldsymbol{\alpha}) < R(\hat{\boldsymbol{\alpha}}, \boldsymbol{\alpha})$ for $k > 0$ and less than some upper value. Thus,

$$\frac{dR(\hat{\boldsymbol{\alpha}}_R, \boldsymbol{\alpha})}{dk} = 2 \sum \frac{\lambda_i(k\alpha_i^2 - \sigma^2)}{(\lambda_i + k)^2}; \tag{8.2.26}$$

at $k = 0$,

$$\left.\frac{dR(\hat{\boldsymbol{\alpha}}_R, \boldsymbol{\alpha})}{dk}\right|_{k=0} = -2\sigma^2 \sum \frac{1}{\lambda_i} < 0.$$

Moreover, it may be seen from (8.2.26) that choosing $k$ such that $(k\alpha_i^2 - \sigma^2) < 0$—for example, $k < \sigma^2/\alpha_M^2$, where $\alpha_M$ is $\max(\alpha_1, \ldots, \alpha_p)$—yields a ridge regression estimator that achieves a smaller risk than the OLS estimator, a result due to Hoerl and Kennard (1970a). As $k$ increases, $R(\hat{\boldsymbol{\alpha}}_R, \boldsymbol{\alpha})$ reaches a minimum and then increases without bound. Although the Hoerl-Kennard theorem assures the existence of an interval of $k$ for which $R(\hat{\boldsymbol{\alpha}}_R, \boldsymbol{\alpha}) < R(\hat{\boldsymbol{\alpha}}, \boldsymbol{\alpha})$, an appropriate value of $k$ must be determined without knowing the $\alpha_i$'s. Always choosing the same value of $k$, that is, choosing $k$ without reference to the data, will not yield a minimax estimator. In that case, for sufficiently large values of at least one $\alpha_i$, $R(\hat{\boldsymbol{\alpha}}_R, \boldsymbol{\alpha})$ will be greater than $R(\hat{\boldsymbol{\alpha}}, \boldsymbol{\alpha}) = \sigma^2 \Sigma\, (1/\lambda_i)$, because the latter does not depend on the $\alpha_i$; see Thisted (1978b). Thus, $k$ must depend on the observations in some way if it is to be minimax. The original treatment of ridge regression, Hoerl and Kennard (1970a) and (1970b), suggested an examination of the ridge trace—a plot of the $\hat{\beta}_{R,i}$ as a function of $k$. In the presence of multicollinearity, the typical ridge trace will display unstable values of the $\hat{\beta}_{R,i}$ for small values of $k$; the smallest value of $k$ consistent with stability is to be chosen in this approach. This method of selecting $k$ is rather subjective because the concept of stability is not well defined; see the discussion of this point in Thisted (1980). The lack of a well-defined value of $k$ also hampers attempts to determine the statistical properties of the estimator.

Other suggestions for data dependent values of $k$ have been offered, and several of these have been examined in Monte Carlo studies [see Vinod (1978) for references] and analytically [especially by Thisted (1976) and (1978b)]. For example, Hoerl, Kennard, and Baldwin (1975) suggested $k = p\hat{\sigma}^2/\|\hat{\boldsymbol{\alpha}}\|^2$, and Hoerl and Kennard (1976) propose $k = (p - 2)\hat{\sigma}^2/\|\hat{\boldsymbol{\alpha}}\|^2$. Thisted (1976) has shown that the former is minimax if and only if

$$\frac{\Sigma_j\, \lambda_j^{-2}}{\lambda_p^{-2}} \geqslant 2 + \frac{p}{2}, \qquad p \geqslant 3, \tag{8.2.27}$$

and the latter is minimax if and only if

$$\frac{\Sigma_j\, \lambda_j^{-2}}{\lambda_p^{-2}} \geqslant 1 + \frac{p}{2}, \qquad p \geqslant 3, \tag{8.2.28}$$

where $\lambda_p$ is the smallest root of $X'X$. (The expression $\Sigma_j\, \lambda_j^{-2}/\lambda_p^{-2}$ is termed the minimaxity index, or MMI.) The proof is in Thisted (1976), who points out that the conditions are difficult to meet when $\lambda_p$ is small—but this is the case of multicollinearity, the situation for which ridge regression was originally devised.

Three sets of data used by Belsley, Kuh, and Welsch (1980, pp. 163–173) suggest that the MMI for typical economics data do not satisfy Equations 8.2.27 or 8.2.28. Their

approach to the detection of multicollinearity is illustrated by estimation of a consumption function, a demand for corporate bonds equation, and an equation that predicts the proportion of income spent on nondurables and services. In each case the MMI is slightly greater than one (and considerably smaller than $1 + p/2$). Thus, in these cases, a ridge regression estimator based either on $k = p\hat{\sigma}^2/\|\hat{\boldsymbol{\alpha}}\|^2$ or $k = (p - 2)\hat{\sigma}^2/\|\hat{\boldsymbol{\alpha}}\|^2$ has a risk function that, for some values of $\boldsymbol{\beta}$, attains a higher value than the risk function of the OLS estimator.

In short, it turns out that ridge regression in principle always improves on OLS whether or not there is a problem of multicollinearity, but that in practice the improvement is more likely to occur when there is little or no multicollinearity. It should be pointed out that the comparison of performance is in terms of mean squared error, and the minimax criterion has been employed; other criteria might imply different conclusions. Empirical Bayes approaches have also been proposed for the estimation of $k$; see Efron and Morris (1972, 1974) and Thisted (1976).

In addition to the ridge regression estimator that we have been discussing, which is called the ordinary ridge estimator (ORE), Hoerl and Kennard (1970a) suggested a generalized ridge estimator (GRE). This estimator is defined by

$$\hat{\boldsymbol{\alpha}}_{\mathrm{GR}} = (\Lambda + K)^{-1}\Lambda\hat{\boldsymbol{\alpha}}, \tag{8.2.29}$$

where $K = \mathrm{diag}\{k_1, \ldots, k_p\}$; that is, in general a different value of $k$ is chosen for each $\alpha_i$, rather than $k_i = k$, for all $i$, as in ORE. The $i$th component of $\hat{\alpha}_{\mathrm{GR}}$ is given by

$$\hat{\alpha}_{\mathrm{GR},i} = \left[\frac{\lambda_i}{\lambda_i + k_i}\right]\hat{\alpha}_i;$$

therefore

$$E(\hat{\alpha}_{\mathrm{GR},i}) = \left[\frac{\lambda_i}{\lambda_i + k_i}\right]\alpha_i,$$

which implies a bias of

$$b_i(k_i) = \frac{-k_i\alpha_i}{\lambda_i + k_i}. \tag{8.2.30}$$

The variance is given by

$$\begin{aligned}\mathrm{Cov}(\hat{\alpha}_{\mathrm{GR}}) &= E[(\hat{\alpha}_{\mathrm{GR}} - E(\hat{\alpha}_{\mathrm{GR}}))(\hat{\alpha}_{\mathrm{GR}} - E(\hat{\alpha}_{\mathrm{GR}}))'] \\ &= \sigma^2(\Lambda + K)^{-1}\Lambda(\Lambda + K)^{-1}.\end{aligned} \tag{8.2.31}$$

The risk function for $\hat{\alpha}_{\mathrm{GR},i}$ under the mean squared error criterion is therefore given by

$$R(\hat{\alpha}_{\mathrm{GR},i}, \alpha_i) = \frac{\sigma^2\lambda_i + \alpha_i^2k_i^2}{(\lambda_i + k_i)^2}. \tag{8.2.32}$$

To compare this risk with that of OLS, subtract $\sigma^2/\lambda_i$ from (8.2.32) to obtain

$$R(\hat{\alpha}_{\mathrm{GR},i}, \alpha_i) - R(\hat{\alpha}_i, \alpha_i) = \frac{k_i(\lambda_i\alpha_i^2k_i - 2\sigma^2\lambda_i - k_i\sigma^2)}{\lambda_i(\lambda_i + k_i)^2}, \tag{8.2.33}$$

which is negative if and only if

$$0 < k_i < \frac{2\sigma^2}{\alpha_i^2 - \sigma^2\lambda_i^{-1}}. \tag{8.2.34}$$

Since $\lambda_i > 0$, a sufficient condition for the dominance of GRE is

$$0 < k_i < \frac{2\sigma^2}{\alpha_i^2}, \tag{8.2.35}$$

and another sufficient condition is

$$0 < k_i \leqslant \frac{\sigma^2}{\alpha_i^2}. \tag{8.2.36}$$

It may be verified that $R(\hat{\alpha}_{GR,i}, \alpha_i)$ is minimized at $k_i = \sigma^2/\alpha_i^2$, and with that choice of $k$,

$$R(\hat{\alpha}_{GR,i}, \alpha_i) = \frac{\sigma^2}{\lambda_i + \sigma^2/\alpha_i^2}.$$

Conditions 8.2.34, 8.2.35, 8.2.36, and the minimizing value of $k_i$ have been used to devise estimators of $k$ in ORE. Several of the suggested $k$'s are harmonic means of upper limits of the $k_i$ that appear in these conditions.[3]

A number of analytic results concerning the performance of generalized ridge estimators have been obtained. Thisted (1978a) shows that $\hat{k}_i$ must not depend on $\hat{\boldsymbol{\alpha}}$ only through $\hat{\alpha}_i$ if it is to dominate OLS; for example, the sample counterpart of (8.2.36), $\hat{k}_i = \hat{\sigma}^2/\hat{\alpha}_i^2$, does not yield a minimax estimator. Minimax GRE's have been developed by Hudson (1974), Berger (1975), and Strawderman (1978). Hudson and Berger propose

$$\hat{k}_i = \frac{(p-2)\sigma^2\lambda_i^2}{\Sigma\, \lambda_j^2\hat{\alpha}_j^2 - (p-2)\sigma^2\lambda_i}, \qquad \text{for known } \sigma^2,$$

which depends on all the $\hat{\alpha}_j$'s.

Strawderman considers the risk function

$$R(\hat{\boldsymbol{\beta}}, \boldsymbol{\beta}) = \frac{1}{\sigma^2} E[(\hat{\boldsymbol{\beta}} - \boldsymbol{\beta})'B(\hat{\boldsymbol{\beta}} - \boldsymbol{\beta})],$$

where $B$ is positive definite. For $p \geqslant 3$, he shows that the GRE,

$$\hat{\boldsymbol{\beta}}_{GR} = \left[I + \frac{asBX'X}{\hat{\boldsymbol{\beta}}'X'X\hat{\boldsymbol{\beta}} + gs + h}\right]^{-1}\hat{\boldsymbol{\beta}},$$

is minimax, where $s = \|\mathbf{y} - X\hat{\boldsymbol{\beta}}\|^2, 0 \leqslant a \leqslant 2(p-2)/(n-p+2)\lambda_M^{-1}, h \geqslant 0, g \geqslant 2p/(n-p+2)$, and $\lambda_M$ is the maximum c.r. of $BX'X$. This estimator is related to an estimator proposed by Efron and Morris (1976). Strawderman notes that the dominating GRE depends on the loss structure because $B$, which plays the role of a weighting matrix

[3]The harmonic mean of the $n$ positive numbers $a_1, \ldots, a_n$ is defined as $n/\Sigma_{i=1}^n (1/a_i)$.

in the risk function, appears in the estimator. Furthermore, no GRE dominates OLS for all choices of $B$. Since in econometric studies there is rarely agreement on the nature of the loss function, the Strawderman estimator may not be generally useful for such applications.

## 8.3 Econometric Applications of James-Stein and Related Estimators

Few econometric applications of James-Stein estimators have appeared. An exception is the expository article by Aigner and Judge (1977). Their approach is to determine whether the James-Stein procedure is capable of improving on OLS in three empirical studies that had been conducted by other researchers. Of particular importance in this connection is whether

$$\frac{\text{tr}(X'X)^{-1}}{d_L} > 2.$$

If not, no $c$ exists that permits the James-Stein estimator to dominate OLS under the "estimation" goal,

$$E[\|\mathbf{b} - \boldsymbol{\beta}\|^2].$$

In view of the multicollinearity often found in economic data, it is important to see whether this condition is met in practice.

The first empirical study is concerned with the commodity structure of U.S. trade. The study, conducted by Baldwin (1971), has "world trade balances" as the dependent variable and nine independent variables (plus an intercept). The value of $[\text{tr}(X'X)^{-1}]/d_L$ is less than 2, generally very close to 1, so that James-Stein does not dominate OLS for these data. Comments about the preliminary test estimator are also made in the article.

The second application is to a study of price-cost margins and industry structure, with reference to the work of Weiss (1974). The dependent variable is gross revenues minus direct costs for each industry, divided by gross revenues. There are 11 independent variables, and the data are from the 1963 Census of Manufactures. For several of the models examined, $[\text{tr}(X'X)^{-1}]/d_L > 2$, which implies that the James-Stein estimators have a lower risk than OLS. Differences between the coefficients estimated by OLS and James-Stein are not great in this example.

A third application is to a study of the Phillips curve, based on the work of Perry (1964). The rate of change in nominal wages is the dependent variable, and there are seven independent variables. Data are quarterly for 1954 through 1962. Most values of $[\text{tr}(X'X)^{-1}]/d_L$ are slightly below 2. Aigner and Judge find little difference between out-of-sample forecasts based on OLS and on James-Stein estimators.

Ridge regression has been rather widely used in econometric applications; the review article by Vinod (1978) contains many references.

## 8.4 Conclusions

We have surveyed a large and rapidly growing body of literature in this part. Since the techniques discussed are relatively new and have not been widely applied, whether they will become generally accepted in applied work is still uncertain. The following summarizes the main points of our discussion.[4]

1. Enlarging the set of possible estimators considered in the conventional approach to regression, which confines itself to unbiased estimators, opens up many interesting possibilities. Adoption of a quadratic loss function, for example, permits comparisons of the performance of biased and unbiased estimators. Since such comparisons are not possible if estimators must be unbiased, potentially useful estimators are never examined. In an econometric application, Trivedi (1978) investigates estimation of distributed lags under a quadratic loss criterion. It should be pointed out that the distributions of the various estimators discussed in this chapter are not known. Accordingly, estimators that perform well under a quadratic loss criterion may not be useful for testing hypotheses or other purposes for which the distribution is needed. Results on estimator performance are sensitive to choice of loss function, and it is rare in econometrics to find a situation where an explicit loss function can be generally agreed upon. In the estimation case, however, the fact that mean squared error reduces to the squared bias plus the variance provides an intuitive justification for its adoption.

2. The James-Stein and related estimators often have good statistical properties compared to the methods usually used in econometrics. It is still too early to tell what their contributions to econometrics will be; more experience with empirical studies is needed, and theoretical extension to typical econometric problems should be undertaken. A recent example of the latter is the use of a Stein-like estimator in the estimation of the reduced form in a simultaneous equation model; see Maasoumi (1978).

3. Recent work has demonstrated the relationship between the James-Stein and ridge regression estimators and has begun to establish their small sample properties. In particular, minimax generalized ridge estimators have been proposed, but their performance depends upon the loss function. It has also been found that ordinary ridge estimators do not dominate OLS when multicollinearity is severe.

4. On the more immediate practical level, results concerning performance of the preliminary test estimator under a quadratic loss criterion are of great importance. Although preliminary test estimators of the type described here have been widely used in practice, they cannot be justified on the usual criterion of linear unbiased minimum variance because omitting a variable "known" to be present in a model introduces bias. The procedure is often adopted when multicollinearity appears to be a problem since variances of estimated coefficients are reduced when equality constraints are placed on a subset of coefficients. In effect, a trade-off of bias for lowered variance is adopted, and the quadratic loss function is a natural representation of that trade-off. Analysis of this estimator shows that some gains in risk are obtained for small departures of the coefficients from hypothesized values, but for the larger departures the preliminary test estimator is worse than the unconstrained estimator. The value of true parameters at which change occurs depends on the $X'X$ matrix and the level of significance employed; in

[4]See Judge and Bock (1978) for an extensive summary of this literature and conclusions.

addition, the more $X'X$ departs from an identity matrix, the smaller is the range over which the risk of the preliminary test estimator is smaller than that of the OLS estimator.

## 8.5 References

Aigner, D. J. and G. G. Judge (1977), ''Application of Pre-Test and Stein Estimators to Economic Data,'' *Econometrica,* **45,** 1279–1288.

Baldwin, R. E. (1971), ''Determinants of the Commodity Structure of U.S. Trade,'' *American Economic Review,* **61,** 126–146.

Belsey, D. A., E. Kuh, and R. E. Welsch (1980), *Regression Diagnostics,* New York: Wiley.

Berger, J. O. (1975), ''Minimax Estimation of Location Vectors for a Wide Class of Densities,'' *Annals of Statistics,* **3,** 1318–1328.

Bock, M. E., T. A. Yancey, and G. G. Judge (1973), ''The Statistical Consequences of Preliminary Test Estimators in Regression,'' *Journal of the American Statistical Association,* **68,** 109–116.

Cooley, T. F. and S. F. LeRoy (1981), ''Identification and Estimation of Money Demand,'' *American Economic Review,* **71,** 825–844.

Efron, B. and C. Morris (1972), ''Limiting the Risk of Bayes and Empirical Bayes Estimators—Part II: The Empirical Bayes Case,'' *Journal of the American Statistical Association,* **67,** 130–139.

Efron, B. and C. Morris (1974), ''Data Analysis Using Stein's Estimator and Its Generalizations,'' R-1394-OEO, The RAND Corporation.

Efron, B. and C. Morris (1976), ''Families of Minimax Estimators of the Mean of a Multivariate Normal Distribution,'' *The Annals of Statistics,* **4,** 11–21.

Greenberg, E. (1980), ''Finite Sample Moments of a Preliminary-Test Estimator in the Case of Possible Heteroscedasticity,'' *Econometrica,* **48,** 1805–1813.

Hoerl, A. E. and R. W. Kennard (1970a), ''Ridge Regression: Biased Estimation for Nonorthogonal Problems,'' *Technometrics,* **12,** 55–67.

Hoerl, A. E. and R. W. Kennard (1970b), ''Ridge Regression: Applications to Nonorthogonal Problems,'' *Technometrics,* **12,** 69–82.

Hoerl, A. E. and R. W. Kennard (1976), ''Ridge Regression: Iterative Estimation of the Biasing Parameter,'' *Communications in Statistics,* **5,** 77–88.

Hoerl, A. E., R. W. Kennard, and K. F. Baldwin (1975), ''Ridge Regression: Some Simulations,'' *Communications in Statistics,* **4,** 105–123.

Hudson, H. M. (1974), ''Empirical Bayes Estimation,'' Ph.D. Thesis, Department of Statistics, Stanford University.

Judge, G. G. and M. E. Bock (1978), *The Statistical Implications of Pre-Test and Stein-Rule Estimators in Econometrics,* Amsterdam: North-Holland.

Leamer, E. E. (1978), *Specification Searches,* New York: Wiley.

Maasoumi, E. (1978), "A Modified Stein-like Estimator for the Reduced Form Coefficients of Simultaneous Equations," *Econometrica,* **46,** 695–703.

Ohtani, K. and T. Toyoda (1980), "Estimation of Regression Coefficients after a Preliminary Test for Homoscedasticity," *Journal of Econometrics,* **12,** 151–159.

Perry, G. L. (1964), "The Determinants of Wage Rate Changes and the Inflation-Unemployment Trade-off for the United States," *Review of Economic Studies,* **31,** 287–308.

Sclove, S. L., C. Morris, and R. Radhakrishnan (1972), "Non-Optimality of Preliminary-Test Estimators for the Mean of a Multivariate Normal Distribution," *The Annals of Mathematical Statistics,* **43,** 1481–1490.

Strawderman, W. E. (1978), "Minimax Adaptive Generalized Ridge Regression Estimators," *Journal of the American Statistical Association,* **73,** 623–627.

Thisted, R. A. (1976), "Ridge Regression, Minimax Estimation and Empirical Bayes Methods," Ph.D. Thesis, Department of Statistics, Stanford Univeristy.

Thisted, R. A. (1978a), "On Generalized Ridge Regression," Technical Report No. 57, Department of Statistics, University of Chicago.

Thisted, R. A. (1978b), "Multicollinearity, Information, and Ridge Regression," Technical Report No. 66, Department of Statistics, University of Chicago.

Thisted, R. A. (1980), "Comment," *Journal of the American Statistical Association,* **75,** 81–86.

Trivedi, P. K. (1978), "Estimation of a Distributed Lag Model Under Quadratic Loss," *Econometrica,* **46,** 1181–1192.

Ullah, A. and S. Ullah (1978), "Double *k*-Class Estimators of Coefficients in Linear Regression," *Econometrica,* **46,** 705–722.

Vinod, H. D. (1978), "A Survey of Ridge Regression and Related Techniques for Improvements over Ordinary Least Squares," *Review of Economics and Statistics,* **60,** 121–131.

Vinod, H. D. (1980), "Improved Stein-Rule Estimator for Regression Problems," *Journal of Econometrics,* **12,** 143–150.

Weiss, L. W. (1974), "The Concentration-Profits Relationship and Antitrust," Columbia Law School *Conference on Industrial Concentration,* Columbia University.

## APPENDIX TO CHAPTER 8

In the text we have dealt with the simplest hypothesis, $\boldsymbol{\beta} = \mathbf{0}$. To permit the analysis of more general restrictions of the form $R\boldsymbol{\beta} = r$, where $R$ is $J \times p$ and $\mathbf{r}$ is $J \times 1$, it is convenient to transform the model to a canonical form. We start with the model $\mathbf{y} = X\boldsymbol{\beta} + \mathbf{e}$, and the estimator will be $\hat{\boldsymbol{\beta}}$ if the hypothesis $R\boldsymbol{\beta} = \mathbf{r}$ is rejected and the restricted estimator,

$$\hat{\boldsymbol{\beta}} - (X'X)^{-1}R'[R(X'X)^{-1}R']^{-1}(R\hat{\boldsymbol{\beta}} - \mathbf{r}) = \hat{\boldsymbol{\beta}} - M(R\hat{\boldsymbol{\beta}} - \mathbf{r}),$$

if the hypothesis is not rejected. Let $P$ be a $p \times p$ nonsingular matrix such that

$$P(X'X)^{-1}P' = I_p,$$

and $Q$ an orthogonal $p \times p$ matrix such that

$$Q(P^{-1})'R'[R(X'X)^{-1}R']^{-1}RP^{-1}Q' = \begin{bmatrix} I_J & 0 \\ 0 & 0 \end{bmatrix}.$$

(Such a $Q$ always exists because

$$\begin{aligned} A &= (P^{-1})'R'[R(X'X)^{-1}R']^{-1}RP^{-1} \\ &= (P^{-1})'R'[RP^{-1}P(X'X)^{-1}P'(P')^{-1}R']^{-1}RP^{-1} \\ &= (P^{-1})'R'[RP^{-1}(P')^{-1}R']^{-1}RP^{-1} \end{aligned}$$

is a symmetric idempotent matrix of rank $J$ whose $J$ nonzero characteristic roots are all equal to one.) Define $W = QP$ and note that

$$W'(X'X)^{-1}W = I.$$

Then rewrite the original model as

$$\begin{aligned} \mathbf{y} = X\boldsymbol{\beta} + \mathbf{e} &= XW^{-1}W\boldsymbol{\beta} + \mathbf{e} \\ &= Z\boldsymbol{\theta} + \mathbf{e}. \end{aligned}$$

To rewrite the constraint, start with

$$\mathbf{r} = R\boldsymbol{\beta} = RW^{-1}\boldsymbol{\theta} = RP^{-1}Q'\boldsymbol{\theta}. \qquad \textbf{(8A.1)}$$

Premultiplying both sides of (8A.1) by the nonsingular matrix

$$Q(P^{-1})'R'[R(X'X)^{-1}R']^{-1}$$

yields

$$\begin{bmatrix} I_J & 0 \\ 0 & 0 \end{bmatrix} \boldsymbol{\theta} = Q(P^{-1})'R'[R(X'X)^{-1}R']^{-1}\mathbf{r} \equiv \mathbf{r}_0.$$

In this form, the OLS estimator is

$$\hat{\boldsymbol{\theta}} = Z'\mathbf{y},$$

and the restricted least squares estimator is

$$\begin{bmatrix} \mathbf{r}_0 \\ \hat{\boldsymbol{\theta}}_{p-J} \end{bmatrix},$$

where $\hat{\boldsymbol{\theta}}_{p-J} = [0, I_{p-J}]\hat{\boldsymbol{\theta}}$.

This completes the reparameterization. This procedure is developed and used in Bock, Yancey, and Judge (1972) to compare OLS, restricted OLS, and preliminary test estimators. (Note that their notation is somewhat different from the one we used.) Also see Aigner and Judge (1977).

## References

Aigner, D. J. and G. G. Judge (1977), "Application of Pre-Test and Stein Estimators to Economic Data," *Econometrica,* **45,** 1279–1288.

Bock, M. E., T. A. Yancey, and G. G. Judge (1972), "The Statistical Consequences of Preliminary-Test Estimators in Regression," *Journal of the American Statistical Association,* **68,** 109–116.

# PART IV

# Topics in Simultaneous Equation Theory

The three chapters of this part deal with identification and estimation of parameters in simultaneous equation models. Chapter 9 takes up several topics in the identification problem that are not usually covered in introductory econometrics courses. Chapter 10 turns to the exact distributions and moments of parameter estimates in equations with two included endogenous variables. Detailed derivations are provided for the exact distribution of the ordinary least squares and two stage least squares methods and for the moments of $k$-class estimators; summaries and references are provided for other estimators. Chapter 11 contains a detailed proof of a theorem on the existence of moments of $k$-class estimators for equations with any number of included endogenous variables as well as summaries and references to other current work in the area of estimation in simultaneous equation models.

# CHAPTER 9

# The Identification Problem

After presenting definitions and other preliminary material we turn to conditions for identification in models containing various combinations of linear and nonlinear variables, parameters, and restrictions. Sections 9.2, 9.3, and 9.4 are concerned with the standard simultaneous equation model; Section 9.5 discusses identification in more general settings; and Section 9.6 briefly mentions additional topics to which further references are given. We assume that the reader is familiar with the material on identification that appears in Johnston (1972) or another textbook at the same level.

## 9.1 Preliminaries

The problem of identification, although of general concern to statisticians, is most often encountered by econometricians in connection with the simultaneous equation model,

$$B\mathbf{y}_t + \Gamma\mathbf{x}_t = \mathbf{u}_t, \qquad t = 1, \ldots, T, \tag{9.1.1}$$

where $B$ is a $G \times G$ nonsingular matrix, $\Gamma$ is $G \times K$, $\mathbf{y}_t$ is a $G \times 1$ vector of endogenous variables, $\mathbf{x}_t$ is a $K \times 1$ vector of predetermined variables, and $\mathbf{u}_t$ is a $G \times 1$ vector of random disturbances. Assuming that the $\mathbf{u}_t$ are independent and identically distributed (which rules out autocorrelated disturbances), the joint density for the sample may be written as

$$f(\mathbf{u}_1, \ldots, \mathbf{u}_T) = f(\mathbf{u}_1) \ldots f(\mathbf{u}_T). \tag{9.1.2}$$

Making the change of variables defined by (9.1.1), we may write

$$p(y; X, B, \Gamma) = |B|^T \prod_{t=1}^{T} f(\mathbf{u}_t), \tag{9.1.3}$$

where $y = (\mathbf{y}_1, \ldots, \mathbf{y}_T)$ and $X = (\mathbf{x}_1, \ldots, \mathbf{x}_T)$. The central question dealt with in the study of identification is whether it is possible to tell the difference between the true $B$ and $\Gamma$ and linear combinations of their rows—$FB$ and $F\Gamma$, where $F$ is any nonsingular matrix—from knowledge of the probability density function of the $\mathbf{y}_t$ and other information. To compute the density in which $FB$ and $F\Gamma$ are the parameters, premultiply (9.1.1) by $F$ to obtain

$$FB\mathbf{y}_t + F\Gamma\mathbf{x}_t = F\mathbf{u}_t \equiv \mathbf{w}_t,$$

where $\mathbf{w}_1, \ldots, \mathbf{w}_T$ has the joint density

$$\begin{aligned} g(\mathbf{w}_1, \ldots, \mathbf{w}_T) &= g(\mathbf{w}_1) \ldots g(\mathbf{w}_T) \\ &= |F^{-1}|^T f(\mathbf{u}_1) \ldots f(\mathbf{u}_T). \end{aligned} \tag{9.1.4}$$

We can also transform from $\mathbf{w}_t$ to $\mathbf{y}_t$, obtaining

$$\begin{aligned} p(y; X, FB, F\Gamma) &= |F|^T|B|^T g(\mathbf{w}_1) \ldots g(\mathbf{w}_T) \\ &= |B|^T f(\mathbf{u}_1) \ldots f(\mathbf{u}_T). \end{aligned} \quad \textbf{(9.1.5)}$$

Comparing (9.1.3) and (9.1.5), we see that $p(y; X, FB, F\Gamma) = p(y; X, B, \Gamma)$, which implies that knowledge of the density alone does not permit us to determine whether the unknown parameters are $(B, \Gamma)$ or $(FB, F\Gamma)$. This discussion motivates the following definition, following Rothenberg (1971):

**Definition**

Two parameter matrices $\alpha^1$ and $\alpha^2$ are *observationally equivalent* if $f(y, \alpha^1) = f(y, \alpha^2)$ for all $y$.

In terms of this definition it can be seen that $(B, \Gamma)$ and $(FB, F\Gamma)$ are observationally equivalent. Identification is next defined.

**Definition**

A parameter matrix $\alpha^0$ is said to be (globally) *identifiable* if there is no other $\alpha^0$ which is observationally equivalent.

In some cases, particularly when nonlinearities are present, we must be content with a weaker form of identifiability:

**Definition**

A parameter matrix $\alpha^0$ is *locally identifiable* if there exists an open neighborhood of $\alpha^0$ containing no other $\alpha$ which is observationally equivalent.

It may be possible to identify observationally equivalent parameter matrices with the use of a priori restrictions on parameters, which come from relevant economic theory. These are written as $\psi_i(\alpha) = 0$. For example, there may be reason to believe that $y_j$ does not belong in the $i$th equation, which yields the *exclusion* restriction, $\beta_{ij} = 0$. Or economic theory may imply a symmetry condition such as $\beta_{ij} = \beta_{ji}$, which would be written as $\beta_{ij} - \beta_{ji} = 0$. Or theory may suggest that certain coefficients sum to unity, giving $\Sigma_i\gamma_{ij} - 1 = 0$. Restrictions may also be nonlinear.

Parameter matrices that satisfy such restrictions are called *admissible*, and the definitions of identifiability and local identifiability should be amended in the presence of such restrictions by requiring that there exist no other $\alpha$ that is both admissible (i.e., satisfies the a priori restrictions) and observationally equivalent to $\alpha^0$. The role of restrictions in identifying the parameters of models such as (9.1.1) is now clear: although $(B, \Gamma)$ and $(FB, F\Gamma)$ are observationally equivalent, for not all $F$ will $(FB, F\Gamma)$ satisfy the restrictions placed on $(B, \Gamma)$, hence such $(FB, F\Gamma)$ are not admissible. If all $F$ other than $F = I$ can be ruled out because the resulting $(FB, F\Gamma)$ fail to satisfy the restrictions, all parameters of the system are identified. And if the restrictions imply, for example, that the first row of $F$ must be the first row of the identity matrix, the first equation is identified. We return to these matters below.

One other preliminary topic should be mentioned—the relationship between the existence of a consistent estimator of a parameter and its identifiability. This question has recently been addressed in a useful short article by Gabrielsen (1978), who proves the following:

**Theorem 9.1.1**

The existence of a consistent estimator for $\boldsymbol{\theta}$ implies its identifiability, but there may be no consistent estimator for an identifiable parameter.

**Proof**

Suppose $\boldsymbol{\theta}$ is not identifiable. Then there are at least two vectors $\boldsymbol{\theta}^1$ and $\boldsymbol{\theta}^2$ that are observationally equivalent. If $\hat{\boldsymbol{\theta}}$ is a consistent estimator for $\boldsymbol{\theta}$, it should converge, in principle, to both $\boldsymbol{\theta}^1$ and $\boldsymbol{\theta}^2$; but this is impossible by the definition of consistency. That is, lack of identifiability implies the lack of a consistent estimator. The fact that the converse is not true is shown by a counterexample. Let

$$y_i = \beta r^i + u_i, \qquad |r| < 1, \qquad i = 1, \ldots, n,$$

where $y_i \sim N(\beta r^i, 1)$. Since knowledge of the density determines $\beta$, $\beta$ is identifiable. Now the least squares estimator of $\beta$,

$$\hat{\beta}_n = \sum_{i=1}^{n} r^i y_i / \sum_{i=1}^{n} r^{2i},$$

converges in probability to the nondegenerate random variable $\hat{\beta}$, where

$$\hat{\beta} \sim N(\beta, (1 - r^2)/r^2),$$

so that $\hat{\beta}_n$ is not consistent for $\beta$. Gabrielsen presents an argument to show that the existence of a consistent estimator would contradict the known result that a test based on $\hat{\beta}_n$ is the uniformly most powerful test for the hypothesis $\beta = 0$ against the alternative $\beta > 0$. □

The theorem is useful in connection with estimation of the reduced form. Upon premultiplying (9.1.1) by $B^{-1}$ and rearranging, we have

$$\begin{aligned}\mathbf{y}_t &= -B^{-1}\Gamma\mathbf{x}_t + B^{-1}\mathbf{u}_t \\ &= \Pi\mathbf{x}_t + \mathbf{v}_t,\end{aligned}$$

where the $G \times K$ matrix $\Pi$ contains the reduced form parameters. Under certain conditions, it is proved in introductory econometrics texts that the least squares regression coefficients obtained by regressing each component of $y$ on all the variables contained in $X$ are consistent estimators of the columns of $\Pi$. Hence $\Pi$ is identifiable.

## 9.2 Identification in Models That Are Linear in Parameters, Variables, and Restrictions

This section is largely based on Richmond (1974), although the notation employed is somewhat different. It generalizes slightly the usual textbook discussion of identification both by permitting cross-equation constraints and by considering the identification of linear combinations of parameters, including individual parameters. The approach, due to Fisher (1966), is algebraic and is related to the concept of "estimable functions," discussed in the statistics literature.

We consider the system of structural equations

$$B\mathbf{y} + \Gamma\mathbf{x} = \mathbf{u}, \tag{9.2.1}$$

where $B$ is $G \times G$, $\Gamma$ is $G \times K$, $\mathbf{y}$ is a $G \times 1$ vector of endogenous variables, $\mathbf{x}$ is a $K \times 1$ vector of exogenous variables, and $\mathbf{u}$ is a $G \times 1$ vector of random disturbances. Before proceeding it will be useful to define the matrix operator, vec($A$):

**Definition**

Let

$$A = \begin{bmatrix} \mathbf{a}_1 \\ \mathbf{a}_2 \\ \cdot \\ \cdot \\ \cdot \\ \mathbf{a}_m \end{bmatrix},$$

where $A$ is $m \times n$ and $\mathbf{a}_i$ is $1 \times n$, $i = 1, \ldots, m$. Then $\text{vec}(A) = [\mathbf{a}_1, \mathbf{a}_2, \ldots, \mathbf{a}_m]$, a $1 \times mn$ vector.

Returning to (9.2.1), we define

$$A = (B, \Gamma) = \begin{bmatrix} \boldsymbol{\alpha}_1 \\ \boldsymbol{\alpha}_2 \\ \cdot \\ \cdot \\ \cdot \\ \boldsymbol{\alpha}_G \end{bmatrix} = \begin{bmatrix} \beta_{11}\ \beta_{12} \cdots \beta_{1G}\ \gamma_{11} \cdots \gamma_{1K} \\ \cdot \\ \cdot \\ \cdot \\ \beta_{G1} \cdots \beta_{GG}\ \gamma_{G1} \cdots \gamma_{GK} \end{bmatrix}$$

$$\begin{aligned} \boldsymbol{\alpha} &= \text{vec}(A) = (\boldsymbol{\alpha}_1, \boldsymbol{\alpha}_2, \ldots, \boldsymbol{\alpha}_G) \\ &= (\beta_{11}, \cdots, \beta_{1G}, \gamma_{11}, \cdots, \gamma_{1K}, \beta_{21}, \ldots, \gamma_{GK}). \end{aligned}$$

$\boldsymbol{\alpha}$ is a $1 \times G(G + K)$ vector of coefficients, and $\boldsymbol{\alpha}_i$ contains the coefficients of the $i$th equation, with the $\beta_{ij}$'s ($j = 1, \ldots, G$) in the first $G$ positions and the $\gamma_{ik}$'s ($k = 1, \ldots, K$) in the remaining positions.

We assume the existence of $R$ linear restrictions among the components of $\boldsymbol{\alpha}$, which may relate parameters in different equations; they will be written as

$$\boldsymbol{\alpha}\boldsymbol{\phi}_j = c_j, \qquad j = 1, \ldots, R, \tag{9.2.3}$$

where $\boldsymbol{\phi}_j$ is $G(G + K) \times 1$ and $c_j$ is a scalar. Define

$$\Phi = [\boldsymbol{\phi}_1, \ldots, \boldsymbol{\phi}_R] \quad \text{and} \quad \mathbf{c} = [c_1, \ldots, c_R], \tag{9.2.4}$$

so that

$$\boldsymbol{\alpha}\Phi = \mathbf{c}, \tag{9.2.5}$$

where $\Phi$ is $G(G + K) \times R$ and $c$ is $1 \times R$.

Defining the $G \times K$ reduced form coefficient matrix as

$$\Pi = -B^{-1}\Gamma \tag{9.2.6}$$

implies

$$B\Pi + \Gamma = 0 \tag{9.2.7}$$

or

$$AW = 0, \tag{9.2.8}$$

where

$$W = \begin{bmatrix} \Pi \\ I \end{bmatrix}, \tag{9.2.9}$$

which has dimension $(G + K) \times K$. In terms of $\boldsymbol{\alpha}$, we may rewrite (9.2.8) as

$$\boldsymbol{\alpha}\begin{bmatrix} W & & & \\ & W & & 0 \\ & & \ddots & \\ 0 & & & W \end{bmatrix} = \boldsymbol{\alpha}[I_G \otimes W] = \boldsymbol{\alpha}W^* = \mathbf{0}, \tag{9.2.10}$$

where $[I_G \otimes W] = W^*$ and $W^*$ is $G(G + K) \times GK$. Bringing together (9.2.5) and (9.2.10), we may write

$$\boldsymbol{\alpha}[W^*, \Phi] = [\boldsymbol{\alpha}W^*, \boldsymbol{\alpha}\Phi] = [\mathbf{0}, \mathbf{c}]. \tag{9.2.11}$$

The last set of equations may be thought of as a system of $GK + R$ equations in the $G(G + K)$ unknown $\alpha_i$'s. If $W^*$ were known, a unique $\boldsymbol{\alpha}$ would exist if and only if $r(W^*, \Phi) = G(G + K)$. This argument proves the following theorem:

**Theorem 9.2.1**

The system (9.2.1) subject to restrictions (9.2.5) is identified if and only if $r(W^*, \Phi) = G(G + K)$.

From a statistical point of view, unique consistent estimators would exist if we had a consistent estimator for $W$ and if the above rank condition is satisfied. As noted above, a consistent estimator is available for $\Pi$, hence for $W^*$. A *necessary* condition for the rank condition to hold is $GK + R \geqslant G(G + K)$, or $R \geqslant G^2$. If the $G$ conventional normalizing conditions are adopted [$\beta_{ii} = 1, i = 1, \ldots, G$], then $G(G - 1)$ additional restrictions are required.

The identifiability condition may also be expressed in terms of the structural parameters. Consider a nonsingular transformation of the original structure,

$$FA = \Delta \equiv \begin{bmatrix} \boldsymbol{\delta}_1 \\ \cdot \\ \cdot \\ \cdot \\ \boldsymbol{\delta}_G \end{bmatrix}, \tag{9.2.12}$$

$$F = \begin{bmatrix} \mathbf{f}_1 \\ \cdot \\ \cdot \\ \cdot \\ \mathbf{f}_G \end{bmatrix}, \tag{9.2.13}$$

where $F$ is $G \times G$, $\boldsymbol{\delta}_i$ is $1 \times (G + K)$, and $\mathbf{f}_i$ is $1 \times G$. Under the transformation, the $i$th transformed equation is given by $\mathbf{f}_i A = \boldsymbol{\delta}_i$. To be an admissible parameter, $\boldsymbol{\delta}_i$ must satisfy the same restrictions as $\boldsymbol{\alpha}_i$; hence,

$$[\mathbf{f}_1 A, \ldots, \mathbf{f}_G A]\Phi = \mathbf{f}A^*\Phi = \mathbf{c}, \tag{9.2.14}$$

where $\mathbf{f} = \text{vec}(\mathbf{F}) \equiv (\mathbf{f}_1, \ldots, \mathbf{f}_G)$ and $A^* = I_G \otimes A$. Since it is assumed that $\mathbf{f} = \text{vec}(\mathrm{I})$ satisfies (9.2.14), a necessary and sufficient condition for identification is contained in the following theorem:

**Theorem 9.2.2**

A necessary and sufficient condition for the identification of (9.2.1) subject to (9.2.5) is $r(A^*\Phi) = G^2$.

The reader should verify that a *necessary* condition for identification is $R \geqslant G^2$, as determined above. To illustrate this result, consider the following system:

$$\beta_{11}y_1 + \beta_{12}y_2 + \gamma_{11}x_1 = u_1$$

$$\beta_{21}y_1 + \beta_{22}y_2 + \gamma_{21}x_1 = u_2,$$

subject to

$$\gamma_{11} - \gamma_{21} = 0$$
$$\beta_{11} - 1 = 0$$
$$\beta_{22} - 1 = 0$$
$$\beta_{12} = 0.$$

The first restriction is a cross-equation restriction; the others each pertain to one equation at a time. Note that only the first equation is identified in the absence of the first restriction. In this case,

$$A^*\Phi = \begin{bmatrix} \beta_{11} & \beta_{12} & \gamma_{11} & 0 & 0 & 0 \\ \beta_{21} & \beta_{22} & \gamma_{21} & 0 & 0 & 0 \\ 0 & 0 & 0 & \beta_{11} & \beta_{12} & \gamma_{11} \\ 0 & 0 & 0 & \beta_{21} & \beta_{22} & \gamma_{21} \end{bmatrix} \begin{bmatrix} 0 & 1 & 0 & 0 \\ 0 & 0 & 0 & 1 \\ 1 & 0 & 0 & 0 \\ 0 & 0 & 0 & 0 \\ 0 & 0 & 1 & 0 \\ -1 & 0 & 0 & 0 \end{bmatrix}$$

$$= \begin{bmatrix} \gamma_{11} & \beta_{11} & 0 & \beta_{12} \\ \gamma_{21} & \beta_{21} & 0 & \beta_{22} \\ -\gamma_{11} & 0 & \beta_{12} & 0 \\ -\gamma_{21} & 0 & \beta_{22} & 0 \end{bmatrix} = \begin{bmatrix} \gamma_{11} & 1 & 0 & 0 \\ \gamma_{11} & \beta_{21} & 0 & 1 \\ -\gamma_{11} & 0 & 0 & 0 \\ -\gamma_{11} & 0 & 1 & 0 \end{bmatrix},$$

from which it may be seen that $r(A^*\Phi) = 4$ unless $\gamma_{11} = 0$; since $G^2 = 4$, the system is identified.

The discussion to this point has been concerned with identification of all the parameters of a model. Occasionally, a researcher may be interested in estimating a linear combination of parameters, which includes the case of a single parameter. Therefore, following Richmond (1974), we next consider the question of the identifiability of a linear combination of the elements of $\boldsymbol{\alpha}$, $\boldsymbol{\alpha}\mathbf{u}'$, where $\mathbf{u}'$ is $G(G + K) \times 1$. To examine this question we require two algebraic lemmas:

**Lemma 9.2.1**

Let $A$ be $m \times n$, $\mathbf{w}$ be $1 \times m$, $\mathbf{b}$ be $1 \times n$, $\mathbf{z}$ be $1 \times n$ and $r(A) = r$. Then *either (a)* $\mathbf{w}A = \mathbf{b}$ has a solution *or* (b) there exists a $\mathbf{z}$ such that $\mathbf{z}A' = \mathbf{0}$ and $\mathbf{b}\mathbf{z}' = 1$, but not both (a) and (b).

**Proof**

The proof is due to Gale (1960, p. 41). (i) Let $\mathbf{w}$ satisfy $\mathbf{w}A = \mathbf{b}$. Then $\mathbf{w}A\mathbf{z}' = \mathbf{b}\mathbf{z}'$, so that we cannot have $A\mathbf{z}' = \mathbf{0}$ and $\mathbf{b}\mathbf{z}' = 1$. (ii) Let $\mathbf{a}_1, \ldots, \mathbf{a}_r$ be a basis for the row space of $A$ (the vector subspace generated by vectors of the form $\mathbf{v}A$, where $\mathbf{v}$ is any

$1 \times m$ vector). Then if $\mathbf{w}A = \mathbf{b}$ has no solution in $\mathbf{w}$, the vectors $\mathbf{a}_1, \ldots, \mathbf{a}_r, \mathbf{b}$ are linearly independent. Accordingly there exists a $\mathbf{z}$ that is orthogonal to each $\mathbf{a}_i$ ($\mathbf{a}_i\mathbf{z}' = 0$, $i = 1, \ldots, r$), but not orthogonal to $\mathbf{b}$. After a possible normalization, we can set $\mathbf{bz}' = 1$. Since all the rows of $A$ may be written as linear combinations of the above basis, we have $A\mathbf{z}' = \mathbf{0}$. □

**Lemma 9.2.2**

Let $A$, $\mathbf{b}$, $\mathbf{w}$, and $\mathbf{z}$ be as in Lemma 9.2.1, and let $\mathbf{u}$ be $1 \times m$. Then $\mathbf{wu}'$ does not depend on $\mathbf{w}$ for each $\mathbf{w}$ satisfying $\mathbf{w}A = \mathbf{b}$ (i.e., if $\mathbf{w}A = \mathbf{b}$, then $\mathbf{wu}'$ depends only on $\mathbf{u}$) if and only if there exists a $\mathbf{z}$ such that $\mathbf{z}A' = \mathbf{u}$.

**Proof**

The proof is due to Richmond (1974). (i) Let $\mathbf{w}$ satisfy $\mathbf{w}A = \mathbf{b}$ and suppose there exists a $\mathbf{z}$ such that $\mathbf{z}A' = \mathbf{u}$. Then $\mathbf{uw}' = \mathbf{z}A'\mathbf{w}' = \mathbf{zb}'$, which is independent of $\mathbf{w}$. (ii) Let $\mathbf{wu}'$ be independent of $\mathbf{w}$ for each $\mathbf{w}$ such that $\mathbf{w}A = \mathbf{b}$, let $\mathbf{w}_1$ satisfy that equation, and let $\mathbf{t}$ be a solution to $\mathbf{t}A = 0$. Then $(\mathbf{w}_1 + \mathbf{t})A = \mathbf{b}$. But if $\mathbf{wu}'$ is independent of $\mathbf{w}$, $\mathbf{w}_1\mathbf{u}'$ must not depend on $\mathbf{t}$, so that $\mathbf{tu}' = 0$. Therefore there is no solution to $\mathbf{t}A = \mathbf{0}$ and $\mathbf{tu}' = 1 = \mathbf{ut}'$, which implies by Lemma 9.2.1 that there exists a solution to $\mathbf{z}A' = \mathbf{u}$. □

If a linear combination of parameters, $\boldsymbol{\alpha}\mathbf{u}'$, is independent of $\boldsymbol{\alpha}$, then for a given $\mathbf{u}'$, the same value of $\boldsymbol{\alpha}\mathbf{u}'$ is obtained whether the parameters are represented by $\boldsymbol{\alpha}$ or by a transformation of $\boldsymbol{\alpha}$. This means that $\boldsymbol{\alpha}\mathbf{u}'$ is identified, even if $\boldsymbol{\alpha}$ itself is not. The previous lemma therefore proves:

**Theorem 9.2.3**

The linear combination of parameters $\boldsymbol{\alpha}\mathbf{u}'$ is identified if and only if there exists a $\mathbf{z}$ such that $[W^*, \Phi]\mathbf{z}' = \mathbf{u}'$; equivalently, if and only if $r(W^*, \Phi, \mathbf{u}') = r(W^*, \Phi)$.

The result may also be expressed in terms of the structural parameters.

**Theorem 9.2.4**

The linear combination of parameters $\boldsymbol{\alpha}\mathbf{u}'$ is identified if and only if there exists $\boldsymbol{\mu}$ such that $A^*\Phi\boldsymbol{\mu} = A^*\mathbf{u}'$; equivalently, $r(A^*\Phi) = r(A^*\Phi, A^*\mathbf{u}')$.

**Proof**

(i) If $\boldsymbol{\alpha}\mathbf{u}'$ is identified, there exists a $\mathbf{z}$ such that $[W^*, \Phi]\mathbf{z}' = \mathbf{u}'$. Since $AW = 0$ implies $A^*W^* = 0$, upon premultiplying $[W^*, \Phi]\mathbf{z}'$ by $A^*$, we obtain $(0, A^*\Phi)\mathbf{z}' = A^*\mathbf{u}'$ or $A^*\Phi[0, I]\mathbf{z}' = \mathbf{A}^*\Phi\boldsymbol{\mu} = A^*\mathbf{u}'$ (where $\boldsymbol{\mu} = [0, I]\mathbf{z}'$), or $r(A^*\Phi, A^*\mathbf{u}') = r(A^*\Phi)$. (ii) If $\mathbf{w}\Phi'A^{*\prime} = \mathbf{u}A^{*\prime}$ has a solution, there exists no $\mathbf{z}$ such that

$$\mathbf{z}A^*\Phi = \mathbf{0} \quad \text{and} \quad \mathbf{u}A^{*\prime}\mathbf{z}' = 1. \tag{9.2.15}$$

Assume $\boldsymbol{\alpha}\mathbf{u}'$ is not identified. Then there is no $\mathbf{t}$ such that

$$\mathbf{t}\begin{bmatrix} W^{*\prime} \\ \Phi' \end{bmatrix} = \mathbf{u},$$

in which case there exists an $\mathbf{s}$ such that $\mathbf{s}[W^*, \Phi] = \mathbf{0}$ and $\mathbf{u}\mathbf{s}' = 1$. The former implies $\mathbf{s}W^* = \mathbf{0}$, or $\mathbf{s}$ is orthogonal to the columns of $W^*$. But we also have $A^*W^* = 0$, that is, the rows of $A^*$ are orthogonal to the columns of $W^*$. Since $r(A^*) = G^2$ and $r(W^*) = GK$, the rows of $A^*$ and $W^*$ comprise a basis for the $G(G + K)$ dimensional space in which $\mathbf{s}$ lies. And since $\mathbf{s}$ is orthogonal to $W^*$, it may be written as $\mathbf{s} = \boldsymbol{\lambda}A^*$, so that we have

$$\mathbf{0} = \mathbf{s}[W^*, \Phi] = \boldsymbol{\lambda}A^*[W^*, \Phi] = [\mathbf{0}, \boldsymbol{\lambda}A^*\Phi],$$

implying $\boldsymbol{\lambda}A^*\Phi = \mathbf{0}$ and $\mathbf{u}A^{*\prime}\boldsymbol{\lambda}' = 1$. Setting $\boldsymbol{\lambda} = \mathbf{z}$ contradicts the nonexistence of a solution for (9.2.15). Therefore $\boldsymbol{\alpha}\mathbf{u}'$ is identified. □

We conclude this section by developing a condition for the identification of the first equation. (By renumbering, any equation may be regarded as the first.) Let $\mathbf{e}_i$ be the $G(G + K) \times 1$ vector with 1 in the $i$th position and 0 elsewhere. Setting $\mathbf{u}'$ equal to $\mathbf{e}_1, \ldots, \mathbf{e}_{G+K}$ in turn, Theorem 9.2.4 implies identification of the first row of $A$ if and only if

$$r([A^*\Phi, \mathbf{A}_i^*]) = r([A^*\Phi]), \qquad i = 1, \ldots, G + K, \tag{9.2.16}$$

where $\mathbf{A}_i^*$ is the $i$th column of $A^*$. These conditions hold if and only if there exist $(G + K)$ $\mathbf{Z}_i$'s, where $\mathbf{Z}_i$ is $R \times 1$, such that

$$\mathbf{A}_i^* = A^*\Phi\mathbf{Z}_i, \qquad i = 1, \ldots, G + K, \tag{9.2.17}$$

or

$$\begin{bmatrix} A \\ 0 \end{bmatrix} = A^*\Phi Z,$$

where $Z = [\mathbf{Z}_1, \ldots, \mathbf{Z}_{G+K}]$ and 0 is $(G^2 - G) \times (G + K)$.

**Theorem 9.2.5**

The first equation of (9.2.1) is identified subject to (9.2.5) if and only if

$$[A^*\Phi][A^*\Phi]^- \begin{bmatrix} A \\ 0 \end{bmatrix} = \begin{bmatrix} A \\ 0 \end{bmatrix}, \tag{9.2.18}$$

where $[A^*\Phi]^-$ denotes the $g$-inverse of $[A^*\Phi]$.

**Proof**

Theorem 6.3.3 of Graybill (1969, p. 104) shows that a necessary and sufficient condition for the existence of a solution in $X$ to $EXB = C$ is $EE^-CB^-B = C$. The theorem follows by setting $Z = X$, $A^*\Phi = E$, $B = I$, and

$$C = \begin{bmatrix} A \\ 0 \end{bmatrix}$$

in (9.2.17). □

If there are no cross-equation restrictions, (9.2.17) reduces to

$$A\Phi^{11}Z = A, \qquad \textbf{(9.2.19)}$$

where $\Phi^{11}$ is the matrix of the first $G + K$ rows of the columns of $\Phi$ that pertain to the first equation and $Z$ is $G \times R$. Applying Theorem 9.2.5 to (9.2.19), we have the necessary and sufficient condition for identifiability,

$$[A\Phi^{11}][A\Phi^{11}]^{-}A = A. \qquad \textbf{(9.2.20)}$$

**Theorem 9.2.6**

A necessary and sufficient condition for identifiability of the first equation, where all restrictions pertaining to that equation are of the form $\boldsymbol{\alpha}_1\Phi^{11} = \mathbf{c}_1$, is $r(A\Phi^{11}) = G$.

**Proof**

(i) If (9.2.20) holds, $r[(A\Phi^{11})(A\Phi^{11})^{-}] = G$, and since $r(AB) \leqslant \min\{r(A), r(B)\}$, and $r(A^{-}) = r(A)$ (Graybill, 1969, p. 99), we have $r(A\Phi^{11}) = G$. (ii) If $r(A\Phi^{11}) = G$, then $(A\Phi^{11})(A\Phi^{11})^{-} = I$ (Graybill, 1969, p. 102), and so (9.2.20) holds. □

Some authors assume the normalization convention $\beta_{11} = 1$, but do not include it in $\Phi^{11}$. In that case the condition is expressed as $r(A\Phi^{11}) = G - 1$; that is, there are $G - 1$ restrictions in addition to $\beta_{11} = 1$. If all restrictions other than $\beta_{11} = 1$ are of the exclusion type, that is, $\beta_{1i} = \gamma_{1j} = 0$ for $R$ values of $i$ and $j$, further simplification is possible. Assume that the restrictions on the first equation take the form of $G_2$ excluded endogenous variables and $K_2$ excluded predetermined variables. Then $R = K_2 + G_2 \geqslant G - 1 = G_1 + G_2 - 1$, where $G_1$ is the number of included endogenous variables. This reduces to the familiar necessary condition for identification, $K_2 \geqslant G_1 - 1$.

## 9.3 Identification in Models That Are Linear in Parameters, Nonlinear in Variables, and Linear in Restrictions

Fisher (1966) takes up the case

$$A\mathbf{q}(\mathbf{x}) = \mathbf{u}, \qquad \textbf{(9.3.1)}$$

where $A$ is an $M \times N^0$ matrix of parameters; $\mathbf{q}(\mathbf{x})$ is an $N^0 \times 1$ vector of functions of $\mathbf{x}$; $\mathbf{x} = (\mathbf{y}, \mathbf{z})$ is vector of $N$ variables, of which the $M$ elements of $\mathbf{y}$ are endogenous and the $N - M$ elements of **z** are exogenous; and **u** is an $M \times 1$ vector of disturbances. The linear model discussed in Section 9.2 is generalized in (9.3.1) to the extent that nonlinear functions of **y** and/or **z** may appear in the model, as well as **y** and **z** themselves. As examples, Fisher presents two models:

$$a_0 + a_1 \log y_1 + a_2 \log y_2 + a_3 z = u_1 \qquad \textbf{(9.3.2)}$$
$$b_0 + b_1 y_1 + b_2 y_2 + b_3 z = u_2$$

and

$$a_0 + a_1 y_1^2 + a_2 y_2^2 + a_3 y_1 y_2 + a_4 z = u_1 \qquad \textbf{(9.3.3a)}$$

$$b_1 y_1 + b_2 y_2 = u_2. \qquad \textbf{(9.3.3b)}$$

In both of these systems $y_1$ and $y_2$ are the endogenous variables and $z$ is the exogenous variable. Each system contains nonlinear functions of the endogenous variables: $\log y_i$ in (9.3.2) and $y_i^2$ and $y_1 y_2$ in (9.3.3). In the absence of information about disturbances, there is an important difference between (9.3.2) and (9.3.3): Squaring (9.3.3b) yields

$$b_1^2 y_1^2 + b_2^2 y_2^2 + 2b_1 b_2 y_1 y_2 = u_2^2,$$

and a linear combination of this equation and (9.3.3a) is observationally equivalent to (9.3.3a). Therefore, Equation 9.3.3a is not identified. In effect, introducing equations that contain nonlinear functions of endogenous variables requires the examination of nonlinear transformations of the equations. [In this example it was necessary to square (9.3.3b).]

For the approach taken by Fisher, it is required that any such relationship be included in the system of equations. Accordingly, Fisher defines

$$\mathbf{A}^* = \begin{bmatrix} A \\ h^1 \\ \cdot \\ \cdot \\ \cdot \\ h^{M^*-M} \end{bmatrix} \qquad \textbf{(9.3.4)}$$

and

$$\mathbf{u}^* = \begin{bmatrix} u \\ \tilde{u}^1 \\ \cdot \\ \cdot \\ \cdot \\ \tilde{u}^{M^*-M} \end{bmatrix}, \qquad \textbf{(9.3.5)}$$

where

$$\mathbf{h}^i \mathbf{q}(\mathbf{x}) = \tilde{u}_i, \qquad i = 1, \ldots, M^* - M, \qquad \textbf{(9.3.6)}$$

$\mathbf{h}^i$ is a $1 \times N^0$ vector of constants, $\tilde{u}_i$ is a function of the random errors, and $M^* - M$ is the number of additional relationships. As an example, in (9.3.3a) we have

$$[a_1\ a_2\ a_3\ 0\ 0\ a_4\ a_0] \begin{bmatrix} y_1^2 \\ y_2^2 \\ y_1 y_2 \\ y_1 \\ y_2 \\ z \\ 1 \end{bmatrix} = u_1,$$

where the column vector in the preceding equation is $\mathbf{q}(\mathbf{x})$. But, as remarked above,

$$[b_1^2\ b_2^2\ 2b_1b_2\ 0\ 0\ 0\ 0] \begin{bmatrix} y_1^2 \\ y_2^2 \\ y_1 y_2 \\ y_1 \\ y_2 \\ z \\ 1 \end{bmatrix} = u_2^2$$

is implied by the second equation of (9.3.3). Therefore,

$$h^1 = [b_1^2\ b_2^2\ 2b_1b_2\ 0\ 0\ 0\ 0] \equiv [c_1\ c_2\ c_3\ c_4\ c_5\ c_6\ c_7]$$

and $\tilde{u}_1 = u_2^2$. No such relationship exists for (9.3.2).

Starting with

$$A^*\mathbf{q}(\mathbf{x}) = \mathbf{u}^*, \qquad \textbf{(9.3.7)}$$

Fisher makes the following assumptions:

1. Equation 9.3.1 can be solved for $\mathbf{y} = G(\mathbf{z}, \mathbf{u})$, where $G(\mathbf{z}, \mathbf{u})$ is continuous in $\mathbf{z}$ and locally unique for $\mathbf{z}$ and $\mathbf{u}$. [This assumption requires that the Jacobian $|\partial\mathbf{q}(\mathbf{x})/\partial\mathbf{y}|$ be nonzero at the values of $\mathbf{z}$ and $\mathbf{u}$ being considered.]
2. The elements of $\mathbf{q}(\mathbf{x})$ are not connected by any linear identity. [All such linear identities can be eliminated before setting up (9.3.7).]
3. The elements of $\mathbf{u}$ are statistically independent of the elements of $\mathbf{z}$.

In addition, a normalizing condition and a set of linear restrictions on the first row of $A$, $\mathbf{A}_1$, of the form

$$\mathbf{A}_1\Phi = \mathbf{0} \qquad \textbf{(9.3.8)}$$

are assumed. A necessary and sufficient condition for identification of $\mathbf{A}_1$ is

$$r(A^*\Phi) = M^* - 1. \qquad \textbf{(9.3.9)}$$

We illustrate this result for Equation 9.3.3a. Normalizing by $a_1 = 1$ and defining $\Phi$ as the matrix of constraints on $\mathbf{A}_1$, we obtain

$$A^*\Phi = \begin{bmatrix} a_1 & a_2 & a_3 & a_5 & a_6 & a_4 & a_0 \\ b_3 & b_4 & b_5 & b_1 & b_2 & b_6 & b_7 \\ c_1 & c_2 & c_3 & c_4 & c_5 & c_6 & c_7 \end{bmatrix} \begin{bmatrix} 0 & 0 \\ 0 & 0 \\ 0 & 0 \\ 1 & 0 \\ 0 & 1 \\ 0 & 0 \\ 0 & 0 \end{bmatrix}$$

$$= \begin{bmatrix} a_5 & a_6 \\ b_1 & b_2 \\ c_4 & c_5 \end{bmatrix} = \begin{bmatrix} 0 & 0 \\ b_1 & b_2 \\ 0 & 0 \end{bmatrix},$$

which implies $r(A^*\Phi) = 1 < M^* - 1 = 2$. Equation 9.3.3a is therefore not identified.

See Fisher's book for a discussion of the size of $M^* - M$, whether or not nonlinearities in variables aid in identification, and how to find the vectors $\mathbf{h}^i$.

## 9.4 Identification in Models That Are Linear in Variables and Parameters and Nonlinear in Restrictions

Wegge (1965) considers the system

$$\mathbf{u}' = A\mathbf{X}', \tag{9.4.1}$$

where $\mathbf{u}$ is a $1 \times M$ vector of disturbances, $E(\mathbf{u}) = \mathbf{0}$, $E(\mathbf{u}'\mathbf{u}) = \Sigma = \{\sigma_{ij}\}$, $A = \{a_{jk}\}$ is $M \times N$, $r(A) = M$, and $\mathbf{X}$ is $1 \times N$. Let

$$\boldsymbol{\delta}^0 = \text{vec}(A, \Sigma),$$

that is

$$\boldsymbol{\delta}^0 = (a_{11}, \ldots, a_{1N}, \sigma_{11}, \ldots, \sigma_{1M}, a_{21}, \ldots, \sigma_{MM}). \tag{9.4.2}$$

Elements of $\boldsymbol{\delta}^0$ will be denoted by $\delta_k^0$, $k = 1, \ldots, M(N + M) = K$.

Restrictions take the form of $R$ continuously differentiable functions

$$\phi_r(\boldsymbol{\delta}) = 0, \qquad r = 1, \ldots, R, \tag{9.4.3}$$

where $\boldsymbol{\delta}$ is an arbitrary parameter point. These restrictions are satisfied by $\boldsymbol{\delta}^0$. It is also assumed that the $\phi_r(\boldsymbol{\delta})$ are symmetric in $\sigma_{ij}$ and $\sigma_{ji}$. [Fisher (1966) takes up the special case where restrictions apply only to individual equations.] In view of the possible nonlinear relationships represented by the $\phi_r(\boldsymbol{\delta})$, we must settle for local identifiability.

The theorem that follows is concerned with identification of the whole system; subsystem identification is also considered in the Wegge article.

**Theorem 9.4.1 (Wegge)**

Let

$$J(T) = \left\{ \frac{\partial \phi_r(\text{vec}(TA,\ T\Sigma T'))}{\partial\ \text{vec}(T)} \right\}, \tag{9.4.4}$$

the $R \times M^2$ Jacobian matrix whose $r$th row consists of the partial derivatives of $\phi_r(\boldsymbol{\delta})$ with respect to each element of vec($T$), and $T$ is an arbitrary $M \times M$ nonsingular matrix. Then if $r(J(I)) = M^2$, $\boldsymbol{\delta}^0 = \text{vec}(A, \Sigma)$ is locally identifiable.[1]

It is known that $\phi_r(\text{vec}(A, \Sigma)) = 0$, $r = 1, \ldots, R$, because the true parameters satisfy the restrictions. If there exists another parameter point, $\boldsymbol{\delta} = \text{vec}(TA,\ T\Sigma T')$, in the neigh borhood of $\boldsymbol{\delta}^0$ that also satisfies the restrictions, we can totally differentiate the system of restrictions with respect to vec($T$) to obtain

$$\begin{bmatrix} d\phi_1 \\ \cdot \\ \cdot \\ \cdot \\ d\phi_R \end{bmatrix} = \begin{bmatrix} \dfrac{\partial\phi_1}{\partial t_1} & \cdots & \dfrac{\partial\phi_1}{\partial t_{M^2}} \\ \cdot & & \cdot \\ \cdot & & \cdot \\ \cdot & & \cdot \\ \dfrac{\partial\phi_R}{\partial t_1} & \cdots & \dfrac{\partial\phi_R}{\partial t_{M^2}} \end{bmatrix} \begin{bmatrix} dt_1 \\ \cdot \\ \cdot \\ \cdot \\ \cdot \\ \cdot \\ \cdot \\ \cdot \\ \cdot \\ dt_{M^2} \end{bmatrix} = \mathbf{0}, \tag{9.4.5}$$

where the partial derivatives are evaluated at $T = I$. $\partial\phi_i/\partial t_j$ is to be interpreted as $\Sigma_k(\partial\phi_i/\partial\delta_k)(\partial\omega_k/\partial t_j)$, where $\omega_k$ is the $k$th element of vec($TA,\ T\Sigma T'$). Since not all $dt_i = 0$, the $M^2$ columns of $J(I)$ are not linearly independent, and $r(J(I)) \neq M^2$. Accordingly, $r(J(I)) = M^2$ implies no solution to (9.4.3) in the neighborhood of $\boldsymbol{\delta}^0$; that is, $\boldsymbol{\delta}^0$ is an "isolated solution" to (9.4.3) and is therefore locally identifiable. □

A discussion of subsets of equations and restrictions, a theorem giving necessary conditions for identification when $r[J(T)]$ is constant for $\text{vec}(T) \in N'_e[\text{vec}(I)]$, and an example are also contained in the Wegge article.

[1]Note that $J(I)$ denotes $J(T)$ evaluated at $T = I$ after the indicated differentiation is performed.

## 9.5 Identification in General Cases

Rothenberg (1971) presents a general discussion of identifiability based partly on the information matrix. He assumes that the density function for $\mathbf{y}$ is a function of a vector of parameters, $\boldsymbol{\alpha}$, contained in $A$, a subset of $m$-dimensional space ($R^m$). The density is denoted by $f(\mathbf{y}, \boldsymbol{\alpha})$. The basic theorem on identifiability requires the following assumptions:

1. $A$ is an open set in $R^m$.
2. For every $\boldsymbol{\alpha} \in A$, $f(\mathbf{y}, \boldsymbol{\alpha}) \geq 0$ and $\int f(\mathbf{y}, \boldsymbol{\alpha})\, d\mathbf{y} = 1$.
3. The sample space, $B = \{\mathbf{y}\colon f(\mathbf{y}, \boldsymbol{\alpha}) > 0\}$, is the same for all $\boldsymbol{\alpha} \in A$.
4. $f(\mathbf{y}, \boldsymbol{\alpha})$ and $\log f(\mathbf{y}, \boldsymbol{\alpha})$ are continuously differentiable functions of $\boldsymbol{\alpha}$ for all $\boldsymbol{\alpha}$ in a convex set containing $A$ and for all $\mathbf{y} \in$ B.
5. The elements of the information matrix

$$R(\boldsymbol{\alpha}) = \{r_{ij}(\boldsymbol{\alpha})\} = E\left[\frac{\partial \log f}{\partial \alpha_i} \cdot \frac{\partial \log f}{\partial \alpha_j}\right] \tag{9.5.1}$$

exist and are continuous functions of all $\boldsymbol{\alpha} \in A$.

To state the theorem we need the following definition:

**Definition**

Let $M(\boldsymbol{\alpha})$ be a matrix of continuous functions of all $\boldsymbol{\alpha} \in A$. Then $\boldsymbol{\alpha}^0 \in A$ is a *regular point* of $M(\boldsymbol{\alpha})$ if there exists an open neighborhood of $\boldsymbol{\alpha}^0$ in which $M(\boldsymbol{\alpha})$ has constant rank.

**Theorem 9.5.1 (Rothenberg)**

Let $\boldsymbol{\alpha}^0$ be a regular point of $R(\boldsymbol{\alpha})$. Then $\boldsymbol{\alpha}^0$ is locally identifiable if and only if $R(\boldsymbol{\alpha}^0)$ is nonsingular.

**Proof**

Define $g(\mathbf{y}, \boldsymbol{\alpha}) = \log f(\mathbf{y}, \boldsymbol{\alpha})$ and $g_i(\mathbf{y}, \boldsymbol{\alpha}) = \partial \log f(\mathbf{y}, \boldsymbol{\alpha})/\partial \alpha_i$. By the multivariate form of the mean value theorem of calculus, there exists an $\boldsymbol{\alpha}^*$ between $\boldsymbol{\alpha}$ and $\boldsymbol{\alpha}^0$, such that

$$g(\mathbf{y}, \boldsymbol{\alpha}) - g(\mathbf{y}, \boldsymbol{\alpha}^0) = \Sigma g_i(\mathbf{y}, \boldsymbol{\alpha}^*)(\alpha_i - \alpha_i^0) \tag{9.5.2}$$

for all $\mathbf{y} \in B$ and all $\boldsymbol{\alpha}$ in a neighborhood of $\boldsymbol{\alpha}^0$. (i) It is now shown that $R(\boldsymbol{\alpha}^0)$ nonsingular implies $\boldsymbol{\alpha}^0$ is identifiable. Suppose $\boldsymbol{\alpha}^0$ is not locally identifiable. Then every open neighborhood of $\boldsymbol{\alpha}^0$ contains an $\boldsymbol{\alpha}^k$ such that $f(\mathbf{y}, \boldsymbol{\alpha}^k) = f(\mathbf{y}, \boldsymbol{\alpha}^0)$ for all $\mathbf{y}$, and since $g(\mathbf{y}, \boldsymbol{\alpha})$ and $g_i(\mathbf{y}, \boldsymbol{\alpha})$ are continuous, every open neighborhood of $\boldsymbol{\alpha}^0$ contains an $\boldsymbol{\alpha}^k$ such that

$$g(\mathbf{y}, \boldsymbol{\alpha}^k) = g(\mathbf{y}, \boldsymbol{\alpha}^0) \tag{9.5.3}$$

for all $\mathbf{y}$. We thus have an infinite sequence of neighborhoods and corresponding $\boldsymbol{\alpha}$'s, $\{\boldsymbol{\alpha}^1, \boldsymbol{\alpha}^2, \ldots, \boldsymbol{\alpha}^k, \ldots\}$, that approach $\boldsymbol{\alpha}^0$. Therefore, for each $\mathbf{y}$, (9.5.2) and (9.5.3) imply

$$\Sigma g_i(\mathbf{y}, \boldsymbol{\alpha}^k)\, d_i^k = 0, \tag{9.5.4}$$

where

$$d_i^k = \frac{\alpha_i^k - \alpha_i^0}{\|\boldsymbol{\alpha}^k - \boldsymbol{\alpha}^0\|}. \tag{9.5.5}$$

The $d_i^k$ $(k = 1, \ldots,)$ are an infinite sequence, and since $\Sigma_i (d_i^k)^2 = 1$, the $d_i^k$ are bounded. By the Bolzano-Weierstrass theorem,[2] the infinite set of real numbers, $d_i^k$, has a limit, $d_i$. Accordingly,

$$\Sigma g_i(\mathbf{y}, \boldsymbol{\alpha}^0) d_i = 0 = [g_1(\mathbf{y}, \boldsymbol{\alpha}^0), \ldots, g_m(\mathbf{y}, \boldsymbol{\alpha}^0)]\mathbf{d}, \tag{9.5.6}$$

where $\mathbf{d}' = (d_1, \ldots, d_m)$. Therefore,

$$0 = E\{\mathbf{d}'[g_1(\mathbf{y}, \boldsymbol{\alpha}^0), \ldots, g_m(\mathbf{y}, \boldsymbol{\alpha}^0)]'[g_1(\mathbf{y}, \boldsymbol{\alpha}^0), \ldots, g_m(\mathbf{y}, \boldsymbol{\alpha}^0)]\} = \mathbf{d}'R(\boldsymbol{\alpha}^0)\mathbf{d}, \tag{9.5.7}$$

which implies $r(R(\boldsymbol{\alpha}^0)) < m$. (ii) Assume $R(\boldsymbol{\alpha}^0)$ singular, that is, $r(R(\boldsymbol{\alpha}^0)) = r < m$ in a neighborhood of $\boldsymbol{\alpha}^0$. Let $c(\boldsymbol{\alpha})$ be a c.v. of $R(\boldsymbol{\alpha})$ associated with a zero c.r. Then, from

$$0 = \mathbf{c}'R\mathbf{c} = E[\Sigma g_i(\mathbf{y}, \boldsymbol{\alpha}) c_i(\boldsymbol{\alpha})]^2, \tag{9.5.8}$$

we must have

$$\Sigma g_i(\mathbf{y}, \boldsymbol{\alpha}) c_i(\boldsymbol{\alpha}) \equiv 0$$

for all $\mathbf{y} \in B$ and $\boldsymbol{\alpha}$ near $\boldsymbol{\alpha}^0$. Since $R(\boldsymbol{\alpha})$ is continuous and has constant rank,

$$[c(\boldsymbol{\alpha})]' = [c_1(\boldsymbol{\alpha}), \ldots, c_m(\boldsymbol{\alpha})]$$

is also continuous. Since we wish to show that there exist values of $\boldsymbol{\alpha}$ other than $\boldsymbol{\alpha}^0$ for which $f(\mathbf{y}, \boldsymbol{\alpha}) = f(\mathbf{y}, \boldsymbol{\alpha}^0)$, we induce variations in $\boldsymbol{\alpha}$ by making it a function of the parameter $t$, that is, $\boldsymbol{\alpha}(t) = [\alpha_1(t), \ldots, \alpha_m(t)]$. In particular, let $\boldsymbol{\alpha}(t)$ solve the system of differential equations

$$\begin{aligned} \frac{\partial \alpha_i(t)}{\partial t} &= c_i(\boldsymbol{\alpha}) \\ \alpha_i(0) &= \alpha_i^0 \end{aligned} \tag{9.5.9}$$

for $0 \leqslant t \leqslant t^*$ and $i = 1, \ldots, m$. Then

$$\begin{aligned} \frac{\partial g(\mathbf{y}, \boldsymbol{\alpha}(t))}{\partial t} &= \Sigma g_i(\mathbf{y}, \boldsymbol{\alpha}(t)) \frac{\partial \alpha_i(t)}{\partial t} \\ &= \Sigma g_i(\mathbf{y}, \boldsymbol{\alpha}(t)) c_i(\boldsymbol{\alpha}(t)). \end{aligned}$$

[2]The theorem states that every bounded infinite set of real numbers has a limit.

But this last term equals zero for small $t$ (where $\boldsymbol{\alpha}$ is close to $\boldsymbol{\alpha}^0$). Therefore

$$\frac{\partial g(\mathbf{y}, \boldsymbol{\alpha}(t))}{\partial t} = 0 \tag{9.5.10}$$

along $\boldsymbol{\alpha}(t)$, $0 \leqslant t \leqslant t^*$, which implies $f(\mathbf{y}, \boldsymbol{\alpha})$ is constant along that portion of $\boldsymbol{\alpha}(t)$, and therefore $\boldsymbol{\alpha}^0$ is not identifiable. □

**Example**

Consider the nonlinear regression model,

$$y_t = h(\boldsymbol{\alpha}, \mathbf{x}_t) + \epsilon_t, \qquad t = 1, \ldots, n, \tag{9.5.11}$$

where $\boldsymbol{\alpha}$ is $1 \times m$. An element of the information matrix, under suitable restrictions on $h(\boldsymbol{\alpha}, \mathbf{x})$—see Rothenberg (1971, p. 581)—is

$$r_{ij}(\boldsymbol{\alpha}) = \Sigma_t h_i(\boldsymbol{\alpha}, \mathbf{x}_t) h_j(\boldsymbol{\alpha}, \mathbf{x}_t), \tag{9.5.12}$$

and so

$$R(\boldsymbol{\alpha}) = HH', \tag{9.5.13}$$

where $h_i(\boldsymbol{\alpha}, \mathbf{x}_t) = \partial h / \partial \alpha_i$ and $H$ is the $m \times n$ matrix $\{h_i(\boldsymbol{\alpha}, \mathbf{x}_t)\}$, $i = 1, \ldots, m$ and $t = 1, \ldots, n$. The theorem implies local identifiability if and only if $r(H(\boldsymbol{\alpha}^0)) = m$.

Virtually the same analysis applies if there are restrictions on $\boldsymbol{\alpha}$,

$$\psi_i(\boldsymbol{\alpha}) = 0, \qquad i = 1, \ldots, k, \tag{9.5.14}$$

where the $\psi_i(\boldsymbol{\alpha})$ are known functions with continuous partial derivatives. Defining the Jacobian matrix for the $\psi_i(\boldsymbol{\alpha})$ as

$$\Psi(\boldsymbol{\alpha}) = \{\Psi_{ij}(\boldsymbol{\alpha})\} = \left\{\frac{\partial \psi_i}{\partial \alpha_j}\right\}$$

and defining

$$V(\boldsymbol{\alpha}) = \begin{bmatrix} R(\boldsymbol{\alpha}) \\ \Psi(\boldsymbol{\alpha}) \end{bmatrix},$$

we have the following:

**Theorem 9.5.2 (Rothenberg)**

Suppose $\boldsymbol{\alpha}^0 \in A'$ [the intersection of $A$ and the solution set of (9.5.14)] is a regular point of both $\Psi(\boldsymbol{\alpha})$ and $V(\boldsymbol{\alpha})$. Then $\boldsymbol{\alpha}^0$ is locally identifiable if and only if $r(V(\boldsymbol{\alpha}^0)) = m$.

**Proof**

The proof is a bit more technical than that of the preceding theorem because of the presence of the restrictions. Suppose $r(\Psi(\boldsymbol{\alpha})) = s$. Then by the implicit function theorem, it is possible to partition $\boldsymbol{\alpha}$ into an $\boldsymbol{\alpha}_1$ with $s$ components and an $\boldsymbol{\alpha}_2$ with $m - s$ components such that

$$\boldsymbol{\alpha}_1 = \mathbf{q}(\boldsymbol{\alpha}_2) \tag{9.5.15}$$

is satisfied for all solutions of (9.5.14) in a neighborhood of $\boldsymbol{\alpha}^0$, where $\mathbf{q}$ is differentiable. Then on this restricted parameter space, $A'$ (technically, a manifold), we may define

$$f^*(\mathbf{y}, \boldsymbol{\alpha}) = f(\mathbf{y}, \mathbf{q}(\boldsymbol{\alpha}_2), \boldsymbol{\alpha}_2). \tag{9.5.16}$$

The information matrix for $\boldsymbol{\alpha}_2$ is

$$r^*_{ij}(\boldsymbol{\alpha}_2) = E\left[\frac{\partial \log f^*}{\partial \alpha_{2i}} \frac{\partial \log f^*}{\partial \alpha_{2j}}\right]. \tag{9.5.17}$$

But since

$$\frac{\partial \log f^*}{\partial \alpha_{2i}} = \sum_{k=1}^{s} \frac{\partial \log f}{\partial \alpha_{1k}} \cdot \frac{\partial q_k(\boldsymbol{\alpha}_2)}{\partial \alpha_{2i}} + \frac{\partial \log f}{\partial \alpha_{2i}} \tag{9.5.18}$$

and

$$r^*_{ij}(\boldsymbol{\alpha}) = \sum_{k=1}^{s} \left[\frac{\partial \log f}{\partial \alpha_{1k}} \frac{\partial q_k(\boldsymbol{\alpha}_2)}{\partial \alpha_{2i}} + \frac{\partial \log f}{\partial \alpha_{2i}}\right] \times \sum_{t=1}^{s} \left[\frac{\partial \log f}{\partial \alpha_{1t}} \frac{\partial q_t(\boldsymbol{\alpha}_2)}{\partial \alpha_{2j}} + \frac{\partial \log f}{\partial \alpha_{2j}}\right], \tag{9.5.19}$$

we have

$$R^*(\boldsymbol{\alpha}) = (Q' \; I)R'R \begin{bmatrix} Q \\ I \end{bmatrix}, \tag{9.5.20}$$

where

$$Q = \left\{\frac{\partial q_i(\boldsymbol{\alpha}_2)}{\partial \alpha_{2j}}\right\}; \tag{9.5.21}$$

$Q$ is $s \times (m - s)$, $I$ is $s \times s$, and $R$ is partitioned to conform with the matrix multiplication indicated in (9.5.20). From (9.5.20), it is easy to see that $R^*(\boldsymbol{\alpha})$ is singular if and only if there exists a nonzero $\mathbf{z}$ with the property

$$R \begin{bmatrix} Q \\ I \end{bmatrix} \mathbf{z} = \mathbf{0}. \tag{9.5.22}$$

It will be shown as a lemma that a nonzero $\mathbf{x}$ of the form

$$\mathbf{x} = \begin{bmatrix} Q \\ I \end{bmatrix} \mathbf{z}$$

exists if and only if $\Psi\mathbf{x} = \mathbf{0}$. Then, suppose a $\mathbf{z}$ satisfying (9.5.22) exists. Set

$$\mathbf{x} = \begin{bmatrix} Q \\ I \end{bmatrix} \mathbf{z},$$

and the lemma to be proved below implies $\Psi\mathbf{x} = \mathbf{0}$. Accordingly, there exists an $\mathbf{x}$ such that

$$\begin{bmatrix} R \\ \Psi \end{bmatrix} \mathbf{x} = V\mathbf{x} = \mathbf{0},$$

showing that $r(V(\boldsymbol{\alpha})) < m$. Therefore $r(V(\boldsymbol{\alpha})) = m$ implies $R^*(\boldsymbol{\alpha})$ is nonsingular. Now suppose that no such $\mathbf{z}$ exists. Then any solution to $R(\boldsymbol{\alpha})\mathbf{x} = \mathbf{0}$ will not have $\mathbf{x}$ of the form

$$\mathbf{x} = \begin{bmatrix} Q \\ I \end{bmatrix} \mathbf{z},$$

hence (by the lemma to be proved) it will not satisfy $\Psi\mathbf{x} = \mathbf{0}$. Therefore

$$\begin{bmatrix} R(\boldsymbol{\alpha}) \\ \Psi(\boldsymbol{\alpha}) \end{bmatrix} \mathbf{x} = \mathbf{0}$$

has no solution in $\mathbf{x}$, and $r(V(\boldsymbol{\alpha})) = m$. In other words, $r(R^*(\boldsymbol{\alpha})) = m - s$ if and only if $r(V(\boldsymbol{\alpha})) = m$. But by Theorem 9.5.1, $\boldsymbol{\alpha}^0$ is identifiable if and only if $R^*(\boldsymbol{\alpha}^0)$ is nonsingular. □

We complete the proof of the theorem by proving the lemma.

**Lemma 9.5.1**

There exists a vector $\mathbf{z}$ such that

$$\mathbf{x} = \begin{bmatrix} Q \\ I \end{bmatrix} \mathbf{z}$$

if and only if $\Psi\mathbf{x} = \mathbf{0}$, where $\boldsymbol{\Psi}$ and $Q$ are as defined above.

**Proof**

By differentiating $\psi_i(\mathbf{q}(\boldsymbol{\alpha}_2), \boldsymbol{\alpha}_2)$ with respect to each of the elements of $\boldsymbol{\alpha}_2$, we obtain the system of equations

$$\mathbf{0} = \frac{\partial\Psi}{\partial\boldsymbol{\alpha}_1}\frac{\partial\mathbf{q}}{\partial\boldsymbol{\alpha}_2} + \frac{\partial\Psi}{\partial\boldsymbol{\alpha}_2} = \frac{\partial\Psi}{\partial\boldsymbol{\alpha}_1} Q + \frac{\partial\Psi}{\partial\boldsymbol{\alpha}_2}. \tag{9.5.23}$$

(i) Let

$$\mathbf{x} = \begin{bmatrix} \mathbf{x}_1 \\ \mathbf{x}_2 \end{bmatrix} = \begin{bmatrix} Q \\ I \end{bmatrix} \mathbf{z} = \begin{bmatrix} Q\mathbf{z} \\ \mathbf{z} \end{bmatrix}, \tag{9.5.24}$$

and partition $\Psi$ as

$$\Psi = \left[\frac{\partial\Psi}{\partial\boldsymbol{\alpha}_1}, \frac{\partial\Psi}{\partial\boldsymbol{\alpha}_2}\right].$$

Then

$$\begin{aligned}\Psi \mathbf{x} &= \frac{\partial \Psi}{\partial \boldsymbol{\alpha}_1}\mathbf{x}_1 + \frac{\partial \Psi}{\partial \boldsymbol{\alpha}_2}\mathbf{x}_2 \\ &= \frac{\partial \Psi}{\partial \boldsymbol{\alpha}_1} Q\mathbf{z} + \frac{\partial \Psi}{\partial \boldsymbol{\alpha}_2}\mathbf{z} \\ &= \left(\frac{\partial \Psi}{\partial \boldsymbol{\alpha}_1} Q + \frac{\partial \Psi}{\partial \boldsymbol{\alpha}_2}\right)\mathbf{z} = \mathbf{0}\end{aligned} \tag{9.5.25}$$

by (9.5.23). (ii) Since $\Psi[{}^{Q}_{I}] = \mathbf{0}$ if $\Psi\mathbf{x} = \mathbf{0}$, the columns of $[{}^{Q}_{I}]$ and $\mathbf{x}$ are in the null space of the columns of $\Psi$. But since $\Psi$ is $k \times m$ of rank $s$, the null space is at most of dimension $m - s$, and $r([{}^{Q}_{I}]) = m - s$. Therefore the columns of $[{}^{Q}_{I}]$ are a basis for that null space, and since $\mathbf{x}$ is also in the space, there exists a $\mathbf{z}$ such that $\mathbf{x} = [{}^{Q}_{I}]\mathbf{z}$. This completes the proof of the lemma and Theorem 9.5.2. □

Rothenberg also discusses the question of global identification, the case where structural parameters depend on the probability density through a reduced form parameter vector, and the linear model with nonlinear restrictions case discussed in Section 9.4.

## 9.6 Other Topics in Identification

Special problems arise when there are lagged endogenous variables and autocorrelation is present in the disturbance terms, because the usual estimators of the reduced form parameters are not consistent. A recent article on that subject, with additional references, is Deistler and Schrader (1979).

The identification problem has been discussed in the context of the Bayesian approach to econometrics. See Kadane (1974) for an introduction and further references.

## 9.7 References

Deistler, M. and J. Schrader (1979), "Linear Models with Autocorrelated Errors: Structural Identifiability in the Absence of Minimality Assumptions," *Econometrica,* **47,** 495–504.

Fisher, F. M. (1966), *The Identification Problem in Econometrics,* New York: McGraw-Hill.

Gabrielsen, A. (1978), "Consistency and Identifiability," *Journal of Econometrics,* **8,** 261–263.

Gale, D. (1960), *The Theory of Linear Economic Models,* New York: McGraw-Hill.

Graybill, F. A. (1969), *Introduction to Matrices with Applications in Statistics,* Belmont, California: Wadsworth.

Johnston, J. (1972), *Econometric Methods,* 2nd ed., New York: McGraw Hill.

Kadane, J. B. (1974), "The Role of Identification in Bayesian Theory," in S. E. Fienberg and A. Zellner, eds., *Studies in Bayesian Econometrics and Statistics,* Amsterdam: North-Holland.

Richmond, J. (1974), "Identifiability in Linear Models," *Econometrica,* **42,** 731–736.

Rothenberg, T. J. (1971), "Identification in Parametric Models," *Econometrica,* **39,** 577–591.

Wegge, L. L. (1965), "Identifiability Criteria for a System of Equations as a Whole," *Australian Journal of Statistics,* **7,** 67–77.

# CHAPTER 10

# The Special Case of Two Included Endogenous Variables: Distribution Theory and Moments

This chapter investigates the distributions of several estimators that have been used in connection with simultaneous equation models in econometrics, concentrating on the special case of equations with two included endogenous variables. The estimators to be considered are ordinary least squares (OLS), two-stage least squares (2SLS), *k*-class estimators, limited information maximum likelihood estimators (LIML), instrumental variable estimators (IV), and one example of a maximum likelihood estimator. After a brief introduction, we take up distribution theory and then turn to moments.

## 10.1 Background

### 10.1.1 Importance of Exact Distribution Theory

The development of simultaneous equation models is the main contribution of econometricians to the broader field of statistics. The interdependent economy depicted by economic theory requires a statistical model that reflects that interdependence, and econometricians began to build and analyze such models more than 40 years ago. Unfortunately, the estimators most frequently employed for this purpose—originally LIML and more recently 2SLS—are rather complicated functions of the underlying random variables, and their exact (or small sample) distributions are extremely difficult to derive. Instead, these and other estimators were defended on such large sample (asymptotic) criteria as consistency and asymptotic efficiency.

Small sample properties were studied largely by means of Monte Carlo experiments. These consist of generating artificial data by adding random disturbances to a known model and then computing estimators from the generated data. A large number of such estimators are computed, each depending on the particular set of random variables generated, and the distribution of the estimators is examined. Comparisons between estimators may be made on the basis of such criteria as the bias, variance, or mean squared error of the generated distributions. The Monte Carlo method is a poor substitute for the actual distribution in many cases. One problem is that the distribution may depend in a complex way on the unknown parameters, but the distributions generated by a Monte Carlo study do not permit a systematic analysis of such dependence. Moreover, computation of the moments of generated distributions of estimators will not reveal the possibility that the moments of the exact distributions do not exist, that is, are infinite. Comparisons on the basis of variances or mean squared error for cases in which expected values and/or variances do not exist will be meaningless, even though numerical values can be computed from Monte Carlo generated experiments.

The analysis of exact distributions and their moments began in the early 1960s, and in recent years substantial progress has been made. A full account of its history and major results prior to 1974 is found in Basmann (1974), who has been a major contributor to its development.

### 10.1.2 Description of the Special Case

This chapter is concerned with estimation of the parameters in a structural equation that contains two endogenous variables and an arbitrary number of exogenous variables. It is further assumed that the equation is identified by means of zero restrictions and that the sample size is greater than the number of exogenous variables. All of the predetermined variables are assumed to be exogenous, that is, there are no lagged endogenous variables included in the system. Finally, there are an arbitrary number of equations (and endogenous variables) in the complete system.

Although somewhat restrictive, equations of this type have been of interest for many years. The simplest Keynesian model, consisting of a consumption function and the GNP identity, is an example. That model was intensively studied by Haavelmo (1947) and was the subject of small sample research by Bergstrom (1962) and Basmann (1961, 1963). The articles that we present generalize the two-equation model by permitting the system to contain an arbitrary number of equations, but continue to assume that only two endogenous variables appear in the equation of interest. Chapter 11 is devoted to more general models.

## 10.2 Distributions of Estimators

This section is divided into two main parts. The first presents a detailed derivation of the exact distribution of OLS and 2SLS estimators, and the second surveys articles containing the distribution theory of other estimators. Since both OLS and 2SLS are special cases of IV and $k$-class estimators, these sections are not mutually exclusive; articles presenting results on IV and $k$-class usually consider the OLS and 2SLS as well. The section also discusses approximations to exact distributions.

### 10.2.1 Distribution Theory for OLS and 2SLS Estimators

Our discussion of the exact distributions of the OLS and 2SLS estimators is based on Sawa (1969); the distributions were derived independently by Richardson (1968). The equation to be estimated takes the form

$$y_{2t} = \alpha + \beta y_{1t} + u_t \qquad (t = 1, \ldots, N), \tag{10.2.1}$$

where $y_{1t}$, $y_{2t}$, and $u_t$ are the $t$th observations on $y_1$, $y_2$, and $u$. As will be shown below, no generality is lost in assuming that there are no exogenous variables in the equation. There are $K$ exogenous variables in the model, $z_{1t}, z_{2t}, \ldots, z_{Kt}$, and without loss of generality it is assumed that

$$\frac{1}{N}\sum_{t=1}^{N}(\mathbf{Z}_t - \overline{\mathbf{Z}})(\mathbf{Z}_t - \overline{\mathbf{Z}})' = I, \tag{10.2.2}$$

where

$$\bar{\mathbf{Z}} = \frac{1}{N}\sum \mathbf{Z}_t \quad \text{and} \quad \mathbf{Z}_t' = [z_{1t}, z_{2t}, \ldots, z_{Kt}].$$

The $u_t$ are assumed to have mutually independent normal distributions with $E(u_t) = 0$, $t = 1, \ldots, N$. We may write the reduced form for $\mathbf{Y}_t' = (y_{1t}, y_{2t})$ as functions of the exogenous variables:

$$\begin{aligned} y_{1t} &= \pi_{10} + \sum_{j=1}^{K} \pi_{1j}z_{jt} + v_{1t} \\ y_{2t} &= \pi_{20} + \sum_{j=1}^{K} \pi_{2j}z_{jt} + v_{2t}, \end{aligned} \tag{10.2.3}$$

where the $\pi_{ij}$ are the reduced form coefficients and the disturbance terms have a bivariate normal distribution,

$$\begin{bmatrix} v_{1t} \\ v_{2t} \end{bmatrix} \sim N_2(\mathbf{0}, \Sigma), \qquad \text{where} \quad \Sigma = \begin{bmatrix} \sigma_{11} & \sigma_{12} \\ \sigma_{12} & \sigma_{22} \end{bmatrix}.$$

The OLS estimator of $\beta$, $\hat{\beta}$, is given by

$$\hat{\beta} = \frac{\Sigma(y_{1t} - \bar{y}_1)(y_{2t} - \bar{y}_2)}{\Sigma(y_{1t} - \bar{y}_1)^2}, \tag{10.2.4}$$

which is the ratio of a covariance to a variance. To determine the probability distribution of this ratio, the Wishart distribution, which is the probability distribution of sample variances and covariances, must be utilized. Moreover, from the specification of the reduced form we see that $E(y_{1t})$ and $E(y_{2t})$ vary with $t$. The required density is therefore the noncentral Wishart distribution (see Appendix E). $E(y_{1t})$ and $E(y_{2t})$ are given by

$$\begin{bmatrix} E(y_{1t}) \\ E(y_{2t}) \end{bmatrix} \equiv \boldsymbol{\mu}_t = \begin{bmatrix} \pi_{10} + \Sigma\pi_{1j}z_{jt} \\ \pi_{20} + \Sigma\pi_{2j}z_{jt} \end{bmatrix}. \tag{10.2.5}$$

To complete the specification of the distribution, we need to derive the means sigma matrix. Since $\mathbf{Y}_t \sim N_2(\boldsymbol{\mu}_t, \Sigma)$, it follows that

$$\Sigma_t\, \mathbf{Y}_t\mathbf{Y}_t' \sim W_2'(\Sigma, N; \Sigma_t\boldsymbol{\mu}_t\boldsymbol{\mu}_t').$$

From (10.2.4), however, it may be seen that $\hat{\beta}$ depends on cross-products and sums of squares of $(y_{it} - \bar{y}_i)$. By (E.2.3) the means sigma matrix may be expressed in terms of the reduced form parameters as

$$\begin{aligned} T = \Sigma(\boldsymbol{\mu}_t - \bar{\boldsymbol{\mu}})(\boldsymbol{\mu}_t - \bar{\boldsymbol{\mu}})' &= N \begin{bmatrix} \Sigma\pi_{1j}^2 & \Sigma\pi_{1j}\pi_{2j} \\ \Sigma\pi_{1j}\pi_{2j} & \Sigma\pi_{2j}^2 \end{bmatrix} \\ &= N \begin{bmatrix} \Sigma\pi_{1j}^2 & \beta\Sigma\pi_{1j}^2 \\ \beta\Sigma\pi_{1j}^2 & \beta^2\Sigma\pi_{1j}^2 \end{bmatrix} \\ &= \begin{bmatrix} \tau^2 & \beta\tau^2 \\ \beta\tau^2 & \beta^2\tau^2 \end{bmatrix}, \end{aligned} \tag{10.2.6}$$

where $\tau^2 = N\Sigma\pi_{1j}^2$. We have used the orthonormality of the $z_{ij}$'s and $\pi_{2j} = \beta\pi_{1j}$ $(j = 1, \ldots, K)$, which follows from the structural equation and the two reduced form equations. Clearly, $r(T) = 1$. Define

$$A = \{a_{ij}\} = \sum_{t=1}^{N} (\mathbf{Y}_t - \overline{\mathbf{Y}})(\mathbf{Y}_t - \overline{\mathbf{Y}})',$$

where $\overline{\mathbf{Y}} = (1/N)\Sigma\mathbf{Y}_t$; then Theorem E.2.1 tells us that

$$\begin{aligned} p(A) &= W_2'(\Sigma, N - 1; T) \\ &= C_1|A|^{(N/2)-2} \exp\left\{-\frac{1}{2} \operatorname{tr} A\,\Sigma^{-1}\right\} \\ &\quad\times (\operatorname{tr}[A\Sigma^{-1}T\Sigma^{-1}])^{-(N-3)/4} \\ &\quad\times 2^{(N-3)/2} \times I_{(N-3)/2}[(\operatorname{tr} A\Sigma^{-1}T\Sigma^{-1})^{1/2}], \end{aligned} \tag{10.2.7}$$

$$C_1 = \frac{\exp\left\{-\frac{1}{2} \operatorname{tr} \Sigma^{-1} T\right\}}{2^{N-1}\pi\Gamma\left(\frac{N}{2} - 1\right) |\Sigma|^{(N-1)/2}}.$$

In this notation, the OLS estimator is

$$\hat{\beta} = \frac{a_{12}}{a_{11}}. \tag{10.2.8}$$

Sawa proceeds by making several transformations for the purpose of finding the distribution of $\hat{\beta}$. The first of these is to simplify the expression tr $A\Sigma^{-1}T\Sigma^{-1}$. To that end, he defines

$$\Psi = \begin{bmatrix} 1 & -\phi \\ 0 & 1 \end{bmatrix}, \tag{10.2.9}$$

where

$$\phi = \frac{\sigma_{22} - \beta\sigma_{12}}{\beta\sigma_{11} - \sigma_{12}} \tag{10.2.10}$$

(assuming $\beta \neq \sigma_{12}/\sigma_{11}$). The $a_{ij}$'s are transformed to $b_{ij}$'s, where

$$B = \{b_{ij}\} = (\Psi')^{-1}A\Psi^{-1}. \tag{10.2.11}$$

The Jacobian of this transformation is one, and it can be verified that tr $A\Sigma^{-1}$ = tr $B\Phi$ and tr $A\Sigma^{-1}T\Sigma^{-1} = \kappa^2 b_{22}$, where

$$\Phi = \{\phi_{ij}\} = \Psi\Sigma^{-1}\Psi' \tag{10.2.12}$$

and

$$\kappa = \frac{\tau(\sigma_{11}\beta - \sigma_{12})}{|\Sigma|}. \tag{10.2.13}$$

After this change of variables, the OLS estimator of $\beta$ is given by

$$\hat{\beta} = \frac{a_{12}}{a_{11}} = \frac{b_{12} - \phi b_{11}}{b_{11}} = r - \phi, \tag{10.2.14}$$

where

$$r = \frac{b_{12}}{b_{11}} = \hat{\beta} + \phi.$$

We next find the distribution of $r$. To do so, make the transformation

$$r = \frac{b_{12}}{b_{11}}, \qquad u = b_{11}, \qquad w = b_{22} - \frac{b_{12}^2}{b_{11}}.$$

Then $b_{11} = u$, $b_{12} = ru$, and $b_{22} = w + r^2u$. The Jacobian of this transformation is $u$. Accordingly, we may derive the joint density of $u$, $r$, $w$ from that of $B$ after making the necessary substitutions in (10.2.7):

$$\begin{aligned} p(u, r, w) &= C_1 w^{(N/2)-2} u^{(N/2)-1} \exp\left\{-\frac{1}{2}\phi_{22}w\right\} \\ &\times \exp\left\{-\frac{1}{2}(\phi_{11} + 2\phi_{12}r + \phi_{22}r^2)u\right\} \\ &\times \sum_{\alpha=0}^{\infty} \frac{\kappa^{2\alpha}(w + r^2u)^\alpha}{\alpha!\Gamma\left[\frac{N-1}{2} + \alpha\right] 2^{2\alpha}}. \end{aligned} \tag{10.2.15}$$

It is necessary to integrate $u$ and $w$ over the range $(0, \infty)$ to find the density for $r$, the variable of interest. The expression $(w + r^2u)^\alpha$ may be expanded by the binomial theorem,

$$(w + r^2u)^\alpha = \sum_{j=0}^{\alpha} \binom{\alpha}{j} w^{\alpha-j} r^{2j} u^j.$$

In this form, the terms containing $w$ and $u$ in (10.2.15) may be written as

$$\sum_{j=0}^{\alpha} \binom{\alpha}{j} w^{N/2+\alpha-j-2} \exp\left\{-\frac{1}{2}\phi_{22}w\right\} u^{N/2+j-1} \times \exp\left\{-\frac{1}{2}(\phi_{11} + 2\phi_{12}r + \phi_{22}r^2)u\right\}. \tag{10.2.16}$$

Since the Gamma function may be written as

$$\Gamma(a) = k^a \int_0^\infty x^{a-1} e^{-kx}\, dx, \tag{10.2.17}$$

integrating $w$ and $u$ over $(0, \infty)$ from (10.2.16) yields

$$\sum_{j=0}^{\alpha} \binom{\alpha}{j} \left(\frac{2}{\phi_{22}}\right)^{N/2+\alpha-j-1} \times \Gamma\left(\frac{N}{2} + \alpha - j - 1\right) \left(\frac{2}{\phi_{11} + 2\phi_{12}r + \phi_{22}r^2}\right)^{N/2+j} \Gamma\left(\frac{N}{2} + j\right). \tag{10.2.18}$$

The following results may be verified, where

$$\xi^2 = \sigma_{22} - \frac{\sigma_{12}^2}{\sigma_{11}}, \qquad \sigma^2 = \sigma_{11},$$

and $\rho = \sigma_{12}/\sigma_{11}$:

$$\begin{aligned}
\phi_{22} &= \frac{\sigma_{11}}{|\Sigma|} = \frac{\sigma^2}{\sigma^2\xi^2} = \frac{1}{\xi^2}, \\
-\frac{1}{2}\operatorname{tr}\Sigma^{-1}T &= -\frac{\tau^2}{2\sigma^2}\left[1 + \frac{\sigma^2(\beta - \rho)^2}{\xi^2}\right], \\
r &= (\hat{\beta} - \rho) + \frac{\xi^2}{\sigma^2(\beta - \rho)}, \\
\kappa &= \frac{\tau(\beta - \rho)}{\xi^2},
\end{aligned} \tag{10.2.19}$$

and

$$\phi_{22}r^2 + 2\phi_{12}r + \phi_{11} = \frac{\sigma^2(\hat{\beta} - \rho)^2 + \xi^2}{|\Sigma|}.$$

Upon making these substitutions and using $r = \hat{\beta} + \phi$, we may write the density for $\hat{\beta}$ as

$$\begin{aligned}
f(\hat{\beta}) = C_2 \sum_{\alpha=0}^{\infty} &\frac{1}{\alpha!\Gamma\left[\dfrac{N-1}{2} + \alpha\right]} \left(\frac{\tau^2(\hat{\beta} - \rho)^2}{2\xi^2}\right)^{\alpha} \sum_{j=0}^{\alpha} \binom{\alpha}{j}\Gamma\left(\frac{N}{2} + \alpha - j - 1\right) \\
&\times \Gamma\left(\frac{N}{2} + j\right)\left(\sigma(\hat{\beta} - \rho) + \frac{\xi^2}{\sigma(\hat{\beta} - \rho)}\right)^{2j}\left(\frac{1}{\sigma^2(\hat{\beta} - \rho)^2 + \xi^2}\right)^{N/2 + j},
\end{aligned} \tag{10.2.20}$$

where

$$C_2 = \frac{\sigma\xi^{N-1}}{\pi\Gamma\left(\dfrac{N}{2} - 1\right)} \exp\left\{-\frac{\tau^2}{2\sigma^2}\left[1 + \frac{\sigma^2(\hat{\beta} - \rho)^2}{\xi^2}\right]\right\}.$$

The density may be written in an alternative form by interchanging the order of summation. To see this, denote the terms in the first summation in (10.2.20) by $g(\alpha)$ and the second as $h(\alpha)$; then

$$\begin{aligned}
\sum_{\alpha=0}^{\infty} g(\alpha) \sum_{j=0}^{\alpha} h(j) &= g(0)h(0) + g(1)[h(0) + h(1)] \\
&\quad + \cdots + g(n)[h(0) + h(1) + \cdots h(n)] + \cdots \\
&= h(0)[g(0) + g(1) + \cdots] + h(1)[g(1) + \cdots] + \cdots \\
&= \sum_{j=0}^{\infty} h(j) \sum_{\alpha=j}^{\infty} g(\alpha) = \sum_{j=0}^{\infty} h(j) \sum_{k=0}^{\infty} g(k)
\end{aligned}$$

where $k = \alpha - j$ or $\alpha = j + k$. Upon making this substitution, with a bit of simplification we have the exact density of the OLS estimator,

$$f(\hat{\beta}) = C_2 \sum_{j=0}^{\infty} \frac{\Gamma\left(\frac{N}{2} + j\right)}{j!} \left(\sigma(\hat{\beta} - \rho) + \frac{\xi^2}{\sigma(\beta - \rho)}\right)^{2j}$$
$$\times \left(\frac{1}{\sigma^2(\hat{\beta} - \rho)^2 + \xi^2}\right)^{N/2 + j} \sum_{k=0}^{\infty} \frac{\Gamma\left(\frac{N}{2} + k - 1\right)}{k!\Gamma\left(\frac{N-1}{2} + k + j\right)} \left(\frac{\tau^2(\beta - \rho)^2}{2\xi^2}\right)^{k+j}, \quad \textbf{(10.2.21)}$$

which may also be expressed as

$$f(\hat{\beta}) = \frac{C_2\Gamma\left(\frac{N}{2} - 1\right)}{[\sigma^2(\hat{\beta} - \rho)^2 + \xi^2]^{N/2}} \sum_{j=0}^{\infty} \frac{\Gamma\left(\frac{N}{2} + j\right)}{j!\Gamma\left(\frac{N-1}{2} + j\right)}$$
$$\times \left(\sigma(\hat{\beta} - \rho) + \frac{\xi^2}{\sigma(\hat{\beta} - \rho)}\right)^{2j} \left(\frac{\theta}{\sigma^2(\hat{\beta} - \rho)^2 + \xi^2}\right)^j$$
$$\times {}_1F_1\left(\frac{N}{2} - 1, \frac{N-1}{2} + j; \theta\right), \quad \textbf{(10.2.22)}$$

where $\theta = \tau^2(\beta - \rho)^2/2\xi^2$ and ${}_1F_1(\ )$ denotes the confluent hypergeometric function (see Appendix F); twice $\theta$ may be interpreted as a noncentrality parameter.

The above derivation assumed $\beta \neq \sigma_{12}/\sigma^2 = \rho$; if $\beta = \rho$, a simpler form is possible since, in that case,

$$\Sigma^{-1}T\Sigma^{-1} = \begin{bmatrix} \delta^2 & 0 \\ 0 & 0 \end{bmatrix},$$

where

$$\delta = \frac{\tau(\sigma_{22} - \beta\sigma_{12})}{|\Sigma|} = \frac{\tau}{\sigma^2}.$$

In the case that $\beta = \rho$,

$$f(\hat{\beta}) = \sigma \exp\left\{-\frac{\tau^2}{2\sigma^2}\right\} \sum_{j=0}^{\infty} \frac{\Gamma\left(\frac{N}{2} + j\right)}{j!\Gamma\left(\frac{N-1}{2} + j\right)} \left(\frac{\tau^2}{2\sigma^2}\right)^j$$
$$\times \left(\frac{\xi^2}{\sigma^2(\hat{\beta} - \rho)^2 + \xi^2}\right)^{N/2+j} \quad \textbf{(10.2.23)}$$

Equations 10.2.22 and 10.2.23 are the exact densities for the OLS estimators of $\beta$ for the special case being considered in this chapter. We discuss their moments and methods of approximation after discussing the distribution of the 2SLS estimator of $\beta$, $\tilde{\beta}$.

For the present case, the 2SLS estimator may be obtained directly from the preceding analysis. We start with the original model:

$$y_{2t} = \alpha + \beta y_{1t} + u_t, \qquad t = 1, \ldots, N. \tag{10.2.1}$$

To find the 2SLS estimator, we apply the method of instrumental variables. First, write (10.2.1) in vector form ($\mathbf{y}_1$, $\mathbf{y}_2$, and $\mathbf{u}$ are $N \times 1$ and $\mathbf{1}$ is a column vector of $N$ ones) as

$$\mathbf{y}_2 = \alpha\mathbf{1} + \beta\mathbf{y}_1 + \mathbf{u}, \tag{10.2.24}$$

and then premultiply (10.2.24) by the $1 \times N$ vectors $(1/\sqrt{N})[\mathbf{Z}_j - \bar{z}_j\mathbf{1}]'$, where $j = 1, \ldots, K$, $\mathbf{Z}_j' = [z_{j1}, \ldots, z_{jN}]$, and $\bar{z}_j = (1/N)\sum_t z_{jt}$, to obtain

$$y_{2j}^* = \beta y_{1j}^* + u_j^*, \qquad j = 1, \ldots, K, \tag{10.2.25}$$

where $y_{ij}^* = (1/\sqrt{N})[\mathbf{Z}_j - \bar{z}_j\mathbf{1}]'\mathbf{y}_i$, $i = 1, 2$, and $\mathbf{u}_j^* = (1/\sqrt{N})[\mathbf{Z}_j - \bar{z}_j\mathbf{1}]'\mathbf{u}$. It should be verified that the 2SLS estimator is given by

$$\tilde{\beta} = \frac{\sum_{j=1}^{K} y_{2j}^* y_{1j}^*}{\sum_{j=1}^{K} y_{1j}^{*2}}. \tag{10.2.26}$$

From the reduced form, we have

$$\begin{aligned} y_{ij}^* &= \frac{1}{N}\sum_t (z_{jt} - \bar{z}_j)\sum_{s=1}^{K} \pi_{is} z_{st} + \frac{1}{N}\sum_t (z_{jt} - \bar{z}_j)v_{it} \\ &= N\pi_{ij} + \frac{1}{N}\sum_t (z_{jt} - \bar{z}_j)v_{it}, \qquad i = 1, 2 \\ &\qquad\qquad\qquad\qquad\qquad\qquad\quad j = 1, \ldots, K. \end{aligned} \tag{10.2.27}$$

In this form, it may be seen that

$$\mathbf{y}_j^* = \begin{bmatrix} y_{1j}^* \\ y_{2j}^* \end{bmatrix} \sim N_2\left(N\begin{bmatrix} \pi_{1j} \\ \pi_{2j} \end{bmatrix}, \Sigma\right), \qquad j = 1, \ldots, K,$$

and the $K$ vectors are independent over the $j$ subscript. Since we are interested in $\Sigma y_{1j}^* y_{2j}^*$ and $\Sigma y_{1j}^{*2}$, we need the distribution of the sums of squares and cross-products. Since the means sigma matrix is given by (10.2.6), it follows that the distribution of $\Sigma_{j=1}^{k} \mathbf{y}_j^*\mathbf{y}_j^{*\prime}$ is given by $W_2'(\Sigma, K; T)$. Accordingly, the exact distribution for the 2SLS estimator is given by (10.2.22) and (10.2.23) with $K$ in place of $N - 1$.

These results must be modified if there are any included exogenous variables. In this case, we have

$$y_{2t} = \beta y_{1t} + \sum_{j=1}^{K_1} \gamma_j z_{jt} + u_t, \tag{10.2.28}$$

where we have assumed that the first $K_1$ exogenous variables are included in this equation. Let

$$Z_1 = \begin{bmatrix} z_{11} & z_{21} & \cdots & z_{K_1 1} \\ \cdot & & & \cdot \\ \cdot & & & \cdot \\ \cdot & & & \cdot \\ z_{1N} & & \cdots & z_{K_1 N} \end{bmatrix}$$

be the $N \times K_1$ matrix of observations on the exogenous variables included in this equation (one of which may be the intercept). Goldberger (1964, p. 194) shows that the OLS estimator of $\beta$ may be found by first regressing $\mathbf{y}_2$ and $\mathbf{y}_1$ on $Z_1$ and then regressing the residuals from the first regression on those from the second. This result implies that

$$\hat{\beta} = \frac{\mathbf{y}_2'[I - Z_1(Z_1'Z_1)^{-1}Z_1']\mathbf{y}_1}{\mathbf{y}_1'[I - Z_1(Z_1'Z_1)^{-1}Z_1']\mathbf{y}_1}. \qquad \textbf{(10.2.29)}$$

Since $[I - Z_1(Z_1'Z_1)^{-1}Z_1']$ is symmetric idempotent of rank $N - K_1$, we may use the following result, which is proved in Appendix E:

If $Q$ is a symmetric idempotent $n \times n$ matrix of rank $q$, and $\mathbf{Z}_i \sim N_n[E(\mathbf{Z}_i), \Sigma]$, then

$$V = Z'QZ \sim W_n'[\Sigma, q; (E(Z))'Q(E(Z))].$$

Therefore,

$$V = \begin{bmatrix} \mathbf{y}_1' \\ \mathbf{y}_2' \end{bmatrix} [I - Z_1(Z_1'Z_1)^{-1}Z_1'][\mathbf{y}_1\mathbf{y}_2] \sim W_2'(\Sigma, N - K_1; T_1), \qquad \textbf{(10.2.30)}$$

where

$$T_1 = \tau_1^2 \begin{bmatrix} 1 & \beta \\ \beta & \beta^2 \end{bmatrix}$$

and

$$\tau_1^2 = N \sum_{j=K_1+1}^{K} \pi_{1j}^2;$$

the $\pi_{1j}$ are the reduced form parameters of the exogenous variables excluded from the first equation. The distribution of $\hat{\beta}$ in the presence of included exogenous variables is, therefore, given by (10.2.22) and (10.2.23), with $N - K_1$ in place of $N - 1$ and $\tau_1$ in place of $\tau$.

The distribution for the 2SLS estimator may be derived from the OLS estimator as above. It may be verified that the relevant Wishart distribution is $W_2'(\Sigma, K_2; T_1)$, where $K_2 = K - K_1$, and the distributions obtained above apply after modifying the degrees of freedom and means sigma matrix appropriately. An interesting special case arises when $K_2 = 1$, which corresponds to the case that the equation is just identified. (The condition for an equation to be just identified is $K_2 = G_1 - 1 = 1$ for the two included endogenous variable case.) For $K_2 = 1$ the 2SLS estimator of $\beta$,

$$\hat{\beta}_{2SLS} = \frac{\mathbf{y}_1'\mathbf{Z}_2(\mathbf{Z}_2'\mathbf{Z}_2)^{-1}\mathbf{Z}_2'\mathbf{y}_2}{\mathbf{y}_1'\mathbf{Z}_2(\mathbf{Z}_2'\mathbf{Z}_2)^{-1}\mathbf{Z}_2'\mathbf{y}_1}, \tag{10.2.31}$$

reduces to

$$\hat{\beta}_{2SLS} = \frac{\mathbf{Z}_2'\mathbf{y}_2}{\mathbf{Z}_2'\mathbf{y}_1}, \tag{10.2.32}$$

since $\mathbf{Z}_2$ is then $N \times 1$. Now, (10.2.32) is a ratio of normally distributed variables, and Fieller's result is applicable. That result, which is found in Appendix D, may be used to obtain the distribution upon replacing the parameters in the general form by the expectations, variances, and covariance of $\mathbf{Z}_2'\mathbf{y}_2$ and $\mathbf{Z}_2'\mathbf{y}_1$. [Mariano and McDonald (1979) show directly that (10.2.22) reduces to the Fieller result for $K_2 = 1$. They also show that the density of the LIML estimator reduces to Fieller's equation.]

Expressions (10.2.22) and (10.2.23) contain two infinite sums and are rather complicated functions of their parameters. Sawa (1969) presents graphs of the densities for $\beta = 0.6$, $\sigma_{11} = \sigma_{22} = 1.0$, and for several values of $N$, $\rho$, and $K$; these are reproduced as Figures 10.1 to 10.5. Figures 10.1 and 10.2 indicate that 2SLS has a smaller bias than OLS, that both are biased in the same direction, and that the distributions are extremely sensitive to the value of $\rho$. Figures 10.3 and 10.4 show that both OLS and 2SLS become more concentrated as $N$ increases, but the mode of the OLS estimator remains at approximately 0.5, while that of the 2SLS estimator drifts toward 0.6. Figure 10.5 illustrates how the 2SLS distribution is affected by $K$; for a fixed $N$ the bias increases with $K$.

Holly and Phillips (1979, p. 1537) use the asymptotic expansion of ${}_1F_1$ to derive an

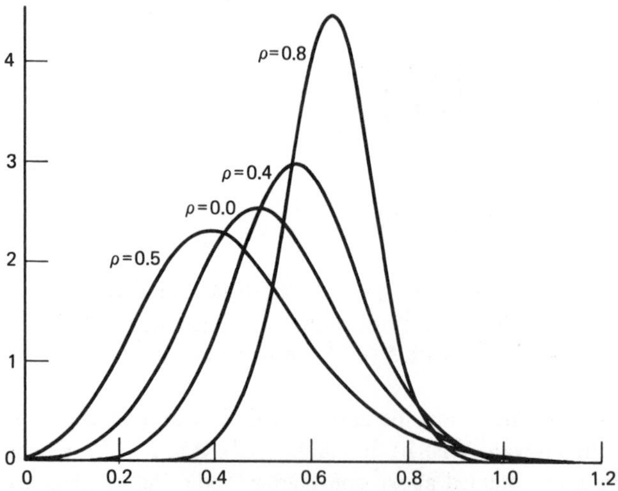


**FIGURE 10.1 Distributions of the OLS estimator for various $\rho$ when $N = 10$. [Reprinted from Sawa (1969), with permission of the publisher. The American Statistical Association.]**

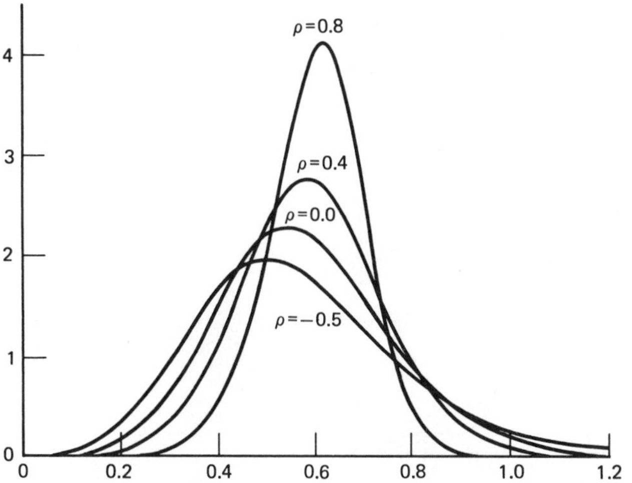


**FIGURE 10.2** Distributions of the 2SLS estimator for various $\rho$ when $N = 10$ and $K = 3$. [Reprinted from Sawa (1969), with permission of the publisher, The American Statistical Association.]

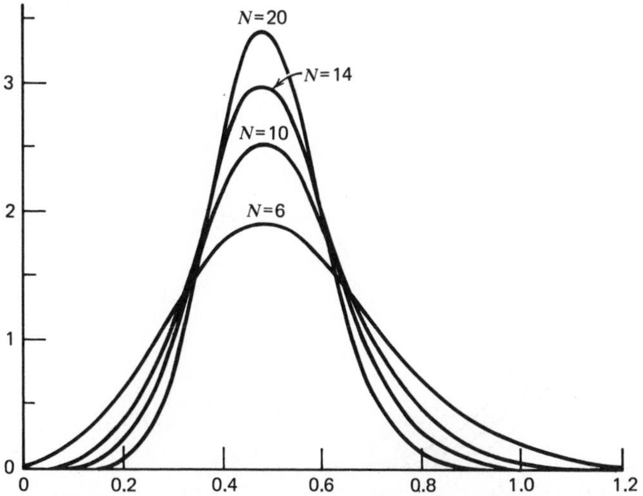


**FIGURE 10.3** Distributions of the OLS estimator for various $N$ when $\rho = 0$. [Reprinted from Sawa (1969), with permission of the publisher, The American Statistical Association.]

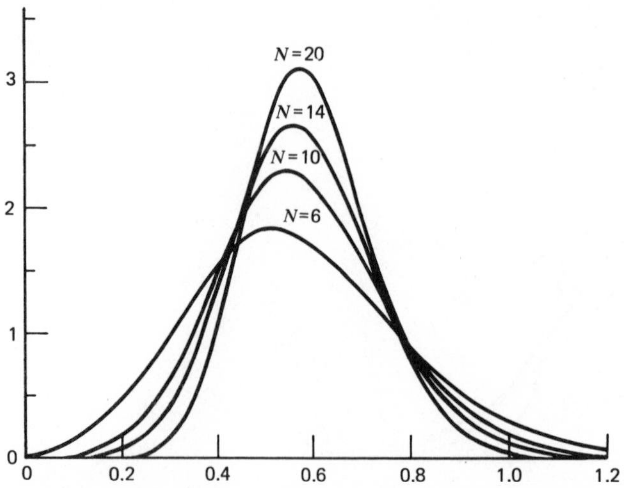


**FIGURE 10.4** Distributions of the 2SLS estimator for various $N$ when $\rho = 0$ and $K = 3$. [Reprinted from Sawa (1969), with permission of the publisher, The American Statistical Association.]

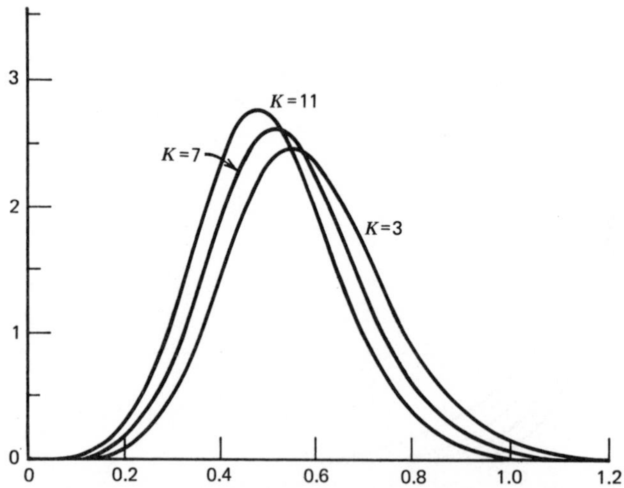


**FIGURE 10.5** Distributions of the 2SLS estimator for various $K$ when $\rho = 0$ and $N = 12$. [Reprinted from Sawa (1969), with permission of the publisher, The American Statistical Association.]

approximation to (10.2.22) in the case of 2SLS. In what follows, we illustrate their result for OLS. Using the first order term in the asymptotic expansion for ${}_1F_1[N/2 - 1, (N - 1)/2 + j; \theta]$ for large $\theta$ (see appendix F), we obtain the following from (10.2.22) after some simplification:

$$f(\hat{\beta}) = \frac{\sigma\xi^{N-1}}{\sqrt{\pi}} \exp\left\{\frac{-\tau^2}{2\sigma^2}\right\} \{\sigma^2(\hat{\beta} - \rho)^2 + \xi^2\}^{-N/2} \times \sum_{j=0}^{\infty} \frac{\Gamma\left(\frac{N}{2} + j\right)}{j!\Gamma\left(\frac{N}{2} - 1\right)} \left\{\left[\sigma(\hat{\beta} - \rho) + \frac{\xi^2}{\sigma(\beta - \rho)}\right]^2 \times \frac{1}{\sigma^2(\hat{\beta} - \rho)^2 + \xi^2}\right\}^j \tag{10.2.33}$$

$$= \frac{\sigma\xi^{N-1}(N - 2)}{2\sqrt{\pi}} \exp\left\{\frac{-\tau^2}{2\sigma^2}\right\} \{\sigma^2(\hat{\beta} - \rho)^2 + \xi^2\}^{-N/2} \times \sum_{j=0}^{\infty} \frac{\Gamma\left(\frac{N}{2} + j\right)}{j!\Gamma\left(\frac{N}{2} - 1\right)} \times \left[\frac{\sigma^4(\hat{\beta} - \rho)^2(\beta - \rho)^2 + 2\sigma^2(\hat{\beta} - \rho)(\beta - \rho)\xi^2 + \xi^4}{\sigma^2(\beta - \rho)^2[\sigma^2(\hat{\beta} - \rho)^2 + \xi^2]}\right]^j. \tag{10.2.34}$$

The last step uses

$$\Gamma\left(\frac{N}{2} - 1\right) = \frac{2}{N - 2}\Gamma\left(\frac{N}{2}\right),$$

which follows from

$$\Gamma\left(\frac{N}{2}\right) = \left(\frac{N}{2} - 1\right)\Gamma\left(\frac{N}{2} - 1\right).$$

Equation 10.2.34 may be simplified by using

$$(1 - x)^{-m} = \sum_{j=0}^{\infty} \frac{\Gamma(m + j)}{j!\Gamma(m)} x^j, \qquad \text{for} \quad |x| < 1.$$

Therefore, if,

$$\frac{|\sigma^4(\hat{\beta} - \rho)^2(\beta - \rho)^2 + 2\sigma^2(\hat{\beta} - \rho)(\beta - \rho)\xi^2 + \xi^4|}{\sigma^2(\beta - \rho)^2[\sigma^2(\hat{\beta} - \rho)^2 + \xi^2]} < 1, \tag{10.2.35}$$

the sum in (10.2.34) may be written as

$$\left(1 - \frac{\sigma^4(\hat{\beta} - \rho)^2(\beta - \rho)^2 + 2\sigma^2(\hat{\beta} - \rho)(\beta - \rho)\xi^2 + \xi^4}{\sigma^2(\beta - \rho)^2[\sigma^2(\hat{\beta} - \rho)^2 + \xi^2]}\right)^{-N/2}. \tag{10.2.36}$$

We can combine the two terms raised to the $-N/2$ power, which yields

$$\begin{aligned}
f(\hat{\beta}) &\sim \frac{\sigma\xi^{N-1}(N-2)}{2\sqrt{\pi}} \exp\left\{\frac{-\tau^2}{2\sigma^2}\right\}\left\{\xi^2 - \frac{2(\hat{\beta}-\rho)}{\beta-\rho}\xi^2 - \frac{\xi^4}{\sigma^2(\beta-\rho)^2}\right\}^{-N/2} \\
&= \frac{\sigma\xi^{N-1}(N-2)}{2\sqrt{\pi}} \exp\left\{\frac{-\tau^2}{2\sigma^2}\right\} \\
&\times \left\{\frac{\xi^2}{\sigma^2(\beta-\rho)^2}[\sigma^2(\beta-\rho)^2 - 2\sigma^2(\hat{\beta}-\rho)(\beta-\rho) - \xi^2]\right\}^{-N/2} \\
&= \frac{\sigma^{N+1}(\beta-\rho)^N(N-2)}{2\sqrt{\pi}\xi} \exp\left\{\frac{-\tau^2}{2\sigma^2}\right\} \\
&\times \{\sigma^2(\beta-\rho)(\beta+\rho-2\hat{\beta}) - \xi^2\}.^{-N/2} \qquad \textbf{(10.2.37)}
\end{aligned}$$

It will be observed that (10.2.37) contains no infinite sums and is readily evaluated for given values of the parameters. Holly and Phillips (1979) show how to deal with the case that (10.2.35) does not hold. Since this is a large $\theta$ expansion, it is of interest to see what parameter values are associated with large values of $\theta$. From the definitions of $\theta$, $\tau^2$, and $\xi^2$, we have

$$\theta = \frac{\tau^2(\beta-\rho)^2}{2\xi^2} = \frac{N\Sigma\pi_{1j}^2(\beta-\rho)^2}{2(\sigma_{22}-\sigma_{12}^2/\sigma_{11})}.$$

Therefore, $\theta$ is large (and the approximation is better) for large sample size, large $\Sigma\pi_{1j}^2$, a large difference between $\beta$ and $\rho$, and a small value of $(\sigma_{22} - \sigma_{12}^2/\sigma_{11})$. The latter is the unexplained variance from the linear regression of $v_{2t}$ on $v_{1t}$, which would be small when these errors are highly correlated.

An alternative form of the exact distributions of OLS and 2SLS has been obtained by Anderson and Sawa (1973). In that paper, normalized forms of the estimators are expressed in terms of a doubly noncentral $F$-distribution. [The ratio of random variables, each of which is distributed as noncentral $\chi^2$ divided by their respective degrees of freedom, is distributed as doubly noncentral $F$. See Johnson and Kotz (1972) for details.] In view of the complicated nature of the distribution, Anderson and Sawa also present approximations to the distribution and density functions of the double $k$-class estimators, which include OLS and 2SLS, for the two included endogenous variable case we have been considering. Starting with the doubly noncentral $F$ distribution mentioned above, they transform the problem to the probability that a certain quadratic form is negative. An asymptotic expansion of the characteristic function of the probability distribution is derived and then inverted to obtain an asymptotic expansion of the original distribution. This is an Edgeworth-type approximation based on the normal distribution and its derivatives. The asymptotic expansion is obtained for large values of the noncentrality parameter, $\boldsymbol{\eta}'\boldsymbol{\eta}$, which corresponds to $\tau_1^2/\sigma^2$ in the Sawa article discussed in detail above. Anderson and Sawa present graphs that compare the exact density of the 2SLS and OLS estimators to a normal approximation and the asymptotic expansion to $O(T^{-1/2})$ for selected parameter values; these are reproduced as Figures 10.6 to 10.9. Figure 10.6 shows that the asymptotic approximation is quite accurate for sample size $T = 20$, and that the normal approximation is reasonably accurate. (The parameter $\alpha$ is a normalized transformation of $\beta$, and $\psi$ is a transformation of the concentration parameter.) But for $T = 10$,

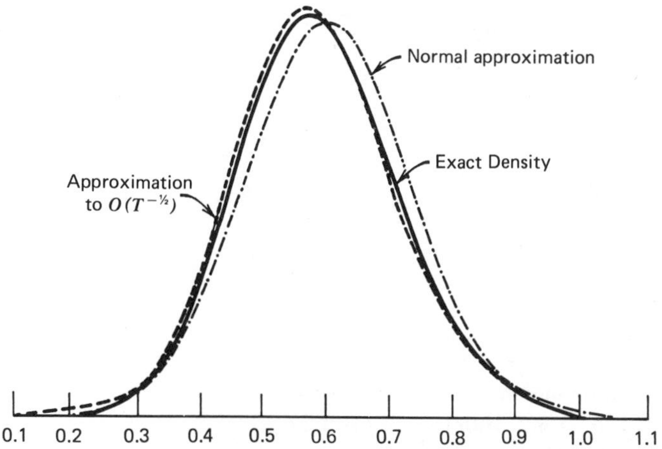


**FIGURE 10.6** **Exact and approximate densities of the two-stage least squares estimator: $T = 20$, $K_1 = 1$, $K_2 = 4$, $\alpha = 0.6$, $\psi = 4$. [Reprinted from Anderson and Sawa (1973), with permission of the publisher, The Econometric Society.]**

Figure 10.7 reveals the inadequacy of the normal approximation, although the approximation to $O(T^{-1/2})$ is still quite good. Figure 10.8 shows the effect on the approximate distribution function of changes in the concentration parameter; they become more concentrated as $\psi$ increases. Figure 10.9 shows that the 2SLS estimator becomes more skewed as $K_2$ increases.

Anderson (1977) comments further on asymptotic expansions. In particular, for 2SLS estimates it is pointed out that large values of the noncentrality parameter ($\tau_1^2/\sigma^2$ in the Sawa notation) may be associated with either large sample size or a small disturbance variance.

Finally, Anderson and Sawa (1979) present tables of the exact distribution of the

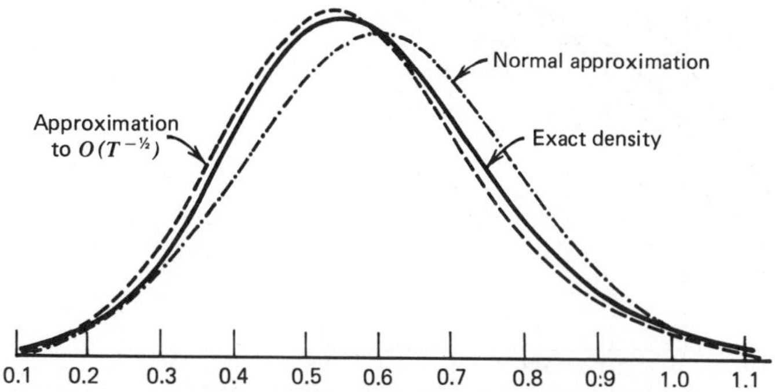


**FIGURE 10.7** **Exact and approximate densities of the two-stage least squares estimator: $T = 10$, $K_1 = 1$, $K_2 = 4$, $\alpha = 0.6$, $\psi = 4$. [Reprinted from Anderson and Sawa (1973), with permission of the publisher, The Econometric Society.]**

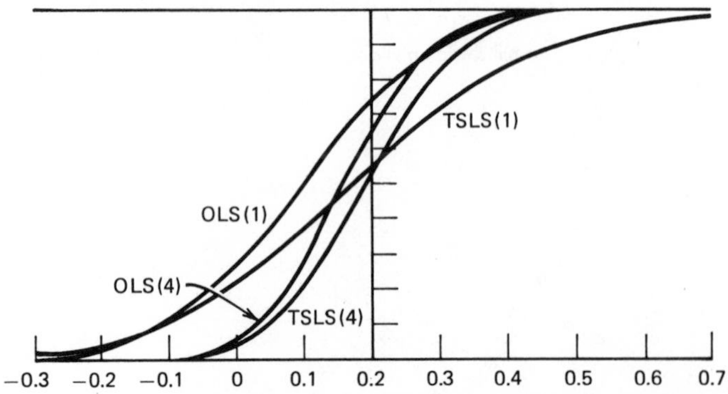


**FIGURE 10.8** **Approximate distributions to $O(T^{-1/2})$; $T = 20$, $K_1 = 0$, $K_2 = 4$, $\alpha = 0.2$. Numbers in parentheses denote values of $\psi$. [Reprinted from Anderson and Sawa (1973), with permission of the publisher, The Econometric Society.]**

2SLS estimate and examine the accuracy of an approximate distribution based on the asymptotic expansion discussed above. The expansion is in terms of $1/\mu$, which is defined in the article and is a function of the noncentrality parameter discussed above. Tables are presented for a wide range of values of the noncentrality parameter and of the number of excluded exogenous variables. An important finding for situations likely to be encountered in practice is that the (standardized) distribution of the 2SLS estimator is more closely concentrated than a normal approximation in overidentified cases. Accordingly, use of the normal approximation will tend to underestimate significance levels.

An alternative approach to approximation may be found in Mariano (1973a). In addition, the work on approximations of instrumental variable estimators by Sargan and Mikhail (1971) may be applied to the OLS and 2SLS estimators.

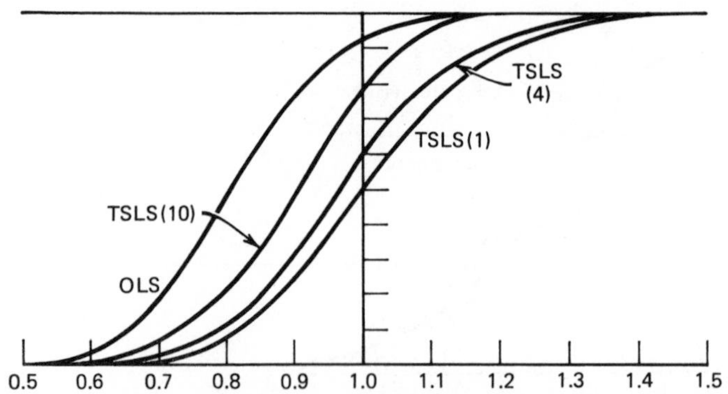


**FIGURE 10.9** **Approximate distributions to $O(T^{-1/2})$; $T = 20$, $K_1 = 0$, $\alpha = 1.0$, $\psi = 4$. Numbers in parentheses denote values of $K_2$. [Reprinted from Anderson and Sawa (1973), with permission of the publisher, The Econometric Society.]**

### 10.2.2 Distributions of Other Estimators

In this section we briefly survey some of the work that has been done on the distri of estimators other than OLS and 2SLS. For the most part we continue to use t included endogenous variable model described above.

**10.2.2a Limited Information Maximum Likelihood (LIML)** Mariano an (1972) obtain the exact distribution of the LIML estimator for the two included endo variable case. The estimator is expressed in terms of two Wishart matrices. An (1974) presents an approximation to the distribution of the LIML estimator. T proximation utilizes a Taylor series expansion and an asymptotic expansion in the size, which appears in the noncentrality parameter. The expansion is in terms normal distribution. Anderson compares the asymptotic expansions of the 2SLS and estimators in terms of the concentration of the distributions around the true para He concludes that large values of $K_2$ (the number of exogenous variables exclude the equation) favor the LIML estimator, and the 2SLS estimator is more concen for small values of $\alpha^2$, where $\alpha = \beta(\omega_{22} - \omega_{12})/\sqrt{|\Omega|}$, and

$$\Omega = \begin{bmatrix} \omega_{11} & \omega_{12} \\ \omega_{12} & \omega_{22} \end{bmatrix}$$

is the covariance matrix of the reduced form disturbances. Anderson and Sawa ( present additional comparisons between 2SLS and LIML estimators, emphasizin these estimators have substantially different small sample properties.

**10.2.2b Instrumental Variables (IV) Estimators** Starting with the two inc endogenous variable case we are considering in this chapter,

$$\mathbf{y}_1 = \beta\mathbf{y}_2 + Z_1\boldsymbol{\gamma}_1 + \mathbf{u}_1 \qquad \textbf{(10.}$$

($\mathbf{y}_1$, $\mathbf{y}_2$, and $\mathbf{u}_1$ are $T \times 1$, $Z_1$ is $T \times K_1$, and $\boldsymbol{\gamma}_1$ is $K_1 \times 1$), an IV estimator is obt by finding a $T \times M$ matrix $X$ that has the properties:

$$\text{(i) plim } \frac{1}{T} X'\mathbf{u}_1 = \mathbf{0} \text{ and}$$

$$\text{(ii) plim } \frac{1}{T} X'Z_1 \text{ is nonsingular.} \qquad \textbf{(10.}$$

Premultiplying (10.2.28) by $X'$ and by $Z_1'$, we obtain the normal equations:

$$\begin{aligned} X'\mathbf{y}_1 &= \beta X'\mathbf{y}_2 + X'Z_1\boldsymbol{\gamma}_1 + X'\mathbf{u}_1 \\ Z_1'\mathbf{y}_1 &= \beta Z_1'\mathbf{y}_2 + Z_1'Z_1\boldsymbol{\gamma}_1 + Z_1'\mathbf{u}_1. \end{aligned} \qquad \textbf{(10.2}$$

Upon dropping the terms involving $\mathbf{u}_1$, solving the second equation for $\boldsymbol{\gamma}_1$, and substituting the resulting expression of $\boldsymbol{\gamma}_1$ into the first equation, we obtain the IV estim for $\beta$:

$$\begin{aligned} \hat{\beta}_{IV} &= \{X'[I - Z_1(Z_1'Z_1)^{-1}Z_1']\mathbf{y}_2\}^{-1} \\ &\times \{X'[I - Z_1(Z_1'Z_1)^{-1}Z_1']\mathbf{y}_1\}. \end{aligned} \qquad \textbf{(10.2.}$$

Different choices for $X$ result in different IV estimators; for example, the choice $X = Z_2$ (the excluded exogenous variables) yields the 2SLS estimator. Several choices have been examined in the literature.

Carter (1976) takes the simple case $\mathbf{X} = \mathbf{w} = Z\mathbf{p}$, where $\mathbf{p}$ and $\mathbf{w}$ are $T \times 1$ vectors and $Z = (Z_1, Z_2)$. It is easily verified that for this case

$$\hat{\beta}_{IV} = \frac{\mathbf{w}'M_1\mathbf{y}_1}{\mathbf{w}'M_1\mathbf{y}_2} \equiv \frac{z_1}{z_2} \tag{10.2.42}$$

where $M_1 = I - Z_1(Z_1'Z_1)^{-1}Z_1'$ and $z_i = \mathbf{w}'M_1\mathbf{y}_1$ $(i = 1, 2)$. Defining

$$\Omega = \begin{bmatrix} \omega_{11} & \omega_{12} \\ \omega_{12} & \omega_{22} \end{bmatrix}$$

as the covariance matrix of the reduced form disturbances, where the reduced form (10.2.3) is written in vector matrix notation as

$$\begin{aligned} \mathbf{y}_1 &= Z\boldsymbol{\pi}_1 + \mathbf{v}_1 \\ \mathbf{y}_2 &= Z\boldsymbol{\pi}_2 + \mathbf{v}_2, \end{aligned} \tag{10.2.43}$$

we have the following:

$$\begin{aligned} E(z_1) &= \mathbf{w}'M_1Z\boldsymbol{\pi}_1 \equiv \mu_1 \\ E(z_2) &= \mathbf{w}'M_1Z\boldsymbol{\pi}_2 \equiv \mu_2 \\ E[(z_1 - \mu_1)^2] &= \omega_{11}\mathbf{w}'M_1\mathbf{w} \equiv \sigma_1^2 \\ E[(z_2 - \mu_2)^2] &= \omega_{22}\mathbf{w}'M_1\mathbf{w} \equiv \sigma_2^2 \\ E[(z_1 - \mu_1)(z_2 - \mu_2)] &= \omega_{12}\mathbf{w}'M_1\mathbf{w} \equiv \sigma_{12}. \end{aligned} \tag{10.2.44}$$

If we assume normality of the error terms, then

$$\begin{bmatrix} z_1 \\ z_2 \end{bmatrix} \sim N_2\left(\begin{bmatrix} \mu_1 \\ \mu_2 \end{bmatrix}, \begin{bmatrix} \sigma_1^2 & \sigma_{12} \\ \sigma_{12} & \sigma_2^2 \end{bmatrix}\right).$$

Accordingly $z_1/z_2$ is the ratio of normally distributed variates; its distribution is given in appendix D.

Phillips (1980) uses $(Z_1, Z_3)$ as instruments, where $Z_3$ is a submatrix of $Z_2$. He derives the distribution of the IV estimator for an arbitrary number of included endogenous variables, but the resulting distributions are very complex. The special cases of two and three included endogenous variables are discussed separately, and some graphs of the density are presented.

Mariano (1977) considers both stochastic and nonstochastic instruments. For the former, he shows that $\hat{\beta}_{IV}$ has the same distribution as a 2SLS estimator in the just identified case; this fact has implications for moments, which are taken up in Section 10.3.2. Stochastic instruments are taken to be of the form $\hat{\mathbf{Y}}_2 = R(R'R)^{-1}R'\mathbf{y}_2$, where $R$ is nonstochastic. Several cases are considered, and some results are presented for the two included endogenous variable case.

Approximations to distributions of IV estimators, when $Z_1$ and a submatrix of $Z_2$ are used as instruments, are presented in Sargan and Mikhail (1971).

**10.2.2c *k*-Class Estimators** Exact distribution functions of *k*-class estimators are presented by Anderson and Sawa (1973) along with approximations based on an Edgeworth-type asymptotic expansion of the distribution function. A second type of approximation is presented by Mariano (1973b), who expresses the estimators in terms of independent bivariate normal variables and applies Taylor series expansions to the distribution function. Finally, Holly and Phillips (1980) utilize a saddlepoint approximation, another type of asymptotic expansion, which has certain advantages over the Edgeworth expansion.

**10.2.2d Maximum Likelihood (ML) Estimators** Bergstrom (1962) considers the distribution of the ML estimator in a special case of the model we have been considering—the two-equation consumption-income model:

$$\begin{aligned} C_t &= \alpha + \beta Y_t + u_t \\ Y_t &= C_t + I_t. \end{aligned} \qquad \textbf{(10.2.45)}$$

In addition to deriving the distribution of the OLS estimator of $\beta$ under the usual assumption of normally distributed erros, Bergstrom finds the distribution of the ML estimator of $\mu = 1/(1 - \beta)$. The ML estimator is obtained from the likelihood function of the reduced form equation,

$$Y_t = \frac{\alpha}{1 - \beta} + \mu I_t + v_t, \qquad \textbf{(10.2.46)}$$

which leads to the OLS estimator $\hat{\mu}$ as the ML estimator. Its distribution is $N(1/(1 - \beta), \sigma^2/T(1 - \beta)^2)$. Since the ML estimator of $g(\mu)$ is $g(\hat{\mu})$, it follows that the ML estimator of $\beta$ is $\hat{\beta}_{ML} = 1 - 1/\hat{\mu}$, and the distribution of $\hat{\beta}_{ML}$ is easily derived from the distribution of $\hat{\mu}$. Some numerical comparisons between OLS and ML are given in the article for selected sample sizes when $\beta = 0.6$ and $\sigma^2 = 0.1$.

## 10.3 Moments and Their Approximations

This section begins with a derivation of the exact moments of *k*-class estimators in the two included endogenous variables case. Since OLS and 2SLS are special cases of this class, their moments and approximations to those moments are discussed there. The second part of the section provides references to articles that consider moments of other estimators.

### 10.3.1 Exact and Approximate Moments of *k*-Class Estimators

This section is based on an article by Sawa (1972), which derives exact moments for the *k*-class estimators, including 2SLS and OLS. Although the moments of the OLS and 2SLS estimators may be computed directly from their distributions—a procedure followed by Sawa (1969) and Richardson (1968)—the 1972 article is discussed here because it uses a different approach and obtains moments for a wider class of estimators. We continue to assume that there are two included endogenous variables.

Sawa starts with the model

$$\mathbf{y}_1 = \mathbf{y}_2 + Z_1\boldsymbol{\gamma}_1 + \mathbf{u}_1, \qquad (10.3.1)$$

from which the reduced form equations for $\mathbf{y}_1$ and $\mathbf{y}_2$ are derived:

$$\begin{aligned}(\mathbf{y}_1, \mathbf{y}_2) &= Z(\boldsymbol{\pi}_1, \boldsymbol{\pi}_2) + (\mathbf{v}_1, \mathbf{v}_2) \\ &= Z_1(\boldsymbol{\pi}_{11}, \boldsymbol{\pi}_{21}) + Z_2(\boldsymbol{\pi}_{12}, \boldsymbol{\pi}_{22}) + (\mathbf{v}_1, \mathbf{v}_2),\end{aligned} \qquad (10.3.2)$$

where $Z_2$ are the exogenous variables excluded from the first equation and $(\mathbf{v}_1, \mathbf{v}_2)$ are the reduced form disturbances, with covariance matrix

$$\Omega = \begin{bmatrix}\omega_{11} & \omega_{12} \\ \omega_{12} & \omega_{22}\end{bmatrix}.$$

Without loss of generality it is assumed that $Z_1'Z_2 = 0$.

The $k$-class estimator of $\beta$, $\hat{\beta}_k$, is the first component of

$$\begin{bmatrix}\mathbf{y}_2'\mathbf{y}_2 - k\hat{\mathbf{v}}_2'\hat{\mathbf{v}}_2 & \mathbf{y}_2'Z_1 \\ Z_1'\mathbf{y}_2 & Z_1'Z_1\end{bmatrix}^{-1}\begin{bmatrix}\mathbf{y}_2'\mathbf{y}_1 - k\hat{\mathbf{v}}_2'\mathbf{y}_1 \\ Z_1'\mathbf{y}_1\end{bmatrix} \qquad (10.3.3)$$

where $\hat{\mathbf{v}}_2 = M\mathbf{y}_2$ and $M = I - Z_1(Z_1'Z_1)^{-1}Z_1' - Z_2(Z_2'Z_2)^{-1}Z_2'$. It may be verified that

$$\hat{\beta}_k = \frac{\mathbf{y}_1'A_k\mathbf{y}_2}{\mathbf{y}_2'A_k\mathbf{y}_2} \qquad (10.3.4)$$

where $A_k = (1 - k)M + Z_2(Z_2'Z_2)^{-1}Z_2'$. The OLS estimator corresponds to $k = 0$, and the 2SLS estimator corresponds to $k = 1$.

Before proceeding further, one special case must be dealt with. One of the assumptions we have been making is that the equation is identified. Since there are two included endogenous variables, this requires that $K_2 \geqslant 1$, where the equality corresponds to the "just identified" case. For $K_2 = 1$, which implies that $Z_2$ is $N \times 1$, as noted in Section 10.2.1 the 2SLS estimator is

$$\hat{\beta}_1 = \frac{\mathbf{y}_1'\mathbf{Z}_2(\mathbf{Z}_2'\mathbf{Z}_2)^{-1}\mathbf{Z}_2'\mathbf{y}_2}{\mathbf{y}_2'\mathbf{Z}_2(\mathbf{Z}_2'\mathbf{Z}_2)^{-1}\mathbf{Z}_2'\mathbf{y}_2} = \frac{\mathbf{y}_1'\mathbf{Z}_2}{\mathbf{y}_2'\mathbf{Z}_2}, \qquad (10.3.5)$$

which is not in the form of (10.3.4). In fact, (10.3.5) is a ratio of normally distributed variables, discussed in Appendix D, and therefore has no finite moments of any order. (And since the 2SLS estimator in the just identified case is also the indirect least squares estimator and the LIML estimator, the same result applies to these.) Accordingly, for the remainder of this section it is assumed that the equation is overidentified; that is, $K_2 \geqslant 2$.

It may be helpful to outline the structure of Sawa's article before presenting details. The first step is to transform $\mathbf{y}_1$ and $\mathbf{y}_2$ to variables with an identity covariance matrix. Next, a lemma is proved that permits computation of the moments of a ratio of two random variables from their joint moment generating function. The application of this lemma to (10.3.4) requires a restriction on the value of $k$, which is presented as a second lemma. The next major step is the computation of the moment generating function of $\mathbf{y}_2'A_k\mathbf{y}_2$ and $\mathbf{y}_1'A_k\mathbf{y}_2$, after which the first lemma is applied to obtain $E(\hat{\beta}_k)$ and $\text{Var}(\hat{\beta}_k)$.

We begin with a transformation of $\mathbf{y}_1$ and $\mathbf{y}_2$ to variables with an identity covariance matrix. To do so, define

$$\Psi = \begin{bmatrix} \xi & 0 \\ \omega\rho & \omega \end{bmatrix}, \tag{10.3.6}$$

where

$$\omega = \sqrt{\omega_{22}}, \qquad \rho = \frac{\omega_{12}}{\omega_{22}}, \qquad \text{and} \quad \xi = \sqrt{\omega_{11} - \frac{\omega_{12}^2}{\omega_{22}}}. \tag{10.3.7}$$

It may be verified that

$$\Omega = \Psi'\Psi. \tag{10.3.8}$$

The linear transformation

$$\begin{aligned}(\mathbf{y}_1^*, \mathbf{y}_2^*) &= (\mathbf{y}_1, \mathbf{y}_2)\Psi^{-1} = Z(\boldsymbol{\pi}_1, \boldsymbol{\pi}_2)\Psi^{-1} + (\mathbf{v}_1, \mathbf{v}_2)\Psi^{-1} \\ &= Z(\boldsymbol{\pi}_1^*, \boldsymbol{\pi}_2^*) + (\mathbf{v}_1^*, \mathbf{v}_2^*)\end{aligned} \tag{10.3.9}$$

creates a disturbance vector with covariance matrix equal to the identity, as may be readily verified. The same transformation applied to the structrual equation yields

$$\mathbf{y}_1^* = \beta^*\mathbf{y}_2^* + Z_1\boldsymbol{\gamma}_1^* + \mathbf{u}^*, \tag{10.3.10}$$

where

$$\beta^* = \frac{\omega(\beta - \rho)}{\xi}, \qquad \boldsymbol{\gamma}_1^* = \xi^{-1}\boldsymbol{\gamma}_1, \qquad \text{and} \quad \mathbf{u}^* = \xi^{-1}\mathbf{u}. \tag{10.3.11}$$

For the $k$-class estimators, the transformation yields

$$\hat{\beta}_k = \rho + \frac{\xi}{\omega}\hat{\beta}_k^*. \tag{10.3.12}$$

Since the moments of $\hat{\beta}_k^*$ are related to the moments of $\hat{\beta}_k$ via (10.3.12), the remainder of the derivation assumes $\Omega = I$, and the asterisks are temporarily dropped.

The following lemma is needed to compute the moments:

**Lemma 10.3.1**

Let $X_1$ be an everywhere positive random variable and $X_2$ be an arbitrary random variable. Assume that the $r$th order moment of $X_2/X_1$, $E[(X_2/X_1)^r]$, exists. Then

$$E\left[\left(\frac{X_2}{X_1}\right)^r\right] = \frac{1}{\Gamma(r)}\int_{-\infty}^{0} (-\theta_1)^{r-1} \left.\frac{\partial^r\phi(\theta_1, \theta_2)}{\partial\theta_2^r}\right|_{\theta_2=0} d\theta_1,$$

where $\phi(\theta_1, \theta_2)$ is the joint moment generating function of $X_1$ and $X_2$.

**Proof**

$$E\left[\left(\frac{X_2}{X_1}\right)^r\right] = \int_{-\infty}^{\infty}\int_0^{\infty} X_2^r\left(\frac{1}{X_1}\right)^r f(X_1, X_2)\, dX_1\, dX_2$$

$$= \int_{-\infty}^{\infty}\int_0^{\infty} X_2^r \frac{1}{\Gamma(r)}\int_0^{\infty} t^{r-1}e^{-X_1 t}\, dt\, f(X_1, X_2)\, dX_1\, dX_2$$

(by 10.2.17)

$$= \frac{1}{\Gamma(r)}\int_{-\infty}^{\infty}\int_0^{\infty} X_2^r \int_{-\infty}^{0} (-\theta_1)^{r-1}e^{\theta_1 X_1}\, d\theta_1 f(X_1, X_2)\, dX_1\, dX_2 \qquad (\theta_1 = -t)$$

$$= \frac{1}{\Gamma(r)}\int_{-\infty}^{0} (-\theta_1)^{r-1}\int_{-\infty}^{\infty}\int_0^{\infty} \frac{\partial^r}{\partial\theta_2^r} e^{\theta_1 X_1 + \theta_2 X_2}\Bigg|_{\theta_2=0} f(X_1, X_2)\, dX_1\, dX_2\, d\theta_1$$

$$= \frac{1}{\Gamma(r)}\int_{-\infty}^{0} (-\theta_1)^{r-1}\frac{\partial^r}{\partial\theta_2^r}\int_{-\infty}^{\infty}\int_0^{\infty} e^{\theta_1 X_1 + \theta_2 X_2} f(X_1, X_2)\, dX_1\, dX_2\Bigg|_{\theta_2=0} d\theta_1$$

$$= \frac{1}{\Gamma(r)}\int_{-\infty}^{\infty} (-\theta_1)^{r-1}\frac{\partial^r\phi(\theta_1, \theta_2)}{\partial\theta_2^r}\Bigg|_{\theta_2=0} d\theta_1. \qquad \textbf{(10.3.13)}$$

The interchange of differentiation and integration is justified by the existence of $E[(X_2/X_1)^r]$. □

The lemma in Sawa's article also claims that a finite value of (10.3.13) is a sufficient condition for the existence of $E[(X_2/X_1)^r]$. Mehta and Swamy (1978) point out that this condition cannot be sufficient for the existence of the moment because, as will be seen below, (10.3.13) is finite when $X_2/X_1$ is the 2SLS estimator of $\beta$ in a just identified equation—an estimator that is the ratio of normal variates, known to have no finite moments. The weaker lemma is still useful for computing moments in view of an article by Kinal (1980), in which necessary and sufficient conditions for the *existence* of moments of $k$-class estimators are established by a different method of proof. (The Kinal article is discussed in Chapter 11.)

In order to apply this lemma to $\hat{\beta}_k$, the denominator must be positive almost everywhere, that is, $\mathbf{y}_2' A_k \mathbf{y}_2 > 0$ except on a set of measure zero. This condition puts a restriction on the value of $k$:

**Lemma 10.3.2**

$A_k$ is positive semidefinite if and only if $k \leqslant 1$.

**Proof**

$$A_k = (1 - k)M + Z_2(Z_2'Z_2)^{-1}Z_2'$$
$$= (1 - k)[I - Z_1(Z_1'Z_1)^{-1}Z_1'] + kZ_2(Z_2'Z_2)^{-1}Z_2',$$

and it is easy to verify that the $K_1$ columns of $Z_1$ are c.v.'s of $A_k$ with c.r.'s equal to zero and the $K_2$ columns of $Z_2$ are c.v.'s of $A_k$ with c.r.'s equal to one. (Remember that $Z_1'Z_2 = 0$.) Finally, since $A_k$ lies in $T$-dimensional space, there exists a matrix $Z_3$, orthogonal to $Z_1$ and $Z_2$; its $T - K_1 - K_2$ columns are c.v.'s of $A_k$ with c.r.'s equal to $1 - k$. Accordingly, $A_k$ may be diagonalized to

$$\Lambda = \begin{bmatrix} 0 & 0 & 0 \\ 0 & I & 0 \\ 0 & 0 & (1-k)I \end{bmatrix} \begin{matrix} K_1 \\ K_2 \\ T - K_1 - K_2 \end{matrix} \qquad (10.3.14)$$
$$\qquad K_1 \quad K_2 \quad T - K_1 - K_2$$

which is positive semidefinite if and only if $k \leqslant 1$. □

Now, by assumption the $T$-dimensional random vectors $\mathbf{y}_1$ and $\mathbf{y}_2$ are mutually independent and

$$\begin{bmatrix} \mathbf{y}_1 \\ \mathbf{y}_2 \end{bmatrix} \sim N_{2T}\left( \begin{bmatrix} \boldsymbol{\mu}_1 \\ \boldsymbol{\mu}_2 \end{bmatrix}, \; I_{2T} \right),$$

where

$$\boldsymbol{\mu}_1 = Z_1\boldsymbol{\pi}_{11} + Z_2\boldsymbol{\pi}_{12}$$
$$\boldsymbol{\mu}_2 = Z_1\boldsymbol{\pi}_{21} + Z_2\boldsymbol{\pi}_{22}. \qquad (10.3.15)$$

Since $E(\mathbf{y}_1) = \beta E(\mathbf{y}_2) + Z_1\boldsymbol{\gamma}_1$, we also have

$$\boldsymbol{\mu}_1 = \beta\boldsymbol{\mu}_2 + Z_1\boldsymbol{\gamma}_1, \qquad (10.3.16)$$

from which it follows that

$$A_k\boldsymbol{\mu}_1 = \beta A_k\boldsymbol{\mu}_2 = Z_2\boldsymbol{\pi}_{12} \qquad (10.3.17)$$

and

$$A_k\boldsymbol{\mu}_2 = Z_2\boldsymbol{\pi}_{22}.$$

The joint m.g.f. of $\mathbf{y}_2'A_k\mathbf{y}_2$ and $\mathbf{y}_1'A_k\mathbf{y}_2$ is defined by

$$\phi(\theta_1, \theta_2) = \int \cdots \int \exp\{\theta_1\mathbf{y}_2'A_k\mathbf{y}_2 + \theta_2\mathbf{y}_1'A_k\mathbf{y}_2\} \times N(\mathbf{y}_1|\boldsymbol{\mu}_1, I)N(\mathbf{y}_2|\boldsymbol{\mu}_2, I)\, d\mathbf{y}_1\, d\mathbf{y}_2, \qquad (10.3.18)$$

where $N(\cdot \mid \boldsymbol{\mu}, I)$ is the normal density with mean $\boldsymbol{\mu}$ and covariance matrix $I$. The values of $\theta_1$ and $\theta_2$ will be assumed to satisfy

$$\theta_2^2 + 2\theta_1 < 1. \qquad (10.3.19)$$

We first assume $0 \leqslant k \leqslant 1$ and take up the case $k > 1$ below. Before working with the integral it is convenient to demonstrate that the quadratic form $Q_k(\theta_1, \theta_2) = I - 2\theta_1A_k - \theta_2^2A_k$ is positive definite for $\theta_1$ and $\theta_2$ satisfying (10.3.19) and $0 \leqslant k \leqslant 1$. Let $\mathbf{x}$ be an arbitrary vector in $T$-dimensional space. Since $[Z_1, Z_2, Z_3]$ is a basis for that space, $\mathbf{x}$ may be expressed as

$$\mathbf{x} = [Z_1, Z_2, Z_3]\boldsymbol{\nu},$$

where $\boldsymbol{\nu}$ is a $T \times 1$ vector. After verifying the following,

$$\begin{aligned} A_k Z_1 &= A_k^2 Z_1 = 0 \\ A_k Z_2 &= A_k^2 Z_2 = Z_2 \\ A_k Z_3 &= (1 - k) Z_3 \quad \text{and} \quad A_k^2 Z_3 = (1 - k)^2 Z_3, \end{aligned} \tag{10.3.20}$$

it is easy to see that

$$\begin{aligned} \mathbf{x}' Q_k \mathbf{x} &= \boldsymbol{\nu}' \begin{bmatrix} Z_1' \\ Z_2' \\ Z_3' \end{bmatrix} Q_k [Z_1, Z_2, Z_3] \boldsymbol{\nu} \\ &= \boldsymbol{\nu}' \begin{bmatrix} I_{K_1} & 0 & 0 \\ 0 & (1 - 2\theta_1 - \theta_2^2) I_{K_2} & 0 \\ 0 & 0 & [1 - 2\theta_1(1 - k) \\ & & - \theta_2^2 (1 - k)^2] I_{K_3} \end{bmatrix} \boldsymbol{\nu}, \end{aligned}$$

where $K_3 = T - K_1 - K_2$. By hypothesis, $1 - 2\theta_1 - \theta_2^2 > 0$. Moreover, for $0 < k < 1$,

$$\begin{aligned} & 1 - 2\theta_1(1 - k) - \theta_2^2(1 - k)^2 \\ & > 1 - 2\theta_1(1 - k) - \theta_2^2(1 - k) \\ & > (1 - k) - 2\theta_1(1 - k) - \theta_2^2(1 - k) \\ & = (1 - k)(1 - 2\theta_1 - \theta_2^2) > 0. \end{aligned} \tag{10.3.21}$$

And at $k = 0$ or $1$, $[1 - 2\theta_1(1 - k) - \theta_2^2(1 - k)^2] > 0$. Therefore $Q_k$ is positive definite under the stated conditions. Finally, let

$$R_k = \begin{bmatrix} I & -\theta_2 A_k \\ -\theta_2 A_k & I - 2\theta_1 A_k \end{bmatrix}. \tag{10.3.22}$$

It may be verified that

$$R_k = (B')^{-1} C B^{-1}, \tag{10.3.23}$$

where

$$B = \begin{bmatrix} I & \theta_2 A_k \\ 0 & I \end{bmatrix} \tag{10.3.24}$$

and

$$C = \begin{bmatrix} I & 0 \\ 0 & I - 2\theta_1 A_k - \theta_2^2 A_k^2 \end{bmatrix}. \tag{10.3.25}$$

We conclude that $R_k$ is positive definite because $C$ is positive definite.

Consider the exponential term in (10.3.18). From

$$N(\mathbf{y}_i|\boldsymbol{\mu}_i, I) = K \exp\left\{-\frac{1}{2}(\mathbf{y}_i - \boldsymbol{\mu}_i)'(\mathbf{y}_i - \boldsymbol{\mu}_i)\right\}(i = 1, 2),$$

it is given by

$$\exp\left\{\theta_1\mathbf{y}_2'A_k\mathbf{y}_2 + \theta_2\mathbf{y}_1'A_k\mathbf{y}_2 - \frac{1}{2}(\mathbf{y}_1 - \boldsymbol{\mu}_1)'(\mathbf{y}_1 - \boldsymbol{\mu}_1) - \frac{1}{2}(\mathbf{y}_2 - \boldsymbol{\mu}_2)'(\mathbf{y}_2 - \boldsymbol{\mu}_2)\right\}. \quad (10.3.26)$$

To perform the integration, we first transform the bracketed expression into the form

$$\begin{bmatrix}\mathbf{y}_1 - \mathbf{a}\\ \mathbf{y}_2 - \mathbf{b}\end{bmatrix}'\begin{bmatrix}E & F\\ F & G\end{bmatrix}\begin{bmatrix}\mathbf{y}_1 - \mathbf{a}\\ \mathbf{y}_2 - \mathbf{b}\end{bmatrix} + f(E, F, G, \mathbf{a}, \mathbf{b}), \quad (10.3.27)$$

where the function $f(E, F, G, \mathbf{a}, \mathbf{b})$ is independent of both $\mathbf{y}_1$ and $\mathbf{y}_2$. We next show how to compute $E$; the other terms are left for the reader to verify. From (10.3.26), the term involving $\mathbf{y}_1'\mathbf{y}_1$ is $-(\frac{1}{2})I$; therefore $E = -(\frac{1}{2})I$. It can also be shown that

$$\begin{aligned} G &= -\frac{1}{2}I + \theta_1 A_k,\\ F &= \frac{1}{2}\theta_2 A_k,\\ \begin{bmatrix}\mathbf{a}\\ \mathbf{b}\end{bmatrix} &= \begin{bmatrix} I & -\theta_2 A_k\\ -\theta_2 A_k & I - 2\theta_1 A_k\end{bmatrix}^{-1}\begin{bmatrix}\boldsymbol{\mu}_1\\ \boldsymbol{\mu}_2\end{bmatrix}\\ &= R_k^{-1}\begin{bmatrix}\boldsymbol{\mu}_1\\ \boldsymbol{\mu}_2\end{bmatrix}, \end{aligned} \quad (10.3.28)$$

and

$$f(E, F, G, \mathbf{a}, \mathbf{b}) = \frac{1}{2}\begin{bmatrix}\boldsymbol{\mu}_1\\ \boldsymbol{\mu}_2\end{bmatrix}' R_k^{-1}\begin{bmatrix}\boldsymbol{\mu}_1\\ \boldsymbol{\mu}_2\end{bmatrix} - \frac{1}{2}\boldsymbol{\mu}_1'\boldsymbol{\mu}_1 - \frac{1}{2}\boldsymbol{\mu}_2'\boldsymbol{\mu}_2. \quad (10.3.29)$$

The partitioned inverse rule, see Goldberger (1964, p. 27), gives the result

$$R_k^{-1} = \begin{bmatrix} I + \theta_2^2 A_k Q_k^{-1} A_k & \theta_2 A_k Q_k^{-1}\\ \theta_2 Q_k^{-1} A_k & Q_k^{-1}\end{bmatrix}. \quad (10.3.30)$$

With this result and Equations 10.3.20, we may rewrite $f(E, F, G, \mathbf{a}, \mathbf{b})$ as

$$f(E, F, G, \mathbf{a}, \mathbf{b}) = -\frac{1}{2}\boldsymbol{\mu}_2'[I - (I + \theta_2\beta A_k)Q_k^{-1}(I + \theta_2\beta A_k)]\boldsymbol{\mu}_2. \quad (10.3.31)$$

The expressions for $E$, $F$, and $G$ and Equation 10.3.31 are substituted into (10.3.26), and then the latter is substituted into (10.3.18), which yields

$$\phi(\theta_1, \theta_2) = \exp\left\{ -\frac{1}{2} \boldsymbol{\mu}_2'[I - (I + \theta_2\beta A_k)Q_k^{-1}(I + \theta_2\beta A_k)]\boldsymbol{\mu}_2 \right\}$$

$$\times \frac{1}{(2\pi)^T} \int \cdots \int \exp\left\{ -\frac{1}{2}\begin{bmatrix} \mathbf{y}_1 - \mathbf{a} \\ \mathbf{y}_2 - \mathbf{b} \end{bmatrix}' R_k \begin{bmatrix} \mathbf{y}_1 - \mathbf{a} \\ \mathbf{y}_2 - \mathbf{b} \end{bmatrix} \right\} d\mathbf{y}_1\, d\mathbf{y}_2, \qquad \textbf{(10.3.32)}$$

and the multiple integral equals

$$(2\pi)^T |R_k|^{-1/2}. \qquad \textbf{(10.3.33)}$$

To complete the evaluation of (10.3.32) we must simplify $|R_k|^{-1/2}$ and (10.3.31). Let the columns of $\Phi_i (i = 1, 2, 3)$ be a set of orthogonal c.v.'s of the symmetric idempotent matrix $Z_i(Z_i'Z_i)^{-1}Z_i'$, that is, $Z_i(Z_i'Z_i)^{-1}Z_i'\Phi_i = \Phi_i$. Then,

$$\Phi_i'\Phi_j = \begin{cases} I_{K_i}, & i = j \\ 0, & i \neq j. \end{cases}$$

With $\Phi \equiv (\Phi_1, \Phi_2, \Phi_3)$ it is easy to verify that

$$\Phi' A_k \Phi = \Lambda,$$
$$\Phi' A_k^2 \Phi = \Lambda^2, \qquad \textbf{(10.3.34)}$$
$$\Phi' \boldsymbol{\mu}_2 = \begin{bmatrix} \boldsymbol{\chi}_1 \\ \boldsymbol{\chi}_2 \\ 0 \end{bmatrix},$$

where

$$\boldsymbol{\chi}_1 = \Phi_1' Z_1 \pi_{21} \quad \text{and} \quad \boldsymbol{\chi}_2 = \Phi_2' Z_2 \pi_{22}. \qquad \textbf{(10.3.35)}$$

We first apply this transformation to

$$\begin{aligned} |R_k| &= |Q_k| = |\Phi'||Q_k||\Phi| \\ &= |\Phi'[I - 2\theta_1 A_k - \theta_2^2 A_k^2]\Phi| \\ &= |I - 2\theta_1 \Lambda - \theta_2^2 \Lambda^2| \\ &= \begin{bmatrix} I_{K_1} & 0 & 0 \\ 0 & (1 - 2\theta_1 - \theta_2^2) I_{K_2} & 0 \\ 0 & 0 & (1 - 2\lambda\theta_1 - \lambda^2\theta_2^2) I_{K_3} \end{bmatrix} \\ &= (1 - 2\theta_1 - \theta_2^2)^{K_2} (1 - 2\lambda\theta_1 - \lambda^2\theta_2^2)^{K_3}, \end{aligned}$$

where $\lambda = 1 - k$. Therefore,

$$|R_k|^{-1/2} = \frac{1}{(1 - 2\theta_1 - \theta_2^2)^{m-n} (1 - 2\lambda\theta_1 - \lambda^2\theta_2^2)^{n}}, \qquad \textbf{(10.3.36)}$$

where

$$m = \frac{T - K_1}{2} \quad \text{and} \quad n = \frac{T - K}{2}.$$

The same approach may be used to simplify (10.3.31). To do so, we use $\Phi'\Phi = I = \Phi\Phi'$ to rewrite the quadratic term:

$$\begin{aligned}
&\boldsymbol{\mu}_2'[I - (I + \theta_2\beta A_k)Q_k^{-1}(I + \theta_2\beta A_k)]\boldsymbol{\mu}_2 \\
&\quad = \boldsymbol{\mu}_2'\Phi\Phi'[I - (\Phi\Phi' + \theta_2\beta\Phi\Phi' A_k\Phi\Phi')Q_k^{-1}(\Phi\Phi' \\
&\qquad + \theta_2\beta\Phi\Phi' A_k\Phi\Phi')]\Phi\Phi'\boldsymbol{\mu}_2 \\
&\quad = \begin{bmatrix} \boldsymbol{\chi}_1 \\ \boldsymbol{\chi}_2 \\ 0 \end{bmatrix}' [I - (I + \theta_2\beta\Lambda)\Phi' Q_k^{-1}\Phi(I + \theta_2\beta\Lambda)] \begin{bmatrix} \boldsymbol{\chi}_1 \\ \boldsymbol{\chi}_2 \\ 0 \end{bmatrix}.
\end{aligned} \tag{10.3.37}$$

Since $\Phi' Q_k^{-1}\Phi = [\Phi' Q_k \Phi]^{-1}$, after more algebra (10.3.37) may be simplified to

$$\boldsymbol{\pi}_{22}' Z_2'\Phi_2\Phi_2' Z_2\boldsymbol{\pi}_{22} - \frac{\boldsymbol{\pi}_{22}' Z_2'\Phi_2\Phi_2' Z_2\boldsymbol{\pi}_{22}(1 + \beta\theta_2)^2}{1 - 2\theta_1 - \theta_2^2}$$

and then to

$$\boldsymbol{\pi}_{22}' Z_2' Z_2\boldsymbol{\pi}_{22} - \frac{\boldsymbol{\pi}_{22}' Z_2' Z_2\boldsymbol{\pi}_{22}(1 + \beta\theta_2)^2}{1 - 2\theta_1 - \theta_2^2}. \tag{10.3.38}$$

The last step follows from

$$\Phi'\Phi = I = \Phi\Phi' = \Phi_1\Phi_1' + \Phi_2\Phi_2' + \Phi_3\Phi_3',$$

which implies

$$Z_2' Z_2 = Z_2'\Phi\Phi' Z_2 = Z_2'\Phi_2\Phi_2' Z_2$$

because $Z_2'\Phi_1 = 0$ and $Z_2'\Phi_3 = 0$.

In order to treat the general case ($\Omega$ not necessarily equal to $I$), it may be seen from (10.3.2) and (10.3.9) that $\boldsymbol{\pi}_{22}^* = \boldsymbol{\pi}_{22}/\omega$. Combining this expression with the result of the previous paragraph, we have

$$\boldsymbol{\pi}_{22}^{*\prime} Z_2'\Phi_2\Phi_2' Z_2\boldsymbol{\pi}_{22}^* = \frac{\boldsymbol{\pi}_{22}' Z_2' Z_2\boldsymbol{\pi}_{22}}{\omega_{22}}, \tag{10.3.39}$$

which also holds for $\Omega = I$, since in that case $\omega_{22} = 1$.

The m.g.f. may therefore be written as

$$\begin{aligned}
\phi(\theta_1, \theta_2) &= \frac{1}{(1 - 2\theta_1 - \theta_2^2)^{m-n}(1 - 2\lambda\theta_1 - \lambda^2\theta_2^2)^n} \\
&\quad \times \exp\left\{ -\delta + \frac{\delta(1 + \beta\theta_2)^2}{1 - 2\theta_1 - \theta_2^2} \right\},
\end{aligned} \tag{10.3.40}$$

where

$$\delta = \frac{\pi'_{22}Z'_2Z_2\pi_{22}}{2\omega_{22}} \tag{10.3.41}$$

is the noncentrality parameter.

We are now ready to apply Lemma 10.3.1 in order to find the moments of the $k$-class estimators. To do so, we differentiate (10.3.40) with respect to $\theta_2$ and evaluate the derivative at $\theta_2 = 0$:

$$\left.\frac{\partial\phi(\theta_1, \theta_2)}{\partial\theta_2}\right|_{\theta_2=0} = \beta\delta g(\theta_1; k, \delta, m + 1, n). \tag{10.3.42}$$

where

$$g(x; k, \delta, p, q) = \frac{2}{(1 - 2x)^{p-q}[1 - 2(1 - k)x]_q} \times \exp\left\{-\delta + \frac{\delta}{1 - 2x}\right\}. \tag{10.3.43}$$

At this point it is useful to reintroduce the asterisk on $\beta$ to reflect the fact that the derivation has proceeded on the assumption that $\Omega = I$. Accordingly, (10.3.42) is rewritten as

$$\left.\frac{\partial\phi(\theta_1, \theta_2)}{\partial\theta_2}\right|_{\theta_2=0} = \beta^*\delta g(\theta_1; k, \delta, m + 1, n). \tag{10.3.42$'$}$$

To find $E(\hat{\beta}_k^*)$, $\theta_1$ must be integrated out of (10.3.42′):

$$E(\hat{\beta}_k^*) = \beta^*\delta G(k, \delta; m + 1, n), \tag{10.3.44}$$

where

$$G(k, \delta; p, q) = \int_{-\infty}^{0} g(x; k, \delta, p, q)\, dx. \tag{10.3.45}$$

To compute the second moment, $E(\hat{\beta}_k^{*2})$, it is necessary to evaluate

$$\begin{aligned}\left.\frac{\partial^2\phi}{\partial\theta_2^2}\right|_{\theta_2=0} &= \delta(1 + 2\beta^2\delta)g(\theta_1; k, \delta, m + 2, n)\\ &\quad + (m - n + \beta^2\delta)g(\theta_1; k, \delta, m + 1, n)\\ &\quad + n(1 - k)^2 g(\theta_1; k, \delta, m + 1, n + 1),\end{aligned} \tag{10.3.46}$$

and Sawa shows that

$$\begin{aligned}(-\theta_1)\left.\frac{\partial^2\phi}{\partial\theta_2^2}\right|_{\theta_2=0} &= -\frac{1}{2}\,[\delta(1 + 2\beta^2\delta)h(m + 1, n)\\ &\quad + (m - n + \beta^2\delta)h(m, n)\\ &\quad + n(1 - k)^2 h(m, n + 1)],\end{aligned}$$

where

$$h(m, n) = \frac{\partial}{\partial \delta} g(x; k, \delta, m, n). \tag{10.3.47}$$

Upon integrating (10.3.47) with respect to $\theta_1$, we have

$$\begin{aligned} E(\hat{\beta}_k^{*2}) &= (\delta + 2\beta_k^{*2}\delta^2)H(k, \delta; m + 1, n) \\ &\quad + (m - n + \beta^{*2}\delta)H(k, \delta; m, n) \\ &\quad + (1 - k)^2 nH(k, \delta; m, n + 1), \end{aligned} \tag{10.3.48}$$

where

$$H(k, \delta; p, q) = -\frac{1}{2}\frac{\partial}{\partial \delta} G(k, \delta; p, q). \tag{10.3.49}$$

Sawa shows that $G(k, \delta; p, q)$ may be expressed in terms of the confluent hypergeometric series:

For $0 \leq k < 1$,

$$G(k, \delta; p, q) = \begin{cases} e^{-\delta} \sum_{j=0}^{\infty} (q)_j k^j \dfrac{\Gamma(p - 1)}{\Gamma(p + j)} {}_1F_1(p - 1; p + j; \delta), & \text{if } p > 1 \\ \infty, & \text{otherwise} \end{cases} \tag{10.3.50}$$

and for $k = 1$,

$$G(1, \delta; p, q) = \begin{cases} e^{-\delta} \dfrac{\Gamma(p - q - 1)}{\Gamma(p - q)} {}_1F_1(p - q - 1; p - q; \delta), & \text{if } p - q > 1 \\ \infty, & \text{otherwise.} \end{cases} \tag{10.3.51}$$

Equations 10.3.42′ and 10.3.48 represent the first and second moments if they exist. To use these expressions we anticipate a result, due to Kinal (1980), that will be proved in Chapter 11: The $r$th moment of the $k$-class estimator of $\beta$ exists if and only if $r < M$, where

$$M = \begin{cases} N - K_1 - G_1 + 2, & \text{for } 0 \leq k < 1 \\ K_2 - G_1 + 2, & \text{for } k = 1. \end{cases}$$

The problem with Sawa's statement of Lemma 10.3.1, which was noted in the text immediately after its proof, appears when (10.3.44) is rewritten using (10.3.51) for $\hat{\beta}_1^*$ with $K_2 = 1$:

$$E(\hat{\beta}_1^*) = \beta^*\delta G\left(1, \delta; \frac{T - K_1}{2} + 1, \frac{T - K_1 - 1}{2}\right).$$

The condition for existence, $p - q > 1$, becomes $(T - K_1)/2 + 1 - (T - K_1 - 1)/$

$2 > 1$, which holds although the moment does not exist. Since Sawa assumes overidentification, that is, $K_2 \geqslant 2$, the conditions given in his article are correct.

Using the relationship $\beta^* = \omega(\beta - \rho)/\xi$, it is easy to obtain the first two moments for $\hat{\beta}_k$ from those for $\hat{\beta}_k^*$ when the latter exist.

$$E(\hat{\beta}_k) = \rho + (\beta - \rho)\delta G(k, \delta; m + 1, n). \qquad \textbf{(10.3.52)}$$

From (10.3.52), we seen that $\hat{\beta}_k$ is biased unless $\beta = \rho$. In addition,

$$E(\hat{\beta}_k^2) = \rho^2 + 2\rho \frac{\xi}{\omega} h_1 + \frac{\xi^2}{\omega^2} h_2, \qquad \textbf{(10.3.53)}$$

where $h_1$ is the right-hand side of (10.3.44) with $\omega(\beta - \rho)/\xi$ in place of $\beta^*$, and $h_2$ is the right-hand side of (10.3.48) with the same change.

Sawa proves a number of other properties of these estimators:

1. If $\beta \neq \rho$ the bias of $\hat{\beta}_k$ is opposite to the sign of $(\beta - \rho)$.
2. The absolute value of the bias is a strictly decreasing and concave function of $k$.
3. No finite moments exist for $k > 1$.

Since the expression for the moments is rather complex, an asymptotic expansion in terms of $\delta$ is derived by Sawa, using the asymptotic expansion of the confluent hypergeometric function. The "bias" of the $k$-class estimator, $b(k)$, derived by comparing $\beta$ with an approximation to $E(\hat{\beta}_k)$ for large $\delta$, is

$$b(k) = (\beta - \rho)(nk - m + 1)\delta^{-1} + O(\delta^{-2}), \qquad 0 \leqslant k \leqslant 1. \qquad \textbf{(10.3.54)}$$

Sawa also presents an asymptotic expansion for the mean squared error:

$$\begin{aligned} \frac{1}{2}\left[\frac{\xi^2}{\omega^2} + (\beta - \rho)^2\right]\delta^{-1} + \Bigg\{\Bigg[n(n + 1)k^2 - 2n\left(m - \frac{3}{2}\right)k \\ + (m - 2)^2\Bigg](\beta - \rho)^2 \\ + (nk^2 - m + 2)\frac{\xi^2}{2\omega^2}\Bigg\}\delta^{-2} + 0\,(\delta^{-3}). \qquad \textbf{(10.3.55)} \end{aligned}$$

The mean squared error and the relative bias are evaluated for various values of $\tau = 2\delta/T$, $T$, $K_1$, and $K_2$ as functions of $k$. Graphs of these functions, due to Sawa, are reproduced as Figures 10.10 to 10.15. Specifications of the cases depicted in the figures are given in Table 10.1. Figures 10.10 and 10.11 illustrate that the relative bias decreases with $k$. Figures 10.12 to 10.15 indicate that the mean squared error is quite sensitive to $\delta$ and $T$, and that the optimal value of $k$ is also sensitive to these parameters. In particular, the choice between OLS and 2SLS is not clear-cut according to this criterion. A similar comparison is given by Richardson and Wu (1971).

Finally, Sawa notes that the above results agree with those obtained by Nagar (1959) and Kadane (1971), who use the approach described in Section 2.3.2, for $0 \leqslant k < 1$. For $k > 1$, however, the Nagar-Kadane method fails to signal the fact that the moments do not exist. Conditions under which the Nagar method yields correct results are discussed in Section 11.3.1.

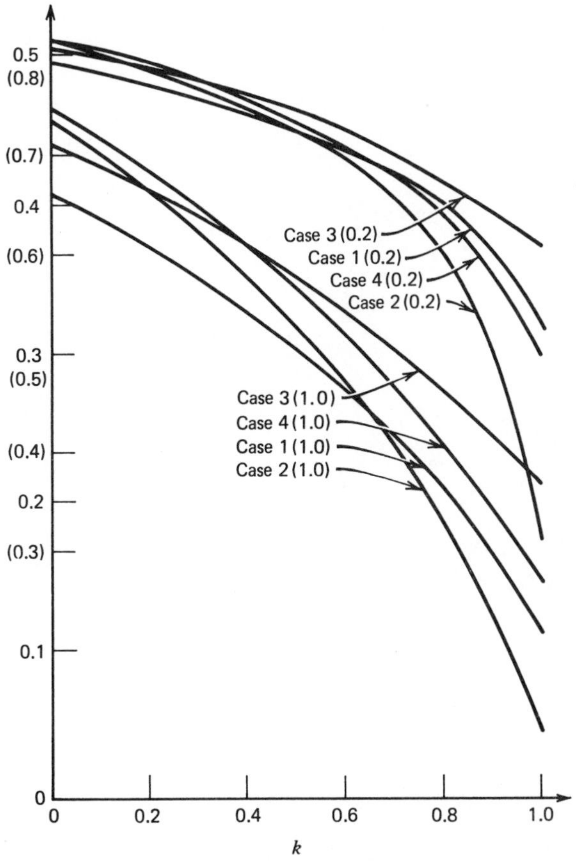


**FIGURE 10.10** **The relative bias for $\tau$ = 0.2 and 1.0. (The parenthesized scales on the vertical axis measure the relative bias for $\tau$ = 0.2.) [Reprinted from Sawa (1972), with permission of the publisher, The Econometric Society.]**

### 10.3.2 Moments of Other Estimators

Mariano and Sawa (1972) show that all moments of the LIML estimator are infinite for the special case being discussed in this chapter. Their approach is to work directly with the density function. Although the moments do not exist, in this and in other cases useful information about the location and dispersion of an estimator's distribution may be obtained from an examination of the moments of an approximating distribution. It should be emphasized that the moments of the approximating distribution may not in general be interpreted as approximations to the moments of the exact distribution; for LIML and other estimators these are infinite, and there is no point in trying to approximate them.

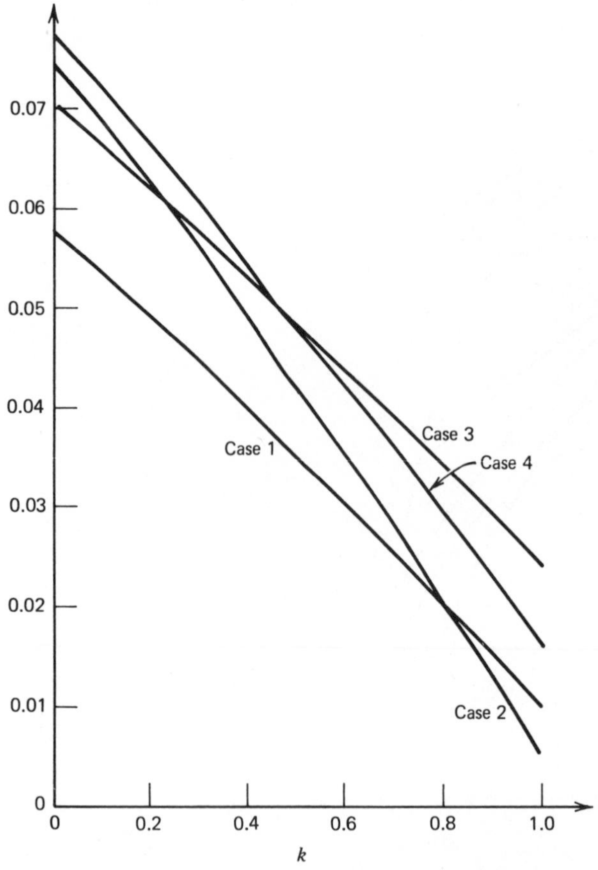


**FIGURE 10.11 The relative bias for $\tau = 10.0$. [Reprinted from Sawa (1972), with permission of the publisher, The Econometric Society.]**

Infinite moments are due to the failure of the density function to approach 0 quickly enough as $|\hat{\beta}| \to \infty$. The approximating distribution may indicate with reasonable accuracy what the density looks like for values for $\hat{\beta}$ near $\beta$.

Anderson (1974) presents an asymptotic expansion of the LIML estimator in the two included endogenous variable case. This expansion is discussed above in Section 10.2.2a. To order $1/\mu$, where $\mu$ is the concentration parameter, the asymptotic expansion may be expressed as

$$p\left[\frac{T\psi\omega_{22}}{\sigma}(\hat{\beta}_{\text{LIML}} - \beta) \leq w\right] = \Phi(w) - \frac{\alpha}{\mu} w^2\phi(w),$$

where $\Phi$ is the standard normal distribution function, $\phi$ is the standard normal density, and $\alpha = (\beta\omega_{22} - \omega_{12})/\sqrt{|\Omega|}$. Thus, if $\alpha = 0$ (or $\beta = \omega_{12}/\omega_{22}$), the approximating density

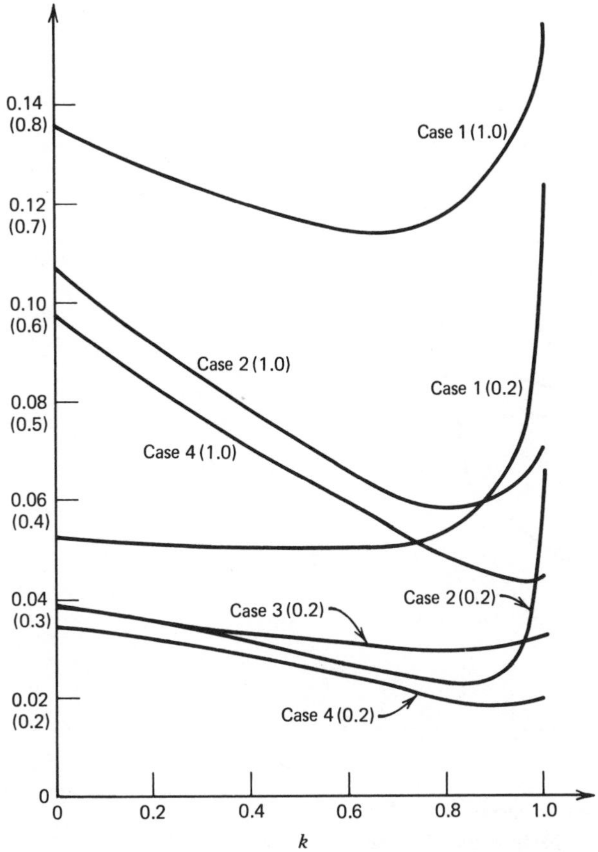


**FIGURE 10.12 The mean squared error for $\tau = 0.2$ and 1.0. (The parenthesized scales on the vertical axis measure the mean squared error for $\tau = 0.2$.) [Reprinted from Sawa (1972), with permission of the publisher, The Econometric Society.]**

is a standard normal distribution with expected value $\beta$. Otherwise, the direction of the "bias" is opposite to the sign of $\alpha$. Anderson also shows that, to order $1/\mu^3$, the median of the distribution of $\hat{\beta}_{\text{LIML}}$ is $\beta$.

Anderson (1977) presents the mean squared error of the LIML estimator, based on the approximating density, to order $1/\mu^2$. It is given by

$$1 + \frac{1}{\mu^2}\left[K_2 + 2 + \frac{K_2^2 - 1}{T - K - 2} + 9\alpha^2\right].$$

We conclude the section with a brief mention of IV estimators. The special case considered by Carter (see Section 10.2.2b) results in a variable distributed as the ratio of normal random variables. As discussed in Appendix D, this distribution has no finite

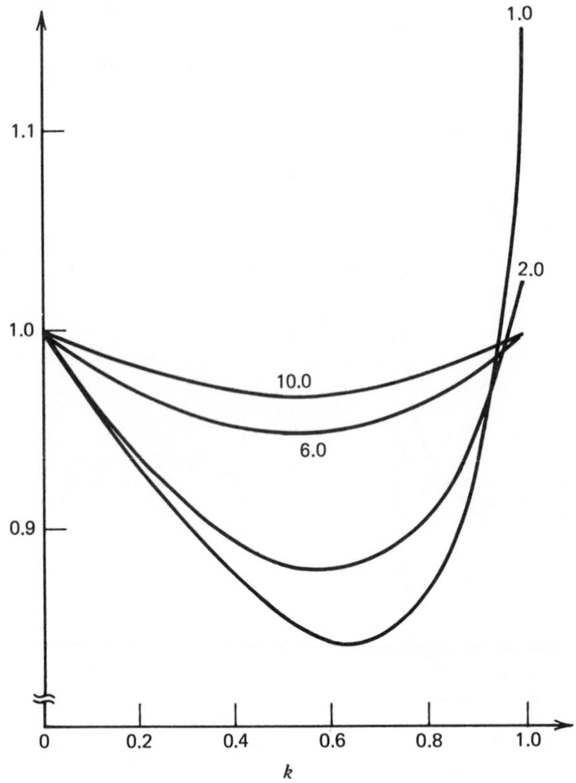


**FIGURE 10.13 The relative mean squared error for various values of noncentrality $\tau$ in case 1. [Reprinted from Sawa (1972), with permission of the publisher, The Econometric Society.]**

moments. Carter applied Geary's approximation (Appendix D) to show that the mean of the approximating distribution is equal to $\beta$, to order $1/\mu_1^2$. Other approximations are given by Mariano (1977) and by Phillips (1980).

## 10.4 Conclusions

Although this chapter has been concerned with the simplest case of simultaneous equation estimation theory—two included endogenous variables and all predetermined variables exogenous—several conclusions seem warranted:

1. The study of small sample properties of simultaneous equation estimators is a lively area of research in which many unsolved problems remain.

2. Many of the estimators proposed for use in simultaneous equation problems turn out to have extremely complex distributions compared to those that arise in single equation

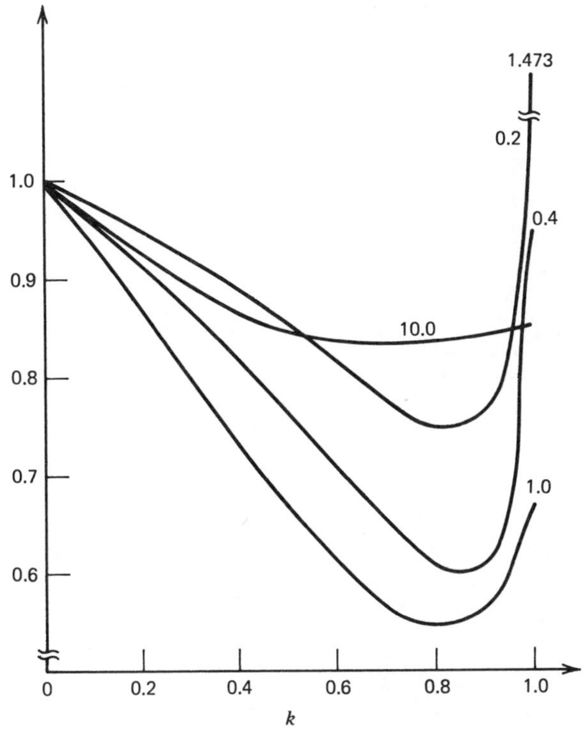


**FIGURE 10.14** **The relative mean squared error for various values of noncentrality $\tau$ in case 2. [Reprinted from Sawa (1972), with permission of the publisher, The Econometric Society.]**

cases. Nevertheless, approximations based on asymptotic expansions make it possible to investigate properties of the distributions, and these can be plotted for specified values of parameters.

3. Although several of the estimators are found to have no finite movements, or only a few finite moments, they are not necessarily inferior to those that have one or more moments. The nonexistence of first and second moments does imply that such estimators cannot be compared to others on the basis of a mean squared error criterion. It is particularly important to be aware of this possibility when using Monte Carlo studies to compare estimators because such studies will not reveal the presence of infinite moments. However, Monte Carlo approximations to the distribution may reveal thick tails, suggesting the possibility that moments do not exist. In any event, choices between estimators need not depend on comparisons of moments. Such properties as speed of convergence to normality or probability of being within a certain distance from the true value of the parameter might also be used, and these do not require the existence of moments.

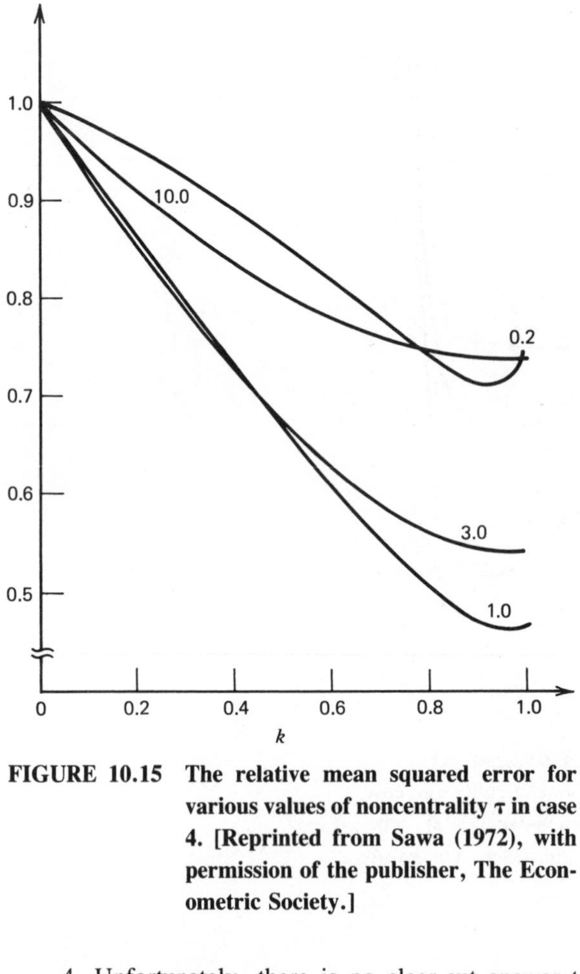


**FIGURE 10.15 The relative mean squared error for various values of noncentrality $\tau$ in case 4. [Reprinted from Sawa (1972), with permission of the publisher, The Econometric Society.]**

4. Unfortunately, there is no clear-cut answer to the "bottom line" question of which is the best estimator. As we have seen, choices among $k$-class, IV, and LIML estimators depend upon the criterion used and on values of both known and unknown parameters. The applied researcher may be able to use results in the articles discussed in this chapter to narrow choices; for example, the performance of the 2SLS estimator is sensitive to $K_2$ (the number of excluded exogenous variables) and the LIML estimator

**TABLE 10.1 Specification of Cases for Figures 10.10 to 10.15**

| Case | $T$ | $K$ | $K_1$ |
|---|---|---|---|
| 1 | 10 | 5 | 2 |
| 2 | 20 | 5 | 2 |
| 3 | 20 | 10 | 3 |
| 4 | 30 | 10 | 3 |

converges to normality faster than the 2SLS estimator. In short, no one estimator can be considered better than the others, and no estimator can be eliminated from consideration on the basis of standard statistical (small sample) criteria.

## 10.5 References

Anderson, T. W. (1974), "An Asymptotic Expansion of the Distribution of the Limited Information Maximum Likelihood Estimate of a Coefficient in a Simultaneous Equation System," *Journal of the American Statistical Association,* **69**, 565–573.

Anderson, T. W. (1977), "Asymptotic Expansions of the Distributions of Estimates in Simultaneous Equations for Alternative Parameter Sequences," *Econometrica,* **45**, 509–518.

Anderson, T. W. and T. Sawa (1973), "Distributions of Estimates of Coefficients of a Single Equation in a Simultaneous System and Their Asymptotic Expansions," *Econometrica,* **41**, 683–714.

Anderson, T. W. and T. Sawa (1979), "Evaluation of the Distribution Function of the Two-Stage Least Squares Estimate," *Econometrica,* **47**, 163–182.

Basmann, R. L. (1961), "A Note on the Exact Finite Sample Frequency Functions of Generalized Classical Linear Estimators in Two Leading Over-Identified Cases," *Journal of the American Statistical Association,* **56**, 619–636.

Basmann, R. L. (1963), "Remarks Concerning the Application of Exact Finite Sample Distribution Functions of GCL Estimators in Econometric Statistical Inference," *Journal of the American Statistical Association,* **58**, 943–976.

Basmann, R. L. (1974), "Exact Finite Sample Distributions for Some Econometric Estimators and Test Statistics: A Survey and Appraisal," Chapter 4 of *Frontiers of Quantitative Economics,* Vol. II, M. D. Intriligator and D. A. Kendrick, eds., Amsterdam: North-Holland, 209–285.

Bergstrom, A. R. (1962), "The Exact Sampling Distributions of Least Squares and Maximum Likelihood Estimators of the Marginal Propensity to Consume," *Econometrica,* **30**, 480–490.

Carter, R. A. L. (1976), "The Exact Distribution of an Instrumental Variables Estimator," *International Economic Review,* **17**, 228–233.

Goldberger, A. S. (1964), *Econometric Theory,* New York: Wiley.

Haavelmo, T. (1947), "Methods of Measuring the Marginal Propensity to Consume," *Journal of the American Statistical Association,* **42**, 105–122.

Holly, A. and P. C. B. Phillips (1979), "A Saddlepoint Approximation to the Distribution of the $k$-Class Estimator of a Coefficient in a Simultaneous System," *Econometrica,* **47**, 1527–1547.

Johnson, N. L. and S. Kotz (1972), *Continuous Multivariate Distributions,* New York: Wiley.

Kadane, J. B. (1971), "Comparison of $k$-Class Estimators When the Disturbances Are Small," *Econometrica,* **39**, 723–738.

Kinal, T. W. (1980), "The Existence of Moments of $k$-Class Estimators," *Econometrica,* **48**, 240–249.

Mariano, R. S. (1973a), "Approximations to the Distribution Functions of the Ordinary Least-Squares and Two-Stage Least-Squares Estimators in the Case of Two Included Endogenous Variables," *Econometrica,* **41**, 67–77.

Mariano, R. S. (1973b), "Approximations to the Distribution Functions of Theil's $k$-Class Estimators," *Econometrica,* **41**, 715–721.

Mariano, R. S. (1977), "Finite Sample Properties of Instrumental Variable Estimators of Structural Coefficients," *Econometrica,* **45**, 487–496.

Mariano, R. S. and J. B. McDonald (1979), "A Note on the Distribution Functions of LIML and 2SLS Structural Coefficients in the Exactly Identified Case," *Journal of the American Statistical Association,* **74**, 847–848.

Mariano, R. S. and T. Sawa (1972), "The Exact Finite-Sample Distribution of the Limited-Information Maximum Likelihood Estimator in the Case of Two Included Endogenous Variables," *Journal of the American Statistical Association,* **67**, 159–163.

Mehta, J. S. and P. A. V. B. Swamy (1978), "The Existence of Moments of Some Simple Bayes Estimators of Coefficients in a Simultaneous Equation Model," *Journal of Econometrics,* **7**, 1–13.

Nagar, A. L. (1959), "The Bias and Moment Matrix of the General $k$-Class Estimators of the Parameters in Simultaneous Equations," *Econometrica,* **27**, 575–595.

Phillips, P. C. B. (1980), "The Exact Distribution of Instrumental Variable Estimators in an Equation Containing $n + 1$ Endogenous Variables," *Econometrica,* **48**, 861–878.

Richardson, D. H. (1968), "The Exact Distribution of a Structural Coefficient Estimator," *Journal of the American Statistical Association,* **63**, 1214–1226.

Richardson, D. H. and De-Min Wu (1971), "A Note on the Comparison of Ordinary and Two-Stage Least Square Estimators," *Econometrica,* **39**, 973–981.

Sargan, J. D. (1974), "The Validity of Nagar's Expansions for the Moments of Econometric Estimators," *Econometrica,* **42**, 169–176.

Sargan, J. D. and W. M. Mikhail (1971), "A General Approximation to the Distribution of Instrumental Varibles Estimates," *Econometrica,* **39**, 131–169.

Sawa, T. (1969), "The Exact Sampling Distribution of Ordinary Least Squares and Two-Stage Least Squares Estimators," *Journal of the American Statistical Association,* **64**, 923–937.

Sawa, T. (1972), "Finite-Sample Properties of the $k$-Class Estimators," *Econometrica,* **40**, 653–680.

# CHAPTER 11

# Moments and Distributions in General Cases

This chapter is concerned with the properties of estimators in situations more general than the cases considered in Chapter 10. Specifically, we take up two types of generalization: the presence of more than two endogenous variables in an equation and the presence of a lagged endogenous variable among the predetermined variables.

The first section of the chapter deals in detail with the existence of moments of $k$-class estimators when there are an arbitrary number of included endogenous variables and briefly notes two other cases; the second surveys small sample distribution theory and approximations for several types of estimators for an arbitrary number of included endogenous variables; the third section examines conditions for the validity of Nagar and Edgeworth approximations for econometric estimators; and the fourth takes up lagged endogenous variables.

## 11.1 Moments of Estimators in Equations That Contain More Than Two Endogenous Variables

This section presents results that generalize upon those reported in Section 10.3 by extending the number of included endogenous variables beyond two. We continue to assume that all predetermined variables are exogenous.

The first subsection considers the existence of moments for $k$-class estimators, and the second discusses existence for three-stage least squares (3SLS) and full information maximum likelihood (FIML) estimators. The third and fourth sections discuss exact moments for two special cases: (i) exactly identified 2SLS estimators with an arbitrary number of included endogenous variables, and (ii) overidentified 2SLS with three included endogenous variables.

### 11.1.1 Existence of Moments of *k*-Class Estimators—Arbitrary Number of Included Endogenous Variables

The topic of this section has been studied by Mariano (1972) and Hatanaka (1973), who confirmed Basmann's conjecture [Basmann (1961, 1963)] that moments of 2SLS estimators exist up to the degree of overidentification. This section is based on Kinal (1980); it assumes the following model: There are $N$ observations, $G$ endogenous variables, and $K$ exogenous variables; $G_1$ endogenous and $K_1$ exogenous variables are included in the first equation; and the $N \times K$ matrix of exogenous variables, $Z$, is normalized so that $Z'Z = I$. The first equation is written as

$$\mathbf{y} = Y_1\boldsymbol{\beta}^* + Z_1\boldsymbol{\gamma} + \mathbf{u} \qquad \textbf{(11.1.1)}$$

where $y$ is $N \times 1$, $Y_1$ is $N \times (G_1 - 1)$, and $Z_1$ is $N \times K_1$. The $N \times 1$ vector of disturbances, $\mathbf{u}$, is assumed to be distributed normally,

$$\mathbf{u} \sim N_N(\mathbf{0}, \omega^2 I).$$

To complete the specification of the model, Kinal utilizes the ''row'' operator on a matrix; it is defined as

$$\text{row}(V, W) = [\mathbf{V}_{(1)}W, \mathbf{V}_{(2)}W, \ldots, \mathbf{V}_{(J)}W], \tag{11.1.2}$$

where $\mathbf{V}_{(j)}$ is the $j$th row of $V$, $V$ is $J \times K$, $W$ is $K \times M$, and row$(V, W)$ is $1 \times JM$. With this operator,

$$\text{row}(Y, I_{G_1}) \sim N_{NG_1}(\text{row}(Z, \Pi), I_N \otimes \Theta), \tag{11.1.3}$$

where $Y = (\mathbf{y}, Y_1)$ and $\Theta$ is the covariance matrix of the reduced form disturbances. In this notation the $n$th row of $Y$, $\mathbf{Y}_{(n)} = (y_{1n}, y_{2n}, \ldots, y_{G_1n})$, has the reduced form representation

$$\mathbf{Y}_{(n)} = \mathbf{Z}_{(n)}\Pi + \mathbf{v}_{(n)}, \tag{11.1.4}$$

and $\mathbf{v}_{(n)} \sim N_{G_1}(\mathbf{0}, \Theta)$. Moreover,

$$\omega^2 = (1\ \boldsymbol{\beta}^{*\prime})\Theta \begin{bmatrix} 1 \\ \boldsymbol{\beta}^* \end{bmatrix},$$

since from

$$\mathbf{Y}_{(n)} \begin{bmatrix} 1 \\ \boldsymbol{\beta}^* \end{bmatrix} = y_{(n)} + \mathbf{Y}_{1(n)}\boldsymbol{\beta}^* = \mathbf{Z}_{(n)}\Pi \begin{bmatrix} 1 \\ \boldsymbol{\beta}^* \end{bmatrix} + \mathbf{v} \begin{bmatrix} 1 \\ \boldsymbol{\beta}^* \end{bmatrix}$$

and

$$y_{(n)} = -\mathbf{Y}_{1(n)}\boldsymbol{\beta}^* + \mathbf{Z}_{1(n)}\boldsymbol{\gamma} + u_{(n)},$$

we have

$$u_{(n)} = \mathbf{v}_{(n)} \begin{bmatrix} 1 \\ \boldsymbol{\beta}^* \end{bmatrix},$$

where $\mathbf{Y}_{1(n)}$ denotes the $n$th row of $Y_1$, and $y_{(n)}$ is the $n$th row of $\mathbf{y}$. Accordingly,

$$E[u_{(n)}^2] = \omega^2 = (1\ \boldsymbol{\beta}^{*\prime})E[\mathbf{v}_{(n)}'\mathbf{v}_{(n)}] \begin{bmatrix} 1 \\ \boldsymbol{\beta}^* \end{bmatrix} = (1\ \boldsymbol{\beta}^{*\prime})\Theta \begin{bmatrix} 1 \\ \boldsymbol{\beta}^* \end{bmatrix}. \tag{11.1.5}$$

To express the $k$-class estimator, define

$$\Lambda_k = (1 - k)(I - Z_1Z_1') + kZ_2Z_2', \qquad 0 \leq k \leq 1, \tag{11.1.6}$$

and

$$r_k = \text{rank}(\Lambda_k) = \begin{cases} N - K_1, & 0 \leq k < 1 \\ K_2, & k = 1, \end{cases} \tag{11.1.7}$$

where $Z_2$ is the $N \times K_2$ matrix of exogenous variables excluded from this equation and $K_2 = K - K_1$. Clearly, $\Lambda_k Z_1 = 0$ (because $Z'Z = I$). Moreover,

$$\hat{\boldsymbol{\beta}}_k^* = -(Y_1'\Lambda_k Y_1)^{-1} Y_1'\Lambda_k \mathbf{y}, \qquad \textbf{(11.1.8)}$$

where $\hat{\boldsymbol{\beta}}_k^*$ is the $k$-class estimator of $\boldsymbol{\beta}^*$.

Before presenting the lengthy and involved details that follow, it is worthwhile to outline the main steps. Starting from (11.1.8), two transformations are made—from $(\mathbf{y}, Y_1)$ to $(\mathbf{w}, W_1)$ and then to $(\mathbf{v}, V_1)$. The first simplifies the equation for $\hat{\boldsymbol{\beta}}_k^*$ into the form $\hat{\boldsymbol{\beta}}_k^* = -(W_1'W_1)^{-1}W_1'\mathbf{w}$, and the second simplifies the covariance of $V_1$ and $\boldsymbol{\epsilon}$ in the transformed regression, $\mathbf{v} = V_1\boldsymbol{\beta} + \boldsymbol{\epsilon}$. With these transformations completed, a lemma is proved concerning the existence of moments of regression coefficients where $V_1$ and $\boldsymbol{\epsilon}$ have the covariance structure of the transformed equation. This is proved by a series of bounds placed on the moments of $\hat{\boldsymbol{\beta}}_k^*$. We now turn to the details of the argument.

The first step is to transform (11.1.8) to a simpler form. Let $Z_3$ be an $(N - K) \times K$ matrix orthogonal to $Z_1$ and $Z_2$. Then it is easy to verify that (i) the columns of $Z_1$ are a set of c.v.'s of $\Lambda_k$ with $K_1$ c.r.'s equal to 0; (ii) the columns of $Z_2$ are c.v.'s of $\Lambda_k$ with $K_2$ c.r.'s equal to 1; and (iii) the columns of $Z_3$ are c.v.'s of $\Lambda_k$ with $N - K$ c.r.'s equal to $(1 - k)$. If we define $D_Z$ as the matrix $(Z_2, Z_3, Z_1)$ normalized so that

$$Z_i'Z_j = \begin{cases} I, & \text{if } i = j \\ 0, & \text{if } i \neq j, \end{cases}$$

we have

$$D_Z'\Lambda_k D_Z = \begin{array}{c} \begin{matrix} N - K_1 & K_1 \end{matrix} \\ \begin{bmatrix} R & 0 \\ 0 & 0 \end{bmatrix} \end{array} \begin{matrix} N - K_1 \\ K_1, \end{matrix} \qquad \textbf{(11.1.9)}$$

where

$$R = \begin{array}{c} \begin{matrix} K_2 & N - K \end{matrix} \\ \begin{bmatrix} I & 0 \\ 0 & (1 - k)I \end{bmatrix} \end{array} \begin{matrix} K_2 \\ N - K. \end{matrix} \qquad \textbf{(11.1.10)}$$

After partitioning $D_Z$ as

$$D_Z = \begin{array}{c} \begin{matrix} r_k & N - r_k \end{matrix} \\ \begin{bmatrix} D_k, & D \end{bmatrix} \end{array} \quad N,$$

where $D_k$ and $D$ are defined implicitly, it is easy to verify that

$$D_k'\Lambda_k D_k = \begin{cases} I_{K_2}, & \text{if } k = 1 \\ R, & \text{if } 0 \leq k < 1, \end{cases} \qquad \textbf{(11.1.11)}$$

$$D_k'D_k = I_{r_k},$$

and

$$D_k'Z_1 = 0.$$

To simplify the expression for $\hat{\boldsymbol{\beta}}_k^*$, Kinal next defines

$$W = R_k^{1/2} D_k' Y = \underset{\quad 1 \qquad\quad G_1 - 1}{\begin{bmatrix} \mathbf{w}, & W_1 \end{bmatrix}} \; r_k \tag{11.1.12}$$

(or $Y = (\mathbf{y}, Y_1) = D_k R_k^{-1/2} W$) and

$$\Psi = R_k^{1/2} D_k' \mathbf{u}, \tag{11.1.13}$$

where $R_k \equiv D_k' \Lambda_k D_k$. After this transformation, we have from (11.1.8)

$$\begin{aligned} \hat{\boldsymbol{\beta}}_k^* &= -(Y_1' \Lambda_k Y_1)^{-1} Y_1' \Lambda_k \mathbf{y} \\ &= -[W_1'(R_k^{-1/2})' D_k' \Lambda_k D_k R_k^{-1/2} W_1]^{-1} \\ &\times [W_1'(R_k^{-1/2})' D_k' \Lambda_k D_k R_k^{-1/2} \mathbf{w}] \\ &= -(W_1' W_1)^{-1} W_1' \mathbf{w} \end{aligned} \tag{11.1.14}$$

since $(R_k^{-1/2})' R_k^{-1/2} = I_{K_2}$ for $k = 1$, and $(R_k^{-1/2})' R R_k^{-1/2} = I_{N-K_1}$, $0 \leqslant k < 1$. Clearly (11.1.14) is the OLS estimator of $\boldsymbol{\beta}^*$ in the equation

$$\mathbf{w} = -W_1 \boldsymbol{\beta}^* + \boldsymbol{\Psi} \tag{11.1.15}$$

because

$$\mathbf{w} + W_1 \boldsymbol{\beta}^* = W \begin{bmatrix} 1 \\ \boldsymbol{\beta}^* \end{bmatrix} = R_k^{1/2} D_k' Y \begin{bmatrix} 1 \\ \boldsymbol{\beta}^* \end{bmatrix} = R_k^{1/2} D_k' Z_1 \boldsymbol{\gamma} + R_k^{1/2} D_k' \mathbf{u} = \mathbf{0} + \boldsymbol{\Psi}.$$

The final step in the transformation is to diagonalize the covariance matrix of $W$. To that end, first note that $E[\boldsymbol{\Psi}] = 0$ and

$$\begin{aligned} \operatorname{Cov}(\boldsymbol{\Psi}) &= E[R_k^{1/2} D_k' \mathbf{u}\mathbf{u}' D_k R_k^{1/2}] \\ &= \omega^2 R_k \end{aligned} \tag{11.1.16}$$

using (11.1.5). Therefore,

$$\boldsymbol{\Psi} \sim N_{r_k}(\mathbf{0}, \omega^2 R_k). \tag{11.1.17}$$

Moreover,

$$\operatorname{row}(W, I_{G_1}) \sim N_{r_k G_1}[\operatorname{row}(R_k^{1/2} D_k', Z\Pi), R_k \otimes \Theta]. \tag{11.1.18}$$

To verify (11.1.18), we require the following lemma:

**Lemma 11.1.1**

$$\begin{aligned} \operatorname{row}(AB, I) &= \operatorname{row}(A, B) \\ &= [\operatorname{row}(A, I)](I \otimes B) \\ &= [\operatorname{row}(B, I)](A' \otimes I), \end{aligned} \tag{11.1.19}$$

where $A$ is $m \times p$, $B$ is $p \times n$, and the identity matrices are of the appropriate dimensions.

**Proof**

Clearly,

$$\text{row}(AB, I) = [\mathbf{A}_{(1)}B, \ldots, \mathbf{A}_{(n)}B] = \text{row}(A, B).$$

We also have

$$[\text{row}(A, I)](I \otimes B) = [\mathbf{A}_{(1)}, \ldots, \mathbf{A}_{(m)}]\begin{bmatrix} B & & & & 0 \\ & B & & & \\ & & \cdot & & \\ & & & \cdot & \\ & & & & \cdot \\ 0 & & & & B \end{bmatrix}$$

$$= [\mathbf{A}_{(1)}B, \ldots, \mathbf{A}_{(m)}B] = \text{row}(A, B),$$

which proves the second equality. For the third,

$$[\text{row}(B, I)](A' \otimes I) = [\mathbf{B}_{(1)}, \ldots, \mathbf{B}_{(p)}]\begin{bmatrix} a_{11}I & \cdots & a_{m1}I \\ \cdot & & \\ \cdot & & \\ \cdot & & \\ a_{1p}I & \cdots & a_{mp}I \end{bmatrix}$$

$$= \left[\sum_{j=1}^{p} a_{1j}\mathbf{B}_{(j)}, \ldots, \sum_{j=1}^{p} a_{mj}\mathbf{B}_{(j)}\right]$$

$$= [\mathbf{A}_{(1)}B, \ldots, \mathbf{A}_{(m)}B].$$ □

Using these results, we have

$$\text{row}(W, I) = \text{row}(R_k^{1/2}D_k'Y, I)$$
$$= \text{row}(R_k^{1/2}D_k', Y); \qquad \textbf{(11.1.20)}$$

hence

$$E[\text{row}(W, I)] = \text{row}(R_k^{1/2}D_k', Z\Pi). \qquad \textbf{(11.1.21)}$$

Moreover

$$\text{Cov}[\text{row}(W, I)] = \text{Cov}[\text{row}(R_k^{1/2}D_k'Y, I)]$$
$$= \text{Cov}[[\text{row}(Y, I)](D_kR_k^{1/2} \otimes I)]. \qquad \textbf{(11.1.22)}$$

Letting $S = D_kR_k^{1/2}$, (11.1.22) becomes

$$\text{Cov}[[\text{row}(Y, I)](S \otimes I)] = (S \otimes I)' \,\text{Cov}[\text{row}(Y, I)](S \otimes I)$$
$$= (S' \otimes I)(I \otimes \Theta)(S \otimes I)$$
$$= S'S \otimes \Theta = R_k \otimes \Theta. \qquad \textbf{(11.1.23)}$$

This completes the derivation of (11.1.18).

Kinal next partitions $\Theta$ and defines $T$ as follows:

$$\Theta = \begin{array}{c} \quad\;\; 1 \quad\;\; G_1 - 1 \\ \left[ \begin{array}{cc} \Theta_{11} & \Theta_{12} \\ \Theta_{21} & \Theta_{22} \end{array} \right] \begin{array}{c} 1 \\ G_1 - 1 \end{array} \end{array},$$

$$T = \begin{array}{c} \qquad\;\; 1 \qquad\qquad\quad G_1 - 1 \\ \left[ \begin{array}{cc} 1 & 0 \\ (\Theta^{11})^{1/2}\,\Theta_{22}^{-1/2}\,\Theta_{21} & (\Theta^{11})^{1/2}\,\Theta_{22}^{1/2} \end{array} \right] \begin{array}{c} 1 \\ G_1 - 1 \end{array} \end{array}, \qquad (11.1.24)$$

where $\Theta^{11} = (\Theta_{11} - \Theta_{12}\Theta_{22}^{-1}\Theta_{21})^{-1}$ is the leading element of $\Theta^{-1}$, and $\Theta_{22}^{1/2}$ has the property that $(\Theta_{22}^{1/2})'\Theta_{22}^{1/2} = \Theta_{22}$. (We know $\Theta_{22}^{1/2}$ exists because $\Theta_{22}$ is positive definite.)

With these definitions we show that $V \equiv (\Theta^{11})^{1/2}WT^{-1}$ has the following distribution:

$$\text{row}(V, I) \sim N_{r_k G_1}(\text{row}(R_k^{1/2}D_k', (\Theta^{11})^{1/2}Z\Pi T^{-1}), R_k \otimes I). \qquad (11.1.25)$$

First, consider $E[\text{row}(V, I)]$.

$$\begin{aligned}
E[\text{row}(V, I)] &= E[\text{row}((\Theta^{11})^{1/2}WT^{-1}, I)] \\
&= \text{row}((\Theta^{11})^{1/2}E[W]T^{-1}, I) \\
&= \text{row}((\Theta^{11})^{1/2}R_k^{1/2}D_k'Z\Pi T^{-1}, I) \\
&= \text{row}((\Theta^{11})^{1/2}R_k^{1/2}D_k'Z\Pi T^{-1}) \\
&= \text{row}(R_k^{1/2}D_k', (\Theta^{11})^{1/2}Z\Pi T^{-1}) \qquad (11.1.26)
\end{aligned}$$

(since $\Theta^{11}$ is a scalar).

Before computing $\text{Cov}(V, I)$ it should be verified that

$$(\Theta^{11})^{-1}T'T = \Theta.$$

Then

$$\begin{aligned}
\text{Cov}[\text{row}(V, I)] &= \text{Cov}[\text{row}((\Theta^{11})^{1/2}WT^{-1}, I)] \\
&= \text{Cov}[[\text{row}(W, I)](I \otimes (\Theta^{11})^{1/2}T^{-1})] \\
&= (I \otimes (\Theta^{11})^{1/2}T^{-1})'\text{Cov}[\text{row}(W, I)](I \otimes (\Theta^{11})^{1/2}T^{-1}) \\
&= (I \otimes (\Theta^{11})^{1/2}T^{-1})'(R_k \otimes \Theta)(I \otimes (\Theta^{11})^{1/2}T^{-1}) \\
&= R_k \otimes \Theta^{11}(T^{-1})'\Theta T^{-1} \\
&= R_k \otimes I_{G_1}. \qquad (11.1.27)
\end{aligned}$$

This completes the derivation of (11.1.25).

If we define $\beta$ from

$$\begin{bmatrix} 1 \\ -\beta \end{bmatrix} = T \begin{bmatrix} 1 \\ \beta^* \end{bmatrix},$$

we have

$$\boldsymbol{\beta} = -\frac{\Theta_{22}^{1/2}\boldsymbol{\beta}^* + \Theta_{22}^{-1/2}\Theta_{21}}{(\Theta_{11} - \Theta_{12}\Theta_{22}^{-1}\Theta_{21})^{1/2}}; \tag{11.1.28}$$

and so from

$$\mathbf{w} = -W_1\boldsymbol{\beta}^* + \boldsymbol{\Psi},$$

or

$$(\mathbf{w}_1, W_1)\begin{bmatrix} 1 \\ \boldsymbol{\beta}^* \end{bmatrix} = \boldsymbol{\Psi},$$

we obtain

$$(\mathbf{w}_1, W_1)T^{-1}T\begin{bmatrix} 1 \\ \boldsymbol{\beta}^* \end{bmatrix} = \boldsymbol{\Psi}$$

and

$$(\Theta^{11})^{1/2}(\mathbf{w}_1, W_1)T^{-1}\begin{bmatrix} 1 \\ -\boldsymbol{\beta} \end{bmatrix} = (\Theta^{11})^{1/2}\,\boldsymbol{\Psi}, \tag{11.1.29}$$

or

$$V\begin{bmatrix} 1 \\ -\boldsymbol{\beta} \end{bmatrix} = \boldsymbol{\epsilon}, \tag{11.1.30}$$

where

$$V = \underset{\phantom{r_k}1\qquad G_1 - 1}{(\mathbf{v}, \qquad V_1)} \quad r_k \tag{11.1.31}$$

and

$$\boldsymbol{\epsilon} = (\theta^{11})^{1/2}\boldsymbol{\Psi}. \tag{11.1.32}$$

Further, since $\boldsymbol{\psi} \sim N_{r_k}(\mathbf{0}, \omega^2 R_k)$, we have

$$\boldsymbol{\epsilon} \sim N_{r_k}(\mathbf{0}, \omega^2\Theta^{11}R_k). \tag{11.1.33}$$

From

$$\text{Cov}[\text{row}(V, I)] = R_k \otimes I,$$

we derive the covariance between the $ng$th element of $V_1$ and the $m$th element of $\boldsymbol{\epsilon}$:

$$\text{Cov}[(V_1)_{ng}, \boldsymbol{\epsilon}_m] = \text{Cov}[(V_1)_{ng}, (\mathbf{v} - V_1\boldsymbol{\beta})_m].$$

Since $\text{Cov}[\text{row}(V, I)] = R_k \otimes I$,

$$\text{Cov}[(V_1)_{ng}, (V_1)_m] = 0 \qquad \text{for} \quad m \neq n. \tag{11.1.34}$$

For $m = n$,

$$\mathrm{Cov}[(V_1)_{ng}, (v_n - \mathbf{V}_{1(n)}\boldsymbol{\beta})] = \mathrm{Cov}[(V_1)_{ng}, -(V_1)_{ng}\beta_g] = -\beta_g(R_k)_{nn}. \quad \textbf{(11.1.35)}$$

We can combine the results for $m = n$ and $m \neq n$ by using the Kronecker delta,

$$\delta_{mn} = \begin{cases} 1 & \text{for } m = n \\ 0 & \text{for } m \neq n, \end{cases}$$

to obtain

$$\mathrm{Cov}[(V_1)_{ng}, \epsilon_m] = -\delta_{mn}(R_k)_{nn}\beta_g. \quad \textbf{(11.1.36)}$$

To summarize the analysis up to this point, note that the original regression,

$$\hat{\boldsymbol{\beta}}_k^* = -(Y_1'\Lambda_k Y_1)^{-1}Y_1'\Lambda_k\mathbf{y},$$

was first transformed to

$$\hat{\boldsymbol{\beta}}_k^* = (W_1'W_1)^{-1}W_1'\mathbf{w}.$$

A transformation of the latter resulted in the equation

$$\hat{\boldsymbol{\beta}}_k = (V_1'V_1)^{-1}V_1'\mathbf{v}, \quad \textbf{(11.1.37)}$$

where $\boldsymbol{\beta}$ and $\boldsymbol{\beta}^*$ are related through (11.1.28). But $\hat{\boldsymbol{\beta}}_k$ can be interpreted as the OLS estimator of $\boldsymbol{\beta}$ in

$$\mathbf{v} = V_1\boldsymbol{\beta} + \boldsymbol{\epsilon}, \quad \textbf{(11.1.38)}$$

where the covariance between $V_1$ and $\boldsymbol{\epsilon}$ assumes the special form given by (11.1.36), a fact that is exploited below. We next turn to the proof of a theorem on the existence of moments of the OLS estimator in equations having the form of (11.1.38) and the covariance structure of (11.1.36).

Let $\mathbf{C} = A\boldsymbol{\beta} + \boldsymbol{\epsilon}$, where $\mathbf{C}$ is $p \times 1$, $A$ is $p \times q$, $\boldsymbol{\beta}$ is $q \times 1$, and $\boldsymbol{\epsilon}$ is $p \times 1$. Assume $\boldsymbol{\epsilon} \sim N_p(\mathbf{0}, N)$, $N = \mathrm{diag}\{\nu_1, \ldots, \nu_p\}$;

$$r(A) = q < p;$$

the $n$th row of $(\mathbf{C}, A)$, $(\mathbf{C}, A)_{(n)}$, is distributed as $N_{q+1}(\boldsymbol{\mu}_{(n)}, s_n I_{q+1})$;

$$E[((\mathbf{C}, A)_{(m)} - \boldsymbol{\mu}_{(m)})'((\mathbf{C}, A)_{(n)} - \boldsymbol{\mu}_{(n)})] = 0, \qquad m \neq n;$$

and $S = \mathrm{diag}\{s_1, \ldots, s_p\}$.

The conditions imply that:

**(i)** The elements of $\mathbf{C}$ are distributed independently of the elements of $A$;

**(ii)** $\nu_n = (1 + \boldsymbol{\beta}'\boldsymbol{\beta})s_n$; and **(11.1.39)**

**(iii)** $\mathrm{Cov}(A_{ng}, \epsilon_m) = -\delta_{mn}s_n\beta_g$. **(11.1.40)**

Result (i) follows directly from the distributional assumption on $(\mathbf{C}, A)_{(n)}$; (ii) follows from noting that $(\mathbf{C} - A\boldsymbol{\beta})_{(n)} = \epsilon_n$ and computing the covariance; and (iii) follows from computing $\mathrm{Cov}[(A_{ng}, (\mathbf{C} - A\boldsymbol{\beta})_{(m)})]$.

**Theorem 11.1.1 (Kinal)**

For the model described above, $E[|b_j|^l]$ is finite if and only if $l < p - q + 1$, where $b_j$ is the $j$th element of the least squares estimator of $\boldsymbol{\beta}$, $\hat{\boldsymbol{\beta}} = (A'A)^{-1}A'\mathbf{C}$.

**Proof**

By the assumptions that have been made, the joint density of the $n$th row of $(\mathbf{C}, A)$ may be written as

$$f[(\mathbf{C}, A)_{(n)}] = (2\pi)^{-(q+1)/2} s_n^{-(q+1)/2}$$
$$\times \exp\left\{-\frac{1}{2}[(\mathbf{C}, A)_{(n)} - \boldsymbol{\mu}_{(n)}]' \frac{1}{s_n} I_{q+1} [(\mathbf{C}, A)_{(n)} - \boldsymbol{\mu}_{(n)}]\right\}. \quad \mathbf{(11.1.41)}$$

Since the rows of $(\mathbf{C}, A)$ are independent, we may multiply the $p$ densities together to obtain

$$f[\mathbf{C}, A)] = (2\pi)^{-p(q+1)/2}|S|^{-(q+1)/2}$$
$$\times \exp\left\{-\frac{1}{2}\sum_{n=1}^{p}\left[((\mathbf{C}, A)_{(n)} - \boldsymbol{\mu}_{(n)})' \frac{1}{s_n} I_{q+1} ((\mathbf{C}, A)_{(n)} - \boldsymbol{\mu}_{(n)})\right]\right\}. \quad \mathbf{(11.1.42)}$$

Partitioning $\boldsymbol{\mu}_{(n)} = [\boldsymbol{\mu}_C, \boldsymbol{\mu}_A]_{(n)}$ to conform to $(\mathbf{C}, A)_{(n)}$, the sum in the exponential of (11.1.42) may be rewritten as

$$\sum_{n=1}^{p}\left[(\mathbf{C} - \boldsymbol{\mu}_C)'_{(n)} \frac{1}{s_n} I(\mathbf{C} - \boldsymbol{\mu}_C)_{(n)}\right] + \sum_{n=1}^{p}\left[(A - \boldsymbol{\mu}_A)'_{(n)} \frac{1}{s_n} I(A - \boldsymbol{\mu}_A)_{(n)}\right]$$
$$= (\mathbf{C} - \boldsymbol{\mu}_C)'S^{-1}(\mathbf{C} - \boldsymbol{\mu}_C) + \mathrm{tr}(A - \boldsymbol{\mu}_A)'S^{-1}(A - \boldsymbol{\mu}_A). \quad \mathbf{(11.1.43)}$$

Upon making this substitution and multiplying by $|b_j|^l$ we obtain

$$E[|b_j|^l] = (2\pi)^{-p(q+1)/2}|S|^{-(q+1)/2}\int_A\int_C |(A'A)^{(j)}A'\mathbf{C}|^l$$
$$\times \exp\left\{-\frac{1}{2}\mathrm{tr}(A - \boldsymbol{\mu}_A)'S^{-1}(A - \boldsymbol{\mu}_A)\right\}$$
$$\times \exp\left\{-\frac{1}{2}(\mathbf{C} - \boldsymbol{\mu}_C)'S^{-1}(\mathbf{C} - \boldsymbol{\mu}_C)\right\} d\mathbf{C}\, dA, \quad \mathbf{(11.1.44)}$$

where $(A'A)^{(j)}$ is the $j$th row of $A'A$, $d\mathbf{C} = \Pi_i d\mathrm{C}_i$, and $dA = \Pi_i\Pi_j\, da_{ij}$. It is convenient for later use to denote the $j$th column of $A'A$ by $(A'A)^{[j]}$ and the $jj$th element of $(A'A)^{-1}$ by $(A'A)^{jj}$. The next step is to transform $\mathbf{C}$ into $b_j$ and $\mathbf{b}$, a $(p - 1) \times 1$ vector, which is integrated out to obtain the joint density of $b_j$ and $A$. The transformation required is

$$\begin{bmatrix} b_j \\ \mathbf{b} \end{bmatrix} = \begin{bmatrix} (A'A)^{(j)}A' \\ HS^{-1/2} \end{bmatrix} \mathbf{C}$$

where $S^{1/2}S^{1/2} = S$ and $H$, which is $(p - 1) \times p$, has the properties

$$A'S^{1/2}H' = 0 \quad \text{and} \quad HH' = I_{p-1}.$$

It should be verified that the inverse of the transformation matrix is given by

$$\begin{bmatrix} (A'A)^{(j)}A' \\ HS^{-1/2} \end{bmatrix}^{-1} = \left[ \frac{SA(A'A)^{[j]}}{\sigma^{*2}}, \; S^{1/2}H' \right],$$

where $\sigma^{*2} = (A'A)^{(j)}A'SA(A'A)^{[j]}$. The Jacobian of the transformation is given by

$$\begin{aligned} J &= \left| \frac{SA(A'A)^{[j]}}{\sigma^{*2}}, \; S^{1/2}H' \right| \\ &= |S^{1/2}| \left| \frac{S^{1/2}A(A'A)^{[j]}}{\sigma^{*2}}, \; H' \right| \\ &= |S^{1/2}| \, |Q|. \end{aligned}$$

But

$$|Q|^2 = |Q'Q| = \frac{1}{\sigma^{*2}};$$

therefore,

$$J = |S^{1/2}|\sigma^*.$$

Moreover,

$$\begin{aligned} \mathbf{C} - \boldsymbol{\mu}_C &= S^{1/2}\left[ \frac{S^{1/2}A(A'A)^{[j]}}{\sigma^{*2}} b_j + H'\mathbf{b} \right] \\ &\quad - S^{1/2}\left[ \frac{S^{1/2}A(A'A)^{[j]}(A'A)^{(j)}A'\boldsymbol{\mu}_C}{\sigma^{*2}} + H'E(\mathbf{b}) \right] \\ &= \frac{SA(A'A)^{[j]}}{\sigma^{*2}} [b_j - (A'A)^{(j)}A'\boldsymbol{\mu}_c] + S^{1/2}H'(\mathbf{b} - E(\mathbf{b})). \end{aligned}$$

Therefore,

$$(\mathbf{C} - \boldsymbol{\mu}_C)'S^{-1}(\mathbf{C} - \boldsymbol{\mu}_C) = \frac{(b_j - (A'A)^{(j)}A'\boldsymbol{\mu}_C)^2}{\sigma^{*2}} + (\mathbf{b} - E(\mathbf{b}))'(\mathbf{b} - E(\mathbf{b})).$$

Integrating out $\mathbf{b}$ yields $(2\pi)^{(p-1)/2}$. The transformed integral (11.1.44) may be written as

$$\begin{aligned} E[|b_j|^l] &= (2\pi)^{-p(q+1)/2}|S|^{-q/2} \int_A \int_{-\infty}^{\infty} |b_j|^l (\sigma^*)^{-1} \\ &\quad \times \exp\left\{ -\frac{1}{2} \operatorname{tr} (A - \mu_A)'S^{-1}(A - \mu_A) \right\} \\ &\quad \times \exp\left\{ -\frac{1}{2} \frac{(b_j - (A'A)^{(j)}A'\boldsymbol{\mu}_C)^2}{\sigma^{*2}} \right\} db_j \, dA. \end{aligned} \tag{11.1.45}$$

For a fixed value of $A$, the following lemma shows that

$$\frac{1}{\sqrt{2\pi}\sigma^*} \int |b_j|^l \exp\left\{ -\frac{1}{2} \frac{(b_j - (A'A)^{(j)}A'\boldsymbol{\mu}_C)^2}{\sigma^{*2}} \right\} db_j \tag{11.1.46}$$

is bounded.

**Lemma 11.1.2**

If $x \sim N(\mu, \sigma^2)$, for any $B > 0$ there exist positive numbers $m(B, l)$ and $M(B, l)$ such that

$$\sigma^l m(\mathrm{B}, \mathrm{l}) \leq E[|x|^l] \leq \sigma^l M(B, l) \qquad \textbf{(11.1.47)}$$

for $|\mu/\sigma| < B$.

**Proof**

Let $l$ be even and $y = (x - \mu)/\sigma$. Then

$$\begin{aligned} E(|x|^l) &= E(x^l) = \frac{1}{\sqrt{2\pi}} \int_{-\infty}^{\infty} (\sigma y + \mu)^l \exp\left\{-\frac{1}{2} y^2\right\} dy \\ &= \sum_{k=0}^{l} \binom{l}{k} \frac{1}{\sqrt{2\pi}} \int_{-\infty}^{\infty} \sigma^{l-k} y^{l-k} \mu^k \exp\left\{-\frac{1}{2} y^2\right\} dy \\ &= \sum_{k=0}^{l} \binom{l}{k} \sigma^l \left(\frac{\mu}{\sigma}\right)^k \frac{1}{\sqrt{2\pi}} \int_{-\infty}^{\infty} y^{l-k} \exp\left\{-\frac{1}{2} y^2\right\} dy. \end{aligned} \qquad \textbf{(11.1.48)}$$

For odd $k$, the integral is zero. For even $k$,

$$\frac{1}{\sqrt{2\pi}} \int_{-\infty}^{\infty} y^{l-k} \exp\left\{-\frac{1}{2} y^2\right\} dy = \frac{(l-k)!}{2^{(l-k)/2} \dfrac{(l-k)}{2}!}; \qquad \textbf{(11.1.49)}$$

see Gnedenko (1973, p. 187). Therefore,

$$E(|x|^l) = \sigma^l \sum_{k=0}^{l} \left(\frac{\mu}{\sigma}\right)^k \frac{l!}{k! 2^{(l-k)/2} \dfrac{(l-k)}{2}!} \qquad \textbf{(11.1.50)}$$

The summation term in (11.1.50) depends on $l$ and $|\mu/\sigma| \equiv B$; it is clearly finite if $B < \infty$ and therefore less than a positive number, $M(B, l)$. Moreover, the term is positive for $B > 0$, and so is greater than a positive number $m(B, l)$.

If $l$ is odd, the above result still follows since

$$|\sigma y + \mu|^l \leq |\sigma y + \mu|^{l+1} + 1,$$

which implies

$$E(|\sigma y + \mu|^l) \leq E(|\sigma y + \mu|^{l+1}) + 1, \qquad \textbf{(11.1.51)}$$

and since $l + 1$ is even when $l$ is odd, we have $E[|x|^l]$ bounded for odd $l$. Accordingly, we can write

$$\sigma^l m(B, l) \leq E(|x|^l) \leq \sigma^l M(B, l). \qquad \square \qquad \textbf{(11.1.52)}$$

For the problem with which we are dealing,

$$\left|\frac{\mu}{\sigma}\right| = \left|\frac{(A'A)^{(j)}A'\boldsymbol{\mu}_C}{\sigma^*}\right|. \tag{11.1.53}$$

Assuming $\| \boldsymbol{\mu}_C \| < \infty$, we need to verify that $0 < |\mu/\sigma| < \infty$. Setting $(A'A)^{(j)}A' = \mathbf{a}$, we have $(A'A)^{(j)} A'\boldsymbol{\mu}_C = \mathbf{a}'\boldsymbol{\mu}_C$. It is well known that

$$\frac{(\mathbf{a}'\boldsymbol{\mu}_C)^2}{(\mathbf{a}'\mathbf{a})(\boldsymbol{\mu}_C'\boldsymbol{\mu}_C)} \leqslant 1, \tag{11.1.54}$$

since the expression on the left-hand side is the square of the cosine of the angle between the vectors $\mathbf{a}$ and $\boldsymbol{\mu}_c$. Therefore

$$\begin{aligned}\frac{(A'A)^{(j)}A'\boldsymbol{\mu}_C}{\sigma^*} &\leqslant \left(\frac{(A'A)^{(j)}A'A(A'A)^{[j]}}{(A'A)^{(j)}A'SA(A'A)^{[j]}}\right)^{1/2} (\boldsymbol{\mu}_C'\boldsymbol{\mu}_C)^{1/2}\\ &\leqslant \frac{(\boldsymbol{\mu}_C'\boldsymbol{\mu}_C)^{1/2}}{s_*^{1/2}},\end{aligned} \tag{11.1.55}$$

where $s_* = \min(s_1, \ldots, s_p)$. Thus, $|\mu/\sigma| < \infty$ when $s_* \neq 0$, and the lemma is applicable. The integral expression (11.1.45) may therefore be bounded as follows:

$$m(B, l)F(\mu_A) \leqslant E(|b_j|^l) \leqslant M(B, l)F(\mu_A), \tag{11.1.56}$$

where

$$\begin{aligned}F(\mu_A) &= (2\pi)^{-pq/2}|S|^{-q/2} \int_A [(A'A)^{(j)}A'SA(A'A)^{[j]}]^{l/2}\\ &\times \exp\left\{-\frac{1}{2}\operatorname{tr}(A - \mu_A)'S^{-1}(A - \mu_A)\right\} dA.\end{aligned} \tag{11.1.57}$$

The existence of moments thus depends on the existence of $F(\mu_A)$. Setting $s^* = \max(s_1, \ldots, s_p)$, we may write

$$s_* \leqslant \frac{(A'A)^{(j)}A'SA(A'A)^{[j]}}{(A'A)^{(j)}A'A(A'A)^{[j]}} \leqslant s^*, \tag{11.1.58}$$

and since it is easily seen that

$$(A'A)^{(j)}A'A(A'A)^{[j]} = (A'A)^{jj}, \tag{11.1.59}$$

we may bound the integral $F(\mu_A)$ by

$$0 \leqslant s_*^{l/2}G(\mu_A) \leqslant F(\mu_A) \leqslant s^{*l/2}G(\mu_A), \tag{11.1.60}$$

where

$$\begin{aligned}G(\mu_A) &= (2\pi)^{-pq/2}|S|^{-q/2} \int_A [(A'A)^{jj}]^{l/2}\\ &\times \exp\left\{-\frac{1}{2}\operatorname{tr}(A - \mu_A)'S^{-1}(A - \mu_A)\right\} dA.\end{aligned} \tag{11.1.61}$$

The next step is to make the transformation

$$A = S^{1/2}B,$$
$$\mu_A = S^{1/2}\mu_B.$$

The Jacobian being $|S|^{q/2}$ (because both $A$ and $B$ have $q$ columns), we can express $G(\mu_A)$ in terms of $B$ as

$$G(S^{1/2}\mu_B) = (2\pi)^{-pq/2}\int_B [(BSB')^{jj}]^{l/2} \times \exp\left\{-\frac{1}{2}\operatorname{tr}(B - \mu_B)'(B - \mu_B)\right\} dB. \tag{11.1.62}$$

By the definitions of $s$ and $s^*$, it follows that

$$s_* I_p \leqslant S \leqslant s^* I_p, \tag{11.1.63}$$

where the inequality $E \leqslant F$ indicates that $E - F$ is nonnegative definite. It then follows that

$$s_* B'B \leqslant B'SB \leqslant s^* B'B \tag{11.1.64}$$

and that

$$s_*(B'SB)^{-1} \leqslant (B'B)^{-1} \leqslant s^*(B'SB)^{-1}, \tag{11.1.65}$$

since $E - F$ nonnegative definite implies that $F^{-1} - E^{-1}$ is nonnegative definite. In that case, the difference between diagonal elements must be nonnegative, and we have

$$s_*(B'SB)^{jj} \leqslant (B'B)^{jj} \leqslant s^*(B'SB)^{jj}. \tag{11.1.66}$$

Applying (11.1.66) to (11.1.62) yields

$$s_*^{l/2} G(S^{1/2}\mu_B) \leqslant \Phi(\mu_B) \leqslant s^{*l/2} G(S^{1/2}\mu_B), \tag{11.1.67}$$

where

$$\Phi(\mu_B) = (2\pi)^{-pq/2}\int_B [(B'B)^{jj}]^{l/2} \exp\left\{-\frac{1}{2}\operatorname{tr}(B - \mu_B)'(B - \mu_B)\right\} dB, \tag{11.1.68}$$

and the existence of $G(S^{1/2}\mu_B)$ depends upon the existence of $\Phi(\mu_B)$.

The next step is to rearrange $B$ so that $j = 1$ and partition $B$ and $\mu_B$ as

$$B = (\mathbf{b}_{(1)}, B_1) \quad \text{and} \quad \mu_B = (\boldsymbol{\mu}_{(1)}, \mu_1).$$

Applying the rule for partitioned inverses, we obtain

$$(B'B)^{11} = [\mathbf{b}'_{(1)}Q\mathbf{b}_{(1)}]^{-1}, \tag{11.1.69}$$

where $Q = I - B_1(B_1'B_1)^{-1}B_1'$, and it follows that

$$\zeta \equiv [(B_1'B_1)^{11}]^{-1} = \mathbf{b}'_{(1)}Q\mathbf{b}_{(1)}. \tag{11.1.70}$$

Now, $Q$ is symmetric idempotent with $r(Q) = p - q + 1$, and since $\mathbf{b}_{(1)}$ and $B_1$ are independently distributed, so are $\mathbf{b}_{(1)}$ and $Q$. Accordingly, $\zeta$ is distributed as noncentral $\chi^2$, conditional on $B_1$, with noncentrality parameter $\boldsymbol{\mu}'_{(1)}Q\boldsymbol{\mu}_{(1)}/2$. Upon making this transformation, (11.1.68) may be rewritten as

$$\begin{aligned}\Phi(\mu_B) &= (2\pi)^{-p(q-1)/2} \int_{B_1} \exp\left\{-\frac{1}{2}\operatorname{tr}(B_1 - \mu_1)'(B_1 - \mu_1)\right\} \\ &\quad \times 2^{-(p-q+1)/2} \exp\left\{-\frac{1}{2}\boldsymbol{\mu}'_{(1)}Q\boldsymbol{\mu}_{(1)}\right\} \\ &\quad \times \int_0^\infty \zeta^{-l/2}\zeta^{(p-q+1-2)/2}\exp\left\{-\frac{1}{2}\zeta\right\} \\ &\quad \times \sum_{i=0}^{\infty} \frac{\left(\frac{1}{4}\boldsymbol{\mu}'_{(1)}Q\boldsymbol{\mu}_{(1)}\zeta\right)^i}{i!\Gamma\left[\frac{p-q+1}{2}+i\right]}\, d\zeta\, dB_1. \end{aligned} \tag{11.1.71}$$

The terms involving the summation index $i$ may be written as

$$\Gamma\frac{1}{\left(\frac{p-q+1}{2}\right)} \sum_{i=0}^{\infty} \frac{\left[\frac{1}{4}\boldsymbol{\mu}'_{(1)}Q\boldsymbol{\mu}_{(1)}\zeta\right]^i}{i!\left(\frac{p-q+1}{2}\right)_i}. \tag{11.1.72}$$

This is a special form of the hypergeometric function; it is denoted by

$${}_0F_1(b; z) = \sum_{i=0}^{\infty} \frac{1}{i!(b)_i} z^i. \tag{11.1.73}$$

This function converges uniformly, permitting the order of integration and summation to be interchanged. Consider the integral for $i = 0$:

$$\int_0^\infty \zeta^{(p-q+1-l)/2-1}\exp\left\{-\frac{1}{2}\zeta\right\} d\zeta. \tag{11.1.74}$$

This integral has the form

$$\int_0^\infty x^n e^{-x/2}\, dx. \tag{11.1.75}$$

To prevent divergence as $x \to \infty$, we must have $n > -1$. Accordingly, a necessary condition for the existence of (11.1.71) is $l < p - q + 1$. It is next shown that this condition is also sufficient. Assuming $l < p - q + 1$, integrate (11.1.71) in terms of gamma functions to obtain

$$\Phi(\mu_B) = \frac{(2\pi)^{p(q-1)/2}}{2^{(p-q+1)/2}} \int_{B_1} \exp\left\{-\frac{1}{2}\,\mu'_{(1)}Q\mu_{(1)}\right\}$$
$$\times \exp\left\{-\frac{1}{2}\,\mathrm{tr}(B_1 - \mu_1)'(B_1 - \mu_1)\right\}$$
$$\times \frac{\Gamma\left(\frac{p-q+1}{2} - \frac{l}{2}\right)}{\Gamma\left(\frac{p-q+1}{2}\right)}$$
$$\times \sum_{i=0}^{\infty} 2^{(p-q+1-l)/2+i} \frac{\left(\frac{1}{4}\mu'_{(1)}Q\mu_{(1)}\right)^i}{i!\left(\frac{p-q+1}{2}\right)_i}$$
$$\times \left(\frac{p-q+1}{2} - \frac{l}{2}\right)_i dB_1. \tag{11.1.76}$$

Because $((p - q + 1)/2 - (l/2))_i \leq ((p - q + 1)/2)_i$, we may bound (11.1.76) from above by removing the terms $((p - q + 1)/2 - (l/2))_i/((p - q + 1)/2)_i$. By cancelling powers of 2 and rearranging, the summation reduces to

$$\sum_{i=0}^{\infty} \frac{\left(\frac{1}{2}\,\mu'_{(1)}Q\mu_{(1)}\right)^i}{i!} = \exp\left\{\frac{1}{2}\,\mu'_{(1)}Q\mu_{(1)}\right\}, \tag{11.1.77}$$

which cancels a term in the first integral. Therefore we end up with

$$\Phi(\mu_B) \leq \frac{\Gamma\left(\frac{p-q+1}{2} - \frac{l}{2}\right)}{\Gamma\left(\frac{p-q+1}{2}\right)} 2^{-l/2}(2\pi)^{-p(q-1)/2}$$
$$\times \int_{B_1} \exp\left\{-\frac{1}{2}\,\mathrm{tr}(B_1 - \mu_1)'(B_1 - \mu_1)\right\} dB_1$$
$$= \frac{\Gamma\left(\frac{p-q+1}{2} - \frac{l}{2}\right)}{\Gamma\left(\frac{p-q+1}{2}\right)} 2^{-l/2}. \tag{11.1.78}$$

It has now been shown that $E(|b_j|^l)$ exists if and only if $l < p - q + 1$. □

To apply this result to the $k$-class estimator, recall that

$$p = r_k = \begin{cases} N - K_1, & \text{if } 0 \leq k < 1 \\ K_2, & \text{if } k = 1 \end{cases}$$

and $q = G_1 - 1$. Therefore, the $l$th moment of the $k$-class estimator exists if and only if

$$l < N - K_1 - G_1 + 2, \qquad \text{for } 0 \leq k < 1$$

and

$$l < K_2 - G_1 + 2, \qquad \text{for } k = 1 \text{ (2SLS)}.$$

Thus, for 2SLS, moments up to the order $K_2 - G_1 + 1$ exist. Since the order condition for identifiability requires $K_2 \geq G_1 - 1$, $K_2 - G_1 + 1$ is the number of overidentifying restrictions, and the result is that the number of finite moments of the 2SLS estimator is equal to the number of overidentifying restrictions. For the remaining members of the $k$-class (including OLS), moments up to the order $N - K_1 - G_1 + 1 = N - (K_1 - G_1 - 1)$ exist. Since $K_1 + G_1 - 1$ is the number of coefficients to be estimated, $N - (K_1 + G_1 - 1)$ is the number of degrees of freedom as conventionally defined.

### 11.1.2 Existence of Moments of Full Information Maximum Likelihood (FIML) Estimators and Three-Stage Least Squares (3SLS) Estimators—Arbitrary Number of Included Endogenous Variables

Sargan (1976, p. 443) notes that in an earlier paper he showed that the FIML has no first moment in general; accordingly it possesses no finite moments of higher order.

Sargan (1978) takes up the question of the existence of moments of 3SLS estimators in an equation with an arbitrary number of included endogenous variables. Two assumptions are imposed in addition to the usual ones: (1) all identifying restrictions pertain to the coefficients of a single equation, that is, there are no cross-equation constraints; and (2) the estimated covariance matrix usually used in 3SLS estimation is replaced either by a nonstochastic matrix or by modifying the estimated matrix so as to bound the ratio of its largest to smallest c.r. Under these restrictions Sargan shows that as many moments exist for the 3SLS estimator as exist for the 2SLS estimator—as many moments as there are overidentifying restrictions.

### 11.1.3 Exact Moments for 2SLS Estimators—Three Included Endogenous Variables

Ullah and Nagar (1974) compute the exact mean for 2SLS estimators when there are three included endogenous variables. By transforming the original problem into one with an identity covariance matrix, they are able to express the expected values of the estimators in terms of expectations of functions of random matrices distributed as noncentral Wishart. The expressions they derive are extremely complicated.

## 11.2 Distribution Theory of Estimators for Equations That Contain More Than Two Endogenous Variables

### 11.2.1 Exactly Identified 2SLS with Three Included Endogenous Variables

Basmann, Brown, Dawes, and Schoepfle (1971) derive the exact density for this case. As might be expected, the joint density for the two coefficients is far too complicated to be useful directly.

### 11.2.2 Instrumental Variables Estimators—Arbitrary Number of Included Endogenous Variables

As mentioned in (10.2.2b) the properties of IV estimators depend on the variables that are used as instruments. Phillips (1980a) investigates the use of the $T \times K_3$ matrix $Z_3$, which is a subset of $Z_2$, the vector of excluded exogenous variables in the model

$$\mathbf{y}_1 = Y_2\boldsymbol{\beta} + Z_1\boldsymbol{\gamma} + \mathbf{u},$$

where $\mathbf{y}_1$ is $T \times 1$, $Y_2$ is $T \times n$, and $Z_1$ is $T \times K_1$. This family of estimators includes 2SLS (where $Z_2 = Z_3$). Phillips utilizes mathematical techniques beyond the scope of this book to derive the exact distributions; references to the necessary background literature are included in his article. Although general results are again extremely complicated, the special case of 2SLS for $n = 1$ and $n = 2$ are investigated in some detail. Graphs of the densities are provided; these indicate that the density is more concentrated for $n = 1$ than for $n = 2$; the density becomes more concentrated as $K_3$ increases, although bias also increases with $K_3$; and the density of $\hat{\beta}_{1,\text{IV}}$ is sensitive to the value of $\beta_{2,\text{IV}}$ and the degree of correlation between the reduced form coefficients in the means sigma matrix.

IV estimators are also studied by Mariano (1977), who distinguishes between nonstochastic instruments (the type studied by Phillips) and stochastic instruments, where $(R'R)^{-1}R'Y_2$ serves as the instrument for $Y_2$, for nonstochastic $R$. It is shown that no moments exist when the number of nonstochastic instruments is equal to the number of coefficients to be estimated. 2SLS and OLS are included in the stochastic category, along with others described in the article.

## 11.3 Validity of Nagar and Edgeworth approximations

### 11.3.1 Nagar Expansions

Nagar (1959) suggested the type of approximation discussed in Section 2.3.2, in which expectations are taken of Taylor series expansions of functions of random variables for the purpose of approximating moments. Examples were provided to show that his method is not applicable in general. Sargan (1974, 1976) considers sufficient conditions for the application of the method and shows that $k$-class estimators and some 3SLS estimators satisfy those conditions under the usual assumptions of normal error terms and in some other cases. Clearly, a necessary condition for the use of the method is that the moments of the estimator exist, and the work reviewed in Section 11.1 is pertinent to that question.

It might be added that Sargan (1974) questions the value of approximating moments in comparison to the value of approximating distributions through the use of Edgeworth and other expansions. The latter provide more useful information for purposes of statistical inference than do the moments and may be applied to a wider set of estimators and distributional assumptions.

### 11.3.2 Edgeworth Expansions

An introduction to Edgeworth approximations may be found in Section 2.2.1; our purpose here is to discuss the question of the applicability of the method to econometric estimators. The general question of conditions under which the method may be used is taken up by Feller (1966) and Chambers (1967); for the case of econometric estimators the main technical articles are those of Sargan (1975, 1976) and Phillips (1977). An important and highly recommended expository article by Phillips (1980b) is the basis of the following discussion.

Sargan and Phillips write the error in an econometric estimator as $\hat{\beta} - \beta = e_T(p, w)$, where $T$ is the sample size, $p$ is a normally distributed vector, and $w$ is a random vector, independent of $p$. Conditions are then placed on $e_T(p, w)$ that permit an Edgeworth expansion and that are met by many of the standard econometric estimators. These included smoothness and invertibility conditions on $e_T(p, w)$ and the existence of bounded moments of all orders of $\sqrt{T}w$. Note that $e_T(p, w)$ need not possess finite moments of all orders, even though $p$ and $w$ are required to do so.

Following Phillips, the approach is conveniently illustrated with 2SLS estimators in the standard model:

$$\mathbf{y}_1 = Y_2\boldsymbol{\beta} + Z_1\boldsymbol{\gamma} + \mathbf{u}, \tag{11.3.1}$$

where $\mathbf{y}_1$ is $T \times 1$, $Y_2$ is $T \times n$, $Z_1$ is $T \times K_1$, and $\mathbf{u} \sim N_T(\mathbf{0}, \sigma^2 I)$. Letting $Z$ be the matrix of all independent variables, the 2SLS estimator of $\boldsymbol{\beta}$ is given by

$$\hat{\boldsymbol{\beta}}_{2SLS} = (Y_2'RY_2)^{-1}(Y_2'R\mathbf{y}_1), \tag{11.3.2}$$

where $R = Z(Z'Z)^{-1}Z' - Z_1(Z_1'Z_1)^{-1}Z_1'$. The relevant reduced form is written as

$$\begin{aligned} \mathbf{y}_1 &= Z\boldsymbol{\pi}_1 + \mathbf{v}_1 \\ Y_2 &= Z\Pi_2 + V_2, \end{aligned} \tag{11.3.3}$$

and the random variables $\mathbf{p}_1$ and $P_2$ are defined as

$$\begin{aligned} \mathbf{p}_1 &= \frac{Z'\mathbf{y}_1}{T} - \frac{Z'Z}{T}\boldsymbol{\pi}_1 = \frac{Z'\mathbf{v}_1}{T} \\ P_2 &= \frac{Z'Y_2}{T} - \frac{Z'Z}{T}\Pi_2 = \frac{Z'V_2}{T}. \end{aligned} \tag{11.3.4}$$

Let $S$ be such that $Z_1 = ZS$. Then we may rewrite (11.3.4) in terms of $p_1$ and $P_2$ to obtain

$$\begin{aligned}\hat{\boldsymbol{\beta}}_{2SLS} = {} & [(P_2 + M\Pi_2)'M^{-1}(P_2 + M\Pi_2) \\ & - (P_2 + M\Pi_2)'S(S'MS)^{-1}S'(P_2 + M\Pi_2)]^{-1} \\ & \times [(P_2 + M\Pi_2)'M^{-1}(\mathbf{p}_1 + M\boldsymbol{\pi}_1) \\ & - (P_2 + M\Pi_2)'S(S'MS)^{-1}S'(\mathbf{p}_1 + M\boldsymbol{\pi}_1)],\end{aligned} \qquad \textbf{(11.3.5)}$$

where $M = T^{-1}Z'Z$.

To apply Sargan's result, set $p = (\mathbf{p}_1, P_2)$ ($w$ does not appear in this application). For a given $h$, the error in $h'\hat{\boldsymbol{\beta}}$ is then $h'$ times expression (11.3.5) minus $\boldsymbol{\beta}$. Since this is a rational function of $p$ that satisfies the requirements of the theorem, an Edgeworth expansion of the probability distribution is valid; the number of moments that may be used in the expansion is equal to the number of overidentifying restrictions.

## 11.4 Lagged Endogenous Variables Included Among the Predetermined Variables

Approximation methods discussed in the previous section have recently been applied to estimators of parameters in equations that contain lagged endogenous variables among the predetermined variables. The main references are papers by Sargan (1976) and Phillips (1977). The expository article by Phillips (1980b) also deals with this subject. He considers the simple model

$$\begin{aligned} C_t &= \alpha Y_t + \beta C_{t-1} + u_t \\ Y_t &= C_t + I_t, \end{aligned} \qquad \textbf{(11.4.1)}$$

where consumption in period $t$, $C_t$, depends on lagged consumption and current income, $Y_t$. The latter is equal to consumption plus investment, $I_t$. It is assumed that $u_t \sim N(0, \sigma_u^2)$; assumptions about $I_t$ will be presented below. With the following definitions,

$$\mathbf{c}' = (C_1, \ldots, C_T),$$

$$\mathbf{c}'_{-1} = (C_0, \ldots, C_{T-1}),$$

$$\mathbf{y}' = (Y_1, \ldots, Y_T),$$

and

$$\mathbf{d}' = (I_1, \ldots, I_T),$$

it should be verified that the OLS estimators of $\alpha$ and $\beta$, $\alpha^*$ and $\beta^*$, are given by

$$\alpha^* = \frac{(\mathbf{c}'_{-1}\mathbf{c}_{-1})(\mathbf{y}'\mathbf{c}) - (\mathbf{y}'\mathbf{c}_{-1})(\mathbf{c}'_{-1}\mathbf{c})}{(\mathbf{y}'\mathbf{y})(\mathbf{c}'_{-1}\mathbf{c}_{-1}) - (\mathbf{y}'\mathbf{c}_{-1})^2} \qquad \textbf{(11.4.2)}$$

and

$$\beta^* = \frac{(\mathbf{y}'\mathbf{y})(\mathbf{c}'\mathbf{c}_{-1}) - (\mathbf{c}'_{-1}\mathbf{y})(\mathbf{y}'\mathbf{c})}{(\mathbf{y}'\mathbf{y})(\mathbf{c}'_{-1}\mathbf{c}_{-1}) - (\mathbf{y}'\mathbf{c}_{-1})^2},$$

which can be rewritten, using $\mathbf{y} = \mathbf{c} + \mathbf{d}$, as

$$\alpha^* = \frac{(\mathbf{c}_{-1}\mathbf{c}_{-1})(\mathbf{c}'\mathbf{c} + \mathbf{d}'\mathbf{c}) - (\mathbf{c}'\mathbf{c}_{-1} + \mathbf{d}'\mathbf{c}_{-1})(\mathbf{c}'_{-1}\mathbf{c})}{(\mathbf{c}'\mathbf{c} + 2\mathbf{d}'\mathbf{c} + \mathbf{d}'\mathbf{d})(\mathbf{c}'_{-1}\mathbf{c}_{-1}) - (\mathbf{c}'\mathbf{c}_{-1} + \mathbf{d}'\mathbf{c}_{-1})^2}$$

and

$$\beta^* = \frac{(\mathbf{c}'\mathbf{c}_{-1})(\mathbf{c}'\mathbf{c} + 2\mathbf{d}'\mathbf{c} + \mathbf{d}'\mathbf{d}) - (\mathbf{c}'\mathbf{c}_{-1} + \mathbf{d}'\mathbf{c}_{-1})(\mathbf{c}'\mathbf{c} + \mathbf{d}'\mathbf{c})}{(\mathbf{c}'\mathbf{c} + 2\mathbf{d}'\mathbf{c} + \mathbf{d}'\mathbf{d})(\mathbf{c}'_{-1}\mathbf{c}_{-1}) - (\mathbf{c}'\mathbf{c}_{-1} + \mathbf{d}'\mathbf{c}_{-1})^2}. \tag{11.4.3}$$

Further straightforward algebra expresses OLS and 2SLS estimators as rational functions of $q_i = (\mathbf{x}'A_i\mathbf{x} - E(\mathbf{x}'A_i\mathbf{x}))/T$ ($i = 1, 2$), where $A_1$ and $A_2$ are defined in the article. The resulting expressions satisfy the conditions of Sargan's theorem for the applicability of Edgeworth expansions. These are presented for $\alpha = 0.2$, $\beta = 0.7$, $\sigma_u^2 = 1.0$ and 0.5, and for both a first and second order autoregressive scheme for generating the $I_t$ series. Results of the calculations are displayed graphically, and the principal findings may be summarized as follows:

1. The median of the 2SLS estimator is closer than the median of the OLS estimator to the true parameter value.
2. The "bias" of the OLS estimator is upward for $\alpha$ and downward for $\beta$.
3. The dispersions of the 2SLS estimators seem somewhat larger than those of the OLS estimators.
4. The results are sensitive to the process generating the $I_t$.

Phillips concludes that the 2SLS estimators are in general superior to the OLS estimators, except that for small sample size ($T = 10$) the probability of outliers is substantial for 2SLS estimates.

## 11.5 Conclusion

This survey of articles in the areas of distribution and approximations theory for simultaneous equation estimators should convince the reader that progress has been made, but that much remains to be done. Because of the extremely complicated form of the distributions it is clear that approximation theory will play a large role, and future econometricians will have to know methods of approximation and how to apply them.

We might also add a word on an aspect of simultaneous equation theory not covered in these chapters—work on the distribution of $t$-statistics and identifiability test statistics. See Sargan (1975) for the former and Basmann, Richardson, and Rohr (1974) for both, as well as references contained therein.

## 11.6 References

Basmann, R. L. (1961), "A Note on the Exact Finite Sample Frequency Functions of Generalized Classical Linear Estimators in Two Leading Over-Indentified Cases," *Journal of the American Statistical Association,* **56**, 619–636.

Basmann, R.L. (1963), "A Note on the Exact Finite Sample Frequency Functions of Generalized Classical Linear Estimators in a Leading Three-Equation Case," *Journal of the American Statistical Association,* **58**, 161–171.

Basmann, R. L., F. L. Brown, W. S. Dawes, and G. K. Schoepfle (1971), "Exact Finite Sample Density Functions of GCL Estimators of Structural Coefficients in a Leading Exactly Identifiable Case," *Journal of the American Statistical Association,* **66**, 122–126.

Basmann, R. L., D. H. Richardson, and R. J. Rohr (1974), "An Experimental Study of Structural Estimators and Test Statistics Associated with Dynamical Econometric Models," *Econometrica,* **42**, 717–730.

Chambers, J. M. (1967), "On Methods of Asymptotic Approximation for Multivariate Distributions," *Biometrika,* **54**, 367–383.

Feller, W. (1966), *An Introduction to Probability Theory and Its Applications,* Vol. II, New York: Wiley.

Gnedenko, B. (1973), *The Theory of Probability,* Moscow: Mir.

Hatanaka, M. (1973), "On the Existence and Approximation Formulae for the Moments of the *k*-Class Estimators," *Economic Studies Quarterly,* **24**, 1–15.

Holly, A. and P. C. B. Phillips (1979), "A Saddlepoint Approximation to the Distribution of the *k*-Class Estimator of a Coefficient in a Simultaneous System," *Econometrica,* **47**, 1527–1547.

Kinal, T. W. (1980), "The Existence of Moments of *k*-Class Estimators," *Econometrica,* **48**, 241–249.

Mariano, R. S. (1972), "The Existence of Moments of the Ordinary Least Squares and Two Stage Least Squares Estimators," *Econometrica,* **40**, 643–652.

Mariano, R. S. (1977), "Finite Sample Properties of Instrumental Variable Estimators of Structural Coefficients," *Econometrica,* **45**, 487–496.

Nagar, A. L. (1959), "The Bias and Moment Matrix of the General *k*-Class Estimators of the Parameters in Simultaneous Equations," *Econometrica,* **27**, 575–595.

Phillips, P. C. B. (1977), "A General Theorem in the Theory of Asymptotic Expansions as Approximations to the Finite Sample Distributions of Econometric Estimators," *Econometrica,* **45**, 1517–1534.

Phillips, P. C. B. (1980a), "The Exact Distribution of Instrumental Variable Estimators in an Equation Containing $n + 1$ Endogenous Variables," *Econometrica,* **48**, 861–878.

Phillips, P. C. B. (1980b), "Finite Sample Theory and the Distributions of Alternative Estimators of the Marginal Propensity to Consume," *Review of Economic Studies,* **47**, 183–224.

Sargan, J. D. (1974), "The Validity of Nagar's Expansion for the Moments of Econometric Estimators," *Econometrica,* **42**, 169–176.

Sargan, J. D. (1975), "Gram-Charlier Approximations Applied to *t* Ratios of *k*-class Estimators," *Econometrica,* **43,** 327–346.

Sargan, J. D. (1976), "Econometric Estimators and the Edgeworth Approximation," *Econometrica,* **44**, 421–448.

Sargan, J. D. (1978), "On the Existence of the Moments of 3SLS Estimators," *Econometrica,* **46**, 1329–1350.

Ullah, A. and A. L. Nagar (1974), "The Exact Mean of the Two Stage Least Squares Estimator of the Structural Parameters in an Equation Having Three Endogenous Variables," *Econometrica,* **42**, 749–758.

# APPENDIX A

# Complex Variables

In applied mathematics, polynomial equations of the form

$$a_0 + a_1Z + a_2Z^2 + \cdots + a_nZ^n = 0$$

often must be solved for $Z$. Equations of this form do not, in general, have solutions if $Z$ is required to be a real number. For example, the equation $1 + Z^2 = 0$ has no solution for real $Z$. To allow solutions to polynomial equations, mathematicians have devised a generalization of the real number system called the *complex number system*. In that system $i$ is defined as the solution to $1 + Z^2 = 0$, that is, $i \equiv \sqrt{-1}$. A complex number $Z$ can be written as

$$Z = X + iY,$$

where $X$ and $Y$ are real numbers. $X$ is referred to as the *real part* of $Z$, $Y$ is referred to as the *imaginary part* of $Z$, and we sometimes write $\text{Re } Z = X$ and $\text{Im } Z = Y$. The "fundamental theorem of algebra" shows that all polynomial equations have solutions if we allow the solutions to be complex numbers.

## A.1 Elementary Properties

We now examine some properties of the complex number system.

**Definition**

*Equality*: Two complex numbers $Z_1 = X_1 + iY_1$ and $Z_2 = X_2 + iY_2$ are said to be equal if and only if $X_1 = X_2$ and $Y_1 = Y_2$. By this definition $Z_1 = 0$ iff $X_1 = 0$ and $Y_1 = 0$.

**Definition**

*Addition*: A complex number $Z_3 = X_3 + iY_3$ is the sum of two complex numbers $Z_1$ and $Z_2$, $Z_1 + Z_2$, if and only if $X_3 = X_1 + X_2$ and $Y_3 = Y_1 + Y_2$. That is

$$Z_3 = Z_1 + Z_2 \quad \text{iff} \quad X_3 = X_1 + X_2 \quad \text{and} \quad Y_3 = Y_1 + Y_2.$$

**Definition**

*Subtraction*: A complex number $Z_3 = X_3 + iY_3$ is the difference of two complex numbers $Z_1$ and $Z_2$, $Z_1 - Z_2$, if and only if

$$X_3 = X_1 - X_2 \quad \text{and} \quad Y_3 = Y_1 - Y_2.$$

**Definition**

*Multiplication*: $Z_3$ is the product of $Z_2$ and $Z_1$ if and only if $Z_3 = X_1X_2 - Y_1Y_2 + i(X_1Y_2 + X_2Y_1)$. This can be seen as follows:

$$\begin{aligned} Z_3 &= Z_1 \cdot Z_2 \\ &= (X_1 + iY_1)(X_2 + iY_2) \\ &= X_1X_2 + iX_1Y_2 + iX_2Y_1 + i^2Y_1Y_2 \\ &= X_1X_2 - Y_1Y_2 + i(X_1Y_2 + X_2Y_1). \end{aligned}$$

Notice that in the computation above, $i$ is treated as a variable, that is, $i$ is treated in the same fashion as $X_1$, and $Y_1$. Note that we have used $i^2 = -1$.

**Definition**

*Inversion*: The inverse of a complex number, $Z_1$, written as $Z_1^{-1}$, or $1/Z_1$, can be written as

$$Z_1^{-1} = \frac{X_1}{X_1^2 + Y_1^2} - \frac{Y_1}{X_1^2 + Y_1^2}\, i.$$

To derive this result, set $Z = Z_1^{-1}$, then

$$\begin{aligned} Z_1 \cdot Z &= (X_1 + iY_1)(X + iY) \\ &= (X_1X - Y_1Y) + i(X_1Y + Y_1X) \\ &= 1 + i0. \end{aligned}$$

We can solve for $X$ and $Y$ by solving the two-equation, two-variable system

$$\begin{aligned} X_1X - Y_1Y &= 1 \\ X_1Y + Y_1X &= 0, \end{aligned}$$

which yields

$$X = \frac{X_1}{X_1^2 + Y_1^2}$$

$$Y = -\frac{Y_1}{X_1^2 + Y_1^2}.$$

**Definition**

*Division*: We say that $Z_3 = Z_2/Z_1$, $Z_1 \neq 0$, if and only if

$$X_3 = \frac{X_1X_2 + Y_1Y_2}{X_1^2 + Y_1^2}$$

and

$$Y_3 = \frac{X_1Y_2 - X_2Y_1}{X_1^2 + Y_1^2}.$$

This can be seen by writing

$$\begin{aligned}
\frac{Z_2}{Z_1} &= Z_2Z_1^{-1} \\
&= (X_2 + iY_2)\left(\frac{X_1}{X_1^2 + Y_1^2} - i\frac{Y_1}{X_1^2 + Y_1^2}\right) \\
&= \frac{X_1X_2 + Y_1Y_2}{X_1^2 + Y_1^2} + i\left(\frac{X_1Y_2 - X_2Y_1}{X_1^2 + Y_1^2}\right).
\end{aligned}$$

Two concepts that are useful in dealing with complex numbers are the *conjugate* and the *modulus* of a complex number. The modulus of a complex number $Z = X + iY$, $|Z|$, is defined as

$$|Z| \equiv \sqrt{X^2 + Y^2},$$

and the conjugate of $Z$, $\bar{Z}$ is

$$\bar{Z} \equiv X - iY.$$

It is easily seen that the product of a complex number and its conjugate is the square of its modulus, that is

$$Z \cdot \bar{Z} = |Z|^2.$$

It is often convenient to write a complex number in the polar form, $Z = re^{i\theta}$, or $X + iY = re^{i\theta}$. To do this, start from the expansion of $e^{\alpha}$,

$$e^{\alpha} = 1 + \alpha + \frac{\alpha^2}{2!} + \frac{\alpha^3}{3!} + \cdots.$$

Then we can write

$$\begin{aligned}
e^{i\theta} &= 1 + (i\theta) + \frac{(i\theta)^2}{2!} + \frac{(i\theta)^3}{3!} + \cdots \\
&= 1 + i\theta - \frac{\theta_2}{2!} - \frac{i\theta^3}{3!} + \frac{\theta^4}{4!} + \frac{i\theta^5}{5!} - \cdots \\
&= \left[1 - \frac{\theta^2}{2!} + \frac{\theta^4}{4!} - \frac{\theta^6}{6!} + \cdots\right] \\
&\quad + i\left[\theta - \frac{\theta^3}{3!} + \frac{\theta^5}{5!} - \frac{\theta^7}{7!} + \cdots\right] \\
&= \cos\theta + i\sin\theta,
\end{aligned}$$

where we have used the expansions for cos θ and sin θ. (Note that $i$ was manipulated as a variable, except that $i^2 = -1$.) Using the above we can write

$$X + iY = re^{i\theta}$$
$$= r[\cos\theta + i\sin\theta].$$

Setting the real and imaginary parts equal yields

$$X = r\cos\theta$$
$$Y = r\sin\theta.$$

Solving this for $r$ and $\theta$ terms of $X$ and $Y$, we have

$$\theta = \tan^{-1}\left(\frac{Y}{X}\right)$$
$$r = (X^2 + Y^2)^{1/2}.$$

Thus, $r = |Z|$, and $\theta$ is called the *argument* of $Z$, denoted by arg $Z$. These equations yield a unique solution for $r$, but not for $\theta$—if $\theta'$ is a solution, $\theta' + 2\pi$ is also a solution. To get a unique solution for $\theta$ we restrict the range of $\theta$ to a range of length $2\pi$; $\theta$ is often restricted to be in the interval $(-\pi, \pi)$. The interval to which $\theta$ is restricted is referred to as the *principal range* of $\theta$.

It is often useful to view complex numbers geometrically. To do so we place the real part of the complex number on the horizontal axis and the imaginary part on the vertical axis. See Figure A.1. Viewed geometrically, addition of complex numbers is just vector addition; see Figure A.2.

The modulus ($r_1$)can be seen in Figure A.3 as the distance from the point to the origin, and $\theta_1$ can be seen to be the angle whose tangent is $Y_1/X_1$.

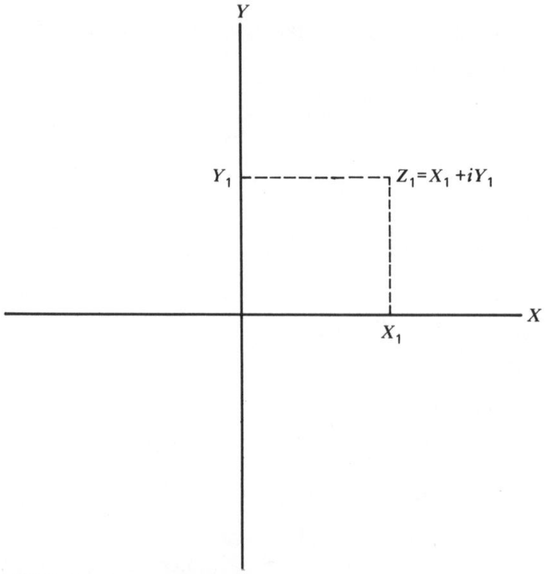


**FIGURE A.1 The complex plane.**

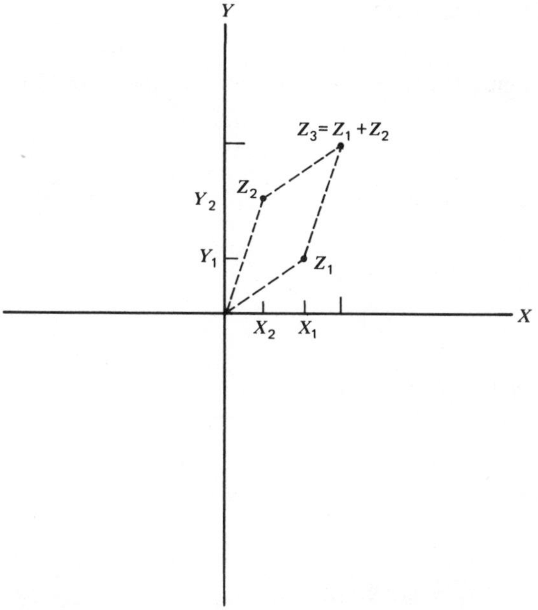


**FIGURE A.2 Addition of complex numbers.**

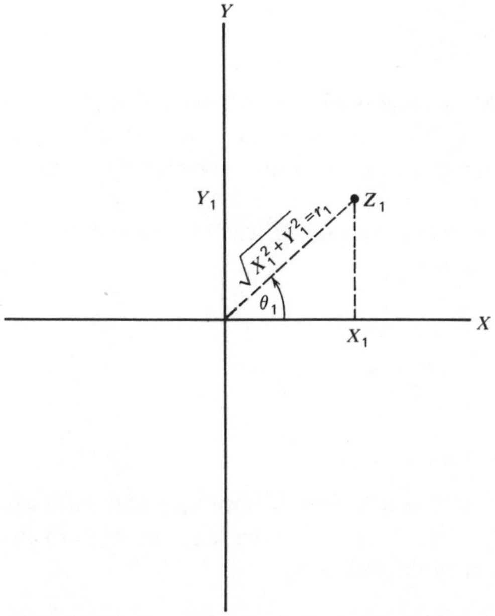


**FIGURE A.3 Modulus and argument of $Z$.**

## A.2 Functions of a Complex Variable

For many purposes it is useful to examine *functions of a complex variable*. We write these as

$$Z_2 = f(Z_1)$$

or

$$X_2 + iY_2 = f(X_1 + iY_1)$$

or

$$X_2 + iY_2 = u(X_1, Y_1) + i\,v(X_1, Y_1).$$

For example

$$\begin{aligned} Z_2 &= f(Z_1) \\ &= (X_1 + iY_1)^2 \\ &= X_1^2 - Y_1^2 + i(2X_1Y_1); \end{aligned}$$

or

$$X_2 + iY_2 = u(X_1, Y_1) + i\,v(X_1, Y_1),$$

where

$$u(X_1, Y_1) = X_1^2 - Y_1^2$$
$$v(X_1, Y_1) = 2X_1Y_1.$$

The theory of functions of a complex variable is a highly developed branch of mathematics that contains many important and interesting theorems. However, since the main body of this text requires only a minimal knowledge of functions of a complex variable, we present only a small amount of this theory.

The first theorem we present contains necessary and sufficient conditions for differentiability of a function of a complex variable.

**Theorem A.2.1**

Let

$$f(Z) = u(X, Y) + i\,v(X, Y)$$

be a function of the complex variable $Z = X + iY$. Then a necessary and sufficient condition for $f(Z)$ to be differentiable at $Z_0 = X_0 + iY_0$ is that the functions $u(X, Y)$ and $v(X, Y)$ be differentiable at $(X_0, Y_0)$ and satisfy the following:

$$\frac{\partial u}{\partial X} = \frac{\partial v}{\partial Y},$$

and

$$\frac{\partial u}{\partial Y} = -\frac{\partial v}{\partial X}$$

at $(X_0, Y_0)$. If these conditions are satisifed we can write

$$f'(Z_0) = \frac{\partial u}{\partial X} + i\frac{\partial v}{\partial X}$$

$$= \frac{\partial v}{\partial Y} - i\frac{\partial u}{\partial Y}.$$

The above necessary and sufficient conditions are referred to as the Cauchy-Riemann equations.

Since the Cauchy-Riemann equations may seem strange, we present an example to show how to use them. We wish to find $f'(Z)$, where $f(Z) = Z^N = (X + iY)^N$.

$$(X + iY)^N = X^N + NX^{N-1}(iY) + \frac{N(N-1)}{2!}X^{N-2}(iY)^2$$

$$+ \frac{N(N-1)(N-2)}{3!}X^{N-3}(iY)^3 + \frac{N(N-1)(N-2)(N-3)}{4!}X^{N-4}(iY)^4$$

$$+ \cdots + \frac{N(N-1)\cdots(N-K+1)}{(K-1)!}X^{N-K}(iY)^K + \cdots$$

$$= X^N - \frac{N(N-1)}{2!}X^{N-2}Y^2$$

$$+ \frac{N(N-1)(N-2)(N-3)}{4!}X^{N-4}Y^4 - \cdots$$

$$+ i[NX^{N-1}Y - \frac{N(N-1)(N-2)}{3!}X^{N-3}Y^3$$

$$+ \frac{N(N-1)(N-2)(N-3)(N-4)}{5!}X^{N-5}Y^5 - \cdots].$$

$$\frac{\partial u(X, Y)}{\partial X} = NX^{N-1} - \frac{N(N-1)(N-2)}{2!}X^{N-3}Y^2$$

$$+ \frac{N\cdots(N-4)}{4!}X^{N-5}Y^4 - \cdots$$

$$\frac{\partial v(X, Y)}{\partial X} = N(N-1)X^{N-2}Y - \frac{N(N-1)(N-2)(N-3)}{3!}X^{N-4}Y^3$$

$$+ \frac{N\cdots(N-5)}{5!}X^{N-6}Y^5 - \cdots$$

$$\frac{\partial u(X, Y)}{\partial Y} = -N(N-1)X^{N-2}Y + \frac{N(N-1)(N-2)(N-3)}{3!}X^{N-4}Y^3 - \cdots$$

$$\frac{\partial v(X, Y)}{\partial Y} = NX^{N-1} - \frac{N(N-1)(N-2)}{2!}X^{N-3}Y^2 + \frac{N\cdots(N-4)}{4!}X^{N-5}Y^4 - \cdots$$

Notice that in this example

$$\frac{\partial u}{\partial X} = \frac{\partial v}{\partial Y} \quad \text{and} \quad \frac{\partial u}{\partial Y} = -\frac{\partial v}{\partial X}.$$

Hence we can write

$$\begin{aligned}
\frac{dZ^N}{dZ} &= \frac{\partial u}{\partial X} + i\frac{\partial v}{\partial X} \\
&= N\left[X^{N-1} - \frac{(N-1)(N-2)}{2!}X^{N-3}Y^2\right. \\
&\quad \left. + \frac{(N-1)\cdots(N-4)}{4!}X^{N-5}Y^4 - \cdots\right] \\
&\quad + iN\left[(N-1)X^{N-2}Y - \frac{(N-1)(N-2)(N-3)}{3!}X^{N-4}Y^3 + \cdots\right] \\
&= N\left[X^{N-1} + (N-1)X^{N-2}(iY) + \frac{(N-1)(N-2)}{2!}X^{N-3}(iY)^2\right. \\
&\quad \left. + \frac{(N-1)(N-2)(N-3)}{3!}X^{N-4}(iY)^3 + \cdots\right] \\
&= N[X + iY]^{N-1} \\
&= NZ^{N-1}.
\end{aligned}$$

This means that $Z^N$ is differentiable with derivative $NZ^{N-1}$. For example, if

$$P(Z) = a_0 + a_1Z + a_2Z^2 + \cdots + a_NZ^N,$$

then

$$\frac{dP(Z)}{dZ} = a_1 + 2a_2Z + 3a_3Z^2 + \cdots + Na_NZ^{N-1}.$$

A function $f(z)$ which is differentiable at every point on a domain $G$ is said to be *analytic* on $G$. Analytic functions can be expanded in a *Taylor series expansion*.

**Theorem A.2.2**

Let $f(z)$ be analytic on a domain $G$. Let $z_0$ be an arbitrary interior point of $G$. Then inside the radius of convergence,

$$\begin{aligned}
f(z) &= \sum_{i=0}^{\infty} \frac{f^{(i)}(z_0)}{i!}(z - z_0)^i \\
&= f(z_0) + f^{(1)}(z_0)(z - z_0) + \frac{f^{(2)}(z_0)(z - z_0)}{2!} + \cdots
\end{aligned}$$

**Proof**

Churchill, Brown, and Verhey (1974, p. 146). □

Therefore, if a function of a complex number is analytic, we can use a Taylor series expansion (or a McClaurin series expansion) in much the same way as with a function of a real variable.

We next present, without proof, the derivatives of a number of common complex functions. Note that in many cases the formula for the derivative of a complex function is the same as the formula for the corresponding real functions.

**Theorem A.2.3**

1. $\frac{d}{dz} z^N = Nz^{N-1};$

2. $\frac{d}{dz}(a_0 + a_1 z + a_2 z^2 + \cdots + a_N z^n) = a_1 + 2a_2 z + \cdots + Na_N z^{N-1};$

3. $\frac{d}{dz} e^{\theta z} = \theta e^{\theta z};$

4. $\frac{d}{dz} \ln(z) = \frac{1}{z};$

5. $\frac{d}{dz} \sin(z) = \cos(z);$

6. $\frac{d}{dz} \cos(z) = -\sin(z);$

7. $\frac{d}{dz} \tan(z) = \sec^2(z).$

**Proof**

Churchill, Brown, and Verhey (1974), pp. 52–72). □

Integration of complex functions is not difficult, but its explanation requires more background than can be included in a brief appendix. Fortunately, in most of the applications contained in this book in which an integral of a function of a complex variable is required, the correct answer will be obtained if $i$ is regarded as a constant with the property that $i^2 = -1$. Deeper analysis of integration in the complex plane is beyond the scope of this book.

## A.3 Reference

Churchill, R. V., J. W. Brown, and R. F. Verhey (1974), *Complex Variables and Application*, New York: McGraw-Hill.

# APPENDIX B

# O, o, and Order in Probability

In doing theoretical econometric work it often happens that certain terms in an equation are small relative to other terms and can therefore be ignored. To do this formally the concept of order in probability has been defined. But before defining order in probability we first define the concept of order as used in the theory of real variables.

**Definition**

Let $\{a_t\}$ and $\{b_t\}$ be sequences of real variables and positive real variables, respectively. Then $a_t$ is of *smaller order* than $b_t$, denoted by

$$a_t = o(b_t),$$

if

$$\lim_{t\to\infty} \frac{a_t}{b_t} = 0.$$

**Definition**

Let $\{a_t\}$ and $\{b_t\}$ be sequences of real variables and positive real variables, respectively. Then $a_t$ is *at most of order* $b_t$, denoted by

$$a_t = O(b_t),$$

if there exists a positive real number $M$ such that $|a_t|/b_t \leq M$ for all $t$.

In determining the order of a sequence the following theorems are useful.

**Theorem B.1**

Let $\{a_t\}$ and $\{b_t\}$ be sequences of real numbers and let $\{c_t\}$ and $\{d_t\}$ be sequences of positive real numbers. If $a_t = o(c_t)$ and $b_t = o(d_t)$, then

$$\text{(i)}\ a_tb_t = o(c_td_t),$$
$$\text{(ii)}\ |a_t|^r = o(c_t^r) \quad \text{for} \quad r > 0,$$
$$\text{(iii)}\ a_t + b_t = o[\max(c_t, d_t)].$$

**Theorem B.2**

Let $\{a_t\}$ and $\{b_t\}$ be sequences of real numbers and let $\{c_t\}$ and $\{d_t\}$ be sequences of positive real numbers. If $a_t = O(c_t)$ and $b_t = O(d_t)$, then

$$\text{(i)}\ a_tb_t = O(c_td_t),$$
$$\text{(ii)}\ |a_t|^r = O(c_t^r) \quad \text{for} \quad r \geq 0,$$
$$\text{(iii)}\ a_t + b_t = O[\max(c_t, d_t)].$$

**Theorem B.3**

Let $\{a_t\}$ and $\{b_t\}$ be sequences of real numbers. Let $\{c_t\}$ and $\{d_t\}$ be sequences of positive real numbers. If $a_t = o(c_t)$ and $b_t = O(d_t)$, then

$$a_t b_t = O(c_t d_t).$$

There are stochastic analogs to these definitions for sequences of random variables.

**Definition**

Let $\{y_t\}$ be a sequence of random variables and $\{a_t\}$ a sequence of nonstochastic positive real variables. Then $y_t$ is of *smaller order in probability* than $a_t$, denoted by

$$y_t = o_p(a_t),$$

if

$$\text{plim}\left(\frac{y_t}{a_t}\right) = 0.$$

**Definition**

Let $\{y_t\}$ be a sequence of random variables and $\{a_t\}$ a sequence of nonstochastic positive real variables. Then $y_t$ is *at most of order in probability* $a_t$, denoted by

$$y_t = O_p(a_t),$$

if, for every $\epsilon > 0$, there is a positive $M(\epsilon)$ such that

$$P\left\{\frac{|y_t|}{a_t} > M(\epsilon)\right\} < \epsilon.$$

Let us examine a few examples of order in probability. Assume $x_t \sim N(0, \sigma^2)$ and consider the sequence,

$$y_t = \frac{x_t}{t}.$$

If follows that $E(y_t) = 0$, $E[y_t - E(y_t)]^2 = \sigma^2/t^2$, and $\lim_{t\to\infty} E[y_t - E(y_t)]^2 = 0$, so that plim $x_t/t = 0$. Thus $x_t$ is of smaller order in probability than $t$, or $x_t = o_p(t)$. Moreover, for the series $x_t$ we have $E(x_t/t) = 0$ and $\lim_t E[x_t/\sqrt{t} - E(x_t/\sqrt{t})]^2 = 0$, so that $x_t$ is also of order smaller than $\sqrt{t}$, that is, $x_t = o_p(t^{1/2})$.

We now examine an example of a sequence of $O_p(a_t)$. Assume $x_t \sim N(\mu, \sigma^2)$ and consider the sequence

$$y_T = \sqrt{T}\frac{(\bar{x}_t - \mu)}{\sigma},$$

where $\bar{x}_T = (1/T)\Sigma_{t=1}^{T} x_t$. Since

$$\frac{\sqrt{T}\,(\bar{x}_T - \mu)}{\sigma} \xrightarrow{d} N(0, 1),$$

$y_T = O_p(\sigma/\sqrt{T})$.

For an excellent discussion of order in probability and related topics, see Fuller (1976).

## B.1 Reference

Fuller, W. A. (1976), *Introduction to Statistical Time Series,* New York: Wiley.

# APPENDIX C

# Characteristic Functions

A characteristic function is a mathematical device used by statisticians to derive properties of functions of a random variable. It is used to transform a density function into a space in which manipulation of the r.v. is easier than in the original space, and then the transformation is inverted back to the space of the density function. Using characteristic functions is analogous to using logarithms. If we were interested in finding the product of $A$ and $B$, we could transform $A$ and $B$ to their logarithms, add the logarithms, and then invert by taking the antilogarithm. This process can be seen diagrammatically as

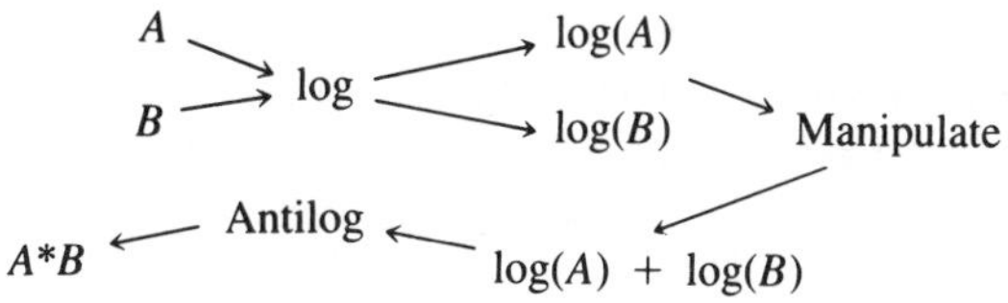


In using characteristic functions, we follow a similar procedure. We first transform the density function into the characteristic function, then we manipulate the characteristic function, and finally we transform back to the density function.

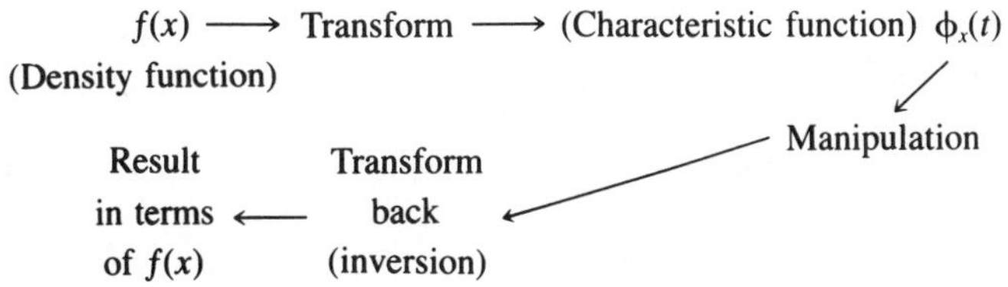


## C.1 Introduction

We begin by defining the *characteristic function* (c.f.).

### Definition

Let $X$ be a random variable with distribution function $F$. The *characteristic function of* $F(x)$, $\phi_x(t)$, is defined as

$$\phi_x(t) \equiv E[e^{itx}].$$

If $X$ is a continuous random variable with density function $f(x)$, then $\phi_x(t) \equiv \int_{-\infty}^{\infty} e^{itx} f(x)\, dx$.[1]

It is sometimes useful to deal with a concept that is closely related to the characteristic function, the *moment generating function* (m.g.f.).

**Definition**

Let $X$ be a random variable with density function $f$. The *moment generating function* $M_x(t)$ is defined as

$$
\begin{aligned}
M_x(t) &= E(e^{tx}) \\
&= \int_{-\infty}^{\infty} e^{tx} f(x)\, dx.
\end{aligned}
$$

Although the moment generating function is simpler than the characteristic function in that it does not use complex numbers, the c.f. is used because it exists for every random variable, while the m.g.f. does not exist for certain r.v.'s. For example, if $X$ has a Cauchy distribution, that is, $X$ has the density function

$$f(x) = \frac{1}{\pi(1 + x^2)}, \qquad -\infty < x < \infty,$$

then the m.g.f. does *not* exist, but the c.f. does.

The definition allows us to find the characteristic function of a given d.f. In some cases, we wish to find the d.f. of a given characteristic function; for this purpose we have the *inversion theorem.*

**Theorem C.1.1**

If $\phi_x(t)$ is the characteristic function of the distribution function $F(x)$, and if $F(x)$ is continuous in $(a - c, a + c)$, then

$$F(a + c) - F(a - c) = \lim_{T\to\infty} \frac{1}{\pi} \int_{-T}^{T} \frac{\sin(ct)}{t} e^{-ita} \phi_x(t)\, dt.$$

If the density function $f(x)$ exists at $x'$, then

$$f(x') = \frac{1}{2\pi} \int_{-\infty}^{\infty} e^{-itx'} \phi_x(t)\, dt.$$

[1]This definition of a characteristic function is somewhat restrictive in that it requires the random variable $X$ to be continuous and to possess a density function. A more advanced treatment would define the characteristic function in terms of the Stieltjes integral. The use of the Stieltjes integral allows the characteristic function to be defined for a random variable even if it is discrete or has no density function.

**Proof**

Wilks (1962, p. 116). □

## C.2 Properties of Characteristic Functions

An important property of characteristic functions is that they are unique.

**Theorem C.2.1**

Let $X$ and $Y$ be random variables with distribution functions $F_x$ and $F_y$ and characteristic functions $\phi_x$ and $\phi_y$. Then $F_y(s) = F_x(s)$ for all real $s$ iff $\phi_x(t) = \phi_y(t)$ for all real $t$.

**Proof**

Wilks (1962, p. 117). □

A major use of this theorem is in proving that two random variables are identically distributed. Showing that two random variables have the same characteristic function is equivalent to showing they are identically distributed.

Perhaps the most useful aspect of characteristic functions is the relationship between convergence of characteristic function and convergence of distribution functions.

**Theorem C.2.2**

Let $\{X_j\}$ be a sequence of random variables with characteristic functions $\{\phi_j(t)\}$. Let $X$ be a random variable with distribution function $F$ and characteristic function $\phi$. Then $X_j \xrightarrow{d} X$ if and only if

$$\lim_{j\to\infty} \phi_j(t) = \phi(t) \quad \text{for every } t \text{ and } \phi(t) \text{ is continuous at } t = 0.$$

**Proof**

Wilks, (1962, p. 122). □

This theorem says that if we can show that the sequence of characteristic functions of a sequence of random variables has a limit, then (1) the sequence of random variables converges in distribution, and (2) the random variable to which the sequence converges is that random variable whose characteristic function is equal to the limit of the sequence of characteristic functions. This is a very useful theorem, since it is often easier to show convergence using characteristic functions than using distribution functions.

We now present a number of results that are useful in proving results with characteristic functions.

**Theorem C.2.3**

Let $Z$ and $X$ be random variables and let $Z = a + bX$, where $a$ and $b$ are constants. Then

$$\phi_z(t) = e^{ita}\, \phi_x(bt)$$

**Proof**

$$\begin{aligned}\phi_z(t) &= E[e^{itz}] \\ &= E[e^{ita} \cdot e^{itbx}] \\ &= e^{ita}\, E[e^{i(tb)x}] \\ &= e^{ita}\, \phi_x(bt).\end{aligned}$$

□

The characteristic function is particularly useful for sums of independent random variables.

**Theorem C.2.4**

Let $X$, $Y$, and $Z$ be random variables. Let $X$ and $Y$ be independent variables, and let $Z = X + Y$. Then

$$\phi_z(t) = \phi_x(t) \cdot \phi_y(t).$$

**Proof**

$$\begin{aligned}\phi_z(t) &= E[e^{itz}] \\ &= E[e^{itx} \cdot e^{ity}] \\ &= E[e^{itx}] \cdot E[e^{ity}] \\ &= \phi_x(t) \cdot \phi_y(t).\end{aligned}$$

□

A similar result can be obtained for linear combinations of independent random variables.

**Theorem C.2.5**

Let $X_i$, $i = 1, \ldots, N$, be independent random variables, let the $\alpha_i$ be constants, and let $Z = \Sigma_{i=1}^{N} \alpha_i X_i$. Then

$$\phi_z(t) = \prod_{i=1}^{N} \phi_{x_i}(\alpha_i t).$$

**Proof**

$$\begin{aligned}
\phi_z(t) &= E[e^{itz}] \\
&= E\left[e^{it\sum_{i=1}^{N}\alpha_i x_i}\right] \\
&= E\left[\prod_{i=1}^{N} e^{it\alpha_i x_i}\right] \\
&= \prod_{i=1}^{N} E[e^{it\alpha_i x_i}] \\
&= \prod_{i=1}^{N} \phi_{x_i}(\alpha_i t).
\end{aligned}$$

□

In statistical work we often want to show that one random variables has the same distribution as another. To do that, we must know the form of the characteristic functions for various random variables. Since the normal distribution is of particular interest in statistical theory, we present several theorems about the c.f.'s of normal variates.

**Theorem C.2.6**

Let $x$ have a $N(0, 1)$ distribution, then

$$\phi_x(t) = e^{-t^2/2}.$$

**Proof**

$$\begin{aligned}
E[e^{itx}] &= \frac{1}{\sqrt{2\pi}} \int_{-\infty}^{\infty} e^{itx}\, e^{-x^2/2}\, dx \\
&= \frac{1}{\sqrt{2\pi}} \int_{-\infty}^{\infty} e^{-1/2[x^2 - 2itx]}\, dx \\
&= \frac{1}{\sqrt{2\pi}} \int_{-\infty}^{\infty} e^{-1/2[x^2 - 2itx - t^2]}\, e^{-t^2/2}\, dx \\
&= e^{-t^2/2} \frac{1}{\sqrt{2\pi}} \int_{-\infty}^{\infty} e^{-1/2(x - it)^2}\, dx \\
&= e^{-t^2/2},
\end{aligned}$$

since the last integral may be regarded as the density of a $N(it, 1)$ variable integrated from $-\infty$ to $\infty$. □

**Theorem C.2.7**

Let $X$ have a $N(\mu, \sigma^2)$ distribution. Then

$$\phi_x(t) = e^{\mu t - \sigma^2 t^2/2}.$$

**Proof**

We can write $X = \mu + \sigma Y$ where $Y$ has a $N(0, 1)$ distribution. Application of Theorem C.2.5 then implies

$$\begin{aligned}\phi_x(t) &= e^{\mu t} \cdot \phi_y(\sigma t) \\ &= e^{\mu t} \cdot e^{-\sigma^2 t^2/2} \\ &= e^{\mu t - \sigma^2 t^2/2}\end{aligned}$$

□

## C.3 Characteristic Functions and Moments

Many times in econometrics we are interested in computing moments of random variables. For this reason, we present some results concerning the relationship between characteristic functions and moments.

**Theorem C.3.1**

Let $X$ be a random variable whose first $r$ moments exist. Then the characteristic function $\phi_x(t)$ is differentiable $r$ times and

$$E(x^n) = (i)^{-n}\, \phi_x^{(n)}(0), \qquad n \leq r,$$

where $\phi_x^n(0)$ is the $n$th derivative of $\phi_x$ evaluated at 0.

**Proof**

$$\phi_x(t) = \int_{-\infty}^{\infty} e^{itx} f(x)\, dx$$

$$\begin{aligned}\phi_x^{(1)}(t) &= \int_{-\infty}^{\infty} \left(\frac{\partial}{\partial t} e^{itx}\right) f(x)\, dx \\ &= \int_{-\infty}^{\infty} ix\, e^{itx} f(x)\, dx.\end{aligned}$$

Hence, at $t = 0$

$$\begin{aligned}\phi_x^{(1)}(0) &= i \int_{-\infty}^{\infty} x\, f(x)\, dx \\ &= i\, E(x).\end{aligned}$$

Moreover,

$$\begin{aligned}\phi_x^{(n)}(t) &= \int_{-\infty}^{\infty} \left[\frac{\partial^n}{(\partial t)^n} e^{itx}\right] f(x)\, dx \\ &= \int_{-\infty}^{\infty} (ix)^n e^{itx} f(x)\, dx,\end{aligned}$$

and at $t = 0$,

$$\begin{aligned}\phi_x^{(n)}(0) &= i^n \int_{-\infty}^{\infty} x^n f(x)\, dx \\ &= i^n E(x^n).\end{aligned}$$

Thus

$$E(x^n) = (i)^{-n}\,\phi_x^{(n)}(0). \qquad \square$$

Note that Theorem C.3.1 requires the existence of the first $r$ moments. Unfortunately, the converse of C.3.1 does not hold. Differentiability of the characteristic function does not imply the existence of the moments. However, if C.3.1 had been written in terms of the m.g.f. rather than the c.f., differentiability would ensure the existence of the moments. This occurs because the existence of the m.g.f. rules out those distributions that violate the converse of C.3.1.

A final theorem that is often useful concerns the approximation of the characteristic function by the moments of a random variable.

### Theorem C.3.2

If the $n$th moment of a random variable $X$ exists, then

$$\phi_x(t) = \sum_{j=0}^{n} \frac{(it)^j}{j!} E(X^j) + o(t^n), \qquad \text{as} \quad t \to 0.$$

### Proof

Approximating $e^{ixt}$ around $t = 0$ with a Taylor series expansion (see Appendix A), we have

$$\phi_x(t) = E[e^{itx}] = \int_{-\infty}^{\infty} f(x)\left[1 + ixt + \frac{(ix)^2t^2}{2} + \frac{(ix)^3t^3}{3!} + \dots + \frac{(ix)^nt^n}{n!} + \frac{t\cdot(t-\epsilon)^n}{(n+1)!}\cdot(i\epsilon)^{n+1}e^{i\epsilon x}\right] dx,$$

where $\epsilon$ is a number between 0 and $t$. Hence

$$\begin{aligned}\phi_x(t) &= \int_{-\infty}^{\infty} f(x)\,dx + it\int_{-\infty}^{\infty} xf(x)\,dx + \frac{(it)^2}{2}\int_{-\infty}^{\infty} x^2f(x)\,dx \\ &\quad + \dots + \frac{(it)^{n-1}}{(n-1)!}\int_{-\infty}^{\infty} x^{n-1}f(x)\,dx \\ &\quad + \frac{(it)^n}{n!}\int_{-\infty}^{\infty} x^n e^{i\epsilon x} f(x)\,dx \\ &= \sum_{j=0}^{n-1}\frac{(it)^j}{j!}E(X^j) + \frac{(it)^n}{n!}E(X^n) \\ &\quad + \frac{(it)^n}{n!}\int_{-\infty}^{\infty} x^n(e^{i\epsilon x} - 1)\,f(x)\,dx.\end{aligned}$$

It can be shown that the integral in the last expression is finite and tends to zero with $t$; therefore, $(it)^n/n!$ times the integral is $o(t_n)$. $\square$

Theorem C.3.2 allows us to approximate a characteristic function by its moments. Assume we know the first moment of a distribution, say $\mu$. Then we can write the characteristic function of $X$ as

$$\phi_x(t) = 1 + i\mu t + o(t),$$

and we can approximate the characteristic function of $X$ by $1 + i\mu t$. Although this result may not seem very powerful, it plays a major role in the proof of the central limit theorem presented in the text. In addition, by using the inversion theorem an approximation to the characteristic function from a few known moments can be used to find an approximation to distribution and density functions.

## C.3 Reference

Wilks, S. S. (1972), *Mathematical Statistics*, New York: Wiley.

# APPENDIX D

# Ratios of Normal Variates

At several points in the discussion of estimators of simultaneous equation parameters, the ratio of normal variates is encountered. It is therefore of interest to determine its distribution, consider the existence of moments, and develop approximations to the distribution. The derivation of the distribution was accomplished by Fieller (1932); we follow the presentation of Gnedenko (1973, pp. 150–152). See also Marsiglia (1965) and Hinkley (1969).

## D.1 Probability Density Function

Suppose that $X$ and $Y$ have a bivariate density given by $p(x, y)$, and we wish to determine the density of $Z = X/Y$. Consider first the distribution function $F(z) = P(X/Y < z)$. For $Y > 0$, $X/Y < z$ implies $X < zY$, and for $Y < 0$ we have $X > zY$. The areas for which $X/Y < z$ are shaded in Figure D.1.

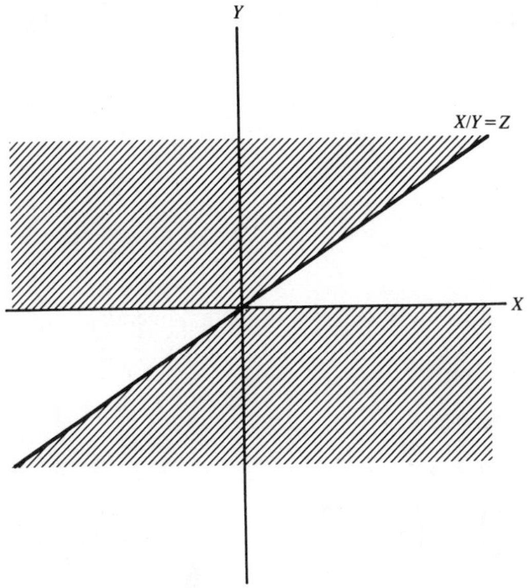


**FIGURE D.1** ***X/Y < z* in shaded regions.**

Therefore, we may write

$$F(z) = \int_{y=0}^{\infty} \int_{x=-\infty}^{zy} p(x, y)\, dx\, dy + \int_{y=-\infty}^{0} \int_{zy}^{\infty} p(x, y)\, dx\, dy. \qquad \textbf{(D.1.1)}$$

To find the density for $z$, we differentiate $F(z)$ with respect to $z$. Using Leibnitz's rule,[1] this is

$$\frac{dF(z)}{dz} = f(z) = \int_0^{\infty} yp(zy, y)\, dy - \int_{-\infty}^{0} yp(zy, y)\, dy = \int_{-\infty}^{\infty} |y| p(zy, y)\, dy. \quad \textbf{(D.1.2)}$$

For the bivariate normal case,

$$p(x, y) = \frac{1}{2\pi\sigma_1\sigma_2(1 - \rho^2)^{1/2}} \times \exp\left\{\frac{1}{2(1 - \rho^2)}\left[\frac{(x - \mu_1)^2}{\sigma_1^2} - \frac{2\rho(x - \mu_1)(x - \mu_2)}{\sigma_1\sigma_2} + \frac{(y - \mu_2)^2}{\sigma_2^2}\right]\right\}. \quad \textbf{(D.1.3)}$$

Applying (D.1.1), we have

$$f(z) = \frac{1}{2\pi\sigma_1\sigma_2(1 - \rho^2)^{1/2}} \int_{-\infty}^{\infty} |y| \exp\left\{\frac{1}{2(1 - \rho^2)}\left[\frac{(zy - \mu_1)^2}{\sigma_1^2} - \frac{2\rho(zy - \mu_1)(y - \mu_2)}{\sigma_1\sigma_2} + \frac{(y - \mu_2)^2}{\sigma_2^2}\right]\right\} dy. \quad \textbf{(D.1.4)}$$

We give details for the integration over $(0, \infty)$; the reader should verify the integration over $(-\infty, 0)$. For convenience, set

$$K = \sigma_1\sigma_2(1 - \rho^2)^{1/2}. \quad \textbf{(D.1.5)}$$

Then

$$f(z) = \frac{1}{2\pi K} \int_0^{\infty} y \exp\left\{-\frac{1}{2K^2}\left[\sigma_2^2(zy - \mu_1)^2 - 2\rho\sigma_1\sigma_2(zy - \mu_1)(y - \mu_2) + \sigma_1^2(y - \mu_2)^2\right]\right\} dy. \quad \textbf{(D.1.6)}$$

To perform the integration we first rewrite the bracketed term in the exponential:

$$\begin{aligned}
[\sigma_2^2 z^2 - 2\rho\sigma_1\sigma_2 z + \sigma_1^2]y^2 &- 2[\sigma_2^2\mu_1 z - \rho\sigma_1\sigma_2 z\mu_2 - \rho\sigma_1\sigma_2\mu_1 + \sigma_1^2\mu_2]y \\
&+ [\sigma_2^2\mu_2^2 - 2\rho\sigma_1\sigma_2\mu_1\mu_2 + \sigma_1^2\mu_2^2] \\
&\equiv Ay^2 - 2By + C \\
&= A\left(y - \frac{B}{A}\right)^2 + \left(C - \frac{B^2}{A}\right).
\end{aligned} \quad \textbf{(D.1.7)}$$

[1]Under appropriate conditions, see Kaplan (1952), the rule states

$$\frac{d}{dt}\int_{a(t)}^{b(t)} f(x, t)\, dx = f[b(t), t]\, b'(t) - f[a(t), t]\, a'(t) + \int_{a(t)}^{b(t)} \frac{\partial f(x, t)}{\partial t}\, dx.$$

Accordingly, (D.1.6) may be written as

$$\frac{1}{2\pi K}\exp\left\{-\frac{1}{2K^2}\left(C-\frac{B^2}{A}\right)\right\}\int_0^\infty y\exp\left\{-\frac{A}{2K^2}\left(y-\frac{B}{A}\right)^2\right\}dy. \tag{D.1.8}$$

To perform the integration, we proceed as follows:

$$\begin{aligned}
&\int_0^\infty y\exp\left\{-\frac{A}{2K^2}\left(y-\frac{B}{A}\right)^2\right\}dy\\
&=\int_0^\infty\left(y-\frac{B}{A}\right)\exp\left\{-\frac{A}{2K^2}\left(y-\frac{B}{A}\right)^2\right\}dy+\frac{B}{A}\int_0^\infty\exp\left\{-\frac{A}{2K^2}\left(y-\frac{B}{A}\right)^2\right\}dy\\
&=-\frac{K^2}{A}\exp\left\{-\frac{A}{2K^2}\left(y-\frac{B}{A}\right)^2\right|_0^\infty\\
&+\frac{B}{A}\left[\int_0^{B/A}\exp\left\{-\frac{A}{2K^2}\left(y-\frac{B}{A}\right)^2dy+\int_{B/A}^\infty\exp\left\{-\frac{A}{2K^2}\left(y-\frac{B}{A}\right)^2dy\right]\right.\right.\\
&=\frac{K^2}{A}\exp\left\{-\frac{B^2}{2K^2}\left\{+\frac{B}{A}\int_0^{B/A}\exp\left\{-\frac{A}{2K^2}\left(y-\frac{B}{A}\right)^2\right\}dy+\frac{\sqrt{2\pi}KB}{2\sqrt{A}\,A}\cdot\right.\right.
\end{aligned} \tag{D.1.9}$$

The integral in (D.1.9) is simplified by making the transformation

$$u=\frac{\sqrt{A}}{K}\left(y-\frac{B}{A}\right). \tag{D.1.10}$$

Then

$$\begin{aligned}
\frac{B}{A}\int_0^{B/A}\exp\left\{-\frac{A}{2K^2}\left(y-\frac{B}{\sqrt{A}}\right)^2\right\}dy&=\frac{B}{A}\frac{K}{\sqrt{A}}\int_{(-B/K)\sqrt{A}}^0\exp\left\{-\frac{1}{2}u^2\right\}du\\
&=-\frac{BK}{A^{3/2}}\int_0^{(-B/K)\sqrt{A}}\exp\left\{-\frac{1}{2}u^2\right\}du.
\end{aligned} \tag{D.1.11}$$

A similar procedure for $-\infty < y < 0$ yields

$$\begin{aligned}
\int_{-\infty}^0 y\exp\left\{-\frac{A}{2K^2}\left(y-\frac{B}{A}\right)^2\right\}dy&=\frac{K^2}{A}\exp\left\{-\frac{\mathrm{B}^2}{2K^2A}\right\}\\
&+\frac{-\mathrm{BK}}{\mathrm{A}^{3/2}}\int_0^{(-B/K)\sqrt{A}}\exp\left\{-\frac{1}{2}u^2\right\}du-\frac{\sqrt{2\pi}KB}{2\sqrt{A}A}\cdot
\end{aligned} \tag{D.1.12}$$

Therefore

$$\begin{aligned}
f(z)&=\frac{\exp\left\{-\frac{1}{2K^2}(C-B^2/A)\right\}}{2\pi K}\left[\frac{2K^2}{A}\exp\left\{\frac{-B^2}{2K^2A}\right\}\right.\\
&\left.+\frac{-2BK}{A^{3/2}}\int_0^{(-B/K)\sqrt{A}}\exp\left\{-\frac{1}{2}u^2\right\}du\right]=\frac{K}{\pi A}\exp\left\{-\frac{C}{2K^2}\right\}\\
&+\exp\left\{-\frac{1}{2K^2}\left(C-\frac{B^2}{A}\right)\right\}\frac{(-B)}{\pi A^{3/2}}\int_0^{(-B/K)\sqrt{A}}\exp\left\{-\frac{1}{2}u^2\right\}du.
\end{aligned} \tag{D.1.13}$$

This rather formidable looking result is easier to grasp if we first consider the case of zero expected values, unit variances, and independent $X$ and $Y$. In that case,

$$K = 1$$
$$A = z^2 + 1$$
$$B = 0$$
$$C = 0;$$

and so

$$f(z) = \frac{1}{\pi(z^2 + 1)}, \tag{D.1.14}$$

which is the Cauchy distribution. This distribution has no finite moments of any order, as may be seen from

$$E(z) = \int_{-\infty}^{\infty} \frac{z}{\pi(z^2 + 1)}\, dz = \int_{-\infty}^{0} \frac{z}{\pi(z^2 + 1)}\, dz + \int_{0}^{\infty} \frac{z}{\pi(z^2 + 1)}\, dz,$$

and the second integral is

$$\lim_{a\to\infty} \int_{0}^{a} \frac{z}{\pi(z^2 + 1)}\, dz = \lim_{a\to\infty} \frac{1}{2\pi} \ln(z^2 + 1) \Big|_{0}^{a} = \infty.$$

Since, after a transformation, general bivariate normal r.v.'s may be expressed as this special case, we have the result that the ratio of normal variates has no finite moments. This is of interest in econometrics because in certain cases an estimator may be shown to reduce to the ratio of normal variates. See Chapter 10 for examples.

## D.2 Geary's Approximation

Geary (1930) showed that the distribution of the ratio of normal variates may be approximated under certain conditions by a normal distribution. Let $E(X) = E(Y) = 0$, and consider the distribution of

$$Z = \frac{b + Y}{a + X}, \tag{D.2.1}$$

where $a$ and $b$ are constants, the variances of $X$ and $Y$ are $\sigma_x^2$ and $\sigma_y^2$, respectively, and let $\rho$, the correlation coefficient, be equal to zero initially. By the method used above, we obtain

$$P(z) = \frac{1}{2\pi\sigma_x\sigma_y} \int_{-\infty}^{\infty} |a + x| \exp\left\{ -\frac{1}{2}\left[\frac{x^2}{\sigma_x^2} + \frac{y^2}{\sigma_y^2}\right]\right\} dx, \tag{D.2.2}$$

where $y = (a + x)z - b$. Breaking up the absolute value term into its positive and negative parts, we have

$$P(z) = \frac{1}{2\pi\sigma_x\sigma_y}\left[\int_{-a}^{\infty} (a + x) \exp\left\{-\frac{1}{2}\left[\frac{x^2}{\sigma_x^2} + \frac{y^2}{\sigma_y^2}\right]\right\} dx - \int_{-\infty}^{-a} (a + x) \exp\left\{-\frac{1}{2}\left[\frac{x^2}{\sigma_x^2} + \frac{y^2}{\sigma_y^2}\right]\right\} dx\right]$$

$$= \frac{1}{2\pi\sigma_x\sigma_y}\int_{-\infty}^{\infty} (a + x) \exp\left\{-\frac{1}{2}\left[\frac{x^2}{\sigma_x^2} + \frac{y^2}{\sigma_y^2}\right]\right\} dx \tag{D.2.3}$$

$$-\frac{1}{\pi\sigma_x\sigma_y}\int_{-\infty}^{-a} (a + x) \exp\left\{-\frac{1}{2}\left[\frac{x^2}{\sigma_x^2} + \frac{y^2}{\sigma_y^2}\right]\right\} dx$$

$$= Q(z) + R(z). \tag{D.2.4}$$

Note that $R(z) > 0$ for all $z$. $Q(z)$ may be evaluated by the transformations

$$x' = x + \frac{(az - b)z\sigma_x^2}{\sigma_y^2 + \sigma_x^2 z^2} \tag{D.2.5}$$

and

$$t = \frac{az - b}{\sqrt{\sigma_y^2 + \sigma_x^2 z^2}} \tag{D.2.6}$$

to obtain

$$p(t) = \frac{1}{\sqrt{2\pi}} e^{-t^2/2}, \tag{D.2.7}$$

which is the standard normal density. From (D.2.4) and (D.2.7) we have

$$1 = \int_{-\infty}^{\infty} P(z)\, dz = \int_{-\infty}^{\infty} Q(z)\, dz + \int_{-\infty}^{\infty} R(z)\, dz$$

$$= \frac{1}{\sqrt{2\pi}}\int_{-a/\sigma_x}^{a/\sigma_x} e^{-t^2/2}\, dt + \int_{-\infty}^{\infty} R(z)\, dz \tag{D.2.8}$$

(Since

$$\lim_{z\to\infty} t = \lim_{z\to\infty} \frac{az - b}{\sqrt{\sigma_y^2 + \sigma_x^2 z^2}} = \frac{a}{\sigma_x} \quad \text{and} \quad \lim_{z\to-\infty} t = \frac{-a}{\sigma_x}\Bigg)$$

$$= 1 - \epsilon + \int_{-\infty}^{\infty} R(z)\, dz, \tag{D.2.9}$$

where $\epsilon$ is defined by

$$\epsilon = 1 - \frac{1}{\sqrt{2\pi}}\int_{-a/\sigma_x}^{a/\sigma_x} e^{-t^2/2}\, dt. \tag{D.2.10}$$

Therefore, $\int_{-\infty}^{\infty} R(z)\,dz$ is the probability that a normal variate is larger in absolute value than $a/\sigma_x$. Since $R(z)$ is a positive function of $z$, we have

$$R(z_1, z_2) \equiv \int_{z_1}^{z_2} R(z)\,dz < \epsilon \tag{D.2.11}$$

for $z_1 \leq z_2$. Letting

$$P(z_1, z_2) \equiv P[z_1 \leqslant z \leqslant z_2], \tag{D.2.12}$$

the above result may be written as

$$Q(z_1, z_2) \equiv \int_{z_1}^{z_2} Q(z)\,dz < P(z_1, z_2) < Q(z_1, z_2) + \epsilon. \tag{D.2.13}$$

For sufficiently large $a/\sigma_x$ (or small $\sigma_x/a$, which is the coefficient of variation of $a + x$), $\epsilon$ may be made arbitrarily small; we therefore have the result that $P(z_1, z_2)$ may be approximated by $Q(z_1, z_2)$. This may be regarded as an asymptotic expansion of $P(z_1, z_2)$ as $a/\sigma_x \to \infty$. The result is easily generalized to nonzero means by redefining $a$ as $a + \mu_n$:

$$x + a = (x - \mu_x) + (a + \mu_x), \tag{D.2.14}$$

and similarly for $y$. Geary also shows that the nonzero covariance case is handled by the transformation

$$z' = \frac{b' + y'}{a + x}, \tag{D.2.15}$$

where

$$y' = \frac{y}{\sigma_y} - \frac{\rho x}{\sigma_x}$$

and

$$b' = \frac{1}{\sigma_y}\left(b - \frac{a\rho\sigma_y}{\sigma_x}\right).$$

Then

$$t = \frac{az' - b'}{\sqrt{1 - \rho^2 + \sigma_x^2 z'^2}} = \frac{az - b}{\sqrt{\sigma^{2x}z^2 - 2\rho\sigma_x\sigma_y z + \sigma_y^2}} \tag{D.2.16}$$

is approximately normally distributed with mean zero and unit standard deviation.

## D.3 Approximations to Moments

Although we have noted that the moments of the ratio of normal distributed variates do not exist, it is possible to develop a type of approximation. Merrill (1928) expresses the ratio as

$$I = \frac{\mu_y + y}{\mu_x + x} = \frac{\mu_y}{\mu_x}\left(1 + \frac{y}{\mu_y}\right)\left(1 + \frac{x}{\mu_x}\right)^{-1} \qquad \textbf{(D.3.1)}$$

and expands the inverse in a series to obtain

$$I = \frac{\mu_y}{\mu_x}\left[1 + \frac{y}{\mu_y} - \frac{x}{\mu_x} - \frac{xy}{\mu_x\mu_y} + \frac{x^2}{\mu_x^2} + \frac{x^2y}{\mu_x^2\mu_y} - \cdots\right]. \qquad \textbf{(D.3.2)}$$

If the means are large and one curtails the normal distribution to eliminate extremely small or large values of $X$ and $Y$, one can drop higher order terms and take expected values of both sides. The result may be interpreted as the moments of the curtailed distribution, and the latter approximates the original distribution when the coefficient of variation of $X$ is small. This procedure is followed by Carter (1976); see Section 10.2.2b. It should be emphasized that the expected value of $Y/X$ does not exist. The expectation of a finite number of terms of (D.3.2) may be regarded as the expected value of an approximating distribution of $Y/X$, which is a good approximation when $\sigma_x/\mu_x$ is small.

## D.4 References

Carter, R. A. L. (1976), "The Exact Distribution of an Instrumental Variables Estimator," *International Economic Review,* **17,** 228–233.

Fieller, E. C. (1932), "The Distribution of the Index in a Normal Bivariate Population," *Biometrika, 24*, 428–440.

Geary, R. C. (1930), "The Frequency Distribution of the Quotient of Two Normal Variates," *Journal of the Royal Statistical Society,* **93,** 442–446.

Gnedenko, B. V. (1973), *The Theory of Probability,* Moscow: Mir Publishers.

Hinkley, D. V. (1969), "On the Ratio of Two Correlated Normal Random Variables," *Biometrika,* **56,** 635–639.

Kaplan, W. (1952), *Advanced Calculus,* Reading: Addison-Wesley.

Marsiglia, G. (1965), "Ratios of Normal Variables and Ratios of Sums of Uniform Variables," *Journal of the American Statistical Association,* **60,** 193–204.

Merrill, A. S. (1928), "Frequency Distribution of an Index When Both the Components Follow the Normal Law," *Biometrika,* **20,** 53–63.

# APPENDIX E

# The Wishart and Noncentral Wishart Distributions

## E.1 Wishart Distribution

The Wishart distribution is discussed in detail by Press (1972), Anderson (1958), and Johnson and Kotz (1972). The following discussion covers the points needed to follow the text; anyone planning to do serious work in theoretical econometrics will need to study multivariate statistics in depth.

Let $\mathbf{X}_t$ be a $p \times 1$ vector whose elements $x_{it}$ are drawn from a joint normal distribution with expected value $\mathbf{0}$ and variance-covariance matrix $\Sigma$; that is, $\mathbf{X}_t \sim N_p(\mathbf{0}, \Sigma)$. Let $\mathbf{X}_1, \mathbf{X}_2, \ldots, \mathbf{X}_N$ be mutually independent and define $X = (\mathbf{X}_1, \mathbf{X}_2, \ldots, \mathbf{X}_N)$. Then $V = XX' = \Sigma \mathbf{X}_t\mathbf{X}_t' = \{\Sigma_t\, x_{it}x_{jt}\}$, the matrix of sums of squares and cross products, follows a $p$-dimensional *Wishart distribution* with scale matrix $\Sigma$ and $N$ degrees of freedom ($p \leq N$). This distribution is denoted by $W_p(\Sigma, N)$. The density is given by

$$p(V) = \frac{C|V|^{(N-p-1)/2}}{|\Sigma|^{N/2}} \exp\left\{-\frac{1}{2} \operatorname{tr} \Sigma^{-1}V\right\}, \tag{E.1.1}$$

where

$$C = \left[2^{Np/2}\pi^{p(p-1)/4} \prod_{j=1}^{p} \Gamma\left(\frac{N+1-j}{2}\right)\right]^{-1}. \tag{E.1.2}$$

An important application of this distribution is to sample variances and covariances of $p$-dimensional normal variates. Thus, if

$$\mathbf{X}_t \sim N_p(\boldsymbol{\mu}, \Sigma), \qquad t = 1, \ldots, N, \qquad \text{and} \quad \bar{\mathbf{X}} = \frac{1}{N}\sum_{t=1}^{N} \mathbf{X}_t,$$

then

$$V = \sum_{t=1}^{N} (\mathbf{X}_t - \bar{\mathbf{X}})(\mathbf{X}_t - \bar{\mathbf{X}})' \quad \text{and} \quad V \sim W_p(\Sigma, N-1).$$

It is easy to verify that the diagonal elements of $1/(N-1)V$ are the sample variances for each of the $p$ components of $\mathbf{X}_t$, and the off-diagonal elements of $1/(N-1)V$ are the covariances between pairs of components of $\mathbf{X}_t$.

## E.2 Noncentral Wishart Distribution

In the cases discussed above $E(\mathbf{X}_t) = \mathbf{0}$ or $\boldsymbol{\mu}$ for $t = 1, \ldots, N$. If $E(\mathbf{X}_t)$ is not constant, the noncentral Wishart distribution must be employed for the distribution of sums of squares and cross products. The following basic information about the distribution is needed for understanding the small sample distribution theory for common simultaneous equation estimators covered in Chapters 10 and 11; more detailed information may be found in Press (1972) and Johnson and Kotz (1972).

Let $\mathbf{X}_t \sim N_p(\boldsymbol{\mu}_t, \Sigma)$ and define the $p \times p$ *means sigma matrix* $T$ by

$$T = \sum_{t=1}^{N} [\boldsymbol{\mu}_t - \bar{\boldsymbol{\mu}}][\boldsymbol{\mu}_t - \bar{\boldsymbol{\mu}}]', \qquad \text{where} \quad \bar{\boldsymbol{\mu}} = \frac{1}{N} \Sigma \boldsymbol{\mu}_t;^{1}$$

then

$$V = \sum_{t=1}^{N} \mathbf{X}_t \mathbf{X}_t'$$

has the $p$-dimensional *noncentral Wishart distribution* with scale matrix $\Sigma$, means sigma matrix $T$, and $N$ degrees of freedom:

$$V \sim W_p'(\Sigma, N; T).$$

If $\boldsymbol{\mu}_t = \mathbf{0}$ for $t = 1, \ldots, N$, then $T = 0$, and the noncentral Wishart reduces to the central Wishart

$$W_p'(\Sigma, N; 0) = W_p(\Sigma, N).$$

The complexity of the distribution increases with the rank of $T$, $r$. For $r = 1$, which is the case needed when there are two included endogenous variables (see Chapter 10), the density takes the following form:

$$W_p'(\Sigma, N; T) = \frac{C|V|^{(N-p-1)/2}}{|\Sigma|^{N/2}} \exp\left\{-\frac{1}{2} \operatorname{tr} \Sigma^{-1} V\right\}$$
$$\times \frac{\exp\left\{-\frac{1}{2} \operatorname{tr} \Sigma^{-1} T\right\}}{\operatorname{tr}(VT)^{(N-2)/4}} I_{(N/2)-1}\,[(\operatorname{tr} V\Sigma^{-1}T\Sigma^{-1})^{1/2}], \qquad \textbf{(E.2.1)}$$

where $C$ is as given in (E.1.2), and $I_\nu(z)$ is a modified Bessel function of the first kind. Although such functions are widely used in differential equations and other branches of mathematics, for present purposes it suffices to note that

$$I_\nu(z) = \left(\frac{1}{2} z\right)^{\nu} \sum_{\alpha=0}^{\infty} \frac{(z^2/4)^{\alpha}}{\alpha!\Gamma(\nu + \alpha + 1)}. \qquad \textbf{(E.2.2)}$$

For $r > 2$, the distributions become extremely complicated; see Press (1972) for further information and references.

Two useful facts concerning the noncentral Wishart distribution are presented in the following theorem.

**Theorem E.2.1**

Let $\mathbf{Z}_t \sim N_p(E(\mathbf{Z}_t), \Sigma)$, $Z = [\mathbf{Z}_1, \ldots, \mathbf{Z}_N]$, $T = (EZ)(EZ)'$, $C$ be a $p \times p$ nonsingular matrix, and $Q$ be a symmetric, idempotent matrix of rank $q$. Then

[1]Some authors define the means sigma matrix as $\Sigma \boldsymbol{\mu}_t \boldsymbol{\mu}_t'$.

(i) $CZZ'C' \sim W_p'(C\Sigma C', N; CTC')$ and

(ii) $Z'QZ \sim W_p'(\Sigma, q; (EZ)'Q(EZ))$.

**Proof**

(i) Let $\mathbf{X}_t \equiv C\mathbf{Z}_t \sim N_p(CE(Z_t), C\Sigma C')$. Then

$$CZZ'C' = \sum_t C\mathbf{Z}_t\mathbf{Z}_t'C' = \sum_t \mathbf{X}_t\mathbf{X}_t' \sim W_p'(C\Sigma C', N; CTC').$$

(ii) Since $Q$ is symmetric idempotent, there exists an orthogonal matrix $R$ such that

$$RQR' = \begin{bmatrix} I_q & 0 \\ 0 & 0 \end{bmatrix}$$

or

$$Q = R'\begin{bmatrix} I_q & 0 \\ 0 & 0 \end{bmatrix}R.$$

Then

$$Z'QZ = Z'R'\begin{bmatrix} I_q & 0 \\ 0 & 0 \end{bmatrix}RZ = U'U,$$

where

$$U' = Z'R'\begin{bmatrix} I_q & 0 \\ 0 & 0 \end{bmatrix}.$$

Let

$$R = \begin{bmatrix} \mathbf{r}_1 \\ \cdot \\ \cdot \\ \cdot \\ \mathbf{r}_p \end{bmatrix};$$

that is, $\mathbf{r}_i$ is the $i$th row of $R$. Then

$$\mathbf{U}_i = \begin{cases} \mathbf{r}_i Z & i = 1, \ldots, q \\ 0 & i = q + 1, \ldots, p, \end{cases}$$

and

$$E\mathbf{U}_i'\mathbf{U}_i = EZ'\mathbf{r}_i'\mathbf{r}_i Z = \Sigma, \qquad i = 1, \ldots, q.$$

Therefore $\mathbf{U}_i \sim N_p(\mathbf{r}_i(EZ), \Sigma)$ and $Z'QZ = \Sigma_{i=1}^q \mathbf{U}_i'\mathbf{U}_i$ is the sum of $q$ independent normal random variables, with common covariance matrix $\Sigma$ and means sigma matrix

$$(E(Z))'R'\begin{bmatrix} I_q & 0 \\ 0 & 0 \end{bmatrix}\begin{bmatrix} I_q & 0 \\ 0 & 0 \end{bmatrix}R(E(Z)) = (E(Z))'Q(E(Z)). \qquad \square$$

As an application of this theorem, consider the distribution of the sample variances and covariances. Assume $\mathbf{X}_t \sim N_p(\boldsymbol{\mu}_t, \Sigma)$ and define $X = [\mathbf{X}_1, \ldots, \mathbf{X}_N]$ and $\mathbf{Y}_t = \mathbf{X}_t - \bar{\mathbf{X}}$, where $\bar{\mathbf{X}} = (1/N)\, \Sigma^N_t \mathbf{X}_t$. Theorem E.2.1 (i) may be used to derive the distribution of $\Sigma \mathbf{Y}_t \mathbf{Y}_t' = YY'$, where $Y = [\mathbf{Y}_1, \ldots, \mathbf{Y}_N]$. $(1/(N-1)YY'$ is the matrix of sample variances and covariances.) Let $\mathbf{1}$ be an $N \times 1$ vector of ones and note that

$$\bar{\mathbf{X}} = \frac{1}{N} X\, \mathbf{1}.$$

Then

$$\begin{aligned}
\Sigma \mathbf{Y}_t \mathbf{Y}_t' &= \Sigma(\mathbf{X}_t - \bar{\mathbf{X}})(\mathbf{X}_t - \bar{\mathbf{X}})' \\
&= \Sigma \mathbf{X}_t \mathbf{X}_t' - \bar{\mathbf{X}} \Sigma \mathbf{X}_t' - \Sigma \mathbf{X}_t \bar{\mathbf{X}}' + N \bar{\mathbf{X}} \bar{\mathbf{X}}' \\
&= \Sigma \mathbf{X}_t \mathbf{X}_t' - N \bar{\mathbf{X}} \bar{\mathbf{X}}' \\
&= XX' - \frac{1}{N} X\, \mathbf{1}\, \mathbf{1}'\, X' \\
&= X\left[I - \frac{1}{N} \mathbf{1}\, \mathbf{1}'\right] X'.
\end{aligned}$$

It is easy to verify that $[I - (1/N)\, \mathbf{1}\, \mathbf{1}']$ is a symmetric idempotent matrix of rank $N - 1$. Therefore by Theorem E.2.1,

$$\begin{aligned}
\sum_{t=1}^{N} (\mathbf{X}_t - \bar{\mathbf{X}})(\mathbf{X}_t - \bar{\mathbf{X}})' &= \sum_{t=1}^{N} \mathbf{X}_t \left[I - \frac{1}{N} \mathbf{1}\, \mathbf{1}'\right] \mathbf{X}_t' \\
&\sim W_p'\left[\Sigma, N-1; \sum_{t=1}^{N} (\boldsymbol{\mu}_t - \bar{\boldsymbol{\mu}})(\boldsymbol{\mu}_t - \bar{\boldsymbol{\mu}})'\right], \qquad \text{(E.2.3)}
\end{aligned}$$

where

$$\bar{\boldsymbol{\mu}} = \sum_{t=1}^{N} \boldsymbol{\mu}_t.$$

Note that if $\boldsymbol{\mu}_t = \boldsymbol{\mu}$ for $t = 1, \ldots, N$, (E.2.3) reduces to the central Wishart distribution, $W_p(\Sigma, N - 1)$, the result noted at the end of Section E.1.

## E.3 References

Anderson, T. W. (1958), *An Introduction to Multivariate Statistical Analysis,* New York: Wiley.

Johnson, N. L. and S. Kotz (1972), *Continuous Multivariate Distributions,* New York: Wiley.

Press, S. J. (1972), *Applied Multivariate Analysis,* New York: Holt, Rinehart & Winston.

# APPENDIX F

# Hypergeometric and Confluent Hypergeometric Functions

## F.1 Hypergeometric Functions

The hypergeometric function is widely used in differential equations and mathematical physics; it is one of the "special functions" that arise frequently in physics. Many of its properties are contained in Chapters 13 and 15 of Abramowitz and Stegun (1965). The following facts will provide sufficient background to follow the text.

The function depends on three parameters $(a, b, c)$ and the variable $z = x + iy$ (which may be complex). For $|z| < 1$, the functions may be expressed as the Gauss hypergeometric series:

$$
\begin{aligned}
{}_2F_1(a, b; c; z) &= \sum_{n=0}^{\infty} \frac{(a)_n(b)_n}{(c)_n} \frac{z^n}{n!} \\
&= \frac{\Gamma(c)}{\Gamma(a)\Gamma(b)} \sum_{n=0}^{\infty} \frac{\Gamma(a+n)\Gamma(b+n)}{\Gamma(c+n)} \frac{z^n}{n!},
\end{aligned}
\qquad \textbf{(F.1.1)}
$$

where

$$
(\alpha)_n = \frac{\Gamma(\alpha + n)}{\Gamma(\alpha)} = (\alpha + n - 1)(\alpha + n - 2) \ldots (\alpha)
$$

and $(\alpha)_0 = 1$. (The first subscript in ${}_2F_1$ indicates the number of parameters in the numerator, and the second the number in the denominator.) This series reduces to a polynomial in $z$ when either $a$ or $b$ is a negative integer. Because of its presence in the denominator, $c$ may not be a negative integer (unless $a$ or $b$ is also a negative integer). Full details on the permitted range of parameters and the behavior of the function for particular values of $z$, as well as relations between hypergeometric functions and other functions and transformations of hypergeometric functions may be found in Abramowitz and Stegun (1965). The function has an integral representation:

$$
{}_2F_1(a, b; c; z) = \frac{\Gamma(c)}{\Gamma(b)\Gamma(c-b)} \int_0^1 t^{b-1} (1-t)^{c-b-1} (1-tz)^{-a} \, dt \qquad \textbf{(F.1.2)}
$$

$$
\operatorname{Re} c > \operatorname{Re} b > 0.
$$

This integral representation is the "analytic continuation" of the series ${}_2F_1(a, b; c; z)$; its value agrees with that of the series over the radius of convergence of the series, and it is defined for a larger set of $z$. By a theorem in complex variables, the representation is unique. It is easy to see the relationship between the integral and the series when $|z| < 1$. In that case,

$$(1 - tz)^{-a} = 1 + atz + \frac{a(a+1)(tz)^2}{2!} + \cdots \tag{F.1.3}$$

Therefore

$$\frac{\Gamma(c)}{\Gamma(b)\Gamma(c-b)} \int_0^1 t^{b-1} (1-t)^{c-b-1} \sum_{j=0}^{\infty} \frac{(a)_j}{j!} z^j t^j \, dt$$

$$= \frac{\Gamma(c)}{\Gamma(b)\,\Gamma(c-b)} \sum_{j=0}^{\infty} \frac{(a)_j}{j!} z^j \times \int_0^1 t^{b+j-1} (1-t)^{c-b-1} \, dt. \tag{F.1.4}$$

The integral is the beta function, $B(b + j, c - b)$, which can be written in terms of gamma functions as

$$B(b+j, c-b) = \frac{\Gamma(b+j)\Gamma(c-b)}{\Gamma(c+j)}.$$

Therefore we have

$$\frac{\Gamma(c)}{\Gamma(b)\Gamma(c-b)} \frac{\Gamma(c-b)}{\Gamma(a)} \sum_{j=0}^{\infty} \frac{\Gamma(a+j)\Gamma(b+j)}{\Gamma(c+j)} \frac{z^j}{j!} = {}_2F_1(a, b; c; z). \tag{F.1.5}$$

Being able to express a result in terms of hypergeometric functions enables the use of the large number of facts that are known about them, for example, derivatives, values for special cases of the arguments, and many relationships between them. In addition, asymptotic expansions for ${}_2F_1(a, b; c; z)$ have been derived as $a$, $b$, $c$, and $z$ become large.

Incidentally, it is interesting to note the relationship between the hypergeometric function we are discussing and the hypergeometric distribution of statistics. The latter is given by

$$f(x) = \frac{\binom{N_1}{x}\binom{N_2}{n-x}}{\binom{N}{n}}, \qquad N = N_1 + N_2.$$

Its c.f. is

$$\sum_{x=0}^{n} e^{itx} \frac{\binom{N_1}{x}\binom{N_2}{n-x}}{\binom{N}{n}} = \frac{\binom{N_2}{n}}{\binom{N}{n}} \sum_{x=0}^{n} \frac{N_1!n!(N_2-n)!}{(N_1-x)!(n-x)!(N_2-n+x)!} \frac{(e^{it})^x}{x!}$$

$$= \frac{\binom{N_2}{n}}{\binom{N}{n}} {}_2F_1(-n_1 - N_1; N_2 - n + 1; e^{it}). \tag{F.1.6}$$

(The last equality is easily verified. It illustrates the fact that ${}_2F_1$ is a polynomial for negative integer values of $a$ or $b$.) Thus the c.f. of the hypergeometric distribution is in the form of a hypergeometric function.

## F.2 Confluent Hypergeometric Functions

The confluent hypergeometric function is a special case of the hypergeometric function; the difference is that only one parameter appears in the numerator of the series expression:

$$ {}_1F_1(a, b; z) = \sum_{n=0}^{\infty} \frac{(a)_n}{(b)_n} \frac{z^n}{n!}. \qquad \textbf{(F.2.1)} $$

If Re $b >$ Re $a > 0$, there is an integral representation:

$$ {}_1F_1(a, b; z) = \frac{\Gamma(b)}{\Gamma(b - a)\Gamma(a)} \int_0^1 e^{zt} t^{a-1} (1 - t)^{b-a-1}\, dt. \qquad \textbf{(F.2.2)} $$

(This is easy to verify; expand $e^{tz}$ in a Taylor series and then write the integrals as beta functions.) This series expansion is valid for all values of $z$. Many relationships between it and other functions, as well as tables, are presented in Abramowitz and Stegun (1965, Chapter 13). To study the exact distribution and moments of various simultaneous equation estimators it is convenient to use the asymptotic expansion of ${}_1F_1$. For applications of interest to us, $z$ will take only real values, denoted by $x$. The asymptotic expansion for large $|x|$ is

$$ {}_1F_1(a, b; x) \sim \frac{\Gamma(b)}{\Gamma(a)} e^x x^{-(b-a)} \sum_{j=0}^{p} \frac{(b - a)_j (1 - a)_j}{j!} x^j. \qquad \textbf{(F.2.3)} $$

See Lebedev (1965, p. 271) for proofs and higher order terms.

## F.3 References


Abramowitz, M. and I. A. Stegun (1965), *Handbook of Mathematical Functions,* New York: Dover.

Lebedev, N. N. (1965), *Special Functions and Their Applications* (Translated and edited by R. A. Silverman), Englewood Cliffs, N.J.: Prentice-Hall.

# Index

*Applied Probability and Statistics (Continued)*

DUNN and CLARK • Applied Statistics: Analysis of Variance and Regression
ELANDT-JOHNSON • Probability Models and Statistical Methods in Genetics
ELANDT-JOHNSON and JOHNSON • Survival Models and Data Analysis
FLEISS • Statistical Methods for Rates and Proportions, *Second Edition*
FRANKEN, KÖNIG, ARNDT, and SCHMIDT • Queues and Point Processes
GALAMBOS • The Asymptotic Theory of Extreme Order Statistics
GIBBONS, OLKIN, and SOBEL • Selecting and Ordering Populations: A New Statistical Methodology
GNANADESIKAN • Methods for Statistical Data Analysis of Multivariate Observations
GOLDBERGER • Econometric Theory
GOLDSTEIN and DILLON • Discrete Discriminant Analysis
GREENBERG and WEBSTER • Advanced Econometrics: A Bridge to the Literature
GROSS and CLARK • Survival Distributions: Reliability Applications in the Biomedical Sciences
GROSS and HARRIS • Fundamentals of Queueing Theory
GUPTA and PANCHAPAKESAN • Multiple Decision Procedures: Theory and Methodology of Selecting and Ranking Populations
GUTTMAN, WILKS, and HUNTER • Introductory Engineering Statistics, *Third Edition*
HAHN and SHAPIRO • Statistical Models in Engineering
HALD • Statistical Tables and Formulas
HALD • Statistical Theory with Engineering Applications
HAND • Discrimination and Classification
HARTIGAN • Clustering Algorithms
HILDEBRAND, LAING, and ROSENTHAL • Prediction Analysis of Cross Classifications
HOAGLIN, MOSTELLER, and TUKEY • Understanding Robust and Exploratory Data Analysis
HOEL • Elementary Statistics, *Fourth Edition*
HOEL and JESSEN • Basic Statistics for Business and Economics, *Third Edition*
HOLLANDER and WOLFE • Nonparametric Statistical Methods
IMAN and CONOVER • Modern Business Statistics
JAGERS • Branching Processes with Biological Applications
JESSEN • Statistical Survey Techniques
JOHNSON and KOTZ • Distributions in Statistics
  Discrete Distributions
  Continuous Univariate Distributions—1
  Continuous Univariate Distributions—2
  Continuous Multivariate Distributions
JOHNSON and KOTZ • Urn Models and Their Application: An Approach to Modern Discrete Probability Theory
JOHNSON and LEONE • Statistics and Experimental Design in Engineering and the Physical Sciences, Volumes I and II, *Second Edition*
JUDGE, HILL, GRIFFITHS, LÜTKEPOHL and LEE • Introduction to the Theory and Practice of Econometrics
JUDGE, GRIFFITHS, HILL and LEE • The Theory and Practice of Econometrics
KALBFLEISCH and PRENTICE • The Statistical Analysis of Failure Time Data
KEENEY and RAIFFA • Decisions with Multiple Objectives
LAWLESS • Statistical Models and Methods for Lifetime Data
LEAMER • Specification Searches: Ad Hoc Inference with Nonexperimental Data
McNEIL • Interactive Data Analysis